Preface

Thank you for purchasing *HACKₑ ₛₐₜ Logical Reasoning*. All of us at Hackers Education Group are confident that this publication will be an invaluable resource as you prepare for the LSAT.

This comprehensive guide to the Logical Reasoning (LR) section was created by a team of experienced instructors and writers with extensive knowledge of the LSAT. It includes clear explanations of core concepts such as conditional and causal reasoning, effective strategies for solving each LR question type, and useful tips to improve performance on test day.

A key feature of *HACKERS LSAT Logical Reasoning* is that each LR question type is presented in its own section with the following elements:

- **An easy-to-understand flow chart that outlines the question-solving process**
- **A step-by-step walkthrough of how to determine the correct answer choice**
- **Information about common tricks used to make incorrect answer choices attractive**
- **Drills to aid in the development of key test-taking skills**
- **Example and practice questions taken from previous administrations of the LSAT**
- **Detailed explanations of these questions and their correct/incorrect answer choices**

Another important feature of this book is the inclusion of two complete LR practice tests composed entirely of actual LSAT questions. Of course, the answer keys for these practice tests contain thorough explanations of the questions and answer choices.

Thank you again for choosing *HACKERS LSAT Logical Reasoning*, and we wish you all the best as you take the first step in achieving your dream of a career in the legal profession.

Contents

HACKERS
LSAT
Logical
Reasoning

Hackers Language
Research Institute

About Hackers

Founded in 1998 by linguistics professor Dr. David Cho, Hackers Education Group has become one of the most successful and trusted educational companies. We are proud to provide innovative and effective learning solutions, including books, classes, and online lectures.

Our team of experts strives to incorporate effective instructional techniques into all of our products and services. Our unique prep programs for standardized tests such as the TOEFL, TOEIC, TEPS, IELTS, GRE, SAT and LSAT are praised by students, and our books are consistently at the top of bestseller lists.

COPYRIGHT © 2020, by Hackers Language Research Institute

January 2, 2020

Hackers Language Research Institute
23, Gangnam-daero 61-gil, Seocho-gu, Seoul, Korea
Inquiries   publishing@hackers.com

ISBN   978-89-6542-341-6 (13740)

Printed in South Korea

2 3 4 5 6 7 8 9 10   26 25 24 23 22 21

Complete LSAT Preparation!
HACKERS ACADEMIA (www.Hackers.ac)
• Accurate diagnostic tests
• Systematic curriculum
• Guided study sessions

Chapter 1

Welcome to the LSAT

Chapter 1: Welcome to the LSAT

Introduction

The LSAT is a standardized test that is required for admission to every American Bar Association-approved law school in the United States, as well as to a growing number of law schools in other countries.

In September 2019, the LSAT moved to a fully digital format. The exam consists of five 35-minute sections: four scored sections and an unscored experimental section. The scored portion of the LSAT includes two Logical Reasoning sections,

	Section	Time	# of Questions
Scored	Logical Reasoning 1	35 minutes	24-26
Scored	Logical Reasoning 2	35 minutes	24-26
Scored	Analytical Reasoning	35 minutes	22-24
Scored	Reading Comprehension	35 minutes	26-28
Unscored	Experimental	35 minutes	22-28
Unscored	Writing Sample	35 minutes	N/A

one Analytical Reasoning section (also known as Logic Games), and one Reading Comprehension section. The unscored experimental section is an additional Logical Reasoning, Analytical Reasoning, or Reading Comprehension section that is used by the Law School Admission Council (LSAC) for research purposes. As the scored sections of the LSAT are presented in random order, it is impossible to identify the experimental section while taking the test. Please note that test-takers will be permitted to take a 15-minute break at the conclusion of the third 35-minute section.

The LSAT is designed to test the skills required to succeed as a law student and lawyer. These include the ability to construct and analyze arguments (Logical Reasoning), organize abstract information and evaluate relationships between variables (Analytical Reasoning), and understand complex written materials (Reading Comprehension). The LSAT does not directly test vocabulary, grammar, or knowledge of particular subjects, making it very difficult to cram for.

The LSAT is the most significant factor in the admissions process. A high LSAT score will increase your chances of being accepted by a prestigious law school and thus affect your future employment opportunities. In addition, your LSAT score will determine whether you qualify for certain scholarships and how much you are eligible to receive. This book will help you achieve the LSAT score needed to embark on your legal career.

Scoring of the LSAT

Each scored question on the LSAT is worth one point. If you answer a question correctly, you will receive one point. If you skip a question or answer it incorrectly, you will not receive a point. This means that there is no penalty for guessing, so it is to your advantage to answer every single question.

The number of questions answered correctly determines your raw score. This is converted into a scaled score of 120 to 180, based on the performance of everyone else who participated in the same test administration. A standardized curve is used to assign a scaled score. The number of correctly answered questions needed to achieve a particular scaled score varies.

Raw Score (# of correct answers)		Scaled Score
Lowest	Highest	
97	100	176~180
93	96	171~175
87	92	166~170
80	86	161~165
71	79	156~160
61	70	151~155
52	60	146~150
42	51	141~145
33	41	136~140
26	32	131~135
20	25	126~130
16	19	121~125
0	15	120

Test Administrations

The LSAT testing year runs from June 1 to May 31. The exact number of administrations varies depending on the year and region. For the 2020-2021 testing year, eight LSAT administrations were scheduled in the United States. Of these, one was a disclosed administration, meaning that in addition to their score, test-takers will be able to access the questions that appeared on the exam, an answer key, and a score conversion chart.

LSAC limits the number of administrations that an individual may participate in. The current policy is as follows:

- no more than three LSATs may be taken within a single testing year
- no more than five LSATs may be taken within the current and past five testing years
- no more than seven LSATs may be taken in total

As most law schools only take into consideration an applicant's highest LSAT score, it is usually worthwhile to retake the LSAT with the aim of getting a higher score. However, it is important to keep in mind that law schools receive all of an applicant's valid LSAT scores. Be sure to check the admissions policies of any law schools you plan to apply to.

Logical Reasoning Section Basics

The Logical Reasoning (LR) section of the LSAT tests one's ability to analyze the logical foundation of an argument or set of facts, reason effectively, and draw inferences. While some knowledge of formal logic (beyond what is presented in this book) can be helpful, it is not required. Success on the LR section is determined by one's ability to read and think critically.

The questions in the LR section all include the same three elements. The first is the stimulus—a short passage that presents either an argument or a set of facts without a conclusion. This is followed by the prompt—a question or incomplete statement regarding the ideas and logical relationships expressed in the stimulus. The final element is the answer choices. There are five of these, and only one is correct. To succeed on the LR section, it is vital to be able to identify the different question types and extract the necessary information from the stimulus.

Here is an example of a typical LR question:

The Prompt

| Directions | | U 🖊 🖊 🖊 🖊 | Aa ⫶≡ 🔅 | Time Remaining: 34:10 |

Safety specialist: When the city of Springfield expanded its network of bicycle-only lanes throughout the city's streets last year, many residents thought that the incidence of accidents involving bicycles would decrease. Recent data shows that there was indeed a slight reduction in accidents involving bicyclists. However, more bicyclists died this year on Springfield's streets than ever before.

The Stimulus

The Answer Choices

7. Which of the following, if true, most helps to resolve the apparent conflict in the safety specialist's statements?

(A) The number of bicyclists on the streets has increased over the last few years.

(B) Bicyclists felt more confident with their own designated lanes and were much less likely to wear helmets.

(C) This year, city hospitals reported more serious injuries to bicyclists than in previous years.

(D) The expansion of the bicycle lane network was an expensive undertaking for the city.

(E) There were significantly more distracted drivers on the road this year than last year.

Progress bar: 1 2 3 4 5 6 7 8 9 10 11 12 13 14 15 16 17 18 19 20 21 22 23 24 25

The example above is presented as it would appear on the digital LSAT. The key features of the interface have been numbered and are explained below.

① **Mark for Review:** Clicking on the flag icon will mark the question for review. A small flag will appear above the corresponding question bubble in the progress bar.

② **Eliminate Answer Choice:** Clicking on one of the bubbles with a diagonal slash through it will cause the corresponding answer choice's text to fade and a bubble with a diagonal slash through it to appear to the left of the answer choice.

③ **Progress Bar:** Clicking on a bubble above a number in the progress bar will open the corresponding question. The progress bar shows which questions have been answered. A white bubble indicates that a question has not been answered, while a black bubble indicates that it has been answered.

④ **Highlight & Underline:** Clicking on the U icon allows sections of text (in the passage, prompt, or answer choices) to be underlined. Clicking on one of the three colored pen icons allows sections of text to be highlighted. Clicking on the eraser icon allows the underlining or highlighting to be removed.

⑤ **Adjust Appearance:** Clicking on these icons allows the font size, line spacing, and screen brightness to be adjusted.

⑥ **Timer:** Clicking on the numbers toggles the display of the time remaining on and off.

The correct answer is (B). This is a Paradox question, a type which is discussed in Chapter 5. For now, it is important to note that this example includes the three parts of every LR question.

Stimulus topics range from business to philosophy to science to economics to art and culture. All the information needed to answer a question is contained in its stimulus—additional knowledge of the topic should not be applied. (The three components of an LR question are covered in detail later in this chapter.)

One of the main skills needed for the LR section is the ability to read both quickly and carefully. In the LR section, test-takers need to catch subtle distinctions, so it is important to read with fine attention to detail. This needs to be done quickly, though. Many test-takers struggle to complete the LR section in the 35 minutes allotted.

The best way to approach an LR question is to read the prompt first, then read the stimulus, and then move on to the answer choices. Reading the answer choices in advance is not helpful as they offer no insight into the information presented in the stimulus, nor do they suggest the best approach for analyzing that information. Likewise, reading the stimulus first is problematic because it is impossible to know what kind of information to be on the lookout for. When test-takers read the stimulus before the prompt, they often have to go back and reread the stimulus to find the details needed to select the correct answer choice, which wastes time. Therefore, one should always read the prompt first as it provides vital information about what to look for while reading the stimulus.

Read the Prompt	**Read the Stimulus**	**Find the Correct Answer**

Having outlined the basic plan of attack for solving LR questions, let's examine how the three components of each question relate to one another. We will begin with the stimulus.

The Stimulus

Arguments vs. Fact Patterns

Every stimulus includes either an argument or a fact pattern. An argument contains at least one proposition that logically supports another one. A proposition that provides support is a premise, while one that receives support is a conclusion. If there are no premises and conclusions, the stimulus is a fact pattern. For example,

> **Han attended the exclusive dance in the Grand Ballroom. All of those who attended this dance are considered to be socialites. Our culture bestows great honor on those considered to be socialites by their peers.**

Here we have three propositions: (1) Han attended the dance, (2) if you attended the dance, you are a socialite, and (3) it is an honor to be considered a socialite. While these propositions are related, they do not support a conclusion. Therefore, this is a fact pattern. If a conclusion were added, such as "Han receives great honor in our culture," then this would be an argument.

Fact patterns are less common than arguments and are generally easier to understand because they are merely factual statements about a particular subject. In contrast, an argument involves complex logical relationships and must be deconstructed to understand its underlying structure and sometimes to identify errors in reasoning. This must be done quickly and carefully in order to receive a high score on the LR section. Let's start by looking at the various elements of an argument and how they fit together.

Parts of an Argument

Premises are propositions that support a conclusion. Premises are also referred to as *evidence* or *supporting details*.

Main conclusions are propositions that are supported by premises and subsidiary conclusions (if any). The main conclusion is the main point of the argument.

Subsidiary conclusions are propositions that are supported by premises and that, in turn, support the main conclusion. In this sense, a subsidiary conclusion is both a premise and a conclusion. The LR section frequently includes arguments with both subsidiary and main conclusions to confuse test-takers. If an argument has more than one conclusion, it will be necessary to determine which one is the main conclusion.

Counter-premises are propositions that contradict premises or conclusions. They bring up points of opposition that the author will later attempt to rebut.

Assumptions are claims that are not explicitly stated in an argument but which must be true for the conclusion to follow logically from the premises. For example,

Since all apples are red, Adam must be eating something red.

The conclusion that Adam must be eating something red does not follow from the premise that all apples are red. What is the missing piece of information? This argument assumes that Adam is eating an apple. Otherwise, how can we know that Adam is eating something red?

Background information is a proposition that is not a premise, counter-premise, or conclusion.

Argument Structure

All arguments include at least one premise and one conclusion. More complex arguments may have multiple premises and conclusions, as well as other components.

How do we know if a proposition is a premise, counter-premise, or conclusion? The most obvious answer is to look at the logical relationships within an argument to determine which propositions are supporting others and which are being supported. However, there is sometimes a quicker way to identify the parts of an argument— checking for indicator words and expressions.

Below is a list of indicators. Please note that this list is not exhaustive. In addition, premises, counter-premises, and conclusions do not always include an indicator, and some indicators can have more than one function.

Premise Indicators	Conclusion Indicators	Counter-Premise Indicators
Since	Thus	But
Because	As a result	However
For	Therefore	In contrast
As	Hence	Yet
After all	So	Despite
Moreover	Consequently	After all
Furthermore	It follows that	On the other hand
In addition	It is clear that	Still
Given that	It implies that	Although
Seeing that	Clearly	Even though
For example	Shows that	Notwithstanding
Due to	For this reason	Whereas
As indicated by	Conclude	In spite of
In that	We may infer	Admittedly
This may be inferred from	Accordingly	
Inasmuch as	It must be that	
Owing to	After all	

Note that a conclusion can also be indicated by the use of specific sentence structures. The two most common are as follows:

The *since A, B* **structure** indicates that the first clause *A* (headed by a premise indicator) is a premise, while the second clause *B* is a conclusion. For example,

Since automobile exhaust is bad for the environment, automobile usage should be limited.

The *A, because B* **structure** indicates that the first clause *A* is a conclusion, while the second clause *B* (headed by a premise indicator) is a premise. For example,

Candidate X will win the election because survey data shows he is the most popular candidate.

Organizational Structure vs. Logical Structure

The organizational structure of an argument is the order in which its component parts, such as premises and conclusions, are presented. The logical structure is the number and types of these parts and their relationships to each other. The logical structure of an argument is not determined by its organizational structure. Whether a proposition is a premise, counter-premise, or conclusion does not depend on its position within the argument. For example, a proposition that is supported by a premise is a conclusion, regardless of whether it appears at the beginning or end of an argument.

The LSAT test-makers often use complex organizational structures to make a question more difficult. Here are the most common ways arguments are organized. The premises are underlined, the conclusions are boldfaced, and the indicator words are italicized.

1. Premise – Premise – Conclusion

Lebron James scored 30 points in his basketball game last week. *Since* in tonight's game he attempted more shots and made a higher percentage of his shots than he did last week, **Lebron must have scored more than 30 points in tonight's game**.

This is the simplest way to order an argument, with the conclusion at the end. Note how the word *since* indicates that what immediately follows is a premise.

2. Conclusion – Premise – Premise

> ***Clearly*, Lebron James scored more than 30 points in tonight's game.** *This may be inferred from* the fact that in tonight's game he attempted more shots and made a higher percentage of his shots than he did in last week's game, in which he scored only 30 points.

This ordering is often the trickiest to spot. Students assume that the conclusion must be near the end and forget to consider that a proposition at the beginning can be the conclusion. Note the indicators *clearly* and *this may be inferred from*.

3. Premise – Conclusion – Premise

> Lebron James attempted more shots and made a higher percentage of his shots in tonight's game than he did last week. ***Therefore*, he must have scored more than 30 points tonight** *because* he scored just 30 points last week.

The conclusion can also be placed between two premises. Note the indicators *therefore* and *because*.

Validity vs. Truth

Valid Arguments

A valid argument is one in which the conclusion must be true if the premises are true—major assumptions are not needed to validate the conclusion, and there are no errors in reasoning. Here is an example of a valid argument:

> **If you are reading this book, you are studying for the LSAT. Everyone studying for the LSAT is super attractive. Therefore, everyone reading this book is super attractive.**

An argument is valid if and only if the truth of the premises guarantees the truth of the conclusion. If our premises are true, that all who read this book must be studying for the LSAT and that the mere act of studying for the LSAT guarantees that one is super attractive, it must be the case that everyone reading this book is super attractive.

Valid arguments do not need to be true. There are likely some people reading this book who are not super attractive. While the conclusion may not be technically true, the argument is still valid because the conclusion follows logically from the premises.

Invalid Arguments

An argument is invalid if the conclusion cannot be properly inferred from the given premises. The invalid arguments in the LR section greatly outnumber the valid ones. Here is an example of an invalid argument:

> **All people living in New York City are very fashionable. John lives in the United States of America. Therefore, John is very fashionable.**

While it may be true that John is fashionable, the conclusion does not follow logically from the premises. This argument requires the assumption that John lives not only in the United States but also in New York City. However, it is possible that John does not live in New York City. For an argument to be invalid, it does not need to be proven false. It only needs to be potentially false.

Logic on the LSAT hinges on validity, not truth. The ability to determine the validity of an argument is one of the most important skills to develop before taking the LSAT. LR questions involve identifying a flaw in the argument, finding an assumption that makes the argument valid, and so on. Invalid arguments are covered in great detail later in this book.

Drill: Stimulus Identification

For each stimulus below, determine the following:
- (a) Does it include an argument or fact pattern?
- (b) Are there any conclusions? If so, list and specify whether they are the main or subsidiary conclusions.
- (c) Are there any premises? If so, list them.
- (d) Are there any counter-premises? If so, list them.

1. According to the local weather channel's forecast, this weekend is expected to be sunny and clear. Since this forecast is rarely incorrect, we can trust that it will probably not rain this weekend. Therefore, we should not expect our golf tournament this weekend to be ruined by the weather.

    (a) _____

    (b) _____

    (c) _____

    (d) _____

2. Thirty graduate students were asked to keep track of their weekly alcohol consumption, including the type and number of beverages they consumed. After a three-month period, it was discovered that the students who had consumed the most alcohol also had the lowest scores on graded assignments. Clearly, consuming alcoholic beverages affects the academic abilities of graduate students.

    (a) _____

    (b) _____

    (c) _____

    (d) _____

3. The effectiveness of the household cleaning agent Germs Be Gone in destroying harmful bacteria has not been proven by any third-party study. If the makers of a household cleaning agent wish to market their product on our television program, they should be willing to have their product undergo numerous tests to show their product's value. Otherwise, if our viewers discovered we were advertising unproven products, our program's integrity would be compromised.

    (a) _____

    (b) _____

    (c) _____

    (d) _____

4. A requirement for any successful sovereign nation is a trusted and fair legal system. In addition, for there to be a fair legal system, law enforcement officers must understand the laws by which their state is governed and apply those laws fairly. Clearly, the nation of Zadia will not remain a successful sovereign nation as its law enforcement officers routinely accept bribes, which interferes with their ability to apply the nation's laws fairly.

    (a) _____

    (b) _____

    (c) _____

    (d) _____

5. Gold analysts predict that if demand for computer circuit boards (of which gold is a chief component) increases, then the price of gold will also increase. If the price of gold increases drastically, the amount available for other uses of gold may steadily decline.

(a) _____

(b) _____

(c) _____

(d) _____

6. The ancient Babylonian ruler Hammurabi was seen by many as a god during his own lifetime. This is indicated by various ancient texts and artworks attributing divinity to him.

(a) _____

(b) _____

(c) _____

(d) _____

7. Nuclear power plants are known to carry with them a risk of a human-error induced nuclear meltdown, which would result in catastrophic environmental damage. However, since the risk of a nuclear meltdown is minimal and the environmental impact from the normal production of nuclear power is less than many other forms of energy, those concerned with damage to the environment should not be overly critical about the construction of new nuclear power plants.

(a) _____

(b) _____

(c) _____

(d) _____

8. Raw meat is high in Vitamin B and many believe it is beneficial for hormonal and reproductive health. For this reason, raw meat should be included in the diet of every adult. Therefore, since promoting a healthy lifestyle is the goal of our restaurant, we should offer at least one dish on our menu that includes raw meat.

(a) _____

(b) _____

(c) _____

(d) _____

9. Despite the fact that John Jackson has remained undefeated in his weight class for over 14 years, he should not be considered for the boxing hall of fame. After all, Jackson has rarely fought challenging opponents and has shied away from title fights that may have affected his undefeated record.

(a) _____

(b) _____

(c) _____

(d) _____

10. Many scholars believe that before the time of European exploration, the various tribes of the Amazon rainforest had little contact with one another and remained genetically isolated. But a recent genetic analysis of descendants of these tribes shows large amounts of admixture and few genetic markers indicating genetic isolation. So, the belief that these tribes had little contact with one another is probably false.

(a) _____

(b) _____

(c) _____

(d) _____

1. **According to the local weather channel's forecast, this weekend is expected to be sunny and clear. Since this forecast is rarely incorrect, we can trust that it will probably not rain this weekend. Therefore, we should not expect our golf tournament this weekend to be ruined by the weather.**

   (a) Argument. There is at least one premise and one conclusion.

   (b) There is both a subsidiary conclusion and a main conclusion here. The main conclusion begins with a conclusion indicator, *therefore*. We know this is the main conclusion because it is supported by the subsidiary conclusion "it will probably not rain this weekend."

   (c) There are two premises. The first sentence does not include a premise indicator, but the weather channel's forecast for sunny and clear weather supports the subsidiary conclusion. The second sentence includes the premise indicator *since*, and the fact that the weather channel's forecast is rarely inaccurate supports the subsidiary conclusion as well.

   (d) No counter-premises.

2. **Thirty graduate students were asked to keep track of their weekly alcohol consumption, including the type and number of beverages they consumed. After a three-month period, it was discovered that the students who had consumed the most alcohol also had the lowest scores on graded assignments. Clearly, consuming alcoholic beverages affects the academic abilities of graduate students.**

   (a) Argument. There is at least one premise and one conclusion.

   (b) The main conclusion begins with the indicator *clearly*.

   (c) The second sentence is a premise stating that students who had consumed the most alcohol had the lowest grades. The first sentence can be regarded as background information because it is used to provide context for the premise.

   (d) No counter-premises.

3. **The effectiveness of the household cleaning agent Germs Be Gone in destroying harmful bacteria has not been proven by any third-party study. If the makers of a household cleaning agent wish to market their product on our television program, they should be willing to have their product undergo numerous tests to show their product's value. Otherwise, if our viewers discovered we were advertising unproven products, our program's integrity would be compromised.**

   (a) Fact pattern. There are no premises or conclusions in this stimulus—just a set of propositions.

   (b) No conclusions.

   (c) No premises.

   (d) No counter-premises.

4. **A requirement for any successful sovereign nation is a trusted and fair legal system. In addition, for there to be a fair legal system, law enforcement officers must understand the laws by which their state is governed and apply those laws fairly. Clearly, the nation of Zadia will not remain a successful sovereign nation as its law enforcement officers routinely accept bribes, which interferes with their**

ability to apply the nation's laws fairly.

(a) Argument. There is at least one premise and one conclusion.

(b) The main conclusion begins with the indicator *clearly*.

(c) There are three premises. The first sentence is a premise stating that a successful sovereign nation requires a trusted and fair legal system. The second premise begins with the premise indicator *in addition* and states that a fair legal system requires law enforcement officers to understand laws and apply them fairly. The third premise appears right after the conclusion and starts with the premise indicator *as*.

(d) No counter-premises.

5. **Gold analysts predict that if demand for computer circuit boards (of which gold is a chief component) increases, then the price of gold will also increase. If the price of gold increases drastically, the amount available for other uses of gold may steadily decline.**

(a) Fact pattern. There are no premises or conclusions in this stimulus—just a set of propositions.

(b) No conclusions.

(c) No premises.

(d) No counter-premises.

6. **The ancient Babylonian ruler Hammurabi was seen by many as a god during his own lifetime. This is indicated by various ancient texts and artworks attributing divinity to him.**

(a) Argument. There is at least one premise and one conclusion.

(b) While there is technically no conclusion indicator, the premise indicator *this is indicated by* in the second sentence implies that the previous proposition is the conclusion the premise is intended to support. The main conclusion here is that Hammurabi was regarded as a god during his lifetime.

(c) The first sentence is a premise stating that various texts and artworks attribute divinity to Hammurabi.

(d) No counter-premises.

7. **Nuclear power plants are known to carry with them a risk of a human-error induced nuclear meltdown, which would result in catastrophic environmental damage. However, since the risk of a nuclear meltdown is minimal and the environmental impact from the normal production of nuclear power is less than many other forms of energy, those concerned with damage to the environment should not be overly critical about the construction of new nuclear power plants.**

(a) Argument. There is at least one premise and one conclusion.

(b) The main conclusion here is that those concerned with damage to the environment should not be overly critical of the construction of new nuclear power plants. There are no conclusion indicators, but a *since premise, conclusion* structure is used.

(c) The second sentence includes the premise that the risk of a nuclear meltdown is minimal and nuclear power has a smaller environmental impact than other forms of energy. It includes the premise indicator *since*.

(d) The word *however* is a counter-premise indicator, but here it is located at the start of the sentence that follows the counter-premise. In this case, *however* indicates that the premise that follows will rebut the counter-premise that precedes it. The counter-premise is that nuclear power plants carry with them the risk of a nuclear meltdown, which would result in catastrophic environmental damage.

8. **Raw meat is high in Vitamin B and many believe it is beneficial for hormonal and reproductive health. For this reason, raw meat should be included in the diet of every adult. Therefore, since promoting a healthy lifestyle is the goal of our restaurant, we should offer at least one dish on our menu that includes raw meat.**

   (a) Argument. There is at least one premise and one conclusion.

   (b) There are two conclusions here. They are signaled by the indicators *for this reason* and *therefore*. To figure out which is the subsidiary conclusion and which is the main conclusion, we must determine which one is used to support the other. Here, the subsidiary conclusion is that raw meat should be included in the diet of every adult, as this is used in support of the main conclusion that raw meat should be offered in the restaurant. The determination that raw meat should be offered in the restaurant does not support the assertion that raw meat should be included in the diet of every adult.

   (c) There are two premises. The first sentence is a premise stating that raw meat has health benefits, which supports the subsidiary conclusion. The first clause of the last sentence contains the indicator *since* and specifies that a goal of the restaurant is to promote a healthy lifestyle. This premise directly supports the main conclusion.

   (d) No counter-premises.

9. **Despite the fact that John Jackson has remained undefeated in his weight class for over 14 years, he should not be considered for the boxing hall of fame. After all, Jackson has rarely fought challenging opponents and has shied away from title fights that may have affected his undefeated record.**

   (a) Argument. There is at least one premise and one conclusion.

   (b) The main conclusion here is that that Jackson should not be considered for the boxing hall of fame. There are no conclusion indicators.

   (c) There are two premises in the second sentence. This sentence begins with the indicator *after all*. The first premise is that Jackson rarely fought challenging opponents, and the second is that he avoided title fights that may have affected his record.

   (d) There is a counter-premise in the first sentence, and it begins with the indicator *despite the fact*. It counters the idea expressed in the conclusion.

10. **Many scholars believe that before the time of European exploration, the various tribes of the Amazon rainforest had little contact with one another and remained genetically isolated. But a recent genetic analysis of descendants of these tribes shows large amounts of admixture and few genetic markers indicating genetic isolation. So, the belief that these tribes had little contact with one another is probably false.**

   (a) Argument. There is at least one premise and one conclusion.

   (b) The main conclusion here begins with the conclusion indicator *so*.

   (c) The second sentence is a premise stating that the genetic analysis of tribal descendants shows genetic admixture and few markers indicating genetic isolation. It begins with *but*, which usually functions as a counter-premise indicator.

(d) The counter-premise here is the first sentence, which is evidence that runs counter to the author's conclusion. It does not include an indicator. Remember, conclusion, premise, and counter-premise indicator words can be very helpful, but ultimately, these argument parts are determined by their relationship to one another.

Prompts and Question Families

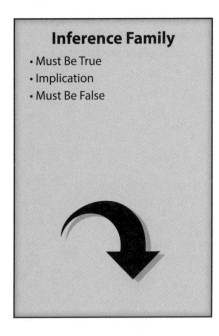

Inference Family

- Must Be True
- Implication
- Must Be False

Classification Family

- Main Point
- Fallacy
- Description
- Mini Description
- Parallel Reasoning
- Parallel Fallacy
- Agree/Disagree

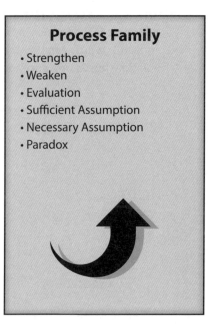

Process Family

- Strengthen
- Weaken
- Evaluation
- Sufficient Assumption
- Necessary Assumption
- Paradox

Logical Reasoning questions can be divided into three main families:

1. The Inference Family
2. The Classification Family
3. The Process Family

LR questions require test-takers to perform a variety of tasks: describe or match the structure of an argument; strengthen or weaken an argument; identify details, inferences, or assumptions; and resolve discrepancies in an argument. The relationship between a question's stimulus, prompt, and answer choices determines which family it belongs to. And, of course, a different approach is required for each family of questions. In later chapters, the question types belonging to each family are examined in detail and methods for solving them are elaborated. First, though, one must become familiar with the different question types and their basic features.

Inference Family

Inference Family questions require test-takers to identify a statement that can be inferred from the stimulus. As the downward arrow indicates, the prompt directs the test-takers to apply the information in the stimulus to the answer choices. The stimulus usually includes a fact pattern.

> 15.81 percent of Logical Reasoning Questions

Must Be True Questions (MBT) – Answering MBT questions involves choosing the answer choice that is true based on the information given in the stimulus. There is no uncertainty involved in MBT questions—the correct answer choice is indisputable.

MBT prompts typically include the following boldfaced expressions:

1. Which one of the following **must be true** on the basis of the information above?

2. If the statements above are true, which one of the following can be **properly inferred**?
3. Which one of the following **follows logically** from the statements above?

Implication Questions (IMP) – Answering IMP questions involves locating the answer choice that is heavily implied by the stimulus, even if it is not certain.

IMP prompts typically include the following boldfaced expressions:

1. Which one of the following is **best illustrated** by the information above?
2. The information above, if true, **most strongly supports** which one of the following?
3. Which one of the following **most logically** completes the argument?

Must Be False Questions (MBF) – Answering MBF questions involves identifying the answer choice that cannot be true based on the information in the stimulus.

MBF prompts typically include the following boldfaced expressions:

1. Which one of the following **cannot be true** on the basis of the information above?
2. If the statements above are true, which one of the following **must be false**?
3. If all of the statements above are true, then each of the following **could be true EXCEPT**?

Classification Family

Classification Family questions require test-takers to identify and classify information presented in the stimulus. The stimulus always includes an argument, and the prompt concerns the relationship between the various parts of the stimulus.

> 38.54 percent of Logical Reasoning Questions

Main Point (MP) – Answering MP questions involves pinpointing the argument's main conclusion. If the argument has multiple conclusions, it is necessary to identify the one that is supported by all the premises and other conclusions.

MP prompts typically include the following boldfaced expressions:

1. Which one of the following **most accurately expresses the main conclusion of the argument**?
2. Which one of the following is **the main point of the argument**?

Fallacy (F) – Answering F questions involves identifying, sometimes in general terms, the logical error or fallacy in an argument. This is the most common type of question in the LR section.

F prompts typically include the following boldfaced expressions:

1. The reasoning in the argument is **flawed** because the argument . . . ?
2. Which one of the following most accurately describes **a flaw** in the argument?
3. The reasoning in the argument is **most vulnerable to criticism** on the grounds that the argument . . . ?
4. The reasoning in the argument is **questionable** because it . . . ?

Description (D) – Answering D questions involves determining, sometimes in general terms, the way in which the argument arrives at its conclusion. These questions concern the reasoning used in the argument and whether that reasoning is valid or invalid.

D prompts typically include the following boldfaced expressions:

1. Which of the following is **a technique of reasoning** used in the argument?
2. The argument **does** which one of the following?
3. The argument **proceeds by** . . . ?

Mini Description (MD) – Answering MD questions involves identifying the role a part of the argument, such as a premise or conclusion, plays in the argument as a whole. The prompt includes a claim from the stimulus and asks about its function.

MD prompts typically include the following boldfaced expressions:

1. The claim that X **plays which one of the following roles** in the argument?
2. Which one of the following **most accurately describes the role** played in the argument by the claim that X?
3. The assertion that X **figures in the argument** in which one of the following ways?

Parallel Reasoning (PR) – Answering PR questions involves selecting the answer choice that contains reasoning most similar in structure to the reasoning in the argument. These questions tend to be the most time-consuming.

PR prompts typically include the following boldfaced expressions:

1. **The reasoning** in the argument above **most closely parallels** that in which one of the following?
2. **The pattern of reasoning** in which of the following is **most similar** to that in the argument above?
3. The argument is **most parallel, in its logical structure**, to which one of the following?

Parallel Fallacy (PF) – PF questions are similar to PR questions, but answering them involves identifying and matching the flawed reasoning in the argument with the flawed reasoning in an answer choice. These questions require a strong ability to recognize logical fallacies.

PF prompts typically include the following boldfaced expressions:

1. **The flawed reasoning** in which one of the following arguments is **most similar** to that in the argument above?
2. Which one of the following displays **an erroneous pattern of reasoning most similar** to that in the argument above?
3. Which one of the following arguments has **a questionable pattern of reasoning most like the reasoning** in the argument above?

Agree/Disagree (A/D) – A/D questions provide the perspectives of two different people. Answering them involves determining what these people agree or disagree about.

A/D prompts typically include the following boldfaced expressions:

1. Which one of the following most accurately express **a point at issue** between X and Y?
2. X's and Y's statement most strongly suggest that they **disagree over** which one of the following propositions?

3. On the basis of their statements, X and Y are committed to **agreeing** about which one of the following?

Process Family

Process Family questions require test-takers to apply a process to the stimulus, which usually includes an argument. As the upward arrow implies, the prompt directs the test-taker to apply the information in the answer choices to the stimulus. For all Process Family questions, it is necessary to assume that each answer choice is true and then identify its effect on the stimulus.

45.65 percent of Logical Reasoning Questions

Strengthen (S) – Answering S questions involves selecting an answer choice that supports the argument.

S prompts typically include the following boldfaced expressions:

1. Which one of the following, if true, **would most strengthen** the argument?
2. Which one of the following, if true, **provides the most support** for the argument?

Weaken (W) – Answering W questions involves selecting an answer choice that undermines the argument. Weaken questions often include arguments with flawed reasoning or unwarranted assumptions.

W prompts typically include the following boldfaced expressions:

1. Which one of the following, if true, **most seriously weakens** the argument?
2. Which one of the following, if true, **most undermines the reasoning** in the argument above?
3. Which one of the following, if true, **most calls into question the reasoning** in the argument?

Evaluation (E) – Answering E questions involves considering whether a question or other piece of information will help with evaluating the validity of the argument.

E prompts typically include the following boldfaced expressions:

1. **The answer to which one of the following questions** would be **most useful in evaluating** the conclusion drawn in the argument?
2. **In evaluating the argument**, it would be **most helpful to know** whether . . . ?
3. **Clarification of which one of the following issues** would **most help in judging the argument** drawn above?

Sufficient Assumption (SA) – Answering SA questions involves identifying a piece of information that, if assumed, would make the argument valid. The correct answer choice for an SA question is often a missing link in the logic chain of the argument.

SA prompts typically include the following boldfaced expressions:

1. The conclusion drawn by **the argument follows logically if which one of the following is assumed**?
2. Which one of the following is **an assumption that would allow the conclusion above to be properly drawn**?
3. The conclusion of the argument is **properly inferred if which one of the following is assumed**?

Necessary Assumption (NA) – Answering NA questions involves selecting an answer choice that must be true for the argument to be valid. The differences between SA and NA questions will be explored at length in Chapter 5.

NA prompts typically include the following boldfaced expressions:

1. The argument **depends on assuming** which one of the following?
2. Which one of the following is **an assumption** on which the argument **depends**?
3. Which one of the following is **an assumption made by the argument**?

Paradox (P) – Answering P questions involves examining an apparent contradiction or unexpected phenomenon in the stimulus and selecting an answer choice that resolves or explains this apparent discrepancy. The stimulus is usually fact pattern.

P prompts typically include the following boldfaced expressions:

1. Which one of the following, if true, **most helps to resolve the apparent discrepancy**?
2. Which one of the following, if true, **best helps to explain why** X?
3. Which one of the following, if true, **most helps to reconcile** X's belief with **the apparently contrary evidence** described above?

Drill: Identify the Prompt

Determine the question type for each of the prompts below.

1. Prompt: The conclusion follows logically if which one of the following is assumed?

   Question Type: _____

2. Prompt: The statements above must strongly support which one of the following?

   Question Type: _____

3. Prompt: The historian's reasoning is flawed in that it . . . ?

   Question Type: _____

4. Prompt: Of the following, which one most accurately expresses the conclusion drawn by the optometrist?

   Question Type: _____

5. Prompt: A point on which Robert's and Kim's views differ is whether . . . ?

   Question Type: _____

6. Prompt: Which one of the following, if true, most helps to explain the unexpected results described above?

   Question Type: _____

7. Prompt: The argument depends on the assumption that . . . ?

   Question Type: _____

8. Prompt: If the statements above are true, which one of the following cannot be true?

   Question Type: _____

9. Prompt: Which of the following can be properly inferred from the information above?

   Question Type: _____

10. Prompt: The reasoning in the argument is most vulnerable to criticism on the grounds that the argument . . . ?

    Question Type: _____

11. Prompt: Which one of the following, if true, most seriously undermines the evidence for the anthropologist's argument?

    Question Type: _____

12. Prompt: The pattern of reasoning in which one of the following arguments is most similar to that in the scientist's argument?

Question Type: _____

13. Prompt: Which of the following is a technique in reasoning used by the statistician?

Question Type: _____

14. Prompt: Which one of the following would it be most helpful to know in order to evaluate the argument?

Question Type: _____

15. Prompt: The assertion that another driver could have later driven by the scene of the accident serves which one of the following functions in the lawyer's argument?

Question Type: _____

16. Prompt: Which one of the following, if true, provides the strongest support for the explanation?

Question Type: _____

17. Prompt: Which one of the following contains flawed reasoning that most closely parallels that in the argument above?

Question Type: _____

18. Prompt: Which one of the following can be logically inferred from the mechanic's statements?

Question Type: _____

19. Prompt: Which one of the following, if assumed, enables the argument's conclusion to be properly inferred?

Question Type: _____

Drill: Identify the Prompt — Answers

1. Sufficient Assumption (SA)

2. Implication (IMP)

3. Fallacy (F)

4. Main Point (MP)

5. Disagree (A/D)

6. Paradox (P)

7. Necessary Assumption (NA)

8. Must Be False (MBF)

9. Must Be True (MBT)

10. Fallacy (F)

11. Weaken (W)

12. Parallel Reasoning (PR)

13. Description (D)

14. Evaluation (E)

15. Mini Description (MD)

16. Strengthen (S)

17. Parallel Fallacy (PF)

18. Implication (IMP)

19. Sufficient Assumption (SA)

If you were not able to accurately identify every question type, don't worry. Plenty of examples are given in the subsequent chapters of this book on individual question types. Note that the LSAT test-makers sometimes use variants and tricks to make questions harder. These are also discussed later in the book.

Notes on Prompts and Question Families

Most – The qualifier *most* is sometimes used in the prompts for Strengthen and Weaken questions, as well as some other question types. For example, a Strengthen prompt might read

> "Which one of the following, if true, provides the **most** support for the writer's conclusion?"

While this seems to point to the possibility that an incorrect answer choice may strengthen an argument, just to a lesser extent than the correct answer choice, this is not the case. There can only be one answer choice that meets the prompt's criteria. For the Strengthen question above, the correct answer choice will inevitably strengthen the writer's argument, while the four incorrect answer choices will not. This applies to all prompts containing the word *most*.

Except and Least – Prompts in the LR section sometimes include *EXCEPT* or *LEAST*. If a prompt says, "Each of the following is an assumption required by the argument EXCEPT," then all four incorrect answer choices will be assumptions necessary for the argument to be valid while the correct answer choice will not be an assumption required by the argument. A common mistake is to believe that the prompt is asking for the polar opposite instead of the logical opposite. For example, it is easy to assume that a Strengthen EXCEPT question is asking for an answer choice that weakens the argument. This is not necessarily correct. The answer to a Strengthen EXCEPT question is the one that does not strengthen the argument. It may weaken the argument, or it may neither strengthen nor weaken the argument.

In a prompt, the word *LEAST* operates in exactly the same way. The Paradox LEAST prompt "Which one of the following, if all of them are true, would be LEAST helpful in resolving the apparent discrepancy between both sets of scientific findings?" will be accompanied by four incorrect answer choices that resolve the paradox and one correct answer choice that does not. The word *LEAST* does not mean that the correct answer choice will resolve the paradox to a lesser extent than the others do (as we would expect based on how least is used in everyday conversation), but rather that it will not resolve the paradox at all.

Principle Questions – Principle questions are not a unique question type but instead act as an additional element in a question type. For example,

> "Which one of the following **principles** most helps to justify the reasoning above?"

A principle is a broad rule or generalization that can be used instead of a specific fact to answer a question. "All students should study for the LSAT" is a principle. Principles are used differently with different question types. Principle Questions are discussed in detail in Chapter 6.

Question Type Frequency – Some question types appear much more frequently than others. The chart on the right was compiled using data from 10 recent LSAT administrations. Note that these numbers are approximate and subject to change.

Question Type Frequency (Per Test)
1. Fallacy (7.4)
2. Strengthen (7.1)
3. Implication (5.8)
4. Necessary Assumption (5.2)
5. Paradox (4.0)
6. Weaken (3.3)
7. Agree/Disagree (2.8)
8. Sufficient Assumption (2.6)
9. Mini Description (2.1)
10. Parallel Reasoning (2.0)
11. Parallel Fallacy (2.0)
12. Main Point (2.0)
13. Must Be True (1.3)
14. Description (1.2)
15. Evaluation (0.9)
16. Must Be False (0.9)

Answer Choices

LR questions always include one correct answer choice and four incorrect answer choices. The correct answer choice always matches the prompt, and the incorrect ones do not match the prompt. For example, the correct answer for a Weaken question is the one that undermines the argument's reasoning, while the four incorrect answer choices do not undermine the argument's reasoning. The recommended approach for answering LR questions is as follows:

Anticipate

After reading the prompt and stimulus (in that order), anticipate what the correct answer choice will be. For some question types, such as Fallacy questions, the answer is easy to anticipate. For other question types, such as Implication questions, many facts are inferable from the argument and anticipating the correct answer choice is more difficult.

Separate

You should then read through the answer choices to locate those that match the answer you anticipated. Separate the answer choices into candidates—those that correspond to your anticipated answer choice—and losers. If you end up with only one candidate, this is most likely the correct answer choice. If you have several candidates, you need to continue to the next step.

Eliminate

If you have more than one candidate, you need to eliminate potentially correct answer choices until only one remains. This process, which varies for each question type, is explored in greater detail in later chapters. If you end up eliminating all the answer choices, you must reread the prompt and stimulus and start this process again from the beginning.

Incorrect Answer Choices

Each LR question type utilizes specific tricks to make incorrect answer choices attractive to test-takers. These are discussed in detail in the relevant sections of this book. However, certain tricks commonly appear in incorrect answer choices for various question types:

Logical Force Error: A statement that is too strong or too weak in terms of logical force.

Broad Claim: A claim that is too broad to be supported by the information in the stimulus.

Invalid Inference: An inference that is based on faulty reasoning.

Irrelevant Information: New information that is not relevant to the stimulus.

Inaccurate Paraphrase: Information from the stimulus that has been altered slightly to make it inaccurate.

Each of these tricks is considered in more detail later in this book. For now, just keep in mind that you are likely to encounter these types of incorrect answer choices frequently.

Guessing

Unlike some other standardized tests, there is no penalty for guessing on the LSAT. Therefore, test-takers should make sure to select an answer choice for every question. A common LSAT myth is that certain answer choices are more commonly correct than others—for example, that (E) has the highest probability of being correct for the final few questions of the LR section. This is not true. There is no optimal guessing strategy except to make sure that you leave no questions blank.

If you are not completely certain about an answer choice or are torn between two or more answer choices, do not spend so much time on the question that you have to rush through subsequent ones. Make your best guess, take note of the question number, and move on. If you have extra time after answering the remaining questions, you can return to those you had to guess on and try to determine the correct answer choices with more certainty. The advantage of this strategy is that if you do not have enough time to return to these questions, you have already marked your guesses on the answer sheet and, therefore, have a chance of getting points for them.

Putting It All Together

To review what we have learned so far, let's look at an LSAT question from a previous administration of the test:

If cold fusion worked, it would provide almost limitless power from very inexpensive raw materials, materials far cheaper than coal or oil. But replacing all the traditional electric generators that use these fuels with cold-fusion power plants would result in a reduction of no more than 25 percent in the average residential electric bill.

Each of the following, if true, would help to resolve the apparent discrepancy between the predictions above EXCEPT:

(A) Cold-fusion power plants would be more expensive to build and maintain than traditional electric generators are.

(B) Environmental regulations now placed on burning coal or fuel oil are less costly than the regulations that would be placed on cold fusion.

(C) Most electric companies would be willing to incorporate cold-fusion technology into their power plants.

(D) Only a relatively small portion of any residential electric bill is determined by the electric company's expenses for fuel.

(E) Personnel costs for the distribution of power to consumers are unrelated to the type of raw materials an electric company uses.

This is a Paradox EXCEPT question. The four incorrect answer choices resolve the paradox, while the correct answer choice does not resolve the paradox. As we read the stimulus, we should be on the lookout for contradictory pieces of information. We should also expect to find a fact pattern in the stimulus as Paradox questions rarely include an argument.

The first step is to read and understand the stimulus. The first proposition states,

> **If cold fusion worked, it would provide almost limitless power from very inexpensive raw materials, materials far cheaper than coal or oil.**

This is pretty straightforward. This first proposition contains a conditional statement (conditional statements are discussed in Chapter 2). The statement provides a condition that, if met, would necessitate an end result. Here, the condition is "if cold fusion worked," and the end result is "it would provide almost limitless power from very inexpensive raw materials." It seems to be the case that if cold-fusion technology were available, cold fusion would be an abundant and inexpensive source of energy compared to coal or oil. Let's continue reading.

> **But replacing all the traditional electric generators that use these fuels with cold-fusion power plants would result in a reduction of no more than 25 percent in the average residential electric bill.**

The first thing we notice is the counter-premise indicator *but*. This signals that the information following it counters the information in the preceding proposition. By replacing the electric generators that use these fuels with cold-fusion power plants, we would only see a 25 percent reduction in the average residential electric bill at the very most.

For Paradox questions, we always need to set our two competing pieces of information against one another. The first is that cold fusion is a very inexpensive source of energy; the second is that switching to cold-fusion power plants would result in only a small reduction in the average power bill. We need to think of ways in which both of these propositions can be true.

Note that the first proposition compares the materials used in cold-fusion energy production to coal and oil. What if it's the case that the electric generators currently in use are actually using cheaper raw materials, such as natural gas? However, the second proposition precludes this with the wording "traditional electric generators that use these fuels." This refers to the electric generators currently in use, which produce energy from coal or oil. We can cut short this line of thinking here.

What else might explain why electric bills would not be significantly reduced if a cheaper energy source were used? Perhaps there are other costs involved in utilizing cold-fusion energy that are passed on to consumers. For example, how much would a cold-fusion power plant cost to construct? Would these plants be more expensive to operate? Having anticipated information that may help to resolve the discrepancy, we can now turn to the answer choices. We will use our anticipated answers to separate candidates from losers.

(A) Cold-fusion power plants would be more expensive to build and maintain than traditional electric generators are.

This is exactly what we anticipated. If cold-fusion power plants were more expensive to build and maintain, the energy they produced would be more costly. This would explain why the reduction in the average residential electric bill would be less than expected. We can add this answer choice to the loser category.

(B) Environmental regulations now placed on burning coal or fuel oil are less costly than the regulations that would be placed on cold fusion.

This is similar to what we originally anticipated. While we did not specify "environmental regulations," it is easy to see that these would introduce new costs into the equation. If the environmental regulations for cold fusion were more costly than those for using coal and oil, the reduction in electric bills might not be significant. We can categorize this answer choice as a loser.

(C) Most electric companies would be willing to incorporate cold-fusion technology into their power plants.

What does this have to do with our anticipated answers? Does the willingness of electric companies matter here? Before going deeper, we can put this in the candidate category.

(D) Only a relatively small portion of any residential electric bill is determined by the electric company's expenses for fuel.

Here, we see that the fuel cost is only a small portion of any electric bill. While not our anticipated answer, this certainly explains why electric bills would only decline by 25 percent. We can put this in the loser category.

(E) Personnel costs for the distribution of power to consumers are unrelated to the type of raw materials an electric company uses.

This answer choice deals with cost, so it seems related to our anticipated answer. However, it indicates that personnel costs are unrelated to the type of raw materials an electric company uses. This means that these costs would be the same for both types of plants. This does not seem to resolve the paradox, but it's a bit unclear. Let's keep this as a candidate.

Our last step is to analyze the two candidates and eliminate the incorrect answer choice. Let's look back at (C).

(C) Most electric companies would be willing to incorporate cold-fusion technology into their power plants.

If most electric companies were willing to incorporate cold-fusion technology into their power plants, would this resolve the paradox that the average electric bill would only be slightly lower when the fuel source is drastically cheaper? It doesn't seem like it would. The stimulus seems to assume that companies would be willing to incorporate the cold-fusion technology due to the words "but replacing . . . with cold-fusion power plants would result in a reduction." (C) does not add any new information that would reconcile the differences between our two competing pieces of information. It looks to be the correct answer. However, we must still go back and consider answer choice (E). If (E) fails to resolve the paradox, it must mean that we did not fully understand the stimulus and should start the whole process over again.

(E) Personnel costs for the distribution of power to consumers are unrelated to the type of raw materials an electric company uses.

As we said in our first pass through, if personnel costs were equal regardless of the raw materials used, it is unlikely that there would be an additional cost for cold-fusion power. However, there does not necessarily need to be an additional cost to reconcile the differences here. For example, assume the raw materials for cold-fusion power cost 5x but coal or oil cost 10x. If these were the only costs involved, you would expect a cost decrease of 50 percent. If we added an additional personnel cost of 10x to both, and fuel and personnel were the only costs, we would have a total cost of 15x for cold-fusion and 20x for oil or coal. Thus, switching from oil or coal to cold-fusion would result in a 25 percent decrease in cost. Therefore, adding an additional equal cost to both sides could account for why the cost reduction is lower than expected. It follows that (E) resolves the paradox, and we can eliminate it as a potential correct answer choice.

The correct answer is (C) as it does not resolve the paradox.

Key Takeaways

Inference Family

The information in the stimulus must be assumed to be true and applied to the answer choices. The stimulus usually includes a fact pattern.

Classification Family

The information in the stimulus must be identified and classified. The stimulus usually includes an argument.

Process Family

The information in the answer choices must be assumed to be true and applied to the stimulus. The stimulus usually includes an argument.

Identify Prompt	Read the prompt and identify the question type. Understanding exactly what the prompt is asking you to do is essential.
Read Stimulus	If the stimulus is a fact pattern, take the time to understand exactly what is being said. If it is an argument, identify the premises, subsidiary conclusion (if any), and main conclusion. Determine whether there are any errors in reasoning.
Anticipate	Anticipate possible answer choices. Some question types, such as Fallacy, Paradox, and Sufficient Assumption, will be easier to do this for than others, such as Implication and Necessary Assumption.
Separate	Read through the answer choices, looking for ones that match your anticipated answer choices. Separate candidates and losers.
Eliminate	Eliminate candidates until you are left with only one. If all candidates are eliminated, start the process over again.

Parts of an Argument

Premise: proposition that supports a conclusion

Main Conclusion: proposition supported by all premises and other conclusions

Subsidiary Conclusion: proposition that is both supported by premises and that supports a main conclusion

Counter-Premise: proposition that rebuts a conclusion or premise

Assumption: unstated information assumed to be true in an argument

Background Information: proposition that is not a premise, conclusion, or counter-premise

Incorrect Answer Choice Tricks

• Logical Force Error
• Broad Claim
• Invalid Inference
• Irrelevant Information
• Inaccurate Paraphrase

Chapter 2

Conditional
Reasoning

Chapter 2: Conditional Reasoning

HACKERS
LSAT *Logical Reasoning*

Introduction

Propositions that appear in the LR section can be categorized as absolute, relational, or conditional statements. The bulk of this chapter is dedicated to conditional statements, the most complex and important of the three. However, it is important to have an understanding of absolute and relational statements as they often appear in the stimulus and answers choices of questions.

Absolute statements simply posit the existence of a fact. For example,

> **The Golden State Warriors won the 2018 NBA championship.**
> **Steve's shirt is on backwards.**
> **This sentence is an absolute statement.**

Causal statements, which are discussed in detail at the end of this chapter, are a form of absolute statement.

As for relational statements, these compare two or more variables. For example,

> **The Golden State Warriors are the best team in the NBA.**
> **Steve is not wearing his shirt the way everyone else is.**
> **This sentence is better written than the previous sentence.**

In the first relational statement, there is a comparative relationship between the Golden State Warriors and every other team in the NBA. In the second statement, Steve is dressed differently than everyone else. Finally, the third sentence asserts that it is better written than the second sentence. All of these statements feature comparisons.

A common trick in the LR section is to present an absolute statement as an incorrect answer choice when a relational statement is supported by the stimulus, and vice versa. For example, for an Implication question that asks us to determine which answer choice is most strongly supported, there is a difference between concluding that "Dr. Chan, an orthopedic surgeon, is the highest paid doctor in her practice" and that "Dr. Chan, an orthopedic surgeon, is highly paid." The first is a relational statement and the second is an absolute statement. The stimulus may suggest that Dr. Chan is highly paid, but this cannot mean that she is the highest paid doctor in her practice unless we know the pay of the other doctors. Conversely, we may be informed that Dr. Chan makes more money than any other doctor in her practice, but we cannot conclude from this that Dr. Chan is highly paid. Perhaps all of the doctors in this practice, including Dr. Chan, receive low salaries. Be sure to clearly distinguish between these two types of statements when attempting to solve a question.

Conditional Statements

Conditional statements assert a specific relationship between two conditions. If one condition is triggered, then the other condition must occur. For example,

If you live in Miami, then you live in Florida.

Conditional reasoning is one of the keys to doing well in the LR section. The information presented in this chapter will help you develop the core skills needed for this section of the test.

This statement does not claim that you live in Miami. Rather, it asserts that if you do live in Miami, it must be the case that you live in Florida. In this example, the first part of the statement is the sufficient condition and the second part is the necessary condition. This classification is not determined by the order in which the conditions appear but by their logical relationship. When the sufficient condition is met, the necessary condition is triggered. We use a → symbol to represent this conditional relationship, as illustrated below:

Miami → Florida

In a conditional statement diagram, the sufficient condition is placed on the left and the necessary condition is placed on the right. This order must always be followed when diagramming conditional statements. Later in this chapter we will consider many valid and invalid inferences that can be drawn from conditional statements. To identify these, a consistent and accurate diagramming system is essential.

The "if . . . then" example diagrammed above is the most basic form of conditional statement. If A is met, then B must follow. However, conditional statements come in many other forms. For example,

Every Californian knows someone who surfs.
Being the best requires a tremendous work ethic.
The top competitor was complimented by all of the judges in the contest.

Whatever the conditional statement's structure might be, there is always a sufficient condition and a necessary condition. Indicator words (which are discussed next) can often be used to identify the sufficient and necessary conditions. If there are no indicator words, transforming the statement into an "if . . . then" statement may make it easier to identify the sufficient and necessary conditions. To do this, one must carefully consider the logical relationships between the ideas expressed in the original statement. For example, the third statement above could not be expressed as "If he was complimented by all of the judges in the contest, then he must be the top competitor." Why? Because this excludes the possibility of anybody else in the competition (or in the world, for that matter) being complimented by all of the judges. Further, this does not match the original sentence, which just says that the top competitor was complimented by all of the judges. Therefore, this sentence has to be expressed as "If he is the top competitor, then he was complimented by all of the judges in the contest." Being the top competitor triggers being complimented by all of the judges.

Again, using an "if . . . then" structure to restate a conditional statement makes it easier to identify the logical relationships between the variables. However, this can be a time-consuming process, so you should use it as a backup method, to be applied only when (1) there are no indicator words, (2) you cannot determine the role of an indicator word, or (3) you want to confirm that you have diagrammed the conditional statement correctly.

Sufficient and Necessary Indicators

What follows is a list of conditional indicators. Some conditional statements contain multiple indicators, while others contain none. The presence of an indicator helps in determining whether a proposition is a conditional statement and also in identifying the sufficient and necessary conditions.

Sufficient Indicators	Necessary Indicators
If	Then
All	Only
Any	Only if
Every	Must
Each	Needs
When	Necessitates
Whenever	Necessary
Who	Requires
Whoever	Demands
In order to	Essential
Sufficient	Entails
Negative Sufficient Indicators	**Negative Necessary Indicators**
Unless	No
Without	None
Except	Not all
Until	

Sufficient Indicators

A sufficient indicator immediately precedes a sufficient condition. In the following examples, the sufficient indicators are italicized and the sufficient conditions are underlined.

> For clarity, spelled-out words and phrases are often used in this book's conditional diagrams. However, you should use shorthand during the test to save time. The first example on the left could be diagrammed as W → G.

My glass is filled with water *whenever* the waitress walks by.
(If the waitress walks by, my glass is filled with water)

Waitress Walks By → Glass Filled

Politicians always lie *if* given the chance to do so.
(If given the chance to do so, then politicians will always lie)

Given the Chance to Lie → Politicians Lie

***All* dogs go to heaven.**
(If it is a dog, then it will go to heaven)

Dog → Go to Heaven

The budget was approved by *every* member of the committee.
(If he is a member of the committee, then he approved the budget)

Member of the Committee → Approve Budget

In order to determine which team goes first, we flip a coin.

(If we want to determine which team goes first, then we should flip a coin)

Determine Which Team Is First → Flip a Coin

Necessary Indicators

Necessary indicators usually immediately precede the necessary condition. In the following examples, the necessary indicators are italicized and the necessary conditions are underlined.

Turning on the flashlight *requires* batteries.

Turn on Flashlight → Batteries

I will go to the movies tonight *only if* someone drives me.

Go to Movies Tonight → Someone Drives Me

If the glove doesn't fit, you *must* acquit.

~~Glove Fits~~ → Acquit

It is *necessary* for a functioning democracy to have a strong legal system.

Functioning Democracy → Strong Legal System

In the third example, the negative sufficient condition (*glove doesn't fit*) is diagrammed as a positive statement that has been crossed out (~~*Glove Fits*~~). This is how you should represent all negative statements when diagramming conditional language. The reason for this will become clear in the Contraposition section of this chapter.

In the final example, the necessary condition *strong legal system* does not directly follow the necessary indicator *necessary*. In some cases, you must determine what the necessary indicator refers to. Here, the word *necessary* refers to *a strong legal system*. Some other indicators, including *required* and *essential*, function in the same way. However, this type of structure is rare.

Special Case — Only

The necessary indicator *only* is a special case in that oftentimes it does not directly refer to the necessary condition. Instead, it often modifies a word or phrase that refers to the necessary condition. Take a look at the following examples:

The *only* time of the year I get to wear this beautiful coat is during the winter.

Wear Beautiful Coat → Winter

Only modifies *time of the year*. What does *time of the year* refer to? *Winter*.

***Only* students with top academic credentials can be accepted into this university.**

Accepted into University → Top Credentials

Only modifies *students*. What does *students* refer to? *Those with top academic credentials.*

The *only* people in this company who are paid too little are the sanitation staff.

Paid Too Little in Company → Sanitation Staff

Only modifies *people*. What does *people* refer to? *The sanitation staff.*

Climbing this advanced rock wall is possible *only* for those in <u>peak physical condition</u>.

Climb Rock Wall → Peak Physical Condition

In the last example, *only* functions as a typical necessary indicator in that it precedes the necessary condition. In this case, *only* directly refers to *those in peak physical condition*, which is the necessary condition.

Remember, if you are struggling to identify the necessary or sufficient condition, convert the sentence into an "if . . . then" statement. The examples above can be rephrased as follows:

If I get to wear this beautiful coat, then it must be winter.

If students are accepted into this university, then they have top academic credentials.

If they are paid too little in this company, then they must be the sanitation staff.

If it is possible for them to climb the advanced rock wall, then they are in peak physical condition.

Although *only* sometimes functions like a typical necessary indicator, it more often modifies a word that refers to the necessary condition. If you see *only* in a conditional statement, you can anticipate such a structure.

Negative Sufficient Indicators

Negative sufficient indicators immediately precede and negate the sufficient condition. Negation is the process of making a negative statement positive or a positive statement negative. This concept is discussed in more detail later in this chapter. Here are several statements containing negative sufficient indicators:

***Until* <u>I find my car keys</u>, I won't be going to the movie theater.**

~~Find Car Keys~~ → ~~Going to Movies~~

I find my car keys follows *until*, which means that it is the sufficient condition and must be negated in the diagram. We can rephrase this statement as "If I do not find my car keys, I will not be going to the movie theater."

Life on Earth could not have started *without* <u>self-replicating RNA molecules</u>.

~~RNA Molecules~~ → ~~Life on Earth~~

What follows *without* is the sufficient condition, and therefore it must be negated.

> A simple trick to use with negative sufficient indicators is to replace *unless/without/except/until* with *if not*. It may sound strange grammatically, but it emphasizes the importance of negating the sufficient condition.

The bicyclist will crash into the stop sign *unless* <u>he does not continue peddling</u>.

Continue Peddling → Bicyclist Crash

This is tricky because what follows *unless* is a negative that could be represented as ~~Continue Peddling~~. However, the same formula applies, and we negate that statement, turning it into a positive and placing it in the sufficient condition position of the diagram.

Strategy A should always be employed *except* for in <u>situations involving business insolvency</u>.

~~Business Insolvency~~ → Strategy A

After *except* we have *situations involving business insolvency*, which we negate and place in the sufficient condition position.

Negative Necessary Indicators

Negative necessary indicators refer to the necessary condition and signal that it must be negated. Statements that include these types of indicators are commonly referred to as NO statements. It is important to note that the necessary condition is always the second term in a NO statement. The negative necessary indicator does not always immediately precede the necessary condition. Consider the following examples:

> **None of the kids on the track team wear glasses.**

> Kids on Track Team → ~~Glasses~~

None negates the second term in the sentence, which is the necessary condition. We can rephrase this statement as "If you are a kid on the track team, then you do not wear glasses."

> **At the bake sale, artificial ingredients were used in *none* of the lemon cakes.**

> Artificial Ingredients → ~~Lemon Cake~~

None negates the second term, which happens to be the term that immediately follows *none*. This statement can be rephrased as "If artificial ingredients were used in the bake sale, then they were not used in the lemon cakes."

> **No current artificial intelligence program can simulate lifelike human conversation.**

> Current AI Programs → ~~Simulate Human Conversation~~

Lastly, *no* negates the second term. This statement can be rephrased as "If it is a current artificial intelligence program, then it cannot simulate lifelike human conversation."

Biconditional Statements — If and Only If

This is a special indicator that does not fit neatly into one category. That's because it comprises *if*, which is a sufficient indicator, and *only if*, which is a necessary indicator. This phrase is thus a combination of the two indicator types and as such indicates both a sufficient and negative condition. For example,

> **I will go bowling if** and only if **they have bowling shoes that fit me.**

Let's look only at the statement's boldfaced words. *If* is a sufficient indicator, so what follows it is the sufficient condition. The statement can be diagrammed as follows:

> Bowling Shoes Fit Me → I Am Going Bowling

This can be rephrased as "If they have bowling shoes that fit me, I will go bowling."

> **I will go bowling** if and **only if they have bowling shoes that fit me.**

Looking at just the boldfaced words, *only if* is a necessary indicator, so we can put what follows in the necessary condition position of our diagram:

> I Am Going Bowling → Bowling Shoes Fit Me

This can be rephrased as "If I'm going bowling, they have bowling shoes that fit me."

What this means is that when *if and only if* appears in a conditional statement, either condition can trigger the other. Therefore, both conditions are sufficient and necessary. We can diagram an *if and only if* statement as follows:

I Am Going Bowling ⟷ Bowling Shoes Fit Me

We use a double-sided arrow to signify that when one of these conditions occurs, so does the other. Note that the order of the terms does not matter.

I Am Going Bowling ⟷ Bowling Shoes Fit Me

is identical to

Bowling Shoes Fit Me ⟷ I Am Going Bowling

Statements such as these are called biconditionals. The sufficient condition and necessary condition of a biconditional can be flipped without being negated. The concept of flipping and negating conditional statements is explained later in this chapter.

Drill: Sufficient and Necessary Condition

Now that you understand the basic features of conditional statements, diagram each of the following statements.

1. Without a properly functioning brake light, you will get a ticket.

   _____

2. A top hat is essential to performing in a Mr. Peanut outfit.

   _____

3. Your performance will be fantastic if you practice enough.

   _____

4. No sodas should be consumed while on a strict diet.

   _____

5. Benji will watch the opening act if and only if he arrives on time.

   _____

6. The only cars worth owning are made in Korea.

   _____

7. Every good calendar includes all seven days of the week.

   _____

8. You will be very cold outside unless you wear a jacket.

   _____

9. None of the restaurants in the area serve vegan food.

   _____

10. I will be able to get to the airport on time only if I drive past the speed limit.

   _____

11. A bath was not given to any of the dogs.

   _____

12. Only medical doctors are allowed to prescribe medication in this country.

_____

13. It is important that we not celebrate until the birthday boy arrives.

_____

14. Getting caught drunk driving is sufficient to require attending a driver's education course.

_____

15. English words are not understood by the staff.

_____

16. The only way to solve our problem is to run away, fast.

_____

Drill: Sufficient and Necessary Condition — Answers

1. **Without a properly functioning brake light, you will get a ticket.**

   ~~Functioning Brake Light~~ → Ticket

   Without is a negative sufficient indicator, meaning that we must negate the sufficient condition.

2. **A top hat is essential to performing in a Mr. Peanut outfit.**

   Performing in Mr. Peanut Outfit → Top Hat

   Essential is a necessary indicator, but it is not used in the typical way here. If the statement were "It is essential to tie your shoes if you want to play baseball," then what follows *essential* would be the necessary condition. However, this sentence says that a top hat *is* essential. When a term is essential, necessary, or required, it is naturally the necessary condition.

3. **Your performance will be fantastic if you practice enough.**

   Practice Enough → Fantastic Performance

   Practice enough follows *if* and is therefore the sufficient condition.

4. **No sodas should be consumed while on a strict diet.**

   Sodas Consumed → ~~Strict Diet~~

   No is a negative necessary indicator. This means that *no* negates the necessary condition, which is always the second term of a NO statement.

5. **Benji will watch the opening act if and only if he arrives on time.**

   Watch Opening Act ⟷ Arrive on Time

   If and only if is a biconditional indicator, meaning that each condition is both sufficient and necessary. In other words, when one condition is met, so is the other.

6. **The only cars worth owning are made in Korea.**

   Cars Worth Owning → Cars Made in Korea

   Only is a necessary indicator but a tricky one to work with. Remember, in many cases you must determine not only which word or phrase *only* modifies, but also what this word or phrase refers to. In this case, *only* modifies *cars*, which refers to *cars made in Korea*. Therefore, *cars made in Korea* is the necessary condition.

7. **Every good calendar includes all seven days of the week.**

   Good Calendar → Includes 7 Days of Week

   Every is a sufficient indicator, so what follows *every* is the sufficient condition.

8. **You will be very cold outside unless you wear a jacket.**

   ~~Wear Jacket~~ → Very Cold

   Unless is a negative sufficient indicator, so what follows *unless* is the sufficient condition and must be negated.

9. **None of the restaurants in the area serve vegan food.**

   Restaurant in Area → ~~Serves Vegan Food~~

   None is a negative necessary indicator. This means that *none* negates the necessary condition, which is the second term because this is a NO statement.

10. **I will be able to get to the airport on time only if I drive past the speed limit.**

    Airport on Time → Drive Past Speed Limit

    Only if is a necessary indicator, so what follows *only if* is the necessary condition.

11. **A bath was not given to any of the dogs.**

    Dogs → ~~Bath~~

    Any is a sufficient indicator, so what follows *any* is the sufficient condition.

12. **Only medical doctors are allowed to prescribe medication in this country.**

    Prescribe Medication → Medical Doctor

    In this example, *only* is a necessary indicator that is functioning in the conventional way. It directly refers to *medical doctors*, which it immediately precedes and which is the necessary condition. To confirm this, we can rephrase this statement using the "if . . . then" structure. Is it "If you are able to prescribe medication, then you are a medical doctor" or "If you are a medical doctor, then you are able to prescribe medication"? The former is correct because while it may be true that medical doctors can prescribe medication, it may not be true that every medical doctor can prescribe medication.

13. **It is important that we not celebrate until the birthday boy arrives.**

    ~~Birthday Boy Arrives~~ → ~~Celebrate~~

    Until is a negative sufficient indicator, so what follows *until* is the sufficient indicator and must be negated.

14. **Getting caught drunk driving is sufficient to require attending a driver's education course.**

    Caught Drunk Driving → Attend Driver's Education Course

    We have two indicator words, which is not uncommon. *Require* is a necessary indicator, so what follows it is the necessary condition. *Sufficient* is a sufficient indicator. It functions in much the same way as *necessary* does in the second question of this drill. If something is sufficient, then it is the sufficient condition.

15. **English words are not understood by the staff.**

    English Words → ~~Understood by Staff~~

    This statement is harder to diagram than the previous ones because there are no indicators. We should therefore turn it into an "if . . . then" statement. Is it "If it is an English word, then the staff do not understand it" or "If the staff do not understand it, then it is an English word"? It is obviously the former. Besides English words, there are surely many other things the staff do not understand, such as quantum physics.

16. **The only way to solve our problem is to run away, fast.**

    Solve Problem → Run Away

    In this case, *only* modifies *way*, and *way* refers to *run away, fast*. Therefore, *run away, fast* is the necessary condition.

Conditional Statement Modifiers

Strength Modification

We have already dealt with conditional statements such as "If it is an apple, then it is delicious." This means that every single apple on the planet is delicious. No exceptions. We call this an ALL statement because it can be rewritten as "All apples are delicious." But what if we want to express this idea less strongly? This is where strength modifiers come into play. Strength modifiers are very important as many LR questions require test-takers to be able to recognize whether a claim is strong, moderate, or weak. Following from this, conditional statements can be classified as ALL, MOST, and SOME statements.

Strength modifiers give us information about conditional relationships. Keep in mind that strength modifiers generally do not function as sufficient or necessary indicators, although there is some overlap.

Further, strength modifiers can be categorized according to degree and quantity. Degree modifiers indicate the likelihood of the sufficient condition leading to the necessary condition. Quantity modifiers indicate the proportion of the sufficient condition that leads to the necessary condition. Refer back to the following chart as your read through this section:

Common Strength Modifiers					
Weak (SOME)		Moderate (MOST)		Strong (ALL)	
Degree	Quantity	Degree	Quantity	Degree	Quantity
May Might Can/Could Occasionally Often	Some Few Several Many Not all Little	Probably Generally Likely Usually Typically	Most Majority Almost all	Always Must Is Are Will	All Every Any No None

Degree Modification

Strong degree modification is a concept we worked with in the previous section. The implication is that when a sufficient condition occurs, the necessary condition must occur. To restate this, the likelihood of the necessary condition occurring is 100 percent. Here are some examples of statements with strong degree modifiers:

Honesty is *always* the best policy.	Best Policy → Honestly
The bar *must* have a happy hour this week.	Bar → Happy Hour This Week
Mr. Jones *is* a rabbi.	Mr. Jones → Rabbi
The Ravens w*ill* win the contest.	Ravens → Win Contest

Note that terms such as *is* and *will* can function as strong degree modifiers in conditional statements when they are not accompanied by another modifier. Conditional statements like these, in which the sufficient condition triggers the necessary condition 100 percent of the time, are called ALL statements.

Moderate degree modification occurs when the probability of the sufficient condition leading to the necessary condition exceeds 50 percent. Here, the previous examples are written using moderate degree modifiers:

Honesty is *usually* the best policy.	Best Policy $\xrightarrow{M}$ Honestly
The bar is *likely* to have a happy hour this week.	Bar $\xrightarrow{M}$ Happy Hour This Week
Mr. Jones is *probably* a rabbi.	Mr. Jones $\xrightarrow{M}$ Rabbi
The Ravens will *likely* win the contest.	Ravens $\xrightarrow{M}$ Win Contest

Note that we use $^M\!\!\to$ to denote moderate strength modifiers. We call any conditional statement containing a moderate strength modifier a MOST statement.

Weak degree modification occurs when the probability of the sufficient condition leading to the necessary condition merely exceeds 0 percent. This means there is a possibility of the event occurring. Here, the previous examples are written using weak degree modifiers:

Honesty is *sometimes* the best policy.	Best Policy $^S\!\!-\!\!^S$ Honestly
The bar *might* have a happy hour this week.	Bar $^S\!\!-\!\!^S$ Happy Hour This Week
Mr. Jones *may* be a rabbi.	Mr. Jones $^S\!\!-\!\!^S$ Rabbi
The Ravens *could* win the contest.	Ravens $^S\!\!-\!\!^S$ Win Contest

We call any conditional statement containing a weak strength modifier a SOME statement. Note that ALL statements and MOST statements are denoted by an arrow, while SOME statements are denoted by an $^S\!\!-\!\!^S$ symbol. This is because SOME statements function like the biconditionals we discussed earlier—each condition is both sufficient and necessary, meaning that we are able to flip these statements without negating them. For example, the last two statements may be rephrased as "A rabbi *may* be Mr. Jones" and "The contest *could* be won by the Ravens." It is unlikely that you will ever have to flip a statement modified by a weak degree modifier to solve an LR question.

Quantity Modification

Strong quantity modification is another concept dealt with in the previous section. The implication is that 100 percent of the sufficient condition leads to the necessary condition. In other words, all constituents of a certain group have a certain quality. Here are a few examples of statements with strong quantity modifiers:

All frogs are amphibians.	Frog $\to$ Amphibian
Everyone who watched the movie enjoyed it.	Watch Movie $\to$ Enjoy
Any wild cat you find is dangerous.	Wild Cat $\to$ Dangerous

These ALL statements imply that 100 percent of the members of the sufficient condition group have a certain quality. That is, 100 percent of the sufficient condition leads to the necessary condition.

Moderate quantity modification occurs when more than 50 percent of the sufficient condition leads to the necessary condition. In other words, most constituents of a certain group have a certain quality. Therefore, a MOST symbol ($^M\!\!\to$) is used to denote this relationship. Here, the previous examples are written using moderate quantity modifiers:

Most frogs are amphibians.	Frog $^M\!\!\to$ Amphibian
The *majority* who watched the movie enjoyed it.	Watch Movie $^M\!\!\to$ Enjoy
Almost all wild cats you find are dangerous.	Wild Cat $^M\!\!\to$ Dangerous

These MOST statements imply that more than 50 percent of the members of the sufficient condition group have a certain quality. That is, more than 50 percent of the sufficient condition leads to the necessary condition.

Note that *almost all* is a moderate quantity modifier because it means less than *all* and signifies a quantity very close to *all*, which is why it is used in MOST statements.

Weak quantity modification occurs when more than 0 percent of the sufficient condition leads to the necessary condition. In other words, some constituents of a certain group have a certain quality. Therefore, a SOME symbol ($^S\!\!-\!\!^S$) is used to denote this relationship. Here, the previous examples are written using weak quantity modifiers:

Some frogs are amphibians.	Frog $^S\!\!-\!\!^S$ Amphibian
A *few* who watched the movie enjoyed it.	Watch Movie $^S\!\!-\!\!^S$ Enjoy
Many wild cats you find are dangerous.	Wild Cat $^S\!\!-\!\!^S$ Dangerous

These SOME statements imply that more than 0 percent of the members of the sufficient condition group have a certain quality. As mentioned previously, the sufficient and necessary conditions of SOME statements can be flipped. For example, the second statement can be read as "Some people who enjoyed the movie watched the movie." You will almost certainly encounter LR questions that require you to flip a statement modified by a weak quantity modifier.

Special Case — Not All

Not all is a special quantity modifier. Like *almost all*, it implies that the quantity is less than 100 percent. However, it does not imply that the quantity is close to 100 percent. *Not all* is generally classified as a weak quantity modifier, but it is important to note that *not all* could in fact mean that the quantity is 0 percent, which distinguishes it from other weak quantity modifiers. Therefore, *not all* can be replaced with *some are not*. For example,

> ***Not all* Leonardo da Vinci's paintings are famous.**

This can be rewritten as

> ***Some* of Leonardo da Vinci's paintings *are not* famous.**

This can be diagrammed as

> LDV's Paintings ^{S}—^{S} ~~Famous~~

A NOT ALL statement is just a SOME statement with the necessary condition negated. The necessary condition is always the second term. The NOT ALL statement above can be flipped to read as "Some things that are not famous are Leonardo da Vinci's Paintings."

Special Case — Few and Little

Few and *little* are most commonly used to create SOME statements. For example,

> **A *few* trees in this forest are sycamores.**

This can be diagrammed as

> Trees ^{S}—^{S} Sycamores

> **Candidate X has a *little* experience.**

This can be diagrammed as

> Candidate X ^{S}—^{S} Experience

However, these terms can also be used to create NOT MOST statements. For example,

> ***Few* trees in this forest are sycamores.**

This can be diagrammed as

> Trees ^{M}→ ~~Sycamores~~

> **Candidate X has *little* experience.**

This can be diagrammed as

> Candidate X ^{M}→ ~~Experience~~

The first of the two statements above implies that the majority of trees in the forest are not sycamores. In fact, it could be the case that none of the trees are sycamores. The second statement implies that Candidate X is inexperienced or even has no experience.

Special Case — No

A NO statement is an ALL statement with the necessary condition negated. Again, the necessary condition is always the second term. For example,

_No_ monkey has the ability to fly.

Monkey → ~~Fly~~

This means that 0 percent of monkeys can fly. In other words, "All monkeys do not have the ability to fly."

Inherent Strength Modifier Inferences

As mentioned earlier, degree and quantity vary by strength modifier category. In terms of degree or quantity, SOME statements exceed 0 percent, MOST statements exceed 50 percent, and ALL statements signify 100 percent. As a result, SOME includes both MOST and ALL, and MOST includes ALL. For example,

Can I have some of your potato chips?

In everyday speech, this would simply be a request for a few chips. In the LR section, however, _some_ means more than 0 percent, so this question can be considered a request to take every single chip. The chart below summarizes the proportion range of the terms in question.

Strength Modifier Category	Proportion
Strong (ALL)	100%
Strong (NO)	0%
Moderate (MOST)	50%< to 100%
Weak (SOME)	0%< to 100%
Weak (NOT ALL)	0% to <100%

Conjunctions and Disjunctions

Conjunctions and disjunctions are common in the LR section, and it is important to understand their roles. You must also learn how to diagram their relationships.

Conjunctions are terms linked by connector words such as _and_. Both terms in a conjunction must be true. A conjunction is also called an AND statement. Consider this example:

Most of the people in this room are consultants and employees of the company.

This can be diagrammed as

People in Room ᴹ→ Consultants AND Employees of Company

This means that over 50 percent of the people in this room are both a consultant and an employee of the company. Let's consider another example:

Neither tomatoes nor onions were put into the salad.

The neither/nor construction functions as a negative AND statement. When you see "neither A nor B," you can rephrase it as "not A and not B." This can be diagrammed as

Rephrase "neither A nor B" as "not A and not B."

Salad → ~~Tomatoes~~ AND ~~Onions~~

Note that even though there is no conditional indicator, we can easily turn this into an "if . . . then" statement. Is it "If you don't have tomatoes and you don't have onions, then it must be this salad" or "If it is this salad, it doesn't have tomatoes or onions"? It is obviously the latter.

Disjunctions are terms linked by connector words such as *or*. One or both of the terms in a disjunction must be true. A disjunction is also called an OR statement. Here is an example:

My workout today could be either push-ups or pull-ups.

This can be diagrammed as

Disjunctions always include the possibility of selecting both options.

Workout → Push-Ups OR Pull-Ups

In everyday speech, this statement would mean that only one of the two exercise options—push-ups or pull-ups—could be part of the workout. But in formal logic, both of the items in a disjunction can be true. Thus, there are three options for the workout: just push-ups, just pull-ups, or both push-ups and pull-ups. It helps to think of *or* as meaning *at least one*.

Special Case – But Not Both

To indicate that only one of two terms can be true, *but not both* is used. Here is an example:

My choice for dinner will be either steak or lobster, but not both.

This means that steak or lobster can be chosen, but not both. It also indicates that one or the other of the options must be chosen. This statement can be broken down into two parts:

Dinner → Steak OR Lobster

Dinner → ~~Steak~~ OR ~~Lobster~~

The first statement indicates that dinner must include at least one of the options while the second statement indicates that dinner must not include at least one of the options. Therefore, we can diagram the complete *but not both* statement as

But not both rarely appears in the LR section, but it has begun appearing more frequently in the Analytical Reasoning section.

Dinner → (Steak OR Lobster) AND (~~Steak~~ OR ~~Lobster~~)

These types of statements rarely appear in the LR section, but you still need to familiarize yourself with them.

Diagram each of the following statements.

1. Many small towns lack both a nightclub and a movie theater.

   _____

2. Practice usually makes perfect unless you practice wrong.

   _____

3. You will recover from your fever and feel better without going to the doctor's office.

   _____

4. If you wear a tie or comb your hair, then you probably won't look unpresentable.

   _____

5. Almost all of the food was eaten by Tomas.

   _____

6. The radio show generally features neither a rapper nor an auctioneer.

   _____

7. Let's go to either the movies or play mini golf tonight, but not both.

   _____

8. Several of Janice's close friends are cats.

   _____

9. Not all waterbeds are comfortable.

   _____

Drill: Strength Modifiers and Conjunctions/Disjunctions — Answers

1. **Many small towns lack both a nightclub and a movie theater.**

   Small Towns ^{S}—^{S} ~~Nightclub~~ AND ~~Movie Theater~~

   Many is a weak quantity modifier, which means that this is a SOME statement. We also have a conjunction. The two terms connected by *and* must be negated because they are preceded by *lack*. This statement can be flipped to read "Some places that do not have a nightclub and do not have a movie theater are small towns."

2. **Practice usually makes perfect unless you practice wrong.**

   ~~Practice Wrong~~ ^{M}→ Practice Makes Perfect

   Unless is a negative sufficient indicator, meaning that we must negate the part that follows and put it on the left side of the diagram. Also included is *usually*, which is a moderate degree modifier, meaning that this is a MOST statement. We can rephrase this statement as "If you do not practice wrong, then practice usually makes perfect."

3. **You will recover from your fever and feel better without going to the doctor's office.**

   ~~Going to Doctor~~ → Recover from Fever AND Feel Better

   Without is a negative sufficient indicator, so we must negate the part that follows it and put this on the left side of the diagram. There is also a conjunction in this statement.

4. **If you wear a tie or comb your hair, then you probably won't look unpresentable.**

   Wear Tie OR Comb Hair ^{M}→ ~~Look Unpresentable~~

   We have a standard "if . . . then" structure here. *Probably* is a moderate degree indicator, which makes this a MOST statement. The sufficient condition includes a disjunction.

5. **Almost all of the food was eaten by Tomas.**

   Food ^{M}→ Eaten by Tomas

   Almost all is a moderate quantity modifier, which makes this a MOST statement. The statement could be rephrased as "Most of the food was eaten by Tomas."

6. **The radio show generally features neither a rapper nor an auctioneer.**

   Radio Show ^{M}→ ~~Rapper~~ AND ~~Auctioneer~~

   Generally is a moderate degree modifier, which makes this a MOST statement. Due to the neither/nor structure, both terms in the conjunction must be negated.

7. **Let's go to either the movies or play mini golf tonight, but not both.**

   Tonight → (Movies OR Mini Golf) AND (~~Movies~~ OR ~~Mini Golf~~)

"Either . . . or . . . but not both" indicates that one option has to be picked, and that doing so precludes picking the other. This statement can be rephrased as "At least one is chosen and at least one is not chosen." *Tonight* is the sufficient condition because performing one of these activities does not necessarily mean that it is currently tonight. These activities could be done on other nights. However, if it is currently tonight, then at least one of the two activities, but not both, is being performed.

8. **Several of Janice's close friends are cats.**

   Janice's Friends ^{S}—^{S} **Cats**

   Several is a weak quantity modifier, which makes this a SOME statement. It can be expressed as either "Some of Janice's close friends are cats" or "Some cats are Janice's close friends."

9. **Not all waterbeds are comfortable.**

   Waterbeds ^{S}—^{S} ~~**Comfortable**~~

   Not all is a special weak quantity modifier in that it negates the second term. *Not all* means *some are not*. Therefore, this SOME statement can be read as "Some waterbeds are not comfortable" or, when flipped, "Some things that are not comfortable are waterbeds."

Conditional Statement Inferences

We have considered the structures of conditional statements and learned how best to identify and diagram them. We have also examined strength modifiers, conjunctions, and disjunctions. We will now begin applying our knowledge of these concepts to LR questions. Conditional statements are important on account of the inferences that can be drawn from them. An inference is a logical conclusion that follows from one or more conditional statements. Valid inferences often help with determining correct answer choices and avoiding trap answer choices, which are often based on invalid inferences. Now that we are able to identify and diagram conditional statements, we can use them to make inferences. In this section, we will examine affirmation, combination, contraposition, and strength modifier inferences.

Affirmation

The most basic type of inference is conditional affirmation. In this case, when a sufficient condition is satisfied, the necessary condition is satisfied as a result. A common mistake among LSAT test-takers is assuming that the sufficient condition has been met when it has not. For example,

If Sarah becomes a librarian, she will pick up reading as a habit.

What can we conclude from this? If the prompt asks us what must be true, the correct answer cannot be "Sarah will pick up reading as a habit." We cannot say for certain that this will happen. What if Sarah chooses not to become a librarian? Thus, we cannot conclude that Sarah will pick up reading as a habit because we do not know if the sufficient condition has been met. In order for us to infer that Sarah will pick up reading as a habit, we need to know that the sufficient condition—Sarah becoming a librarian—has been satisfied.

Combination

LR questions often contain more than one conditional statement. When they do, the conditional statements almost always relate to one another somehow. The most basic way to combine conditional statements is to create a logic chain. For this to be done, the sufficient condition of an ALL statement must be identical to the necessary condition of another ALL statement. For example,

All of my classmates are math majors. Math majors enjoy solving equations.

This can be diagrammed as

    Classmates → Math Majors
    Math Majors → Enjoy Solving Equations

The sufficient condition in the second statement (Math Majors) is identical to the necessary condition in the first statement. Therefore, we can create a logic chain:

    Classmates → Math Majors → Enjoy Solving Equations

If you are my classmate, you are a math major, and if you are a math major, you enjoy solving equations. We can shorten this by stating that if you are my classmate, you enjoy solving equations, or

Classmates → Enjoy Solving Equations

This is a valid inference. Note that these are ALL statements. A logic chain cannot be created if one or both of the statements are SOME statements. Neither can a logic chain be created with two MOST statements. However, it is possible to combine an ALL and a MOST statement to create a logic chain, a process that is discussed in detail later in this chapter (in Strength Modifier Inferences).

Contraposition

Being able to find the contrapositive of a conditional statement is essential to success on the LR section. Usually, to determine the contrapositive of a conditional statement, the sufficient and necessary conditions must be flipped and negated to create a logically equivalent statement. For example,

To live in Miami, you must live in Florida.

Must indicates a necessary condition, so we know that living in Florida is a necessary condition resulting from living in Miami. This can be diagrammed as

Miami → Florida

If you live in Miami, it must be true that you also live in Florida. What else can we figure out from this? Let's try flipping and negating the conditional statement. First, we flip it:

Florida → Miami

Then we negate both sides:

~~Florida → Miami~~

We can read this as "If you do not live in Florida, then you do not live in Miami." This is a valid inference that follows from our original conditional statement. How can you live in Miami if you do not live in Florida? Because we cannot meet the necessary condition (of living in Florida), we cannot meet the sufficient condition (of living in Miami). When a necessary condition is negated, the sufficient condition must also be negated. Let's look at a more complex example:

The only way to get good grades on a school exam is to study hard or cheat off a smart neighbor.

As explained previously, *only* is a necessary indicator that often modifies a word that directly refers to the necessary condition. In this example, *only* modifies *way*, which refers to studying hard or cheating off a smart neighbor. *Way* does not refer to getting good grades on an exam. Therefore, the disjunction is in the necessary condition and getting good grades is the sufficient condition.

Good Exam Grade → Study Hard OR Cheat Off Neighbor

As there is a disjunction in the necessary condition, finding the contrapositive is tricky. Assume we simply flipped and negated the statement as we did previously:

~~Study Hard OR Cheat Off Neighbor → Good Exam Grade~~

This reads "If you don't study hard or you don't cheat off your neighbor,

> When finding the contrapositive of a conditional statement that contains a conjunction or disjunction, we must negate the AND to an OR or vice versa.

you won't be able to get a good exam grade." This is not a valid inference because a disjunction in the sufficient condition results in only one part (not studying hard or not cheating off a neighbor) being needed to trigger the necessary condition, not both. So, this inference could mean that a student who does not study hard will not receive a good exam grade. But not studying hard does not preclude the student from cheating off a neighbor. A valid inference must state that both parts of the sufficient condition must be satisfied in order to trigger the necessary condition. This can be expressed as follows:

~~Study Hard~~ AND ~~Cheat Off Neighbor~~ → ~~Good Exam Grade~~

This is a valid inference. But why? According to the original statement, either studying hard or cheating (or both) will result in a good grade. Therefore, it follows that if you do not study hard and you do not cheat off your neighbor, you will not get a good grade. We must retain the meaning of the original statement, and both parts of the sufficient condition in the contrapositive must be satisfied for the necessary condition to be triggered.

Therefore, to find the contrapositive, the conjunctions and disjunctions in the conditional statement must be negated as well. An OR statement must be turned into an AND statement, and vice versa. Let's look at another example:

As long as you keep your hand in the air and don't let someone else flag the car down first, you'll be able to hail a taxi.

Hand in Air AND ~~Let Someone Steal~~ → Hail Taxi

If you satisfy both conditions (keeping your hand in the air and not letting someone else nab the taxi in front of you), you'll be able to hail the taxi. Let's flip and negate:

~~Hail Taxi~~ → ~~Hand in Air~~ OR Let Someone Steal

This reads, "If you are not able to hail a taxi, then you must have not kept your hand in the air, or you must have let someone steal your taxi." This is a valid inference. Failure to achieve the necessary condition of hailing the taxi means that one of the parts of the sufficient condition was not satisfied.

Note that all of the previous examples are ALL statements. As was mentioned, it is not possible to find the contrapositive of a MOST or SOME statement. For example,

The majority of pets are not domesticated cats.

This can be diagrammed as

Pets ^{M}→ ~~Cats~~

When this is flipped and negated, we get

Cats ^{M}→ ~~Pets~~

This means that the majority of domesticated cats are not pets, which is not a valid inference because it is not logically equivalent to the original statement. This applies to SOME statements as well.

However, we can find the contrapositive of a biconditional. Consider the following example:

A person is a vegetarian if and only if that person does not eat meat.

This statement can be diagrammed as

Vegetarian ⟷ ~~Eat Meat~~

Since each condition is both sufficient and necessary in a biconditional, the conditions do not need to be flipped to find the contrapositive. It is only necessary to negate them:

~~Vegetarian~~ ⟷ Eat Meat

This statement can be read as both "If you are not a vegetarian, you eat meat" and "If you eat meat, you are not a vegetarian." Both of these are valid inferences.

Flipped Reasoning — Invalid Inferences

Flipped reasoning is a form of fallacious reasoning commonly employed in the LR section to trick test-takers. It appears in arguments and answer choices alike. Flipped reasoning occurs when a conditional statement is flipped but not negated. This results in an invalid inference. Consider the following example:

The warrior beetle has a large thorax and a thick outer skeleton. Any insect with a thick outer skeleton is able to pick up more than 10 times its body weight. Therefore, if an insect can lift 10 times its body weight, it must be a warrior beetle.

There are two conditional statements acting as premises in this argument. The first is

Warrior Beetle → Large Thorax AND Thick Skeleton

The second is

Thick Skeleton → Pick Up >10x Body Weight

Since Thick Skeleton is in the necessary condition of the first premise and the sufficient condition of the first premise, we can infer that

Warrior Beetle → Thick Skeleton → Pick Up >10x Body Weight

or simply

Warrior Beetle → Pick Up >10x Bodyweight

The example above flips this valid inference without negating it to reach the conclusion that "an insect that can lift 10 times its body weight must be a warrior beetle." This can be diagrammed as

Pick Up >10x Bodyweight → Warrior Beetle

To make this a valid inference, it must be negated:

~~Pick Up >10x Bodyweight~~ → ~~Warrior Beetle~~

This reads, "If an insect cannot pick up more than 10 times its bodyweight, it must not be a warrior beetle," which is a valid inference.

Always make sure to both flip AND negate a conditional statement to find the valid contrapositive.

Negated Reasoning — Invalid Inferences

Negated reasoning is also used to trick test-takers. Negated reasoning occurs when the conditional statement is negated but not flipped. For example,

A hero can be considered a superhero only if he or she has a superpower and has no fear of danger.

My friend Jeff, who saved a baby from a burning building, is not a superhero, so it must be the case that he feels fear in the face of danger.

The first premise is a complex conditional statement. It can be diagrammed as

Superhero → Superpower AND ~~Feel Fear of Danger~~

The second premise is that Jeff, who performed a heroic action, is not a superhero. This can be diagrammed as

~~Superhero~~

The argument concludes that because Jeff is not a superhero, he must feel fear in the face of danger. This is negated reasoning. If we negate both sides of the conditional statement without flipping it, we get

~~Superhero~~ → ~~Superpower~~ OR Feel Fear of Danger

Using this negated reasoning, either Jeff does not have a superpower or Jeff feels fear in the face of danger. However, it is perfectly possible that Jeff, while not a superhero, does not feel fear in the face of danger. The correct contrapositive is

~~Superpower~~ OR Feel Fear of Danger → ~~Superhero~~

This reads as "If you do not have a superpower or you feel fear in the face of danger, you must not be a superhero." Jeff may not have a superpower, but that does not mean that he fears danger.

Flipped reasoning and negated reasoning are common on the LSAT. Be wary of these invalid inferences!

Drill: Contraposition

Diagram the contrapositive for each of the following statements.

1. Without a map, there is no way we can find the destination.

   _____

2. Revenue will be increased only if we raise the price of tickets.

   _____

3. If the storm arrives, it will pass through Smithtown, Holly Oaks, or both.

   _____

4. No turkeys can fly for long distances.

   _____

5. Our country will enter a financial crisis if taxes are not raised or expenditures are not decreased.

   _____

6. The only way to enjoy a movie is to watch the whole thing and stay off your phone.

   _____

7. The only way to cure Disease X is with Medication A or Medication B, but not both.

   _____

8. Josh will not be able to fit into his suit for the wedding, unless he goes on a diet.

   _____

9. Our team will lose if and only if our star player Karen is injured.

   _____

Drill: Contraposition — Answers

1. **Without a map, there is no way we can find the destination.**

   Statement: ~~Map~~ → ~~Find Destination~~

   Contrapositive: Find Destination → Map

   Without is a negative sufficient indicator, meaning that whatever it refers to is placed on the left side of the diagram and negated.

2. **Revenue will be increased only if we raise the price of tickets.**

   Statement: Revenue Increase → Raise Ticket Price

   Contrapositive: ~~Raise Ticket Price~~ → ~~Revenue Increase~~

   Only if is a necessary indicator, so what follows *only if* is placed on the right side of the diagram.

3. **If the storm arrives, it will pass through Smithtown, Holly Oaks, or both.**

   Statement: Storm Arrives → Smithtown OR Holly Oaks

   Contrapositive: ~~Smithtown~~ AND ~~Holly Oaks~~ → ~~Storm Arrives~~

   Remember that OR negates to AND, and vice versa.

4. **No turkeys can fly for long distances.**

   Statement: Turkey → ~~Fly Long Distance~~

   Contrapositive: Fly Long Distance → ~~Turkey~~

   No negates the necessary condition.

5. **Our country will enter a financial crisis if taxes are not raised or expenditures are not decreased.**

   Statement: ~~Raise Taxes~~ OR ~~Decrease Expenditures~~ → Financial Crisis

   Contrapositive: ~~Financial Crisis~~ → Raise Taxes AND Decrease Expenditures

   If indicates the sufficient condition, so what follows it is placed on the left side of the diagram.

6. **The only way to enjoy a movie is to watch the whole thing and stay off your phone.**

   Statement: Enjoy Movie → Watch Whole Movie AND Stay Off Phone

   Contrapositive: ~~Watch Whole Movie~~ OR ~~Stay Off Phone~~ → ~~Enjoy Movie~~

   Only is a special necessary indicator. When *only* is used, the necessary condition is often whatever the word modified by *only* refers to. Here, *only* modifies *way*, which refers to the measures that must be taken so as to enjoy a movie: watching the whole thing and staying off your phone. Therefore, this is the necessary condition.

7. **The only way to cure Disease X is with Medication A or Medication B, but not both.**

   Statement: Cure Disease X → (Med A OR Med B) AND (~~Med A~~ OR ~~Med B~~)

Contrapositive: (Med A AND Med B) OR (Med A AND Med B) → Cure Disease X

This is the trickiest problem in the set. *Only* modifies *way*, which refers to *Medication A or Medication B*. Therefore, the latter is the necessary condition. However, the inclusion of *but not both* complicates the situation. To cure Disease X, we must select one of the two medications and not select the other medication. When we find the contrapositive, OR turns to AND, and vice versa.

8. **Josh will not be able to fit into his suit for the wedding, unless he goes on a diet.**

   Statement: Diet → Fit Into Suit

   Contrapositive: Fit Into Suit → Diet

   Unless, like *without*, is a negative sufficient indicator. What follows *unless* is negated and placed on the left side of the diagram.

9. **Our team will lose if and only if our star player Karen is injured.**

   Statement: Team Loses ⟷ Karen Injured

   Contrapositive: Team Loses ⟷ Karen Injured

   If and only if indicates that each condition is both necessary and sufficient, which we denote with a double arrow. Since flipping a biconditional does not affect its meaning, we can simply negate both sides to find the contrapositive.

Strength Modifier Inferences

Earlier in this chapter, we discussed ALL, MOST, and SOME statements and their inherent inferences. Valid inferences can also be made by combining these statements. There are five ways to combine these statements to make valid modifier inferences.

ALL and SOME

This combination is the most commonly tested modifier inference in the LR section. To make a valid inference, the sufficient condition of both statements must be the same. For example,

Some college students drink alcohol. Every college student takes an introductory math class.

These two statements can be diagrammed as

College Students ^{S}—^{S} Drink Alcohol
College Students $\rightarrow$ Take Intro Math

Note how the sufficient condition for both statements is the same. That means that we can conclude a SOME statement from the two necessary conditions. If some college students drink alcohol and all college students take an introductory math course, then it must be the case that some people who drink alcohol are taking an introductory math course:

Drink Alcohol ^{S}—^{S} Take Intro Math

To reiterate, when the sufficient conditions are the same, we can infer a SOME statement from an ALL and a SOME statement.

Let's look at another example:

To be a judge, you must wear a black robe. Many people who wear black robes are magicians.

These statements can be diagrammed as

Judge $\rightarrow$ Black Robe
Black Robe ^{S}—^{S} Magicians

Since the sufficient conditions are not the same, we cannot combine these statements. If we took the contrapositive of the first statement, we would get Black Robe in the sufficient condition, which does not match either. Therefore, we cannot conclude that some judges are magicians. That would be a very interesting yet invalid inference.

Let's consider one last example:

Not many boxers have all of their teeth. People with missing teeth are considered attractive in many cultures.

These statements can be diagrammed as

Boxers ^{S}—^{S} ~~All Teeth~~
~~All Teeth~~ $\rightarrow$ Attractive

At first glance, it seems as if the sufficient conditions are different. However, remember that SOME statements can be flipped without being negated, which is why we do not denote them with an arrow. So, we can flip the first

SOME statement to line up our sufficient conditions.

All Teeth ˢ—ˢ Boxers
All Teeth → Attractive

We can conclude from this that some boxers are considered attractive in many cultures.

ALL and MOST

There are two ways to combine ALL and MOST statements. The first method is similar to that used to combine ALL and SOME statements. When the sufficient conditions are the same, a SOME statement can be inferred. For example,

Most politicians are liars. Mentally sane people do not become politicians.

This can be diagrammed as

Politicians ᴹ→ Liars
Mentally Sane → Politicians

We then find the contrapositive of the second statement to match our sufficient conditions:

Politicians ᴹ→ Liars
Politicians → Mentally Sane

We can then infer that if most politicians are liars and no politicians are mentally sane, then some liars are not mentally sane:

Liars ˢ—ˢ Mentally Sane

It is also possible to infer a MOST statement by combining an ALL and a MOST statement to create a logic chain (discussed earlier in the Combination section). For example,

Criminal lawyers tend to be intelligent. Intelligent people know that learning is a lifelong process.

This can be diagrammed as

Criminal Lawyers ᴹ→ Intelligent
Intelligent → Learning Is Lifelong Process

When the necessary condition of a MOST statement is identical to the sufficient condition of an ALL statement, we can infer a MOST statement. This can be done by creating a logic chain:

Criminal Lawyers ᴹ→ Intelligent → Learning Is Lifelong Process

If most criminal lawyers are intelligent, and all intelligent people know that learning is a lifelong process, then it must be the case that most criminal lawyers know that learning is a lifelong process. This is represented by combining the two ends of the chain.

Criminal Lawyers ᴹ→ Learning is Lifelong Process

This is the only modifier inference that results in a MOST statement, which is an important point to remember.

MOST and MOST

MOST and MOST statements can be combined like ALL and SOME statements. When the sufficient conditions of two MOST statements are the same, a SOME statement can be inferred from the necessary conditions. For example,

Most basketball players are tall. Generally, basketball players can jump high.

This can be diagrammed as

Basketball Players $^M\!\!\rightarrow$ Tall
Basketball Players $^M\!\!\rightarrow$ Jump High

Let's think about this for a moment. If most (over 50 percent of) basketball players are tall and most can also jump high, there must be at least some overlap between the two groups of basketball players. So, it must be the case that at least some people who are tall can jump high, which can be diagrammed as

Tall $^S\!\!-\!\!^S$ Jump High

This is a valid inference drawn from two MOST statements. However, consider the following:

Most sodas are flavored after fruits. Most orders from Benson's fast-food restaurant include sodas.

This is diagrammed as

Soda $^M\!\!\rightarrow$ Fruit-Flavored
Benson Fast-Food Orders $^M\!\!\rightarrow$ Sodas

It may seem like we can combine the two into a logic chain, as follows:

Benson Fast-Food Orders $^M\!\!\rightarrow$ Sodas $^M\!\!\rightarrow$ Fruit-Flavored

However, we cannot infer anything from these MOST statements. Even if, let's say, 90 percent of sodas are fruit-flavored, Benson's may still only serve cola-flavored sodas. We cannot conclude that most or even some orders from Benson's include fruit-flavored sodas.

ALL and ALL

We can combine two ALL statements to get a SOME statement. For example,

Actors will not be cast for this new movie unless they are famous. All of the actors in this movie are good-looking.

This can be diagrammed as

~~Famous~~ $\rightarrow$ ~~Actors in New Movie~~
Actors in New Movie $\rightarrow$ Good-Looking

If we find the contrapositive of the first statement, we end up with two identical sufficient conditions:

Actors in New Movie $\rightarrow$ Famous
Actors in New Movie $\rightarrow$ Good-Looking

Therefore, since we have two identical sufficient conditions, we can infer a SOME statement. It must be the case that some famous people are good-looking, which can be diagrammed as

Famous ^{S}—^{S} Good-Looking

We know this is true because all of the actors in the new movie are both famous and good looking. We cannot say that most or all of the famous people in the world are good-looking, or that most or all of the good-looking people in the world are famous, but because of what we know about the actors in this new movie, we can conclude that some famous people are good-looking and that some good-looking people are famous.

As was discussed in the Combination section of this chapter, two ALL statements can be combined to create a logic chain. Another ALL statement can be inferred by combining the ends of this chain.

No Valid Inferences between MOST and SOME/SOME and SOME

Without additional information, there is no way to combine a MOST and SOME statement to produce a valid inference. For example,

Most Americans own cars. Some Americans have traveled to Antarctica.

This can be diagrammed as

Americans ^{M}→ Own Car
Americans ^{S}—^{S} Antarctica

We cannot conclude that some people who have traveled to Antarctica own cars. It could be the case that every person who has traveled to Antarctica belongs to the minority of Americans who do not own a car. No valid inferences can be drawn between the MOST statement and SOME statement above.

Likewise, no valid inferences can be made between two SOME statements. If we said,

Some fruits are green. Some candies are green.

this could be diagrammed as

Fruits ^{S}—^{S} Green
Candies ^{S}—^{S} Green

Even if we flip both SOME statements to get similar sufficient conditions, no valid inferences follow. It is not the case that some fruits are candies or some candies are fruits, at least based on the information given.

Review: Strength Modifier Inferences

This chart shows the valid and invalid strength modifier combinations and inferences:

		VALID		INVALID
ALL + SOME	✓	$A \rightarrow B$ $\underline{A \; {}^{S}\!\!-\!\!{}^{S} C}$ $B \; {}^{S}\!\!-\!\!{}^{S} C$		$A \rightarrow B$ $\underline{B \; {}^{S}\!\!-\!\!{}^{S} C}$ $A \; {}^{S}\!\!-\!\!{}^{S} C$ ✗
ALL + MOST	✓	$A \xrightarrow{M} B$ $\underline{A \rightarrow C}$ $B \; {}^{S}\!\!-\!\!{}^{S} C$		
	✓	$A \xrightarrow{M} B$ $\underline{B \rightarrow C}$ $A \xrightarrow{M} C$		$A \rightarrow B$ $\underline{B \xrightarrow{M} C}$ $A \xrightarrow{M} C$ ✗
MOST + MOST	✓	$A \xrightarrow{M} B$ $\underline{A \xrightarrow{M} C}$ $B \; {}^{S}\!\!-\!\!{}^{S} C$		$A \xrightarrow{M} B$ $\underline{B \xrightarrow{M} C}$ $A \; {}^{S}\!\!-\!\!{}^{S} C$ ✗
ALL + ALL	✓	$A \rightarrow B$ $\underline{A \rightarrow C}$ $B \; {}^{S}\!\!-\!\!{}^{S} C$		

Drill: Valid Inferences

For each problem, diagram all of the valid inferences that can be drawn from the fact pattern, including contrapositives. If there are no valid inferences, write *None*.

1. Only if we raise the minimum wage will worker pay increase. But if we raise the minimum wage, the cost of consumer goods will increase. When the cost of consumer goods increases, the middle class is hurt.

   _____

   _____

2. Karim is running a marathon on Monday. Karim is usually able to complete the marathon with a good time. When someone is able to complete the marathon with a good time, they receive a medal.

   _____

   _____

3. Some chefs snack on the job. All chefs know how to make delicious pastries.

   _____

   _____

4. Most citizens of Country X adore the president. Generally, the citizens of Country X are avid tennis fans.

   _____

   _____

5. No newborn baby is able to speak in full sentences. Some computer programs are able to speak in full sentences.

   _____

   _____

6. The king always allows his subjects to plead their case, unless they disrespect the crown. Some people who are not allowed to plead their case are verbally abusive.

   _____

   _____

7. Most of the people who enter the raffle don't win anything. Lee just entered the raffle.

   _____

   _____

8. Ivan will not join the chess club only if the dues are expensive. Natasha will join the club if and only if Ivan joins the club. If Natasha joins the club, she will become an enthusiastic chess player.

_____

_____

9. The majority of the world's billionaires live in developed countries. Most people who live in developed countries have running water.

_____

_____

10. Many movies end with a twist. A lot of movies have happy endings.

_____

_____

11. The majority of farmers work hard. The majority of farmers also work long hours. All people who work long hours must be dedicated to their job.

_____

_____

12. All writers use proper grammar. Some people who use proper grammar correct others' grammar.

_____

_____

13. To be an actor, you must have a presentable headshot. Most people with presentable headshots got them from a professional photographer. Without makeup and good light, you cannot have a presentable headshot.

_____

_____

14. Some primates have tremendous upper-body strength. All humans are considered primates. Many primates have sharp canines.

_____

_____

15. Not all salads contain vegetables. If a meal does not contain vegetables, Binh will not eat it.

_____

_____

16. Several of the job applicants to this company have great résumés. No one with less than three years' experience applied for a job with this company. Many of the job applicants spoke multiple languages.

_____

_____

Drill: Valid Inferences — Answers

1. **Only if we raise the minimum wage will worker pay increase. But if we raise the minimum wage, the cost of consumer goods will increase. When the cost of consumer goods increases, the middle class is hurt.**

   Statements: Worker Pay Increase → Raise Minimum Wage

   Raise Minimum Wage → Cost of Goods Increases

   Cost of Goods Increases → Middle Class Hurt

   Inferences: Worker Pay Increase → Middle Class Hurt

   ~~Middle Class Hurt → Worker Pay Increase~~

   This is a basic combination inference involving ALL statements. We can create the chain Worker Pay Increase → Raise Minimum Wage → Cost of Goods Increase → Middle Class Hurt to infer that Worker Pay Increase → Middle Class Hurt. This reads as "If worker pay increases, then the middle class will be hurt."

2. **Karim is running a marathon on Monday. Karim is usually able to complete the marathon with a good time. When someone is able to complete the marathon with a good time, they receive a medal.**

   Statements: Karim $^M\rightarrow$ Complete w/ Good Time

   Complete w/ Good Time → Medal

   Inferences: Karim $^M\rightarrow$ Medal

   Here, the necessary condition of the MOST statement is combined with the sufficient condition of the ALL statement. We can create the chain Karim $^M\rightarrow$ Complete w/ Good Time → Medal, which reads as "Karim usually receives a medal at the marathon."

3. **Some chefs snack on the job. All chefs know how to make delicious pastries.**

   Statements: Chefs ^{S}—^{S} Snack on Job

   Chefs → Delicious Pastries

   Inferences: Snack on Job ^{S}—^{S} Delicious Pastries

   Because the sufficient conditions are the same, we are able to combine the SOME and ALL statements to get "Some people who snack on the job know how to make delicious pastries."

4. **Most citizens of Country X adore the president. Generally, the citizens of Country X are avid tennis fans.**

   Statements: Citizens $^M\rightarrow$ Adore President

   Citizens $^M\rightarrow$ Avid Tennis Fans

   Inferences: Adore President ^{S}—^{S} Avid Tennis Fans

   The sufficient conditions of the two MOST statements are the same, so we can combine the necessary conditions to create a SOME statement that reads "Some people who adore the president are avid tennis fans."

5. **No newborn baby is able to speak in full sentences. Some computer programs are able to speak in full sentences.**

Statements: Newborn Baby → ~~Speak Full Sentences~~

Computer Programs ^S—^S Speak Full Sentences

Inferences: Computer Programs ^S—^S ~~Newborn Baby~~

No negates the necessary condition of the first conditional statement. The contrapositive of the first statement is Speak Full Sentences → ~~Newborn Baby~~. If we flip the second statement (remember, a SOME statement can be flipped without being negated), we end up with two identical sufficient conditions. We can now infer a SOME statement from the two necessary conditions. This can be read as "Some computer programs are not newborn babies."

6. **The king always allows his subjects to plead their case, unless they disrespect the crown. Some people who are not allowed to plead their case are verbally abusive.**

Statements: ~~Disrespect Crown~~ → Plead Case

~~Plead Case~~ ^S—^S Verbally Abusive

Inferences: Disrespect Crown ^S—^S Verbally Abusive

Unless is a negative sufficient indicator, so Disrespect Crown is negated and placed in the sufficient condition position. As with the previous question, by finding the contrapositive of the first statement, we are able to match identical sufficient indicators and infer a SOME statement from the two necessary conditions. This reads as "Some people who disrespect the crown are verbally abusive."

7. **Most of the people who enter the raffle don't win anything. Lee just entered the raffle.**

Statements: Enter Raffle ^M→ ~~Win~~

Lee → Enter Raffle

Inferences: None

We can only make inferences if the necessary condition of the MOST statement is identical to the sufficient condition of the ALL statement or if both sufficient conditions are identical. Neither case applies here. The fact that most people do not win the raffle does not mean that Lee will not win the raffle.

8. **Ivan will not join the chess club only if the dues are expensive. Natasha will join the club if and only if Ivan joins the club. If Natasha joins the club, she will become an enthusiastic chess player.**

Statements: ~~Ivan Joins~~ → Expensive Dues

Natasha Joins ⟷ Ivan Joins

Natasha Joins → Natasha Becomes Enthusiastic Chess Player

Inferences: ~~Expensive Dues~~ → Natasha Becomes Enthusiastic Chess Player

~~Natasha Becomes Enthusiastic Chess Player~~ → Expensive Dues

The presence of *if and only if* in the second statement indicates that it is a biconditional. By finding the contrapositive of the first statement, we can create the following logic chain: ~~Expensive Dues~~ → Ivan Joins → Natasha Joins → Natasha Becomes Enthusiastic Chess Player. Questions in the LR section tend to focus on inferences that result from combining the ends of a logic chain. The main inference reads, "If dues are not expensive, then Natasha will become an enthusiastic chess player."

9. **The majority of the world's billionaires live in developed countries. Most people who live in developed countries have running water.**

Statements: World's Billionaires $^M\!\!\rightarrow$ Live in Developed Countries

Live in Developed Countries $^M\!\!\rightarrow$ Running Water

Inferences: None

To combine two MOST statements, it is necessary for the sufficient conditions to match. Therefore, there are no possible inferences here.

10. **Many movies end with a twist. A lot of movies have happy endings.**

Statements: Movies $^S\!\!-\!\!^S$ End w/ Twist

Movies $^S\!\!-\!\!^S$ Happy Ending

Inferences: None

Many and *a lot* indicate SOME statements. We are unable to infer anything from two SOME statements.

11. **The majority of farmers work hard. The majority of farmers also work long hours. All people who work long hours must be dedicated to their job.**

Statements: Farmers $^M\!\!\rightarrow$ Work Hard

Farmers $^M\!\!\rightarrow$ Work Long Hours

Work Long Hours $\rightarrow$ Dedicated to Job

Inferences: Work Hard $^S\!\!-\!\!^S$ Work Long Hours

Farmers $^M\!\!\rightarrow$ Dedicated to Job

Dedicated to Job $^S\!\!-\!\!^S$ Work Hard

Dedicated to Job $^S\!\!-\!\!^S$ Work Long Hours

Here, we can combine the first two MOST statements to infer a SOME statement. Next, we can combine the necessary condition of the second MOST statement with the sufficient condition of the ALL statement to infer a MOST statement. We can then combine the second inference and with the first and second statements to get our third and fourth inferences. The inferences, respectively, read as, "Some people who work hard work long hours," "Most farmers are dedicated to their job," "Some people who are dedicated to their job work hard," and "Some people who are dedicated to their job work long hours."

12. **All writers use proper grammar. Some people who use proper grammar correct others' grammar.**

Statements: Writers $\rightarrow$ Use Proper Grammar

Use Proper Grammar $^S\!\!-\!\!^S$ Correct Others' Grammar

Inferences: None

ALL and SOME statements can only be combined if their sufficient conditions match. That is not the case here.

13. **To be an actor, you must have a presentable headshot. Most people with presentable headshots got them from a professional photographer. Without makeup and good lighting, you cannot have a presentable headshot.**

Statements: Actor $\rightarrow$ Presentable Headshot

Presentable Headshot $^M\!\!\rightarrow$ Professional Photographer

~~Makeup OR Good Lighting~~ $\rightarrow$ ~~Presentable Headshot~~

Inferences: Professional Photographer $^S\!\!-\!\!^S$ Makeup AND Good Lighting

The first two statements cannot be combined because the MOST statement's necessary condition does not match the ALL statement's sufficient condition. In addition, these statements' sufficient conditions do not match. Be careful diagramming the third statement, as *without* is a negative sufficient indicator. So, it not only negates the terms in the sufficient condition but also negates AND to OR. The contrapositive of the third statement is Presentable Headshot → Makeup AND Good Lighting. Since this sufficient condition matches that of the second statement, we can infer a SOME statement from the two necessary conditions that reads, "Some professional photographers make use of makeup and lighting."

14. **Some primates have tremendous upper-body strength. All humans are considered primates. Many primates have sharp canines.**

    Statements: Primates ^{S}—^{S} Tremendous Upper Body Strength

    Humans → Primates

    Primates ^{S}—^{S} Sharp Canines

    Inferences: None

    We cannot combine an ALL statement with a SOME statement unless the sufficient conditions are identical, which is not the case here. Additionally, a set of SOME statements can never yield a valid inference.

15. **Not all salads contain vegetables. If a meal does not contain vegetables, Binh will not eat it.**

    Statements: Salads ^{S}—^{S} ~~Vegetables~~

    ~~Vegetables~~ → ~~Binh~~

    Inferences: Salads ^{S}—^{S} ~~Binh~~

    A NOT ALL statement is a SOME statement with the second term negated. We can flip the first statement so that ~~Vegetables~~ is the sufficient condition for both statements, which allows us to infer a SOME statement from the two necessary conditions. This reads, "Some salads will not be eaten by Binh."

16. **Several of the job applicants to this company have great résumés. No one with less than three years' experience applied for a job with this company. Many of the job applicants spoke multiple languages.**

    Statements: Job Applicants ^{S}—^{S} Great Résumés

    < 3 Years' Experience → ~~Job Applicants~~

    Job Applicants ^{S}—^{S} Spoke Multiple Languages

    Inferences: Great Résumés ^{S}—^{S} ~~< 3 Years' Experience~~

    Spoke Multiple Languages ^{S}—^{S} ~~< 3 Years' Experience~~

    The first sentence is a SOME statement. *No* negates the necessary condition of the second statement. The contrapositive of the second statement is Job Applicants → ~~< 3 Years' Experience~~. Now the sufficient conditions of all three statements match. We cannot combine the two SOME statements, but when the sufficient conditions of an ALL and a SOME statement are identical, we can infer a SOME statement from the two necessary conditions. We can combine the first statement with the second and the second statement with the third to get "Some people with great résumés do not have less than three years' experience" and "Some people who speak multiple languages do not have less than three years' experience."

Problem Set: Conditional Statements

Now it is time to try your hand at some actual LR questions. All of these questions have appeared on previous administrations of the LSAT. These questions are very challenging, and you will have to apply all of the skills you have learned in this chapter to solve them.

1. Biologist: We know the following things about plant X. Specimens with fuzzy seeds always have long stems but never have white flowers. Specimens with curled leaves always have white flowers, and specimens with thorny seedpods always have curled leaves. A specimen of plant X in my garden has a long stem and curled leaves.

   From the biologist's statements, which one of the following can be properly inferred about the specimen of plant X in the biologist's garden?

   (A) It has white flowers and thorny seedpods.
   (B) It has white flowers but lacks thorny seedpods.
   (C) It has white flowers but lacks fuzzy seeds.
   (D) It has fuzzy seeds and thorny seedpods.
   (E) It lacks both white flowers and fuzzy seeds.

2. Many successful graphic designers began their careers after years of formal training, although a significant number learned their trade more informally on the job. But no designer ever became successful who ignored the wishes of a client.

   If all of the statements above are true, which one of the following must also be true?

   (A) All graphic designers who are unsuccessful have ignored the wishes of a client.
   (B) Not all formally trained graphic designers ignore client's wishes.
   (C) The more attentive a graphic designer is to a client's wishes, the more likely the designer is to be successful.
   (D) No graphic designers who learn their trade on the job will ignore client's wishes.
   (E) The most successful graphic designers learn their trade on the job.

3. Ethicist: Every moral action is the keeping of an agreement, and keeping an agreement is nothing more than an act of securing mutual benefit. Clearly, however, not all instances of agreement-keeping are moral actions. Therefore, some acts of securing mutual benefit are not moral actions.

   The pattern of reasoning in which one of the following arguments is most similar to that in the ethicist's argument?

   (A) All calculators are kinds of computer, and all computers are devices for automated reasoning. However, not all devices for automated reasoning are calculators. Therefore, some devices for automated reasoning are not computers.
   (B) All exercise is beneficial, and all things that are beneficial promote health. However, not all things that are beneficial are forms of exercise. Therefore, some exercise does not promote health.
   (C) All metaphors are comparisons, and not all comparisons are surprising. However, all metaphors are surprising. Therefore, some comparisons are not metaphors.
   (D) All architecture is design and all design is art. However, not all design is architecture. Therefore, some art is not design.
   (E) All books are texts, and all texts are documents. However, not all texts are books. Therefore, some documents are not books.

4. All parrots can learn to speak a few words and phrases. Not all parrots have equally pleasant dispositions, though some of those native to Australia can be counted on for a sweet temper. Almost any parrot, however, will show tremendous affection for an owner who raised the bird from a chick by hand-feeding it.

If the statements above are true, then which one of the following must be true?

(A) Some parrots that can learn to speak are sweet tempered.
(B) If a parrot is not native to Australia, then it will be sweet tempered only if it is hand-fed as a chick.
(C) The sweetest-tempered parrots are those native to Australia.
(D) Australia is the only place where one can find birds that can both learn to speak and be relied on for a sweet temper.
(E) All species of pet birds that are native to Australia can be counted on for a sweet temper.

5. All highly successful salespersons are both well organized and self-motivated, characteristics absent from many salespersons who are not highly successful. Further, although only those who are highly successful are well known among their peers, no salespersons who are self-motivated regret their career choices.

If all of the statements above are true, which one of the following must be true?

(A) No self-motivated salespersons who are not highly successful are well organized.
(B) All salespersons who are well organized but not highly successful are self-motivated.
(C) No salespersons who are well known among their peers regret their career choices.
(D) All salespersons who are not well organized regret their career choices.
(E) All salespersons who do not regret their career choices are highly successful.

6. "Good hunter" and "bad hunter" are standard terms in the study of cats. Good hunters can kill prey that weigh up to half their body weight. All good hunters have a high muscle-to-fat ratio. Most wild cats are good hunters, but some domestic cats are good hunters as well.

If the statements above are true, which one of the following must also be true?

(A) Some cats that have a high muscle-to-fat ratio are not good hunters.
(B) A smaller number of domestic cats than wild cats have a high muscle-to-fat ratio.
(C) All cats that are bad hunters have a low muscle-to-fat ratio.
(D) Some cats that have a high muscle-to-fat ratio are domestic.
(E) All cats that have a high muscle-to-fat ratio can kill prey that weigh up to half their body weight.

1. **Correct Answer (C).** *Prep Test 40, Section 1, Question 24.*

The first step is to read the prompt and identify this as an MBT question based on the words *properly inferred*. This question type is discussed in more detail in the next chapter. For now, simply note that the prompt asks which of the answer choices contains information that must be true about the specimen of plant X in the garden. The stimulus includes a fact pattern with multiple conditional statements, and these need to be diagrammed. Here are the conditional statements, in order of appearance:

Conditional Statement 1: Specimens with fuzzy seeds always have long stems
Conditional Statement 2: Specimens with fuzzy seeds never have white flowers
Conditional Statement 3: Specimens with curled leaves always have white flowers
Conditional Statement 4: Specimens with thorny seedpods always have curled leaves

We can diagram these conditional statements as follows:

> S1: Fuzzy Seeds → Long Stems
> S2: Fuzzy Seeds → ~~White Flowers~~
> S3: Curled Leaves → White Flowers
> S4: Thorny Seedpods → Curled Leaves

We are concerned about what is true regarding the specimen of plant X in the garden. We know that it has long stems and curled leaves, so we should focus on the conditional statements that mention these features first and look for any inferences we can make that will provide us with additional information.

The first conditional statement has Long Stems as its necessary condition. However, we need Long Stems as the sufficient condition to learn anything about the specimen in the garden. We can flip the necessary and sufficient conditions, but then we have to negate both. This gives us the contrapositive ~~Long Stems~~ → ~~Fuzzy Seeds~~. So, if plant X does not have long stems, it does not have fuzzy seeds. However, this information does not help us because we know that the specimen in the garden has long stems.

Let's turn to the statements that mention curled leaves. The fourth statement has the same problem as the first one—Curled Leaves is the necessary condition. Finding the contrapositive of this statement will not help us. However, Curled Leaves is the sufficient condition of the third statement. This provides us with new information. If plant X has curled leaves, it has white flowers. Therefore, we now know the specimen in the garden has white flowers.

This is not enough to find the correct answer choice. However, the contrapositive of the second statement is White Flowers → ~~Fuzzy Seeds~~. This means that the specimen in the garden does not have fuzzy seeds.

We should therefore anticipate a correct answer choice involving white flowers but no fuzzy seeds, and this turns out to be answer choice (C). As we know which terms must be included in the correct answer choice, there is no need to go through all of the answer choices.

2. **Correct Answer (B).** *Prep Test 41, Section 1, Question 21.*

This is also an MBT question, and the stimulus includes a fact pattern with conditional statements. Here are the conditional statements, in order of appearance:

Conditional Statement 1: Many successful graphic designers . . . formal training
Conditional Statement 2: Although a significant number . . . more informally on the job
Conditional Statement 3: No designer ever became successful who ignored the . . . client

The first statement includes the weak quantity modifier *many*, which means it is a SOME statement. The next statement is also a SOME statement as it includes the modifier *significant number*. Lastly, the *no* in our third statement functions as a strong quantity modifier that negates the necessary condition.

We can diagram these three conditional statements as follows:

> S1: Successful Designers ^{S}—^{S} Formal Training
> S2: Successful Designers ^{S}—^{S} Informal Training
> S3: Successful Designers → ~~Ignore Wishes of Client~~

Although all three statements have the same sufficient condition, the two SOME statements cannot be combined. However, we can combine a SOME statement and an ALL statement. Combining the first and third statements gives us the inference ~~Ignore Wishes of Client~~ ^{S}—^{S} Formal Training. This reads as, "Some designers who do not ignore the wishes of a client have formal training." Combining the second and third statements results in ~~Ignore Wishes of Client~~ ^{S}—^{S} Informal Training. We now have two inferences, and we should anticipate these as possible correct answer choices.

As both inferences are SOME statements, the correct answer choice must be a SOME statement as well. This means that any answer choice with an ALL or MOST statement can be eliminated. A savvy test-taker would scan the answers, identify (B) as the only answer choice that contains a SOME statement, select it, and move on. However, we will go over each answer choice for the sake of practice.

(A) All graphic designers who are unsuccessful have ignored the wishes of a client.

This can be diagrammed as ~~Successful Designers~~ → Ignore Wishes of Client. This is an invalid inference drawn from the third statement, based on negated reasoning. The contrapositive of the third statement is actually Ignore Client Wishes → ~~Successful Designers~~. This is a loser.

(B) Not all formally trained graphic designers ignore client's wishes.

This matches one of our anticipated answer choices. Remember that a NOT ALL statement is a SOME statement with the necessary condition negated. This can be diagrammed as Formal Training ^{S}—^{S} ~~Ignore Wishes of Client~~. This is a candidate.

(C) The more attentive a graphic designer is to a client's wishes, the more likely the designer is to be successful.

This is not a conditional statement but a relational statement. *The more attentive* and *the more likely* are relational terms and are not mentioned in the stimulus. This is another loser.

(D) No graphic designers who learn their trade on the job will ignore client's wishes.

No negates the necessary condition, so this can be diagrammed as Informal Training → ~~Ignore Wishes of Client~~. As an ALL statement that does not match our anticipated answers, this is another loser.

(E) The most successful graphic designers learn their trade on the job.

This is another relational statement as it contains *the most successful*. The only categories discussed in the fact pattern are *successful* and *unsuccessful*. In addition, there is no indication that the most successful designers learn their trade informally. This is also a loser.

As (B) is the only candidate, it must be the correct answer choice.

3. **Correct Answer (E).** *Prep Test 57, Section 3, Question 20.*

This is a PR question. If it took you a very long time to solve, don't worry. PR questions tend to require more time than other question types. Additionally, this is a very difficult question. PR questions ask you not only to identify the structure of an argument but also to find an answer choice with an equivalent structure. The argument includes several conditional statements that function as premises as well as a conclusion:

Premise 1: Every moral action is the keeping of an agreement
Premise 2: The keeping of an agreement is . . . act of securing mutual benefit
Premise 3: Not all instances of agreement-keeping are moral actions
Conclusion: Some acts of securing mutual benefit are not moral actions

These can be diagrammed as

> P1: Moral Action → Keeping Agreement
> P2: Keeping Agreement → Securing Mutual Benefit
> P3: Keeping Agreement ^{S}—^{S} ~~Moral Actions~~
> _____
> C: Securing Mutual Benefits ^{S}—^{S} ~~Moral Actions~~

Note that the conclusion only depends on combining the second and third premises. Since the sufficient conditions of the ALL statement and the SOME statement are the same, we can infer a SOME statement from the necessary conditions, which is what the argument concludes. Therefore, this is a valid argument.

We now need to identify the answer choice by finding an argument that has the same structure. Representing an argument in an abstract manner often makes it easier to understand its underlying structure. The premises of this argument can be expressed as follows:

> P1: a → b
> P2: b → c
> P3: b ^{S}—^{S} a
> _____
> C: c ^{S}—^{S} a

The first two premises form the logic chain a → b → c. The third is a SOME statement, and the conclusion is a SOME statement inferred from the second and third premises. It is difficult to anticipate an answer choice for this type of question. The next step is to separate the answer choices into candidates and losers. Any answer choice that includes a MOST statement or that does not have two ALL statements and two SOME statements would be a loser. As none of the answer choices meet these criteria, we have to go through them one by one.

(A) **All calculators are kinds of computer, and all computers are devices for automated reasoning. However, not all devices for automated reasoning are calculators. Therefore, some devices for automated reasoning are not computers.**

> P1: Calculators (a) → Computers (b)
> P2: Computers (b) → Automated Reasoning (c)
> P3: Automated Reasoning (c) ^{S}—^{S} ~~Calculators (a)~~
> _____
> C: Automated Reasoning (c) ^{S}—^{S} ~~Computers (b)~~

Not only does this argument have a different structure, but it is also invalid. There is no way to conclude a SOME statement about ~~Computers~~. Since the argument in the stimulus is valid, the correct answer choice must also be valid. This is a loser.

(B) **All exercise is beneficial, and all things that are beneficial promote health. However, not all things that are beneficial are forms of exercise. Therefore, some exercise does not promote health.**

P1: Exercise (a) → Beneficial (b)
P2: Beneficial (b) → Promote Health (c)
P3: Beneficial (b) ^S—^S ~~Exercise~~ (a)
C: Exercise (a) ^S—^S ~~Promote Health~~ (c)

This is almost what we want, but it is invalid. Because the second and third premises have the same sufficient indicator, a SOME statement can be inferred between the two necessary conditions: Promote Health ^S—^S ~~Exercise~~. The conclusion in this argument negates this valid inference. This is a loser.

(C) All metaphors are comparisons, and not all comparisons are surprising. However, all metaphors are surprising. Therefore, some comparisons are not metaphors.

P1: Metaphors (a) → Comparisons (b)
P2: Comparisons (b) ^S—^S ~~Surprising~~ (c)
P3: Metaphors (a) → Surprising (c)
C: Comparisons (b) ^S—^S ~~Metaphors~~ (a)

Although this is a valid argument, the first three terms do not connect in a logic chain like the terms in the original argument. The fact that this answer choice has a different argument structure makes it a loser.

(D) All architecture is design and all design is art. However, not all design is architecture. Therefore, some art is not design.

P1: Architecture (a) → Design (b)
P2: Design (b) → Art (c)
P3: Design (b) ^S—^S ~~Architecture~~ (a)
C: Art (c) ^S—^S ~~Design~~ (b)

Here, the logic chain of a → b → c is intact. However, an invalid inference is made in the conclusion. As the second and third premises have the same sufficient condition, it is possible to conclude that Art ^S—^S ~~Architecture~~. The conclusion that Art ^S—^S ~~Design~~ is invalid, making this an incorrect answer choice. This is another loser.

(E) All books are texts, and all texts are documents. However, not all texts are books. Therefore, some documents are not books.

P1: Books (a) → Texts (b)
P2: Texts (b) → Documents (c)
P3: Texts (b) ^S—^S ~~Books~~ (a)
C: Documents (c) ^S—^S ~~Books~~ (a)

This argument is both valid and matches the structure of the original argument. We have the logic chain a → b → c, and the conclusion is a SOME statement validly inferred from the second and third premises, which have identical sufficient conditions. This is the correct answer choice.

---

4. **Correct Answer (A).** *Prep Test 43, Section 2, Question 22.*

This is an MBT question, and the stimulus includes a fact pattern with conditional statements. These can be diagrammed as follows:

Conditional Statement 1: Parrots → Learn to Speak
Conditional Statement 2: Parrots ^S—^S ~~Good Disposition~~
Conditional Statement 3: Australian Parrots ^S—^S Good Disposition
Implied Relationship: Australian Parrots → Parrots
Conditional Statement 4: Hand Fed from Chick ^M→ Good Disposition

When diagramming conditional statements, the same terms should be used to describe phrases that are almost identical. For example, Good Disposition describes *pleasant dispositions*, *sweet temper*, and *tremendous affection* in the diagrams above. In addition, it is important to take note of and diagram any implied relationships. For this question, we know that if it is an Australian parrot, it is still a type of parrot, so we can diagram this as well.

Now we can begin to look for inferences. The fourth statement is useless to us because its sufficient condition does not match any of the others, and it is not part of a logic chain. As all the other statements are ALL or SOME statements, we should look for ALL statements with identical sufficient or necessary conditions and SOME statements with identical sufficient conditions in order to make valid inferences. By doing this, we can anticipate the following answers:

Anticipated Answer 1

S1: Parrots → Learn to Speak
S2: Parrots ^{S}—^{S} ~~Good Disposition~~
Inf: Learn to Speak ^{S}—^{S} ~~Good Disposition~~

This reads as "Some parrots that can learn to speak do not have good dispositions."

Anticipated Answer 2

S1: Parrots → Learn to Speak
IR: Australian Parrots → Parrots
Inf: Australian Parrots → Learn to Speak
S3: Australian Parrots ^{S}—^{S} Good Disposition
Inf: Learn to Speak ^{S}—^{S} Good Disposition

This reads as "Some parrots that can learn to speak have good dispositions."

The second anticipated answer is a little trickier than the first one. We can link the first statement with the implied relationship to infer Australian Parrots → Learn to Speak. We can then combine this inference with the third statement to infer a SOME statement from the two necessary conditions.

We now have two anticipated answers to look for in the answer choices. Note that the contrapositives of Parrots → Learn to Speak, Australian Parrots → Parrots, Australian Parrots → Learn to Speak, and Hand Fed from Chick ^{M}→ Good Disposition are possible correct answer choices as well. However, when the fact pattern includes complex conditional statements with multiple strength modifiers, simple contrapositives are hardly ever being tested. Let's take a look at the answer choices.

(A) Some parrots that can learn to speak are sweet tempered.

This matches Anticipated Answer 2. The good thing about anticipating answers for MBT questions with conditional language is that when you find a match, there is no point in going through the normal process of separating candidates and losers and then eliminating answers choices. We know for a fact that this must be true, so we can move on. However, for the sake of practice, we will now review the rest of the answer choices.

(B) If a parrot is not native to Australia, then it will be sweet tempered only if it is hand-fed as a chick.

This is a bit tricky to diagram. *Only if* indicates that Hand Fed from Chick is the necessary condition, but what about the sufficient condition? There are a few different elements in the sufficient condition. For the sufficient condition to be triggered, we must have a parrot, but not an Australian parrot, that has a good disposition. This can be diagrammed as

Parrot AND ~~Australian Parrot~~ AND Good Disposition → Hand Fed from Chick

As this cannot be inferred from the fact pattern, it is a loser.

(C) The sweetest-tempered parrots are those native to Australia.

This is a relational statement and therefore cannot be the correct answer to an MBT question involving conditional statements. The fact pattern says that some parrots from Australia are sweet-tempered, but that does not necessarily mean the sweetest parrots on the planet come from Australia. This is far too strong of a statement to be the correct answer choice. This is a loser.

(D) Australia is the only place where one can find birds that can both learn to speak and be relied on for a sweet temper.

Again, this is far too strong. How do we know that Australia is the only place with birds like this? We only know that Australia is one place where there are some parrots with these qualities. This statement can be diagrammed as

Learn to Speak AND Good Disposition → Australia

This cannot be inferred from the fact pattern. This is another loser.

(E) All species of pet birds that are native to Australia can be counted on for a sweet temper.

This statement can be diagrammed as

Australian Pet Birds → Good Disposition.

Even if we substitute Pet Birds for Parrots, this is far too strong. The third proposition only says that some Australian parrots have a good disposition. This is also a loser.

As (A) is the only candidate, it has to be the correct answer choice.

---

5. **Correct Answer (C).** *Prep Test 40, Section 1, Question 22.*

This is another MBT question that includes a fact pattern with conditional statements. These can be diagrammed as follows:

S1: Highly Successful → Well Organized AND Self-Motivated
S2: ~~Highly Successful~~ ˢ—ˢ ~~Well Organized~~ AND ~~Self-Motivated~~
S3: Well Known → Highly Successful
S4: Self-Motivated → ~~Regret Career Choices~~

A few remarks on how this was diagrammed: In the second statement, *characteristics absent* refers to *well organized and self-motivated*, and *many* indicates a SOME statement. In the third statement, *only* modifies *those*, which refers to the necessary condition, *highly successful*. To confirm this is correct, we can create an "if . . . then" statement. Is it "If you are well known, you must be highly successful," or is it "If you are highly successful, you must be well known"? Here, it is the former. Lastly, in the fourth statement, the *no* at the beginning of the sentence negates the necessary condition.

The next step is to combine statements. There are three ALL statements and one SOME statement. The SOME statement shares terms with the contrapositives of the first, third, and fourth statements. However, the contrapositive of the first ALL statement includes a disjunction rather than the conjunction in the SOME statement:

S1: ~~Well Organized~~ OR ~~Self-Motivated~~ → ~~Highly Successful~~
S2: ~~Well Organized~~ AND ~~Self-Motivated~~ ˢ—ˢ ~~Highly Successful~~

Therefore, these statements can be combined. Even if the sufficient conditions were identical, we would only be able to infer that "Some people who are not highly successful are not highly successful," which is obviously useless. We can then move on to combining the SOME statement with the contrapositive of the third ALL statement:

S2: ~~Highly Successful~~ ˢ—ˢ ~~Well Organized~~ AND ~~Self-Motivated~~
S3: ~~Highly Successful~~ → ~~Well Known~~

As the sufficient conditions are identical, we can infer a SOME statement from the necessary conditions. This is that "Some salespersons who are not well organized and not self-motivated are not well known," which can be diagrammed as follows:

~~Well Organized~~ AND ~~Self-Motivated~~ ˢ—ˢ ~~Well Known~~

This is a valid inference.

We should now combine the SOME statement with the contrapositive of the fourth ALL statement:

S2: ~~Well Organized~~ AND ~~Self-Motivated~~ ᔆ—ᔆ ~~Highly Successful~~
S4: Self-Motivated → ~~Regret Career Choices~~

As the sufficient conditions are not identical, we cannot combine these two statements.

We can now turn to the ALL statements. We are looking for identical necessary and sufficient conditions to link these statements together. The link between the first and third statements is easy to spot:

S1: Highly Successful → Well Organized AND Self-Motivated
S3: Well Known → Highly Successful
Logic Chain: Well Known → Highly Successful → Well Organized AND Self-Motivated
Inf: Well Known → Well Organized AND Self-Motivated
Inf: ~~Well Organized~~ OR ~~Self-Motivated~~ → ~~Well Known~~

We can then combine the first inference with the fourth statement:

Inf: Well Known → Well Organized AND Self-Motivated
S4: Self-Motivated → ~~Regret Career Choices~~
Logic Chain: Well Known → Highly Successful → Well Organized AND Self-Motivated → ~~Regret Career Choices~~
Inf: Well Known → ~~Regret Career Choices~~
Inf: Regret Career Choices → ~~Well Known~~

Note that there is a conjunction in the first inference that can be linked to only one of the terms in the fourth statement. This is acceptable when forming a logic chain.

We should anticipate a correct answer choice that states Well Known → ~~Regret Career Choices~~ or its contrapositive, Regret Career Choices → ~~Well Known~~. Note that any of the other inferences we made or their contrapositives could theoretically be the correct answer choice. However, it is common for the LSAT to test an inference based on the ends of a logic chain (especially a complex one such as this). Let's turn to the answer choices now.

(A) No self-motivated salespersons who are not highly successful are well organized.

No negates the necessary condition, and there is a conjunction in the sufficient condition. This can be diagrammed as follows:

Self-Motivated AND ~~Highly Successful~~ → ~~Well Organized~~

The only thing we know about people who are not well organized (through the contrapositive of the first proposition) is that they are not highly successful. This answer choice is a result of flipped reasoning. Additionally, being self-motivated does not correspond to not being well organized. Therefore, this is a loser.

(B) All salespersons who are well organized but not highly successful are self-motivated.

The sufficient condition is indicated by *all* and includes a conjunction. This can be diagrammed as follows:

Well Organized AND ~~Highly Successful~~ → Self-Motivated

This is similar to the previous answer choice. The only way to have Well Organized or ~~Highly Successful~~ as the sufficient condition is to form the contrapositive of the third proposition, which allows us to infer that if you are not highly successful, you are not well known among your peers. This does not match (B), so (B) is a loser.

(C) No salespersons who are well known among their peers regret their career choices.

This matches our anticipated answer choice. *No* negates the necessary condition, which can be diagrammed as follows:

Well Known → ~~Regret Career Choices~~

This is a candidate.

(D) All salespersons who are not well organized regret their career choices.

This can be diagrammed as follows:

~~Well Organized~~ → Regret Career Choices

Regret Career Choices cannot be the necessary condition; only ~~Regret Career Choices~~ can. Additionally, the only inference that can be made about salespersons who are not well organized is that they are not highly successful and thus (from the contrapositive of the third proposition) not well known among their peers. Therefore, this answer choice is a loser.

(E) All salespersons who do not regret their career choices are highly successful.

This can be diagrammed as follows:

~~Regret Career Choices~~ → Highly Successful

The full logic chain of the fact pattern is

Well Known → Highly Successful → Well Organized AND Self-Motivated → ~~Regret Career Choices~~

Therefore, we know that Highly Successful → ~~Regret Career Choices~~. This answer choice is the flipped version of a valid inference. It is a loser.

As (C) is the only candidate, it has to be the correct answer choice.

---

6. **Correct Answer (D).** *Prep Test 54, Section 2, Question 16.*

This is another MBT question that includes a fact pattern with conditional statements. We can diagram this fact pattern as follows:

S1: Good Hunters → Kill Prey Half Bodyweight
S2: Good Hunters → High Muscle-Fat Ratio
S3: Wild Cats ^{M}→ Good Hunters
S4: Domestic Cats ^{S}—^{S} Good Hunters

The conditional statements here are relatively easy to diagram, but the first one may be tricky because of a lack of indicator words. It is best to convert it into an "if . . . then" statement, which reads as "If they are good hunters, they must be able to kill prey up to half of their bodyweight."

After diagramming these conditional statements, our next step is to combine them. There are ALL, MOST, and SOME statements, so all five ways to make inferences with strength modifiers must be considered. It is also possible to form logic chains with ALL statements. Let's look at each inference that can be made:

S1: Good Hunters → Kill Prey Half Bodyweight S2: Good Hunters → High Muscle-Fat Ratio Inf: Kill Prey Half Bodyweight ^{S}—^{S} High Muscle-Fat Ratio This inference reads as "Some things that can kill prey up to half of their bodyweight have a high muscle-to-fat ratio."	We can infer a SOME statement from the necessary conditions of the two ALL statements with identical sufficient conditions.

S1: Good Hunters → Kill Prey Half Bodyweight S3: Wild Cats ^{M}→ Good Hunters Inf: Wild Cats ^{M}→ Kill Prey Half Bodyweight This inference reads as "Most wild cats can kill prey up to half of their bodyweight."	We can infer a MOST statement from the sufficient condition of the ALL statement and the necessary condition of the MOST statement because these are identical.

S2: Good Hunters → High Muscle-Fat Ratio S3: Wild Cats ^{M}→ Good Hunters Inf: Wild Cats ^{M}→ High Muscle-Fat Ratio This inference reads as "Most wild cats have high muscle-to-fat ratios."	Again, we can infer a MOST statement from the sufficient condition of the ALL statement and the necessary condition of the MOST statement because these are identical.

S1: Good Hunters → Kill Prey Half Bodyweight S4: Domestic Cats ^{S}—^{S} Good Hunters Inf: Domestic Cats ^{S}—^{S} Kill Prey Half Bodyweight This inference reads as "Some domestic cats can kill prey up to half of their bodyweight."	If we flip the SOME statement, its sufficient condition matches that of the ALL statement. We can then infer a SOME statement from the necessary conditions.

S1: Good Hunters → High Muscle-Fat Ratio S4: Domestic Cats ^{S}—^{S} Good Hunters Inf: Domestic Cats ^{S}—^{S} High Muscle-Fat Ratio This inference reads as "Some domestic cats have a high muscle-to-fat ratio."	Again, we can flip the SOME statement so that its sufficient condition matches that of the ALL statement. We can then infer a SOME statement from the necessary conditions.

We now have five inferences that we can anticipate seeing in the answer choices.

(A) Some cats that have a high muscle-to-fat ratio are not good hunters.

This can be diagrammed as follows:

High Muscle-Fat Ratio ^{S}—^{S} ~~Good Hunters~~

While this may be true, it is not inferable from our conditional statements. The second statement says that all good hunters have a high muscle-to-fat ratio. Therefore, it may be possible that every cat with a high muscle-to-fat ratio is a good hunter. So, we cannot conclude that some of these cats are not good hunters. This is a loser.

(B) A smaller number of domestic cats than wild cats have a high muscle-to-fat ratio.

This is a relational statement that does not correspond to any of the statements in the stimulus or to any of our inferences. Therefore, this is a loser.

(C) All cats that are bad hunters have a low muscle-to-fat ratio.

This can be diagrammed as follows:

~~Good Hunters~~ → ~~High Muscle-Fat Ratio~~.

This is the negated version of the second conditional statement. This is a loser.

(D) Some cats that have a high muscle-to-fat ratio are domestic.

This is one of our anticipated answer choices. It can be diagrammed as follows:

High Muscle-Fat Ratio ^S—^S Domestic Cats

This is a candidate.

(E) All cats that have a high muscle-to-fat ratio can kill prey that weigh up to half their body weight.

Lastly, this can be diagrammed as follows:

High Muscle-Fat Ratio → Kill Prey Half Bodyweight

This is close to our anticipated answer High Muscle-Fat Ratio ^S—^S Kill Prey Half Bodyweight, but it is far too strong. We know that good hunters have both qualities, but we cannot conclude that all cats with one quality also have the other. It could be the case that animals that are not good hunters have one, but not both, of these qualities. This is a loser.

As (D) is the only candidate, it has to be the correct answer choice.

Causal Reasoning

A causal statement is a special type of absolute statement that expresses a cause-and-effect relationship. Although causal reasoning is not as common as conditional reasoning in the LR section, it does play an important role in certain question types.

About 35 percent of Strengthen and Weaken questions involve causal reasoning. It also appears less frequently in Fallacy, Parallel Sufficient Assumption, Necessary Assumption, Parallel Reasoning, and Description questions.

Causal reasoning has a very high burden of proof. To conclude that A caused B, you must rule out all other factors or variables. Maybe C caused B. Maybe B actually caused A. Maybe both A and C caused B. Or perhaps C caused both A and B. As this process of ruling out borders on being impossible, LR arguments that have a causal statement as a conclusion are almost always invalid. Let's look at an example:

> **Fossil evidence shows that dinosaurs went extinct approximately 65 million years ago. Around this time, there is evidence that a large asteroid crashed into Earth, disrupting the planet's geological homeostasis. Therefore, the asteroid caused the dinosaurs to go extinct.**

The argument can be outlined as follows:

> P1: Dinosaurs went extinct approximately 65 million years ago.
> P2: Large asteroid crashed into Earth approximately 65 million years ago.
> C: Large Asteroid CAUSE Dinosaurs to go extinct.

CAUSE is used to denote a causal relationship. This statement implies that an asteroid was the cause of the dinosaurs' extinction. This argument is invalid. The first premise shows an event occurring, the second premise shows an event occurring at the same time, and the conclusion states that one of these caused the other. Just because two events happen at the same time does not imply a causal relationship. It could simply be a coincidence that both events happened concurrently. Or, it could be that the mass extinction caused the asteroid to hit Earth. If this seems implausible, remember that the reasoning used here is the same as that used in the argument—both events occurred at the same time; therefore, one caused the other. As it is almost impossible to state that one factor is the sole cause of another, an argument with a causal relationship in its conclusion is almost always invalid.

The only exception to this rule is if the causal conclusion is the result of a logic chain created by linking two causal premises. For example,

> **The accident at the Chernobyl nuclear plant in 1986 put residents at risk of developing cancer. We know this because exposure to above-normal levels of nuclear radiation causes a higher rate of cancer, and residents living near the power plant at this time were exposed to unusually high levels of radiation due to an accident at the Chernobyl site.**

This is a valid argument, and it can be outlined as follows:

> P1: Higher level of exposure to nuclear radiation CAUSE Higher risk of cancer
> P2: Accident at Chernobyl CAUSE Higher level of exposure to nuclear radiation
> C: Accident at Chernobyl CAUSE Higher risk of cancer

The conclusion of this argument is the first causal statement. The first causal premise is easy to spot but the second is a bit tricky. There are many words and phrases that can indicate causality, a few of which are listed in the box on the right. In this case, we have the indicator *due to*, meaning that high levels of radiation were the result of the accident at the Chernobyl site.

Causal Indicators	
Causes	Because of
Made	Contributed to
Leads to	Responsible for
Due to	Was a factor
Played a role in	Result of
Produced	Reason for
Effected by	Achieved by

Like conditional statements, causal statements can be linked together to form a logic chain. The logic chain in this argument can be expressed as follows:

Accident at Chernobyl CAUSE Higher Radiation Exposure CAUSE Higher Risk Cancer

The conclusion of the argument is an inference that results from combining the end of this logic chain. As the premises of an argument are always assumed to be true, this is a valid conclusion.

Note that logic chains based on causal statements are very rare, which means that most arguments with a causal statement as the conclusion are invalid. Causal reasoning is explored in greater detail in later chapters. For now, note the ways in which it is possible to undermine a causal conclusion for a Fallacy or Weaken question and the ways in which it is possible to support a causal conclusion for a Strengthen, Sufficient Assumption, or Necessary Assumption question:

Undermining a Causal Relationship	**Supporting a Causal Relationship**
1. **Alternative Cause**: Identify another possible cause of the effect. This could be a third factor which causes both the effect and the original cause.	1. **Eliminate Alternative Causes**: Remove the possibility that another factor caused the effect.
2. **Reversed Cause and Effect**: Show that instead of A CAUSE B, the relationship is actually B CAUSE A.	2. **Same Cause, Same Effect**: Find another instance in which both the cause and effect occur.
3. **Same Cause, No Effect**: Find an instance in which the cause occurs but the effect does not occur.	3. **No Cause, No Effect**: Find another instance in which neither the cause nor the effect occur.
4. **Same Effect, No Cause**: Find an instance in which the effect occurs but the cause does not occur.	

Key Takeaways

Valid Inferences		Invalid Inferences	
Combination Inferences	**Contrapositive Inferences**	**Flipped Reasoning**	**Negated Reasoning**
$A \rightarrow B$ $\underline{B \rightarrow C}$ $A \rightarrow C$	$\underline{A \rightarrow B}$ $\overline{B} \rightarrow \overline{A}$ $\underline{A \rightarrow B \text{ AND } C}$ $\overline{B} \text{ OR } \overline{C} \rightarrow \overline{A}$	$\underline{A \rightarrow B}$ $B \rightarrow A$ $\underline{A \rightarrow B \text{ AND } C}$ $B \text{ AND } C \rightarrow A$	$\underline{\overline{A} \rightarrow \overline{B}}$ $A \rightarrow B$ $\underline{A \rightarrow B \text{ AND } C}$ $\overline{A} \rightarrow \overline{B} \text{ OR } \overline{C}$

Strength Modifier Inferences	
ALL **+** **SOME**	$A \rightarrow B$ $\underline{A \ {}^{s}\!\!-\!\!{}^{s}\ C}$ $B \ {}^{s}\!\!-\!\!{}^{s}\ C$
ALL **+** **MOST**	$A \xrightarrow{M} B$ $\underline{A \rightarrow C}$ $B \ {}^{s}\!\!-\!\!{}^{s}\ C$
	$A \xrightarrow{M} B$ $\underline{B \rightarrow C}$ $A \xrightarrow{M} C$
MOST **+** **MOST**	$A \xrightarrow{M} B$ $\underline{A \xrightarrow{M} C}$ $B \ {}^{s}\!\!-\!\!{}^{s}\ C$
ALL **+** **ALL**	$A \rightarrow B$ $\underline{A \rightarrow C}$ $B \ {}^{s}\!\!-\!\!{}^{s}\ C$

Sufficient Indicators		Necessary Indicators	
If	Whenever	Then	Necessary
All	Who	Only	Requires
Any	Whoever	Only if	Demands
Every	In order to	Must	Essential
Each	Sufficient	Needs	Entails
When		Necessitates	

Negative Sufficient Indicators		Negative Necessary Indicators	
Unless	Except	No	None
Without	Until	Not all	

Strength Modifier Indicators					
Weak (SOME)		Moderate (MOST)		Strong (ALL)	
Degree	Quantity	Degree	Quantity	Degree	Quantity
May	Some	Probably	Most	Always	All
Might	Few	Generally	Majority	Must	Every
Can/Could	Several	Likely	Almost all	Is	Any
Occasionally	Many	Usually		Are	No
Often	Not all	Typically		Will	None
	Little				

Strength Modifier Category	Proportion
Strong (ALL)	100%
Strong (NO)	0%
Moderate (MOST)	50%< to 100%
Weak (SOME)	0%< to 100%
Weak (NOT ALL)	0% to <100%

Chapter 3

Inference
Family

Chapter 3: Inference Family

HACKERS
LSAT *Logical Reasoning*

Overview

Inference Family

In this chapter, you will learn how to identify and solve Inference Family questions.

Inference Family questions ask you to find the answer choice that is inferable from the propositions in the stimulus, which are assumed to be true. The stimulus usually includes a fact pattern rather than an argument.

The three question types in this family—Must Be True (MBT), Implication (IMP), and Must Be False (MBF)—are examined in detail in separate sections. Each section includes step-by-step instructions on how to solve the question type, detailed analyses of example questions, and drills to help you develop key skills. In addition, you will get to tackle practice questions taken from previous administrations of the LSAT. The methods for solving these practice questions are explained thoroughly in the answer keys.

Must Be True

Must Be True
Implication
Must Be False

Must Be True

≈ 1.3 questions per test

Example Prompts

If the statements above are true, which one of the following *must be true*?

Which of the following can be *properly inferred* from the statements above?

Which of the following statements *follows logically* from the set of statements above?

Take These Steps

Read the stimulus, which usually includes a fact pattern. Does it include conditional language?

Yes → Does the stimulus include multiple conditional statements?

No ↓

Summarize the stimulus. Consider the relationships between the propositions, focusing on the strongest propositions. Anticipate a paraphrase of a proposition or a weak statement supported by the stimulus.

Yes ↓

Summarize the stimulus, diagramming the conditional statements. Anticipate a valid inference, a contrapositive, a paraphrase of a conditional statement or other proposition, or a weak statement supported by the stimulus.

No ↓

Summarize the stimulus, diagramming the conditional statement. Anticipate a paraphrase of this statement, its contrapositive, a paraphrase of another proposition, or a weak statement supported by the stimulus.

Answer Choices

Correct Answer Choices	**Incorrect Answer Choices**
Statements that are definitely true based on the stimulus	Statements that are not necessarily true based on the stimulus
Accurate paraphrases of propositions or summaries of the stimulus	Inaccurate paraphrases of propositions
Valid inferences or contrapositives	Invalid inferences or contrapositives
Often statements that are weak in logical force	Irrelevant information or broad claims not supported by the stimulus
	Statements that are too strong in logical force

Must Be True (MBT) questions ask you to find the answer choice that must be true based on the information in the stimulus. Though MBT questions have started appearing less often on the LSAT, they remain important.

It is necessary to pay close attention to the language used in an MBT question. Whether an answer choice is correct or incorrect is often determined by a single word or phrase, such as a strength or degree modifier. In fact, a defining characteristic of this question type is the lack of flexibility in terms of the relationship between the correct answer choice and the stimulus. If a statement may be true but may also be false, it cannot be the correct answer choice. Therefore, it is vital to focus on the wording of an MBT question. MBT questions typically include a fact pattern rather than an argument.

How to Solve Must Be True Questions

The first step is to look for conditional language. Most MBT questions include one or more conditional statements.

If There Is Conditional Language

Most MBT questions include a stimulus with conditional language. Initially, you should always diagram these statements to ensure that you fully understand the relationships they express. Once you become adept at conditional reasoning, you can skip this step to save time. Remember to look for sufficient and necessary indicators as well as strength modifiers.

> Make sure you fully understand Chapter 2 before moving on to this section. Conditional reasoning is used extensively in MBT questions.

If there is only one conditional statement, anticipate a paraphrase of this statement or its contrapositive being the correct answer choice. You should also pay close attention to how the propositions—including the conditional statement—fit together. The correct answer choice is sometimes a statement that is justified by the information in the stimulus. In rare cases, it is simply a paraphrase of a proposition.

If there is more than one conditional statement, check if these statements can be joined together to form a logic chain. If so, there is a high likelihood that the correct answer choice will be related to the inference that can be made by combining the ends of this chain. For example,

$$C \rightarrow D$$
$$\cancel{C} \rightarrow \cancel{B}$$
$$\underline{A \rightarrow B}$$
$$A \rightarrow B \rightarrow C \rightarrow D$$

By finding the contrapositive of the second statement, we are able to connect $A \rightarrow B \rightarrow C \rightarrow D$. The ends of the logic chain are $A \rightarrow D$. In this case, the answer choice is likely to be $A \rightarrow D$ or its contrapositive, $\cancel{D} \rightarrow \cancel{A}$. Can the answer choice be another link in the chain or its contrapositive, such as $B \rightarrow D$ or $\cancel{C} \rightarrow \cancel{A}$? Yes. However, the ends of the chain are more likely to be tested in an LR question.

You should also check for any strength modifier inferences that can be made by combining the sufficient and necessary conditions of compatible statements. Remember, there are five valid combinations:

ALL + SOME = SOME
ALL + MOST = SOME
ALL + MOST = MOST
MOST + MOST = SOME
ALL + ALL = MOST

Valid strength modifier inferences and their contrapositives are oftentimes the basis of the correct answer choice.

Sometimes, we are faced with multiple conditional statements that cannot be linked in a logic chain or combined to make strength modifier inferences. In this situation, a paraphrase of one of these statements or its contrapositive may very well be the correct answer choice. Less commonly, the correct answer choice is simply a statement that is supported by the information in the stimulus.

Let's look at an example:

> When uncontrollable factors such as a lack of rain cause farmers' wheat crops to fail, fertilizer and seed dealers, as well as truckers and mechanics, lose business, and fuel suppliers are unable to sell enough diesel fuel to make a profit.
>
> Which one of the following claims follows logically from the information above?
>
> (A) If several of the businesses that sell to farmers do not prosper, it is because farming itself is not prospering.
> (B) If rainfall is below average, those businesses that profit from farmers' purchases tend to lose money.
> (C) Farmers are not responsible for the consequences of a wheat crop's failing if wheat growth has been affected by lack of rain.
> (D) A country's dependence on agriculture can lead to major economic crises.
> (E) The consequences of a drought are not restricted to the drought's impact on farm productivity.

The word *when* appears in the first line, indicating the sufficient condition of a conditional statement. In addition, the presence of *cause* signals that there is a causal relationship within the sufficient condition. The conditional statement can be diagrammed as

Uncontrollable Factors CAUSE Wheat Crops Fail → Certain Businesses Adversely Affected

This is the only conditional statement in the stimulus, and, in fact, the stimulus does not include any other propositions. So, the diagram above functions as a summary of the stimulus as well. We should now anticipate potential correct answer choices. The correct answer choice could simply be a statement supported by the stimulus. However, as causal reasoning rarely appears in a conditional statement, it is more likely that the correct answer choice will be a paraphrase of the conditional statement or its contrapositive, which can be diagrammed as

~~Certain Businesses Adversely Affected~~ → Uncontrollable Factors ~~CAUSE~~ Wheat Crops Fail

Let's look at the answer choices one by one.

(A) If several of the businesses that sell to farmers do not prosper, it is because farming itself is not prospering.

Although the word *if* makes this answer choice appear to be a conditional statement, the phrase *it is because* indicates that it is a causal statement, which can be diagrammed as

~~Farming Prospering~~ CAUSE ~~Other Business Prosper~~

This is not an accurate paraphrase of the stimulus, which states that if wheat crops fail, then fertilizer and seed dealers, mechanics, and truckers are negatively affected. (A) makes the much broader claim that when these businesses are not prospering, this is because farmers are not prospering. This is not necessarily true. A variety of other factors, such as bad management, could prevent the other businesses from prospering. In addition, *not prosper* is not synonymous with *adversely affected*. Finally, the phrase *several of the businesses that sell to farmers* is imprecise. This could mean the businesses mentioned in the stimulus, but it could also mean something else. This answer choice can be placed in the loser category.

(B) If rainfall is below average, those businesses that profit from farmers' purchases tend to lose money.

This matches our anticipated answer choice. Furthermore, the inclusion of the phrase *tend to* weakens the statement, making it more attractive as a correct answer choice. For now, we will consider this a candidate.

(C) Farmers are not responsible for the consequences of a wheat crop's failing if wheat growth has been affected by lack of rain.

The word *responsible* is a red flag. Where in the stimulus is responsibility mentioned? This is irrelevant information. This answer choice is a loser.

(D) A country's dependence on agriculture can lead to major economic crises.

This answer choice is too broad. While the stimulus does state that the failure of wheat crops affects other businesses, it does not discuss agriculture in general (i.e. other types of crops). In addition, we cannot say with certainty that an economic crisis will occur because several types of businesses have been negatively affected. Although this statement could be true based on the information in the stimulus, it does not necessarily have to be true. Therefore, this answer choice is a loser as well.

(E) The consequences of a drought are not restricted to the drought's impact on farm productivity.

This matches our anticipated answer choice. It is saying that a drought can affect things other than farm productivity, which seems to be an accurate paraphrase of the conditional statement. This is a second candidate.

We now need to eliminate one of our two candidates. Let's look back at (B). One thing to consider is that this answer choice includes the wording *rainfall is below average*, while the stimulus refers to *lack of rain*. *Lack of rain* is much stronger than *rainfall is below average*. *Rainfall is below average* may indicate rainfall levels that are slightly lower than normal rather than the complete absence or serious shortfall of rain indicated by *lack of rain*. This discrepancy is sufficient to eliminate (B).

The wording in answer choice (E) holds up as *drought* means an extended period of dryness with little or no rain. The rest of this answer choice matches the original statement as well—if wheat crop failures caused by a lack of rain have negative effects on other businesses, then the consequences of a drought are not limited to farmers. This is the correct answer choice.

If There Is No Conditional Language

If there are no conditional statements, summarize the stimulus and focus on the relationships between the propositions. Try to understand how these ideas fit together and anticipate an answer choice that expresses a particularly strong relationship or resolves an apparent contradiction. Also consider how the propositions can be reworded, as the answer choice may be a paraphrase of an individual proposition or of the stimulus as a whole. Keep in mind that it is very difficult to anticipate the correct answer choice of an MBT stimulus with no conditional language. Fortunately, these are very rare.

Looking at the Answer Choices

The correct answer choice of an MBT question is always a statement that is necessarily true based on the information in the stimulus. Keep in mind that there can be no doubt about this—if it may possibly be false, it cannot be the correct answer choice.

Also, the correct answer choice will almost always be weak in logical force. This is because a weak statement is much easier to prove true than a strong one. For example, less evidence is required to support the weak claim "some people are good" than for the strong claim "all people are good." To prove the first one, all that is needed are a few examples of good people. For the second one, you would need to establish that there are no bad people at all. What makes a claim weak? A big tip-off is a SOME statement rather than a MOST or an ALL statement. However, a statement can be strong even if it does not include a strength modifier. For example, the claim "people can live anywhere" is stronger than "people can live in many places."

Incorrect answer choices often include a logical force error. In this case, the statement presented as an answer choice is too strong to be proven true by the information in the stimulus.

In addition, incorrect answer choices commonly present irrelevant information. In these cases, it is important to remember that you should not apply outside knowledge to LR questions. Whether or not an answer choice is factually true is not important—what matters is whether it is true based on the information in the stimulus. If an answer choice focuses on information that is not included in the stimulus, it is almost certainly incorrect because of the near impossibility of determining whether or not this information is true based only on the stimulus.

You should also watch out for answer choices that make claims that are too broad. These types of answer choices can be tricky because they often present a claim that is potentially true based on the stimulus. Remember the basic rule of MBT questions—the correct answer choice is necessarily true. A claim that is broader than what is stated in the stimulus could be true but does not have to be true, so it cannot be the correct answer choice.

Finally, be on the lookout for inaccurate paraphrases of propositions. Incorrect answer choices often appear to be restatements of propositions, but include one or two slight differences in meaning that make them inaccurate.

Drill: Must Be True

After identifying this as an MBT question, read the stimulus. Underline all sufficient indicators, necessary indicators, and strength modifiers.

In the troposphere, the lowest level of Earth's atmosphere, the temperature decreases as one progresses straight upward. At the top, the air temperature ranges from -50 degrees Celsius over the poles to -85 degrees Celsius over the equator. At that point the stratosphere begins, and the temperature stops decreasing and instead increases as one progresses straight upward through the stratosphere. The stratosphere is warmed by ozone. When an ozone particle absorbs a dose of ultraviolet sunlight, heat is generated.

If you see any conditional statements, diagram them below. Diagram the contrapositives as well.

_____

_____

_____

_____

_____

_____

Summarize the stimulus, paying close attention to the relationships between propositions.

_____

_____

_____

_____

_____

_____

For each answer choice below, determine whether it must be true. Then, explain why or why not.

(A) The troposphere over the poles is thicker than the troposphere over the equator.

_____

_____

_____

(B) It is warmer at the top of the stratosphere over the poles than it is at the top of the stratosphere over the equator.

_____

_____

_____

(C) The temperature in the middle part of the stratosphere over the North Pole is at least as great as the temperature in the middle part of the stratosphere over the equator.

_____

_____

_____

(D) The temperature at any point at the top of the stratosphere is at least as great as the temperature at the top of the troposphere directly beneath that point.

_____

_____

_____

(E) Depletion of the earth's ozone layer would increase the air temperature in the stratosphere and decrease the air temperature in the troposphere.

_____

_____

_____

Drill: Must Be True — Answers

Stimulus:

In the troposphere, the lowest level of Earth's atmosphere, the temperature decreases as one progresses straight upward. At the top, the air temperature ranges from -50 degrees Celsius over the poles to -85 degrees Celsius over the equator. At that point the stratosphere begins, and the temperature stops decreasing and instead increases as one progresses straight upward through the stratosphere. The stratosphere is warmed by ozone. When an ozone particle absorbs a dose of ultraviolet sunlight, heat is generated.

Diagram:

There is one conditional statement:

Ozone Absorbs UV → Heat Generated

Its contrapositive can be diagrammed as

~~Heat Generated~~ → ~~Ozone Absorbs UV~~

Summary:

In the troposphere, the temperature decreases as you travel upwards. Once you reach the stratosphere, the temperature increases as you travel upwards. This upper layer, the stratosphere, is warmed by ozone due to the interaction of ozone particles and ultraviolet radiation, which creates heat.

Answer Choices:

(A) **The troposphere over the poles is thicker than the troposphere over the equator.**

This is a relational statement that is not necessarily true. It introduces new information. We know the temperature at the top of the troposphere over the poles and equator, but there is no information about the thickness of the troposphere.

(B) **It is warmer at the top of the stratosphere over the poles than it is at the top of the stratosphere over the equator.**

This is another relational statement that cannot be definitively established as true because it presents new information. The bottom layer of the stratosphere is -50 degrees Celsius over the poles and -85 over the equator. We know the temperatures are higher at the top of the stratosphere, but we cannot determine how fast the temperature increases over both locations.

(C) **The temperature in the middle part of the stratosphere over the North Pole is at least as great as the temperature in the middle part of the stratosphere over the equator.**

This is also a relational statement. As it introduces new information, it may not be true. We do not know the temperature of the middle part of the stratosphere above either location, so we cannot make this comparison.

(D) **The temperature at any point at the top of the stratosphere is at least as great as the temperature at the top of the troposphere directly beneath that point.**

This must be true. Since the temperature increases once the stratosphere is reached, every point of the stratosphere must be warmer than the top of the troposphere.

(E) **Depletion of the earth's ozone layer would increase the air temperature in the stratosphere and decrease the air temperature in the troposphere.**

Finally, this statement is false. It contradicts the conditional statement, which claims that ozone warms the stratosphere. Therefore, more ozone would produce more heat in this layer of the atmosphere.

Problem Set: Must Be True

1. There are two kinds of horror stories: those that describe a mad scientist's experiments and those that describe a monstrous beast. In some horror stories about monstrous beasts, the monster symbolizes a psychological disturbance in the protagonist. Horror stories about mad scientists, on the other hand, typically express the author's feeling that scientific knowledge alone is not enough to guide human endeavor. However, despite these differences, both kinds of horror stories share two features: they describe violations of the laws of nature and they are intended to produce dread in the reader.

   If the statements above are true, which one of the following would also have to be true?

   (A) All descriptions of monstrous beasts describe violations of the laws of nature.
   (B) Any story that describes a violation of a law of nature is intended to invoke dread in the reader.
   (C) Horror stories of any kind usually describe characters who are psychologically disturbed.
   (D) Most stories about mad scientists express the author's antiscientific views.
   (E) Some stories that employ symbolism describe violations of the laws of nature.

2. The law of the city of Weston regarding contributions to mayoral campaigns is as follows: all contributions to these campaigns in excess of $100 made by nonresidents of Weston who are not former residents of Weston must be registered with the city council. Brimley's mayoral campaign clearly complied with this law since it accepted contributions only from residents and former residents of Weston.

   If the statements above are true, then which one of the following statements must be true?

   (A) No nonresident of Weston contributed in excess of $100 to Brimley's campaign.
   (B) Some contributions to Brimley's campaign in excess of $100 were registered with the city council.
   (C) No contributions to Brimley's campaign needed to be registered with the city council.
   (D) All contributions to Brimley's campaign that were registered with the city council were in excess of $100.
   (E) Brimley's campaign did not register any contributions with the city council.

3. To face danger solely because doing so affords one a certain pleasure does not constitute courage. Real courage is manifested only when a person, in acting to attain a goal, perseveres in the face of fear prompted by one or more dangers involved.

Which one of the following statements can be properly inferred from the statements above?

(A) A person who must face danger in order to avoid future pain cannot properly be called courageous for doing so.
(B) A person who experiences fear of some aspects of a dangerous situation cannot be said to act courageously in that situation.
(C) A person who happens to derive pleasure from some dangerous activities is not a courageous person.
(D) A person who faces danger in order to benefit others is acting courageously only if the person is afraid of that danger.
(E) A person who has no fear of the situations that everyone else would fear cannot be said to be courageous in any situation.

4. Historian: One traditional childrearing practice in the nineteenth century was to make a child who misbehaved sit alone outside. Anyone passing by would conclude that the child had misbehaved. Nowadays, many child psychologists would disapprove of this practice because they believe that such practices damage the child's self-esteem and that damage to children's self-esteem makes them less confident as adults. However, no one disagrees that adults raised under that traditional practice were, on average, as confident as adults not so raised.

Which one of the following can be properly inferred from the historian's statements?

(A) The beliefs of many present-day child psychologists about the consequences of loss of self-esteem are incorrect.
(B) Some of the most confident adults, as well as some of the least confident adults, were raised under the traditional practice in question.
(C) With the traditional childrearing practice, passersby did not always make correct inferences about children's behavior by observing them outdoors.
(D) The most confident adults are those who developed the highest level of self-esteem in childhood.
(E) If children's loss of self-esteem makes them less confident as adults, then the traditional childrearing practice in question did not tend to cause significant loss of self-esteem.

5. Trust, which cannot be sustained in the absence of mutual respect, is essential to any long-lasting relationship, personal or professional. However, personal relationships, such as marriage or friendship, additionally require natural affinity. If a personal relationship is to endure, it must be supported by the twin pillars of mutual respect and affinity.

If the statements above are true, then which one of the following must also be true?

(A) A friendship supported solely by trust and mutual respect will not be long-lasting.
(B) In the context of any professional relationship, mutual respect presupposes trust.
(C) If a personal relationship is supported by mutual respect and affinity, it will last a long time.
(D) Personal relationships, such as marriage or friendship, are longer-lasting than professional relationships.
(E) Basing a marriage on a natural affinity will ensure that it will endure.

6. Most serious students are happy students, and most serious students go to graduate school. Furthermore, all students who go to graduate school are overworked.

Which one of the following can be properly inferred from the statements above?

(A) Most overworked students are happy students.
(B) Some happy students are overworked.
(C) All overworked students are serious students.
(D) Some unhappy students go to graduate school.
(E) All serious students are overworked.

7. If the price it pays for coffee beans continues to increase, the Coffee Shoppe will have to increase its prices. In that case, either the Coffee Shoppe will begin selling noncoffee products or its coffee sales will decrease. But selling noncoffee products will decrease the Coffee Shoppe's overall profitability. Moreover, the Coffee Shoppe can avoid a decrease in overall profitability only if its coffee sales do not decrease.

Which one of the following statements follows logically from the statements above?

(A) If the Coffee Shoppe's overall profitability decreases, the price it pays for coffee beans will have continued to increase.
(B) If the Coffee Shoppe's overall profitability decreases, either it will have begun selling noncoffee products or its coffee sales will have decreased.
(C) The Coffee Shoppe's overall profitability will decrease if the price it pays for coffee beans continues to increase.
(D) The price it pays for coffee beans cannot decrease without the Coffee Shoppe's overall profitability also decreasing.
(E) Either the price it pays for coffee beans will continue to increase or the Coffee Shoppe's coffee sales will increase.

Problem Set: Must Be True — Answers

1. **Correct Answer (E).** *Prep Test 42, Section 2, Question 16.*

Our first step is to read the stimulus and look for conditional language. The first proposition is background information that identifies two different types of horror stories—those about mad scientists and those about monstrous beasts. The second proposition provides more information about the first type and includes the weak strength modifier *some*. The third proposition describes the second type of horror story and includes the moderate strength modifier *typically*. The final sentence of the stimulus describes features common to both story types. To make it easier to identify inferences, the last proposition can be expressed as two conditional statements. If we do this, the four conditional statements in this stimulus can be diagrammed as follows:

> S1: Monstrous Beast Story ^{S}—^{S} Symbolizes Disturbance in Protagonist
> S2: Mad Scientist Story $^M\rightarrow$ Scientific Knowledge Not Enough
> S3: Mad Scientist Story $\rightarrow$ Violation of Nature AND Intended Dread
> S4: Monstrous Beast Story $\rightarrow$ Violation of Nature AND Intended Dread

Although these statements cannot be linked to form a logic chain, several strength modifier inferences can be made. Because the sufficient conditions of the first and fourth statements are identical, a SOME statement can be inferred between their necessary conditions. This is also true of the third and fourth statements. These inferences can be diagrammed as follows:

> Inf: Symbolizes Disturbance in Protagonist ^{S}—^{S} Violation of Nature AND Intended Dread
> Inf: Scientific Knowledge Not Enough ^{S}—^{S} Violation of Nature AND Intended Dread

These two inferences can be restated, respectively, as "Some stories that symbolize a psychological disturbance in the protagonist describe violations of the laws of nature and are intended to produce dread" and "Some stories that express the author's feeling that scientific knowledge is not enough to guide human endeavor describe violations of the laws of nature and are intended to produce dread."

We should anticipate one of these inferences (or their contrapositives) as being the correct answer choice. Although there are other possibilities, such as a paraphrase or contrapositive of one of the statements, the correct answer choice is likely to be an inference if one can be made. As both of our inferences are SOME statements, we should look for a SOME statement in the answer choices. (A) and (B) are ALL statements, and (C) and (D) are MOST statements. We will therefore look at answer choice (E) first.

(E) Some stories that employ symbolism describe violations of the laws of nature.

This matches one of our anticipated answer choices. Symbolizing a psychological disturbance involves the use of symbolism, and at least some of these stories describe violations of the laws of nature. Because this answer choice states our first inference and the rest of the answer choices are ALL and MOST statements, we will move on to the next question. If you can identify the correct answer choice quickly and with a high degree of certainty, do not waste time going through all of the remaining answer choices.

2. **Correct Answer (C).** *Prep Test 57, Section 2, Question 25.*

This is an unusual MBT question in that it includes an argument rather than a fact pattern. There is one conditional statement, marked by the indicators *all* and *must*. We can diagram it as

> Nonresident Contribution over $100 + ~~Former Resident~~ $\rightarrow$ Register w/ City Council

A contribution over $100 from a nonresident who is not a former resident needs to be registered. The argument's conclusion states that that Brimley's campaign complied with the law since it accepted contributions only from residents and former residents of Weston. Note that *only* here does not indicate a necessary condition but excludes the possibility of other people contributing. The argument can be outlined as follows:

P1: Law: Nonresident Contribution over $100 + ~~Former Resident~~ → Register w/ City Council
P2: Brimley's campaign only accepted contributions from residents and former residents

C: Brimley's campaign complied with law

This seems rather straightforward. Brimley's campaign must have complied with the law because it only accepted contributions from residents and former residents, and the law applies to nonresidents who are not former residents.

We should anticipate a paraphrase of the conditional statement (or its contrapositive) or of one of the other statements. The correct answer choice may also be a weak statement supported by the stimulus.

(A) No nonresident of Weston contributed in excess of $100 to Brimley's campaign.

This answer choice introduces irrelevant information. The argument states that Brimley's campaign accepted donations from former residents (i.e. nonresidents) of Weston. There is no indication of the amounts these former residents donated. Therefore, this answer choice is not necessarily true based on the information in the passage. It can be put in the loser category.

(B) Some contributions to Brimley's campaign in excess of $100 were registered with the city council.

Why would Brimley's campaign need to register any contributions? It only accepted money from residents and former residents and, therefore, was not legally required to register any contributions. There is no mention of any other requirement related to the registration of contributions. We can consider this a loser.

(C) No contributions to Brimley's campaign needed to be registered with the city council.

This matches one of our anticipated answer choices. It is a statement that seems to be supported by the stimulus. Brimley accepted contributions only from people whose contributions did not need to be registered. We will consider this a candidate.

(D) All contributions to Brimley's campaign that were registered with the city council were in excess of $100.

Based on the stimulus, none of the contributions Brimley's campaign received were required to be registered with the city council, regardless of whether they were in excess of $100. We can consider this a loser.

(E) Brimley's campaign did not register any contributions with the city council.

This matches one of our anticipated answer choices. It is very similar to (C), so we will consider it a candidate.

This means that we must eliminate one of the two candidates. The difference between the two possible correct answer choices is that (C) says that no contributions needed to be registered, while (E) states that the campaign did not register any contributions. (E) is a much stronger statement than (C) because it excludes the possibility that Brimley's campaign registered contributions even if there was no requirement to do so. This means that while (E) is very likely true, there is a small chance that it might not be. In contrast, (C) is definitely true based on the stimulus. Therefore, (C) is the correct answer choice.

3. **Correct Answer (D).** *Prep Test 54, Section 2, Question 25.*

The second sentence of the stimulus includes a conditional statement with the necessary indicator *only*. It can be diagrammed as follows:

Real Courage → Attain Goal AND Perseveres Over Fear Prompted by Danger

Here, *only* refers to the qualities that must be present when a person shows real courage. These qualities in themselves do not make someone courageous. Note that although the stimulus does not contain *and*, expressing the terms in the necessary condition as a conjunction makes their relationship easier to understand. The first sentence of this stimulus provides background information related to the conditional statement—it tells us what does not necessarily constitute courage. The stimulus, therefore, only contains one important bit of information, the conditional statement. We should anticipate a correct answer choice that restates this conditional statement or its contrapositive:

~~Attain Goal~~ OR ~~Perseveres Over Fear Prompted by Danger~~ → ~~Real Courage~~

Note that since Real Courage is not the necessary condition, there are no qualities here that definitively prove that someone has Real Courage. However, there are qualities that show that someone has ~~Real Courage~~; namely, not attaining a goal or not persevering in the face of fear prompted by danger.

(A) A person who must face danger in order to avoid future pain cannot properly be called courageous for doing so.

To claim that someone is not courageous, we need to show that he or she is not attaining a goal or not persevering in the face of fear. In this answer choice, "avoid future pain" seems like a goal, and there is no reference to fear. Therefore, this is a loser.

(B) A person who experiences fear of some aspects of a dangerous situation cannot be said to act courageously in that situation.

This answer choice suggests that experiencing fear prevents a person from being courageous. This does not match the stimulus, which actually requires the experience of fear (otherwise a person could not persevere in the face of it). This is another loser.

(C) A person who happens to derive pleasure from some dangerous activities is not a courageous person.

This answer choice is an inaccurate paraphrase of the first sentence of the stimulus. It leaves out the idea of facing danger solely for pleasure. There is nothing to prevent a person from deriving pleasure from a dangerous activity and yet still feeling fear and persevering over this fear. This can be classified as a loser.

(D) A person who faces danger in order to benefit others is acting courageously only if the person is afraid of that danger.

This matches our anticipated answer choice. This is a conditional statement, as indicated by the term *only if*. What follows *only if* is the necessary condition. The diagram is as follows:

Real Courage + Attain Goal (Benefit Others) + Face Danger → Fear

This can be restated as "If you exhibit real courage while attaining a goal and facing danger, then you must have been afraid of that danger." This seems to match the stimulus, which states that for a person to exhibit real courage, he or she must be trying to attain a goal and persevering over the fear of danger. This answer choice is a candidate.

(E) A person who has no fear of the situations that everyone else would fear cannot be said to be courageous in any situation.

This seems to express that a person with no fear cannot persevere over fear, meaning that he or she can never be courageous. However, you should immediately note that this answer choice specifies "situations that everyone else would fear." What if a person has a unique fear that is not shared by other people? In this case, he or she would have the opportunity to show real courage. This is a loser.

As (D) is the only candidate, it has to be the correct answer choice.

4. **Correct Answer (E).** *Prep Test 40, Section 3, Question 11.*

There are no conditional statements in this stimulus. Therefore, we should summarize the stimulus to make sure we understand what is being said. It states that while many child psychologists believe that the traditional childrearing practice described damages children's self-esteem and makes them less confident as adults, adults raised under that traditional practice were, on average, just as confident as adults not raised under the traditional practice. There seems to be a discrepancy here. Would we not expect the adults who experienced this practice as children to be less confident than other adults?

The child psychologists have two beliefs: (1) This traditional practice lowers self-esteem, and (2) Low self-esteem makes children less confident as adults. At least one of these beliefs has to be wrong. We should anticipate a correct answer choice that must be true and is related to this apparent contradiction.

(A) The beliefs of many present-day child psychologists about the consequences of loss of self-esteem are incorrect.

This is not necessarily true. It could be that they are wrong about the practice causing a loss of self-esteem in children and right about low self-esteem in childhood negatively affecting confidence in adulthood. In other words, it could be the case that belief (1) is incorrect but belief (2) is correct. We can consider this a loser.

(B) Some of the most confident adults, as well as some of the least confident adults, were raised under the traditional practice in question.

This answer choice introduces irrelevant information. There is nothing in the stimulus about the most and least confident adults. Instead, the average of a group is being discussed. This is a loser.

(C) With the traditional childrearing practice, passersby did not always make correct inferences about children's behavior by observing them outdoors.

Again, this answer choice includes irrelevant information. We have no reason to believe that there were occasions in which a passerby made an incorrect inference about the child's behavior. This answer choice is a loser.

(D) The most confident adults are those who developed the highest level of self-esteem in childhood.

Again, this answer choice includes irrelevant information. This is a relational statement that is not supported by the stimulus. Even if the child psychologists are correct that low self-esteem in childhood leads to less confidence as an adult, there is no indication that children with the highest levels of self-esteem become the most confident adults. In addition, we cannot even be sure that the child psychologists' theory is correct. We can consider this a loser.

(E) If children's loss of self-esteem makes them less confident as adults, then the traditional childrearing practice in question did not tend to cause significant loss of self-esteem.

This matches our anticipated answer choice. It states that if belief (2) is correct, then belief (1) must be incorrect. This is a true statement, and it resolves the contradiction that we noticed in the stimulus. Note that this answer choice is not saying the one belief is correct or incorrect—that would be too strong of a statement. Instead, it simply says that if one of the beliefs is true, the other one must be false. This is our correct answer choice.

5. **Correct Answer (A).** *Prep Test 45, Section 1, Question 8.*

This stimulus includes several conditional statements that are easy to identify because of the use of indicators such as *essential*, *require*, *if*, and *must*. These statements can be diagrammed as follows:

> S1: Trust → Mutual Respect
> S2: Long-Lasting Relationship → Trust
> S3: Personal Relationship → Natural Affinity
> S4: Personal Relationship Endure → Mutual Respect AND Natural Affinity

The first sentence of the stimulus actually includes two conditional statements. For the first one, Trust is the sufficient condition and Mutual Respect is the necessary condition. The second conditional statement in this sentence includes the indicator *essential*. If Trust is essential, it is the necessary condition, and Long-Lasting Relationship is the sufficient one. In the next sentence, Personal Relationships require Natural Affinity, indicating that Natural Affinity is the necessary condition and Personal Relationship is the sufficient one. In the last statement, *must* indicates that Mutual Respect AND Natural Affinity is the necessary condition.

The first two conditional statements can be combined to create a logic chain:

> Long-Lasting Relationship → Trust → Mutual Respect

As none of the other statements can be used to make inferences, we can anticipate a correct answer choice based on the ends of this logic chain, Long-Lasting Relationship → Mutual Respect, or the contrapositive, ~~Mutual Respect~~ → ~~Long-Lasting Relationship~~. Other possible correct answer choices include a paraphrase or contrapositive of any of the other conditional statements, especially the fourth conditional statement, which is the most complex. The contrapositive of the fourth conditional statement is ~~Mutual Respect~~ OR ~~Natural Affinity~~ → ~~Personal Relationship Endure~~.

(A) A friendship supported solely by trust and mutual respect will not be long-lasting.

This matches one of our anticipated answer choices. It states that friendship, which is a personal relationship, will not be long-lasting if it is supported solely by trust and mutual respect. This must be true based on the contrapositive of the fourth conditional statement, which states that if there is no natural affinity, a personal relationship will not endure. Although this answer choice is not a direct paraphrase, it must be true based on the stimulus. Therefore, it can be classified as a candidate.

(B) In the context of any professional relationship, mutual respect presupposes trust.

Here, *presupposes* is a necessary indicator that functions in a manner similar to *necessitates*. This answer choice can be diagrammed as follows:

> Mutual Respect → Trust

This is an invalid inference, as it is based on flipped reasoning. Here, the first conditional statement is flipped but not negated. This answer choice is a loser.

(C) If a personal relationship is supported by mutual respect and affinity, it will last a long time.

This answer choice can be diagrammed as follows:

> Mutual Respect AND Natural Affinity → Personal Relationship Endure

This is the flipped version of our fourth statement, and is therefore an invalid inference. We can classify this answer choice as a loser.

(D) Personal relationships, such as marriage or friendship, are longer-lasting than professional

relationships.

This is a relational statement comparing personal and professional relationships. The passage does not touch upon this, so we can consider this answer choice to be a loser.

(E) Basing a marriage on a natural affinity will ensure that it will endure.

As a marriage is a personal relationship, this answer choice can be diagrammed as

Natural Affinity → Personal Relationship Endure

As this is an incomplete flipped version of the fourth conditional statement, (E) is clearly a loser.

As (A) is the only candidate, it has to be the correct answer choice.

6. **Correct Answer (B).** *Prep Test 41, Section 3, Question 25.*

This stimulus includes several conditional statements with strength modifiers such as *most* and *all*. The diagrams are as follows:

S1: Serious Students ^{M}→ Happy Students
S2: Serious Students ^{M}→ Graduate School
S3: Graduate School → Overworked

We can make several inferences here. We can combine the two MOST statements to create a SOME statement from their necessary conditions, as follows:

Inf1: Happy Students ^{S}—^{S} Graduate School

Next, we can combine the necessary condition of the second MOST statement with the sufficient condition of the ALL statement to create a MOST statement:

Inf2: Serious Students ^{M}→ Overworked

As the inferences we have made share terms with the original statements, it is possible to make additional inferences. As the first inference is a SOME statement, it can be flipped without being negated. This results in identical sufficient conditions for the first statement and the first inference, allowing us to infer a SOME statement from the necessary conditions:

Inf3: Overworked ^{S}—^{S} Happy Students

Note that we could have also inferred this from combining the first statement and the second inference.

Lastly, we should note that the second statement and the second inference are MOST statements with identical sufficient conditions. We can combine them to create the following SOME statement:

Inf4: Graduate Students ^{S}—^{S} Overworked

What we have to work with are the conditional statements in the stimulus as well as our inferences, as follows:

S1: Serious Students ^{M}→ Happy Students
S2: Serious Students ^{M}→ Graduate School
S3: Graduate School → Overworked
Inf1: Happy Students ^{S}—^{S} Graduate School
Inf2: Serious Students ^{M}→ Overworked
Inf3: Overworked ^{S}—^{S} Happy Students
Inf4: Graduate Students ^{S}—^{S} Overworked

We can anticipate any of these inferences (or their contrapositives) as being the correct answer choice. We may also see a paraphrase of the ALL statement or its contrapositive. Among the answer choices, we notice one ALL statement, two MOST statements, and two SOME statements. We will want to look at the SOME statements first, as three of our four inferences are SOME statements. Answer choice (B) immediately stands out as a direct paraphrase of our third inference:

(B) Some happy students are overworked.

We can select it and move on to our next question. With MBT questions that rely heavily on conditional language and strength modifiers, there is no need to spend time reviewing all of the answer choices when you see one that clearly restates a valid inference.

---

7. **Correct Answer (C).** *Prep Test 51.5, Section 3, Question 22.*

There are several conditional statements in this stimulus, and some include indicators such as *if* and *only if*. The diagrams are as follows:

S1: Bean Price Increase → Shop Price Increase
S2: Shop Price Increase → Noncoffee Products OR Coffee Sales Decrease
S3: Noncoffee Products → Shop Profitability Decrease
S4: ~~Shop Profitability Decrease → Coffee Sales Decrease~~

In the first sentence, what follows *if* is the sufficient condition, and the second clause is the necessary condition. The next sentence begins with *in that case*, which refers to the necessary condition of the previous sentence. If Shop Price Increase, then the Coffee Shoppe will either sell noncoffee products or its coffee sales will decrease. If the first option is carried out (selling noncoffee products), then the shop's overall profitability will decrease. Lastly, what follows *only if* is the necessary condition, and the preceding clause is the sufficient condition.

Next, we must look for valid inferences. We can link the first, second, and third statements with the contrapositive of the fourth statement to create the following logic chains:

Bean Price Increase → Shop Price Increase → Noncoffee Products → Shop Profitability Decrease

OR

Bean Price Increase → Shop Price Increase → Coffee Sales Decrease → Shop Profitability Decrease

We can draw the same inference based on the ends of both logic chains:

Bean Price Increase → Shop Profitability Decrease

The inevitable result of the shop paying more for coffee beans is a decrease in its overall profitability. Since LSAT questions frequently involve the ends of logic chains, we can expect the correct answer choice to be either this inference or its contrapositive, ~~Shop Profitability Decrease → Bean Price Increase~~.

Of course, we should also be on the lookout for restatements of the conditional statements. Let's move on to the answer choices.

(A) If the Coffee Shoppe's overall profitability decreases, the price it pays for coffee beans will have continued to increase.

This answer choice can be diagrammed as

Shop Profitability Decrease → Bean Price Increase

This is the flipped version of our anticipated answer choice. This is a loser.

(B) If the Coffee Shoppe's overall profitability decreases, either it will have begun selling noncoffee products or its coffee sales will have decreased.

This answer choice can be diagrammed as

Shop Profitability Decrease → Noncoffee Products OR Coffee Sales Decrease

This is an invalid inference. Shop Profitability Decrease is not the sufficient condition of any of the statements or of the inference, so we cannot infer anything from the shop's overall profitability decreasing. We can categorize this answer choice as a loser.

(C) The Coffee Shoppe's overall profitability will decrease if the price it pays for coffee beans continues to increase.

This matches our anticipated answer choice. It can be diagrammed as

Bean Price Increase → Shop Profitability Decrease

This is a candidate.

(D) The price it pays for coffee beans cannot decrease without the Coffee Shoppe's overall profitability also decreasing.

This answer choice can be diagrammed as

~~Shop Profitability Decrease~~ → ~~Bean Price Decrease~~

This is a tricky answer choice because it is very similar to the contrapositive of the inference. However, it is an invalid inference on account of a slight difference. This answer choice has bean prices not decreasing as the necessary condition, whereas the contrapositive of the inference has bean prices not increasing as the necessary condition. This is a loser.

(E) Either the price it pays for coffee beans will continue to increase or the Coffee Shoppe's coffee sales will increase.

This answer choice states Bean Price Increase OR Coffee Sales Increase. Although the stimulus states Bean Price Increase → Coffee Sales Decrease, this does not necessarily mean that ~~Bean Price Increase~~ → Coffee Sales Increase. Coffee sales could decrease for another reason, or they could stay at the same level. This is a loser.

As (C) is the only candidate, it has to be the correct answer choice.

Implication

Must Be True
Implication
Must Be False

Implication

≈ 5.8 questions per test

Example Prompts

Which one of the following is *most strongly supported* by the information above?

Which of the following is *best illustrated* by the statements above?

Which one of the following *most logically* completes the argument?

Take These Steps

Read the stimulus, which usually includes a fact pattern. Does it include an incomplete argument?

Does it include an unusual circumstance?

No →

Yes ↓

No →

Does it include conditional language?

Yes ↓   No ↓

Yes (incomplete argument) →
Outline the argument, diagramming the conditional statements. Anticipate a possible conclusion to the argument based on this information.

Summarize the stimulus, diagramming the conditional statements. Anticipate a plausible explanation for the unusual circumstance in the stimulus. Take note of any clues related to this in the stimulus.

Summarize the stimulus, diagramming the conditional statements. Anticipate a valid inference, a contrapositive, a paraphrase of a proposition, or a weak statement supported by the stimulus.

Summarize the stimulus. Consider the relationships between the propositions, focusing on the strongest propositions. Anticipate a paraphrase of a proposition or a weak statement supported by the stimulus.

Answer Choices

Correct Answer Choices	Incorrect Answer Choices
Statements strongly supported by the stimulus	Statements not strongly support by the stimulus
Accurate paraphrases of propositions or summaries of the stimulus	Inaccurate paraphrases of propositions
Valid inferences or contrapositives	Invalid inferences or contrapositives
Explanations of unusual circumstances or possible conclusions to arguments	Irrelevant information or broad claims not supported by the stimulus
Often statements that are weak in logical force	Opinions presented as facts
	Statements that are too strong in logical force

Implication (IMP) questions are similar to MBT questions, but there is one important difference—IMP questions do not require the same degree of certainty. Whereas the correct answer choice for an MBT must necessarily be true based on the information in the stimulus, the correct answer choice for an IMP question only needs to have a significant possibility of being true. In other words, IMP questions are more flexible with regard to the relationship between the correct answer choice and the stimulus.

There are two distinct subtypes of IMP questions: incomplete argument and unusual circumstance. The first asks you to find the most likely conclusion to an argument, while the second requires that you resolve an apparent discrepancy or contradiction. In addition, IMP questions may simply ask you to find the answer choice that is most strongly supported by the information in the stimulus. The majority of IMP questions include fact patterns, but arguments appear more frequently in IMP questions than they do in other types of Inference questions.

How to Solve Implication Questions

Conditional language is less common in IMP questions than in MBT and MBF questions. Regardless of whether conditional statements are included, all IMP questions fall into one of the following three categories.

If There Is an Incomplete Argument

The stimulus for this type of IMP question always includes an argument with one or more premises and possibly subsidiary conclusions as well. It also includes a conclusion indicator followed by a partial conclusion and _____. The prompt usually asks which answer choice most logically completes the argument. You must consider the content of the premises as well as their relationships with each other to determine the most likely conclusion for the argument. As you read the stimulus, ask yourself what argument the author is trying to make.

Let's look at an example:

> Advertisers have learned that people are more easily encouraged to develop positive attitudes about things toward which they originally have neutral or even negative attitudes if those things are linked, with pictorial help rather than exclusively through prose, to things about which they already have positive attitudes. Therefore, advertisers are likely to _____.
>
> Which one of the following most logically completes the argument?
>
> (A) use little if any written prose in their advertisements
> (B) try to encourage people to develop positive attitudes about products that can be better represented pictorially than in prose
> (C) place their advertisements on television rather than in magazines
> (D) highlight the desirable features of the advertised product by contrasting them pictorially with undesirable features of a competing product
> (E) create advertisements containing pictures of things most members of the target audience like

This stimulus includes only one premise, which states that advertisers have learned that people will develop positive attitudes toward products if those products are linked through pictures—not just prose—to other products they feel positively about. Looking at the incomplete conclusion, we can see that the correct answer choice will be about how advertisers are likely to capitalize on this. Accordingly, we can anticipate that the correct answer choice will be about using images to advertise products. Let's look at the answer choices:

(A) use little if any written prose in their advertisements

It seems very probable that advertisers will use pictures to promote products, but this does not mean that they are likely to limit the use of prose—especially to this extent. The premise suggests that pictures are used to supplement prose rather than replace it. We can consider this a loser.

(B) try to encourage people to develop positive attitudes about products that can be better represented pictorially than in prose

This suggests that advertisers are likely to focus on products that can be better represented through pictures than through prose. There is no information about this in the stimulus. This answer choice also ignores a key idea in the stimulus; namely, that the products being promoted must be linked through pictures to products customers already have a positive attitude toward. This is a loser.

(C) place their advertisements on television rather than in magazines

This answer choice introduces irrelevant information. There is nothing in the stimulus about television being a better medium for advertisements than magazines. This is a loser.

(D) highlight the desirable features of the advertised product by contrasting them pictorially with undesirable features of a competing product

This answer choice introduces irrelevant information. There is nothing in the stimulus about comparing desirable and undesirable features of competing products. (D) is also a loser.

(E) create advertisements containing pictures of things most members of the target audience like

This matches our anticipated answer choice. Advertisers are likely to create ads with pictures of things that the consumers like. This is the correct answer choice.

If There Is an Unusual Circumstance

An IMP question may include a stimulus with an unusual circumstance. This means that there is a discrepancy or contradiction that must be resolved. For this type of question, you should identify the competing facts in the stimulus and anticipate an explanation that accounts for them. Keep in mind that the stimulus itself often includes a clue regarding this explanation.

Let's look at an example:

> In the recent election, a country's voters overwhelmingly chose Adler over Burke. Voters knew that Burke offered more effective strategies for dealing with most of the country's problems. Moreover, Burke has a long public record of successful government service

that testifies to competence and commitment. It was well known, however, that Burke's environmental policy coincided with the interests of the country's most dangerous polluter, whereas Adler proposed a policy of strict regulation.

Which one of the following is most strongly supported by the information above?

(A) Throughout their respective political careers, Adler has been more committed to taking measures to protect the country's environment than Burke has been.
(B) Voters realized that their country's natural resources are rapidly being depleted.
(C) The concern of the country's voters for the environment played an important role in Adler's election.
(D) Offering effective strategies for dealing with a country's problems is more important in winning an election than having a long record of successful government service.
(E) In every respect other than environmental policy, Burke would have served the country better than Adler will.

The stimulus includes an unusual circumstance—Adler overwhelmingly won the election, even though Burke should have been more favored by the voters because he has more effective policies for dealing with the nation's problems and a long record of public service. There is also some information about the two candidates' environmental policies—Burke's coincided with the country's most dangerous polluter, while Adler was in favor of strict environmental regulation. Although no mention is made of how voters viewed this issue, it seems reasonable to suppose that it played a major role in the election, and that Adler won because of his environmental policy. This would resolve the unusual circumstance. Does this necessarily have to be true? No. It could be the case that something else about Adler appealed to voters. Maybe he seemed much more genuine and honest. Maybe he was endorsed by another popular politician. There are many other possibilities. But, looking at the information in the stimulus, it seems highly likely that Adler's stance on the environment played at least some role in his victory. We should anticipate a correct answer choice related to this.

(A) Throughout their respective political careers, Adler has been more committed to taking measures to protect the country's environment than Burke has been.

This matches our anticipated answer choice. However, it may be too broad to be the correct answer choice. We only have information about Adler's and Burke's proposed environmental policies at the time of the election. However, we will consider it as a candidate for now.

(B) Voters realized that their country's natural resources are rapidly being depleted.

This answer choice is definitely too broad. The country's natural resources are not mentioned in the stimulus. There could be other environmental concerns that are important to voters. This is a loser.

(C) The concern of the country's voters for the environment played an important role in Adler's election.

This matches our anticipated answer choice. Although Burke's strategies and record should have appealed to voters, his opponent won. The only variable in the stimulus that can account for this is their different environmental policies. This answer choice is a candidate.

(D) Offering effective strategies for dealing with a country's problems is more important in winning an election than having a long record of successful government service.

This is a relational statement that is not supported by the stimulus. We can infer that having a strict environmental policy is more important than having effective strategies or a long public record, but there is no information that allows us to compare having effective strategies and having a long record. This is a loser.

(E) In every respect other than environmental policy, Burke would have served the country better than Adler will.

This is another answer choice that is too broad. First, just because voters preferred Adler's environmental policy, this does not mean it is in the best interest of the country. It could be that Burke's environmental policy would better serve the country's interests. Second, the stimulus said that voters believed Burke had more effective strategies for most (not all) of the country's problems. This means that there could be some nonenvironmental problems that Burke did not have effective strategies for. But this answer choice states that Burke would have served his country better with regard to every issue other than environmental ones. We can categorize (E) as a loser.

We have two candidates, (A) and (C), so we need to eliminate one. (A) is a much broader claim than (C). We have no clear information about Burke's and Adler's positions throughout the course of their political careers. What if Burke had been in favor of environmental regulation early in his career? What if Adler had never cared about environmental issues until the recent election? This answer choice involves too much uncertainty, so we can eliminate it. This means that (C) has to be the correct answer choice. Even though it has a possibility of being false, it is the only answer choice that is strongly supported by the stimulus.

If There Is Neither an Incomplete Argument nor an Unusual Circumstance

Finally, the stimulus of an IMP question may contain neither an incomplete argument nor an unusual circumstance. In this case, the stimulus is almost always a fact pattern. A stimulus such as this will occasionally involve conditional reasoning. You should diagram the conditional statements and then attempt to make valid inferences. If there are statements that can be linked to form a logic chain, anticipate a correct answer choice that is an inference based on the ends of the chain or its contrapositive. You should also look for valid strength modifier inferences and anticipate one of these or one of their contrapositives as being the correct answer choice. Occasionally, the correct answer choice is simply a paraphrase of one of the statements, a contrapositive of one of the statements, or a claim that is supported by the statements.

More commonly, the stimulus does not include conditional language. This makes it very difficult to anticipate the correct answer choice. In this case, you should summarize the stimulus and then look for restatements of individual propositions or of the stimulus as a whole in the answer choices. The correct answer may also be a statement that is supported by the stimulus.

When answering an IMP question that has a fact-pattern stimulus, it is important to remember the distinction between IMP and MBT questions made at the beginning of this section. The correct answer choice to an IMP question does not necessarily have to be true—it just needs to be strongly supported by the information in the stimulus.

Let's look at an example:

> Journalists agree universally that lying is absolutely taboo. Yet, while many reporters claim that spoken word ought to be quoted verbatim, many others believe that tightening a quote from a person who is interviewed is legitimate on grounds that the speaker's remarks would have been more concise if the speaker had written them instead. Also, many reporters

believe that, to expose wrongdoing, failing to identify oneself as a reporter is permissible, while others condemn such behavior as a type of lying.

Which one of the following is most supported by the information above?

(A) Reporters make little effort to behave ethically.
(B) There is no correct answer to the question of whether lying in a given situation is right or wrong.
(C) Omission of the truth is the same thing as lying.
(D) Since lying is permissible in some situations, reporters are mistaken to think that it is absolutely taboo.
(E) Reporters disagree on what sort of behavior qualifies as lying.

The first step is to summarize the stimulus. Despite the presence of several strength modifiers, this stimulus does not include any useful conditional statements. The propositions are simply presenting reporters' opinions about several journalism-related issues. Journalists universally agree that lying is wrong, but some claim that spoken words should be quoted verbatim while others think that cleaning up a quote is permissible. Some reporters feel that it is sometimes acceptable to fail to identify oneself as a reporter, while others think this is a form of lying. An important consideration is that the propositions in this stimulus are mostly opinions. For example, even though all journalists agree that lying is taboo, this does not mean that *lying is taboo* is strongly supported by the stimulus— this is the opinion of the journalists, not a fact. We should anticipate a correct answer choice that is a restatement of an individual proposition or of the stimulus as a whole, or one that is supported by the stimulus.

(A) Reporters make little effort to behave ethically.

This answer choice includes irrelevant information. The amount of effort reporters make to behave ethically is not discussed in the stimulus. We can consider it a loser.

(B) There is no correct answer to the question of whether lying in a given situation is right or wrong.

Just because journalists are undecided about the question of whether lying in a given situation is right or wrong does not mean that there is no correct answer. This is another loser.

(C) Omission of the truth is the same thing as lying.

This is not supported by the stimulus. The journalists disagree about whether omitting the truth should be considered lying. Even if they were in agreement, we would still be dealing with an opinion, not a fact. This belongs in the loser category.

(D) Since lying is permissible in some situations, reporters are mistaken to think that it is absolutely taboo.

We cannot say that lying is permissible in some situations. First, the stimulus includes only opinions about this issue, not facts. Second, it is implied that the journalists who hold the opinion that concealing one's identity is permissible in some situations do not consider it to be lying. Therefore, we cannot even say that some people think lying is permissible in some situations. This answer choice is a loser.

(E) Reporters disagree on what sort of behavior qualifies as lying.

This matches one of our anticipated answer choices. It involves the opinions of journalists. Given the contents of the stimulus, this is a good sign. One thing we know for certain from the stimulus is that reporters hold different opinions about what constitutes lying. This answer choice is strongly supported by the stimulus and therefore has to be correct.

Looking at the Answer Choices

The correct answer choice of an IMP question is a statement that is strongly supported by the stimulus. If the stimulus is an incomplete argument, the correct answer choice is a possible conclusion. If the stimulus includes an unusual circumstance, the correct answer choice addresses it. Regardless, correct answer choices for IMP questions all tend to make weak claims rather than strong ones. You should always select the answer choice with the weakest language if you are unable to select between multiple candidates.

Incorrect answers choices for IMP questions also contain tricks such as introducing irrelevant details or making broad claims that are not supported by the stimulus. You should also watch out for opinions from the stimulus stated as facts in the answer choices. For example, if the stimulus states, "All members of this political party believe that democracy is the best form of government," an incorrect answer choice may claim, "Democracy is the best form of government." At first glance, this seems like a candidate because it appears to be a restatement of a proposition from the stimulus. However, the first statement conveys the opinion of a group of people, while the second mistakenly treats this opinion as fact. Just because someone believes something does not make it true.

After identifying this as an IMP question, read the stimulus.

In modern "brushless" car washes, cloth strips called mitters have replaced brushes. Mitters are easier on most cars' finishes than brushes are. This is especially important with the new clear-coat finishes found on many cars today, which are more easily scratched than older finishes are.

Does this stimulus contain an incomplete argument? If so, what conclusion is the argument attempting to advance?

_____

_____

_____

Does this stimulus contain an unusual circumstance? If so, what would be a plausible explanation for this circumstance?

_____

_____

_____

_____

If you see any conditional statements, diagram them below. Diagram the contrapositives as well.

_____

_____

_____

_____

Summarize the stimulus, paying close attention to the relationships between propositions.

_____

_____

_____

_____

For each answer choice below, determine whether it is strongly supported. Then, explain why or why not.

(A) When car washes all used brushes rather than mitters, there were more cars on the road with scratched finishes than there are today.

_____

_____

_____

(B) Modern "brushless" car washes were introduced as a direct response to the use of clear-coat finishes on cars.

_____

_____

_____

(C) Modern "brushless" car washes usually do not produce visible scratches on cars with older finishes.

_____

_____

_____

(D) Brushes are more effective than mitters and are preferred to cleaning cars with older finishes.

_____

_____

_____

(E) More cars in use today have clear-coat finishes rather than older finishes.

_____

_____

_____

Stimulus:

In modern "brushless" car washes, cloth strips called mitters have replaced brushes. Mitters are easier on most cars' finishes than brushes are. This is especially important with the new clear-coat finishes found on many cars today, which are more easily scratched than older finishes are.

Incomplete argument:

It does not include an incomplete argument.

Unusual circumstance:

It does not include an unusual circumstance.

Diagram:

There are no conditional statements.

Summary:

Modern car washes use mitters, which are easier on car finishes than brushes. This is especially important for newer cars with clear-coat finishes, as these get scratched more easily than older finishes.

Answer Choices:

(A) **When car washes all used brushes rather than mitters, there were more cars on the road with scratched finishes than there are today.**

This is not supported. We can assume that when car washes had brushes, most cars had older finishes. However, there is no information in the stimulus about whether older finishes tended to get scratched by brushes.

(B) **Modern "brushless" car washes were introduced as a direct response to the use of clear-coat finishes on cars.**

This is a causal relationship that is not supported by the stimulus. Based on the stimulus, we cannot infer that clear-coat finishes CAUSE the introduction of mitters. It could be the other way around. Or, there may be another cause.

(C) **Modern "brushless" car washes usually do not produce visible scratches on cars with older finishes.**

This is supported. If mitters are easier on most cars' finishes than brushes, and clear-coat finishes are more easily scratched than older finishes, it would make sense that mitters usually do not produce visible scratches on older finishes. Does this necessarily have to be true? No. But it is strongly supported by the stimulus, which is sufficient for an IMP question.

(D) **Brushes are more effective than mitters and are preferred to cleaning cars with older finishes.**

This is not supported. It is a relational statement that introduces new information about the efficacy of brushers and mitters.

(E) **More cars in use today have clear-coat finishes rather than older finishes.**

This is not supported. It is new information. The frequency of each type of finish is not discussed in the stimulus.

Problem Set: Implication

1. Although fiber-optic telephone cable is more expensive to manufacture than copper telephone cable, a telephone network using fiber-optic cable is less expensive overall than a telephone network using copper cable. This is because copper cable requires frequent amplification of complex electrical signals to carry them for long distances, whereas the pulses of light that are transmitted along fiber-optic cable can travel much farther before amplification is needed.

The above statements, if true, most strongly support which one of the following?

(A) The material from which fiber-optic cable is manufactured is more expensive than the copper from which copper cable is made.

(B) The increase in the number of transmissions of complex signals through telephone cables is straining those telephone networks that still use copper cable.

(C) Fiber-optic cable can carry many more signals simultaneously than copper cable can.

(D) Signals transmitted through fiber-optic cable travel at the same speeds as signals transmitted through copper cable.

(E) The cost associated with frequent amplification of signals traveling through copper cable exceeds the extra manufacturing cost of fiber-optic cable.

2. Cardiologist: Coronary bypass surgery is commonly performed on patients suffering from coronary artery disease when certain other therapies would be as effective. Besides being relatively inexpensive, these other therapies pose less risk to the patient since they are less intrusive. Bypass surgery is especially debatable for single-vessel disease.

The cardiologist's statements, if true, most strongly support which one of the following?

(A) Bypass surgery is riskier than all alternative therapies.

(B) Needless bypass surgery is more common today than previously.

(C) Bypass surgery should be performed when more than one vessel is diseased.

(D) Bypass surgery is an especially expensive therapy when used to treat single-vessel disease.

(E) Sometimes there are equally effective alternatives to bypass surgery that involve less risk.

3. Early urban societies could not have been maintained without large-scale farming nearby. This is because other methods of food acquisition, such as foraging, cannot support populations as dense as urban ones. Large-scale farming requires irrigation, which remained unfeasible in areas far from rivers or lakes until more recent times.

Which one of the following is most strongly supported by the information above?

(A) Most people who lived in early times lived in areas near rivers or lakes.

(B) Only if farming is possible in the absence of irrigation can societies be maintained in areas far from rivers or lakes.

(C) In early times it was not possible to maintain urban societies in areas far from rivers or lakes.

(D) Urban societies with farms near rivers or lakes do not have to rely upon irrigation to meet their farming needs.

(E) Early rural societies relied more on foraging than on agriculture for food.

4. Philosopher: Nations are not literally persons; they have no thoughts or feelings, and, literally speaking, they perform no actions. Thus, they have no moral rights or responsibilities. But no nation can survive unless many of its citizens attribute such rights and responsibilities to it, for nothing else could prompt people to make the sacrifices national citizenship demands. Obviously, then, a nation _____.

Which one of the following most logically completes the philosopher's argument?

(A) cannot continue to exist unless something other than the false belief that the nation has moral rights motivates its citizens to make sacrifices

(B) cannot survive unless many of its citizens have some beliefs that are literally false

(C) can never be a target of moral praise or blame

(D) is not worth the sacrifices that its citizens make on its behalf

(E) should always be thought of in metaphorical rather than literal terms

5. In response to several bacterial infections traced to its apple juice, McElligott now flash pasteurizes its apple juice by quickly heating and immediately rechilling it. Intensive pasteurization, in which juice is heated for an hour, eliminates bacteria more effectively than does any other method, but is likely to destroy the original flavor. However, because McElligott's citrus juices have not been linked to any bacterial infections, they remain unpasteurized.

The statements above, if true, provide the most support for which one of the following claims?

(A) McElligott's citrus juices contain fewer infectious bacteria than do citrus juices produced by other companies.
(B) McElligott's apple juice is less likely to contain infectious bacteria than are McElligott's citrus juices.
(C) McElligott's citrus juices retain more of the juices' original flavor than do any pasteurized citrus juices.
(D) The most effective method for eliminating bacteria from juice is also the method most likely to destroy flavor.
(E) Apple juice that undergoes intensive pasteurization is less likely than McElligott's apple juice is to contain bacteria.

6. Certain bacteria that produce hydrogen sulfide as a waste product would die if directly exposed to oxygen. The hydrogen sulfide reacts with oxygen, removing it and so preventing it from harming the bacteria. Furthermore, the hydrogen sulfide tends to kill other organisms in the area, thereby providing the bacteria with a source of food. As a result, a dense colony of these bacteria produces for itself an environment in which it can continue to thrive indefinitely.

Which one of the following is most strongly supported by the information above?

(A) A dense colony of the bacteria can indefinitely continue to produce enough hydrogen sulfide to kill other organisms in the area and to prevent oxygen from harming the bacteria.
(B) The hydrogen sulfide produced by the bacteria kills other organisms in the area by reacting with and removing oxygen.
(C) Most organisms, if killed by the hydrogen sulfide produced by the bacteria, can provide a source of food for the bacteria.
(D) The bacteria can continue to thrive indefinitely only in an environment in which the hydrogen sulfide they produce has removed all oxygen and killed other organisms in the area.
(E) If any colony of bacteria produces hydrogen sulfide as a waste product, it thereby ensures that it is both provided with a source of food and protected from harm by oxygen.

7. Editorialist: News media rarely cover local politics thoroughly, and local political business is usually conducted secretively. These factors each tend to isolate local politicians from their electorates. This has the effect of reducing the chance that any particular act of resident participation will elicit a positive official response, which in turn discourages resident participation in local politics.

Which one of the following is most strongly supported by the editorialist's statements?

(A) Particular acts of resident participation would be likely to elicit a positive response from local politicians if those politicians were less isolated from their electorate.

(B) Local political business should be conducted less secretively because this would avoid discouraging resident participation in local politics.

(C) The most important factor influencing a resident's decision as to whether to participate in local politics is the chance that the participation will elicit a positive official response.

(D) More-frequent thorough coverage of local politics would reduce at least one source of discouragement from resident participation in local politics.

(E) If resident participation in local politics were not discouraged, this would cause local politicians to be less isolated from their electorate.

8. Market Analyst: According to my research, 59 percent of consumers anticipate paying off their credit card balances in full before interest charges start to accrue, intending to use the cards only to avoid carrying cash and writing checks. This research also suggests that in trying to win business from their competitors, credit card companies tend to concentrate on improving the services their customers are the most interested in. Therefore, my research would lead us to expect that _____.

Which one of the following most logically completes the market analyst's argument?

(A) most consumers would be indifferent about which company's credit card they use

(B) credit card companies would not make the interest rate they charge on cards the main selling point

(C) most consumers would prefer paying interest on credit card debts over borrowing money from banks

(D) most consumers would ignore the length of time a credit card company allows to pay the balance due before interest accrues

(E) the most intense competition among credit card companies would be over the number of places that they can get to accept their credit cards

1. **Correct Answer (E).** *Prep Test 47, Section 3, Question 1.*

This stimulus does not involve an incomplete argument. However, it includes an unusual circumstance. We will begin by summarizing the stimulus, diagramming the conditional statements in the process. Note that this stimulus is an argument with a counter-premise, premises, and a conclusion. It can be outlined as follows:

> CP: Fiber-optic telephone cables are more expensive than copper telephone cable.
> P1: Copper Cable → Frequent Amplification
> P2: Fiber-Optic Cable → Less Frequent Amplification
> ———————————————————————————————————————
> C: Overall, fiber-optic network is less expensive than copper-cable network.

The unusual circumstance is apparent in the counter-premise and conclusion. If fiber-optic cables are more expensive than copper ones, why is a fiber-optic network less expensive than a copper-cable one? The two premises provide a clue. Copper cables require more frequent amplification of signals than fiber-optic cables. If the amplification process somehow adds to the cost of the network, then this resolves our unusual circumstance. We can anticipate a correct answer choice related to this.

(A) The material from which fiber-optic cable is manufactured is more expensive than the copper from which copper cable is made.

At first glance, this answer choice seems like a restatement of the counter-premise. However, it introduces a new detail—the material from which fiber-optic cables are made is more expensive. This is not supported by the stimulus. Other factors related to the manufacturing process could make fiber-optic cables more expensive. We can consider this answer choice a loser.

(B) The increase in the number of transmissions of complex signals through telephone cables is straining those telephone networks that still use copper cable.

This answer choice presents irrelevant information. There is nothing in the stimulus about the number of signal transmissions straining networks. This is a loser.

(C) Fiber-optic cable can carry many more signals simultaneously than copper cable can.

This introduces irrelevant information. The stimulus claims that amplification is needed more frequently for copper cables than for fiber-optic cables because pulses of light can travel farther along fiber-optic cables before amplification is needed. However, there is no indication that this affects the number of signals that can be transmitted simultaneously. This answer choice is a loser.

(D) Signals transmitted through fiber-optic cable travel at the same speeds as signals transmitted through copper cable.

This answer choice also includes irrelevant information. Speed is not mentioned anywhere in the stimulus. As a result, it is impossible to determine whether signals travel through the two types of cable at the same speed or at different speeds. This answer choice is a loser.

(E) The cost associated with frequent amplification of signals traveling through copper cable exceeds the extra manufacturing cost of fiber-optic cable.

This matches our anticipated answer choice. The costs related to the amplification of signals for copper cables are greater than the additional cost of manufacturing fiber-optic cables. This accounts for the copper-cable networks being more expensive. Although this answer choice does not necessarily have to be true, it is strongly supported by the stimulus and resolves the unusual circumstance. This has to be the correct answer choice.

2. **Correct Answer (E).** *Prep Test 44, Section 2, Question 2.*

This stimulus includes neither an incomplete argument nor an unusual circumstance. Conditional statements are also absent. Therefore, we should simply summarize the stimulus. It states that coronary bypass surgery is a treatment commonly used on people suffering from coronary artery disease despite there being other therapies that are less expensive, less risky, and yet just as effective. Bypass surgery seems to be a more controversial option when the patient has single diseased vessel. We should anticipate an answer choice that is a paraphrase of a proposition or that is supported by the stimulus.

(A) Bypass surgery is riskier than all alternative therapies.

This is too broad of a claim. We know that bypass surgery is riskier than some unspecified therapies, but we do not know if it is the riskiest of all available therapies. Here, a relational statement from the stimulus is expressed as an absolute statement. This is a loser.

(B) Needless bypass surgery is more common today than previously.

This is irrelevant information. We know nothing about how common bypass surgery was in the past; we only know that it is common now. This is also a loser.

(C) Bypass surgery should be performed when more than one vessel is diseased.

This is too strong of a claim. The use of *should* suggests that bypass surgery must always be used when more than one vessel is diseased. Although the stimulus implies that bypass surgery can be used in this situation, it also states that other methods are as effective in treating coronary artery disease in general. It also states that these methods are less costly and less risky. This implies that they can be used to treat at least some patients with multiple diseased arteries. As this answer choice includes a logical force error, we can consider it a loser.

(D) Bypass surgery is an especially expensive therapy when used to treat single-vessel disease.

This claim is not supported by the stimulus. The last proposition states that bypass surgery is especially debatable when used to treat single-vessel disease. This may be because it is too expensive or because it is too risky. There may even be another reason. This is a loser.

(E) Sometimes there are equally effective alternatives to bypass surgery that involve less risk.

This matches one of our anticipated answer choices. According to the stimulus, there are less risky therapies that are just as effective as bypass surgery. In addition, this is a weak claim because of the use of *sometimes*. As this is the only candidate, it has to be the correct answer choice.

3. **Correct Answer (C).** *Prep Test 52, Section 3, Question 14.*

This stimulus has neither an incomplete argument nor an unusual circumstance. However, it does include conditional statements. These statements can be diagrammed as follows:

    S1: ~~Large Scale Farming~~ → ~~Early Urban Society~~
    S2: Foraging → ~~Early Urban Society~~
    S3: Large Scale Farming → Irrigation
    S4: Irrigation → ~~Far from River~~ OR ~~Far from Lake~~

In the first sentence, *without* is a negative sufficient indicator—what follows it must be negated before being placed on the left side of the diagram. The second conditional statement does not include any indicators, but it can be rephrased as "If the food acquisition method is foraging, then it cannot support an early urban society." The third statement includes the necessary indicator *requires*. Finally, the fourth statement can be rephrased as "If irrigation occurs, then it must be in areas not far from rivers or not far from lakes." Note that *which* refers to *irrigation* in the preceding clause.

We should now look for valid inferences. We cannot make any strength modifier inferences. However, we can connect the contrapositive of the first statement with the third and fourth statements to create the following logic chain:

Early Urban Society → Large Scale Farming → Irrigation → ~~Far from River~~ OR ~~Far from Lake~~

We can then link the ends of this chain to make the following inference and its contrapositive:

Early Urban Society → ~~Far from River~~ OR ~~Far from Lake~~
Far from River AND Far from Lake → ~~Early Urban Society~~

We should anticipate the correct answer choice being based on one of these inferences. They can be rephrased as "If there was early urban society, then it must not have been far from a river or not far from a lake" and "If it is far from a river and far from a lake, then there could not have been early urban society."

(A) Most people who lived in early times lived in areas near rivers or lakes.

This answer choice seems to be supported by the stimulus. If all urban societies were near rivers or lakes, then it is reasonable to suppose that most people lived close to these bodies of water. Although it is not one of our anticipated answer choices, we will keep it as a candidate.

(B) Only if farming is possible in the absence of irrigation can societies be maintained in areas far from rivers or lakes.

If we assume that the *farming* and *societies* mentioned in this answer choice are the same as the *large-scale farming* and *urban societies* discussed in the stimulus, then this answer choice directly contradicts the stimulus, which states the large-scaling farming requires irrigation. If the terms in the answer choice mean something else, then this is irrelevant information. Either way, this answer choice is a loser.

(C) In early times it was not possible to maintain urban societies in areas far from rivers or lakes.

This matches one of our anticipated answer choices. It expresses the contrapositive of the inference based on combining the ends of the logic chain. This is a candidate.

(D) Urban societies with farms near rivers or lakes do not have to rely upon irrigation to meet their farming needs.

This directly contradicts the stimulus, which states that irrigation was necessary for the large-scale farming that was a requirement for early urban societies. This is a loser.

(E) Early rural societies relied more on foraging than on agriculture for food.

This answer choice includes irrelevant information. Nothing is mentioned in the stimulus about rural societies. We can consider this a loser.

We will now attempt to eliminate one of the candidates. Looking back at (A), we can see that it includes an inaccurate paraphrase: *early urban society* is rephrased as *people living in early times*. We do not know what proportion of people living in early times lived in urban societies. If most people were not members of urban societies, then it is possible that most people did not live near rivers or lakes. Therefore, we can eliminate (A) and choose answer choice (C).

4. Correct Answer (B). *Prep Test 51.5, Section 3, Question 16.*

The stimulus includes an incomplete argument. It can be outlined as follows:

> P1: Nations are not persons.
> SC: Nations have no moral rights or responsibilities.
> P2: ~~Many Citizens Attribute Rights~~ OR ~~Responsibilities to Nation~~ → ~~Nation Survive~~
> C: Obviously, then, a nation _____.

There is a subsidiary conclusion in the second sentence, marked by the indicator *thus*. The third sentence is a conditional statement, and it includes the negative sufficient indicator *unless*. Its contrapositive can be diagrammed as follows:

> Nation Survive → Many Citizens Attribute Rights AND Responsibilities to Nation

The conclusion begins with *obviously, then, a nation*. What do we know about a nation? We know that if it survives, citizens attribute rights and responsibilities to it. But this contradicts the subsidiary conclusion, which states that nations have no moral rights or responsibilities. We should anticipate a correct answer choice that can function as a conclusion while resolving this apparent contradiction.

(A) cannot continue to exist unless something other than the false belief that the nation has moral rights motivates its citizens to make sacrifices

This is not supported by the stimulus. The conditional statement says that for a nation to survive, citizens must ascribe rights and responsibilities to it. This answer choice says that something other than this false belief must be ascribed. Therefore, this answer is a loser.

(B) cannot survive unless many of its citizens have some beliefs that are literally false

This matches our anticipated answer choice. This answer explains the contradiction we noticed in the stimulus. In order for a nation to survive, citizens must believe that a nation has rights and responsibilities. However, the stimulus clearly states that nations do not have rights and responsibilities. Therefore, the beliefs of the citizens must be false. This is a candidate.

(C) can never be a target of moral praise or blame

This answer choice introduces new information. *Moral praise or blame* is different from *moral rights or responsibilities*. This is a loser.

(D) is not worth the sacrifices that its citizens make on its behalf

This is too broad of a claim. It may be true that a nation is not worth the sacrifices of its citizens, but there is nothing in the stimulus to support this. We can consider this answer choice as a loser.

(E) should always be thought of in metaphorical rather than literal terms

This is too strong of a claim. Ascribing rights and responsibilities to a nation as you would to a person could be considered an example of thinking of a nation in metaphorical terms. And based on the stimulus, it may be possible to argue that this should be done. However, the inclusion of *always* makes this answer choice incorrect. Nothing in the stimulus supports the claim that a person should never think of a nation in literal terms. This answer choice is a loser.

As (B) is the only candidate, it has to be the correct answer choice.

5. **Correct Answer (E).** *Prep Test 52, Section 1, Question 24.*

The stimulus includes neither an incomplete argument nor an unusual circumstance. Conditional statements are also absent. Therefore, we should summarize the stimulus and anticipate an answer choice that is supported by it or that is a paraphrase of a proposition.

According to the stimulus, McElligott is now flash pasteurizing its apple juice after bacterial infections were linked to this product. There is a process called intensive pasteurization that eliminates bacteria more effectively than any other method, including flash pasteurization. However, intensive pasteurization is likely to destroy the original flavor. McElligott's citrus juices have not been linked to bacterial infections, so they have not been pasteurized by any method.

(A) McElligott's citrus juices contain fewer infectious bacteria than do citrus juices produced by other companies.

This claim is not supported by the stimulus. We know nothing about the citrus juices produced by other companies and very little about McElligott's citrus juices. This is a loser.

(B) McElligott's apple juice is less likely to contain infectious bacteria than are McElligott's citrus juices.

Again, this answer choice is not supported by the stimulus. There is too much uncertainty.

It is implied that McElligott's citrus juices contain little or no bacteria because they have not been linked to bacterial infections. However, we do not know how effective the flash pasteurization process is at eliminating bacteria from the apple juice. This answer choice is a loser.

(C) McElligott's citrus juices retain more of the juices' original flavor than do any pasteurized citrus juices.

This matches one of our anticipated answer choices. It is a statement supported by the stimulus. McElligott's citrus juice is not pasteurized, so there is no risk of a loss of flavor through pasteurization. We will consider this a candidate for now.

(D) The most effective method for eliminating bacteria from juice is also the method most likely to destroy flavor.

This answer choice seems attractive at first. We know that intensive pasteurization is the most effective method for removing bacteria and that it destroys flavor. However, this answer choice includes a logical force error. The stimulus says that intensive pasteurization is likely to destroy flavor, whereas (D) says it is most likely to destroy flavor. We cannot know from the stimulus that all other methods of pasteurization are less likely to destroy flavor than intensive pasteurization. Therefore, this answer choice is a loser.

(E) Apple juice that undergoes intensive pasteurization is less likely than McElligott's apple juice is to contain bacteria.

This matches one of our anticipated answer choices. We know that intensive pasteurization is the most effective method for eliminating bacteria and that McElligott's apple juice is flash pasteurized. That being said, it may be possible for an apple juice undergoing intensive pasteurization to start with a higher bacteria level—meaning that even following pasteurization it will contain more bacteria than McElligott's. But note that this answer choice makes a weak claim—it includes the modifier *less likely*. As a result, it seems to be supported by the stimulus. We will consider it a candidate.

We now need to eliminate either (C) or (E). Looking back at (C) with a more critical eye, it becomes apparent that although intensive pasteurization may be likely to destroy flavor, we do not know anything about other methods of pasteurization in this regard. Other citrus juices may be pasteurized in a way that eliminates more of their flavor. In addition, the wording of (C) is much stronger than that of (E). (C) says that the citrus juice *retains more*, not *is likely to contain more*, which would match the strength of *less likely* in (E). There is too much uncertainty concerning other pasteurization methods to pick (C), so we can eliminate it and select (E).

6. **Correct Answer (A).** *Prep Test 52, Section 3, Question 23.*

The stimulus contains neither an incomplete argument nor an unusual circumstance. There is a conditional statement, though. It can be diagrammed as follows:

Directly Exposed to Oxygen → Bacteria that Produce HS Die

There are no other conditional statements in the stimulus, which means that we should now summarize the stimulus. Note that this stimulus includes an argument rather than a fact pattern. It seems to be the case that hydrogen sulfide is very helpful to certain bacteria as it removes oxygen and kills other organisms, which then become a source of food. Thus, the bacteria receive both protection and nourishment. The stimulus concludes that a dense colony of these bacteria can create an environment in which they can thrive indefinitely. We should anticipate a correct answer choice that is a paraphrase or the contrapositive of our conditional statement, a paraphrase of another proposition, or a claim that is supported by the stimulus.

(A) **A dense colony of the bacteria can indefinitely continue to produce enough hydrogen sulfide to kill other organisms in the area and to prevent oxygen from harming the bacteria.**

This matches one of our anticipated answer choices. It seems to be a paraphrase of the argument's conclusion with additional details from the other parts of the stimulus included. A dense colony of bacteria can survive indefinitely, and its ability to survive hinges on producing hydrogen sulfide for protection and nourishment. This answer choice is a candidate.

(B) **The hydrogen sulfide produced by the bacteria kills other organisms in the area by reacting with and removing oxygen.**

This answer choice is not supported by the stimulus. Hydrogen sulfide reacts with and removes oxygen, but this is not specified as the cause of other organisms dying. Maybe they die through contact with the hydrogen sulfide. This is a loser.

(C) **Most organisms, if killed by the hydrogen sulfide produced by the bacteria, can provide a source of food for the bacteria.**

This answer choice includes a logical force error. Based on the information in the stimulus, we cannot know that most organisms that die from hydrogen sulfide provide a source of food for the bacteria, just that some do. This is another loser.

(D) **The bacteria can continue to thrive indefinitely only in an environment in which the hydrogen sulfide they produce has removed all oxygen and killed other organisms in the area.**

This is the flipped version of answer choice (A). The stimulus implies that if bacteria are able to remove oxygen and kill other organisms for food, then they will survive indefinitely. This answer choice says that if they survive indefinitely, then they must be able to remove all oxygen and kill other organisms for food. What if there are other conditions that allow the bacteria to survive indefinitely? We can consider this a loser.

(E) If any colony of bacteria produces hydrogen sulfide as a waste product, it thereby ensures that it is both provided with a source of food and protected from harm by oxygen.

This is another logical force error. We cannot know whether any bacteria that produce hydrogen sulfide are provided with food and protection because the stimulus only discusses certain bacteria that produce hydrogen sulfide. This is also a loser.

As (A) is the only candidate, it has to be the correct answer choice.

7. **Correct Answer (D).** *Prep Test 51.5, Section 2, Question 22.*

The stimulus contains neither an incomplete argument nor an unusual circumstance. Conditional language is also absent. However, there are causal relationships between the propositions, which means that they can be joined together to form the following causal chain:

> Lack of Thorough News or Secretive Politics CAUSE Politicians Isolated from Electorate CAUSE Small Chance of Response to Resident Participation CAUSE Discourage Participation

As we can do with a logic chain, we can combine the ends, which results in:

> Lack of Thorough News or Secretive Politics CAUSE Discourage Participation

Although the correct answer choice may well be a paraphrase of another causal relationship in the chain or simply a paraphrase of a proposition, we should anticipate the causal statement above as the most likely correct answer choice. Note that we do not need to worry about a contrapositive—causal statements do not have contrapositives.

(A) Particular acts of resident participation would be likely to elicit a positive response from local politicians if those politicians were less isolated from their electorate.

This answer choice contains a logical force error. We know that feeling isolated from the electorate decreases the chances of a politician responding positively to a particular act of resident participation. If feeling isolated leads to a decrease, then we can say that not feeling isolated would not lead to a decrease, and, therefore, that acts of resident participation would be more likely to elicit a positive response. However, note the use of the word *likely* in (A). This means that over 50 percent of acts of resident participation would receive a positive response, which is too strong of a claim based on the information in the stimulus. Therefore, this answer choice is a loser.

(B) Local political business should be conducted less secretively because this would avoid discouraging resident participation in local politics.

Be careful when an answer choice includes *should*. This word conveys as value judgment. If a proposition stated that discouraging resident participation should be avoided, then this answer choice would be possible. However, the stimulus simply describes a situation—no judgments are made. Therefore, this answer choice is also a loser.

(C) The most important factor influencing a resident's decision as to whether to participate in local politics is the chance that the participation will elicit a positive official response.

This answer choice includes a logical force error. *The most important factor* is too strong. The stimulus indicates that the prospect of drawing a favorable official response is a factor influencing resident participation, but there is no indication that this is the most significant factor. We can categorize this answer choice as a loser.

(D) More-frequent thorough coverage of local politics would reduce at least one source of discouragement from resident participation in local politics.

This matches one of our anticipated answer choices. (D) states that additional thorough coverage would reduce one source of discouragement from resident participation. This is closely related to what we got by combining the ends of the causal chain: Lack of Thorough News or Secretive Politics CAUSE Discourage Participation. This is a candidate.

(E) If resident participation in local politics were not discouraged, this would cause local politicians to be less isolated from their electorate.

This answer choice is an attempt to express the contrapositive of part of the causal chain. However, a causal statement does not have a contrapositive. For example, "Playing loud music causes people to dance" does not mean that "Not dancing causes people to not play loud music." This answer choice is a loser.

As (D) is the only candidate, it has to be the correct answer choice.

---

8. **Correct Answer (B).** *Prep Test 59, Section 2, Question 24.*

The stimulus includes an incomplete argument, so we should outline the argument and then anticipate a possible conclusion. The argument can be outlined as follows:

P1: Most customers plan to pay off credit card balances to avoid interest.
P2: Credit card companies concentrate on services customers are most interested in.
C: Therefore, my research would lead us to expect that _____.

We should anticipate a correct answer choice related to credit card companies focusing on the group of customers who pay off their balances to avoid interest.

(A) most consumers would be indifferent about which company's credit card they use

This does not match our anticipated answer choice, but it seems possible. Why would customers care which credit card they use if they are not planning on paying interest? We will keep this as a candidate for now.

(B) credit card companies would not make the interest rate they charge on cards the main selling point

This matches our anticipated answer choice. If most consumers do not plan on paying interest, credit card companies are unlikely to focus on interests rates when promoting their cards. If they do, their main selling point will not appeal to most customers. This is another candidate.

(C) most consumers would prefer paying interest on credit card debts over borrowing money from banks

This answer choice introduces irrelevant information. We know nothing about the preferences of consumers with regard to borrowing money from banks. This is a loser.

(D) most consumers would ignore the length of time a credit card company allows to pay the balance due before interest accrues

This answer choice is not supported by the stimulus. If customers prefer to pay credit card balances before interest accrues, then they are likely to be concerned about the length of time companies allow before interest is charged. This is another loser.

(E) the most intense competition among credit card companies would be over the number of places that they can get to accept their credit cards

This answer choice includes irrelevant information. There is nothing in the passage about places where particular credit cards are accepted. This is a loser.

We now must eliminate one of our candidates. Looking at (A) more critically, we can see a couple of issues. First, there may be other factors besides interest rates that determine which credit cards consumers prefer, such as reward points or annual fees. Second, this is a MOST statement, meaning that it is relatively difficult to prove. In contrast, (B) is a SOME statement, and it is more strongly supported by the stimulus. Remember, when in doubt, select the weaker statement. We can eliminate (A) and choose (B).

Must Be False

INFERENCE FAMILY

Must Be True
Implication
Must Be False

Must Be False

≈ 0.9 questions per test

Example Prompts

If the statements above are true, then which of the following *must be false*?

Based on the information above, which one of the following *cannot be true*?

If the statements above are true, each of the following *could be true EXCEPT*:

Take These Steps

Read the stimulus, which usually includes a fact pattern. Does it include conditional language?

Yes →

Does the stimulus include multiple conditional statements?

No ↓

Summarize the stimulus. Consider the relationships between the propositions, focusing on the strongest propositions. Anticipate a strong claim that directly contradicts a proposition or a relationship between propositions.

Yes ↓

Summarize the stimulus, diagramming the conditional statements. Anticipate a strong claim that contradicts a combination or strength modifier inference, a proposition, a contrapositive, or a relationship between propositions.

No ↓

Summarize the stimulus, diagramming the conditional statement. Anticipate a strong claim that contradicts the conditional statement, its contrapositive, another proposition, or a relationship between propositions.

Answer Choices

Correct Answer Choices	Incorrect Answer Choices
Statements that are definitely false based on the stimulus	Statements that are not necessarily false based on the stimulus
Statements that contradict valid inferences, contrapositives, propositions, or relationships between propositions	Accurate paraphrases of propositions
Often statements that are strong in logical force	Valid inferences or contrapositives
	Irrelevant information or broad claims not supported by the stimulus
	Statements that are too weak in logical force

Must Be False (MBF) questions ask you to determine which answer choice can definitely be proven false using the information in the stimulus. If the answer choice is potentially false or cannot be proven to be true, this is not enough. It must directly contradict the information in the stimulus, meaning that it has no possibility of being true. If an answer choice could be false but also could be true, it cannot be the correct answer choice. This is why one of the MBF prompts states, "each of the following could be true EXCEPT."

As with MBT questions, MBF questions are usually fact patterns, and you must assume that all propositions are true. MBF questions often include conditional language.

How to Solve Must Be False Questions

Most MBF questions include conditional statements. Therefore, the first step toward solving an MBF question is to identify the conditional language, if any. As mentioned earlier, when you are certain that you have identified the correct answer choice, you may want to simply mark it and move on to save time. This is particularly useful for MBF questions because an answer choice that is necessarily false is always the correct answer choice.

If There Is Conditional Language

Diagram all of the conditional statements. Then look for valid combination and strength modifier inferences. You should also take note of all the contrapositives. The correct answer choice usually directly contradicts a conditional statement, inference, or contrapositive. In rare cases, it may contradict a nonconditional proposition in the stimulus. Keep in mind that the correct answer choice needs to be more than just an invalid inference or inaccurate paraphrase. The answer choice must be necessarily false based on the information in the stimulus. Let's look at an example:

> All bookworms wear glasses. If you wear glasses, you look smart.
>
> If the statements above are true, then which of the following must be false?
>
> (A) Most bookworms look smart.
> (B) All people who look smart are bookworms.
> (C) Some bookworms do not look smart.
> (D) Most people who wear glasses are bookworms.
> (E) Becoming a bookworm causes people to look smart.

This argument can be outlined as follows:

    S1: Bookworm → Glasses
    S2: Glasses → Look Smart

We can then combine these two statements to create the following logic chain and inference based on the ends of the chain:

    Bookworm → Glasses → Look Smart
    Bookworm → Look Smart

Now, let's consider the answer choices. Remember, we are looking for the one that must be false based on the stimulus.

(A) Most bookworms look smart.

This not only could be true, it is true. If all bookworms look smart, then most must look smart. Remember, *most* (>50%) is inclusive of *all* (100%). This is a loser.

(B) All people who look smart are bookworms.

This could be true. It is an invalid inference based on flipped reasoning, but that does not mean that it must be false. It may be the case that everyone who looks smart is a bookworm and every bookworm looks smart. We cannot prove that (B) is true, based on the stimulus, but neither can we prove that it is false. This is another loser.

(C) Some bookworms do not look smart.

This must be false. If all bookworms look smart, it cannot be the case that some do not. This directly violates the inference we made from the ends of the logic chain. This is a candidate.

(D) Most people who wear glasses are bookworms.

This could be true. This statement cannot be proven, but it does not contradict anything in the stimulus. This is a loser.

(E) Becoming a bookworm causes people to look smart.

This could be true too. This answer choice implies a causal relationship between becoming a bookwork and looking smart. The stimulus does not support (E), but neither does it include any information that precludes (E). This is also a loser.

As (C) is the only candidate, it has to be the correct answer choice.

If There Is No Conditional Language

When there are no conditional statements, which is uncommon for MBF questions, summarize the stimulus, paying careful attention to the relationships between the propositions. Anticipate a strong statement that directly contradicts a proposition or a relationship between propositions. This type of question is very difficult to anticipate a correct answer choice for.

Looking at the Answer Choices

The correct answer choice is always a statement that is definitely false based on the information in the stimulus. Further, the correct answer choice directly contradicts a proposition or valid inference. Unlike MBT and IMP questions, MBF questions tend to have strong claims as correct answer choices. This is because a strong claim is easier to prove false than a weak claim is.

The incorrect answer choices often make invalid inferences, introduce new information, or make broad claims. These may be attractive because they cannot be proven true, but neither can they be proven false. You should always keep in mind that you are looking for an answer choice that must be false, based on the information in the stimulus.

If you are having problems identifying a correct answer choice, it sometimes helps to ask yourself whether an answer choice could be true. If it has the possibility of being true, it cannot be the correct answer.

Drill: Must Be False

After identifying this as an MBF question, read the stimulus.

Two things are true of all immoral actions. First, if they are performed in public, they offend public sensibilities. Second, they are accompanied by feelings of guilt.

If you see any conditional statements, diagram them below. Diagram the contrapositives as well.

_____

_____

_____

_____

_____

Summarize the stimulus, paying close attention to the relationships between propositions.

_____

_____

_____

_____

_____

For each answer choice below, determine whether it could be true. Then, explain why or why not.

(A) Some immoral actions that are not performed in public are not accompanied by feelings of guilt.

_____

_____

_____

(B) Immoral actions are wrong solely by virtue of being accompanied by feelings of guilt.

_____

_____

_____

(C) Some actions that offend public sensibilities if they are performed in public are not accompanied by feelings of guilt.

_____

_____

_____

(D) Some actions that are accompanied by feelings of guilt are not immoral, even if they frequently offend public sensibilities.

_____

_____

_____

(E) Every action performed in public that is accompanied by feelings of guilt is immoral.

_____

_____

_____

Drill: Must Be False — Answers

Stimulus:

Two things are true of all immoral actions. First, if they are performed in public, they offend public sensibilities. Second, they are accompanied by feelings of guilt.

Diagram:

There are two conditional statements in the stimulus. The first is indicated by the word *if*. The second follows conceptually from the word *all*.

Immoral Action AND In Public → Offend Public

Immoral Action → Feelings of Guilt

These cannot be combined to make any inferences.

Summary:

The phrase *two things are true of all* indicates that two necessary conditions are triggered by an immoral action. First, when an immoral action is performed in public, it offends public sensibilities. Second, an immoral action is accompanied by feelings of guilt.

Answer Choices:

(A) **Some immoral actions that are not performed in public are not accompanied by feelings of guilt.**

This could not be true. This statement can be diagrammed as

Immoral Actions AND ~~In Public~~ ^{S}—^{S} ~~Feelings of Guilt~~

This directly contradicts the second conditional statement. All immoral actions are accompanied by feelings of guilt, whether performed in public or not.

(B) **Immoral actions are wrong solely by virtue of being accompanied by feelings of guilt.**

This could be true. It includes new information—the stimulus does not specify what makes immoral actions wrong. Therefore, this answer choice does not contradict the stimulus.

(C) **Some actions that offend public sensibilities if they are performed in public are not accompanied by feelings of guilt.**

This could be true. We know that immoral actions, whether performed in public or not, are accompanied by feelings of guilt. However, we do not know if the actions mentioned in this answer choice are moral or immoral. Therefore, it could be true that they are not accompanied by guilt.

(D) **Some actions that are accompanied by feelings of guilt are not immoral, even if they frequently offend public sensibilities.**

This could be true. There could be actions that bring on guilt but are not immoral, regardless of whether they offend public sensibilities or not.

(E) **Every action performed in public that is accompanied by feelings of guilt is immoral.**

This could be true. It may be the case that only immoral actions performed in public are accompanied by feelings of guilt and that other actions performed in public are not accompanied by guilt.

Problem Set: Must Be False

1. Those who have the ability to fully concentrate are always of above-average intelligence. Also, being successfully trained in speed-reading will usually be accompanied by an increased ability to concentrate.

   If the statements above are true, then each of the following could be true EXCEPT:

   (A) Some people can speed-read, and are able to fully concentrate, but are of below-average intelligence.
   (B) All people who can speed-read are of above-average intelligence.
   (C) Many people of above-average intelligence are unable to fully concentrate.
   (D) Some people with little ability to concentrate are of below-average intelligence, but can speed-read.
   (E) All people who can speed-read are able to concentrate to some extent.

2. Journalist: Recent studies have demonstrated that a regular smoker who has just smoked a cigarette will typically display significantly better short-term memory skills than a nonsmoker, whether or not the nonsmoker has also just smoked a cigarette for the purposes of the study. Moreover, the majority of those smokers who exhibit this superiority in short-term memory skills will do so for at least eight hours after having last smoked.

   If the journalist's statements are true, then each of the following could be true EXCEPT:

   (A) The short-term memory skills exhibited by a nonsmoker who has just smoked a cigarette are usually substantially worse than the short-term memory skills exhibited by a nonsmoker who has not recently smoked a cigarette.
   (B) The short-term memory skills exhibited by a nonsmoker who has just smoked a cigarette are typically superior to those exhibited by a regular smoker who has just smoked a cigarette.
   (C) The short-term memory skills exhibited by a nonsmoker who has just smoked a cigarette are typically superior to those exhibited by a regular smoker who has not smoked for more than eight hours.
   (D) A regular smoker who, immediately after smoking a cigarette, exhibits short-term memory skills no better than those typically exhibited by a nonsmoker is nevertheless likely to exhibit superior short-term memory skills in the hours following a period of heavy smoking.
   (E) The short-term memory skills exhibited by a regular smoker who last smoked a cigarette five hours ago are typically superior to those exhibited by a regular smoker who has just smoked a cigarette.

3. On the basis of relatively minor morphological differences, some scientists suggest that Neanderthals should be considered a species distinct from Cro-Magnons, the forerunners of modern humans. Yet the fact that the tools used by these two groups of hominids living in different environments were of exactly the same type indicates uncanny behavioral similarities, for only if they faced the same daily challenges and met them in the same way would they have used such tools. This suggests that they were members of the same species, and that the morphological differences are due merely to their having lived in different environments.

If the statements above are true, then each of the following could be true EXCEPT:

(A) Morphological differences between the members of two populations do not guarantee that the two populations do not belong to the same species.

(B) The daily challenges with which an environment confronts its inhabitants are unique to that environment.

(C) There are greater morphological differences between Cro-Magnons and modern humans than there are between Cro-Magnons and Neanderthals.

(D) Use of similar tools is required if members of two distinct groups of tool-making hominids are to be considered members of the same species.

(E) Through much of their coexistence, Cro-Magnons and Neanderthals were geographically isolated from one another.

1. **Correct Answer (A).** *Prep Test 41, Section 3, Question 10.*

The stimulus includes two conditional statements, as signaled by the indicators *always* and *usually*. The statements can be diagrammed as follows:

> S1: Ability to Fully Concentrate $\rightarrow$ Above-Average Intelligence
> S2: Speed-Reading $^M\!\!\rightarrow$ Increase Ability to Concentrate

Note that while the sufficient condition of the first statement and the necessary condition of the second statement look similar, they actually express distinct ideas. These statements cannot be combined to create any inferences. Therefore, we should anticipate an answer choice that contradicts either of these statement or their contrapositives.

(A) Some people can speed-read, and are able to fully concentrate, but are of below-average intelligence.

This matches one of our anticipated answer choices. It can be diagrammed as

> Speed-Reading AND Ability to Fully Concentrate $^S\!\!-\!\!^S$ ~~Above Average Intelligence~~

This directly contradicts the first conditional statement, which states that those with the ability to fully concentrate have above-average intelligence. No one able to fully concentrate can have below-average intelligence. This is a candidate.

(B) All people who can speed-read are of above-average intelligence.

This is not a valid inference, but it does not contradict either of the conditional statements. It could be true that all people who can speed-read are of above-average intelligence. It could also be the case that they are all of below-average intelligence. This answer choice could be true, so it is a loser.

(C) Many people of above-average intelligence are unable to fully concentrate.

This is an invalid inference based on the first conditional statement. However, it does not contradict the statement, so this answer choice could be true. It is a loser.

(D) Some people with little ability to concentrate are of below-average intelligence, but can speed-read.

The second statement says that the ability to speed-read usually boosts a person's ability to concentrate. This answer choice does not contradict that statement because a person could have a very little ability to concentrate to begin with. This answer choice could be true. Therefore, it is a loser.

(E) All people who can speed-read are able to concentrate to some extent.

The ability to speed-read usually boosts your ability to concentrate. This means that even if a person has no ability, speed-reading will increase it. Therefore, all people who can speed-read can concentrate to some extent. This answer choice could be true, so it is another loser.

As (A) is the only candidate, it has to be the correct answer choice.

2. **Correct Answer (B).** *Prep Test 52, Section 1, Question 18.*

The stimulus does not include any conditional statements. It can be summarized as follows: smokers who have recently smoked a cigarette typically exhibit better short-term memory skills than nonsmokers, even if those nonsmokers recently smoked as well. The majority of these smokers display improved memory for up to eight hours. We know that smokers typically have better short-term memory after smoking a cigarette than nonsmokers, so we can anticipate that the answer will be that nonsmokers, whether having recently smoked a cigarette or not, usually have better memories than smokers who have smoked a cigarette in the past eight hours.

(A) **The short-term memory skills exhibited by a nonsmoker who has just smoked a cigarette are usually substantially worse than the short-term memory skills exhibited by a nonsmoker who has not recently smoked a cigarette.**

We do not know how nonsmokers who have smoked compare to those who have not. This is irrelevant information, so this answer choice could be true. It is a loser.

(B) **The short-term memory skills exhibited by a nonsmoker who has just smoked a cigarette are typically superior to those exhibited by a regular smoker who has just smoked a cigarette.**

This matches our anticipated answer choice. The stimulus states that the short-term memory skills of smokers who have recently smoked a cigarette are typically superior to those of nonsmokers, whether they have smoked a cigarette or not. This answer choice contradicts this, so it must be false. (B) is a candidate.

(C) **The short-term memory skills exhibited by a nonsmoker who has just smoked a cigarette are typically superior to those exhibited by a regular smoker who has not smoked for more than eight hours.**

This is irrelevant information. We know nothing about regular smokers who have not smoked in the past eight hours. This answer choice could be true. It is a loser.

(D) **A regular smoker who, immediately after smoking a cigarette, exhibits short-term memory skills no better than those typically exhibited by a nonsmoker is nevertheless likely to exhibit superior short-term memory skills in the hours following a period of heavy smoking.**

There is no indication that the improvement in short-term memory occurs immediately after smoking. Therefore, it may occur hours later. Also, the stimulus makes no reference to heavy smoking. This answer choice could be true, so it is a loser.

(E) **The short-term memory skills exhibited by a regular smoker who last smoked a cigarette five hours ago are typically superior to those exhibited by a regular smoker who has just smoked a cigarette.**

This introduces irrelevant information. The stimulus does not compare smokers who have just smoked with smokers who smoked five hours earlier. Again, it could be the case the improvement in memory skills occurs hours after smoking a cigarette. This answer choice could be true. It is another loser.

As (B) is the only candidate, it has to be the correct answer choice.

3. **Correct Answer (B).** *Prep Test 56, Section 3, Question 22.*

We have one conditional statement here, indicated by the words *only if*. Note that the stimulus is an argument, which is rare among MBF questions. We can outline it as follows:

P1: Similar Tools
P2: Different Environments
P3: Similar Tools → Same Daily Challenges AND Same Solutions
C: Cro-Magnons and Neanderthals were members of same species.

We can anticipate a statement that directly violates our conditional statement or its contrapositive, but we should also be on the lookout for a contradiction of another premise or the conclusion of the argument.

(A) Morphological differences between the members of two populations do not guarantee that the two populations do not belong to the same species.

When an answer choice uses double negatives or confusing language, try to rephrase it. This is saying that two populations with morphological differences may belong to the same species. This not only could be true but must be true based on the stimulus. It is a loser.

(B) The daily challenges with which an environment confronts its inhabitants are unique to that environment.

This matches one of our anticipated answer choices. According to the first two premises, Cro-Magnons and Neanderthals used similar tools and lived in different environments. The conditional statement says that if they used similar tools, they faced the same challenges and found the same solutions. Therefore, they faced the same daily challenges despite living in different environments. This means that daily challenges are not unique to a particular environment. This answer choice contradicts the information in the stimulus, so it must be false. This is a candidate.

(C) There are greater morphological differences between Cro-Magnons and modern humans than there are between Cro-Magnons and Neanderthals.

This is irrelevant information. The stimulus does not discuss modern humans or the extent of the morphological differences between Cro-Magnons and Neanderthals. Therefore, this answer choice could be true. It is a loser.

(D) Use of similar tools is required if members of two distinct groups of tool-making hominids are to be considered members of the same species.

This is an invalid inference, but it does not contradict any of the information in the stimulus. It could be the case that members of the same species must use the same tools. If this is so, Cro-Magnons and Neanderthals could be the same species. This answer choice could be true, so it is another loser.

(E) Through much of their coexistence, Cro-Magnons and Neanderthals were geographically isolated from one another.

If Cro-Magnons and Neanderthals lived in different environments, they are likely to have been geographically isolated from each other. This answer choice does not contradict anything in the stimulus, so it could be true. It is also a loser.

As (B) is the only candidate, it has to be the correct answer choice.

Key Takeaways

15.81% of LR Questions

Must Be True (MBT) – 2.57% of LR Questions
Implication (IMP) – 11.46% of LR Questions
Must Be False (MBF) – 1.78% of LR Questions

Example Prompts

MBT: The statements above, if true, most strongly support which one of the following?

MBT: Which of the following must be true based on the information above?

MBT: Which of the following can be properly inferred from the statements above?

IMP: Which of the following is best illustrated by the information above?

IMP: Which one of the following most logically completes the argument?

IMP: Which one of the following is most strongly supported by the information above?

MBF: If the statements above are true, then each of the following could be true EXCEPT:

MBF: Based on the information above, which one of the following cannot be true?

MBF: If the statements above are true, then which of the following must be false?

The information in the stimulus must be assumed to be true and applied to the answer choices. The stimulus usually includes a fact pattern.

IMP Subtypes

Incomplete Argument: The stimulus includes an incomplete argument. You must select an answer choice that logically completes the argument based on the information in the stimulus.

Unusual Circumstance: The stimulus includes a contradiction or a discrepancy. You must find the answer choice that best resolves the competing facts in the stimulus.

Correct Answer Choices

MBT: Statements that must be true based on the stimulus

IMP: Statements that are strongly supported by the stimulus

MBF: Statements that must be false based the stimulus

Incorrect Answers Choices

Could Be False: Statements that could be false (MBT, IMP)

Could Be True: Statements that could be true (MBF)

Broad Claims: Claims that go beyond what is stated in the stimulus (MBT, IMP, MBF)

Irrelevant Information: New information that is not relevant to the stimulus (MBT, IMP, MBF)

Invalid Inferences: Conditional inferences that are based on flipped or negated reasoning (MBT)

Opinions: Points of view expressed in the stimulus that are presented as fact (IMP)

Logical Force Errors: Statements that are too strong, considering the wording of the stimulus (MBT, IMP)

Inaccurate Paraphrases or Descriptions: Statements that inaccurately describe or paraphrase an element of the argument (IMP)

Chapter 4

Classification
Family

Chapter 4: Classification Family

Overview

Classification Family

In this chapter, you will learn how to identify and solve Classification Family questions.

Classification Family questions ask you to find the answer choice that correctly classifies information in the stimulus, which always includes an argument rather than a fact pattern.

The seven question types in this family—Main Point (MP), Fallacy (F), Description (D), Mini Description (MD), Parallel Reasoning (PR), Parallel Fallacy (PF), and Agree/Disagree (A/D)—are examined in detail in separate sections later in this chapter. Each section includes step-by-step instructions on how to solve the question type, detailed analyses of example questions, and drills to help you develop key skills. In addition, you will get to tackle practice questions taken from previous administrations of the LSAT. The methods for solving these practice questions are explained thoroughly in the answer key.

Main Point

Main Point

≈ 2.0 questions per test

Example Prompts

Which one of the following *most accurately expresses the main point of the argument?*

Of the following, which one *most accurately expresses the main conclusion?*

Which one of the following *most accurately expresses the conclusion of the argument?*

Take These Steps

Read the stimulus, which always includes an argument. Look for conclusion or counter-premise indicators. If there are no indicators, determine which statements are supported by the others. Is there more than one conclusion?

No

Anticipate a paraphrase of the main conclusion. The correct answer choice may also include supporting details.

Yes

Determine which conclusion is supported by all other premises and does not provide support to any other conclusion. This is the main conclusion. Anticipate a paraphrase of the main conclusion. The correct answer choice may also include supporting details.

Answer Choices

Correct Answer Choices	Incorrect Answer Choices
Statements that are definitely true based on the stimulus	Statements that are not necessarily true based on the stimulus
Accurate paraphrases of main conclusions that may include supporting details from the premises	Incomplete or inaccurate paraphrases of main conclusions
	Paraphrases of subsidiary conclusions or premises
	Irrelevant information or broad claims not supported by the stimulus

Chapter 4

For MP questions, test-takers must select the answer choice that restates the main conclusion of the argument. Being able to quickly identify the main conclusion of an argument is essential here. If you are having trouble differentiating between the various parts of an argument—such as premise, counter-premise, subsidiary conclusion, and main conclusion—take some time to review the relevant sections of Chapter 1.

As the correct answer choice of an MP question is always an accurate and complete paraphrase of the conclusion, it must be true based on the information in the argument. This means that any potentially false answer choice is incorrect and can be eliminated. Also, note that the correct answer choice sometimes includes supporting details as well as a paraphrase of the main conclusion. This is done to increase the overall difficulty of the question.

How to Solve Main Point Questions

MP questions are relatively easy to solve if the argument includes only one conclusion, and this is marked by an indicator. However, they can be challenging if there are multiple conclusions or if the conclusion is difficult to identify due to a lack of indicators.

The first step toward solving an MP question is to read the argument carefully and note any conclusion or counter-premise indicators. The main conclusion of an MP question often appears at the beginning or in the middle of an argument. If it appears in the middle, it is sometimes preceded by a counter-premise indicator such as *but*, *yet*, or *however*. This shows that the conclusion refutes an earlier statement. Alternatively, there may be a conclusion indicator or no indicator at all. Many arguments contain both main and subsidiary conclusions, increasing the overall difficulty of the question.

> Review the premise, conclusion, and counter-premise indicators introduced in Chapter 1.

If There Is Only One Conclusion

If there is only one conclusion, underline it and anticipate a paraphrase of this statement as being the correct answer choice. As mentioned previously, the correct answer choice may include details from other parts of the argument. Consider the following example:

> **Many nutritionists believe that red meat is bad for overall health. This belief is mistaken. Red meat boosts the body's autoimmune response and provides large amounts of protein, which help in repairing the body. Red meat can be consumed in moderate amounts without negatively affecting overall health.**

The conclusion is that the belief (*that red meat is bad for overall health*) is mistaken. The rest of the argument backs this up. The correct answer choice may not be a simple paraphrase of this statement, though. It might also include supporting details. For example, the correct answer choice could be "The belief that red meat is bad for your health is wrong because it can be consumed in moderate amounts without being unhealthy." This answer choice is correct not on account of the additional details but because it accurately paraphrases the main conclusion of the argument.

Let's look at an example:

> Dietitian: Many diet-conscious consumers are excited about new "fake fat" products
> designed to give food the flavor and consistency of fatty foods, yet without fat's harmful
> effects. Consumers who expect the new fat substitute to help them lose weight are

likely to be disappointed, however. Research has shown that when people knowingly or unknowingly eat foods containing "fake fat," they tend to take in at least as many additional calories as are saved by eating "fake fat."

Which one of the following most accurately expresses the conclusion of the dietitian's argument?

(A) People tend to take in a certain number of daily calories, no matter what types of food they eat.
(B) Most consumers who think that foods with "fake fat" are more nutritious than fatty foods are destined to be disappointed.
(C) "Fake fat" products are likely to contribute to obesity more than do other foods.
(D) "Fake fat" in foods is probably not going to help consumers meet weight loss goals.
(E) "Fake fat" in foods is indistinguishable from genuine fat by most consumers on the basis of taste alone.

Our first step is to look for conclusion or counter-premise indicators. Here, we have *however*. Although this is a counter-premise indicator, it sometimes precedes a conclusion that counters an earlier statement. This seems to be the case here. Many consumers are excited about "fake fat" products, but the dietitian states that they will probably be disappointed if they expect the product to help them lose weight. The argument can be outlined as follows:

P1: "Fake fat" products are designed to have less harmful effects than those with real fat.
P2: When people eat "fake fat," they take in at least as many additional calories as are saved.
C: Consumers will probably be disappointed in "fake fat's" ability to help them lose weight.

As this argument has only one conclusion, we do not have to worry about differentiating between subsidiary and main conclusions. We can simply underline the conclusion and anticipate a paraphrase as being the correct answer choice.

(A) People tend to take in a certain number of daily calories, no matter what types of food they eat.

This answer choice is related to the second premise, not the conclusion. In addition, it could be false because the argument states that people tend to take in at least as many additional calories as are saved when they eat "fake fat." This suggests more calories than usual may be consumed. We can categorize this answer choice as a loser.

(B) Most consumers who think that foods with "fake fat" are more nutritious than fatty foods are destined to be disappointed.

This is a tricky answer choice because it nearly matches the conclusion. However, it includes an equivocation error—the stimulus says that consumers think that "fake fat" helps them lose weight, but this answer choice states that they think foods containing it are more nutritious than fatty foods. It could be that "fake fat" is more nutritious even though it may not lead to weight loss. This statement could be false, so it is a loser.

(C) "Fake fat" products are likely to contribute to obesity more than do other foods.

This answer choice is a relational statement, comparing "fake fat" products' and other foods' contributions to obesity. This is new information, which means that this answer choice is potentially false and, therefore, a loser.

(D) "Fake fat" in foods is probably not going to help consumers meet weight loss goals.

Chapter 4 Classification Family **157**

This matches our anticipated answer choice. This answer choice restates the information in the conclusion. It even matches the strength of the conclusion due to *probably*. This is a candidate.

> **(E) "Fake fat" in foods is indistinguishable from genuine fat by most consumers on the basis of taste alone.**

This answer choice is related to the first premise, not the conclusion. In addition, it could be false because it claims that that "fake fat" is indistinguishable from real fat. However, the stimulus only says that "fake fat" is designed to match the flavor and consistency of real fat. It is possible that "fake fat" does not function as designed. This is a loser.

As (D) is the only candidate, it has to be the correct answer choice.

If There Are Multiple Conclusions

If the argument includes multiple conclusions, you need to identify the main conclusion. Remember, the main conclusion is supported by all of the premises of the argument and does not provide support for any other conclusion. Do not confuse it with a subsidiary conclusion, which receives support from premises but also supports the main conclusion.

Once you have identified the main conclusion, underline it and anticipate a paraphrase of this statement as being the correct answer choice. Consider the following:

> **Monica will do better on this exam than Stuart. Monica scored higher on a recent IQ test than Stuart; therefore, she is more intelligent than Stuart. Additionally, Monica studied very hard for this exam.**

The second sentence of this argument includes the conclusion indicator *therefore*. This means that the second clause of this sentence is a conclusion. But is it the main conclusion? No, because it provides support for the first statement of the stimulus.

> P1: Monica scored higher than Stuart on a recent IQ test.
> SC: Monica is more intelligent than Stuart.
> P2: Monica studied very hard for this exam.
> C: Monica will do better on this exam than Stuart.

The two premises and the subsidiary conclusion all support the conclusion that Monica will do better on the exam than Stuart. As this conclusion does not provide support for any other statement, it is the main conclusion. The correct answer choice must be a paraphrase of this statement.

Here's an example:

> Australia has considerably fewer species of carnivorous mammals than any other continent does but about as many carnivorous reptile species as other continents do. This is probably a consequence of the unusual sparseness of Australia's ecosystems. To survive, carnivorous mammals must eat much more than carnivorous reptiles need to; thus carnivorous mammals are at a disadvantage in ecosystems in which there is relatively little food.
>
> Which one of the following most accurately expresses the main conclusion of the argument?
>
> (A) Australia has considerably fewer species of carnivorous mammals than any other

continent does but about as many carnivorous reptile species as other continents do.

(B) In ecosystems in which there is relatively little food, carnivorous mammals are at a disadvantage relative to carnivorous reptiles.

(C) The unusual sparseness of Australia's ecosystems is probably the reason Australia has considerably fewer carnivorous mammal species than other continents do but about as many carnivorous reptile species.

(D) The reason that carnivorous mammals are at a disadvantage in ecosystems in which there is relatively little food is that they must eat much more in order to survive than carnivorous reptiles need to.

(E) Because Australia's ecosystems are unusually sparse, carnivorous mammals there are at a disadvantage relative to carnivorous reptiles.

This is a difficult question. We have one conclusion indicator here, *thus*. What follows is a conclusion, but is it the argument's main conclusion? To be the main conclusion, the statement must be supported by all the premises and not provide support to any other conclusions. Let's see if that is the case here.

We are presented with a strange fact, that Australia has fewer carnivorous mammals but as many carnivorous reptiles as other continents, which is explained as a consequence of the unusual sparseness of Australia's ecosystems. The argument goes on to explain that carnivorous mammals must eat much more than reptiles, which results in carnivorous mammals being at a disadvantage when there is relatively little food. This conclusion, that carnivorous mammals are at a disadvantage when there is little food, actually supports another statement in the argument, that the low number of carnivorous mammals is explained by the unusual sparseness of the ecosystem. The argument can be outlined as follows:

P1: Carnivorous mammals need more food than carnivorous reptiles.
SC: Carnivorous mammals are at a survival disadvantage in sparse environments.
C: The ratio of carnivorous mammals to reptiles is a consequence of unusual sparseness.

The conclusion preceded by *thus* is actually a subsidiary conclusion, used to support the main conclusion that the presence of fewer carnivorous mammals than expected is due to Australia's unusual sparseness.

(A) Australia has considerably fewer species of carnivorous mammals than any other continent does but about as many carnivorous reptile species as other continents do.

This answer choice presents background information that the main conclusion tries to explain. (A) is a loser.

(B) In ecosystems in which there is relatively little food, carnivorous mammals are at a disadvantage relative to carnivorous reptiles.

This is a paraphrase of the subsidiary conclusion. We can consider this answer choice a loser.

(C) The unusual sparseness of Australia's ecosystems is probably the reason Australia has considerably fewer carnivorous mammal species than other continents do but about as many carnivorous reptile species.

This is a paraphrase of the main conclusion. It even matches the strength of the conclusion due to *probably*. Let's keep it as a candidate and examine the other answer choices.

(D) The reason that carnivorous mammals are at a disadvantage in ecosystems in which there is relatively little food is that they must eat much more in order to survive than carnivorous reptiles

need to.

This is a paraphrase of the subsidiary conclusion combined with information from the premise that supports that conclusion. We can consider (D) a loser.

(E) **Because Australia's ecosystems are unusually sparse, carnivorous mammals there are at a disadvantage relative to carnivorous reptiles.**

Again, this is a paraphrase of our subsidiary conclusion. (E) is another loser.

As (C) is the only candidate, it has to be the correct answer choice.

Looking at the Answer Choices

To reiterate, the correct answer choice of an MP question is always a complete and accurate paraphrase of the argument's main conclusion. In some cases, details from the argument are included with the paraphrase to increase the difficulty level.

Incorrect answer choices are commonly paraphrases of other parts of the argument, such as premises or subsidiary conclusions. Note that the accuracy of these paraphrases does not matter—these answer choices are always incorrect. Other incorrect answer choices include partial or inaccurate paraphrases of the main conclusion. And some incorrect answer choices even introduce new information that is not relevant to the stimulus or make a broad claim that is not supported by the stimulus.

As the correct answer choice must be true, any answer choice that is potentially false, based on the information in the stimulus, is incorrect and thus can be eliminated.

Drill: Main Point

Read the stimulus. Identify the various parts of the argument and underline the main conclusion.

In practice the government will have the last word on what an individual's rights are, because its police will do what its officials and courts say. But that does not mean that the government's view is necessarily the correct view; anyone who thinks it is must believe that persons have only such moral rights as the government chooses to grant, which means that they have no moral rights at all.

Counter-premise:

_____

_____

_____

Premise:

_____

_____

_____

Subsidiary Conclusion:

_____

_____

_____

Main Conclusion:

_____

_____

_____

Indicate whether each answer choice could be false. Select the one that accurately restates the main conclusion.

(A) Individuals have no rights at all unless the government says that they do.

   Could it be false?   Yes ☐   No ☐

(B) What government officials and courts say an individual's rights are may not be correct.

   Could it be false?   Yes ☐   No ☐

(C) Individuals have rights unless the government says that they do not.

   Could it be false?   Yes ☐   No ☐

(D) The police always agree with government officials and the courts about what an individual's rights are.

   Could it be false?   Yes ☐   No ☐

(E) One should always try to uphold one's individual rights against the government's view of what those rights are.

   Could it be false?   Yes ☐   No ☐

Chapter 4

Paraphrase the main conclusion.

Stimulus:

In practice the government will have the last word on what an individual's rights are, because its police will do what its officials and courts say. But that does not mean that the government's view is necessarily the correct view; anyone who thinks it is must believe that persons have only such moral rights as the government chooses to grant, which means that they have no moral rights at all.

Counter-premise:

"In practice the government will have the last word on what an individual's rights are, because its police will do what its officials and courts say." This is information supporting the view that the government's view is always correct.

Premise:

"anyone who thinks [that the government's view is necessarily correct] must believe that persons have only such moral rights as the government chooses to grant." This supports the following line.

Subsidiary Conclusion:

"they have no moral rights at all." This is indicated by the words *which means that*, indicating the words preceding this line support it as a conclusion.

Main Conclusion:

"But that does not mean that the government's view is necessarily the correct view." Often, the conclusion is indicated by counter-premise indicator words, which express disagreement with a prior viewpoint.

Answer Choices:

(A) **Individuals have no rights at all unless the government says that they do.**

Could it be false? Yes ■ No □

This could be false because the argument says that the government's view on rights is not necessarily correct.

(B) **What government officials and courts say an individual's rights are may not be correct.**

Could it be false? Yes □ No ■

This must be true. As a restatement of the main conclusion, (B) must be the correct answer choice.

(C) **Individuals have rights unless the government says that they do not.**

Could it be false? Yes ■ No □

This could be false because the government's view on rights is not necessarily correct.

(D) **The police always agree with government officials and the courts about what an individual's rights are.**

Could it be false? Yes ■ No □

This could be false because we do not know whether the police agree with government officials. This is new information.

(E) **One should always try to uphold one's individual rights against the government's view of what those rights are.**

Could it be false? Yes ■ No □

This could be false. The use of *should* implies obligation, which is not discussed in the argument. Thus, this answer choice introduces new information.

Paraphrase the main conclusion.

The fact that the government dictates what actions people can take does not mean that the government has a correct view on people's rights.

1. Statistician: Two major studies found no causal link between medical procedure X and disorder Y, but these studies are flawed. One study looked at 1,000 people who had undergone procedure X and the other study looked at 1,100 people who had undergone procedure X. But because disorder Y occurs in only .02 percent of the population, researchers would need to include many more than 1,100 people in a study to detect even a doubling of the rate of disorder Y.

Which one of the following most accurately expresses the main conclusion of the statistician's argument?

(A) Contrary to the findings of two major studies, there is reason to think that procedure X causes disorder Y.

(B) Two studies that discovered no causal link between procedure X and disorder Y are unsound.

(C) Researchers should conduct more-extensive studies of procedure X to determine whether the procedure is causally linked with disorder Y.

(D) The two studies cited did not reach a conclusion as to whether disorder Y results from procedure X.

(E) Despite the opinions of many medical experts, it has not been established that there is a causal link between procedure X and disorder Y.

2. Citizen: The primary factor determining a dog's disposition is not its breed but its home environment. A bad owner can undo generations of careful breeding. Legislation focusing on specific breeds of dogs would not address the effects of human behavior in raising and training animals. As a result, such breed-specific legislation could never effectively protect the public from vicious dogs. Moreover, in my view, the current laws are perfectly adequate.

Which one of the following most accurately expresses the conclusion drawn by the citizen?

(A) The public would not be effectively protected from violent dogs by breed-specific legislation.

(B) A good home environment is more important than breeding to a dog's disposition.

(C) The home environment of dogs would not be regulated by breed-specific legislation.

(D) Irresponsible dog owners are capable of producing dogs with bad dispositions regardless of generations of careful breeding.

(E) The vicious-dog laws that are currently in effect do not address the effects of human behavior in raising and training dogs.

3. Prediction, the hallmark of the natural sciences, appears to have been made possible by reducing phenomena to mathematical expressions. Some social scientists also want the power to predict accurately and assume they ought to perform the same reduction. But this would be a mistake; it would neglect data that are not easily mathematized and thereby would only distort the social phenomena.

Which one of the following most accurately expresses the main conclusion of the argument?

(A) The social sciences do not have as much predictive power as the natural sciences.
(B) Mathematics plays a more important role in the natural sciences than it does in the social sciences.
(C) There is a need in the social sciences to improve the ability to predict.
(D) Phenomena in the social sciences should not be reduced to mathematical formula.
(E) Prediction is responsible for the success of the natural sciences.

Problem Set: Main Point — Answers

1. **Correct Answer (B).** *Prep Test 41, Section 1, Question 5.*

Reading the stimulus, we notice the counter-premise indicator *but* in the first and third sentences. Oftentimes in MP questions, a counter-premise indicator such as *but* is used to introduce a conclusion that refutes a preceding statement. The first sentence states that a study found no causal link between a procedure and a disorder, but these studies are flawed. What follows *but* may be the conclusion; however, we should check the rest of the stimulus. The two studies looked at 1,000 and 1,100 people, but more people would have to be studied to detect a significant increase in the disorder. This information supports the previous statement that these studies are flawed. There is only one conclusion in this argument—"these studies are flawed"—and we should anticipate a paraphrase of this statement as being the correct answer choice.

(A) Contrary to the findings of two major studies, there is reason to think that procedure X causes disorder Y.

This answer choice does not match our paraphrase of the conclusion. This is a loser.

(B) Two studies that discovered no causal link between procedure X and disorder Y are unsound.

This matches our anticipated answer choice. The studies, which discovered no causal link between procedure X and disorder Y, are flawed. Let's consider this a candidate.

(C) Researchers should conduct more-extensive studies of procedure X to determine whether the procedure is causally linked with disorder Y.

Researchers *should*? Always watch out for the word *should*. The statistician only says that the studies are flawed and that more-extensive studies would have to be carried out to identify a causal link. There is no reference to an obligation to conduct such studies. This is a loser.

(D) The two studies cited did not reach a conclusion as to whether disorder Y results from procedure X.

The conclusion states that there is no causal link between X and Y, not that a conclusion about a link could not be made. This is a loser.

(E) Despite the opinions of many medical experts, it has not been established that there is a causal link between procedure X and disorder Y.

While this might be true, it is not the conclusion of the argument. This is a loser.

As (B) is the only candidate, it has to be the correct answer choice.

2. **Correct Answer (A).** *Prep Test 47, Section 3, Question 6.*

Looking at the stimulus, we notice the conclusion indicator *as a result*. What follows this phrase is a conclusion. The first two sentences of the stimulus include premises that support this conclusion. Note the use of *moreover* in the last sentence. This is a premise indicator, so you may think that what follows is additional support for the conclusion. However, what follows *moreover* is actually background information—the citizen's opinion about current laws, which is not directly related to the argument. We should look for an answer choice that is a paraphrase of the argument's only conclusion, "breed-specific legislation could never effectively protect the public from vicious dogs."

(A) The public would not be effectively protected from violent dogs by breed-specific legislation.

This matches our anticipated answer choice. This is a candidate.

(B) A good home environment is more important than breeding to a dog's disposition.

This is an accurate paraphrase of the first premise in the argument. As it does not restate the conclusion, this answer choice is a loser.

(C) The home environment of dogs would not be regulated by breed-specific legislation.

This too is a paraphrase of a premise rather than of the conclusion. (C) is a loser.

(D) Irresponsible dog owners are capable of producing dogs with bad dispositions regardless of generations of careful breeding.

This paraphrases part of a premise. (D) goes in the loser category.

(E) The vicious-dog laws that are currently in effect do not address the effects of human behavior in raising and training dogs.

This is new information. Additionally, this statement may well be false, as the citizen states that the current laws are perfectly adequate, which implies that the effects of human behavior have been addressed. This answer choice is a loser.

As (A) is the only candidate, it has to be the correct answer choice.

3. **Correct Answer (D).** *Prep Test 42, Section 4, Question 10.*

Like the first question in this set, this argument uses the counter-premise indicator *but* to present its conclusion. The argument says that prediction in the natural sciences has been made possible by reducing phenomena to mathematical expressions and that some social scientists want to follow suit. The argument concludes that this would be a mistake because such a reduction would result in the neglect of data that are not easily mathematized. An accurate paraphrase of this conclusion might be "It would be a mistake for social scientists to reduce social phenomena to mathematical expression." Let's look for something like this among the answer choices.

(A) The social sciences do not have as much predictive power as the natural sciences.

This is a relational statement. We know nothing about the relative predictive power of the social and natural sciences. This is a loser.

(B) Mathematics plays a more important role in the natural sciences than it does in the social sciences.

This is implied by the argument. However, it is not related to the conclusion, which makes (B) a loser.

(C) There is a need in the social sciences to improve the ability to predict.

This is a paraphrase of information in a premise, not the conclusion. (C) is a loser.

(D) Phenomena in the social sciences should not be reduced to mathematical formula.

This matches our anticipated answer. It is an accurate paraphrase of the conclusion, so we will consider it a candidate.

(E) Prediction is responsible for the success of the natural sciences.

This is far too broad. Prediction may or may not be responsible for the success of the natural sciences. More importantly, this claim is not related to the conclusion. This is a loser.

As (D) is the only candidate, it has to be the correct answer choice.

Fallacy

CLASSIFICATION FAMILY

Main Point
Fallacy
Description
Mini Description
Parallel Reasoning
Parallel Fallacy
Agree/Disagree

Fallacy

≈ 7.4 questions per test

Example Prompts

Which one of the following most accurately describes *a flaw* in the argument?

The reasoning in the argument is *questionable* because it . . .

The reasoning in the argument is *most vulnerable* to criticism on the grounds that it . . .

Take These Steps

Read the stimulus, which always includes an argument. Identify the main conclusion, subsidiary conclusions (if any), and premises. Consider the logical relationships between these parts to determine how the main conclusion is supported.

Determine the error in reasoning committed to reach the conclusion. The argument always includes a logical fallacy.

Anticipate a description of the logical fallacy. There may be multiple answer choices based on the same type of fallacy. Therefore, you must anticipate one that paraphrases the relevant content from the argument.

Answer Choices

Correct Answer Choices	Incorrect Answer Choices
Complete and accurate descriptions of fallacies that occur in the argument	Descriptions of fallacies that do not occur in the argument
	Incomplete or inaccurate descriptions of fallacies that occur in the argument
	Descriptions of parts of the argument that are not flawed
	Irrelevant information

Fallacies are among the most important concepts in the LR section. Not only do F questions appear more often than any other question type (approximately eight per test), but the fallacies detailed in this section also play an important role in other questions types, most notably Parallel Fallacy, Strengthen, Weaken, Necessary Assumption, and Description. Accordingly, you should expect to encounter 10 to 15 fallacy-related arguments on the LSAT.

As F questions make use of abstract language in the answer choices to describe the errors in reasoning that occur in the argument, the correct answer choice can often be accurately anticipated. As multiple candidates are rare, you can usually select the answer choice that matches what you anticipated and move on.

How to Solve Fallacy Questions

The first step toward solving an F question is to identify the premises, subsidiary conclusions (if any), and main conclusion. Then examine the logical relationships between these parts of the argument to determine how the conclusion has been reached.

The next step is to identify the error in reasoning committed by the argument. You will need to become familiar with a variety of logical fallacies, and these will be examined in detail later in this section.

Once you have identified the fallacy, you should anticipate a correct answer choice that accurately expresses the flawed reasoning in the argument. Often, answer choices that express a particular type of fallacy use similar language. This can make it easier to identify the correct answer choice. However, it is important to note that some incorrect answer choices are related to the same type of fallacy as the correct answer choice. This means that you have to carefully consider each answer choice and determine how it relates to the argument.

Looking at the Answer Choices

Answer choices for F questions often include complex language that refers to the abstract logic of an argument. Therefore, it is important to become familiar with the typical wordings of the answer choices that express each type of fallacy. These wordings are included below in the descriptions of the common fallacy types.

The correct answer choice accurately and completely describes the error of reasoning that occurs in the argument. Sometimes, it simply points out the fallacy without referring to the content of the argument. In other cases, it indicates the fallacy but also includes specific details from the argument.

A common type of trap answer choice describes valid reasoning in the argument. Such incorrect answer choices can be attractive if you have not accurately anticipated the fallacy because they accurately describe a logical relationship in the argument. Another common type of incorrect answer choice expresses the appropriate fallacy but inaccurately describes how it applies to the argument. Finally, F questions also frequently contain incorrect answer choices that describe fallacies not mentioned in the argument or that introduce new information.

Common Fallacy Types

The chart below features the fallacies that appear most often in F questions. Although the Big Six come up most frequently, the others are common as well.

The Big Six	Other Common Fallacies	
Sampling	Absence of Evidence	False Comparison
Selection	Composition	Proportion
Conditional Reasoning	Strength Modifier	Inappropriate Authority
Causal Reasoning	Ad Hominem	Circular Reasoning
Equivocation		
Questionable Assumption		

Note that this list is not exhaustive—you may encounter other forms of invalid reasoning. However, these are the fallacies you are most likely to be tested on. We will now examine each of them in detail.

Sampling Fallacy

Always be suspicious about an LR question that uses a survey, poll, or study to reach its conclusion. A Sampling Fallacy occurs when an argument

> **One of the Big Six Fallacies**

reaches an invalid conclusion about a group based on data gathered from an inappropriate sample. This fallacy can occur in two ways:

1. A conclusion about a group is made based on data from a sample that is not representative of the group. This is by far the most common type of Sampling Fallacy. For example,

> **American researchers conducted a poll outside of a Texas church on Sunday afternoon. The poll results were surprising. Of the respondents, 98 percent claimed they believed in God. Therefore, the vast majority of the Americans believe in God.**

A credible poll must sample a group likely to be representative of the majority. Here, though, the poll was conducted outside of a church, where people who believe in God are far more likely to be encountered than in other places. We cannot make a conclusion about the general public based on this sample.

2. A conclusion is based on a sample that is biased regarding the results of the survey, poll, or study or that does not understand what is being asked. For example,

> **Advertisement: You'll love Yellow Delicious bananas! We conducted a poll on over 500 of our shareholders who overwhelmingly responded that Yellow Delicious bananas are the best bananas on the market!**

The members of the sample group have a clear financial interest in Yellow Delicious bananas, so they are biased with regard to the results of the poll. This means that the data cannot be used to make a conclusion about the general population.

Sampling Fallacy answer choices typically include the following boldfaced expressions:
- The reasoning in the argument is flawed in that the argument generalizes from **a sample that is unlikely to be representative** of public sentiment.
- The reasoning in the argument is flawed in that the argument relies on evidence **drawn from a sample** that may have a reason to be **biased**.
- The reasoning in the argument is flawed in that **the argument** uses evidence from **a sample too small** to be **representative of the group** it purports to make a conclusion about.

Let's look at an example:

> The enthusiastic acceptance of ascetic lifestyles evidenced in the surviving writings of
> monastic authors indicates that medieval societies were much less concerned with monetary

gain than are contemporary Western cultures.

The reasoning in the argument is most vulnerable to criticism on the grounds that the argument

(A) employs the imprecise term "ascetic"
(B) generalizes from a sample that is likely to be unrepresentative
(C) applies contemporary standards inappropriately to medieval societies
(D) inserts personal opinions into what purports to be a factual debate
(E) advances premises that are inconsistent

The phrase indicates *that* is a conclusion indicator. What precedes this expression is the premise that supports the conclusion. The argument claims that because monastic authors enthusiastically accepted ascetic lifestyles, medieval societies cared less about monetary gain.

This argument reaches a conclusion about medieval societies as a whole based on the writings of monastic authors—a group of people who are likely to have different beliefs than the other members of society. We should look for an answer choice that expresses this fallacy.

(A) employs the imprecise term "ascetic"

Although the term *ascetic* is imprecise, it corresponds to the phrase *much less concerned with monetary gain*.

(B) generalizes from a sample that is likely to be unrepresentative

This answer choice describes the erroneous reasoning in the argument. (B) has to be the correct answer choice.

(C) applies contemporary standards inappropriately to medieval societies

The argument does not apply contemporary standards to medieval societies.

(D) inserts personal opinions into what purports to be a factual debate

The argument does not describe a factual debate.

(E) advances premises that are inconsistent

There is only one premise in the argument.

Selection Fallacy

A Selection Fallacy occurs when an argument concludes that an option must be selected based on the assumption that there are a number of options to

One of the Big Six Fallacies

choose from. Arguments containing Selection Fallacies often fail to consider a full list of options or to grant that more than one option can be selected. This fallacy can occur in two ways:

1. The list of options is not exhaustive. This is the case when the argument fails to establish that the options presented are the only ones that can be selected from. For example,

   Nation X is in a financial crisis. One way to fix this is to decrease spending. The only way we can decrease spending is to lower military expenditures. In conclusion, in order to fix the financial crisis, we must decrease military expenditures.

The argument specifies that one way to deal with the financial crisis is to reduce spending. It goes on to say that the only way to decrease spending is to lower military spending. The argument concludes that military spending must be lowered. What about other ways to cope with the financial crisis, such as increasing taxes? The argument does not establish that decreasing spending is the only way to fix the crisis—just that it is one way to do so. The list of options presented is not exhaustive.

2. The options are not mutually exclusive. This is the case when two or more options are assumed to be mutually exclusive when in fact they could both be selected. For example,

> **Jane and Joe could not have robbed the store. If Jane robbed the store, she'd be too short to turn off the silent alarm on the ceiling. If Joe robbed the store, he'd be too large to fit through the crawl space to get to the vault.**

The argument provides evidence that neither Jane nor Joe could have robbed the store without assistance. However, there is no reason to believe it had to be either one or the other—they could have worked together to rob the store. The argument falsely assumes that the two options cannot both be selected.

Selection Fallacy answer choices typically include the following boldfaced expressions:
- The reasoning in the argument is flawed in that the argument fails to consider that **both factors could jointly** affect the outcome.
- The reasoning in the argument is flawed in that the argument confuses **an adequate solution with a required one**.
- The reasoning in the argument is flawed in that the argument ignores the possibility that there are **other options available to be selected**.

Let's look at an example:

> Administrator: Because revenue fell by 15 percent this year, the university needs to reduce next year's budget. This could be accomplished by eliminating faculty positions. It could also be accomplished by reducing faculty salaries. Since we will not eliminate any faculty positions, we must reduce faculty salaries.

> The administrator's reasoning is flawed because the administrator

> (A) presumes, without providing justification, that more money would be saved by reducing faculty salaries than would be saved by eliminating faculty positions

> (B) presumes, without providing justification, that the budget cannot be reduced unless faculty positions are eliminated or faculty salaries are reduced

> (C) ignores the possibility that, though budget cuts will be needed, they will not need to be as high as 15 percent

> (D) presumes, without providing justification, that some faculty members will leave their jobs rather than accept a reduced salary

> (E) ignores the possibility that the budget could be reduced by eliminating some faculty positions and reducing the remaining faculty members' salaries

The word *since* indicates a premise followed by a conclusion. The conclusion is that faculty salaries must be reduced. Why? Because the budget must be reduced. The administrator lists two ways to achieve this: eliminating faculty positions and reducing faculty salaries. The administrator goes on to say that as positions will not be eliminated, salaries must be reduced. However, the administrator does not indicate that these are the only options. If other methods can be used to lower the budget, faculty salaries need not be affected. Let's look for an answer choice that expresses this error.

> **(A) presumes, without providing justification, that more money would be saved by reducing faculty salaries than would be saved by eliminating faculty positions**

This is a relational statement comparing the savings that would result from the two options presented by the administrator. The argument does not make this comparison.

> **(B) presumes, without providing justification, that the budget cannot be reduced unless faculty positions are eliminated or faculty salaries are reduced**

This has to be the correct answer choice. The argument presumes there are only two options to choose from.

> **(C) ignores the possibility that, though budget cuts will be needed, they will not need to be as high as 15 percent**

The argument does not specify that a budget decrease of 15 percent is required.

> **(D) presumes, without providing justification, that some faculty members will leave their jobs rather than accept a reduced salary**

The argument does not discuss how faculty will react to a salary reduction.

> **(E) ignores the possibility that the budget could be reduced by eliminating some faculty positions and reducing the remaining faculty members' salaries**

The relevant premise, which must be accepted as true, specifies that positions will not be eliminated.

Conditional Reasoning Fallacy

This fallacy has been discussed in previous chapters, but we will review it once more in the context of F questions. A Conditional Reasoning Fallacy typically involves a conclusion that is an invalid contrapositive of a premise. It can occur in two ways:

> **One of the Big Six Fallacies**

1. A conditional statement is flipped but not negated to infer an invalid conclusion (flipped reasoning). For example,

> **In order to build muscle, it is necessary to exercise. Exercising is beneficial for your health for other reasons as well. So, if you exercise, you will build muscle.**

The first premise can be diagrammed as Build Muscle → Exercise. This premise is flipped but not negated to infer an invalid conclusion, which can be expressed as Exercise → Build Muscle.

2. A conditional statement is negated but not flipped to infer an invalid conclusion (negated reasoning). For example,

> **The martial arts tournament includes top-notch competitors. Every competitor is extremely well trained in martial arts. Therefore, if you are not competing in this tournament, you must not be well trained in martial arts.**

The first premise can be diagrammed as Competitor → Well Trained in Martial Arts. The conclusion can be expressed as ~~Competitor~~ → ~~Well Trained in Martial Arts~~. This is an invalid inference because the premise has been negated but not flipped.

Conditional Reasoning Fallacy answer choices typically include the following boldfaced expressions:
- The reasoning in the argument is flawed in that the argument fails to recognize that **failure to satisfy one sufficient condition precludes a different sufficient condition** from being satisfied that will bring about the result.
- The reasoning in the argument is flawed in that the argument presumes, without providing justification, that if **certain events each produce a particular result, then no other event is sufficient to produce that result**.
- The reasoning in the argument is flawed in that the argument assumes without warrant that just because **satisfying a given condition is enough to ensure a result, satisfying that condition is necessary for that result**.

Let's look at an example:

> If Agnes's research proposal is approved, the fourth-floor lab must be cleaned out for her use. Immanuel's proposal, on the other hand, requires less space. So if his proposal is approved, he will continue to work in the second-floor lab. Only those proposals the director supports will be approved. So since the director will support both proposals, the fourth-floor lab must be cleaned out.
>
> The argument's reasoning is flawed because the argument
>
> (A) presumes, without providing justification, that the fourth-floor lab is bigger than the second-floor lab
> (B) fails to consider the possibility that a proposal will be rejected even with the director's support
> (C) presumes, without providing justification, that the director will support both proposals with equal enthusiasm
> (D) fails to consider the possibility that Immanuel will want to move to a bigger lab once his proposal is approved
> (E) presumes, without providing justification, that no lab other than the fourth-floor lab would be adequate for Agnes's research

The argument has a *since premise, conclusion* structure. The conditional statements can be diagrammed as follows:

P1: Agnes's Proposal Approved → 4F Lab Cleaned
P2: Immanuel's Proposal Approved → Continue 2F
P3: Proposal Approved → Director Support
_____
C: Director Support → Agnes's Proposal Approved → 4F Lab Cleaned

The conclusion includes an invalid inference. The third premise states that for a proposal to be approved, the director must support it. However, this does not mean that a proposal supported by the director must be approved. The conclusion is based on flipped reasoning, and we should anticipate a description of this logical flaw in the correct answer choice.

(A) presumes, without providing justification, that the fourth-floor lab is bigger than the second-floor lab

This includes information implied in the second premise, but it is not a logical error.

(B) fails to consider the possibility that a proposal will be rejected even with the director's support

This describes the fallacy we identified in the argument. Support from the director does not guarantee that a proposal will be approved. This has to be the correct answer choice.

(C) presumes, without providing justification, that the director will support both proposals with equal enthusiasm

This is irrelevant information. Enthusiasm is not discussed in the argument.

(D) fails to consider the possibility that Immanuel will want to move to a bigger lab once his proposal is approved

This is irrelevant information as well.

(E) presumes, without providing justification, that no lab other than the fourth-floor lab would be adequate for Agnes's research

This includes an accurate restatement of an idea expressed in the first premise. It is not a logical error.

Causal Reasoning Fallacy

Causal reasoning was introduced in Chapter 2. Causal Reasoning fallacies occur when the argument relies on insufficient evidence to conclude that one

> One of the Big Six Fallacies

factor caused another. Whenever causal reasoning is present in a Fallacy question, it is inevitably tested. A Causal Reasoning Fallacy can occur in three different ways:

1. The argument concludes a cause and effect relationship from a correlation. This is the most common way in which a Causal Reasoning Fallacy occurs and is the basis of the other two ways. For example,

> **Temperatures in California this summer were higher than any other year on record. California also experienced a plague of forest fires this summer. It must have been the record heat that produced the forest fires in California this summer.**

Just because record temperatures and forest fires occurred during the same season does not mean that Hot Temperature CAUSE Forest Fires. In order to determine this, we would need to rule out every other potential cause of the forest fires.

2. The argument concludes that one factor caused another, when a third factor is more likely to have played a role. So, instead of A CAUSE B, it is actually C CAUSE B or C CAUSE A AND B. For example,

> **Researchers were surprised to find that on days when ice cream sales were highest in Chicago, murders tended to be more likely. The researchers concluded that the consumption of ice cream must give people murderous tendencies.**

As in the first example, the conclusion of this argument mistakes correlation for causation. However, the argument also implies that a third factor may be involved. A correct answer choice might be something like "The argument fails to consider that high temperatures caused both an increase in ice cream consumption and an increase in murders."

3. Cause and effect can be reversed. Instead of A CAUSE B, it is B CAUSE A. For example,

It has been well established that people who drink coffee in the morning have trouble sleeping at night. Therefore, having a morning coffee must cause people to have sleep troubles.

Again, correlation does not equal causation. However, the argument also suggests that the causal relationship between the two factors should be reversed. It is much more likely that not sleeping well at night causes people to drink coffee.

Causal Reasoning Fallacy answer choices typically include the following boldfaced expressions:
- The reasoning in the argument is flawed in that the argument concludes that one phenomenon **caused** another only from evidence that shows **that both factors occurred at the same time**.
- The reasoning in the argument is flawed in that the argument fails to consider that another **factor may be the cause behind the result**.
- The reasoning in the argument is flawed in that the argument determines that Factor A **caused** Factor B only from evidence that the two **factors are correlated**.
- The reasoning in the argument is flawed in that the argument presumes, without providing justification, that because Factor A and Factor B **are associated** with one another, **one factor must be the cause of the other**.

Let's look at an example:

Scientist: While studying centuries-old Antarctic ice deposits, I found that several years of relatively severe atmospheric pollution in the 1500s coincided with a period of relatively high global temperatures. So it is clear in this case that atmospheric pollution did cause global temperatures to rise.

The reasoning in the scientist's argument is most vulnerable to criticism on the grounds that the argument

(A) presumes, without providing justification, that a rise in global temperatures is harmful
(B) draws a general conclusion based on a sample that is likely to be unrepresentative
(C) inappropriately generalizes from facts about a specific period of time to a universal claim
(D) takes for granted that the method used for gathering data was reliable
(E) infers, merely from a claim that two phenomena are associated, that one phenomenon causes the other

In this argument, the conclusion is indicated by the phrase *so it is clear*. The following clause, which states that atmospheric pollution caused global temperatures to rise, is the conclusion. The evidence supporting this claim is that a period of high pollution coincided with high temperatures. Faulty causation is at play here. It is just as likely that another factor, such as a volcanic eruption, caused both to increase or that the rise in temperatures resulted in increased pollution.

(A) presumes, without providing justification, that a rise in global temperatures is harmful

The argument does not state that a rise in global temperatures is harmful.

(B) draws a general conclusion based on a sample that is likely to be unrepresentative

This answer choice describes a Sampling Fallacy. The scientist does not make a claim about a larger group based on a sample.

(C) inappropriately generalizes from facts about a specific period of time to a universal claim

The scientist does not make a universal claim. He makes a claim about a specific period of time (several years in the 1500s).

(D) takes for granted that the method used for gathering data was reliable

This is new information. There is no indication that the method used to gather data was unreliable.

(E) infers, merely from a claim that two phenomena are associated, that one phenomenon causes the other

This answer choice describes the same Causal Reasoning Fallacy that we identified in the argument. (E) has to be the correct answer choice.

Equivocation Fallacy

Equivocation Fallacies involve a shift in the meaning of a key concept or term as an argument develops. Equivocations commonly appear in the incorrect answer choices of many question types on the LSAT. In Fallacy questions, Equivocation Fallacies can occur in two ways:

One of the Big Six Fallacies

1. The argument switches from using one term or concept to using a similar, yet distinct, term or concept. This is the most common version of an Equivocation Fallacy. For example,

   Our clothing company is aiming to increase its profits next quarter. By advertising more on television channels teenagers are most likely to watch, we can attract more customers in a key demographic, bringing in more revenue. Therefore, advertising is likely to help us meet our goal.

In this argument the first premise states that the goal is to increase profits, and the conclusion says that advertising will help the clothing company meet this goal. The problem is that the second premise specifies that advertising will result in more revenue, which is different from profit. It is possible that advertising will be costly, so even if it brings in more revenue, it may not lead to an increase in profits. The argument equivocates between *profit* and *revenue*.

2. The argument uses an important term in different ways. The term is used equivocally, making the conclusion invalid. Here's an example:

   When the president of the company is on vacation, hiring and firing decisions are delegated to the employee with the most seniority. Since Marsha is the only senior citizen working at the company, she should have the hiring and firing decisions delegated to her.

Here, the argument equivocates between two different meanings of the word *senior*. The first usage concerns the number of years worked at a company, and the second has to do with age. This shift in meaning invalidates the conclusion.

Equivocation Fallacy answer choices typically include the following boldfaced expressions:
- The reasoning in the argument is flawed in that the argument allows an important term to **shift in meaning** throughout the argument.
- The reasoning in the argument is flawed in that the argument makes **an irrelevant shift** from discussing

Concept A to discussing Concept B.

- The reasoning in the argument is flawed in that the argument draws a conclusion based on **equivocal language**.

Let's look at an example:

> Beck: Our computer program estimates municipal automotive use based on weekly data. Some staff question the accuracy of the program's estimates. But because the figures it provides are remarkably consistent from week to week, we can be confident of its accuracy.
>
> The reasoning in Beck's argument is flawed in that it
>
> (A) fails to establish that consistency is a more important consideration than accuracy
> (B) fails to consider the program's accuracy in other tasks that it may perform
> (C) takes for granted that the program's output would be consistent even if its estimates were inaccurate
> (D) regards accuracy as the sole criterion for judging the program's value
> (E) fails to consider that the program could produce consistent but inaccurate output

This argument has a *because premise, conclusion* structure. It concludes that we can be confident in the computer program's accuracy because it provides consistent figures from week to week. However, *consistency* and *accuracy* are similar yet distinct concepts. Something can be both consistent and inaccurate. Equivocating between these two terms creates an error of reasoning in the argument. We can anticipate the correct answer choice being related to this error.

(A) fails to establish that consistency is a more important consideration than accuracy

Beck does not claim that consistency is more important than accuracy.

(B) fails to consider the program's accuracy in other tasks that it may perform

The argument does not indicate that other tasks are performed, and Beck speaks only to the accuracy of the program's estimate of municipal automotive use.

(C) takes for granted that the program's output would be consistent even if its estimates were inaccurate

Beck does not take for granted that if the estimates were inaccurate, the program would still be consistent. He considers accuracy and consistency to be the same.

(D) regards accuracy as the sole criterion for judging the program's value

The program's value is not discussed; only its consistency and accuracy are.

(E) fails to consider that the program could produce consistent but inaccurate output

This has to be the correct answer choice. Beck blurs the meanings of the two terms.

Questionable Assumption Fallacy

One of the Big Six Fallacies

Though not explicitly stated in the argument, an assumption is a claim that must be true for the conclusion to follow logically from the premises. Arguments that depend on minor assumptions can be valid. However, when the conclusion depends on a major or implausible assumption—one that creates a significant logical gap—the argument can no longer be considered valid. This is a Questionable Assumption Fallacy, and it can occur in two ways:

1. The argument contains a significant gap in reasoning that is not addressed. This occurs when the premises do not directly lead to the conclusion, and a large assumption is needed to make the argument valid. For example,

    The Penguins are set to play in the National Hockey Tournament. Teams that win the National Hockey Tournament usually see endorsement deals awarded to their star players, larger fan attendance in the games following the tournament, and many other perks. Sam is a player on the Penguins, so he will receive an endorsement deal.

This argument is missing two critical components. First, in order for this argument to be valid, we must assume that the Penguins will actually win the National Hockey Tournament. The second necessary assumption is that Sam is actually a star player. As there are two questionable assumptions, this argument is invalid.

2. The argument contains a gap in reasoning and evidence that the gap is unlikely to be addressed. In other words, an assumption is made that seems to contradict one or more of the premises in the argument. This does not need to be a significant gap in logic because the argument includes evidence that the assumption cannot be true. For example,

    Anthropological evidence suggests that Neanderthals had a more primitive culture than early Homo sapiens. While Neanderthals used tools, made art, and manipulated the environment around them, Homo sapiens were better able to perform these tasks. This is all very surprising since Neanderthals were more intelligent than Homo sapiens. We know this because the brain and skull of Neanderthals were 10 percent larger than those of Homo sapiens.

This argument concludes that Neanderthals were more intelligent than Homo sapiens because their brain and skull were larger. This may seem to be a reasonable assumption, but the second premise suggests that Homo sapiens were better at tasks that require intelligence. This throws into question the central assumption that brain and skull size determines intelligence.

Questionable Assumption Fallacy answer choices typically include the following boldfaced expressions:
- The reasoning in the argument is flawed in that the argument **presumes, without providing justification, that . . .**
- The reasoning in the argument is flawed in that the argument **takes for granted that** . . .
- The reasoning in the argument is flawed in that the argument offers evidence that appears to **undermine an important assumption** being made.

Let's look at an example:

> Over 90 percent of the human brain currently serves no purpose, as is evident from the fact that many people with significant brain damage show no discernible adverse effects. So, once humans begin to tap into this tremendous source of creativity and innovation, many problems that today seem insurmountable will be within our ability to solve.
>
> Which one of the following most accurately describes a flaw in the argument?
>
> (A) The argument presumes, without providing justification, that the effects of brain damage

are always easily detectable.

(B) The argument presumes, without providing justification, that the only reason that any problem remains unsolved is a lack of creativity and innovation.

(C) The argument infers that certain parts of the brain do nothing merely on the basis of the assertion that we do not know what they do.

(D) The argument infers that problems will be solved merely on the basis of the claim that they will be within our ability to solve.

(E) The argument presumes, without providing justification, that the currently unused parts of the brain are a potential source of tremendous creativity and innovation.

The indicator *so* precedes the conclusion that when humans begin to utilize the unused portion of the brain, which is a source of creativity and innovation, they will be able to solve daunting problems. The evidence for this is that over 90 percent of the brain currently serves no purpose. The conclusion contains an idea that seemingly comes out of nowhere. Where do we get this tremendous source of creativity and innovation? The argument assumes that the 90 percent of the brain that currently serves no purpose is a source of creativity and innovation. This is a large leap to take in order for the argument to make sense without any supporting information. The assumption is very questionable.

(A) The argument presumes, without providing justification, that the effects of brain damage are always easily detectable.

This is irrelevant information. The argument does not say it is easy to detect brain damage.

(B) The argument presumes, without providing justification, that the only reason that any problem remains unsolved is a lack of creativity and innovation.

The argument implies that these two qualities will help us solve more problems. It does not say that they can be used to solve any problem.

(C) The argument infers that certain parts of the brain do nothing merely on the basis of the assertion that we do not know what they do.

This is not true. The argument specifies that we know that 90 percent of the brain is not relied on because people with brain damage often display no negative effects.

(D) The argument infers that problems will be solved merely on the basis of the claim that they will be within our ability to solve.

This is irrelevant information. The argument does not discuss whether or not problems will be solved. It only talks about the ability to solve them.

(E) The argument presumes, without providing justification, that the currently unused parts of the brain are a potential source of tremendous creativity and innovation.

This has to be the correct answer choice. The argument makes the questionable assumption that the unused portion of the brain is a possible source of creativity and innovation.

Absence of Evidence Fallacy

Absence of Evidence Fallacies occur when there is insufficient evidence to support a conclusion. This fallacy can occur in three ways:

1. The argument claims that something is true because it has not been proven false. For example,

> **You've failed to explain how I performed this magic trick. Therefore, it must really be magic.**

| P: You cannot prove it is false. |
| C: So, it must be true. |

Just because the trick has not been proven to not be magic does not mean that it is magic.

2. The argument claims that something is false because it cannot be proven true. For example,

> **Enthusiasts have combed through the Himalayan Mountains and have not yet found a Yeti. This means that the Yeti does not exist.**

| P: You cannot prove it is true. |
| C: So, it must be false. |

Just because a Yeti has not been found does not mean that Yetis do not exist.

3. The argument claims that something is false because a piece of supporting evidence is false. This can weaken an argument but is insufficient to invalidate it. For example,

| P: Your premise is false. |
| C: Your conclusion is false. |

> **The suspected bank robber claimed that he couldn't have been the culprit because he was at a baseball game. Video footage shows he was nowhere near the baseball stadium. We can conclude that he must have been the one who robbed the bank.**

The fact that he did not attend the game weakens the robber's argument, but it does not necessarily mean that he robbed the bank.

Absence of Evidence Fallacy answer choices typically include the following boldfaced expressions:
- The reasoning in the argument is flawed in that the argument takes for granted that the fact that a claim has **not been demonstrated to be false establishes that it is true**.
- The reasoning in the argument is flawed in that the argument **fails to provide evidence** to justify the claim being made.
- The reasoning in the argument is flawed in that the argument confuses **lack of evidence for truth with evidence for falsity**.

Let's look at an example:

> Industrialist: Environmentalists contend that emissions from our factory pose a health risk to those living downwind. The only testimony presented in support of this contention comes from residents of the communities surrounding the factory. But only a trained scientist can determine whether or not these emissions are dangerous, and none of the residents are scientists. Hence our factory's emissions present no health risk.

The reasoning in the industrialist's argument is flawed because the argument

(A) impugns the motives of the residents rather than assessing the reasons for their contention
(B) does not consider the safety of emissions from other sources in the area
(C) presents no testimony from scientists that the emissions are safe
(D) fails to discuss the benefits of the factory to the surrounding community
(E) equivocates between two different notions of the term "health risk"

The indicator *hence* precedes the conclusion that the factory's emissions present no health risk. This conclusion is based on the fact that the only testimony that the emissions may be harmful comes from residents who are not trained scientists. This premise works against the idea that the emissions present a health risk, but it does not prove that the emissions do not present a health risk. It just indicates that there is no evidence of a health risk. This is an example of the first variety of Absence of Evidence Fallacy.

(A) impugns the motives of the residents rather than assessing the reasons for their contention

The argument does not impugn the motives of the residents.

(B) does not consider the safety of the emissions from other sources in the area

The argument is only concerned about the emissions from the factory. It does not discuss other sources.

(C) presents no testimony from scientists that the emissions are safe

This has to be the correct answer choice. The industrialist has no proof that the emissions are safe. He can only show that opponents of the factory have not proved they are unsafe.

(D) fails to discuss the benefits of the factory to the surrounding community

The argument's sole concern is the emissions from the factory. It does not mention other benefits, such as employment.

(E) equivocates between two different notions of the term "health risk"

The term *health risk* is used consistently throughout the argument.

False Comparison Fallacy

Comparisons are commonly used in the LR section as an argumentative device. Valid comparisons of similar items, situations, or ideas can either provide support for a conclusion or function as the conclusion of an argument. However, an invalid comparison is a logical error that can weaken an argument. False Comparison Fallacies can occur in two ways:

1. An argument compares items, situations, or ideas that are significantly different. For example,

> **Ron is busy working from home, so he doesn't have the time to play video games with his son today. It must be true also that if a fire were to start, Ron would be too busy to put it out.**

Playing video games and putting out a fire are significantly different actions. The former is a recreational activity, while the latter is a response to a dangerous situation. Even if Ron is too busy to play video games, it is likely that he would take the time to put out a fire.

2. An argument makes an incomplete comparison between two similar things. For example,

> **An SUV has a number of advantages: it includes a lot of storage space, it has a lot of legroom, and it is very safe. Accordingly, SUVs are better than sedans.**

The argument mentions several advantages of SUVs. However, the comparison between SUVs and sedans is incomplete. The argument mentions none of the advantages and disadvantages of sedans. Neither are any of the disadvantages of SUVs mentioned. Without this information, it is impossible to make a valid comparison between the two types of vehicles.

False Comparison Fallacy answer choices typically include the following boldfaced expressions:
- The reasoning in the argument is flawed in that the argument **treats as similar two cases that are different in a critical respect**.
- The reasoning in the argument is flawed in that the argument ignores the possibility that **the relationship between the two items is not comparable**.

Let's look at an example:

Because the statement "all gray rabbits are rabbits" is true, it follows by analogy that the statement "all suspected criminals are criminals" is also true.

The reasoning above is flawed because it fails to recognize that

(A) the relationship between being a criminal and being a rabbit is not of the same kind as that between being suspected and being gray

(B) the relationship between being suspected and being a rabbit is not of the same kind as that between being gray and being a criminal

(C) the relationship between being a gray rabbit and being a rabbit is not of the same kind as that between being a suspected criminal and being a criminal

(D) not all rabbits are gray

(E) not all criminals are suspected

The conclusion starts with the indicator *it follows*. The argument employs the term *analogy* to say that if one relationship is true, the other must also be true. This is an invalid comparison because the two relationships are significantly different. A gray rabbit is by definition a rabbit, while a suspected criminal only has the potential to be a criminal. We can anticipate a correct answer choice that addresses this invalid comparison.

(A) the relationship between being a criminal and being a rabbit is not of the same kind as that between being suspected and being gray

This is close to what we expected to see, but the terms have been mixed up. The argument does not discuss the relationship between being a criminal and being a rabbit.

(B) the relationship between being suspected and being a rabbit is not of the same kind as that between being gray and being a criminal

Again, this is close, but the argument does not discuss the relationship between being suspected and being a rabbit.

(C) the relationship between being a gray rabbit and being a rabbit is not of the same kind as that between being a suspected criminal and being a criminal

This has to be the correct answer choice. It describes the two relationships being compared and states that they are different.

(D) not all rabbits are gray

The argument does not assume this.

(E) not all criminals are suspected

The argument does not assume this.

Composition Fallacy

This fallacy occurs when the argument assumes that a whole group has the same qualities as a part of that group. It is not possible to make a conclusion about a whole group based on evidence about a part of that group, and vice versa. Composition Fallacies can occur in two ways:

1. **Whole to Part:** The argument uses evidence that a whole has a certain quality in order to conclude that a part of that whole has the same quality. For example,

    It would be dangerous to open up the enclosures in this zoo and let all the animals roam free. Therefore, it would also be dangerous to let Seth the Sloth out of his enclosure.

This argument takes evidence of the whole (all the animals in the zoo) having a quality and applies it to a part of that whole (the sloth). It is not necessarily true that letting Seth the Sloth out of his enclosure would be dangerous.

2. **Part to Whole:** The argument uses evidence that a part (or multiple parts) of a whole has a certain quality to conclude that the whole must have that property. For example,

    Vitamin C is an important vitamin in this multivitamin pill. Because vitamin C is not dangerous when consumed in large quantities, neither is this multivitamin pill.

We cannot infer that since a part of a whole has a quality, the whole has that quality as well. The multivitamin contains other ingredients besides vitamin C, and some of these may be dangerous when consumed in large quantities.

Composition Fallacy answer choices typically include the following boldfaced expressions:
- The reasoning in the argument is flawed in that the argument improperly draws an inference about **a whole from a premise about individual parts**.
- The reasoning in the argument is flawed in that the argument assumes what is true of **the constituent elements of a whole is also true of the whole**.
- The reasoning in the argument is flawed in that the argument justifies **a generalization about the group** from evidence that only speaks to **part of that group**.

Let's look at an example:

> Pundit: The average salary for teachers in our society is lower than the average salary for athletes. Obviously, our society values sports more than it values education.

The reasoning in the pundit's argument is questionable because the argument

(A) presumes, without providing justification, that sports have some educational value

(B) fails to consider that the total amount of money spent on education may be much greater than the total spent on sports

(C) fails to consider both that most teachers are not in the classroom during the summer and that most professional athletes do not play all year

(D) compares teachers' salaries only to those of professional athletes rather than also to the salaries of other professionals

(E) fails to compare salaries for teachers in the pundit's society to salaries for teachers in other societies

The pundit argues that since the average teacher is paid less than the average athlete, our society values sports more than education. The argument jumps from comparing two parts (teachers to athletes) to two wholes (education to sports). Remember, a whole does not necessarily have a characteristic just because a part does. It could be the case that spending on education exceeds spending on sports, even if athletes are paid more than teachers. This is a Part-to-Whole Composition Fallacy.

(A) presumes, without providing justification, that sports have some educational value

The argument does not presume this.

(B) fails to consider that the total amount of money spent on education may be much greater than the total spent on sports

This has to be the correct answer choice. The argument fails to consider that the whole may have a quality that is not shared by a part of the whole.

(C) fails to consider both that most teachers are not in the classroom during the summer and that most professional athletes do not play all year

This suggests that teachers and athletes have something in common. (C) is not the flaw in the argument.

(D) compares teachers' salaries only to those of professional athletes rather than also to the salaries of other professionals

The argument reaches a conclusion about the comparative value of education and sports. This conclusion does not require that teachers' salaries be compared with those of other professionals.

(E) fails to compare the salaries for teacher in the pundit's society to salaries for teachers in other societies

This is not relevant to the conclusion of the argument. There is no need to compare teachers in the pundits' society with those in other societies.

Proportion Fallacy

Proportion Fallacies confuse proportions with absolute amounts. A premise about a proportion cannot be used to reach a conclusion about an absolute amount, and a premise about an absolute amount cannot support a conclusion about a proportion. These questions can be intimidating because they appear to require mathematical operations, but this is not the case. Although some math is employed below, this is just to demonstrate that proportions and absolute amounts can never be compared. Math is never needed to solve this type of fallacy question. Here is an example of an argument with a Proportion Fallacy:

Nation X has a varied economy with many different industries. While the nation's economy has grown by 50 percent in the past 30 years, not every industry has grown. For example, the oil industry used to represent 26 percent of the country's GDP, while now it only represents 20 percent.

The argument states that the oil industry has not grown. The increase in the size of a particular industry is an absolute number. However, the argument provides a proportion (percentage of GDP) as evidence that the oil industry has not grown. The following chart shows how the oil industry could have increased in absolute terms and yet still account for a smaller portion of the overall economy:

	30 Years Ago	Today
Economy of Nation X	$100 billion	$150 billion
Oil Industry of Nation X	$26 billion (26% of GDP)	$30 billion (20% of GDP)

Even though the value of the oil industry has increased by $4 billion, it now makes up a smaller share of Nation X's GDP. This is because the overall economy has grown by 50 percent—from $100 billion to $150 billion—meaning that the oil industry now accounts for a smaller proportion of the economy. This example illustrates the difference between a proportion and an absolute amount. There are two ways in which a Proportion Fallacy can occur:

1. A proportion supports a conclusion about an absolute amount. For example,

    Smartphone producer SD Limited gained additional market share this year, which means it must have sold more smartphones this year than last.

2. An absolute amount supports a conclusion about a proportion. For example,

    CEO Jack Davies received a $10,000 salary increase this year while janitor Lisa Smith received a $3,000 salary increase. Therefore, Jack received a larger percentage increase in salary.

Proportion Fallacy answer choices typically include the following boldfaced expressions:
*   The reasoning in the argument is flawed in that the argument fails to consider the possibility that a decrease in **amount** coincides with a decrease in **percentage**.
*   The reasoning in the argument is flawed in that the argument assumes that an increase in **proportion** guarantees an increase in **number**.

Let's look at an example:

> Consumer advocate: There is ample evidence that the model of car one drives greatly affects the chances that one's car will be stolen. The model of car stolen most often in our country last year, for example, was also the model stolen most often in the preceding year.

The consumer advocate's reasoning is most vulnerable to criticism on the grounds that it

(A) fails to address adequately the possibility that the model of car that was stolen most often last year was the most common model of car in the consumer advocate's country
(B) fails to address adequately the possibility that the age of a car also greatly affects its chances of being stolen
(C) fails to address adequately the possibility that the car model that was stolen most often last year was stolen as often as it was because it has a high resale value
(D) presumes, without providing justification, that someone considering whether or not to steal a particular car considers only what model the car is
(E) presumes, without providing justification, that the likelihood of a car's being stolen should override other considerations in deciding which car one should drive

The conclusion of this argument is that some car models have a higher chance of being stolen. However, the evidence only tells us that a specific model was stolen the most number of times, not that this model has the highest chance of being stolen. This is a Proportion Fallacy because the consumer advocate confuses an amount in the premise with a proportion in the conclusion. Even if Ferraris are more likely to be stolen, Toyota Corollas may be stolen more often because there are far more of them on the road.

(A) fails to address adequately the possibility that the model of car that was stolen most often last year was the most common model of car in the consumers advocate's country

This has to be the correct answer choice. The argument does not address the possibility that the number of times a car is stolen may depend partly on popularity rather than likelihood of being stolen.

(B) fails to address adequately the possibility that the age of a car also greatly affects its chances of being stolen

Car ages are not discussed in the argument.

(C) fails to address adequately the possibility that the car model that was stolen most often last year was stolen as often as it was because it has a high resale value

This is not a flaw in the argument. It is a reason why the car might be more likely to be stolen.

(D) presumes, without providing justification, that someone considering whether or not to steal a particular car considers only what model the car is

The argument does not presume that car thieves only care about the model of the car.

(E) presumes, without providing justification, that the likelihood of a car's being stolen should override other considerations in deciding which car one should drive

The argument does not discuss which factors should be considered when choosing a car to drive.

Strength Modifier Fallacy

Strength modifiers are discussed in great detail in Chapter 2. Strength Modifier Fallacies occur when an invalid inference is drawn from one or more statements containing degree or quantity strength modifiers.

Strength Modifier Fallacies can occur in two ways:

1. An invalid strength modifier inference is made by combining two conditional statements. For example,

Some tall people are good at basketball. Some basketball players are famous. Therefore, all tall people are famous.

Be sure to review the valid strength modifier inferences (covered in Chapter 2):

$$
\begin{array}{cc}
\begin{array}{c} \text{ALL} \\ + \\ \text{SOME} \end{array} &
\begin{array}{c} A \rightarrow B \\ \underline{A \;{}^S\!\!-\!\!{}^S\, C} \\ B \;{}^S\!\!-\!\!{}^S\, C \end{array}
\end{array}
$$

$$
\begin{array}{cc}
\begin{array}{c} \text{ALL} \\ + \\ \text{MOST} \end{array} &
\begin{array}{c} A \;{}^M\!\!\rightarrow B \\ \underline{A \rightarrow C} \\ B \;{}^S\!\!-\!\!{}^S\, C \end{array}
\end{array}
$$

ALL + MOST	$A \xrightarrow{M} B$ $B \rightarrow C$ $A \xrightarrow{M} C$
MOST + MOST	$A \xrightarrow{M} B$ $A \xrightarrow{M} C$ $B \; {}^{S}\underline{\quad}{}^{S} \; C$
ALL + ALL	$A \rightarrow B$ $A \rightarrow C$ $B \; {}^{S}\underline{\quad}{}^{S} \; C$

2. An invalid inherent strength modifier inference is made based on a single conditional statement. A conclusion cannot be stronger in logical force than the premise that supports it. This means that SOME statements cannot be used to support MOST or ALL statements, and MOST statements cannot be used to support ALL statements. For example,

Most people never need surgery. As a result, there is no need for surgeons.

Strength Modifier Fallacy answer choices typically include the following boldfaced expressions:
- The reasoning in the argument is flawed in that the argument confuses **the chance of an event happening with the necessity of it happening**.
- The reasoning in the argument is flawed in that the argument concludes that something **never occurs** on the grounds that it **usually never occurs**.
- The reasoning in the argument is flawed in that the argument contains a premise that does not support **the strength of the conclusion**.

Let's look at an example:

On some hot days the smog in Hillview reaches unsafe levels, and on some hot days the wind blows into Hillview from the east. Therefore, on some days when the wind blows into Hillview from the east, the smog in Hillview reaches unsafe levels.

The reasoning in the argument is flawed in that the argument

(A) mistakes a condition that sometimes accompanies unsafe levels of smog for a condition that necessarily accompanies unsafe levels of smog
(B) fails to recognize that one set might have some members in common with each of two others even though those two other sets have no members in common with each other
(C) uses the key term "unsafe" in one sense in a premise and in another sense in the conclusion
(D) contains a premise that is implausible unless the conclusion is presumed to be true
(E) infers a particular causal relation from a correlation that could be explained in a variety of other ways

The stimulus contains the conclusion indicator *therefore* and multiple SOME statements. The argument can be outlined as follows:

Hot Days ^{S}—^{S} High Smog
Hot Days ^{S}—^{S} Wind from East
High Smog ^{S}—^{S} Wind from East

As two SOME statements can never be combined to create a valid inference, this argument includes a Strength Modifier Fallacy. We can anticipate a correct answer choice that addresses this flaw in the argument.

> **(A) mistakes a condition that sometimes accompanies unsafe levels of smog for a condition that necessarily accompanies unsafe levels of smog**

This answer choice describes a Conditional Reasoning Fallacy.

> **(B) fails to recognize that one set might have some members in common with each of two others even though those two other sets have no members in common with each other**

This has to be the correct answer choice. Hot Days overlaps with High Smog and Wind from East, but this does not mean that High Smog and Wind from East overlap. Again, you cannot combine two SOME statements.

> **(C) uses the key term "unsafe" in one sense in a premise and in another sense in the conclusion**

This answer choice describes an Equivocation Fallacy.

> **(D) contains a premise that is implausible unless the conclusion is presumed to be true**

This answer choice describes a Circular Reasoning Fallacy (will be discussed later in this section).

> **(E) infers a particular causal relation from a correlation that could be explained in a variety of other ways**

This answer choice describes a Causal Reasoning Fallacy.

Inappropriate Authority Fallacy

An appeal to authority can be a valid method for supporting a conclusion. However, when the opinion of an unsuitable person or group is used to bolster an argument, it is an Inappropriate Authority Fallacy. There are two ways in which this can occur:

1. An authority in one field expresses an opinion concerning another field. For example,

> **My chiropractor helps me keep my spine in proper alignment, which really improves my athletic performance. Recently, he gave me a nutrition program I can use to add muscle while staying lean. It is clear that I should follow this nutrition program if I want to improve my athletic performance even further.**

We cannot assume that the chiropractor is a nutrition expert as well as a chiropractic expert. Therefore, even if the chiropractor's treatments improve the patient's athletic performance, we cannot conclude that the chiropractor's nutrition plan will too. This type of Inappropriate Authority Fallacy typically involves an opinion given by an expert about a field somewhat related to his or her area of expertise (yet different).

2. The opinion is given by a nonexpert. This includes surveys of large groups of people with no specialized knowledge about the subject they are giving their opinion on. For example,

> **Survey: We asked 1,000 Americans to pick the language most difficult for an English speaker to**

learn. The most commonly selected answer was Japanese. So, at least when it comes to American English speakers, the hardest language to learn is Japanese.

There is nothing to indicate that the people surveyed have attempted to learn Japanese or are knowledgeable enough about the process of language acquisition to provide an informed opinion.

Inappropriate Assumption Fallacy answer choices typically include the following boldfaced expressions:
- The reasoning in the argument is flawed in that the argument depends on **the opinions** of people whose **knowledge of the subject matter** is not shown to be strong enough to support their general **opinion**.
- The reasoning in the argument is flawed in that the argument takes evidence that a claim is **believed to be true** by many to constitute **relevant evidence** that the claim is in fact true.

Let's look at an example:

> Hospital Executive: At a recent conference on nonprofit management, several computer experts maintained that the most significant threat faced by large institutions such as universities and hospitals is unauthorized access to confidential data. In light of this testimony, we should make the protection of our clients' confidentiality our highest priority.
>
> The hospital executive's argument is most vulnerable to which one of the following objections?
>
> (A) The argument confuses the causes of a problem with the appropriate solutions to that problem.
> (B) The argument relies on the testimony of experts whose expertise is not shown to be sufficiently broad to support their general claim.
> (C) The argument assumes that a correlation between two phenomena is evidence that one is the cause of the other.
> (D) The argument draws a general conclusion about a group based on data about an unrepresentative sample of that group.
> (E) The argument infers that a property belonging to large institutions belongs to all institutions.

The phrase *in light of this testimony* indicates that what follows is the conclusion. The hospital executive backs up the claim that client confidentiality should be the highest priority with opinions from several computer experts. Why would computer experts be knowledgeable about client confidentiality? We should anticipate a correct answer choice that describes this issue.

(A) The argument confuses the causes of a problem with the appropriate solutions to that problem.

This answer choice describes a Conditional Reasoning Fallacy.

(B) The argument relies on the testimony of experts whose expertise is not shown to be sufficiently broad to support their general claim.

This has to be the correct answer choice. We are not sure that these particular experts can determine that protection of privacy should be prioritized.

(C) The argument assumes that a correlation between two phenomena is evidence that one is the cause of the other.

This answer choice describes a Causal Reasoning Fallacy.

(D) The argument draws a general conclusion about a group based on data about an unrepresentative sample of that group.

This answer choice describes a Sampling Fallacy.

(E) The argument infers that a property belonging to large institutions belongs to all institutions.

This answer choice describes a Part-to-Whole Composition Fallacy.

Ad Hominem Fallacy

An Ad Hominem Fallacy involves an attack on the source of a claim rather than the claim itself. This type of reasoning is always invalid in LR questions. Even if the source's credibility is completely undermined, the source's information could still be accurate. Ad Hominem Fallacies are usually easy to spot. They come in two varieties:

1. The source's character is attacked in an effort to invalidate a claim. This reasoning is erroneous because the value of a claim does not hinge on the value of its source. If an argument is solely based on an attack on someone's character, it is invalid. For example,

   Dr. Hoffman's claim that the proposed tax will hurt our economy is clearly false. We know this because, while Dr. Hoffman may have a Ph.D. in economics, he obtained that degree from a for-profit online university mill known for "selling" degrees.

If Dr. Hoffman were debating a better-educated professor on the subject, a layperson could use the information about the professors' alma maters to evaluate their credibility, but this has no bearing on the claim about the proposed tax. Dr. Hoffman may not be an expert, but this does not prove that the proposed tax will not hurt the economy.

2. The source's behavior is shown to be inconsistent with the source's advice or claim. This does not nullify the advice or claim. A person's thoughts and actions are not always perfectly aligned. For example,

   If smoking is really that bad for your health, you wouldn't be doing it. Surely it can't be as bad as you make it out to be.

The person in question may be a hypocrite, but performing an action that is inconsistent with a statement does not make this statement untrue.

Ad Hominem Fallacy answer choices typically include the following boldfaced expressions:
   • The reasoning in the argument is flawed in that the argument undermines **the source** of a claim rather than **the claim itself**.
   • The reasoning in the argument is flawed in that the argument uses irrelevant information about **a person's character** rather than criticizing the opposing **viewpoint** itself.

Let's look at an example:

   Politician: Most of those at the meeting were not persuaded by Kuyler's argument, nor
      should they have been, for Kuyler's argument implied that it would be improper to

enter into a contract with the government; and yet—as many people know—Kuyler's company has had numerous lucrative contracts with the government.

Which one of the following describes a flaw in the politician's argument?

(A) It concludes that an argument is defective merely on the grounds that the argument has failed to persuade anyone of the truth of its conclusion.

(B) It relies on testimony that is likely to be biased.

(C) It rejects an argument merely on the grounds that the arguer has not behaved in a way that is consistent with the argument.

(D) It rejects a position merely on the grounds that an inadequate argument has been given for it.

(E) It rejects an argument on the basis of an appeal to popular opinion.

The politician concludes that those at the meeting should not be persuaded by Kuyler's argument, which implied that it would be improper to enter into a contract with the government. The politician offers Kuyler's inconsistent behavior as evidence that his argument is invalid. This is an Ad Hominem Fallacy. Kuyler's argument is not invalidated just because he acts in a manner that is inconsistent with it.

(A) It concludes that an argument is defective merely on the grounds that the argument has failed to persuade anyone of the truth of its conclusion.

The argument's failure to persuade most people is part of the conclusion, not the evidence for the conclusion. This answer choice also uses the term *anyone*, while the argument says *most*.

(B) It relies on testimony that is likely to be biased.

The politician refers to Kuyler's words and behavior to undermine, not support, his argument.

(C) It rejects an argument merely on the grounds that the arguer has not behaved in a way that is consistent with the argument.

This has to be the correct answer choice. The politician dismisses Kuyler's argument wholly on account of the latter's behavior.

(D) It rejects a position merely on the grounds that an inadequate argument has been given for it.

The specifics of Kuyler's argument are not discussed.

(E) It rejects an argument on the basis of an appeal to popular opinion.

Again, the fact that most people were not persuaded is part of the conclusion, not a premise.

Circular Reasoning Fallacy

An argument employs circular reasoning when its premise and conclusion are logically identical (even if phrased differently). In other words, circular reasoning occurs when an argument's conclusion is a restatement of the evidence for that conclusion. This fallacy can be tricky to identify, so it is important to be on the lookout for conclusions that restate one or more of their supporting premises.

> Circular Reasoning Fallacies rarely appear in arguments, but descriptions of this fallacy frequently appear in incorrect answer choices for questions that include other types of fallacies.

Here's an example of circular reasoning:

In his autobiography, John says he is a very honest person. This must be true because the book also claims he never told a lie.

P: John never told a lie.
C: John is a very honest person.

In this argument, the premise and conclusion are identical. If you accept the premise as true, the conclusion must be accepted as well. Often, different words or phrases are used in the premises and conclusion to trick the reader into thinking that each part of the argument discusses a different topic.

Circular Reasoning Fallacy answer choices typically include the following boldfaced expressions:
- The reasoning in the argument is flawed in that the argument **presupposes what it seeks to establish**.
- The reasoning in the argument is flawed in that the argument **concludes** something **indistinguishable** from **the evidence used to support it**.

Let's look at an example:

The typological theory of species classification, which has few adherents today, distinguishes species solely on the basis of observable physical characteristics, such as plumage color, adult size, or dental structure. However, there are many so-called "sibling species," which are indistinguishable on the basis of their appearance but cannot interbreed and thus, according to the mainstream biological theory of species classification, are separate species. Since the typological theory does not count sibling species as separate species, it is unacceptable.

The reasoning in the argument is most vulnerable to criticism on the grounds that

(A) the argument does not evaluate all aspects of the typological theory
(B) the argument confuses a necessary condition for species distinction with a sufficient condition for species distinction
(C) the argument, in its attempt to refute one theory of species classification, presupposes the truth of an opposing theory
(D) the argument takes a single fact that is incompatible with a theory as enough to show that theory to be false
(E) the argument does not explain why sibling species cannot interbreed

This argument includes the *since premise*, *conclusion* structure. Therefore, the conclusion is that the typological theory is unacceptable. The evidence for this is that birds that belong to the same species according to the typological theory are members of different species according to the mainstream theory. The argument assumes that the mainstream theory is correct (and, therefore, that the typological theory is incorrect) and uses this to support the conclusion that the typological theory is incorrect. This is a Circular Reasoning Fallacy. The truth of the conclusion cannot be stated or assumed in a premise.

(A) the argument does not evaluate all aspects of the typological theory

This may be true, but the argument does not require that all parts of the theory be evaluated.

(B) the argument confuses a necessary condition for species distinction with a sufficient condition for

species distinction

This answer choice describes a Conditional Reasoning Fallacy.

> **(C) the argument, in its attempt to refute one theory of species classification, presupposes the truth of an opposing theory**

This has to be the correct answer choice. The argument tries to refute the typological theory by claiming that it is incompatible with the mainstream theory, which is assumed to be correct.

> **(D) the argument takes a single fact that is incompatible with a theory as enough to show that theory to be false**

This is not fallacious. In addition, the argument does not do this—it assumes that one theory is correct and another is incorrect without relying on evidence.

> **(E) the argument does not explain why sibling species cannot interbreed**

It is not necessary for the argument to explain this.

Drill: Identify the Fallacy in the Argument

Identify the type of fallacy in each argument.

1. I will not go hiking with you if my phone is dead. If this Internet article is correct, installing this application on my phone will drastically extend its battery life. Since I'll be able to go hiking without my phone dying, I will be able to go hiking with you.

_____

2. As a baseball pitcher, Yuki is superior to Kenzo. Therefore, Yuki can throw a baseball farther than Kenzo can.

_____

3. Children, such as Asa, are not allowed into the movie unless a parent accompanies them. Asa's mother has agreed to accompany her, so Asa will be allowed into the movie.

_____

4. Chen must not attend Harvard University. I assumed that he went to that school when I saw him wearing a Harvard T-shirt, but Chen told me that he had received the shirt from this father.

_____

5. Students should be sure to read every page of the books they reference in their thesis papers. Reference books, like the introductory textbook to this course, are meant to provide information on a subject, and neglecting to read every page of the introductory textbook would leave a student very unprepared for the class.

_____

6. If I'm going to pay off my credit card balance this year, I must spend less on restaurants or get a raise at work. Since neither alone will allow me to pay off my bill, I won't be able to do so this year.

_____

7. Congressman Matthews claims that this bill will help solve copyright infringement issues. But it will not solve anything. Congressman Matthews bragged on social media about illegally downloading movies, so we can't trust his opinion on the matter.

_____

8. A study was conducted in which 1,000 unpaid college volunteers were given Medication X. The medication was designed to decrease social inhibition and promote a feeling of bonding with other classmates. The medication was shown to be successful, as the students in the study were much more likely than their peers to be involved in extracurricular activities.

_____

9. My uncle suggests that we travel to his beach house by bus or by boat. Since I am deathly afraid of water, we must travel by bus.

_____

10. The only solution to a bad hangover is water and Vitamin Z. Vitamin Z reduces the harmful effects of alcohol and prepares the body for rehydration. As a result, taking water and vitamin Z will cure a bad hangover.

_____

11. Chad Maxwell, a decorated army veteran with multiple medals and honors bestowed upon him, supports this new spending bill that will increase funding for the army in specific key areas. Since Maxwell supports this bill, you can be sure that it is the right bill for our country.

_____

12. Department Store A provides better-value products than Department Store B. We know this because a survey was conducted at Department Store A in which the vast majority of respondents agreed with that sentiment.

_____

13. The shopping plaza's sales must have been devastated by the recent hurricane. The grocery store, which normally accounts for 40 percent of the shopping plaza's sales, was the only business to see increased sales.

_____

14. A mail poll was conducted in which the question was posed, "Do you often respond back to unsolicited letters?" To our astonishment, 100 percent of participants responded "Yes." The effectiveness of mail polls has been thoroughly underestimated.

_____

15. Our law gives judges the discretion to sentence guilty parties to a range of prison time, even if not specifically recommended by the jury. Therefore, the judge's decision to give Mr. Harrison 20 years of community service is not improper.

_____

16. Long periods of drinking alcohol produce tremendous damage to the spleen. We know this because most people who are diagnosed with spleen conditions are alcoholics.

_____

17. This arts committee is in charge of funding and planning various cultural projects across the city. We know that the committee must be against traditional values as that is exactly the sentiment their last art exhibit portrayed.

_____

18. Most television actresses can cry on demand. Generally, television actresses begin their careers acting in television commercials. This means that the majority of television actresses that can cry on demand begin their careers acting in television commercials.

_____

19. Hulk Hogan was the most popular wrestler in the 1970s. We know this because Hulk Hogan was better received than any other wrestler during this time.

_____

1. Questionable Assumption Fallacy

2. Equivocation Fallacy

3. Conditional Reasoning Fallacy

4. Absence of Evidence Fallacy

5. False Comparison Fallacy

6. Selection Fallacy

7. Ad Hominem Fallacy

8. Causal Reasoning Fallacy

9. Selection Fallacy

10. Conditional Reasoning Fallacy

11. Inappropriate Authority Fallacy

12. Sampling Fallacy

13. Proportion Fallacy

14. Sampling Fallacy

15. Equivocation Fallacy

16. Causal Reasoning Fallacy

17. Composition Fallacy

18. Strength Modifier Fallacy

19. Circular Reasoning Fallacy

Drill: Identify the Fallacy in the Answer Choices

The following is a list of mock answer choices, each of which describes a specific fallacy. Below each answer choice, write the name of the fallacy.

1. conflates the chances of an event occurring with the amount of times that event has occurred

2. generalizes from what may be an unrepresentative sample

3. fails to consider whether the opinion relied on is an appropriate opinion for that particular subject

4. ignores the possibility that both options can be undertaken simultaneously

5. mistakes a condition necessary for a certain result as sufficient to bring about that result

6. ignores the possibility that not all of the options are being considered

7. rejects a claim because of evidence undermining the source of that claim

8. fails to consider if a given result may be caused by an alternative phenomenon

9. presumes, without providing justification, that the evidence given necessarily supports the argument's conclusion

10. allows the meaning of an important concept to shift during the course of the argument

11. confuses an adequate solution to produce a certain outcome with a required solution to produce that outcome

_____

12. presupposes what it sets out to establish

_____

13. assumes that just because an event is possible, it must be probable

_____

14. infers that each member of a group must have a certain quality on the basis of that group itself having that quality

_____

15. mistakes a result for the factor that produced that result

_____

16. takes for granted that evidence presented appears to undermine an assumption being made

_____

17. ambiguously uses a key term

_____

18. fails to consider that the participants questioned may be biased toward the subject asked of them

_____

19. rejects a claim on the basis of certain evidence of that claim being defeated

_____

20. presumes, without justification, that relationships between the two variables are analogous

_____

1. Proportion Fallacy

2. Sampling Fallacy

3. Inappropriate Authority Fallacy

4. Selection Fallacy

5. Conditional Reasoning Fallacy

6. Selection Fallacy

7. Ad Hominem Fallacy

8. Causal Reasoning Fallacy

9. Questionable Assumption Fallacy

10. Equivocation Fallacy

11. Conditional Reasoning Fallacy

12. Circular Reasoning Fallacy

13. Strength Modifier Fallacy

14. Composition Fallacy

15. Causal Reasoning Fallacy

16. Questionable Assumption Fallacy

17. Equivocation Fallacy

18. Sampling Fallacy

19. Absence of Evidence Fallacy

20. False Comparison Fallacy

Problem Set: Fallacy

1. Psychologist: A study of 436 university students found that those who took short naps throughout the day suffered from insomnia more frequently than those who did not. Moreover, people who work on commercial fishing vessels often have irregular sleep patterns that include frequent napping, and they also suffer from insomnia. So it is very likely that napping tends to cause insomnia.

The reasoning in the psychologist's argument is most vulnerable to criticism on the grounds that the argument

(A) presumes, without providing justification, that university students suffer from insomnia more frequently than do members of the general population
(B) presumes that all instances of insomnia have the same cause
(C) fails to provide a scientifically respectable definition for the term "napping"
(D) fails to consider the possibility that frequent daytime napping is an effect rather than a cause of insomnia
(E) presumes, without providing justification, that there is such a thing as a regular sleep pattern for someone working on a commercial fishing vessel

2. Columnist: The failure of bicyclists to obey traffic regulations is a causal factor in more than one quarter of the traffic accidents involving bicycles. Since inadequate bicycle safety equipment is also a factor in more than a quarter of such accidents, bicyclists are at least partially responsible for more than half of the traffic accidents involving bicycles.

The columnist's reasoning is flawed in that it

(A) presumes, without providing justification, that motorists are a factor in less than half of the traffic accidents involving bicycles
(B) improperly infers the presence of a causal connection on the basis of a correlation
(C) fails to consider the possibility that more than one factor may contribute to a given accident
(D) fails to provide the source of the figures it cites
(E) fails to consider that the severity of injuries to bicyclists from traffic accidents can vary widely

3. Researcher: People with certain personality disorders have more theta brain waves than those without such disorders. But my data show that the amount of one's theta brain waves increases while watching TV. So watching too much TV increases one's risk of developing personality disorders.

A questionable aspect of the reasoning above is that it

(A) uses the phrase "personality disorders" ambiguously
(B) fails to define the phrase "theta brain waves"
(C) takes correlation to imply a causal connection
(D) draws a conclusion from an unrepresentative sample of data
(E) infers that watching TV is a consequence of a personality disorder

4. The average length of stay for patients at Edgewater Hospital is four days, compared to six days at University Hospital. Since studies show that recovery rates at the two hospitals are similar for patients with similar illnesses, University Hospital could decrease its average length of stay without affecting quality of care.

The reasoning in the argument is most vulnerable to criticism on the grounds that the argument

(A) equates the quality of care at a hospital with patient's average length of stay
(B) treats a condition that will ensure the preservation of quality of care as a condition that is required to preserve quality of care
(C) fails to take into account the possibility that patients at Edgewater Hospital tend to be treated for different illnesses than patients at University Hospital
(D) presumes, without providing justification, that the length of time patients stay in the hospital is never relevant to the recovery rates of these patients
(E) fails to take into account the possibility that patients at University Hospital generally prefer longer hospital stays

5. Humans are supposedly rational: in other words, they have a capacity for well-considered thinking and behavior. This is supposedly the difference that makes them superior to other animals. But humans knowingly pollute the world's precious air and water and, through bad farming practices, deplete the soil that feeds them. Thus, humans are not rational after all, so it is absurd to regard them as superior to other animals.

The reasoning above is flawed in that it

(A) relies crucially on an internally contradictory definition of rationality
(B) takes for granted that humans are aware that their acts are irrational
(C) neglects to show that the irrational acts perpetrated by humans are not also perpetrated by other animals
(D) presumes, without offering justification, that humans are no worse than other animals
(E) fails to recognize that humans may possess a capacity without displaying it in a given activity

6. If the play were successful, it would be adapted as a movie or revived at the Decade Festival. But it is not successful. We must, regrettably, conclude that it will neither become a movie nor be revived at the Decade Festival.

The argument's reasoning is flawed because the argument

(A) fails to draw the conclusion that the play will not both be adapted as a movie and be revived at the Decade Festival, rather than that it will do neither

(B) fails to explain in exactly what way the play is unsuccessful

(C) equates the play's aesthetic worth with its commercial success

(D) presumes, without providing justification, that there are no further avenues for the play other than adaptation as a movie or revival at the Decade Festival

(E) fails to recognize that the play's not satisfying one sufficient condition does not preclude its satisfying a different sufficient condition for adaptation as a movie or revival at the Decade Festival

7. Fishing columnist: When an independent research firm compared the five best-selling baits, it found that Benton baits work best for catching trout. It asked a dozen top anglers to try out the five best-selling baits as they fished for speckled trout in a pristine northern stream, and every angler had the most success with a Benton bait. These results show that Benton is the best bait for anyone who is fishing for trout.

Each of the following describes a flaw in the reasoning in the fishing columnist's argument EXCEPT:

(A) The argument overlooks the possibility that some other bait is more successful than any of the five best-selling baits.

(B) The argument overlooks the possibility that what works best for expert anglers will not work best for ordinary anglers.

(C) The argument overlooks the possibility that the relative effectiveness of different baits changes when used in different locations.

(D) The argument overlooks the possibility that two best-selling brands of bait may be equally effective.

(E) The argument overlooks the possibility that baits that work well with a particular variety of fish may not work well with other varieties of that fish.

8. The peppered moth avoids predators by blending into its background, typically the bark of trees. In the late nineteenth century, those peppered moths with the lightest pigmentation had the greatest contrast with their backgrounds, and therefore were the most likely to be seen and eaten by predators. It follows, then, that the darkest peppered moths were the least likely to be seen and eaten.

Which one of the following most accurately describes a flaw in the reasoning of the argument?

(A) The argument overlooks the possibility that light peppered moths had more predators than dark peppered moths.

(B) The argument takes for granted that peppered moths are able to control the degree to which they blend into their backgrounds.

(C) The argument presumes, without providing justification, that all peppered moths with the same coloring had the same likelihood of being seen and eaten by a predator.

(D) The argument overlooks the possibility that there were peppered moths of intermediate color that contrasted less with their backgrounds than the darkest peppered moths did.

(E) The argument presumes, without providing justification, that the only defense mechanism available to peppered moths was to blend into their backgrounds.

9. Some classes of animal are so successful that they spread into virtually every ecosystem, whereas others gradually recede until they inhabit only small niches in geographically isolated areas and thereby become threatened. Insects are definitely of the former sort and ants are the most successful of these, ranging from the Arctic Circle to Tierra del Fuego. Hence, no species of ant is a threatened species.

The argument is flawed because it takes for granted that

(A) the Arctic Circle and Tierra del Fuego do not constitute geographically isolated areas

(B) because ants do not inhabit only a small niche in a geographically isolated area, they are unlike most other insects

(C) the only way a class of animal can avoid being threatened is to spread into virtually every ecosystem

(D) what is true of the constituent elements of a whole is also true of the whole

(E) what is true of a whole is also true of its constituent elements

10. If violations of any of a society's explicit rules routinely go unpunished, then that society's people will be left without moral guidance. Because people who lack moral guidance will act in many different ways, chaos results. Thus, a society ought never to allow any of its explicit rules to be broken with impunity.

The reasoning in the argument is most vulnerable to criticism on the grounds that the argument

(A) takes for granted that a society will avoid chaos as long as none of its explicit rules are routinely violated with impunity

(B) fails to consider that the violated rules might have been made to prevent problems that would not arise even if the rules were removed

(C) infers, from the claim that the violation of some particular rules will lead to chaos, that the violation of any rule will lead to chaos

(D) confuses the routine nonpunishment of violations of a rule with sometimes not punishing violations of the rule

(E) takes for granted that all of a society's explicit rules result in equally serious consequences when broken

11. Student: The publications of Professor Vallejo on the origins of glassblowing have reopened the debate among historians over whether glassblowing originated in Egypt or elsewhere. If Professor Vallejo is correct, there is insufficient evidence for claiming, as most historians have done for many years, that glassblowing began in Egypt. So, despite the fact that the traditional view is still maintained by the majority of historians, if Professor Vallejo is correct, we must conclude that glassblowing originated elsewhere.

Which one of the following is an error in the student's reasoning?

(A) It draws a conclusion that conflicts with the majority opinion of experts.

(B) It presupposes the truth of Professor Vallejo's claims.

(C) It fails to provide criteria for determining adequate historical evidence.

(D) It mistakes the majority view for the traditional view.

(E) It confuses inadequate evidence for truth with evidence for falsity.

12. A television manufacturing plant has a total of 1,000 workers, though an average of 10 are absent on any given day for various reasons. On days when exactly 10 workers are absent, the plant produces televisions at its normal rate. Thus, it is reasonable to assume that the plant could fire 10 workers without any loss in production.

The argument is most vulnerable to criticism on the grounds that it

(A) ignores the possibility that if 10 workers were fired, each of the remaining workers would produce more televisions than previously
(B) fails to show that the absentee rate would drop if 10 workers were fired
(C) takes for granted that the normal rate of production can be attained only when no more than the average number of workers are absent
(D) overlooks the possibility that certain workers are crucial to the production of televisions
(E) takes for granted that the rate of production is not affected by the number of workers employed at the plant

13. Historian: Flavius, an ancient Roman governor who believed deeply in the virtues of manual labor and moral temperance, actively sought to discourage the arts by removing state financial support for them. Also, Flavius was widely unpopular among his subjects, as we can conclude from the large number of satirical plays that were written about him during his administration.

The historian's argumentation is most vulnerable to criticism on the grounds that it

(A) fails to consider the percentage of plays written during Flavius's administration that were not explicitly about Flavius
(B) treats the satirical plays as a reliable indicator of Flavius's popularity despite potential bias on the part of the playwrights
(C) presumes, without providing evidence, that Flavius was unfavorably disposed toward the arts
(D) takes for granted that Flavius's attempt to discourage the arts was successful
(E) fails to consider whether manual labor and moral temperance were widely regarded as virtues in ancient Rome

14. Some anthropologists argue that the human species could not have survived prehistoric times if the species had not evolved the ability to cope with diverse natural environments. However, there is considerable evidence that *Australopithecus afarensis*, a prehistoric species related to early humans, also thrived in a diverse array of environments, but became extinct. Hence, the anthropologists' claim is false.

The reasoning in the argument is most vulnerable to criticism on the grounds that the argument

(A) confuses a condition's being required for a given result to occur in one case with the condition's being sufficient for such a result to occur in a similar case

(B) takes for granted that if one species had a characteristic that happened to enable it to survive certain conditions, at least one related extinct species must have had the same characteristic

(C) generalizes, from the fact that one species with a certain characteristic survived certain conditions, that all related species with the same characteristic must have survived exactly the same conditions

(D) fails to consider the possibility that *Australopithecus afarensis* had one or more characteristics that lessened its chances of surviving prehistoric times

(E) fails to consider the possibility that, even if a condition caused a result to occur in one case, it was not necessary to cause the result to occur in a similar case

15. Columnist: Several recent studies show, and insurance statistics confirm, that more pedestrians are killed every year in North American cities when crossing with the light than when crossing against it. Crossing against the light in North American cities is therefore less dangerous than crossing with the light.

The columnist's reasoning is most vulnerable to criticism on the grounds that it

(A) relies on sources that are likely to be biased in their reporting

(B) presumes, without providing justification, that because two things are correlated there must be a causal relationship between them

(C) does not adequately consider the possibility that a correlation between two events may be explained by a common cause

(D) ignores the possibility that the effects of the types of actions considered might be quite different in environments other than the ones studied

(E) ignores possible differences in the frequency of the two actions whose risk is being assessed

Problem Set: Fallacy — Answers

1. **Correct Answer (D).** *Prep Test 52, Section 1, Question 2.*

Fallacy Type: Causal Reasoning Fallacy

The conclusion, indicated by *so*, states that it is very likely that Napping CAUSE Insomnia. The argument's evidence for this comes from two studies that show a correlation between frequent naps and insomnia in two different environments. Both studies show evidence of two variables being correlated, but that does not mean that one causes the other. The assumption of a causal connection between napping and insomnia is, therefore, a Causal Reasoning Fallacy. It could very well be the case that a third factor is causing both napping and insomnia. It could also be the case that instead of Napping CAUSE Insomnia, it is really that Insomnia CAUSE Napping. In other words, students and people who work on commercial fishing boats may take frequent naps throughout the day because they do not sleep properly at night. We should anticipate a correct answer choice that addresses the Causal Reasoning Fallacy in the argument.

(A) presumes, without providing justification, that university students suffer from insomnia more frequently than do members of the general population

The psychologist never explicitly or implicitly states this. (A) is a loser.

(B) presumes that all instances of insomnia have the same cause

The psychologist never states this either. It could be the case that napping is just one possible cause of insomnia. This is another loser.

(C) fails to provide a scientifically respectable definition for the term "napping"

Such a definition is not necessary for the argument to be valid. We can consider this answer choice to be a loser.

(D) fails to consider the possibility that frequent daytime napping is an effect rather than a cause of insomnia

This matches our anticipated answer choice. It is possible that cause and effect are reversed. (D) is a candidate.

(E) presumes, without providing justification, that there is such a thing as a regular sleep pattern for someone working on a commercial fishing vessel

The phrase *irregular sleep patterns* refers to sleep patterns that are outside of the norm. Whether or not people working on fishing boats can have a regular sleep pattern does not affect the validity of the argument. This is a loser.

As (D) is the only candidate, it has to be the correct answer choice.

2. **Correct Answer (C).** *Prep Test 57, Section 3, Question 10.*

Fallacy Type: Selection Fallacy

This argument includes a *since premise, conclusion* structure and can be outlined as follows:

P1: Bicyclists Failing to Obey Traffic Regulations CAUSE > 1/4 of Accidents w/ Bicycles
P2: Inadequate Bicycle Safety Equipment CAUSE > 1/4 of Accidents w/ Bicycles
C: Bicyclists responsible for more than 1/2 of Accidents w/ Bicycles

This argument seems valid at first glance. Causal statements that function as premises are valid and assumed to be true. In addition, the two categories of bicycle accidents equal more than 1/2 when combined. However, it is unclear whether these categories of accidents are exclusive. They may overlap. Consider this example:

More than 1/4 of my drinks at the party included club soda. Additionally, more than 1/4 of my drinks at the party included vodka. Therefore, club soda and vodka made up more than 1/2 of my drinks.

We do not know whether these categories are exclusive. It could be the case that every drink that included club soda also included vodka. Therefore, it is not necessarily true that both ingredients accounted for more than 1/2 of the drinks.

There could be a similar overlap between accidents caused by bicyclists failing to obey traffic regulations and those caused by bicyclists with inadequate safety equipment. In short, the argument assumes that the two categories are exclusive, which is not necessarily true. We should anticipate a correct answer choice that addresses a Selection Fallacy.

(A) presumes, without providing justification, that motorists are a factor in less than half of the traffic accidents involving bicycles

Whether motorists are a factor or not does not affect whether bicyclists are a factor. An accident can have more than one cause. In addition, the argument does not discuss how often motorists are a factor. This is a loser.

(B) improperly infers the presence of a causal connection on the basis of a correlation

This answer choice describes a Causal Reasoning Fallacy. As mentioned above, the causal statements are premises, not conclusions, so there cannot be a Causal Reasoning Fallacy. (B) is also a loser.

(C) fails to consider the possibility that more than one factor may contribute to a given accident

This matches our anticipated answer choice. The argument does not consider that an accident can have more than one contributing factor, which is why the columnist thinks that each type of accident must be exclusive. This is a candidate.

(D) fails to provide the source of the figures it cites

No argument is required to specify the source of its claims. This is a loser.

(E) fails to consider that the severity of injuries to bicyclists from traffic accidents can vary widely

The severity of injuries is not relevant to the conclusion. This is a loser.

As (C) is the only candidate, it has to be the correct answer choice.

3. **Correct Answer (C).** *Prep Test 41, Section 3, Question 13.*

Fallacy Type: Causal Reasoning Fallacy

The conclusion of this argument is indicated by the word *so*. The argument concludes that watching too much TV increases the risk of developing personality disorders; in other words, Too Much TV CAUSE Personality Disorders. Remember, a causal relationship does not require the inclusion of the word *cause*. It can be any relationship in which one factor results in another factor. Here, the evidence for a causal conclusion is that there is a correlation between personality disorders and increased theta brain waves, and that the amount of theta brain waves increases when a person watches TV. Thus, we have a Causal Reasoning Fallacy. A correlation between two factors does not mean that one causes the other.

(A) uses the phrase "personality disorders" ambiguously

This answer choice describes an Equivocation Fallacy. Although *personality disorders* is not defined, its meaning does not seem to change throughout the argument. This is a loser.

(B) fails to define the phrase "theta brain waves"

It is true that this term is not defined, but this does not affect the validity of the argument. (B) is a loser.

(C) takes correlation to imply a causal connection

This matches our anticipated answer choice. A Causal Reasoning Fallacy is described clearly and directly. (C) is a candidate.

(D) draws a conclusion from an unrepresentative sample of data

This answer choice describes a Sampling Fallacy. There is no reason to think that the data presented by the researcher is unrepresentative. This is a loser.

(E) infers that watching TV is a consequence of a personality disorder

The answer choice describes a Causal Reasoning Fallacy, but it inaccurately restates the content of the argument. The research claims the exact opposite—that personality disorders are a consequence of watching too much TV. This is a loser.

As (C) is the only candidate, it has to be the correct answer choice.

---

4. **Correct Answer (C).** *Prep Test 52, Section 3, Question 16.*

Fallacy Type: False Comparison Fallacy

This argument uses the *since premise, conclusion* structure to argue that since Edgewater Hospital and University Hospital have similar recovery rates for similar illnesses, the latter could decrease its average length of stay without affecting quality of care. This is because average length of stay for patients at Edgewater Hospital is four days while at University Hospital it is six days. The conclusion is based on a false comparison: it assumes that both hospitals treat the same types of illnesses with the same frequency. What if a larger proportion of University Hospital's patients have serious illnesses than Edgewater Hospital's? This would explain why the hospitals' average length of stay differs though they have similar recovery rates for similar illnesses. We do not know whether these two hospitals are similar enough to be compared. Thus, we should look for an answer choice that describes a False Comparison Fallacy.

(A) equates the quality of care at a hospital with patient's average length of stay

The argument does not equate the two. It concludes that since the recovery rates are similar for similar illnesses, quality of care will be unaffected if the length of stay changes. This is a loser.

(B) treats a condition that will ensure the preservation of quality of care as a condition that is required to preserve quality of care

This answer choice describes a Conditional Reasoning Fallacy. There are no conditional statements in the argument. This is also a loser.

(C) fails to take into account the possibility that patients at Edgewater Hospital tend to be treated for different illnesses than patients at University Hospital

This matches our anticipated answer choice. The argument does not consider that each hospital may deal with certain illnesses more often than the other. If this were the case, the average length of stay would not be the same, regardless of recovery rates. This is a candidate.

(D) presumes, without providing justification, that the length of time patients stay in the hospital is never relevant to the recovery rates of these patients

The argument does not presume this. The argument actually equates the length of time patients stay in the hospital with recovery rates. This is a loser.

(E) fails to take into account the possibility that patients at University Hospital generally prefer longer hospital stays

Patient preference regarding length of hospital stay has no bearing on recovery rates. This is also a loser.

As (C) is the only candidate, it has to be the correct answer choice.

5. **Correct Answer (E).** *Prep Test 54, Section 2, Question 15.*

Fallacy Type: Equivocation Fallacy

The indicator word *thus* precedes the subsidiary conclusion that humans are not rational after all, with the phrase *so* it showing that this subsidiary conclusion supports the main conclusion (that it is absurd to regard humans as superior to other animals). The evidence for the subsidiary conclusion is that humans act irrationally. The argument can be outlined as follows:

> P1: *Rational* means having the capacity for well-considered thinking and behavior. This is supposedly what makes humans superior to animals.
> P2: Humans knowingly commit acts that do not seem well-considered.
> SC: Humans are not rational.
> C: Humans are not superior.

This seems like a good argument at first glance. However, it includes an equivocation—the meaning of the term *rational* changes throughout. Initially, *rational* is defined simply as the capacity for well-considered thinking and behavior. Having the capacity to do something does not mean that you always do it—just that you have the ability to do it. However, the subsidiary conclusion states that people are not rational because they do not always exhibit well-considered thinking and behavior. Initially, *rational* refers to "having the capacity for well-considered thinking and behavior," but it comes to mean "always exhibiting well-considered thinking and behavior." We can anticipate a correct answer choice that describes this Equivocation Fallacy.

(A) relies crucially on an internally contradictory definition of rationality

The definition of *rational* in the first sentence does not include an internal contradiction. This is a loser.

(B) takes for granted that humans are aware that their acts are irrational

Whether or not humans are aware that their actions are irrational is not addressed in the argument. This is a loser.

(C) neglects to show that the irrational acts perpetrated by humans are not also perpetrated by other animals

It does not matter if irrational acts are perpetrated by other animals. The argument's conclusion is that humans are not superior to other animals, not that other animals are superior to humans. This is a loser.

(D) presumes, without offering justification, that humans are no worse than other animals

The argument does not presume this. The conclusion states that humans are not superior to other animals. This means that they could theoretically be worse than animals. We can consider this answer choice a loser.

(E) fails to recognize that humans may possess a capacity without displaying it in a given activity

This matches our anticipated answer choice. The definition of *rational* in the first sentence does not require that humans always act in a well-considered manner. Further on, though, the argument states that humans are not rational because they do not always exhibit well-considered thinking and actions. (E) has to be the correct answer choice.

6. **Correct Answer (E).** *Prep Test 45, Section 1, Question 13.*

Fallacy Type: Conditional Reasoning Fallacy

This argument contains conditional statements. It can be outlined as follows:

P1: Successful Play → Adapted as Movie OR Revived at Festival
P2: ~~Successful Play~~
C: ~~Successful Play~~ → ~~Adapted as Movie~~ AND ~~Revived at Festival~~

The conditional statement tells us that if a play is successful, it will either become a movie or be revived at the Decade Festival. The contrapositive of this statement can be diagrammed as follows:

~~Adapted as Movie~~ AND ~~Revived at Festival~~ → ~~Successful Play~~

However, the conclusion has negated the first premise of the argument without flipping it. This is not a valid inference. The fact that a play is not successful does not mean that it will not be adapted into a movie and not revived at the festival. For example, even if a play is not successful, it may be liked by a director who then decides to make a movie based on it. This argument includes a Conditional Reasoning Fallacy—specifically, negated reasoning. We should look for an answer choice that describes this flaw in the argument.

(A) fails to draw the conclusion that the play will not both be adapted as a movie and be revived at the Decade Festival, rather than that it will do neither

The answer choice accurately describes the conclusion, which uses a *neither/nor* structure to indicate that both options will not occur. However, this is not a flaw in the argument. (A) is a loser.

(B) fails to explain in exactly what way the play is unsuccessful

It is not necessary for the argument to do this. (B) is a loser.

(C) equates the play's aesthetic worth with its commercial success

This answer choice describes an Equivocation Fallacy. The argument does even discuss these two concepts. This is also a loser.

(D) presumes, without providing justification, that there are no further avenues for the play other than adaptation as a movie or revival at the Decade Festival

The argument does not presume this. It only concludes that the two avenues specified are not possible. We can put this in the loser category.

(E) fails to recognize that the play's not satisfying one sufficient condition does not preclude its satisfying a different sufficient condition for adaptation as a movie or revival at the Decade Festival

This matches our anticipated answer choice. Not triggering the sufficient condition of the first premise does not mean that the play will not be adopted as a movie and not be revived at the festival. There are other sufficient conditions that could trigger these terms. In other words, the conclusion of the argument is invalid because it is negated but not flipped. This has to be the correct answer choice.

7. **Correct Answer (D).** *Prep Test 40, Section 3, Question 19.*

Fallacy Type: Sampling Fallacy

This question includes an EXCEPT prompt, which is rare for F questions. The argument concludes that Benton is the best bait for anyone who fishes for trout. This claim is supported by a study comparing the five best-selling baits. The argument shows that when a dozen top anglers fished for speckled trout in a pristine northern stream using these baits, they had the most success with Benton's product. There are a number of Sampling Fallacies here. Each incorrect answer choice must accurately describe one of these Sampling Fallacies, while the correct answer choice must not.

(A) The argument overlooks the possibility that some other bait is more successful than any of the five best-selling baits.

We cannot conclude that Benton is the best bait when only five baits were compared. This answer choice describes a Sampling Fallacy in the argument, so it is a loser.

(B) The argument overlooks the possibility that what works best for expert anglers will not work best for ordinary anglers.

We cannot conclude that Benton is the best for all anglers based on the results achieved by top anglers. This answer choice accurately describes a Sampling Fallacy in the argument. It is a loser.

(C) The argument overlooks the possibility that the relative effectiveness of different baits changes when used in different locations.

We cannot conclude that Benton is the best bait for catching trout in any environment based on the results in one particular environment (a pristine northern stream). As this answer choice accurately describes a Sampling Fallacy in the argument, it is a loser.

(D) The argument overlooks the possibility that two best-selling brands of bait may be equally effective.

This answer choice does not describe a flaw in the argument. The argument clearly states that Benton was more effective than any of the other five best-selling baits. If two of them were equally effective, the argument's claim would remain valid. As this answer choice does not describe a fallacy in the argument, it has to be the correct answer choice.

(E) The argument overlooks the possibility that baits that work well with a particular variety of fish may not work well with other varieties of that fish.

We cannot conclude that Benton is the best bait for trout in general based on its effectiveness with a particular type of trout. This answer choice accurately describes a Sampling Fallacy in the argument. It is a loser.

8. **Correct Answer (D).** *Prep Test 59, Section 3, Question 20.*

Fallacy Type: Selection Fallacy

The phrase *it follows, then* precedes the conclusion that the darkest moths were the least likely to be seen and eaten. This is supported by the fact that the moths with the lightest pigmentation contrasted the most with tree bark, making them more likely to be seen and eaten. The argument assumes that if the lightest moths were in the most danger, the darkest moths must have been the least threatened. This is not necessarily the case, though. For example, assume that there are moths with five different shades, as represented by the following spectrum:

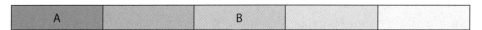

If the tree bark were the color of the square marked A, the lightest moths would stand out the most and the darkest moths would blend in the best. The conclusion would be valid in this case. However, if the tree bark were the color of the square marked B, the lightest and darkest moths would both stand out. The moth best suited to this situation would be light gray. The argument assumes that moths are either dark or light, without taking in consideration intermediate colors. This is a Selection Fallacy, as the argument takes dark and light to be the only options. We should look for an answer choice that expresses this fallacy.

    (A) The argument overlooks the possibility that light peppered moths had more predators than dark peppered moths.

The argument does not overlook this as it explicitly states that light peppered moths were more likely to be seen and eaten. This is a loser.

    (B) The argument takes for granted that peppered moths are able to control the degree to which they blend into their backgrounds.

The argument does not assume this. (B) is also a loser.

    (C) The argument presumes, without providing justification, that all peppered moths with the same coloring had the same likelihood of being seen and eaten by a predator.

The argument presumes that coloring affected the likelihood of being seen and eaten by a predator, but it does not claim that it was the only factor. We can classify this answer choice as a loser.

    (D) The argument overlooks the possibility that there were peppered moths of intermediate color that contrasted less with their backgrounds than the darkest peppered moths did.

This matches our anticipated answer choice. The argument does not consider other options. Instead, it assumes that the darkest moths were the least threatened because the lightest moths were in the most danger. This is a candidate.

    (E) The argument presumes, without providing justification, that the only defense mechanism available to peppered moths was to blend into their backgrounds.

The argument does not presume this. (E) is another loser.

As (D) is the only candidate, it has to be the correct answer choice.

9. **Correct Answer (E).** *Prep Test 48, Section 1, Question 17.*

Fallacy Type: Composition Fallacy

The conclusion that no ant species is threatened is preceded by the indicator *hence*. The support for this claim is that, as a class of animals, insects are so successful that they have spread into virtually every ecosystem. With their extensive range, ants are the most successful type of insect. The argument can be broken down even more simply: since ants in general are very successful, every species of ant is also successful. This is a Whole-to-Part Composition Fallacy. We cannot conclude that every species of ant is successful based on the fact that ants as a whole are very successful. The correct answer choice must describe this fallacy.

(A) the Arctic Circle and Tierra del Fuego do not constitute geographically isolated areas

Whether these regions are isolated or not does not affect the validity of the argument. The conclusion is that ants are not threatened, not that they are geographically isolated. We can consider this answer choice to be a loser.

(B) because ants do not inhabit only a small niche in a geographically isolated area, they are unlike most other insects

The argument does not state that other insects only inhabit small niches in geographically isolated areas. Neither does it claim that ants are unlike other insects. This is also a loser.

(C) the only way a class of animal can avoid being threatened is to spread into virtually every ecosystem

This is too strong of a claim, based on the information in the argument. Threatened species only inhabit small, geographically isolated areas, but some nonthreatened species may be in the same situation. This is a loser.

(D) what is true of the constituent elements of a whole is also true of the whole

This answer choice describes a Composition Fallacy. We will consider it as a candidate.

(E) what is true of a whole is also true of its constituent elements

This one also describes a Composition Fallacy, so it is a candidate as well.

Let's look at our two candidates. Answer choice (D) describes a Part-to-Whole Composition Fallacy. For this to be the correct answer choice, the argument would have to claim that because no species of ant is threatened, ants are the most successful insect. However, the argument actually claims the opposite—no species is threatened because ants are the most successful insect. This is a Whole-to-Part Composition Fallacy. Thus, (E) has to be the correct answer choice.

10. **Correct Answer (D).** *Prep Test 41, Section 1, Question 22.*

Fallacy Type: Strength Modifier Fallacy

The conclusion of this argument follows the indicator *thus*—a society ought never to allow any of its rules to be broken with impunity because when violations of society's rules routinely go unpunished, the society's people are left without moral guidance, and people without moral guidance bring about chaos. The argument can be outlined as follows:

> P1: Rules Routinely Violated but Unpunished → ~~Moral Guidance~~
> P2: ~~Moral Guidance~~ → Act in Many Different Ways
> P3: Act in Many Different Ways → Chaos Results
> C: ~~Rules Violated but Unpunished~~

The problem here is that the scope of the argument is changed by certain words. The first word that is important to note is *routinely*. *Routinely* means *frequently*. When rules routinely go unpunished, a chain reaction is set off, resulting in chaos. However, the conclusion states that a society ought never to allow any of its rules to be broken with impunity. To rephrase the argument in a simpler way: when rule violations routinely go unpunished, chaos frequently results, so every single rule violation should be punished. The conclusion that is supported is that rules should not routinely go unpunished, not that every rule breaker should be punished. This is a Strength Modifier Fallacy in the sense that a weak premise (routinely) is given to support a strong conclusion (never).

(A) takes for granted that a society will avoid chaos as long as none of its explicit rules are routinely violated with impunity

The argument does not assume that routine failure to punish rule violations is the only sufficient condition that leads to chaos. Other things could lead to chaos as well. This is a loser.

(B) fails to consider that the violated rules might have been made to prevent problems that would not arise even if the rules were removed

The argument states that when rule violations go unpunished, society is left without moral guidance. There is no discussion of the specific rules and types of rules that may or may not be effective. This is also a loser.

(C) infers, from the claim that the violation of some particular rules will lead to chaos, that the violation of any rule will lead to chaos

This matches our anticipated answer choice. We can consider it a candidate.

(D) confuses the routine nonpunishment of violations of a rule with sometimes not punishing violations of the rule

This also matches our anticipated answer choice. We have a second candidate.

(E) takes for granted that all of a society's explicit rules result in equally serious consequences when broken

The argument does not assume this. The argument is concerned with routine nonpunishment of rules, not with the consequences that follow from specific rules being violated. This is a loser.

We now need to eliminate a candidate. Upon closer examination, answer choice (C) does not actually match our anticipated answer. The argument addresses the issue of routine nonpunishment of rule violations in general. It is not concerned with a few specific rules. We can therefore eliminate (C).

(D) matches our anticipated answer choice because it claims that the argument confuses routine nonpunishment with sometimes not punishing a rule breaker. The argument's conclusion does just this by stating that no rule should be broken without punishment. This has to be the correct answer choice.

11. **Correct Answer (E).** *Prep Test 54, Section 2, Question 22.*

Fallacy Type: Absence of Evidence Fallacy

The argument claims that Professor Vallejo has reopened the debate about the origins of glassblowing. If Vallejo is correct, then there is not enough evidence to claim that glassblowing began in Egypt, as most historians believe. The argument then concludes that if Vallejo is correct, we must conclude that glassblowing originated outside of Egypt. There is a subtle flaw in this argument. There is a conditional statement in the premise that is very similar to, but not quite the same as, a conditional statement in the conclusion.

P: Vallejo is Correct → Not Enough Evidence to Claim It Comes from Egypt

C: Vallejo is Correct → Not from Egypt

This is an Absence of Evidence Fallacy. If Vallejo is correct, there is not enough evidence to definitively say glassblowing originated in Egypt, but that does not mean we can definitively say that it did not originate in Egypt.

(A) It draws a conclusion that conflicts with the majority opinion of experts.

Drawing a conclusion that conflicts with experts' views is fine, as long as you have evidence for that conclusion. In addition, the argument draws no such conclusion. (A) is a loser.

(B) It presupposes the truth of Professor Vallejo's claims.

This answer choice describes a Circular Reasoning Fallacy. (B) is a loser.

(C) It fails to provide criteria for determining adequate historical evidence.

The argument remains valid whether or not it provides criteria for determining adequate evidence. This is also a loser.

(D) It mistakes the majority view for the traditional view.

According to the argument, the majority view and the traditional view are the same. We can categorize this answer choice as a loser.

(E) It confuses inadequate evidence for truth with evidence for falsity.

This matches our anticipated answer choice. The student takes a lack of evidence that glassblowing originated in Egypt as evidence that it did not originate in Egypt. This is classic Absence of Evidence Fallacy language. (E) has to be the correct answer choice.

12. **Correct Answer (B).** *Prep Test 40, Section 3, Question 23.*

Fallacy Type: Questionable Assumption Fallacy

Indicated by *thus*, the conclusion is that the plant could fire 10 of its 1,000 workers without any loss in production. The basis for this is that 10 employees on average are absent each day, and that this does not affect the rate of production. The assumption is that if 10 workers were fired, there would be no change in the number of workers present on any given day; in other words, once the employees were fired, there would be no more absences. This seems doubtful, though. It is likely that some of the remaining 990 workers would be absent each day, meaning that there would be less workers available than before. This may have a negative effect on production. We should anticipate an answer choice that describes this Questionable Assumption Fallacy.

(A) ignores the possibility that if 10 workers were fired, each of the remaining workers would produce more televisions than previously

If this were a possibility, then the argument would not be flawed. It would account for why television production would remain the same with potentially less workers at the plant. This is a loser.

(B) fails to show that the absentee rate would drop if 10 workers were fired

This matches our anticipated answer choice. The argument assumes that the absentee rate would drop to zero, without considering the possibility of continued absences. This is a candidate.

(C) takes for granted that the normal rate of production can be attained only when no more than the average number of workers are absent

The argument does not discuss attaining a normal production rate. It also assumes that no workers will be absent. (C) is a loser.

(D) overlooks the possibility that certain workers are crucial to the production of televisions

This may be the correct answer choice. If employees who are crucial to making televisions were fired, the production rate would decline. We now have two candidates.

(E) takes for granted that the rate of production is not affected by the number of workers employed at the plant

The argument does not assume that the rate of production is not affected by the number of workers. It assumes that firing 10 people would not negatively impact production. This is a loser.

Looking back at the candidates, (D) can be eliminated. Although it states a possible assumption, it is beyond the scope of the argument. Specific types of workers are not mentioned. It may even be the case that the plant will fire 10 workers who have no role in production. (B) is more closely related to the content of the argument, so it has to be the correct answer choice.

---

13. **Correct Answer (B).** *Prep Test 57, Section 2, Question 26.*

Fallacy Type: Sampling Fallacy

The historian concludes that Flavius was widely unpopular among his subjects based on the fact that a large number of satirical plays were written about him during his administration. By itself, the connection between his popularity and his depiction in theater does not seem inappropriate. However, the background information presented earlier in the passage states that Flavius actively sought to discourage the arts by removing their financial support, which suggests bias on the part of the playwrights in regard to Flavius. Therefore, the sample (playwrights) cannot represent the general population. That is, the argument includes a Sampling Fallacy.

(A) fails to consider the percentage of plays written during Flavius's administration that were not explicitly about Flavius

This has no bearing on the validity of the argument. (A) is a loser.

(B) treats the satirical plays as a reliable indicator of Flavius's popularity despite potential bias on the part of the playwrights

This matches our anticipated answer choice. The number of satirical plays may not be a reliable indicator of Flavius's popularity among the general public if the writers of those plays were biased. A sample must be representative of the group a conclusion is being made about and cannot be tainted by bias. (B) is a candidate.

(C) presumes, without providing evidence, that Flavius was unfavorably disposed toward the arts

The argument provides evidence to support this claim. It states that Flavius tried to discourage the arts by removing their state funding. This is also a loser.

(D) takes for granted that Flavius's attempt to discourage the arts was successful

The degree of success of Flavius's attempt is not relevant to the argument. This is a loser.

(E) fails to consider whether manual labor and moral temperance were widely regarded as virtues in ancient Rome

This has no impact on the validity of the argument. (E) is another loser.

As (B) is the only candidate, it has to be the correct answer choice.

14. **Correct Answer (A).** *Prep Test 51.5, Section 3, Question 25.*

Fallacy Type: Conditional Reasoning Fallacy

The argument concludes that the anthropologists' claim is false. The claim in question is that the human species could not have survived prehistoric times without having evolved the ability to adapt to different environments. The word *if* indicates the sufficient condition of a conditional statement, which can be diagrammed as follows:

~~Ability to Adapt to Diversity~~ → ~~Survive~~

The contrapositive of this statement is as follows:

Survive → Ability to Adapt to Diversity

The argument then provides evidence to invalidate this claim. It states that a prehistoric species related to early humans had the ability to adapt to diverse environments but was ultimately wiped out. How does this disprove the anthropologists' claim? It doesn't. The argument implies that because this species had the ability to adapt but did not survive, then the anthropologists' claim is invalidated. But the anthropologists do not argue that the ability to adapt ensures survival. Rather, they argue that without the ability to adapt, a species will not survive. The argument confuses what is necessary for survival with what is sufficient for survival. This is a Conditional Reasoning Fallacy that employs flipped reasoning. The answer choice for this type of fallacy is difficult to anticipate, but we know to look for answer choices with conditional language.

(A) confuses a condition's being required for a given result to occur in one case with the condition's being sufficient for such a result to occur in a similar case

This answer choice includes the term *sufficient*, so it is a candidate.

(B) takes for granted that if one species had a characteristic that happened to enable it to survive certain conditions, at least one related extinct species must have had the same characteristic

There are no conditional indicators, so this is a loser.

(C) generalizes, from the fact that one species with a certain characteristic survived certain conditions, that all related species with the same characteristic must have survived exactly the same conditions

No generalization occurs in the argument. Neither does it include any terms related to conditional reasoning. This is a loser.

(D) fails to consider the possibility that *Australopithecus afarensis* had one or more characteristics that lessened its chances of surviving prehistoric times

There is no conditional language here, so we can consider (D) a loser.

(E) fails to consider the possibility that, even if a condition caused a result to occur in one case, it was not necessary to cause the result to occur in a similar case

This answer choice includes *necessary*, so it is a candidate.

We now have to eliminate one of the two candidates. (E) actually describes a causal relationship rather than a conditional relationship. It says that if a condition (Ability to Adapt to Diversity) caused a result (Survival) in one case, it was not necessary to cause the result in a similar case. In other words, Ability to Adapt to Diversity does not CAUSE (and is not a sufficient condition to trigger) Survival.

Returning to (A), we can see that this answer choice better describes the fallacy in the argument. The argument confuses a condition being required to bring about a given result (Ability to Adapt to Diversity) in one case with a condition being sufficient to cause a result (Survival) in another case. (A) has to be the correct answer choice.

Conditional Reasoning Fallacy questions can be very difficult. Upon recognizing this fallacy, scan for conditional language to reduce the number of possible answer choices.

15. Correct Answer (E). *Prep Test 50, Section 4, Question 22.*

Fallacy Type: Proportion Fallacy

The conclusion that crossing against the light is more dangerous for pedestrians than crossing with the light is indicated by *therefore*. The evidence for this is that several sources show that more pedestrians are killed when crossing with the light than when crossing against it. There are several terms here that can help us identify the fallacy: *studies, statistics, more pedestrians, and less dangerous*. The words *studies* and *statistics* should alert us to the possibility that the argument includes a Sampling Fallacy.

The premise talks about one category (crossing with the light) resulting in more pedestrian deaths than a second category (crossing against the light). The conclusion states that one category (crossing with the light) is less dangerous than the other. The problem is that *more pedestrians* refers to the amount of pedestrians killed, while *less dangerous* refers to the likelihood of getting killed. To put it another way, the premise refers to an amount while the conclusion refers to a proportion. Thus, we have a Proportion Fallacy. If you are having trouble seeing the fallacy here, consider the following example:

> **The number of people killed in car accidents this year was greater than the number of people who died in bear-wrestling matches. Therefore, it is far more dangerous to drive a car than it is to wrestle a bear.**

The fallacy is easier to see here. Though more people are killed crossing with the light, this does not necessarily mean that it is more dangerous on a case-by-case basis than crossing against the light. It is most likely the case that more people in North America cross with the light than against the light. We should therefore look for an answer choice that describes this Proportion Fallacy.

(A) relies on sources that are likely to be biased in their reporting

This describes a Sampling Fallacy. The presence of *insurance statistics* in the argument may make this answer choice attractive, but it is incorrect for two reasons. The first is that insurance companies have no reason to be biased against people who cross with the light. Crossing against the light is illegal, and it is unlikely that insurance companies would want to encourage people to do this. The second reason is that insurance statistics are not the actual source of the claim—they are just used to confirm the claim, which is based on recent studies. (A) is a loser.

(B) presumes, without providing justification, that because two things are correlated there must be a causal relationship between them

This describes a Causal Reasoning Fallacy, which does not occur in the argument. (B) is a loser.

(C) does not adequately consider the possibility that a correlation between two events may be

explained by a common cause

This also describes a Causal Reasoning Fallacy. We can consider (C) a loser.

(D) ignores the possibility that the effects of the types of actions considered might be quite different in environments other than the ones studied

This answer choice is implying that the relationship studied might not exist in other environments. However, the studies present evidence from North American cities, and the argument makes a conclusion about North American cities. Therefore, there is no reason to consider other environments. This answer choice describes a Sampling Fallacy but not the one present in the argument. (D) is also a loser.

(E) ignores possible differences in the frequency of the two actions whose risk is being assessed

This matches our anticipated answer choice. The argument ignores the relative frequency of two types of actions. If the frequency is the same, the argument's conclusion would be valid. However, we do not know how often pedestrians cross against the light and with the light. Therefore, this has to be the correct answer choice.

Description

Description
≈ 1.2 questions per test

Example Prompts

Which one of the following *most accurately describes the method of reasoning*?

The argument *proceeds by* . . .

The argument employs which one of the following a*rgumentative strategies*?

Person A *responds to* Person B by . . .

Take These Steps

Read the stimulus, which always includes an argument. Is there more than one viewpoint presented?

Yes

Identify the parts of the argument and how they relate to each other. Focus on how the second viewpoint undermines the conclusion of the first viewpoint. Anticipate a complete and accurate description of how this is done, using abstract language.

No

Identify the parts of the argument and how they relate to each other. Focus on how the conclusion is supported by the premises. Anticipate a complete and accurate description of the structure of the argument, using abstract language.

Answer Choices

Correct Answer Choices	Incorrect Answer Choices
Statements that use abstract language to describe logical relationships	Statements that use abstract language to describe logical relationships
Accurate and complete descriptions of how the argument is developed (one-viewpoint argument)	Descriptions of argumentative structures that do not occur in the argument
Accurate and complete descriptions of how one viewpoint undermines the other (two-viewpoint argument)	Partial or inaccurate descriptions of argumentative structures that do not occur in the argument
	Descriptions of fallacies that do not occur in the argument

To solve D questions, it is necessary to identify the logical relationships between the various parts of an argument or determine how one viewpoint attempts to invalidate another. In both cases, the answer choices use abstract terms to describe logical relationships and rarely include specific content from the argument. This means that it is relatively easy to anticipate correct answer choices for this question type. As with F questions, upon finding an answer choice that clearly matches your anticipated answer choice, you can select it and move on to the next question. Very rarely are there multiple candidates that need to be eliminated.

How to Solve Description Questions

The first step toward solving a D question is to determine whether the argument includes one or two viewpoints. In a one-viewpoint argument, a single author provides support for a conclusion without presenting any detailed explanations of competing viewpoints. A two-viewpoint argument comes in two forms. The first involves two different authors presenting competing perspectives on an issue. The second involves only one author, but the position of another person is presented and discussed in detail.

Once the number of viewpoints has been determined, the next step is to identify the argumentative structure. If there is one viewpoint, you will need to focus on how the argument is developed to reach its conclusion. If there are two viewpoints, you will need to figure out how the second viewpoint attempts to invalidate the first.

This question type has a number of recurring argumentative structures (discussed in detail below). However, it is important to note that D questions have many other argumentative structures, so you will likely encounter ones not described in this section.

If There Is One Viewpoint in the Argument

If the argument only expresses one viewpoint, you should identify the parts of the argument and then determine how they relate to each other logically. Focus on how the author develops the premises to support the conclusion and anticipate a correct answer choice that describes this in abstract terms.

For one-viewpoint arguments, three common argumentative structures appear:

1. **Making a comparison or analogy:** This is when the argument compares two relationships to advance its conclusion. Note that D question answer choices frequently include the term *analogy* or a variation thereof. Here is an example of this argumentative structure:

> **There is probably life on Planet X. We know this because it has similar oxygen and carbon levels to Earth, which supports life.**

2. **Applying a principle:** This occurs when an argument applies a general rule or principal to a specific set of facts in order to reach a conclusion. For example,

> **The municipal code states that street festivals may only take place on Saturday, Sundays, or national holidays. As Tuesday is a national holiday, we will be able to hold our street festival on that day.**

3. **Using an example:** This involves using one or more specific examples to support a general conclusion. For example,

> **Planes are more expensive but quicker than trains, and trains are more expensive but quicker than automobiles. It is clear that more expensive modes of transportation are generally faster than less**

expensive modes of transportation.

This type of argumentative structure is the most common among one-viewpoint arguments. However, as mentioned previously, you will probably encounter others, including
- Rejecting alternative options
- Appealing to an authority

Let's look at an example:

> Professor: A person who can select a beverage from among 50 varieties of cola is less free than one who has only these 5 choices: wine, coffee, apple juice, milk, and water. It is clear, then, that meaningful freedom cannot be measured simply by the number of alternatives available; the extent of the differences among the alternatives is also a relevant factor.

> The professor's argument proceeds by

> (A) supporting a general principle by means of an example
> (B) drawing a conclusion about a particular case on the basis of a general principle
> (C) supporting its conclusion by means of an analogy
> (D) claiming that whatever holds for each member of a group must hold for the whole group
> (E) inferring one general principle from another, more general, principle

This is a one-viewpoint argument. The indicator *it is clear* precedes the conclusion that meaningful freedom is not measured simply by the number of alternatives but by the extent of those alternatives. The first sentence in the argument is an example of this principle and provides support for the conclusion. Therefore, the argument uses an example to support a general principle. We should look for a correct answer choice that describes this.

(A) supporting a general principle by means of an example

This matches our anticipated answer choice. A general principle—that freedom cannot be measured by the number of choices but should instead be measured by the extent of the differences among those choices—is supported by a hypothetical example. Remember, a hypothetical example is still an example. This answer choice is a candidate.

(B) drawing a conclusion about a particular case on the basis of a general principle

This is the opposite of what occurs in the argument. The conclusion is a general principle that is supported by an example, not the other way around. (B) is a loser.

(C) supporting its conclusion by means of an analogy

There is no analogy in the argument. The example includes a comparison between people who have different beverage options, but this is not an analogy. Analogies are comparisons between two sets of relationships that support a conclusion. This is a loser.

(D) claiming that whatever holds for each member of a group must hold for the whole group

This describes a Part-to-Whole Composition Fallacy, which is not present in the argument. This is also a loser.

(E) inferring one general principle from another, more general, principle

The example is not a general example. In addition, the conclusion is more general than the example. This is a loser.

As (A) is the only candidate, it has to be the correct answer choice.

If There Are Two Viewpoints in the Argument

If there are two viewpoints in the argument, first analyze the argument to determine how the conclusion expressed in the first viewpoint is supported. Then, focus on how the second viewpoint undermines that conclusion. You should anticipate a correct answer choice that describes how this is done.

For two-viewpoint arguments, three common argumentative structures appear:

> When the argument has two authors, it is very common to see a fallacy in the first viewpoint. When this is the case, the second viewpoint almost inevitably focuses on this error in reasoning. Refer to explanations of the common fallacies in the previous section of this chapter.

1. **Undermining a premise:** This occurs when the second viewpoint presents information that undermines one or more of the premises used to support the conclusion of the first viewpoint. For example,

   > **During the recent school staff meeting, the cafeteria manager suggested that the cafeteria should no longer offer personalized pizza for lunch as pizza sales were low, which indicates that students are not interested in eating personalized pizza for lunch. However, it is more likely that the long wait times for the personalized pizza is the cause of the low sales as students have a limited amount of time to purchase and eat their food.**

2. **Challenging an assumption:** This is when the second viewpoint argues that an assumption that the first viewpoint relies on is unfounded. For example,

   > **Jesse: Grass-fed beef is healthier to consume than grain-fed beef. Grain-fed cows are usually kept in feedlots where they are injected with artificial hormones to encourage growth. This leads to unhealthy levels of artificial hormones in the meat that comes from these cows.**

   > **Tang: I agree that using artificial hormones on cows can lead to harmful substances in the beef they produce. However, grass-fed cows are usually injected with artificial hormones as well.**

Here, Jesse makes the assumption that grass-fed cows, unlike grain-fed cows, are not usually injected with artificial hormones. Tang responds by challenging that assumption.

3. **Rejecting a claim on insufficient evidence:** This occurs either when the second viewpoint claims that the first viewpoint has not provided enough evidence to support a conclusion or when the second viewpoint claims that the evidence provided is irrelevant. For example,

   > **Professor Trejo claims that physicists are the hardest-working academics at our university. I am not disputing that claim. However, Professor Trejo has failed to provide a comparison with academics in other fields, such as biologists and chemists.**

These are the most common argumentative structures for two-viewpoint arguments. Others that you may encounter include
- Appealing to an authority
- Using a counter-example

- Pointing out a fallacy
- Offering new evidence
- Suggesting a different causal conclusion
- Clarifying a previous statement
- Using a proposed line of reasoning to make a ridiculous conclusion

Let's look at an example:

Gamba: Muñoz claims that the Southwest Hopeville Neighbors Association overwhelmingly opposes the new water system, citing this as evidence of citywide opposition. The association did pass a resolution opposing the new water system, but only 25 of 350 members voted, with 10 in favor of the system. Furthermore, the 15 opposing votes represent far less than 1 percent of Hopeville's population. One should not assume that so few votes represent the view of the majority of Hopeville's residents.

Of the following, which one most accurately describes Gamba's strategy of argumentation?

(A) questioning a conclusion based on the results of a vote, on the grounds that people with certain views are more likely to vote
(B) questioning a claim supported by statistical data by arguing that statistical data can be manipulated to support whatever view the interpreter wants to support
(C) attempting to refute an argument by showing that, contrary to what has been claimed, the truth of the premises does not guarantee the truth of the conclusion
(D) criticizing a view on the grounds that the view is based on evidence that is in principle impossible to disconfirm
(E) attempting to cast doubt on a conclusion by claiming that the statistical sample on which the conclusion is based is too small to be dependable

Although there is only one author, this is a two-viewpoint argument. Gamba presents the viewpoint of another person—Muñoz—who claims that the SHNA's opposition to the new water system indicates citywide opposition. Gamba argues against this, saying that only a small proportion of the members of the SHNA voted, and that this number represents less than 1 percent of the city's population. Gamba implicitly suggests that Muñoz has committed a Sampling Fallacy in that the result of the vote does not represent the view of the majority of residents. This counters Muñoz's claim that the vote is evidence of citywide opposition. What we have here is the undermining of a premise (the evidence of the vote) or the pointing out of a fallacy. We should anticipate a correct answer choice that describes either of these methods of countering an argument.

(A) questioning a conclusion based on the results of a vote, on the grounds that people with certain views are more likely to vote

The first part of this answer choice characterizes the argument correctly, but the second part does not. Gamba does not discuss who is more likely to vote. This is a loser.

(B) questioning a claim supported by statistical data by arguing that statistical data can be manipulated to support whatever view the interpreter wants to support

This is only partially accurate. Gamba does not argue that statistical data can be manipulated in this way. (B) is also a loser.

(C) attempting to refute an argument by showing that, contrary to what has been claimed, the truth of the premises does not guarantee the truth of the conclusion

This is not what we anticipated, but it seems to be true at first glance. Part of Gamba's argument is that even if the sample were accurate, the conclusion could not follow because the sample was too small. Let's consider this as a candidate.

(D) criticizing a view on the grounds that the view is based on evidence that is in principle impossible to disconfirm

Gamba does not suggest that the evidence is impossible to disconfirm. This is a loser.

(E) attempting to cast doubt on a conclusion by claiming that the statistical sample on which the conclusion is based is too small to be dependable

This matches one of our anticipated answer choices, so it is a candidate.

We will now eliminate ones of the candidates. (C) is tempting, but it mischaracterizes Muñoz's viewpoint. Muñoz does not claim that the sample vote guarantees that the majority of city residents hold the same view. He says that it is evidence that the city holds this view. Therefore, "contrary to what has been claimed" is inaccurate. (C) is not the correct answer choice.

Answer choice (E) accurately describes how Gamba casts doubt on the conclusion by undermining the premise that the sample represents citywide opinion. It is also true that the reason this sample does not represent the city is that it is too small to be representative. (E) has to be the correct answer choice.

Looking at the Answer Choices

As is the case with F questions, D questions include answer choices that use abstract language to describe logical relationships. However, D answer choices are less likely to include specific details from the stimulus. As mentioned before, for single-viewpoint arguments, you should anticipate a correct answer choice that fully and accurately describes how the argument reaches its conclusion. For arguments with two viewpoints, the correct answer choice describes how the second viewpoint undermines the first.

Incorrect answer choices often describe an argumentative structure that does not actually occur in the argument. It is also common for an incorrect answer choice to inaccurately or partially describe an argumentative structure that does appear. You will also encounter answer choices that describe a fallacy that does not actually occur in the argument.

Drill: Identify the Prevalent Argumentative Structure in the Answer Choices

The following is a list of mock answer choices, each of which describes one of the common argumentative structures mentioned earlier in this section. Below each answer choice, write the name of the argumentative structure in question.

1. attempts to invalidate the argument by questioning the truth of its evidence

   _____

2. uses a case in which evidence is available to make a conclusion about an analogous case in which direct evidence is unavailable

   _____

3. questions a presupposition that the argument is based off of

   _____

4. provides a specific instance to illustrate a general claim

   _____

5. attacking the strength of the analogy on which the opposing argument is based

   _____

6. demonstrates that a certain protocol would be adopted in one situation in order to support the claim that that protocol should be adopted in a similar situation

   _____

7. uses a general guideline to infer a conclusion about specific facts

   _____

8. challenges the conclusion of the argument by claiming it is not supported by verifiable data

   _____

9. describes a situation meant to show the truth of a broader principle

   _____

10. claims there is inherent uncertainty that the argument refuses to acknowledge

   _____

1. Undermining a premise

2. Making a comparison or analogy

3. Challenging an assumption

4. Using an example

5. Undermining a premise

6. Making a comparison or analogy

7. Applying a principle

8. Rejecting a claim on insufficient evidence

9. Using an example

10. Challenging an assumption

1. Phoebe: There have been many reported sightings of strange glowing lights, but a number of these sightings have a straightforward, natural explanation. They occurred clustered in time and location around the epicenters of three earthquakes, and so were almost certainly earthquake lights, a form of ball lightning caused by stresses in the ground.

   Quincy: I am skeptical that the association between the lights and the earthquakes is anything more than a coincidence. The theory that ground stresses related to earthquakes can cause any kind of lightning is extremely speculative.

   In responding to Phoebe, Quincy

   (A) takes a correlation to be a causal relation
   (B) challenges the accuracy of the data about sightings that Phoebe takes for granted
   (C) criticizes Phoebe's explanation as unsubstantiated
   (D) offers an explanation of the glowing lights different from Phoebe's
   (E) accuses Phoebe of introducing irrelevant information

2. Yang: Yeast has long been known to be a leaven, that is, a substance used in baking to make breads rise. Since biblical evidence ties the use of leavens to events dating back to 1200 B.C., we can infer that yeast was already known to be a leaven at that time.

   Campisi: I find your inference unconvincing; several leavens other than yeast could have been known in 1200 B.C.

   Campisi counters Yang's argument by

   (A) suggesting that an alternative set of evidence better supports Yang's conclusion
   (B) questioning the truth of a presumption underlying Yang's argument
   (C) denying the truth of Yang's conclusion without considering the reason given for that conclusion
   (D) pointing out that the premises of Yang's argument more strongly support a contrary conclusion
   (E) calling into question the truth of the evidence presented in Yang's argument

3. Economist: A country's trade deficit may indicate weakness in its economy, but it does not in itself weaken that economy. So restricting imports to reduce a trade deficit would be like sticking a thermometer into a glass of cold water in the hope of bringing down a patient's feverish temperature.

The economist's argument employs which one of the following techniques?

(A) claiming that a crucial assumption entails a falsehood
(B) demonstrating that an analogy explicitly used to establish a certain conclusion is faulty
(C) appealing to an analogy in order to indicate the futility of a course of action
(D) calling into question the authority on the basis of which a claim is made
(E) showing that a recommended course of action would have disastrous consequences

4. Anne: Halley's Comet, now in a part of its orbit relatively far from the Sun, recently flared brightly enough to be seen by telescope. No comet has ever been observed to flare so far from the Sun before, so such a flare must be highly unusual.

Sue: Nonsense. Usually no one bothers to try to observe comets when they are so far from the Sun. This flare was observed only because an observatory was tracking Halley's Comet very carefully.

Sue challenges Anne's reasoning by

(A) pointing out that Anne's use of the term "observed" is excessively vague
(B) drawing attention to an inconsistency between two of Anne's claims
(C) presenting evidence that directly contradicts Anne's evidence
(D) offering an alternative explanation for the evidence Anne cites
(E) undermining some of Anne's evidence while agreeing with her conclusion

1. **Correct Answer (C).** *Prep Test 41, Section 3, Question 9.*

Argumentative Structure: Rejecting a claim on insufficient evidence

As there are two authors, this is obviously a two-viewpoint argument. Phoebe claims that the presence of strange glowing lights has a natural explanation, concluding that they were almost certainly earthquake lights—a form of ball lightning caused by ground stresses. Quincy responds by claiming that the association between the lights and earthquakes is just a coincidence, criticizing Phoebe's evidence as being extremely speculative. This can be interpreted as Quincy rejecting Phoebe's claim based on insufficient evidence or Quincy pointing out a Causal Reasoning Fallacy in her argument. We should anticipate a correct answer choice that describes one of these two methods for discrediting an argument.

(A) takes a correlation to be a causal relation

At first glance, this seems attractive because it describes a Causal Reasoning Fallacy. However, it is Phoebe who commits this error, not Quincy. This is a loser.

(B) challenges the accuracy of the data about sightings that Phoebe takes for granted

Quincy does not challenge the accuracy of the data. Instead, he claims that the data fails to support Phoebe's conclusion. This is a loser.

(C) criticizes Phoebe's explanation as unsubstantiated

This matches one of our anticipated answer choices. (C) is a candidate.

(D) offers an explanation of the glowing lights different from Phoebe's

Quincy does not offer another explanation of the glowing lights. This is a loser.

(E) accuses Phoebe of introducing irrelevant information

Quincy does not claim the information is irrelevant. This is also a loser.

As (C) is the only candidate, it has to be the correct answer choice.

2. **Correct Answer (B).** *Prep Test 41, Section 3, Question 12.*

Argumentative Structure: Challenging an assumption

The presence of two authors indicates that this is a two-viewpoint argument. The phrase *we can infer* indicates that Yang's conclusion is that yeast was used as a leaven in biblical times. To support this conclusion, he refers to biblical evidence that ties the use of leavens to events dating back to 1200 B.C. Yang assumes that yeast was one of the leavens used back then. Campisi points out that this assumption is invalid; there were other leavens that could have been used in 1200 B.C. besides yeast. Thus, Campisi challenges an assumption. We can anticipate an answer choice that describes this.

(A) suggesting that an alternative set of evidence better supports Yang's conclusion

Campisi does not provide alternative evidence to support Yang's conclusion. This is a loser.

(B) questioning the truth of a presumption underlying Yang's argument

This matches our anticipated answer choice. Yang presumes that yeast was the only leaven in use in 1200 B.C., whereas Campisi suggests that this might not be correct. (B) is a candidate.

(C) denying the truth of Yang's conclusion without considering the reason given for that conclusion

Campisi does consider the reason for Yang's conclusion. He suggests that an underlying assumption may be invalid. This is a loser.

(D) pointing out that the premises of Yang's argument more strongly support a contrary conclusion

Campisi does not point out that another conclusion is better supported by the premises. This is also a loser.

(E) calling into question the truth of the evidence presented in Yang's argument

This is very similar to (B), so let's consider it a candidate.

We now need to eliminate one of our two candidates. Upon returning to (B) and (E), we find a slight difference. Campisi does not actually question the truth of the premise—he questions the underlying assumption that is required for the premise to support the conclusion. He does not suggest that the premise is false; rather, he says that an invalid assumption is required to support the conclusion. Therefore, (B) has to be the correct answer choice.

3. **Correct Answer (C).** *Prep Test 59, Section 3, Question 14.*

Argumentative Structure: Making a comparison or analogy

There is one author presenting a single viewpoint, so this is a one-viewpoint argument. What follows the indicator *so* is the conclusion, which compares restricting imports to reduce a trade deficit with sticking a thermometer in cold water to bring down a fever. This analogy is used to explain why restricting imports to reduce a trade deficit is unwise; doing so would affect an economic indicator without affecting the economy itself. The first sentence is a premise that helps us understand the analogy. We should anticipate a correct answer choice about making a comparison or an analogy. As mentioned earlier, the correct answer choice for this type of argumentative structure always includes *analogy* or a similar term. By scanning the answer choices for this wording, we are able to pick out (B) and (C).

(B) demonstrating that an analogy explicitly used to establish a certain conclusion is faulty

The analogy is actually in the conclusion of the argument. This is a loser.

(C) appealing to an analogy in order to indicate the futility of a course of action

The economist thinks that this course of action, restricting imports to reduce a trade deficit, is pointless. Certainly, sticking a thermometer in cold water to bring down a fever serves no purpose. This is the correct answer choice.

4. **Correct Answer (D).** *Prep Test 40, Section 1, Question 4.*

Argumentative Structure: Undermining a premise

This is a two-viewpoint argument with two authors. In the first viewpoint, *so* precedes the conclusion that a flare must be highly unusual because no comet has ever been observed to flare so far from the Sun before. Anne commits a Proportion Fallacy here. Her premise is about the number of times a flare has been observed, but her conclusion is about the likelihood of the flare occurring. Sue says that people do not usually bother to observe comets far from the Sun, and that this flare was only observed because Halley's Comet was being tracked very carefully. She has undermined the flawed premise by offering an alternative explanation. We can anticipate a correct answer choice that describes this.

(A) pointing out that Anne's use of the term "observed" is excessively vague

Sue does not do this. This answer choice centers on an Equivocation Fallacy. It is a loser.

(B) drawing attention to an inconsistency between two of Anne's claims

Sue does not point out an inconsistency between two claims. She suggests a different explanation for the flare being seen. This is a loser.

(C) presenting evidence that directly contradicts Anne's evidence

Sue does not present new evidence. She provides an alternative explanation for an existing premise. This is also a loser.

(D) offering an alternative explanation for the evidence Anne cites

This matches our anticipated correct answer choice. It is a candidate.

(E) undermining some of Anne's evidence while agreeing with her conclusion

While Sue does undermine some of Anne's evidence, she does not agree with the conclusion, as indicated by the word *nonsense*. This answer choice is incorrect.

Answer choice (D) is the only candidate, so it has to be correct.

Mini Description

CLASSIFICATION FAMILY

Main Point
Fallacy
Description
Mini Description
Parallel Reasoning
Parallel Fallacy
Agree/Disagree

Mini Description

≈ 2.1 questions per test

Example Prompts

The *assertion* that _____ *figures in the argument* in which one of the following ways?

Which one of the following *most accurately describes the role* played in the argument by the claim that _____?

The reference to _____ *plays which one of the following roles* in the argument?

Take These Steps

Read the stimulus, which always includes an argument. Locate the claim presented in the prompt and then identify the argument's main conclusion.

Determine the function of the claim and its relationship to the parts of the argument. Usually, the claim is a premise, counter-premise, conclusion, background detail, opposing viewpoint, or example.

Anticipate a full and accurate description of the claim's role. The correct answer choice likely includes a combination of abstract language used to describe the function of the claim and specific details from the argument.

Answer Choices

Correct Answer Choices	**Incorrect Answer Choices**
Complete and accurate descriptions of the function of the claim presented in the prompt	Complete and accurate descriptions of the function of other claims
	Descriptions of a function that does not appear in the argument
	Incomplete or inaccurate descriptions of the function of the claim presented in the prompt

Mini Description (MD) questions are much narrower in focus than D questions because they ask about the specific role of a single claim rather than about the argument as a whole. The claim is often a main conclusion, subsidiary conclusion, premise, or counter-premise. However, it is sometimes background information, an opposing viewpoint, or an example.

MD questions always include arguments, and these tend to be more complex than those of other questions types. Being able to quickly and accurately identify the various parts of an argument and determine how they relate to each other is vital for solving for MD questions.

How to Solve Mini Description Questions

The first step toward solving an MD question is to locate the claim in the argument. After doing so, read through the argument carefully to identify its main conclusion.

The next step is to determine the function of the claim. In many cases, it is a premise, counter-premise, or conclusion. However, the claim can also take the form of background information that provides the context necessary to understand an argument, an opposing viewpoint that is discredited by the argument, or an example that illustrates a premise, among others. Regardless, you must determine the claim's logical relationship to the rest of the argument and then anticipate an answer choice that completely and accurately describes this relationship.

It is important to note that the correct answer choice tends to be very specific. For example, rather than simply state that the claim is a premise, the answer choice may specify that it is a premise that supports the subsidiary conclusion. Therefore, you need to reach a full understanding of how the claim relates to the rest of the argument before you turn to the answer choices.

Let's look at an example:

> Scientist: Isaac Newton's *Principia*, the seventeenth-century work that served as the cornerstone of physics for over two centuries, could at first be understood by only a handful of people, but a basic understanding of Newton's ideas eventually spread throughout the world. This shows that the barriers to communication between scientists and the public are not impermeable. Thus recent scientific research, most of which also [can be described only in language that seems esoteric to most contemporary readers], may also become part of everyone's intellectual heritage.
>
> Which one of the following most accurately describes the role played in the scientist's argument by the claim that recent scientific research can often be described only in language that seems esoteric to most contemporary readers?
>
> (A) It is raised as a potential objection to the argument's main conclusion, but its truth is called into doubt by the preceding statements.
> (B) It is a premise that supports the argument's main conclusion by suggesting that the results of recent scientific research are only superficially different from claims made in Newton's *Principia*.
> (C) It is cited as further evidence for the conclusion that the barriers to communication between scientists and the public are not impermeable.
> (D) It is a claim that serves mainly to help establish the relevance of the preceding statements to the argument's final conclusion.

(E) It serves to cast doubt on an alleged similarity between Newton's *Principia* and recent scientific research.

After identifying this as an MD question and reading the stimulus, we need to locate the claim presented in the prompt. Before analyzing the function of this claim, we should identify the conclusion of the argument. We have two conclusion indicators, *thus* and *this shows that*. Both of the signaled statements are conclusions, but which is the subsidiary conclusion and which is the main conclusion? To determine this, we must figure out which conclusion supports the other. Consider the following:

P: Barriers to communication between science and public are not impermeable.

C: Therefore, recent scientific research that seems esoteric may also become part of everyone's intellectual heritage.

OR

P: Recent scientific research that seems esoteric may also become part of everyone's intellectual heritage.

C: Therefore, barriers to communication between scientists and the public are not impermeable.

The first option seems most likely because it matches the example earlier in the argument—just as Newton's findings came to be understood by a large number of people, recent research will become part of everyone's intellectual heritage. So, the last sentence is the main conclusion. What precedes it is the subsidiary conclusion. The argument can be outlined as follows:

P: *Principia* could initially be understood by few because of its complexity, but now, society generally has a basic understanding of the work's ideas.

SC: Therefore, communication barriers between scientists and citizens are not impermeable.

C: Thus, recent scientific research that also seems complicated to many may also become part of everyone's basic understanding.

So, how does the claim that scientific research seems esoteric to most contemporary readers function in the argument? It is part of the main conclusion, and it serves to connect the conclusion to an earlier example by showing a similarity between recent research and Newton's book. *Principia* was initially difficult for people to understand, and so is modern research.

We should anticipate an answer choice that specifies that the claim is part of the main conclusion or that points out that it connects the conclusion to an earlier example.

(A) **It is raised as a potential objection to the argument's main conclusion, but its truth is called into doubt by the preceding statements.**

The first part of this answer choice seems plausible. The main conclusion states that recent research may become part of the public's intellectual heritage. Stating that this research is esoteric to many people could be a potential objection to this conclusion. However, the claim is actually part of the conclusion. In addition, the second part of the answer choice is clearly inaccurate. The claim is not called into doubt at all by the preceding statements. We can consider this a loser.

(B) **It is a premise that supports the argument's main conclusion by suggesting that the results of recent scientific research are only superficially different from claims made in Newton's *Principia*.**

The claim is not a premise supporting the main conclusion—it is part of the conclusion. In addition, the claim does not suggest that recent research is only superficially different from *Principia*; rather, it points out a similarity between the two. (B) is a loser.

(C) It is cited as further evidence for the conclusion that the barriers to communication between scientists and the public are not impermeable.

Evidence is another way of saying *premise*. The claim is not a premise. Furthermore, the content of this answer choice is based on the subsidiary conclusion. (C) is a loser.

(D) It is a claim that serves mainly to help establish the relevance of the preceding statements to the argument's final conclusion.

This matches one of our anticipated answer choices. The claim helps connect the main conclusion to the previous statement about *Principia*. (D) can be considered a candidate.

(E) It serves to cast doubt on an alleged similarity between Newton's *Principia* and recent scientific research.

The claim does not cast doubt on a similarity between recent research and *Principia* but, instead, points out a shared characteristic. This answer choice is a loser.

As (D) is the only candidate, it has to be the correct answer choice.

Looking at the Answer Choices

The correct answer choice of an MD question is always a complete and accurate description of the role of the claim presented in the prompt. It almost always includes a combination of abstract language and specific content from the argument.

The fact that MD questions usually begin with a statement such as *it is a premise* or *it is a conclusion* often makes it easy to eliminate answer choices that were not anticipated. That is, if a claim is part of the conclusion, then an answer choice beginning with *it is a premise* cannot be correct. Sometimes, the terms *conclusion*, *premise*, and so on are used in the answer choices. Other times, though, these types of terms are paraphrased to raise the difficulty level. The following is a nonexhaustive list of the alternative wordings used in answer choices:

Main Conclusion:
- claim/position/generalization/view/assertion supported by . . .

Subsidiary Conclusion:
- claim/position/assertion/evidence that supports the . . .

Premise:
- supports the claim that . . .
- show that . . .
- is offered as a reason/evidence why . . .

Counter-premise:
- evidence for the viewpoint that the argument attempts to undermine/counter
- a possible objection to the claim set forth in the argument

Background Information:
- a claim compatible with either accepting or rejecting the argument's conclusion
- information meant to contextualize the argument
- information central to both the opposing viewpoint and the viewpoint advocated by the argument
- irrelevant information

Example:
- an illustration of the reasoning used to support the author's viewpoint

Opposing Viewpoint:
- a claim/position/generalization/view/assertion that the argument intends to undermine/counter

Incorrect answer choices for MD questions often correctly identify the specific function of the claim presented in the prompt but misidentify its relationship to the other part of an argument. For example, the claim may be correctly identified as a premise but incorrectly described as supporting a subsidiary conclusion. Another common trick is to accurately describe how the claim relates to another part of the argument but to misidentify the former. For instance, the answer choice may accurately state that a claim supports the main conclusion but incorrectly identify the claim as an example rather than a premise. Finally, an incorrect answer choice may describe the function of a claim that does not appear in the prompt or even discuss a function that does not actually appear in the argument. For example, an answer choice may describe the role of a subsidiary conclusion even though the argument only includes a main conclusion.

Drill: Mini Description Argument Parts

Mark each part of the argument, as specified.

Draw a line through the ~~counter-premise~~, if applicable.
Underline the <u>subsidiary conclusion</u>, if applicable.
Double underline the <u>main conclusion</u>.
Bracket the [premise(s)].
Double bracket [[background information]], if applicable.

1. Many companies have a strict dress code to ensure a professional work environment. However, universities are not companies. Since one of the goals of a university is to help students develop creativity and individuality, students should be free to express themselves. Therefore, universities should not have a strict dress code for students.

2. Research shows that the human body releases large amounts of oxytocin, a hormone responsible for relaxation and comfort, when cuddling. Since Giant Blue Teddy Bears are so great to cuddle with, your significant other is sure to appreciate one as a valentine's Day gift!

3. Technological obsolescence is inevitable in a capitalistic society. Although technological innovation often makes products cheaper, the end result of frenzied innovation is the loss of jobs in certain industries because these industries have become obsolete or workers are being replaced by automated processes.

Drill: Mini Description Argument Parts — Answers

1. ~~Many companies have a strict dress code to ensure a professional work environment~~. However, [[universities are not companies.]] Since [one of the goals of a university is to help students develop creativity and individuality], students should be free to express themselves. Therefore, <u>universities should not have a strict dress code for students</u>.

2. [Research shows that the human body releases large amounts of oxytocin, a hormone responsible for relaxation and comfort, when cuddling]. Since [Giant Blue Teddy Bears are so great to cuddle with], <u>your significant other is sure to appreciate one as a Valentine's Day gift</u>!

3. [[Technological obsolescence is inevitable in a capitalistic society]]. Although ~~technological innovation often makes products cheaper~~, <u>the end result of frenzied innovation is the loss of jobs in certain industries</u> because [these industries have become obsolete or workers are being replaced by automated processes].

1. It is well documented that people have positive responses to some words, such as "kind" and "wonderful," and negative responses to others, such as "evil" and "nausea." Recently, psychological experiments have revealed that people also have positive or negative responses to many nonsense words. This shows that people's responses to words are conditioned not only by what the words mean, but also by how they sound.

The claim that people have positive or negative responses to many nonsense words plays which one of the following roles in the argument?

(A) It is a premise offered in support of the conclusion that people have either a positive or negative response to any word.

(B) It is a conclusion for which the only support provided is the claim that people's responses to words are conditioned both by what the words mean and by how they sound.

(C) It is a generalization partially supported by the claim that meaningful words can trigger positive or negative responses in people.

(D) It is a premise offered in support of the conclusion that people's responses to words are engendered not only by what the words mean, but also by how they sound.

(E) It is a conclusion supported by the claim that people's responses under experimental conditions are essentially different from their responses in ordinary situations.

2. Teacher: Participating in organized competitive athletics may increase a child's strength and coordination. As critics point out, however, it also instills in those children who are not already well developed in these respects a feeling of inferiority that never really disappears. Yet, since research has shown that adults with feelings of inferiority become more successful than those free of such anxieties, funding for children's athletic programs should not be eliminated.

Which one of the following most accurately describes the role played in the teacher's argument by the assertion that participating in organized competitive athletics may increase a child's strength and coordination?

(A) It is mentioned as one possible reason for adopting a policy for which the teacher suggests an additional reason.

(B) It is a claim that the teacher attempts to refute with counterarguments.

(C) It is a hypothesis for which the teacher offers additional evidence.

(D) It is cited as an insufficient reason for eliminating funding for children's athletic programs.

(E) It is cited as an objection that has been raised to the position that the teacher is supporting.

3. It is now a common complaint that the electronic media have corroded the intellectual skills required and fostered by the literary media. But several centuries ago the complaint was that certain intellectual skills, such as the powerful memory and extemporaneous eloquence that were intrinsic to oral culture, were being destroyed by the spread of literacy. So, what awaits us is probably a mere alteration of the human mind rather than its devolution.

The reference to the complaint of several centuries ago that powerful memory and extemporaneous eloquence were being destroyed plays which one of the following roles in the argument?

(A) evidence supporting the claim that the intellectual skills fostered by the literary media are being destroyed by the electronic media

(B) an illustration of the general hypothesis being advanced that intellectual abilities are inseparable from the means by which people communicate

(C) an example of a cultural change that did not necessarily have a detrimental effect on the human mind overall

(D) evidence that the claim that the intellectual skills required and fostered by the literary media are being lost is unwarranted

(E) possible evidence, mentioned and then dismissed, that might be cited by supporters of the hypothesis being criticized

4. Pain perception depends only partly on physiology. During World War II a significantly lower percentage of injured soldiers requested morphine than did civilians recuperating from surgery. The soldier's response to injury was relief, joy at being alive, even euphoria; to the civilians, surgery was a depressing, calamitous event. So it would seem that the meaning one attaches to a wound can affect the amount of pain one perceives.

The claim that pain perception depends only partly on physiology figures in the argument in which one of the following ways?

(A) It is an assumption on which the argument depends.

(B) It undermines the argument's main conclusion.

(C) It summarizes a position that the argument is meant to discredit.

(D) It is information that the argument takes for granted.

(E) It is the main conclusion of the argument.

5. Nutritionist: Because humans have evolved very little since the development of agriculture, it is clear that humans are still biologically adapted to a diet of wild foods, consisting mainly of raw fruits and vegetables, nuts and seeds, lean meat, and seafood. Straying from this diet has often resulted in chronic illness and other physical problems. Thus, the more our diet consists of wild foods, the healthier we will be.

The claim that humans are still biologically adapted to a diet of wild foods plays which one of the following roles in the nutritionist's argument?

(A) It is a conclusion for which the only support offered is the claim that straying from a diet of wild foods has often resulted in chronic illness and other physical problems.

(B) It is a premise for which no justification is provided, but which is used to support the argument's main conclusion.

(C) It is a phenomenon for which the main conclusion of the nutritionist's argument is cited as an explanation.

(D) It is an intermediate conclusion for which one claim is offered as support, and which is used in turn to support the argument's main conclusion.

(E) It is a premise offered in support of the claim that humans have evolved very little since the development of agriculture.

6. Philosopher: Graham argues that since a person is truly happy only when doing something, the best life is a life that is full of activity. But we should not be persuaded by Graham's argument. People sleep, and at least sometimes when sleeping, they are truly happy, even though they are not doing anything.

Which one of the following most accurately describes the role played in the philosopher's argument by the claim that at least sometimes when sleeping, people are truly happy, even though they are not doing anything?

(A) It is a premise of Graham's argument.

(B) It is an example intended to show that a premise of Graham's argument is false.

(C) It is an analogy appealed to by Graham but that the philosopher rejects.

(D) It is an example intended to disprove the conclusion of Graham's argument.

(E) It is the main conclusion of the philosopher's argument.

Problem Set: Mini Description — Answers

1. **Correct Answer (D).** *Prep Test 42, Section 2, Question 2.*

   After locating the stated claim, we need to identify the conclusion. The phrase *this shows that* indicates that the conclusion is that people's responses to words depend not only on what they mean but also how they sound. This is supported by two premises: people have positive or negative responses to words with positive or negative connotations, and recent physiological experiments have shown that people have positive or negative responses to many nonsense words. The claim in the prompt is the second premise; therefore, we can anticipate a correct answer choice that states that the claim is a premise that supports the conclusion.

   (A) **It is a premise offered in support of the conclusion that people have either a positive or negative response to any word.**

   This matches our anticipated answer choice. The phrase *it is a premise* makes this answer choice a candidate.

   (B) **It is a conclusion for which the only support provided is the claim that people's responses to words are conditioned both by what the words mean and by how they sound.**

   As this answer choice describes a conclusion, it is a loser.

   (C) **It is a generalization partially supported by the claim that meaningful words can trigger positive or negative responses in people.**

   Our claim is not a generalization. Neither is it supported by another claim (which would make it a conclusion). This is another loser.

   (D) **It is a premise offered in support of the conclusion that people's responses to words are engendered not only by what the words mean, but also by how they sound.**

   This matches our anticipated answer choice. The phrase *it is a premise* is used, so we can consider this a candidate.

   (E) **It is a conclusion supported by the claim that people's responses under experimental conditions are essentially different from their responses in ordinary situations.**

   The phrase *it is a conclusion* indicates that this answer choice is a loser.

   We must now eliminate one of the two candidates. Let's look at (A) first. This answer choice seems to match what we anticipated—the claim is a premise that supports the conclusion. However, the conclusion stated in (A)—that people have a positive or negative response to any word—does not match the content of the argument. This answer choice can be eliminated.

   In contrast, (D) not only correctly identifies the role of the claim but also accurately restates the conclusion the claim supports. (D) has to be the correct answer choice.

2. **Correct Answer (A).** *Prep Test 42, Section 4, Question 3.*

   After locating the stated claim in the first sentence, we must look for the argument's conclusion. The last sentence contains a *since premise, conclusion* structure, so we can gather that the argument's conclusion is that funding for children's athletic programs should not be eliminated. The conclusion is supported by a premise that counters the viewpoint that some children who play sports develop a feeling of inferiority.

How does the claim in the first sentence fit into the argument? Although it appears to be a premise at first glance, the argument does not actually use the information in this claim to support the conclusion. Instead, this statement functions as background information that could serve as additional evidence for the conclusion, even though it is not actually used. We should anticipate a correct answer choice that states that the claim is background information that may provide additional support for the conclusion.

(A) It is mentioned as one possible reason for adopting a policy for which the teacher suggests an additional reason.

This matches our anticipated answer choice. The fact that sports may increase a child's strength and coordination is one possible reason for adopting a policy of preserving funding for children's athletic programs (even though the teacher uses another reason to support the conclusion in the argument). (A) is a candidate.

(B) It is a claim that the teacher attempts to refute with counterarguments.

The teacher does not try to refute the claim. This is a loser.

(C) It is a hypothesis for which the teacher offers additional evidence.

The claim seems to be a factual statement rather than a hypothesis, and the teacher does not offer additional evidence to support it. This is also a loser.

(D) It is cited as an insufficient reason for eliminating funding for children's athletic programs.

This is close to our anticipated answer choice, but the inclusion of the term *insufficient* makes it incorrect. The argument is not concerned with whether the claim is a sufficient or insufficient reason. This is also a loser.

(E) It is cited as an objection that has been raised to the position that the teacher is supporting.

The teacher supports retaining funding for sport programs, and this claim could be used to support the teacher's position. This answer choice is a loser.

As (A) is the only candidate, it has to be the correct answer choice.

3. **Correct Answer (C).** *Prep Test 51.5, Section 2, Question 11.*

The claim is the second statement of the argument, while the conclusion is that our future probably entails a mere alteration of the human mind rather than regression. The conclusion is preceded by the indicator *so*. The first sentence presents the opposing viewpoint that electronic media has corroded intellectual skills. The claim is an example that counters this viewpoint, and, as a result, provides support for the conclusion. This means that it functions as a premise supporting the conclusion. We should anticipate a correct answer choice that describes this relationship using a term such as *example*, *premise*, or *evidence*.

(A) evidence supporting the claim that the intellectual skills fostered by the literary media are being destroyed by the electronic media

This answer choice includes the term *evidence*. However, the claim is not evidence that intellectual skills are regressing. Rather, the claim supports the conclusion that the human mind is not devolving. This is a loser.

(B) an illustration of the general hypothesis being advanced that intellectual abilities are inseparable from the means by which people communicate

This claim is not an illustration of a hypothesis. In addition, the hypothesis described in this answer choice is not stated in the argument. We can consider (B) a loser.

(C) an example of a cultural change that did not necessarily have a detrimental effect on the human mind overall

This matches our anticipated answer choice. If the claim is an example of a cultural change that did not have a detrimental effect on the human mind, then it supports the conclusion that the human mind will probably not devolve. (C) is a candidate.

(D) evidence that the claim that the intellectual skills required and fostered by the literary media are being lost is unwarranted

This matches our anticipated answer choice as well. The claim is evidence for the conclusion, and the conclusion counters the viewpoint that the intellectual skills required and fostered by the literary media are being corroded. We can consider (D) a candidate.

(E) possible evidence, mentioned and then dismissed, that might be cited by supporters of the hypothesis being criticized

The claim is not dismissed, and it does support the opposing viewpoint that is countered by the conclusion. This is a loser.

We now have to eliminate one of the two candidates. (D) seems like a strong candidate, but it has one significant issue—the conclusion does not actually state that that the intellectual skills fostered by literary media are not being lost. The alteration of the human mind may well involve the loss of some of these skills. This is sufficient to disqualify this answer choice, meaning that (C) has to be the correct answer choice.

4. **Correct Answer (E).** *Prep Test 40, Section 3, Question 6.*

The claim is the first sentence of the argument. The word *so* indicates that the last sentence is a conclusion. The evidence for the conclusion is that a lower percentage of World War II soldiers requested morphine than did civilians and that each group reacted to their injuries differently. However, it is immediately unclear how the first sentence figures into this; it does not support the premise in the second sentence, and it does not support the conclusion in the last sentence. In fact, it seems to be a conclusion, meaning that we need to determine which is the subsidiary conclusion and which is the main conclusion. Let's outline the two options:

P: The meaning one attaches to a wound can affect the amount of pain one perceives.
C: Therefore, pain perception depends only partly on physiology.

OR

P: Pain perception depends only partly on physiology.
C: Therefore, the meaning one attaches to a wound can affect the amount of pain one perceives.

The first option makes more sense. The meaning one attaches to a wound can affect pain levels, so it must be the case that pain perception depends only partly on physiology. In the second option, the premise is related to the conclusion but does not actually provide evidence to support it.

We should therefore anticipate a correct answer choice that refers to the argument's main conclusion. We can hone in on (B) and (E), the only answer choices that include these terms.

We now need to eliminate one of the two candidates. (B) says that the claim undermines the main conclusion, which is not true—the claim is the main conclusion. As (E) describes the claim's function in clear language, it has to be the correct answer choice. If there is an answer choice that accurately describes the function of the claim using only abstract language (i.e. it does not include content from the argument), you can simply select it and move on.

5. **Correct Answer (D).** *Prep Test 42, Section 4, Question 18.*

The claim is the second clause of the first sentence, and it is preceded by the conclusion indicator *it is clear that.* However, the final sentence also begins with a conclusion indicator (*thus*). Therefore, we need to determine which is the main conclusion and which is the subsidiary one. Let's look at the two options:

P: Humans are still biologically adapted to a diet of wild foods.		P: The more our diet consists of wild foods, the better.
C: Therefore, the more our diet consists of wild foods, the better.	OR	C: Therefore, humans are still biologically adapted to a diet of wild foods.

It seems clear that the first option works better. Humans are adapted to wild foods, which is why we should include a lot of wild food in our diet. The assertion that we should consume a lot of wild foods does not necessarily support the conclusion that humans are still biologically adapted to those foods.

The claim is therefore the subsidiary conclusion and the last sentence is the main conclusion. We should anticipate an answer choice that describes this function, possibly using terms like *subsidiary conclusion* or *intermediary conclusion.* Note that less direct language, such as *claim/position/assertion/evidence that supports the main conclusion* is also possible.

(A) **It is a conclusion for which the only support offered is the claim that straying from a diet of wild foods has often resulted in chronic illness and other physical problems.**

Although the claim is a conclusion, it is not supported by the premise that straying from a diet of wild foods has often resulted in chronic illness and other physical problems. These details actually support the main conclusion. This is a loser.

(B) **It is a premise for which no justification is provided, but which is used to support the argument's main conclusion.**

A subsidiary conclusion is technically a premise as it supports another conclusion. However, there is evidence to support the subsidiary conclusion. We can consider this answer choice a loser.

(C) **It is a phenomenon for which the main conclusion of the nutritionist's argument is cited as an explanation.**

The claim is not a phenomenon that needs explaining. This is also a loser.

(D) **It is an intermediate conclusion for which one claim is offered as support, and which is used in turn to support the argument's main conclusion.**

This matches our anticipated answer choice. The claim is an intermediate conclusion as it is supported by a premise and it supports the main conclusion. (D) is a candidate.

(E) **It is a premise offered in support of the claim that humans have evolved very little since the development of agriculture.**

The fact that humans have evolved very little supports the stated claim, which is a subsidiary conclusion. This is a loser.

As (D) is the only candidate, it has to be the correct answer choice.

6. **Correct Answer (B).** *Prep Test 52, Section 3, Question 17.*

The claim is in the last sentence. The conclusion is in the middle of the argument and begins with the counter-premise indicator *but*, which means that it counters the opposing viewpoint stated in the first sentence. The philosopher states that people are sometimes truly happy when they are sleeping, even though that means they are doing nothing at all. This refutes Graham's premise that a person is truly happy only when doing something. The claim is therefore evidence for the conclusion that we should not be persuaded by Graham's argument. More specifically, it is an example that undermines Graham's premise that you can only be truly happy when doing something. We should anticipate a correct answer choice that describes this function.

(A) It is a premise of Graham's argument.

The claim refutes a premise of Graham's argument. This is a loser.

(B) It is an example intended to show that a premise of Graham's argument is false.

This matches our anticipated answer choice. The claim is an example showing that Graham's premise that you can only be truly happy when doing something is false. Let's consider (B) a candidate.

(C) It is an analogy appealed to by Graham but that the philosopher rejects.

The claim is not an analogy, and it is used to support the philosopher's argument, not Graham's. We can consider this a loser.

(D) It is an example intended to disprove the conclusion of Graham's argument.

This also matches our anticipated answer choice. The claim supports the conclusion that we should not be persuaded by Graham's argument. (D) is a candidate.

(E) It is the main conclusion of the philosopher's argument.

The claim is not the conclusion of the argument. This is a loser.

We must eliminate either (B) or (D). The problem with (D) is that the philosopher's argument is not necessarily that Graham's conclusion is wrong but that Graham's conclusion is unfounded because the premise is not necessarily true. The stated claim undermines the premise of Graham's argument, but it is not used to disprove Graham's conclusion. It is perfectly possible that the philosopher would agree that even though sometimes people are truly happy while sleeping, the best life is a life full of activity. Therefore, we can eliminate (D) and select (B).

Parallel Reasoning

Parallel Reasoning

≈ 2.0 questions per test

Example Prompts

The reasoning in the argument above *most closely parallels* that in which of the following?

The pattern of reasoning in which one of the following arguments is *most similar* to that in the argument above?

Take These Steps

Read the stimulus, which always includes an argument. Identify the main conclusion, subsidiary conclusions (if any), and premises. Does the argument contain multiple conditional statements?

No →

Check the strength of the conclusion and determine if it includes prescriptive language. Eliminate incorrect answer choices containing conclusions that do not match these features. Determine the argumentative structure of the argument. If it does not match one of the common argumentative structures, create an abstract paraphrase. Anticipate a correct answer choice that matches the argumentative structure of the stimulus.

Yes ↓

Outline the argument, diagramming all conditional statements. Note any strength modifiers, conjunctions, or disjunctions, and eliminate incorrect answer choices that do not include these features. Anticipate a correct answer choice that matches the argumentative structure of the stimulus.

Answer Choices

Correct Answer Choices	**Incorrect Answer Choices**
Arguments with the same argumentative structure and validity	Arguments with a different argumentative structure or validity
Arguments with a conclusion that has the same strength and use of prescriptive language	Arguments that include a conclusion with a different strength and use of prescriptive language
Arguments that include the same conditional language, such as strength modifiers, conjunctions, and disjunctions	Arguments that include slight deviations in argumentative structure, such as weaker conclusions, different strength modifiers, and conjunctions instead of disjunctions

Parallel Reasoning (PR) questions are similar to D questions in that both require that you identify and summarize the underlying structure of an argument. However, PR questions are more complex because the answer choices do not include a clear description of an argumentative structure. Instead, each answer choice is a short argument. You must select the one with an argumentative structure that corresponds to that of the argument in the stimulus. The argument is almost always a valid one, although invalid arguments do occasionally appear. PR questions are generally more complicated and time-consuming than other types of LR questions.

How to Solve Parallel Reasoning Questions

The first step toward solving a PR question is to identify the conclusion and supporting premises. Next, determine whether the argument includes multiple conditional statements. Approximately half of all PR questions include arguments with conditional reasoning.

If There Are Multiple Conditional Statements

For a PR question with multiple conditional statements, the first step is to outline the argument, making sure to diagram all the conditional statements. Next, take note of any strength modifiers, conjunctions, and disjunctions. After doing so, you should anticipate a correct answer choice that matches the stimulus with regard to the following:
- validity of argument
- number of premises
- relationship between conclusion and premises
- number and types of terms within premises
- strength of conditional statements
- presence of conjunctions or disjunctions

It is usually necessary to outline and diagram the answer choices as well. Note that the parts of the argument may appear in a different order. For example, if the conclusion appears at the beginning of the stimulus, it may appear in the middle or at the end of the answer choice. In addition, the topics of the stimulus and answer choice need not be related.

PR questions with multiple conditional statements can be stressful because of the amount of time required to outline and diagram both the stimulus and answer choices. However, because the correct answer choice must closely match the structure of the original argument, it is often easy to eliminate answer choices. In most cases, you can quickly scan through the answer choices to eliminate ones that do not match the original, based on obvious factors like the strength of the premises or the presence of conjunctions or disjunctions.

Let's look at an example:

> Every new play that runs for more than three months is either a commercial or a critical success. Last year, all new plays that were critical successes were also commercial successes. Therefore, every new play that ran for more than three months last year was a commercial success.
>
> The pattern of reasoning in which one of the following arguments is most similar to that in the argument above?

(A) Most new restaurants require either good publicity or a good location in order to succeed. But most restaurants with a good location also receive good publicity. Hence, a restaurant that has a good location is guaranteed to succeed.

(B) Every best-selling cookbook published last year is both well written and contains beautiful photographs. The cookbook Cynthia Cleveland published last year is well written and contains beautiful photographs. Therefore, Cleveland's cookbook is a best seller.

(C) All students at the Freeman School of Cooking study either desserts or soups in their second year. This year, all Freeman students studying soups are also studying desserts. Therefore, every second-year student at Freeman is studying desserts this year.

(D) Chefs who become celebrities either open their own restaurants or write books about their craft, but not both. John Endicott is a celebrated chef who opened his own restaurant. Therefore, Endicott does not write books about his craft.

(E) Every catering service in Woodside Township will accept both residential and business catering assignments. Peggy's Fine Foods is a catering service that will not accept business catering assignments. Hence, Peggy's Fine Foods is not in Woodside Township.

The argument can be outlined as follows:

P1: New Play Run >3 Months → Commercial Success OR Critical Success
P2: Critical Success → Commercial Success
_____
C: New Play >3 Months → Commercial Success

This is a valid argument. If every new play is either option A or option B, and all option Bs are also option As, then every new play has to be option A.

To match this argument, the correct answer choice must include two ALL statement premises (one with a disjunction) and an ALL statement conclusion. Obviously there are other requirements, but an answer choice that does not include these elements or that includes other elements—such as a SOME or MOST statement or a conjunction—is incorrect and can be eliminated immediately.

(A) Most new restaurants require either good publicity or a good location in order to succeed. But most restaurants with a good location also receive good publicity. Hence, a restaurant that has a good location is guaranteed to succeed.

The presence of two MOST statements allows us to eliminate this answer choice. In addition, notice how there are two MOST statement premises and an ALL statement conclusion. This is an invalid inference, meaning that (A) includes an invalid argument. As the original argument is valid, this answer choice is a definite loser.

(B) Every best-selling cookbook published last year is both well written and contains beautiful photographs. The cookbook Cynthia Cleveland published last year is well written and contains beautiful photographs. Therefore, Cleveland's cookbook is a best seller.

The presence of a conjunction allows us to quickly eliminate this answer choice. This is a loser.

(C) **All students at the Freeman School of Cooking study either desserts or soups in their second year. This year, all Freeman students studying soups are also studying desserts. Therefore, every second-year student at Freeman is studying desserts this year.**

This matches our anticipated answer choice. There are two ALL statement premises, one containing a disjunction, and one ALL statement conclusion. Though not necessarily the correct answer choice, (C) is a candidate.

(D) **Chefs who become celebrities either open their own restaurants or write books about their craft, but not both. John Endicott is a celebrated chef who opened his own restaurant. Therefore, Endicott does not write books about his craft.**

The inclusion of the phrase *but not both* is enough to disqualify this answer choice. The argument in the stimulus contains a disjunction, and the argument is structured in such a way that both options must occur. On a side note, the first premise in the answer choice uses the term *chefs who become celebrities*, while the second premise states that John Endicott is a *celebrated chef*. These are not identical terms, which mean the argument includes an equivocation error. (D) is a loser.

(E) **Every catering service in Woodside Township will accept both residential and business catering assignments. Peggy's Fine Foods is a catering service that will not accept business catering assignments. Hence, Peggy's Fine Foods is not in Woodside Township.**

This answer choice includes a conjunction, so it is a loser.

This leaves us with (C). By focusing on two of the most obvious requirements, we were able to eliminate all the incorrect answer choices without having to diagram them. Usually, it is only possible to eliminate two or three answer choices this way. Still, this saves a tremendous amount of time.

If There Are Not Multiple Conditional Statements

When the argument does not include more than one conditional statement, begin by identifying the conclusion. Check whether it is a strong, moderate, or weak statement and whether it includes any prescriptive language such as *should* or *ought*. The conclusion of the correct answer choice must include the same features. Focusing on the conclusion is a useful way to eliminate incorrect answer choices.

Also determine how the premises support the conclusion as the correct answer choice must have a matching argumentative structure. In many cases, it will be one of the argumentative structures that commonly appear in D questions:

- Appealing to an authority
- Using a counter-example
- Pointing out a fallacy
- Offering new evidence
- Undermining a premise
- Challenging an assumption
- Rejecting a claim on insufficient evidence
- Suggesting a different causal conclusion
- Clarifying a previous statement
- Using a proposed line of reasoning to make a ridiculous conclusion

However, you will often encounter argumentative structures that do not fit into one of these categories. When this happens, you should attempt to develop an *abstract paraphrase*. This is a short, simple statement describing the argumentative structure in abstract terms. The advantage of this approach is that it allows you to quickly compare the argumentative structure of the stimulus with that of an answer choice. Here are a few examples:

Argument	Abstract Paraphrase
Purchasing this machine will allows us to boost our production output and increase revenue. However, the annual cost of this machine would be greater than any revenue increase. Therefore, we should not purchase this machine.	"Bad outweighs the good"
Mechanics that cannot provide either cheap service or fast service generally go out of business. Many successful mechanics are able to provide cheap service or fast service, but not both. Therefore, a mechanic's service can be successful, even it is not cheap.	"Unnecessary to do both to succeed"
If one wants to develop an appreciation for classical music, it is often counterproductive to begin by attending a full classical concerto, as that can be overwhelming. It is better to watch a scene from a favorite movie that contains classical music and appreciate how the music moves the narrative.	"Best to start with small exposure"
We cannot conclude that Homo Erectus was responsible for ancient stone tools found in Lamont Cave. After all, other hominid species are known to have lived near this cave.	"Insufficient evidence"

Developing an effective abstract paraphrase takes practice. The key is that it should not be too broad or too narrow. Be flexible when comparing the answer choices to an abstract paraphrase. It may be the case that no answer choice is a perfect match, but that one has an argumentative structure that is similar enough to make it the correct answer choice.

Let's look at an example:

> The local radio station will not win the regional ratings race this year. In the past ten years the station has never finished better than fifth place in the ratings. The station's manager has not responded to its dismal ratings by changing its musical format or any key personnel, while the competition has often sought to respond to changing tastes in music and has aggressively recruited the region's top radio personalities.
>
> The reasoning in which one of the following is most similar to that in the argument above?
>
> (A) Every swan I have seen was white. Therefore all swans are probably white.
> (B) A fair coin was fairly flipped six times and was heads every time. The next flip will probably be heads too.
> (C) All lions are mammals. Therefore Leo, the local zoo's oldest lion, is a mammal too.
> (D) Recently stock prices have always been lower on Mondays. Therefore they will be lower this coming Monday too.
> (E) Only trained swimmers are lifeguards, so it follows that the next lifeguard at the local pool will be a trained swimmer.

The conclusion in the first sentence is a strong statement that specifies that the local radio station will not win the regional ratings race. We know this is the conclusion because the rest of the argument provides supporting evidence; for instance, the station has never finished better than fifth place and it has not made any meaningful changes. There are no conditional statements, and the stimulus does not have one of the argumentative structures previously reviewed. Therefore, we should come up with an abstract paraphrase. Why will the local radio station not win the race? According to the argument, it has lost in the past and nothing has changed. Based on this, we can create the abstract paraphrase

"If it happened in the past and nothing has changed, it will continue to happen."

We should anticipate a correct answer choice with a similar argumentative structure and with a conclusion that is a strong statement.

(A) Every swan I have seen was white. Therefore all swans are probably white.

The inclusion of the term *probably* makes the conclusion of this answer choice weaker than the one in the stimulus. In addition, the argumentative structure does not match our abstract paraphrase. There is no time element or absence of change element. Therefore, this is a loser.

(B) A fair coin was fairly flipped six times and was heads every time. The next flip will probably be heads too.

The conclusion is a weaker statement because of the inclusion of *probably*. Also, the argumentative structure does not match the abstract paraphrase. A fair coin has a 50 percent chance of being heads each time it is flipped. There is no connection between the number of times it came up heads in the past and the outcome of the next flip. In contrast, the fact that the radio station has lost in the past and made no changes is a good indicator that it will lose again. This answer choice is a loser.

(C) All lions are mammals. Therefore Leo, the local zoo's oldest lion, is a mammal too.

The conclusion is a strong statement. However, the argument provides a general rule and then applies it to a specific example. This does not match our abstract paraphrase. (C) is also a loser.

(D) Recently stock prices have always been lower on Mondays. Therefore they will be lower this coming Monday too.

This matches our anticipated answer choice. The conclusion is a strong statement. In addition, it includes the necessary time element from the abstract paraphrase. However, it does not include the absence of change element. But maybe the abstract paraphrase is too specific. We will consider this answer choice a candidate.

(E) Only trained swimmers are lifeguards, so it follows that the next lifeguard at the local pool will be a trained swimmer.

The conclusion is an ALL statement that simply affirms the premise, which states that Lifeguard → Trained Swimmer. If this is true, then it follows that the lifeguard at the local pool is a trained swimmer. While this argument is valid, it does not match our abstract paraphrase. This is a loser.

As answer choice (D) is the only candidate, it has to be the correct answer choice.

Looking at the Answer Choices

As mentioned earlier, PR questions include answer choices that are short arguments. The correct answer choice matches the argumentative structure of the stimulus.

Incorrect answer choices commonly include slight deviations from the argumentative structure of the stimulus. When the stimulus includes multiple conditional statements, the incorrect answer choices commonly have premises or conclusions that are stronger or weaker than those in the stimulus, conjunctions instead of disjunctions (and vice versa), and so on. It is also typical for incorrect answer choices to include an invalid argument when the stimulus includes a valid argument. If the stimulus does not include multiple conditional statements, always check the conclusion first. Often, incorrect answer choices have a conclusion that is a stronger or weaker statement than the one in the stimulus or that fails to use prescriptive language when the conclusion of the stimulus does so.

In addition, incorrect answer choices—regardless of whether they include multiple conditional statements—often have a topic that is similar to that in the stimulus but have a different argumentative structure. Remember, the topics do not need to match.

Drill: Abstract Paraphrase

For each short argument, provide an abstract paraphrase of the argumentative structure. Ensure that it is not too broad or narrow.

1. For good reason, computer hardware companies usually hire employees with knowledge of many technological fields other than computing. This is because customers who buy high-end computer hardware are interested in these fields and having employees who can relate better to customers' interests is good for business. This is true even if these employees lack the social skills to interact with other customers.

   _____

2. The research conducted by Dr. Peters is important but it in no way proves his hypothesis regarding mesothelioma contraction. Such a conclusion would affect millions of dollars in legal settlements from those who contracted mesothelioma during their employment, and we need extraordinary evidence before we can make such a consequential claim.

   _____

3. The only energy drink I will have is Voltage Energy. It includes just the right amount of caffeine and taurine, the substances that make energy drinks so effective. Other companies overload their drinks with these ingredients, which can cause negative side effects such as dizziness and nausea.

   _____

4. The French Falcons will win in this year's international tournament. After all, the Falcons won the tournament last year.

   _____

5. Karina is not responsible for the car accident. Even though she was driving 10 mph above the speed limit, Ivan pulled out of his driveway without looking, which would have caused the collision between the two even if Karina had not been speeding.

   _____

Drill: Abstract Paraphrase — Answers

1. When interacting with customers, similar interests is sometimes more important than social skills.

2. Extraordinary claims require extraordinary evidence.

3. Too much of a good thing can result in negative consequences.

4. What has happened in the past will continue to happen in the future.

5. A party is not responsible for a consequence that would have arisen without that party's bad action.

Note that your responses may not match these exactly. There are many ways to phrase an abstract paraphrase.

Problem Set: Parallel Reasoning

1. Team captain: Winning requires the willingness to cooperate, which in turn requires motivation. So you will not win if you are not motivated.

The pattern of reasoning in which one of the following is most similar to that in the argument above?

(A) Being healthy requires exercise. But exercising involves risk of injury. So, paradoxically, anyone who wants to be healthy will not exercise.

(B) Learning requires making some mistakes. And you must learn if you are to improve. So you will not make mistakes without there being a noticeable improvement.

(C) Our political party will retain its status only if it raises more money. But raising more money requires increased campaigning. So our party will not retain its status unless it increases its campaigning.

(D) You can repair your own bicycle only if you are enthusiastic. And if you are enthusiastic, you will also have mechanical aptitude. So if you are not able to repair your own bicycle, you lack mechanical aptitude.

(E) Getting a ticket requires waiting in line. Waiting in line requires patience. So if you do not wait in line, you lack patience.

2. Often, a product popularly believed to be the best of its type is no better than any other; rather, the product's reputation, which may be independent of its quality, provides its owner with status. Thus, although there is no harm in paying for status if that is what one wants, one should know that one is paying for prestige, not quality.

Which one of the following arguments is most similar in its reasoning to the argument above?

(A) Often, choosing the best job offer is a matter of comparing the undesirable features of the different jobs. Thus, those who choose a job because it has a desirable location should know that they might be unhappy with its hours.

(B) Most people have little tolerance for boastfulness. Thus, although one's friends may react positively when hearing the details of one's accomplishments, it is unlikely that their reactions are entirely honest.

(C) Those beginning a new hobby sometimes quit it because of the frustrations involved in learning a new skill. Thus, although it is fine to try to learn a skill quickly, one is more likely to learn a skill if one first learns to enjoy the process of acquiring it.

(D) Personal charm is often confused with virtue. Thus, while there is nothing wrong with befriending a charming person, anyone who does so should realize that a charming friend is not necessarily a good and loyal friend.

(E) Many theatrical actors cannot enjoy watching a play because when they watch others, they yearn to be on stage themselves. Thus, although there is no harm in yearning to perform, such performers should, for their own sakes, learn to suppress that yearning.

3. The fact that people who exercise vigorously are sick less often than average does not prove that vigorous exercise prevents illness, for whether one exercises vigorously or not depends in part on one's preexisting state of health.

The reasoning in which one of the following arguments is most similar to that in the argument above?

(A) Having strong verbal skills encourages people to read more, so the fact that habitual readers tend to be verbally skilled does not prove that reading produces verbal skill.

(B) Musical and mathematical skills are often produced by the same talent for perceiving abstract patterns, so the fact that some mathematicians are not skilled musicians does not prove that they lack the talent that can produce musical skill.

(C) Since how people choose to dress often depends on how their friends dress, the fact that a person chooses a style of dress does not prove that he or she truly prefers that style to any other.

(D) The fact that taller children often outperform other children at basketball does not show that height is a decisive advantage in basketball, for taller children tend to play basketball more frequently than do other children.

(E) The fact that two diseases have similar symptoms does not establish that they have the same underlying cause, for dissimilar causes can have similar effects.

4. To get the free dessert, one must order an entrée and a salad. But anyone who orders either an entrée or a salad can receive a free soft drink. Thus, anyone who is not eligible for a free soft drink is not eligible for a free dessert.

The reasoning in the argument above is most similar to the reasoning in which one of the following arguments?

(A) To get an executive position at Teltech, one needs a university diploma and sales experience. But anyone who has worked at Teltech for more than six months who does not have sales experience has a university diploma. Thus, one cannot get an executive position at Teltech unless one has worked there for six months.

(B) To be elected class president, one must be well liked and well known. Anyone who is well liked or well known has something better to do than run for class president. Therefore, no one who has something better to do will be elected class president.

(C) To grow good azaleas, one needs soil that is both rich in humus and low in acidity. Anyone who has soil that is rich in humus or low in acidity can grow blueberries. So, anyone who cannot grow blueberries cannot grow good azaleas.

(D) To drive to Weller, one must take the highway or take Old Mill Road. Anyone who drives to Weller on the highway will miss the beautiful scenery. Thus, one cannot see the beautiful scenery without taking Old Mill Road to Weller.

(E) To get a discount on ice cream, one must buy frozen raspberries and ice cream together. Anyone who buys ice cream or raspberries will get a coupon for a later purchase. So, anyone who does not get the discount on ice cream will not get a coupon for a later purchase.

5. Some visitors to the park engage in practices that seriously harm the animals. Surely, no one who knew that these practices seriously harm the animals would engage in them. So it must be concluded that some of the visitors do not know that these practices seriously harm the animals.

The pattern of reasoning exhibited by which one of the following arguments is most similar to that exhibited by the argument above?

(A) Some of the people who worked on the failed project will be fired. Everyone in this department played an important part in that project. Therefore some people in this department will be fired.

(B) Some of the people who signed the petition were among the mayor's supporters. Yet the mayor denounced everyone who signed the petition. Hence the mayor denounced some of her own supporters.

(C) Some of the people polled live outside the city limits. However, no one who can vote in city elections lives outside the city. Therefore some of the people polled cannot vote in the upcoming city election.

(D) All of the five original planners are responsible for this problem. Yet none of the original planners will admit responsibility for the problem. Thus some of the people responsible for the problem will not admit responsibility.

(E) Some members of the Liberal Party are in favor of the proposed ordinance. But all members of the city council are opposed to the proposed ordinance. Hence some members of the city council are not Liberals.

6. Landscape architect: If the screen between these two areas is to be a hedge, that hedge must be of either hemlocks or Leyland cypress trees. However, Leyland cypress trees cannot be grown this far north. So if the screen is to be a hedge, it will be a hemlock hedge.

In which one of the following is the pattern of reasoning most similar to that in the landscape architect's argument?

(A) If there is to be an entrance on the north side of the building, it will have to be approached by a ramp. However, a ramp would become impossibly slippery in winter, so there will be no entrance on the north side.

(B) If visitors are to travel to this part of the site by automobile, there will be a need for parking spaces. However, no parking spaces are allowed for in the design. So if visitors are likely to come by automobile, the design will be changed.

(C) The subsoil in these five acres either consists entirely of clay or consists entirely of shale. Therefore, if one test hole in the area reveals shale, it will be clear that the entire five acres has a shale subsoil.

(D) Any path along this embankment must be either concrete or stone. But a concrete path cannot be built in this location. So if there is to be a path on the embankment, it will be a stone path.

(E) A space the size of this meadow would be suitable for a playground or a picnic area. However, a playground would be noisy and a picnic area would create litter. So it will be best for the area to remain a meadow.

Problem Set: Parallel Reasoning — Answers

1. **Correct Answer (C).** *Prep Test 57, Section 2, Question 19.*

There are two necessary indicators, *requires* and *if*, and the conclusion indicator *so*. The argument can be outlined as:

P1: Winning → Cooperation
P2: Cooperation → Motivation
C: ~~Motivation~~ → ~~Winning~~

Which in turn indicates that the preceding clause, *willingness to cooperate*, is what requires motivation.

The necessary condition of the first premise matches the sufficient condition of the second premise, creating the logical chain Winning → Cooperation → Motivation. The ends of this chain can be combined to create the inference Winning → Motivation. The contrapositive of this inference (~~Motivation~~ → ~~Winning~~) is the conclusion of the argument.

We are looking for an answer choice that combines two ALL statements to create a logical chain. Its conclusion should be an inference based on combining the ends of this chain. Note that it does not matter whether the conclusion is the contrapositive of this inference or not.

Before diagramming, it is worth checking if there are any answer choices that can be easily eliminated. Unfortunately, there are not. All of the conclusions in the answer choices are conditional statements, and none include prescriptive language. In addition, there are no MOST statements, SOME statements, conjunctions, or disjunctions. Therefore, we must diagram the answer choices.

(A) **Being healthy requires exercise. But exercising involves risk of injury. So, paradoxically, anyone who wants to be healthy will not exercise.**

Stimulus Argument Diagram	Answer Choice Argument Diagram
P1: Winning → Cooperation	P1: Healthy → Exercise
P2: Cooperation → Motivation	P2: Exercise → Risk of Injury
C: ~~Motivation~~ → ~~Winning~~	C: Healthy → ~~Exercise~~

This answer choice does not match the stimulus. If the conclusion were Healthy → Risk of Injury or ~~Risk of Injury~~ → ~~Healthy~~, then it would be correct. Also, the argument is invalid because the conclusion contradicts a premise. (A) is a loser.

(B) **Learning requires making some mistakes. And you must learn if you are to improve. So you will not make mistakes without there being a noticeable improvement.**

Stimulus Argument Diagram	Answer Choice Argument Diagram
P1: Winning → Cooperation	P1: Learning → Mistakes
P2: Cooperation → Motivation	P2: Improve → Learning
C: ~~Motivation~~ → ~~Winning~~	C: ~~Improve~~ → ~~Mistakes~~

In the answer choice, the logical chain begins with the second premise rather than the first, but this is not a factor when comparing arguments. However, the answer choice includes an argument that is invalid due to negated reasoning. The conclusion should be Improve → Mistakes or ~~Mistakes~~ → ~~Improve~~. We can put this in the loser category.

(C) **Our political party will retain its status only if it raises more money. But raising more money** requires increased campaigning. So our party will not retain its status unless it increases its campaigning.

Stimulus Argument Diagram	Answer Choice Argument Diagram
P1: Winning → Cooperation P2: Cooperation → Motivation C: ~~Motivation → Winning~~	P1: Status → Money P2: Money → Campaigning C: ~~Campaigning → Status~~

This matches our anticipated answer choice. Note that *unless* is a negative sufficient indicator, which means that the sufficient condition that follows it must be negated. This argumentative structure matches that of the stimulus perfectly. (C) is a candidate.

(D) You can repair your own bicycle only if you are enthusiastic. And if you are enthusiastic, you will also have mechanical aptitude. So if you are not able to repair your own bicycle, you lack mechanical aptitude.

Stimulus Argument Diagram	Answer Choice Argument Diagram
P1: Winning → Cooperation P2: Cooperation → Motivation C: ~~Motivation → Winning~~	P1: Repair Bike → Enthusiastic P2: Enthusiastic → Mechanical Aptitude C: ~~Repair Bike → Mechanical Aptitude~~

This answer choice is invalid because its conclusion is based on negated reasoning. It is a loser.

(E) Getting a ticket requires waiting in line. Waiting in line requires patience. So if you do not wait in line, you lack patience.

Stimulus Argument Diagram	Answer Choice Argument Diagram
P1: Winning → Cooperation P2: Cooperation → Motivation C: ~~Motivation → Winning~~	P1: Ticket → Waiting P2: Waiting → Patience C: ~~Waiting → Patience~~

As the conclusion is the negated version of the second premise, the argument is invalid. This is also a loser.

As answer choice (C) is the only candidate, it has to be the correct answer choice.

2. **Correct Answer (D).** *Prep Test 47, Section 1, Question 15.*

This argument does not include conditional statements. The word *thus* indicates that the conclusion is that there is no harm in paying for status if that is what one wants, but one should know that one is paying for prestige, not quality. Note the word *should* in the conclusion. The conclusion of the correct answer choice must also contain prescriptive language, such as *should* or *ought*. Knowing this, we can scan through the answer choices and quickly eliminate (B) and (C).

We now need to determine the argumentative structure of the stimulus. The conclusion is supported by the claim that many products provide their owners with status regardless of their quality. The argument does not match any of the common argumentative structures, so we need to create an abstract paraphrase:

"Understand what you are actually getting."

Now let's look at the remaining answer choices:

(A) Often, choosing the best job offer is a matter of comparing the undesirable features of the different jobs. Thus, those who choose a job because it has a desirable location should know that they might be unhappy with its hours.

This matches our anticipated answer choice. The argument states that people should compare the negative features of jobs to select the best one. In other words, they must truly understand the consequences of selecting a particular job. (A) is a candidate.

(D) Personal charm is often confused with virtue. Thus, while there is nothing wrong with befriending a charming person, anyone who does so should realize that a charming friend is not necessarily a good and loyal friend.

This also matches our anticipated answer choice. The argument states that there is nothing wrong with befriending someone with one characteristic as long as you realize that the friend may not have another characteristic. We now have two candidates.

(E) Many theatrical actors cannot enjoy watching a play because when they watch others, they yearn to be on stage themselves. Thus, although there is no harm in yearning to perform, such performers should, for their own sakes, learn to suppress that yearning.

This argument does not have a clear relationship to our abstract paraphrase. (E) is a loser.

We now have to eliminate one of our two candidates. (D) seems like a much closer match. It includes the phrase *there is nothing wrong with*, which is almost the same as the phrase *there is no harm in* in the stimulus. We could make our abstract paraphrase more specific to include this idea:

"There is nothing wrong with picking that option as long as you actually understand what you are getting."

This abstract paraphrase allows us to eliminate (A), so (D) has to be the correct answer choice.

---

3. **Correct Answer (A).** *Prep Test 40, Section 1, Question 23.*

The stimulus does not include any conditional statements. The word *for* indicates that the statement after it explains the one before it. This means that the conclusion is that the fact that there is a correlation between exercising vigorously and being sick less often does not prove that Exercise CAUSE Less Illness. Note that *prevents* functions like CAUSE + negative term. The conclusion is supported by the fact that whether or not one exercises depends on one's current state of health.

This is a common argumentative structure. The author suggests a different causal conclusion or, to be more specific, that a causal relationship may be reversed.

Before we look for this argumentative structure in the answer choices, let's eliminate all answer choices with conclusions that do not express a causal relationship. (C) and (D) can be eliminated, leaving (A), (B), and (E) to choose from.

(A) Having strong verbal skills encourages people to read more, so the fact that habitual readers tend to be verbally skilled does not prove that reading produces verbal skill.

This matches our anticipated answer choice. The conclusion of (A) is that a correlation between habitual readers and strong verbal skills does not prove that reading improves verbal skills (having strong verbal skills could cause a person to read more). (A) is a candidate.

(B) Musical and mathematical skills are often produced by the same talent for perceiving abstract patterns, so the fact that some mathematicians are not skilled musicians does not prove that

they lack the talent that can produce musical skill.

This answer choice claims that musical and mathematical skills often spring from the same talent. However, the argument does not actually offer another causal conclusion. Instead, the conclusion is an inference based on the causal relationship in the premise. (B) is a loser.

(E) The fact that two diseases have similar symptoms does not establish that they have the same underlying cause, for dissimilar causes can have similar effects.

This answer choice argues that even if two diseases have the same symptoms, they may not have the same cause. This does not match the stimulus. (E) is a loser.

As (A) is the only candidate, it has to be the correct answer choice.

4. **Correct Answer (C).** *Prep Test 54, Section 4, Question 25.*

This argument includes multiple conditional statements, as indicated by the words *must* and *anyone*. The argument can be outlined as

P1: Free Dessert → Entrée AND Salad
P2: Entrée OR Salad → Free Drink
C: ~~Free Drink~~ → ~~Free Dessert~~

The necessary condition of the first statement can connect to the sufficient condition of the second statement even though they are not technically identical because AND is inclusive of OR. If an entrée and salad are ordered, this triggers both options in the sufficient condition of the second statement.

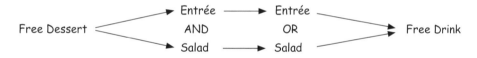

From the premises, we can infer that Free Dessert → Free Drink or its contrapositive ~~Free Drink~~ → ~~Free Dessert~~, which is the conclusion of the argument. In the answer choices, we must look for (1) a conditional premise with a conjunction, (2) a conditional premise with a disjunction, and (3) a conditional conclusion that validly connects the ends of a logical chain. We should scan the answer choices to eliminate any that do not include a conditional premise with a conjunction and a conditional premise with a disjunction. (A) can be eliminated because it does not include a disjunction; (D) can be eliminated because it does not have a conjunction. We now need to diagram the remaining answer choices.

(B) To be elected class president, one must be well liked and well known. Anyone who is well liked or well known has something better to do than run for class president. Therefore, no one who has something better to do will be elected class president.

Stimulus Argument Diagram	Answer Choice Argument Diagram
P1: Free Dessert → Entrée AND Salad	P1: Class President → Liked AND Known
P2: Entrée OR Salad → Free Drink	P2: Liked OR Known → Something Better to Do
C: ~~Free Drink~~ → ~~Free Dessert~~	C: Something Better to do → ~~Class President~~

Although the premises of this answer choice match those of the conclusion, the conclusion is invalid. The sufficient condition of the conclusion needs to be negated because of the negative necessary indicator *no*. This is a loser.

(C) To grow good azaleas, one needs soil that is both rich in humus and low in acidity. Anyone who has soil that is rich in humus or low in acidity can grow blueberries. So, anyone who

cannot grow blueberries cannot grow good azaleas.

Stimulus Argument Diagram	Answer Choice Argument Diagram
P1: Free Dessert → Entrée AND Salad P2: Entrée OR Salad → Free Drink C: ~~Free Drink~~ → ~~Free Dessert~~	P1: Grow Azaleas → Humus AND Low Acidity P2: Humus OR Low Acidity → Blueberries C: ~~Blueberries~~ → ~~Grow Azaleas~~

This matches our anticipated answer choice. It includes the three elements we are looking for. Note that the conclusion is the contrapositive of the linkage between the first and last terms of the chain. (C) is a candidate.

(E) **To get a discount on ice cream, one must buy frozen raspberries and ice cream together. Anyone who buys ice cream or raspberries will get a coupon for a later purchase. So, anyone who does not get the discount on ice cream will not get a coupon for a later purchase.**

Stimulus Argument Diagram	Answer Choice Argument Diagram
P1: Free Dessert → Entrée AND Salad P2: Entrée OR Salad → Free Drink C: ~~Free Drink~~ → ~~Free Dessert~~	P1: Ice Cream Discount → Raspberries AND Ice Cream P2: Ice Cream OR Raspberries → Coupon C: ~~Ice Cream Discount~~ → ~~Coupon~~

The premises match those of the stimulus, but the conclusion is invalid. It is the negated version of an inference made by combining the ends of the logical chain. (E) is a loser.

(C) is the only candidate, so it has to be the correct answer choice.

5. Correct Answer (C). *Prep Test 45, Section 1, Question 25.*

This is one of the toughest Parallel Reasoning questions that has appeared on the LSAT. It includes multiple conditional statements, as indicated by the presence of the strength modifiers *some*, *no one*, and *some*. The argument can be outlined as

P1: Visitors ^{S}—^{S} Engage in Practices that Harm
P2: Know Practices Harm → ~~Engage in Practices that Harm~~
C: Visitors ^{S}—^{S} ~~Know Practices Harm~~

The conclusion has been reached by flipping the first conditional statement and finding the contrapositive of the second conditional statement:

P1: Engage in Practices that Harm ^{S}—^{S} Visitors
P2: Engage in Practices that Harm → ~~Know Practices Harm~~
C: Visitors ^{S}—^{S} ~~Know Practices Harm~~

When the sufficient condition of a SOME statement matches the sufficient condition of an ALL statement, we can infer a SOME statement between the necessary conditions.

In the answer choices, we want to look for (1) a SOME statement premise, (2) an ALL statement premise, and (3) a conclusion that infers a SOME statement from the contrapositive of an ALL statement and a SOME statement. Remember, it is not enough for an answer choice to have the same conclusion as the stimulus; it must reach that conclusion through the same reasoning.

We can quickly scan the answer choices and eliminate any that lack the first two elements. This helps us eliminate (D), which includes two ALL statement premises. Let's diagram each of the remaining answer choices.

(A) **Some of the people who worked on the failed project will be fired. Everyone in this**

department played an important part in that project. Therefore some people in this department will be fired.

Stimulus Argument Diagram	Answer Choice Argument Diagram
P1: Visitors ^{S}—^{S} Engage in Practices that Harm P2: Know Practices Harm → ~~Engage in Practices that Harm~~ C: Visitors ^{S}—^{S} ~~Know Practices Harm~~	P1: Work Failed Project ^{S}—^{S} Fired P2: Department → Work Failed Project C: Department ^{S}—^{S} Fired

The conclusion of this answer choice is invalid. The premises have different sufficient conditions, so no valid inferences can be made. (A) is a loser.

(B) Some of the people who signed the petition were among the mayor's supporters. Yet the mayor denounced everyone who signed the petition. Hence the mayor denounced some of her own supporters.

Stimulus Argument Diagram	Answer Choice Argument Diagram
P1: Visitors ^{S}—^{S} Engage in Practices that Harm P2: Know Practices Harm → ~~Engage in Practices that Harm~~ C: Visitors ^{S}—^{S} ~~Know Practices Harm~~	P1: Signed Petition ^{S}—^{S} Supporters P2: Signed Petition → Mayor Denounced C: Mayor Denounced ^{S}—^{S} Supporters

This matches our anticipated answer choice. The conclusion is a valid SOME statement that results from combining the identical sufficient conditions of a SOME statement and an ALL statement. (B) is a candidate.

(C) Some of the people polled live outside the city limits. However, no one who can vote in city elections lives outside the city. Therefore some of the people polled cannot vote in the upcoming city election.

Stimulus Argument Diagram	Answer Choice Argument Diagram
P1: Visitors ^{S}—^{S} Engage in Practices that Harm P2: Know Practices Harm → ~~Engage in Practices that Harm~~ C: Visitors ^{S}—^{S} ~~Know Practices Harm~~	P1: People Polled ^{S}—^{S} Outside City Limit P2: Vote → ~~Outside City Limit~~ C: People Polled ^{S}—^{S} ~~Vote~~

This matches our anticipated answer choice. The conclusion is a SOME statement inferred from the identical sufficient conditions of a SOME and an ALL statement. Note that the contrapositive of the second premise must be found to make this inference. (C) is a candidate.

(E) Some members of the Liberal Party are in favor of the proposed ordinance. But all members of the city council are opposed to the proposed ordinance. Hence some members of the city council are not Liberals.

Stimulus Argument Diagram	Answer Choice Argument Diagram
P1: Visitors ^{S}—^{S} Engage in Practices that Harm P2: Know Practices Harm → ~~Engage in Practices that Harm~~ C: Visitors ^{S}—^{S} ~~Know Practices Harm~~	P1: Liberal Party ^{S}—^{S} In Favor of Ordinance P2: City Council → ~~In Favor of Ordinance~~ C: City Council ^{S}—^{S} ~~Liberal Party~~

The conclusion is invalid. By flipping the SOME statement and finding the contrapositive of the ALL statement, we can infer a SOME statement between the two sufficient conditions. However, the SOME statement that is concluded in this argument is that City Council ^S—^S ~~Liberal Party~~, whereas the valid conclusion is ~~City Council~~ ^S—^S Liberal Party. Therefore, (E) is a loser.

Now we must eliminate either (B) or (C). What makes this difficult is that both include the required elements from the stimulus. However, (C) has two elements that answer (B) lacks. Firstly, its second premise is a NO statement, which negates the second term. Second, in order to arrive at the conclusion, it is necessary to find the contrapositive of the second statement. These two elements make answer choice (C) most similar to the argument in the stimulus. The first chapter of this book states that there are always four incorrect answer choices and one correct answer choice, and that the word *most* in the prompt is inconsequential. However, there are very rare exceptions to the rule, with this question being one of them.

6. **Correct Answer (D).** *Prep Test 51, Section 1, Question 5.*

There is only one conditional statement in this argument, so there is no need to diagram it. The first premise states that there are only two options, while the second premise rejects one of the options. The argument concludes that the remaining option must be selected. This common one-viewpoint argumentative structure is called *rejecting alternative options*. The argument concludes that if only A or B can be selected, and B does not work, then we must select A. We can anticipate an answer choice with a similar structure.

(A) If there is to be an entrance on the north side of the building, it will have to be approached by a ramp. However, a ramp would become impossibly slippery in winter, so there will be no entrance on the north side.

This answer choice does not present options that can be rejected. It presents us with an action and concludes that this action cannot be undertaken. (A) is a loser.

(B) If visitors are to travel to this part of the site by automobile, there will be a need for parking spaces. However, no parking spaces are allowed for in the design. So if visitors are likely to come by automobile, the design will be changed.

Again, there are no options to choose from. This is also a loser.

(C) The subsoil in these five acres either consists entirely of clay or consists entirely of shale. Therefore, if one test hole in the area reveals shale, it will be clear that the entire five acres has a shale subsoil.

This is a very tricky answer choice. The stimulus claims that because it cannot be option B, it must be option A. This answer choice claims that since tests show that the subsoil is option A, then all of the subsoil must be option A. We do not arrive at option A by rejecting option B as we do in the stimulus. Therefore, (C) is a loser.

(D) Any path along this embankment must be either concrete or stone. But a concrete path cannot be built in this location. So if there is to be a path on the embankment, it will be a stone path.

This matches our anticipated answer choice. We are presented with two options. One option is rejected, and it is concluded that the other option must be selected. (D) is a candidate.

(E) A space the size of this meadow would be suitable for a playground or a picnic area. However, a playground would be noisy and a picnic area would create litter. So it will be best for the area to remain a meadow.

In this answer choice, the second premise does not eliminate an option; it provides a reason not to pick either option. The argument concludes that neither will be picked. (E) is a loser.

As (D) is the only candidate, it has to be the correct answer choice.

Parallel Fallacy

Parallel Fallacy

≈ 2.0 questions per test

Example Prompts

The flawed reasoning in the argument above *most closely parallels* that in which of the following?

The questionable pattern of reasoning in which of the following arguments is *most similar* to that in the argument above?

Take These Steps

Read the stimulus, which always includes an argument. Identify the main conclusion, subsidiary conclusions (if any), and premises. Consider the logical relationships between these parts to determine how the main conclusion is supported.

Determine the error in reasoning committed to reach the conclusion. The argument always includes a logical fallacy. If you do not recognize the fallacy type, create an abstract paraphrase.

Anticipate a correct answer choice that is an invalid argument containing the same fallacy as the one in the stimulus.

Answer Choices

Correct Answer Choices	**Incorrect Answer Choices**
Invalid arguments containing the same fallacy	Valid arguments
	Invalid arguments containing a different fallacy
	Invalid arguments containing the same general type of fallacy but a different subtype

Parallel Fallacy (PF) questions always include a stimulus with an argument, and the answer choices are short arguments. However, PF questions are fairly easy to solve. There is no need to match premises, terms, or other aspects of argumentative structure. It is only necessary to determine the fallacy in the stimulus and find the answer choice that commits the same fallacy. In a way, PF questions are an extension of F questions. Be sure to review the fallacies listed in the F question section of this chapter as they play an important role in PF questions.

How to Solve Parallel Fallacy Questions

As with an F question, the first step toward solving a PF question is to identify the various parts of the argument, including the premises, subsidiary conclusions, and main conclusion. Next, you need to consider their logical relationships and determine how the conclusion is supported.

Once you have done this, it is time to pinpoint which fallacy has been committed. If there are conditional or causal statements, you can expect to find a conditional or causal fallacy. If not, look for one of the other fallacies described earlier in this chapter. If the fallacy in the argument does not match any that you are familiar with, try to make an abstract paraphrase of the error of reasoning. Make sure that this abstract paraphrase is not too broad or narrow. However, you will rarely (if ever) have to make an abstract paraphrase because the fallacy almost always turns out to be one of those explained in the F question section of this chapter.

Let's look at an example:

My suspicion that there is some truth to astrology has been confirmed. Most physicians I have talked to believe in it.

The flawed pattern of reasoning in the argument above is most similar to that in which one of the following?

(A) Professor Smith was convicted of tax evasion last year. So I certainly wouldn't give any credence to Smith's economic theories.

(B) I have come to the conclusion that several governmental social programs are wasteful. This is because most of the biology professors I have discussed this with think that this is true.

(C) Quantum mechanics seems to be emerging as the best physical theory we have today. Most prominent physicists subscribe to it.

(D) Most mechanical engineers I have talked to say that it is healthier to refrain from eating meat. So most mechanical engineers are vegetarians.

(E) For many years now, many people, some famous, have reported that they have seen or come in contact with unidentified flying objects. So there are probably extraterrestrial societies trying to contact us.

The conclusion, that there is some truth to astrology, is stated in the first sentence. It is supported by the premise that most of the physicians the author has talked to believe in it. Does the premise support the conclusion? Not necessarily. The conclusion is based on the reliability of physicians with regard to whether or not astrology is true. Why would physicians be knowledgeable about this subject? This is an Inappropriate Authority Fallacy. We should seek an answer choice that includes this fallacy.

(A) Professor Smith was convicted of tax evasion last year. So I certainly wouldn't give any credence to Smith's economic theories.

This is an Ad Hominem Fallacy because it attacks the source of the argument instead of the argument itself (Smith's economic theories). (A) is a loser.

(B) I have come to the conclusion that several governmental social programs are wasteful. This is because most of the biology professors I have discussed this with think that this is true.

This matches our anticipated answer choice. (B)'s argument concludes that several governmental social programs are wasteful based on the opinions of most of the biologists the author has talked to. Social programs are not likely to have anything to do with biology, so this argument includes an Inappropriate Authority Fallacy. (B) is a candidate.

(C) Quantum mechanics seems to be emerging as the best physical theory we have today. Most prominent physicists subscribe to it.

This is a valid argument. The fact that most expert physicists subscribe to quantum mechanics over other physical theories is evidence that it is the best physical theory. Physicists are appropriate authorities with regard to quantum mechanics. (C) is a loser.

(D) Most mechanical engineers I have talked to say that it is healthier to refrain from eating meat. So most mechanical engineers are vegetarians.

This argument includes an Equivocation Fallacy. The argument jumps from the concept of *refraining from eating meat* to that of *abstaining from eating meat* (being a vegetarian). (D) is a loser.

(E) For many years now, many people, some famous, have reported that they have seen or come in contact with unidentified flying objects. So there are probably extraterrestrial societies trying to contact us.

This argument includes a Questionable Assumption Fallacy. First, one must assume that the UFO-related reports are true. Second, one must assume that because people have come into contact with UFOs, the hypothetical extraterrestrials are trying to make contact. (E) is a loser.

As (B) is the only candidate, it has to be the correct answer choice.

Looking at the Answer Choices

Like PR questions, PF questions include short arguments as answer choices. The correct answer choice is always an invalid argument containing the same fallacy as the one in the stimulus.

Incorrect answer choices may not even include a fallacy—that is, they may be valid arguments. In addition, they may be invalid arguments containing a completely different fallacy. A common trick is the inclusion of a fallacy that is of the same general type as the one in the stimulus, but that is a different subtype. For example, if both the stimulus and correct answer choice include a Part-to-Whole Composition Fallacy, an incorrect answer choice might include a Whole-to-Part Composition Fallacy.

Drill: Parallel Fallacy

Identify the fallacy in the argument below. Then, determine which of the short arguments that follow include the same fallacy.

The rich in this country are paying far too little in taxes. Because of tax loopholes, the top 1 percent are only paying an effective tax rate of 27 percent on their income, while the middle class are paying an effective tax rate of 30 percent. There is no reason why I, as a middle-class citizen, should be paying more taxes to the government every year than a billionaire! This is why we need tax reform immediately.

Fallacy Type: _____

	Parallel Fallacy?
1. Most of the dogs I have rescued from the animal shelter have had violent tendencies. Therefore, most dogs have violent tendencies.	
2. Automobile accidents kill more people each year than sharks do. Therefore, you are more likely to die from a car accident than a shark attack.	
3. The dinosaurs were probably killed by the emergence of small mammals, such as rodents. After all, the fossil record shows a proliferation of these small mammals around the same time dinosaurs went extinct.	
4. I was correct when I said I can eat more food than you. You only finished half of your order of ribs while I finished all of my onion rings.	
5. Teachers in this country should not complain about their salary being too low. After all, teachers in less-wealthy countries make far less money than teachers in this country.	
6. Cancer rates have been declining year after year. This is a good thing, because it shows that the number of people dying from cancer is decreasing.	

Drill: Parallel Fallacy — Answers

Fallacy Type: Proportion Fallacy

The argument includes a Proportion Fallacy; specifically, evidence about proportions is used to justify a conclusion about an absolute amount. The argument reasons that because the wealthy do not pay as high a proportion of their income as the middle class does, the middle class must be paying a higher absolute amount to the government.

	Parallel Fallacy?
1. **Most of the dogs I have rescued from the animal shelter have had violent tendencies. Therefore, most dogs have violent tendencies.** This includes a Sampling Fallacy. The argument uses information about a sample of dogs that are unlikely to be representative of all dogs to reach a conclusion about dogs in general.	No
2. **Automobile accidents kill more people each year than sharks do. Therefore, you are more likely to die from a car accident than a shark attack.** This includes a Proportion Fallacy, but one in which the premises are about an absolute number and the conclusion is about a proportion. This does not match the argument above. Here, the number of deaths from cars and sharks are used to infer that a person is more likely to be killed by a car than by a shark, without considering the relative frequency of these two events.	No
3. **The dinosaurs were probably killed by the emergence of small mammals, such as rodents. After all, the fossil record shows a proliferation of these small mammals around the same time dinosaurs went extinct.** This includes a Causation Fallacy. The argument mistakes correlation for causation. The fact that small mammals emerged in large numbers at the same time that dinosaurs went extinct does not mean that the emergence caused the extinction. Many other factors could be involved in the extinction, and it may have even caused the emergence of large numbers of small mammals.	No
4. **I was correct when I said I can eat more food than you. You only finished half of your order of ribs while I finished all of my onion rings.** This includes a Proportion Fallacy. The premise is about the proportion of an order that was eaten while the conclusion is about the absolute amount of food that can be eaten. This argument has the exact same fallacy as that in the argument above.	Yes
5. **Teachers in this country should not complain about their salary being too low. After all, teachers in less-wealthy countries make far less money than teachers in this country.** This includes a Comparison Fallacy. It is not clear whether the comparison between teachers in this country and teachers in less-wealthy countries is appropriate because there is a significant difference between the two groups—the wealth of their countries of residence.	No
6. **Cancer rates have been declining year after year. This is a good thing, because it shows that the number of people dying from cancer is decreasing.** This includes a Proportion Fallacy. The premise is about the proportion of people getting cancer while the conclusion is about the absolute number of people dying from cancer. The argument above includes the exact same fallacy.	Yes

Problem Set: Parallel Fallacy

1. A psychiatrist argued that there is no such thing as a multiple personality disorder on the grounds that in all her years of clinical practice, she had never encountered one case of this type.

   Which one of the following most closely parallels the questionable reasoning cited above?

   (A) Anton concluded that colds are seldom fatal on the grounds that in all his years of clinical practice, he never had a patient who died of a cold.

   (B) Lyla said that no one in the area has seen a groundhog and so there are probably no groundhogs in the area.

   (C) Sauda argued that because therapy rarely had an effect on her patient's type of disorder, therapy was not warranted.

   (D) Thomas argued that because Natasha has driven her car to work every day since she bought it, she would probably continue to drive her car to work.

   (E) Jerod had never spotted a deer in his area and concluded from this that there are no deer in the area.

2. We should accept the proposal to demolish the old train station, because the local historical society, which vehemently opposes this, is dominated by people who have no commitment to long-term economic well-being. Preserving old buildings creates an impediment to new development, which is critical to economic health.

   The flawed reasoning exhibited by the argument above is most similar to that exhibited by which one of the following arguments?

   (A) Our country should attempt to safeguard works of art that it deems to possess national cultural significance. These works might not be recognized as such by all taxpayers, or even all critics. Nevertheless, our country ought to expend whatever money is needed to procure all such works as they become available.

   (B) Documents of importance to local heritage should be properly preserved and archived for the sake of future generations. For, if even one of these documents is damaged or lost, the integrity of the historical record as a whole will be damaged.

   (C) You should have your hair cut no more than once a month. After all, beauticians suggest that their customers have their hair cut twice a month, and they do this as a way of generating more business for themselves.

   (D) The committee should endorse the plan to postpone construction of the new expressway. Many residents of the neighborhoods that would be affected are fervently opposed to that construction, and the committee is obligated to avoid alienating those residents.

   (E) One should not borrow even small amounts of money unless it is absolutely necessary. Once one borrows a few dollars, the interest starts to accumulate. The longer one takes to repay, the more one ends up owing, and eventually a small debt has become a large one.

3. Opposition leader: Our country has the least fair court system of any country on the continent and ought not to be the model for others. Thus, our highest court is the least fair of any on the continent and ought not to be emulated by other countries.

The flawed reasoning in which one of the following arguments is most similar to that in the opposition leader's argument?

(A) The residents of medium-sized towns are, on average, more highly educated than people who do not live in such towns. Therefore, Maureen, who was born in a medium-sized town, is more highly educated than Monica, who has just moved to such a town.

(B) At a certain college, either philosophy or engineering is the most demanding major. Therefore, either the introductory course in philosophy or the introductory course in engineering is the most demanding introductory-level course at that college.

(C) For many years its superior engineering has enabled the Lawson Automobile Company to make the best racing cars. Therefore, its passenger cars, which use many of the same parts, are unmatched by those of any other company.

(D) Domestic cats are closely related to tigers. Therefore, even though they are far smaller than tigers, their eating habits are almost the same as those of tigers.

(E) If a suit of questionable merit is brought in the first district rather than the second district, its chances of being immediately thrown out are greater. Therefore, to have the best chance of winning the case, the lawyers will bring the suit in the second district.

4. Dana intentionally watered the plant every other day. But since the plant was a succulent, and needed dry soil, the frequent watering killed the plant. Therefore Dana intentionally killed the plant.

Which one of the following arguments exhibits a flawed pattern of reasoning most similar to the flawed pattern of reasoning exhibited in the argument above?

(A) Jack stole $10 from Kelly and bet it on a race. The bet returned $100 to Jack. Therefore Jack really stole $100 from Kelly.

(B) Celeste knows that coffee is grown in the mountains in Peru and that Peru is in South America. Therefore Celeste should know that coffee is grown in South America.

(C) The restaurant owner decided to take an item off her restaurant's menu. This decision disappointed Jerry because that item was his favorite dish. Therefore the restaurant owner decided to disappoint Jerry.

(D) The heavy rain caused the dam to break, and the breaking of the dam caused the fields downstream to be flooded. Therefore the heavy rain caused the flooding of the fields.

(E) The power plant raised the water temperature, and whatever raised the water temperature is responsible for the decrease in fish. Therefore the power plant is responsible for the decrease in fish.

5. Evidence suggests that we can manufacture a car with twice the fuel efficiency of a normal car, and it has been shown that we can produce a car that meets safety standards for side-impact crashes. So we can make a car that does both.

The flawed reasoning in the argument above is most similar to that in which one of the following?

(A) Since there is no dishwasher currently available that uses energy efficiently and there is no dishwasher currently available that effectively cleans pans, no dishwasher currently available is well engineered. For, to be well engineered, a dishwasher must use energy efficiently and clean pans effectively.

(B) Kameko might catch a cold this winter and she might go outside without a hat this winter. Therefore, it is possible that Kameko will catch a cold because she goes outside without a hat this winter.

(C) Susan says that it is cold outside, and Nathan says that it is snowing; therefore, it is both cold and snowing outside.

(D) It is possible to write a best-selling novel and it is possible to write one that appeals to the critics. Therefore, an author could write a critically acclaimed novel that gains a large readership.

(E) There are machines that brew coffee and there are machines that toast bread. And it is possible to make a machine that does both. So there will someday be a machine that does both.

6. Books that present a utopian future in which the inequities and sufferings of the present are replaced by more harmonious and rational social arrangements will always find enthusiastic buyers. Since gloomy books predicting that even more terrifying times await us are clearly not of this genre, they are unlikely to be very popular.

The questionable pattern of reasoning in which one of the following arguments is most similar to that in the argument above?

(A) Art that portrays people as happy and contented has a tranquilizing effect on the viewer, an effect that is appealing to those who are tense or anxious. Thus, people who dislike such art are neither tense nor anxious.

(B) People who enjoy participating in activities such as fishing or hiking may nevertheless enjoy watching such spectator sports as boxing or football. Thus, one cannot infer from someone's participating in vigorous contact sports that he or she is not also fond of less violent forms of recreation.

(C) Action movies that involve complicated and dangerous special-effects scenes are enormously expensive to produce. Hence, since traditional dramatic or comedic films contain no such scenes, it is probable that they are relatively inexpensive to produce.

(D) Adults usually feel a pleasant nostalgia when hearing music they listened to as adolescents, but since adolescents often like music specifically because they think it annoys their parents, adults rarely appreciate the music that their children will later listen to with nostalgia.

(E) All self-employed businesspeople have salaries that fluctuate with the fortunes of the general economy, but government bureaucrats are not self-employed. Therefore, not everyone with an income that fluctuates with the fortunes of the general economy is a government bureaucrat.

7. Most of the employees of the Compujack Corporation are computer programmers. Since most computer programmers receive excellent salaries from their employers, at least one Compujack employee must receive an excellent salary from Compujack.

Which one of the following arguments exhibits a flawed pattern of reasoning most similar to the flawed pattern of reasoning exhibited by the argument above?

(A) Most gardeners are people with a great deal of patience. Since most of Molly's classmates are gardeners, at least one of Molly's classmates must be a person with a great deal of patience.

(B) Most of Molly's classmates are gardeners. Since most gardeners are people with a great deal of patience, some of Molly's classmates could be people with a great deal of patience.

(C) Most gardeners are people with a great deal of patience. Since most of Molly's classmates are gardeners, at least one of Molly's classmates who is a gardener must be a person with a great deal of patience.

(D) Most gardeners are people with a great deal of patience. Since most of Molly's classmates who garden are women, at least one female classmate of Molly's must be a person with a great deal of patience.

(E) Most of Molly's classmates are gardeners with a great deal of patience. Since most of Molly's classmates are women, at least one female classmate of Molly's must be a gardener with a great deal of patience.

Problem Set: Parallel Fallacy — Answers

1. **Correct Answer (E).** *Prep Test 57, Section 2, Question 8.*

Fallacy: Absence of Evidence

The psychiatrist concludes that multiple personality disorder does not exist because she has never encountered it in her practice. Her claim is that because she herself cannot prove that it exists, it must not exist. This is an Absence of Evidence Fallacy. Just because something has not been proven true does not mean that it must be false. We should anticipate an answer choice that includes this fallacy.

> **(A) Anton concluded that colds are seldom fatal on the grounds that in all his years of clinical practice, he never had a patient who died of a cold.**

This argument includes a Sampling Fallacy. Although it appears similar to the argument in the stimulus, there is a key difference—Anton does not claim that colds do not exist but rather that they are rarely fatal. He bases this claim on the fact that none of his patients have ever died of a cold. We cannot be certain that the patients he has encountered are representative of the general population. This answer choice is a loser.

> **(B) Lyla said that no one in the area has seen a groundhog and so there are probably no groundhogs in the area.**

Like the previous answer choice, (B) does not claim that groundhogs do not exist in the area. Instead, it reaches a conclusion about the likelihood of groundhogs being in the area. Absence of Evidence Fallacies are concerned with whether something is true or false, not whether it is likely or unlikely. (B) is also a loser.

> **(C) Sauda argued that because therapy rarely had an effect on her patient's type of disorder, therapy was not warranted.**

This argument includes a Strength Modifier Fallacy. The premise is a MOST statement and the conclusion is an ALL statement. An ALL statement conclusion must be supported by an ALL statement premise. (C) is a loser.

> **(D) Thomas argued that because Natasha has driven her car to work every day since she bought it, she would probably continue to drive her car to work.**

This argument assumes that what has been happening will continue in the future. There is no conclusion that something does not exist, based on a lack of evidence. (D) is another loser.

> **(E) Jerod had never spotted a deer in his area and concluded from this that there are no deer in the area.**

This matches our anticipated answer choice. Jerod has not seen deer in his area, so he concludes that deer must not exist in his area. In other words, he has not proved that a claim is true, so he concludes that it must be false. This has to be the correct answer choice.

2. **Correct Answer (C).** *Prep Test 51.5, Section 3, Question 20.*

Fallacy: Ad Hominem

The first sentence includes the *conclusion*, *because premise* structure. We should note the use of the word *should* in the conclusion. The argument concludes that the proposal to demolish the old train station should be accepted because the local historical society opposes it. The argument goes on to say that the historical society has no commitment to long-term economic well-being and that preserving the building creates an impediment to new development, a factor critical to economic health. While the argument provides a reason as to why the building should not be preserved (it creates an impediment to new development), the main support for this claim is that the historical society, which may be biased, opposes the destruction of the building. This is an Ad Hominem Fallacy, as the argument attacks the supporters of the claim that the building must be preserved instead of attacking the claim itself. We should look for an answer choice containing the same fallacy.

(A) Our country should attempt to safeguard works of art that it deems to possess national cultural significance. These works might not be recognized as such by all taxpayers, or even all critics. Nevertheless, our country ought to expend whatever money is needed to procure all such works as they become available.

There is no attack on the source of a claim in this argument. (A) is a loser.

(B) Documents of importance to local heritage should be properly preserved and archived for the sake of future generations. For, if even one of these documents is damaged or lost, the integrity of the historical record as a whole will be damaged.

Here too, there is no attack on the source of a claim. (B) is also a loser.

(C) You should have your hair cut no more than once a month. After all, beauticians suggest that their customers have their hair cut twice a month, and they do this as a way of generating more business for themselves.

This matches our anticipated answer choice. The claim that people should get their hair cut twice a month is attacked based on the fact that its source is beauticians, who have a possible bias. This is an Ad Hominem Fallacy. (C) is a candidate.

(D) The committee should endorse the plan to postpone construction of the new expressway. Many residents of the neighborhoods that would be affected are fervently opposed to that construction, and the committee is obligated to avoid alienating those residents.

This argument does the opposite of what the argument in the stimulus does. It supports a claim because of its source. (D) is a loser.

(E) One should not borrow even small amounts of money unless it is absolutely necessary. Once one borrows a few dollars, the interest starts to accumulate. The longer one takes to repay, the more one ends up owing, and eventually a small debt has become a large one.

There is no attack on the source of a claim in this argument. (E) is a loser.

As (C) is the only candidate, it has to be the correct answer choice.

3. **Correct Answer (B).** *Prep Test 47, Section 1, Question 21.*

Fallacy: Composition

The word *thus* indicates that the conclusion is that the highest court is the least fair of any country on the continent and ought not to be a model for others. The support for this is that the country has the least fair court system on the continent and this court system should not be the model for others. This is a Whole-to-Part Composition Fallacy. Just because the whole (the court system) has a certain quality does not mean that the part (the highest court) also has that quality. We should anticipate a correct answer choice that includes the same fallacy.

(A) The residents of medium-sized towns are, on average, more highly educated than people who

do not live in such towns. Therefore, Maureen, who was born in a medium-sized town, is more highly educated than Monica, who has just moved to such a town.

This argument includes an Equivocation Fallacy. The meaning of the phrase *on average* has shifted. Maureen is assumed to be more highly educated than Monica because she is a long-term resident of a medium-sized town. However, the premise states that residents of these towns are on average more highly educated. It does not state that all residents are more highly educated. (A) is a loser.

(B) At a certain college, either philosophy or engineering is the most demanding major. Therefore, either the introductory course in philosophy or the introductory course in engineering is the most demanding introductory-level course at that college.

This matches our anticipated answer choice. If the whole (a major in philosophy or engineering) is the most demanding major, that does not necessarily mean that a part of that whole (the introductory-level course) is the most demanding introductory-level course. This is a Whole-to-Part Composition Fallacy, and thus (B) is a candidate.

(C) For many years its superior engineering has enabled the Lawson Automobile Company to make the best racing cars. Therefore, its passenger cars, which use many of the same parts, are unmatched by those of any other company.

This argument includes a False Comparison Fallacy. The premise provides information about racing cars, while the conclusion is about passenger cars. Without additional information, we cannot say that one type of car the company produces is the best just because another type of car it produces is the best. (C) is a loser.

(D) Domestic cats are closely related to tigers. Therefore, even though they are far smaller than tigers, their eating habits are almost the same as those of tigers.

This argument includes a Questionable Assumption Fallacy. The argument assumes that just because tigers and domestic cats are closely related they have the same eating habits. (D) is also a loser.

(E) If a suit of questionable merit is brought in the first district rather than the second district, its chances of being immediately thrown out are greater. Therefore, to have the best chance of winning the case, the lawyers will bring the suit in the second district.

This argument includes an Equivocation Fallacy. The phrases *chances of being immediately thrown out are greater* and *the best chance of winning the case* are treated as if they have the same meaning. This is a loser.

As (B) is the only candidate, it has to be the correct answer choice.

4. **Correct Answer (C).** *Prep Test 56, Section 2, Question 7.*

Fallacy: Questionable Assumption

The indicators *since* and *therefore* make it easy to identify the premise and conclusion. The argument concludes that Dana intentionally killed the plant based on the premise that she intentionally watered the plant every other day and this action resulted in the plant dying. The word *intentionally* implies that Dana's purpose was to kill the plant, which is not supported by the premise. The assumption is that if you intentionally perform an action, you also intend for the consequences of that action to occur. This is a Questionable Assumption Fallacy. We should anticipate a correct answer choice containing the same fallacy.

(A) Jack stole $10 from Kelly and bet it on a race. The bet returned $100 to Jack. Therefore Jack really stole $100 from Kelly.

This answer choice does not involve a questionable assumption. (A) is a loser.

(B) Celeste knows that coffee is grown in the mountains in Peru and that Peru is in South America. Therefore Celeste should know that coffee is grown in South America.

This is also a valid argument. If Celeste knows that coffee is grown in Peru and that Peru is in South America, then she should know that coffee is grown South America. (B) is a loser as well.

(C) The restaurant owner decided to take an item off her restaurant's menu. This decision disappointed Jerry because that item was his favorite dish. Therefore the restaurant owner decided to disappoint Jerry.

This matches our anticipated answer choice. The restaurant owner decided to take an item off the menu, and the consequence was that Jerry was disappointed. The argument concludes that the restaurant owner decided to disappoint Jerry. Here, we have the same questionable assumption, that if you intend to do something (take an item off the menu), then you also intend for the consequences to occur (disappointing Jerry). (C) is a candidate.

(D) The heavy rain caused the dam to break, and the breaking of the dam caused the fields downstream to be flooded. Therefore the heavy rain caused the flooding of the fields.

This is a valid argument. If Heavy Rain CAUSE Dam to Break and Dam to Break CAUSE Downstream Flood, then we can link the two to conclude that Heavy Rain CAUSE Downstream Flood. (D) is a loser.

(E) The power plant raised the water temperature, and whatever raised the water temperature is responsible for the decrease in fish. Therefore the power plant is responsible for the decrease in fish.

This too is a valid argument. The premise states that whatever raised the water temperature is responsible for the decrease in fish. The first premise says that the power plant raised the water temperature, so the power plant must be responsible for the decrease in fish. (E) is a loser.

As (C) is the only candidate, it has to be the correct answer choice.

5. **Correct Answer (D).** *Prep Test 40, Section 1, Question 20.*

Fallacy: Selection

The word *so* indicates the conclusion that it is possible to make a car that both meets certain safety standards and has twice the fuel efficiency of a normal car. This is a Selection Fallacy. Being able to select option A or option B does not necessarily mean that both options can be selected at the same time. Let's look for a Selection Fallacy in the answer choices.

(A) Since there is no dishwasher currently available that uses energy efficiently and there is no dishwasher currently available that effectively cleans pans, no dishwasher currently available is well engineered. For, to be well engineered, a dishwasher must use energy efficiently and clean pans effectively.

This is a valid argument. If a well-engineered dishwasher must have two specific qualities, and no dishwasher has either of these qualities, then there are no well-engineered dishwashers. This is a loser.

(B) Kameko might catch a cold this winter and she might go outside without a hat this winter. Therefore, it is possible that Kameko will catch a cold because she goes outside without a hat this winter.

The conclusion states that it is possible that Kameko Outside Without Hat CAUSE Kameko Catch Cold. We cannot infer a causal relationship based on the premise that two separate factors are possible. This is also a loser.

(C) Susan says that it is cold outside, and Nathan says that it is snowing; therefore, it is both cold and snowing outside.

This matches our anticipated answer choice. The argument concludes that two options are occurring at the same time based on reports of two different options occurring. (C) is a candidate.

(D) It is possible to write a best-selling novel and it is possible to write one that appeals to the critics. Therefore, an author could write a critically acclaimed novel that gains a large readership.

This also matches our anticipated answer choice. The argument concludes that an author could write a novel with two qualities based on the premise that it is possible to write a novel with either quality. (D) is a candidate.

(E) There are machines that brew coffee, and there are machines that toast bread. And it is possible to make a machine that does both. So there will someday be a machine that does both.

The argument concludes that a machine will be built that has both qualities based on the premise that it is possible to make a machine that has both qualities. Just because something is possible does not mean it will happen. This is a loser.

We must now eliminate one of our two candidates. Looking back at (C), we can see it is wrong for two reasons. First, there is an issue with the relationship between the two options. In order for it to be snowing, it must be cold outside. Second, the premise does not state that each option is possible; instead, it present reports from two sources, Susan and Nathan. One or both of these individuals could be providing inaccurate information. We can eliminate (C).

(D) claims that two options are possible and then concludes that it is possible to have both at the same time. This matches the fallacy in the stimulus. (D) has to be the correct answer choice.

6. **Correct Answer (C).** *Prep Test 52, Section 3, Question 24.*

Fallacy: Conditional Reasoning

The argument concludes that books that do not present a utopian future are unlikely to be popular. The support for this comes from a conditional statement in the first sentence, indicated by the sufficient indicator *always*. The argument can be represented as

> P1: Books w/ Utopian Future → Enthusiastic Buyers
> P2: Gloomy Books Predicting Terrible Times → ~~Books w/ Utopian Future~~
> C: ~~Books w/ Utopian Future~~ → ~~Enthusiastic Buyers~~

It is important to use similar terms whenever possible. For instance, we should diagram *unlikely to be popular* as ~~Enthusiastic Buyers~~.

The argument includes a Conditional Reasoning Fallacy. The conclusion negates the first premise without flipping it (negated reasoning). We should therefore look for an answer choice that includes the same error in reasoning.

(A) Art that portrays people as happy and contented has a tranquilizing effect on the viewer, an effect that is appealing to those who are tense or anxious. Thus, people who dislike such art are neither tense nor anxious.

The first statement includes a conditional statement, which can be rephrased as "If art portrays people as happy and contented, then it has a tranquilizing effect on the viewer." However, the argument does not conclude with the negated version of this statement. This answer choice is a loser.

(B) People who enjoy participating in activities such as fishing or hiking may nevertheless enjoy watching such spectator sports as boxing or football. Thus, one cannot infer from someone's participating in vigorous contact sports that he or she is not also fond of less violent forms of recreation.

The premises are not conditional statements, so this argument does not include a Conditional Reasoning Fallacy. (B) is also a loser.

(C) Action movies that involve complicated and dangerous special-effects scenes are enormously expensive to produce. Hence, since traditional dramatic or comedic films contain no such scenes, it is probable that they are relatively inexpensive to produce.

This matches our anticipated answer choice. The argument can be outlined as

P1: Action Movies w/ Special Effects → Expensive
P2: Traditional Drama or Comedy → ~~Action Movies w/ Special Effects~~
C: ~~Action Movies w/ Special Effects~~ → ~~Expensive~~

The conclusion is an inference based on negated reasoning. The first premise has been negated but not flipped. (C) is a candidate.

(D) Adults usually feel a pleasant nostalgia when hearing music they listened to as adolescents, but since adolescents often like music specifically because they think it annoys their parents, adults rarely appreciate the music that their children will later listen to with nostalgia.

The premises are not conditional statements, so this argument does not include a Conditional Reasoning Fallacy. (D) is a loser.

(E) All self-employed businesspeople have salaries that fluctuate with the fortunes of the general economy, but government bureaucrats are not self-employed. Therefore, not everyone with an income that fluctuates with the fortunes of the general economy is a government bureaucrat.

This argument is a little tricky, so we will outline it:

P1: Self-Employed Businesspeople → Fluctuating Salaries
P2: Government Bureaucrats → ~~Self-Employed Businesspeople~~
C: Fluctuating Salaries ^{S}—^{S} ~~Government Bureaucrat~~

If we find the contrapositive of the second statement, we have two ALL statements with identical sufficient conditions. This allows us to infer a SOME statement between their necessary conditions. Note that *not everyone* is the same as *not all*, which can be treated as *some are not*. The argument is valid, making (E) a loser.

As (C) is the only candidate, it has to be the correct answer choice.

---

7. **Correct Answer (A).** *Prep Test 49, Section 4, Question 24.*

Fallacy: Strength Modifier

This argument uses a *since premise, conclusion* structure to conclude that at least one employee must receive an excellent salary from the company. Both of the premises are MOST statements. The argument can be outlined as

P1: Employees of Compujack $^M\!\!\rightarrow$ Computer Programmers
P2: Computer Programmers $^M\!\!\rightarrow$ Excellent Salaries
C: Employees of Compujack $^S\!\!-\!\!^S$ Excellent Salaries

The conclusion infers a SOME statement from the two MOST statement premises. However, this is a Strength Modifier Fallacy. Two MOST statements can only be combined when they have identical sufficient conditions. In this argument, the necessary condition of the first premise matches the sufficient condition of the second premise. These two premises cannot be combined. We should anticipate a correct answer choice that contains two MOST statement premises and a SOME statement conclusion.

(A) Most gardeners are people with a great deal of patience. Since most of Molly's classmates are gardeners, at least one of Molly's classmates must be a person with a great deal of patience.

P1: Gardeners $^M\!\!\rightarrow$ Great Patience
P2: Molly's Classmates $^M\!\!\rightarrow$ Gardeners
C: Molly's Classmates $^S\!\!-\!\!^S$ Great Patience

This matches our anticipated answer choice. The argument includes two MOST statements, each with a different sufficient condition, from which a SOME statement has been inferred. (A) is a candidate.

(B) Most of Molly's classmates are gardeners. Since most gardeners are people with a great deal of patience, some of Molly's classmates could be people with a great deal of patience.

P1: Molly's Classmates $^M\!\!\rightarrow$ Gardeners
P2: Gardeners $^M\!\!\rightarrow$ Great Patience
C: Molly's Classmates $^S\!\!-\!\!^S$ Could Great Patience

This is close to what we are looking for. The conclusion is a SOME statement inferred from two MOST statements, each with a different sufficient condition. However, the conclusion includes an additional element—the term *could*. The stimulus states that that some employees must receive excellent salaries, whereas the conclusion of this argument states that some classmates could have great patience. (B) is a loser.

(C) Most gardeners are people with a great deal of patience. Since most of Molly's classmates are gardeners, at least one of Molly's classmates who is a gardener must be a person with a great deal of patience.

P1: Gardeners $^M\!\!\rightarrow$ Great Patience
P2: Molly's Classmates $^M\!\!\rightarrow$ Gardeners
C: Molly's Classmate + Gardeners $^S\!\!-\!\!^S$ Great Patience

The conclusion of this answer choice is different from than that of the stimulus. Two terms are included in the sufficient condition rather than one. (C) is a loser.

(D) Most gardeners are people with a great deal of patience. Since most of Molly's classmates who garden are women, at least one female classmate of Molly's must be a person with a great deal of patience.

P1: Gardeners $^M\!\!\rightarrow$ Great Patience
P2: Molly's Classmates + Gardeners $^M\!\!\rightarrow$ Women
C: Molly's Classmates + Gardener + Women $^S\!\!-\!\!^S$ Great Patience

The structure of this argument differs from that of the stimulus. (D) is also a loser.

(E) **Most of Molly's classmates are gardeners with a great deal of patience. Since most of Molly's classmates are women, at least one female classmate of Molly's must be a gardener with a great deal of patience.**

P1: Molly's Classmates $^M\!\!\longrightarrow$ Gardeners + Great Patience
P2: Molly's Classmates $^M\!\!\longrightarrow$ Women
_____
C: Molly's Classmates + Women $^S\!\!-\!^S$ Gardeners + Great Patience

The structure of this argument does not match that of the stimulus. We can consider (E) a loser.

As (A) is the only candidate, it has to be the correct answer choice.

Agree/Disagree

Main Point
Fallacy
Description
Mini Description
Parallel Reasoning
Parallel Fallacy
Agree/Disagree

Agree/Disagree
≈ 2.8 questions per test

Chapter 4

Example Prompts

On the basis of their statements, A and B are committed to *agreeing* about which one of the following?

A and B *disagree* about the truth of which one of the following?

Which of the following most accurately expresses *the point at issue* between A and B?

Take These Steps

Read the first argument, identifying the premises, subsidiary conclusions (if any), and main conclusion.

Read the second argument, identifying the premises, subsidiary conclusions (if any), and main conclusion. Pay close attention to any expressions that indicate agreement or disagreement with claims in the first argument.

If there is not a clear point of agreement or disagreement or you cannot find a match for your anticipated answer choice, review each answer choice to determine whether the authors would agree or disagree with it. For Agree questions, anticipate an answer choice that both authors would agree with. For Disagree questions, anticipate an answer choice that one author would agree with and one author would disagree with.

For an Agree question, identify any points of agreement between the two arguments. For a Disagree question, identify any points of disagreement. If there is a single, clear point of agreement or disagreement, anticipate an answer choice that expresses this point.

Answer Choices

Correct Answer Choices	**Incorrect Answer Choices**
For Agree questions, statements both authors would agree with	For Agree questions, statements one author would disagree with
For Disagree questions, statements one author would agree with and one author would disagree with	For Disagree questions, statements both authors would agree or disagree with
	Statements for which the position of one or both of the authors is unclear (usually including irrelevant information, a claim that is too broad, a claim that is too narrow, or prescriptive language)

Agree/Disagree (A/D) questions always include two arguments presented by two different authors. Each author has a distinct position regarding a particular issue. The prompt asks you to identify the answer choice that expresses a point related to this issue that both authors would agree with or that one author would agree with and the other would disagree with. Thus, this question type has two subtypes: Agree questions and Disagree questions. Agree prompts include the word *agree* or a variation thereof, while Disagree prompts include the word *disagree*, the phrase *point at issue*, or some variation thereof. The same basic method can be used to solve both subtypes.

How to Solve Agree/Disagree Questions

Once you have read the prompt and determined whether you are dealing with an Agree or Disagree question, read the first argument and identify the premises and conclusion. Then, read the second argument, focusing on the points that either agree or disagree with those of the first argument. These may be related to the background information, premises, or conclusion of either argument. Keep in mind that there may be more than one point of agreement or disagreement, which makes it more difficult to identify the correct answer choice. When reading through the second argument, look for expressions that indicate agreement (such as *it is true that* and *it seems likely that*) or disagreement (such as *however*, *but*, and *on the contrary*). These may refer to points made in the first argument.

If you are able to identify a clear point of agreement or disagreement, you should anticipate a correct answer choice that states this point. Quickly scan the answer choices. If you find one that clearly expresses the point of agreement or disagreement, you can select it and move on. If not, you need to go through the answer choices one by one, determining whether the authors would agree or disagree with them. As you do this, write A or D on the left side of your scratch paper to indicate whether the first author would agree or disagree with the statement, and do the same on the right side regarding the second author. If it is unclear how an author would feel about a statement, write a question mark. If it is an agree question, the correct answer choice is the one with two As. If is a disagree question, the correct answer choice is the one with an A and a D.

Note that in rare cases, answer choices are phrased in a neutral manner, making it impossible to determine whether the authors would agree or disagree with them. Consider the following example:

> **John: Rich people do not have to worry about how to make ends meet. Therefore, having a lot of money invariably makes a person happy.**

> **Beth: But many wealthy people are not happy with their lives. Therefore, having money does not necessarily result in happiness.**

If this stimulus were for a Disagree question, a typical prompt and correct answer choice would be

> **John and Beth disagree about the truth of which one of the following?**

> **(A) Having money always makes people happy.**

Looking at this statement, we can clearly see that John would agree with it, and Beth would disagree with it. However, the question and answer choice could be something like

> **John and Beth disagree over**

> **(A) whether money always makes people happy**

The answer choice is worded in such a way that you cannot say whether the authors would agree or disagree with it. For these types of questions, the correct answer choice is often a clear paraphrase of the point of agreement or disagreement in the stimulus, making it easy to identify the correct answer choice without going through all of the answer choices. However, if you do have to review multiple answer choices, simply reword each one slightly to make a statement that each author would have to agree or disagree with. For example, the answer choice above could be rephrased as:

(A) money always makes people happy

Worded this way, it is clear that John would agree with the statement and Beth would not. Therefore, this would be the correct answer choice.

Let's look at a full example:

> Maria: Popular music is bad art because it greatly exaggerates the role love plays in everyday life and thereby fails to represent reality accurately.
>
> Theo: Popular music is not supposed to reflect reality; it performs other artistic functions, such as providing consoling fantasies and helping people create some romance in their often difficult lives. You should understand popular music before you condemn it.
>
> The dialogue provides the most support for the claim that Maria and Theo disagree over whether
>
> (A) most good art creates consoling illusions
> (B) some bad art exaggerates the role love plays in everyday life
> (C) art should always represent reality as it could be, not as it is
> (D) art need not represent reality accurately to be good art
> (E) popular music should not be considered to be an art form

Reading the prompt, we can see that this is a Disagree question. The first argument uses a *conclusion, because premise* structure to conclude that popular music is bad art. The term *thereby* indicates another conclusion—that popular music fails to represent reality accurately. This is a subsidiary conclusion meant to explain why popular music is bad art. Maria's argument is that because popular music greatly exaggerates the role love plays in everyday life, it fails to represent reality accurately, which means that it is bad art.

Theo's first statement is that popular music is not supposed to reflect reality. This is his conclusion, and he supports it by saying that popular music performs other artistic functions, such as providing fantasies and helping people create romance in their lives. He then states that Maria should understand popular music before she condemns it. This is background information.

Now that we are clear about the arguments, we need to find the point of disagreement. Theo does not actually disagree with Maria's conclusion that popular music is bad art; rather, he disagrees with the premise that supports her conclusion. He claims that popular music's failure to represent reality accurately does not make it bad art. The point of disagreement here is whether art can be said to be good or bad based on how accurately it represents reality. We can anticipate an answer choice that expresses this. Scanning the answer choices, we can see that (D) is a direct match. However, we will review all of the answer choices for practice.

?   **(A) most good art creates consoling illusions**   ?

We cannot say for sure whether Maria would disagree with this. It may be the case that art can contain both consoling illusions and fail to represent reality accurately. This statement is also too specific for Theo to agree with. We know he believes that art that offers consoling illusions is not necessary bad art, but does he believe that most good art creates consoling illusions? (A) is a loser.

A   **(B) some bad art exaggerates the role love plays in everyday life**   ?

Maria would agree with this. Maria claims that popular music exaggerates the role love plays in everyday life and that popular music is bad art, which means that some bad art exaggerates the role love plays in everyday life. However, we cannot say for sure that Theo would disagree with this. Theo believes that good art need not be realistic. But he may think that there is some bad art that is not realistic. Since we are uncertain about Theo's opinion, we can consider (B) a loser.

?   **(C) art should always represent reality as it could be, not as it is**   ?

We cannot know for sure where the speakers would stand on this statement because it is too broad. It concerns what all art should always do. Thus, it is too strong for Theo to agree with, and we do not know where Maria stands on the function of art in general. (C) is a loser.

D   **(D) art need not represent reality accurately to be good art**   A

This matches our anticipated answer choice. Maria would disagree with this statement. Her argument is that art that does not represent reality accurately is bad art, which is the exact opposite of this statement. Theo would agree with this statement, since he believes that art may be good or bad regardless of how accurately it depicts reality or whether it exaggerates the role love plays in everyday life. Because Maria would disagree with the statement and Theo would agree with it, (D) is a candidate.

D   **(E) popular music should not be considered to be an art form**   D

Maria states that popular music is bad art, which implies that she thinks it is a form of art. So she would disagree with this statement. Theo would disagree with this statement as well. He says that popular music performs other artistic functions, which implies that he believes that popular music is an art form. (E) is a loser.

As (D) is the only candidate, it has to be the correct answer choice.

Looking at the Answer Choices

The correct answer choices are either a statement that both authors would agree with (Agree questions) or a statement that one would agree with and the other would disagree with (Disagree questions). The position of each author with regard to a statement must be unambiguous. The most common trick answer choices for this question type are statements that fail to align with the position of one or both of the authors. Such statements often introduce new information or are too broad or too specific. If you can only say that an author would probably agree or disagree with a statement, it is incorrect. You must be able to say that an author would definitely agree or disagree.

Drill: Agree/Disagree

Underline the main conclusion of each argument. Then, indicate whether Tom and Vinny would agree (A) or disagree (D) with the statements below. If it is unclear, write a question mark.

	Tom: Jack Meeks is the greatest boxer who has ever lived. At the peak of his career, he went undefeated for a string of 27 fights, going up against the best fighters in his division. He may have lost later in his career, but he should not be judged on his fighting ability when he was close to retirement. Vinny: He lost to many fighters early in his career as well, which is important to consider. Jack Meeks was the greatest middleweight fighter who ever lived, but the middleweight division is notoriously less talented than other divisions. There have been many fighters in other divisions much more deserving of being called "the greatest boxer who has ever lived."	
Tom		**Vinny**
	Jack Meeks was the greatest middleweight boxer who ever lived.	
	Fighters should be judged on their fighting ability toward the end of their careers.	
	No fighter will ever be greater than Jack Meeks.	
	Jack Meeks could have beaten the average heavyweight fighter.	
	It is important to consider the early fights a fighter lost when assessing how great of a boxer that fighter was.	
	Jack Meeks went undefeated for a string of 27 fights.	
	The middleweight division is notoriously less talented than other divisions.	
	In the prime of his career, Jack Meeks was the greatest boxer who ever lived.	
	There are many other fighters besides Jack Meeks more deserving of being called "the greatest fighter who has ever lived."	
	Jack Meeks was in his prime during the end of his career.	

Tom: Jack Meeks is the greatest boxer who has ever lived. At the peak of his career, he went undefeated for a string of 27 fights, going up against the best fighters in his division. He may have lost later in his career, but he should not be judged on his fighting ability when he was close to retirement.

Vinny: He lost to many fighters early in his career as well, which is important to consider. Jack Meeks was the greatest middleweight fighter who ever lived, but the middleweight division is notoriously less talented than other divisions. There have been many fighters in other divisions much more deserving of being called "the greatest boxer who has ever lived."

Tom		Vinny
A	Jack Meeks was the greatest middleweight boxer who ever lived.	A
D	Fighters should be judged on their fighting ability toward the end of their careers.	?
A	No fighter will ever be greater than Jack Meeks.	D
?	Jack Meeks could have beaten the average heavyweight fighter.	?
?	It is important to consider the early fights a fighter lost when assessing how great of a boxer that fighter was.	A
A	Jack Meeks went undefeated for a string of 27 fights.	?
?	The middleweight division is notoriously less talented than other divisions.	A
A	In the prime of his career, Jack Meeks was the greatest boxer who ever lived.	?
D	There are many other fighters besides Jack Meeks more deserving of being called "the greatest fighter who has ever lived."	A
D	Jack Meeks was in his prime during the end of his career.	?

1. Antonio: One can live a life of moderation by never deviating from the middle course. But then one loses the joy of spontaneity and misses the opportunities that come to those who are occasionally willing to take great chances, or to go too far.

   Marla: But one who, in the interests of moderation, never risks going too far is actually failing to live a life of moderation: one must be moderate even in one's moderation.

   Antonio and Marla disagree over

   (A) whether it is desirable for people occasionally to take great chances in life
   (B) what a life of moderation requires of a person
   (C) whether it is possible for a person to embrace other virtues along with moderation
   (D) how often a person ought to deviate from the middle course in life
   (E) whether it is desirable for people to be moderately spontaneous

2. Carolyn: The artist Marc Quinn has displayed, behind a glass plate, biologically replicated fragments of Sir John Sulston's DNA, calling it a "conceptual portrait" of Sulston. But to be a portrait, something must bear a recognizable resemblance to its subject.

   Arnold: I disagree. Quinn's conceptual portrait is a maximally realistic portrait, for it holds actual instructions according to which Sulston was created.

   The dialogue provides most support for the claim that Carolyn and Arnold disagree over whether the object described by Quinn as a conceptual portrait of Sir John Sulston

   (A) should be considered to be art
   (B) should be considered to be Quinn's work
   (C) bears a recognizable resemblance to Sulston
   (D) contains instructions according to which Sulston was created
   (E) is actually a portrait of Sulston

3. Sherrie: Scientists now agree that nicotine in tobacco is addictive inasmuch as smokers who try to stop smoking suffer withdrawal symptoms. For this reason alone, tobacco should be treated the same way as other dangerous drugs. Governments worldwide have a duty to restrict the manufacture and sale of tobacco.

Fran: By your own admission, "addictive" is broad enough to include other commonly consumed products, such as coffee and soft drinks containing caffeine. But of course the manufacture and sale of these products should not be restricted.

The dialogue above lends the most support to the claim that Sherrie and Fran disagree with each other about which one of the following statements?

(A) The manufacture and sale of all drugs should be regulated by governments.
(B) Coffee and soft drinks that contain caffeine should not be regulated by governments.
(C) Agreement by scientists that a substance is addictive justifies government restrictions on products containing that substance.
(D) Scientists are not proper authorities with respect to the question of whether a given substance is addictive.
(E) Scientists and governments have a duty to cooperate in regulating drugs to protect the public health.

4. Logan: Newspapers have always focused on ephemeral matters while ignoring important societal changes. For this and other reasons, old newspapers are useless to both amateur and professional historians.

Mendez: But news stories, along with popular art, provide a wealth of information about what the people of an era thought and felt.

On the basis of their statements, Logan and Mendez are committed to disagreeing over whether

(A) newspapers accurately report the most important changes taking place in a society
(B) the study of previous eras should include investigations of the conventions of newspaper reporting
(C) popular art is an important source of information about what the people of previous eras thought and felt
(D) newspapers ought to focus more on the types of stories they have glossed over in the past
(E) newspaper reports from former eras are useful sources of material for understanding the past

5. Marc: The fact that the people of our country look back on the past with a great deal of nostalgia demonstrates that they regret the recent revolution.

Robert: They are not nostalgic for the recent past, but for the distant past, which the prerevolutionary regime despised; this indicates that although they are troubled, they do not regret the revolution.

Their dialogue provides the most support for the claim that Marc and Robert agree that the people of their country

(A) tend to underrate past problems when the country faces troubling times

(B) are looking to the past for solutions to the country's current problems

(C) are likely to repeat former mistakes if they look to the country's past for solutions to current problems

(D) are concerned about the country's current situation, and this is evidenced by their nostalgia

(E) tend to be most nostalgic for the things that are the farthest in their past

6. Taylor: Researchers at a local university claim that 61 percent of the information transferred during conversation is communicated through nonverbal signals. But this claim, like all such mathematically precise claims, is suspect, because claims of such exactitude could never be established by science.

Sandra: While precision is unobtainable in many areas of life, it is commonplace in others. Many scientific disciplines obtain extremely precise results, which should not be doubted merely because of their precision.

The statements above provide the most support for holding that Sandra would disagree with Taylor about which one of the following statements?

(A) Research might reveal that 61 percent of the information taken in during a conversation is communicated through nonverbal signals.

(B) It is possible to determine whether 61 percent of the information taken in during a conversation is communicated through nonverbal signals.

(C) The study of verbal and nonverbal communication is an area where one cannot expect great precision in one's research results.

(D) Some sciences can yield mathematically precise results that are not inherently suspect.

(E) If inherently suspect claims are usually false, then the majority of claims made by scientists are false as well.

7. Claude: Because of the relatively high number of middle-aged people in the workforce, there will be fewer opportunities for promotion into upper-management positions. Since this will decrease people's incentive to work hard, economic productivity and the quality of life will diminish.

Thelma: This glut of middle-aged workers will lead many people to form their own companies. They will work hard and thus increase economic productivity, improving the quality of life even if many of the companies ultimately fail.

On the basis of their statements, Claude and Thelma are committed to agreeing about which ones of the following?

(A) The quality of life in a society affects that society's economic productivity.
(B) The failure of many companies will not necessarily have a negative effect on overall economic productivity.
(C) How hard a company's employees work is a function of what they think their chances for promotion are in that company.
(D) The number of middle-aged people in the workforce will increase in the coming years.
(E) Economic productivity will be affected by the number of middle-aged people in the workforce.

1. **Correct Answer (B).** *Prep Test 51.5, Section 3, Question 7.*

This is a Disagree question. Antonio concludes that one loses the joy of spontaneity and misses certain opportunities by living a life of moderation. Marla begins her argument with the word *but*, indicating she disagrees with a point made by Antonio. She concludes that by never taking risks, one is not actually living a life of moderation. Marla does not address the merits of living a life of moderation but instead disputes Antonio's definition of what living a life of moderation entails (never deviating from the middle course and never taking great chances or going too far). Marla says a person who never risks going too far is not living a life of moderation. This is the point of disagreement—what is required for a person to live a life of moderation.

Looking at the prompt and answer choices, we can see that this question is one of the rare types we discussed previously—the answer choices are not statements each author would agree or disagree with. Instead, they are possible points of disagreement. Fortunately, after scanning the answer choices, we can see that (B) clearly states the point of disagreement we identified in the stimulus. This is the correct answer choice. However, we will go through all of the answer choices for practice.

A   **(A) whether it is desirable for people occasionally to take great chances in life**   ?

If we delete *whether*, this statement becomes one that the authors can agree or disagree with. Antonio would agree that it is desirable to sometimes take great chances, but it is unclear what Marla's position would be. Therefore, this is a loser.

A   **(B) what a life of moderation requires of a person**   D

As mentioned before, this is the correct answer choice. Antonio thinks that a life of moderation requires never taking risks, while Marla thinks that one must be moderate in one's moderation and therefore sometimes take risks. They disagree about what a life of moderation involves. Just to make sure, we could rephrase this as "a life of moderation requires that a person never take risks" to create a statement that the authors could agree or disagree with. Antonio would agree with the new statement, and Marla would disagree with it.

?   **(C) whether it is possible for a person to embrace other virtues along with moderation**   ?

Again, omitting *whether* creates a statement that the authors could agree or disagree with. However, we know neither author's position because this answer choice introduces new information. Other virtues are not discussed in the stimulus. This is a loser.

?   **(D) how often a person ought to deviate from the middle course in life**   ?

We can eliminate this answer choice without rephrasing it on account of the phrase *how often*, which makes the answer choice too specific. It is implied that Antonio believes that great chances should be taken, but we do not know how often he thinks this should be done. Marla never address whether one should or should not live a life of moderation or take chances. (D) is a loser.

?   **(E) whether it is desirable for people to be moderately spontaneous**   ?

Again, deleting *whether* gives us a statement the authors could agree or disagree with. However, neither has a clear position regarding this point. It is implied that Antonio thinks that it is desirable to sometimes be spontaneous, but it is unclear if Antonio thinks it is desirable to be moderately spontaneous. More importantly, we have no information about how Marla feels regarding the benefits of living a moderate life. (E) is a loser.

2. Correct Answer (E). *Prep Test 51.5, Section 3, Question 3.*

This is a Disagree question. Carolyn concludes that a portrait must bear a resemblance to its subject, implying that the conceptual portrait of Sulston is not actually a portrait (since fragments of DNA do not bear a recognizable resemblance to a subject). Arnold explicitly disagrees with this statement, stating that the object in question is a maximally realistic portrait because it holds the actual instructions according to which Sulston was created. The point of disagreement here seems to be whether or not it is necessary for a portrait to bear a resemblance to its subject in order to be a portrait. Looking at the answer choices, there does not seem to be a clear match, so we have to check them one by one.

?   **(A) should be considered to be art**   ?

Neither Carolyn nor Arnold discuss whether the object should be considered art or provide a definition of art. This is a loser.

A   **(B) should be considered to be Quinn's work**   A

Both Carolyn and Arnold credit the work to Quinn. There is no reason to believe that either would view this object as not being Quinn's work. (B) is a loser.

D   **(C) bears a recognizable resemblance to Sulston**   ?

This is similar to our anticipated answer choice. Unfortunately, while we know that Carolyn would disagree with this statement, it is not clear whether Arnold also think that the object does not have a recognizable resemblance to Sulston. He just says that a portrait does not need to resemble its subject. This may imply that he does not think the object resembles Sulston, but we cannot know his position with certainty. Thus, (C) is a loser.

A   **(D) contains instructions according to which Sulston was created**   A

Carolyn and Arnold would both agree with this statement. Carolyn states that the object includes Sulston's DNA, and Arnold states that it has the instructions according to which Sulston was created (DNA, in other words). This is a loser.

D   **(E) is actually a portrait of Sulston**   A

Carolyn would disagree with this statement. She says that a portrait must resemble its subject. The object consists of DNA fragments and, therefore, does not resemble its subject. So, it is not a portrait, according to Carolyn. Arnold would agree with this statement. He considers the object to be a maximally realistic portrait. This has to be the correct answer choice.

3. Correct Answer (C). *Prep Test 42, Section 2, Question 13.*

This is a Disagree question. Sherrie's conclusion is that governments worldwide have a duty to restrict the manufacture and sale of tobacco. Her support for this claim is that nicotine is addictive and that tobacco should be treated the same way as other dangerous drugs. Fran responds with an argumentative technique called *using a proposed line of reasoning to reach a ridiculous conclusion*. Fran argues that many products are addictive, including coffee and soft drinks, and it would be ridiculous for the government to restrict these products. The point of disagreement here is whether a product with addictive properties needs to be regulated by the government. Looking through the answer choices, it is clear that (C) expresses this point of disagreement. However, we will go through all of the answer choices.

? **(A) The manufacture and sale of all drugs should be regulated by governments.** ?

This is irrelevant information. Whether all drugs should be regulated is not discussed in either argument. (A) is a loser.

? **(B) Coffee and soft drinks that contain caffeine should not be regulated by governments.** A

Fran would agree with this statement. However, we cannot say with any certainty whether Sherrie would agree or disagree with it. (B) is a loser.

A **(C) Agreement by scientists that a substance is addictive justifies government restrictions on products containing that substance.** D

This has to be the correct answer choice. Sherrie's argument is based upon the idea that scientific agreement on a substance's addictiveness justifies government restriction of nicotine. Fran disagrees, claiming that if this statement were true, it would lead to coffee and soft drinks being regulated, which should not happen.

D **(D) Scientists are not proper authorities with respect to the question of whether a given substance is addictive.** ?

Sherrie uses scientific agreement on addiction as the basis of her argument, so we know that she would disagree with this statement. However, Fran does not mention scientists or who would have the authority to determine addictiveness. Therefore, this is a loser.

? **(E) Scientists and governments have a duty to cooperate in regulating drugs to protect the public health.** ?

This is irrelevant information. Neither argument discusses the duty of scientists and governments to cooperate. (E) is a loser.

4. **Correct Answer (E).** *Prep Test 40, Section 3, Question 16.*

This is a Disagree question. The phrase *for this and other reasons* indicates that what follows it is the conclusion and what precedes it is a premise. Therefore, Logan concludes that old newspapers are useless to both amateur and professional historians because newspapers have always focused on ephemeral matters while ignoring important societal changes. Mendez uses the word *but* to show that he is disagreeing with this conclusion and to introduce the evidence for his position. He claims that news stories provide a wealth of information as to what people of a particular era thought and felt. The point of disagreement between the two is whether old newspapers are useless for historians. Looking through the answer choices, we can see that (E) expresses this point clearly. We will go through all of them, though.

D **(A) newspapers accurately report the most important changes taking place in a society** ?

Logan explicitly disagrees with this statement in his premise. Although it is likely that Mendez would agree with this statement, we cannot say for certain because the inclusion of the phrase *the most important changes* makes the statement too specific. (A) is a loser.

? **(B) the study of previous eras should include investigations of the conventions of newspaper reporting** ?

This answer choice includes irrelevant information. Neither argument discusses the conventions of newspaper reporting, so we cannot determine whether Logan or Mendez would agree or disagree with this statement. Therefore, (B) is a loser.

? **(C) popular art is an important source of information about what the**   A
     people of previous eras thought and felt

Mendez would agree with this statement, but we do not know how Logan would feel about it because he does not discuss popular art. This is a loser.

? **(D) newspapers ought to focus more on the types of stories they have**   ?
     glossed over in the past

This statement includes prescriptive language, which is not present in either argument. In addition, it seems to be making a judgment about the role newspapers should take now or in the future, which is something neither Logan nor Mendez discuss. (D) is a loser.

D **(E) newspaper reports from former eras are useful sources of material for**   A
     understanding the past

This has to be the correct answer choice. Logan explicitly disagrees with this statement in his argument while Mendez explicitly agrees with this statement in his argument.

---

5. **Correct Answer (D).** *Prep Test 43, Section 2, Question 19.*

This is an Agree question. Marc claims that because people in the country look back on the past with nostalgia, they must regret the recent revolution. Robert disagrees, claiming that they look back with nostalgia at the distance past, not the recent past, and that the distance past was despised by the prerevolutionary regime. The point of agreement here is difficult to specify. It seems to be that both Marc and Robert agree that people of their country are looking back on the past with nostalgia, although they disagree on how far back in the past they are actually looking. As no answer choice clearly matches this, we have to look at each one.

? **(A) tend to underrate past problems when the country faces troubling**   ?
     times

This is irrelevant information. We do not know whether Marc and Robert feel that the people of their country underrate past problems. This is a loser.

A **(B) are looking to the past for solutions to the country's current problems**   A

This is related to our anticipated answer choice. And based on the argument, it certainly seems as if Marc and Robert think that people in their country are looking to the past for remedies to their ongoing problems. This is a candidate.

? **(C) are likely to repeat former mistakes if they look to the country's past**   ?
     for solutions to current problems

Again this answer choice introduces irrelevant information, making it impossible to determine whether Marc or Robert would agree with it. (C) is a loser.

A **(D) are concerned about the country's current situation, and this is**   A
     evidenced by their nostalgia

This is also related to our anticipated answer choice. Marc would agree with this because he believes that people in his country regret the recent revolution, which means they are concerned about the country's current situation. Robert would also agree with this because he believes that the people of his country are troubled and long for the distant past. (D) is a candidate.

> ? **(E) tend to be most nostalgic for the things that are the farthest in their** ?
> **past**

This answer choice is too specific. Marc makes no mention of this while Robert only talks about nostalgia for the distant past, not the most distant past. (E) is a loser.

We now must eliminate one of our two candidates. Looking back at answer choice (B), we may not be able to say with certainty that Marc and Robert would agree with it. The phrase *solutions to problems* is a little too specific. We can eliminate this answer choice. In contrast, (D) perfectly matches the arguments in the stimulus. (D) has to be the correct answer choice.

6. **Correct Answer (D).** *Prep Test 51.5, Section 2, Question 16.*

This is a Disagree question. Taylor states that 61 percent of the information transferred during a conversation is communicated nonverbally. This is background information. Taylor then concludes that this claim is suspect because precise claims can never be established by science. Sandra states that precision is unobtainable in many areas of life but is commonplace in others, such as in many scientific disciplines. Based on this, she concludes that one should not necessarily doubt a claim because of its precision. The point of disagreement here seems to be whether a mathematically precise claim is necessarily suspect. Looking through the answer choices, we can see that (D) is a match. However, we will go through all of the answer choices.

> A **(A) Research might reveal that 61 percent of the information taken in** ?
> **during a conversation is communicated through nonverbal signals.**

Taylor specifically states that this claim is suspect, meaning that it may or may not be true. He would agree with (A) because it includes *might*. Sandra does not address this claim, so we cannot know whether she would agree with it. (A) is a loser.

> D **(B) It is possible to determine whether 61 percent of the information taken** ?
> **in during a conversation is communicated through nonverbal signals.**

Taylor specifically states that this sort of precise claim is suspect and could never be established by science. Sandra does not address this claim directly, so we do not know her position. (B) is a loser.

> A **(C) The study of verbal and nonverbal communication is an area where** ?
> **one cannot expect great precision in one's research results.**

Taylor would agree with this, as he concludes that claims of this exactitude could never be established by science. However, we have no information about Sandra's position on this subject. Therefore, (C) is also a loser.

> D **(D) Some sciences can yield mathematically precise results that are not** A
> **inherently suspect.**

This has to be the correct answer choice. Taylor would disagree with this statement as he believes that all mathematically precise results are suspect. Sandra would agree with (D) because she says many scientific disciplines obtain extremely precise results, and these results should not be doubted based on their precision.

? (E) If inherently suspect claims are usually false, then the majority of ?
claims made by scientists are false as well.

This statement introduces irrelevant information. Neither argument discusses whether suspect claims are usually false, let alone whether claims made by scientists are usually false because suspect claims are usually false. (E) is a loser.

7. Correct Answer (E). *Prep Test 47, Section 1, Question 25.*

This is an Agree question. The first argument has a *since premise, conclusion* structure. Claude concludes that economic activity and the quality of life will decrease. His evidence for this claim is that there is a high number of middle-aged people in the workforce, which will result in fewer opportunities for promotion, decreasing people's incentive to work hard. Thelma argues that the glut of middle-aged workers will lead many people to form their own companies, thus improving economic productivity and the quality of life. The conclusions of these arguments are radically different, so we must look to the premises for a point of agreement. They both seem to agree that there is a high number of middle-aged people in the workforce. Looking through the answer choices, we cannot find one that clearly expresses this point. Therefore, we must go through all of them.

? (A) The quality of life in a society affects that society's economic ?
productivity.

This is irrelevant information. Neither argument directly addresses the relationship between quality of life and economic productivity. (A) is a loser.

? (B) The failure of many companies will not necessarily have a negative A
effect on overall economic productivity.

It is not clear whether Claude would agree with this statement as he does not discuss this issue. However, Thelma would agree with it. She believes that it is possible that many companies will fail but that economic productivity will still increase—meaning that the failure of these companies will not necessarily have a negative impact on the economy. (B) is also a loser.

A (C) How hard a company's employees work is a function of what they think ?
their chances for promotion are in that company.

Claude would agree with this statement because he believes that fewer opportunities for promotion will decrease people's incentive to work hard. However, it is not clear whether Thelma agrees that whether employees work hard or not is dependent on their chances of being promoted. We can categorize this answer choice as a loser.

? (D) The number of middle-aged people in the workforce will increase in the ?
coming years.

This is irrelevant information. Neither argument discusses whether the number of middle-aged people in the workforce will increase, decrease, or stay the same. (D) is a loser.

A (E) Economic productivity will be affected by the number of middle-aged A
people in the workforce.

Claude believes that economic productivity will decrease because of the high number of middle-aged people in the workforce. Thelma thinks the high number of middle-aged people in the workforce will cause economic productivity to increase. Although they disagree about the exact result of having many middle-aged workers, they both agree that it will affect economic productivity in some way. This has to be the correct answer choice.

Key Takeaways

38.54% of LR Questions

Example Prompts

MP: Which one of the following most accurately expresses the conclusion of the argument?

MP: Of the following, which one most accurately expresses the main conclusion?

F: Which one of the following most accurately describes a flaw in the argument?

F: The reasoning in the argument is questionable because it . . .

D: Which one of the following most accurately describes the method of reasoning?

D: The argument employs which one of the following argumentative strategies?

MD: Which one of the following most accurately describes the role played in the argument by the claim that ____?

MD: The reference to ____ plays which one of the following roles in the argument?

PR: The reasoning in the argument above most closely parallels that in which of the following?

PR: The pattern of reasoning in which one of the following arguments is most similar to that in the argument above?

PF: The questionable pattern of reasoning in which of the following arguments is most similar to that in the argument above?

PF: The flawed reasoning in the argument above most closely parallels that in which of the following?

A/D: Which of the following most accurately expresses the point at issue between A and B?

A/D: A and B disagree about the truth of which one of the following?

Main Point (MP) – 3.95%
Fallacy (F) – 14.64%
Description (D) – 2.37%
Mini Description (MD) – 4.15%
Parallel Reasoning (PR) – 3.95%
Parallel Fallacy (PF) – 3.95%
Agree/Disagree (A/D) – 5.53%

Common Argumentative Structures

Making a comparison or analogy
Applying a principle
Using an example
Undermining a premise
Challenging an assumption
Rejecting a claim on insufficient evidence

 The prompt directs you to identify and classify information presented in the stimulus. You must understand the relationships between the various parts of an argument.

Big Six Common Fallacies

Sampling Fallacy – Occurs when an invalid conclusion is reached about a group based on data gathered from an inappropriate sample

Selection Fallacy – Occurs when the fact that there may be other options to select from or two options cannot both be selected at the same time is not considered

Conditional Reasoning Fallacy – Occurs when an invalid inference is made based on conditional statements

Causal Reasoning Fallacy – Occurs when an argument concludes a causal relationship from a correlation

Equivocation Fallacy – Occurs when the meaning of a term or concept shifts, or two similar terms or concepts are used interchangeably

Questionable Assumption Fallacy – Occurs when an argument is not supported by its premises because contains a significant gap in reasoning

Correct Answer Choices

MP: Accurate paraphrases of the main conclusion

F: Accurate descriptions of the fallacy

D (one viewpoint): Accurate descriptions of the argumentative structure

D (two viewpoints): Accurate descriptions of how one viewpoint undermines the other

MD: Accurate descriptions of the function of a claim

PR: Arguments with the same argumentative structure

PF: Invalid arguments with the same fallacy

A/D (Agree Question): Statements both authors would agree with

A/D (Disagree question): Statements one author would agree with and the other would disagree with

Incorrect Answers Choices

Could Be False: Statements that could be false (MP, A/D)

Broad Claims: Claims that go beyond what is stated in the stimulus (MP, A/D)

Irrelevant Information: Information that is not relevant to the stimulus (MP, A/D)

Inaccurate Paraphrase or Description: Statements that inaccurately describe or paraphrase an element of the argument (MP, F, D, MD)

Incorrect Paraphrase or Description: Statements that describe or paraphrase the wrong element of the argument or an element that is not present (MP, F, D, MD)

Mismatched Arguments: Arguments that do not match the argumentative structure of the stimulus (PR) or that do not include the same fallacy (PF)

Chapter 5

Process Family

Chapter 5: Process Family

Process Family

In this chapter, you will learn how to identify and solve Process Family questions.

Process Family questions ask you to apply a specific process to the information in the stimulus. As you read the answer choices, you must assume each to be true and determine which answer choice correctly applies the process specified in the prompt to the stimulus. All Process Family questions include arguments except for Paradox questions, which usually include fact patterns.

The six question types in this family—Strengthen (S), Weaken (W), Evaluation (E), Sufficient Assumption (SA), Necessary Assumption (NA), and Paradox (P)—are examined in detail in separate sections of this chapter. Each section includes step-by-step instructions on how to solve the question type, detailed analyses of example questions, and drills to help you develop key skills. In addition, you will get to tackle practice questions taken from previous administrations of the LSAT. The methods for solving these practice questions are explained thoroughly in the answer key.

Strengthen

PROCESS FAMILY

Strengthen
Weaken
Evaluation
Sufficient Assumption
Necessary Assumption
Paradox

Strengthen
≈ 7.1 questions per test

Example Prompts

Which one of the following, if true, *most strengthens* the argument?

If true, which one of the following *most strongly supports* the argument?

Which one of the following, if true, *most helps to support* the argument?

Take These Steps

Read the stimulus, which will always include an argument. Identify the main conclusion, subsidiary conclusions (if any), and premises. Does the argument contain a causal conclusion?

No → Does the argument include an assumption, comparison, or fallacy?

ASSUMPTION | COMPARISON | FALLACY

Yes → Anticipate a statement that eliminates an alternative cause of the effect, has the same cause and same effect, or has no same cause and no same effect.

ASSUMPTION → Anticipate a clear statement that validates the assumption required by the argument.

COMPARISON → Anticipate an explanation of why the comparison is appropriate, why an option is favored, or why an option is disfavored.

FALLACY → Anticipate information that eliminates or greatly reduces the significance of the logical error in the argument.

Answer Choices

Correct Answer Choices	**Incorrect Answer Choices**
Statements that strengthen the argument	Statements that do not strengthen the argument
Statements that address a causal conclusion, assumption, comparison, or fallacy in the argument	Statements that weaken the argument
	Irrelevant information

Strengthen (S) questions ask you to select the answer choice that strengthens the argument in the stimulus. The correct answer choice usually addresses a specific weakness in the argument by providing additional support for the conclusion. Each answer choice presents new information. You must assume this information is true and determine whether it strengthens the argument.

Arguments always include one of the following elements (listed in order of frequency):

- Causal conclusion
- Assumption
- Logical fallacy
- Comparison

Note that there can be some overlap between the logical fallacy category and the others. For example, an argument with a causal conclusion may or may not include a Causal Reasoning Fallacy. However, this is not an issue when it comes to selecting the correct answer choice. The process for strengthening an argument with a causal conclusion, for instance, remains the same whether or not the argument also includes a Causal Reasoning Fallacy.

How to Solve Strengthen Questions

The first step toward solving an S question is to identify the argument's premises and conclusion. You must then determine how the conclusion is supported by the premises and identify weaknesses in the argument. As causal conclusions, assumptions, and comparisons are easy to identify, you should check for these elements first.

If There Is a Causal Conclusion

Arguments with causal conclusions are the type that appears most often in S questions. They are easy to identify because a causal conclusion always states that A CAUSE B. Remember, the word *cause* may or may not be present. There are a number of causal indicators, including

causes	because of
made	contributed to
leads to	responsible for
due to	was a factor
played a role in	result of
produced	reason for
effected by	achieved by

When an argument includes a causal conclusion, you can be confident that the correct answer choice provides evidence to support the cause-and-effect relationship expressed in the conclusion. This is the case even if the argument includes a Causal Reasoning Fallacy. As is discussed at the end of Chapter 2, an argument with a causal conclusion is valid if the conclusion has been arrived at by connecting the ends of a causal chain. If the first premise states that A CAUSE B and the second premise states that B CAUSE C, then the conclusion that A CAUSE C is valid. Whether the argument is valid or invalid has no bearing on the correct answer choice in an S question.

When a causal conclusion is present, the correct answer strengthens the argument by eliminating an *alternative cause*, presenting an example of *same cause, same effect*, or presenting an example of *no cause, no effect*. Consider the following:

At the start of the year, City X instituted a new traffic law that imposed hefty fines on drivers caught using mobile phones. This year, the number of traffic accidents has reached a record low, decreasing 30 percent since last year. It is clear that the reduction in accidents is due to the new traffic law.

This argument concludes that New Traffic Law CAUSE Reduction in Accidents because these two factors occurred during the same time period. In other words, it assumes causation from correlation, which is the first type of Causal Reasoning Fallacy discussed in Chapter 4. If this were a real LSAT question, we would anticipate a correct answer choice that strengthens the causal conclusion by presenting new information that falls into one of the three following categories:

Eliminate an Alternative Cause: The argument would be strengthened if it were shown that a potential alternative cause of the effect could not have been the actual cause of the effect. For example,

City X has not seen a decreased number of drivers on its roads.

This statement eliminates the possibility that the 30 percent decrease in accidents was actually caused by a decrease in the number of drivers (rather than the new traffic law). With the elimination of the possibility that this alternative factor was the actual cause of the reduction in traffic accidents, the argument is strengthened.

Same Cause, Same Effect: Introducing a similar case in which the same cause-and-effect relationship is present would also strengthen the argument. For example,

City Y also instituted a similar law this year and saw a reduction in traffic accidents.

This statement shows that the same cause-and-effect relationship occurred in a similar situation. This information would strengthen the argument.

No Cause, No Effect: Introducing a similar case in which the specific cause-and-effect relationship is absent would strengthen the relationship as well. For example,

City Z, which has not enacted any new traffic laws this year, has not seen a reduction in traffic accidents.

This statement demonstrates that the effect is unlikely to occur without the cause. This information would strengthen the argument.

Let's look at a full example:

On the Caribbean island of Guadeloupe, a researcher examined 35 patients with atypical Parkinson's disease and compared their eating habits to those of 65 healthy adults. She found that all of the patients with atypical Parkinson's regularly ate the tropical fruits soursop, custard apple, and pomme cannelle, whereas only 10 of the healthy adults regularly ate these fruits. From this, she concluded that eating these fruits causes atypical Parkinson's.

Which one of the following, if true, most strengthens the researcher's reasoning?

(A) For many of the atypical Parkinson's patients, their symptoms stopped getting worse, and in some cases actually abated, when they stopped eating soursop, custard apple, and pomme cannelle.

(B) Of the healthy adults who did not regularly eat soursop, custard apple, and pomme cannelle, most had eaten each of these fruits on at least one occasion.

(C) In areas other than Guadeloupe, many people who have never eaten soursop, custard apple, and pomme cannelle have contracted atypical Parkinson's.

(D) The 10 healthy adults who regularly ate soursop, custard apple, and pomme cannelle ate significantly greater quantities of these fruits, on average, than did the 35 atypical Parkinson's patients.

(E) Soursop, custard apple, and pomme cannelle contain essential vitamins not contained in any other food that is commonly eaten by residents of Guadeloupe.

The argument concludes that Eating Certain Tropical Fruit CAUSE Atypical Parkinson's, based on a correlation between the regular consumption of certain tropical fruits and the occurrence of the disease in adults. This is a typical correlation-to-causation error. We should anticipate a correct answer choice that eliminates an *alternative cause*, shows *same cause, same effect*, or shows *no cause, no effect*.

(A) For many of the atypical Parkinson's patients, their symptoms stopped getting worse, and in some cases actually abated, when they stopped eating soursop, custard apple, and pomme cannelle.

This matches one of our anticipated answer choices. It shows that when patients stopped eating the tropical fruit, the Parkinson's symptoms went away. This is a perfect example of *no cause, no effect*. (A) is a candidate.

(B) Of the healthy adults who did not regularly eat soursop, custard apple, and pomme cannelle, most had eaten each of these fruits on at least one occasion.

This answer choice actually weakens the argument by showing that the healthy adults also ate the tropical fruits on at least one occasion. This is a case of *same cause, no effect*, a method used to weaken an argument based on causal reasoning. (B) is a loser.

(C) In areas other than Guadeloupe, many people who have never eaten soursop, custard apple, and pomme cannelle have contracted atypical Parkinson's.

This answer choice shows *no cause, same effect*, another method for weakening an argument with a causal conclusion. (C) is a loser.

(D) The 10 healthy adults who regularly ate soursop, custard apple, and pomme cannelle ate significantly greater quantities of these fruits, on average, than did the 35 atypical Parkinson's patients.

This is another example of *same cause, no effect*, as the healthy adults consumed significantly more of the fruits than the adults who had Parkinson's. (D) is a loser.

(E) Soursop, custard apple, and pomme cannelle contain essential vitamins not contained in any other food that is commonly eaten by residents of Guadeloupe.

This information is irrelevant to the conclusion. It may explain why residents of Guadeloupe want to eat these fruits, but it neither strengthens nor weakens the claim that the fruits cause Parkinson's disease. (E) is a loser.

As (A) is the only candidate, it has to be the correct answer choice.

If There Is an Assumption

If the conclusion of an argument is dependent on a significant assumption for its validity, the correct answer choice is likely related to this. Whether or not the assumption can be considered a Questionable Assumption Fallacy does not matter (except for the fact that larger assumptions are easier to spot than smaller ones). You must identify the assumption required by the argument and anticipate a correct answer choice that validates this assumption.

Let's look at an example:

> Editor: Many candidates say that if elected they will reduce governmental intrusion into voters' lives. But voters actually elect politicians who instead promise that the government will provide assistance to solve their most pressing problems. Governmental assistance, however, costs money, and money can come only from taxes, which can be considered a form of governmental intrusion. Thus, governmental intrusion into the lives of voters will rarely be substantially reduced over time in a democracy.
>
> Which one of the following, if true, would most strengthen the editor's argument?
>
> (A) Politicians who win their elections usually keep their campaign promises.
> (B) Politicians never promise what they really intend to do once in office.
> (C) The most common problems people have are financial problems.
> (D) Governmental intrusion into the lives of voters is no more burdensome in nondemocratic countries than it is in democracies.
> (E) Politicians who promise to do what they actually believe ought to be done are rarely elected.

The word *thus* indicates the conclusion that governmental intrusion into the lives of voters is not likely to be reduced in a democracy. The premise that supports this claim is that voters elect politicians who promise that the government will provide assistance for their problems, and this assistance can be considered a form of governmental intrusion. The first sentence acts as a counter-premise—it states that candidates say they will reduce governmental intrusion.

This argument relies on an assumption. The premise speaks to what the politicians promise to do while the conclusion speaks to what will actually happen once they are elected. The fact that politicians promise governmental assistance does not mean that they will provide it once they are in office. We should anticipate a correct answer choice that states that if politicians promise something, they keep their promise once in office.

(A) Politicians who win their elections usually keep their campaign promises.

This matches our anticipated answer choice. If politicians who win their elections usually keep their campaign promises, the argument is valid. This answer choice explicitly states the assumption that underlies the argument. (A) is a candidate.

(B) Politicians never promise what they really intend to do once in office.

This answer choice states the opposite of what we anticipated, and it weakens the argument by implying that governmental intrusions may not occur. (B) is a loser.

(C) The most common problems people have are financial problems.

This information is irrelevant to the conclusion, which focuses on governmental intrusion. (C) is a loser.

(D) Governmental intrusion into the lives of voters is no more burdensome in nondemocratic countries than it is in democracies.

This is irrelevant information. The argument does not discuss nondemocratic countries. (D) is a loser.

(E) Politicians who promise to do what they actually believe ought to be done are rarely elected.

Like (B), this answer choice weakens the argument by stating that the politicians who promise to provide assistance for voters' most pressing problems are likely to renege. (E) is a loser.

As (A) is the only candidate, it has to be the correct answer choice.

If There Is a Comparison

If the argument includes a comparison in a premise or in the conclusion, you should anticipate a correct answer choice that strengthens the argument by explaining why the comparison is appropriate, why the favored option is favored, or why the disfavored option is disfavored. Note that when it comes to selecting the correct answer choice, it does not matter whether the comparison in the argument results in a False Comparison Fallacy.

Let's look at an example:

Skeletal remains of early humans indicate clearly that our ancestors had fewer dental problems than we have. So, most likely, the diet of early humans was very different from ours.

Which one of the following, if true, most strengthens the argument?

(A) A healthy diet leads to healthy teeth.
(B) Skeletal remains indicate that some early humans had a significant number of cavities.
(C) The diet of early humans was at least as varied as is our diet.
(D) Early humans had a shorter average life span than we do, and the most serious dental problems now tend to develop late in life.
(E) Diet is by far the most significant factor contributing to dental health.

This argument concludes that the diet of early humans was probably very different from that of modern humans. The evidence for this is that our ancestors had fewer dental problems than we have. The argument makes a comparison between the dental problems of two groups in order to conclude that the diets of these groups are very different. As this argument does not include a favored or disfavored option, we know that the correct answer choice must strengthen the argument by showing that the comparison is valid. Therefore, we can anticipate a correct answer choice that explains why dental problems are closely linked to diet.

(A) A healthy diet leads to healthy teeth.

This matches our anticipated answer choice. If a healthy diet leads to healthy teeth, it would make sense to assume that our diet is different from that of our ancestors since we have more dental problems. (A) is a candidate.

(B) Skeletal remains indicate that some early humans had a significant number of cavities.

If we assume that the phrase a *significant number of cavities* indicates more cavities than modern humans have, this answer choice seems to contradict the premise that early humans clearly had fewer dental problems than we have. In effect, the argument is weakened. Even if the phrase does not indicate that early humans had more cavities than we do, this answer choice does not strengthen the argument. Therefore, it is a loser.

(C) The diet of early humans was at least as varied as is our diet.

This is irrelevant information. The argument does not discuss the extent to which the diets are varied. (C) is a loser.

(D) Early humans had a shorter average life span than we do, and the most serious dental problems now tend to develop late in life.

This tells us that it is inappropriate to compare early and modern humans. (D) weakens the argument, so it is a loser.

(E) Diet is by far the most significant factor contributing to dental health.

This matches our anticipated answer choice. If diet is the most significant factor with regard to dental health, then it is appropriate to compare the two groups. (E) is a candidate.

We now need to eliminate one of the two candidates. Let's return to (A). There seems to be a slight issue with this answer choice—it only deals with a healthy diet and healthy teeth, while the argument discusses dental problems. Just because a healthy diet leads to healthy teeth, this does not mean that an unhealthy diet leads to more dental problems. It could be the case that neither group had healthy teeth, but early humans still had fewer cavities than modern ones. Because of this, we can eliminate (A) and select (E).

If There Is a Fallacy

If the argument does not include a causal conclusion, assumption, or comparison, it must include a logical fallacy. In this case, the correct answer choice presents information that eliminates or greatly reduces the significance of the error in reasoning. Therefore, the first step toward solving this type of question is to identify the specific fallacy in the argument. Then, you must determine what type of information is required to fix the error in reasoning. You should anticipate a correct answer choice that provides these details. All of the fallacies discussed in Chapter 4 appear in this type of question. However, the Big Six are the most common:

The Big Six	
Sampling	An argument reaches an invalid conclusion about a group based on data gathered from an inappropriate sample. To fix this fallacy, a correct answer choice must show that the sample is actually representative of the group.
Selection	An argument concludes that an option must be selected, based on the premise that there is a limited number of options to choose from. To fix this fallacy, a correct answer choice must show that the list of options is exhaustive or exclusive.
Conditional Reasoning	An argument includes a conclusion that is an invalid inference drawn from conditional statements. To fix this fallacy, a correct answer choice must provide evidence that the inference is valid.
Causal Reasoning	An argument concludes that one factor caused another, based on insufficient evidence. To fix this fallacy, a correct answer choice must provide additional evidence to support the causal conclusion. *See previous explanation on how to solve S questions with arguments that contain a causal conclusion.*
Equivocation	An argument includes an important term or concept that undergoes a shift in meaning or two different terms or concepts that are used interchangeably. To fix this fallacy, a correct answer choice must show that the term or concept is being used consistently or that the two different terms or concepts have the same meaning.
Questionable Assumption	An argument includes a logical gap that is not addressed or one for which there is evidence that it will not be addressed. The gap should be significant enough to make the argument invalid. To fix this fallacy, a correct answer choice must validate the assumption required by the argument. *See previous explanation on how to solve S questions with arguments that contain an assumption.*

Let's look at an example:

> TV meteorologist: Our station's weather forecasts are more useful and reliable than those of the most popular news station in the area. After all, the most important question for viewers in this area is whether it will rain, and on most occasions when we have forecast rain for the next day, we have been right. The same cannot be said for either of our competitors.

Which one of the following, if true, most strengthens the meteorologist's reasoning?

(A) The meteorologist's station forecast rain more often than did the most popular news station in the area.
(B) The less popular of the competing stations does not employ any full-time meteorologists.
(C) The most popular news station in the area is popular because of its investigative news reports.
(D) The meteorologist's station has a policy of not making weather forecasts more than three days in advance.
(E) On most of the occasions when the meteorologist's station forecasts that it would not rain, at least one of its competitors also forecast that it would not rain.

The meteorologist concludes that the station's weather forecasts are more useful and reliable than those of the most popular news station in the area. What is the evidence for this conclusion? The argument states that on most occasions when the station has forecast rain for the next day, it has been correct. This premise is about the proportion of accurate forecasts rather than the amount. The TV meteorologist is committing a Proportion Fallacy. For the conclusion that the station's forecasts are more useful and reliable than its competitors' to be valid, the station would need to have made at least the same number of forecasts as the competitors. We should anticipate a correct answer choice that fixes this Proportion Fallacy by providing this information.

(A) The meteorologist's station forecast rain more often than did the most popular news station in the area.

This matches our anticipated answer choice. If the meteorologist's station forecast rain more often and more accurately than did the most popular news station, the claim that the meteorologist's station is more useful and reliable becomes much stronger. (A) is a candidate.

(B) The less popular of the competing stations does not employ any full-time meteorologists.

This is irrelevant information. The argument does not discuss the employment of full-time meteorologists, and this information does not address the fallacy in the argument. (B) is a loser.

(C) The most popular news station in the area is popular because of its investigative news reports.

This is irrelevant information. We are not concerned with the stations' popularity or about programs other than weather forecasts. (C) is a loser.

(D) The meteorologist's station has a policy of not making weather forecasts more than three days in advance.

This would not strengthen the argument and could perhaps weaken it (people may not consider a forecast to be useful if it is not received very far in advance). We can consider (D) a loser.

(E) On most of the occasions when the meteorologist's station forecasts that it would not rain, at least one of its competitors also forecast that it would not rain.

This weakens the argument by showing that the station's forecasts match those of its competitors. (E) is a loser.

As (A) is the only candidate, it has to be the correct answer choice.

Looking at the Answer Choices

The correct answer choice is always a statement that strengthens the argument by presenting new information. It may provide details that support a premise in the argument or include an entirely new premise that supports the conclusion.

Incorrect answer choices often weaken the argument through the methods discussed in the next section of this chapter. However, you should note that incorrect answer choices do not have to weaken the argument—an answer choice is incorrect if it does not strengthen the argument. A common trick is the inclusion of irrelevant information in an incorrect answer choice. Many test-takers find such answer choices difficult to eliminate because they do not actually weaken the argument.

Drill: Strengthen

The following short arguments include causal conclusions. For each, write three statements using each of the following methods to strengthen an argument: eliminate an *alternative cause*, show *same cause, same effect*, and show *no cause, no effect*.

1. New research has shown that "joint cracking," or the routine bending of a person's joints to produce a cracking or popping sound, is responsible for the development of arthritis in that specific area in a person's later years. This was shown by survey data in which adults who suffer from arthritis of the hand were far more likely to report being frequent knuckle crackers in their 20s.

2. Over the last two years, Nation X has sponsored an aggressive ad campaign informing the public about the dangers of alcohol. This campaign contributed greatly to reducing alcohol consumption in the country. We can see this clearly because alcohol sales in the country are 15 percent lower this year than they were before the campaign.

3. The consumption of undercooked meat often leads to food poisoning or other acute illnesses. The neighborhood taco restaurant is known for employing cooks who do not know how to properly cook food or prepare meals. Therefore, Jerry's current food poisoning must have been caused by eating lunch at the restaurant that day.

1. **Causal Conclusion:** Joint Cracking CAUSE Arthritis

   Example of Elimination of an Alternative Cause: Adults who suffer from hand arthritis were no more likely to have jobs involving routine physical labor than adults who do not suffer from hand arthritis.

   Example of Same Cause, Same Effect: Evidence shows that adults who suffer from neck arthritis are much more likely than other adults to have cracked their neck joints when they were younger.

   Example of No Cause, No Effect: The same study shows that people who reported never having cracked their finger joints had an almost nonexistent rate of hand arthritis.

2. **Causal Conclusion:** Ad Campaign CAUSE Reduction in Alcohol Consumption

   Example of Elimination of an Alternative Cause: Alcohol sales accurately reflect the amount of alcohol consumption in Country X.

   Example of Same Cause, Same Effect: Surveys show that the people who were most frequently exposed to the ad campaign showed the largest decrease in alcohol consumption.

   Example of No Cause, No Effect: Country Y did not run an ad campaign during the same time period and did not experience a decline in alcohol consumption.

3. **Causal Conclusion:** Lunch at Taco Restaurant CAUSE Food Poisoning

   Example of Elimination of an Alternative Cause: Jerry did not eat any undercooked meat for breakfast.

   Example of Same Cause, Same Effect: Jerry's friend, Martha, who joined Jerry for lunch, also contracted food poisoning that day.

   Example of No Cause, No Effect: This was the first time Jerry ate at the restaurant and also the first time he suffered from food poisoning.

1. A typical gasoline-powered lawn mower emits about as much air-polluting material per hour of use as does an automobile. Collectively, such mowers contribute significantly to summer air pollution. Since electric mowers emit no air pollutants, people can help reduce air pollution by choosing electric mowers over gasoline ones whenever feasible.

Which one of the following, if true, provides the most support for the argument?

(A) Lawns help to clean the air, replacing pollutants with oxygen.

(B) Electric lawn mowers are more expensive to purchase and maintain than are gasoline mowers.

(C) Producing the power to run an electric mower for an hour causes less air pollution than does running an automobile for an hour.

(D) Most manufacturers of gasoline lawn mowers are trying to redesign their mowers to reduce the emission of air pollutants.

(E) Lawn mowers are used for fewer hours per year than are automobiles.

2. In contemplating major purchases, businesses often consider only whether there is enough money left from monthly revenues after paying monthly expenses to cover the cost of the purchase. But many expenses do not occur monthly; taking into account only monthly expenses can cause a business to over expand. So the use of a cash-flow statement is critical for all businesses.

Which one of the following, if true, most strengthens the argument?

(A) Only a cash-flow statement can accurately document all monthly expenses.

(B) Any business that has over expanded can benefit from the use of a cash-flow statement.

(C) When a business documents only monthly expenses it also documents only monthly revenue.

(D) A cash-flow statement is the only way to track both monthly expenses and expenses that are not monthly.

(E) When a business takes into account all expenses, not just monthly ones, it can make better decisions.

3. Poor nutrition is at the root of the violent behavior of many young offenders. Researchers observed that in a certain institution for young offenders, the violent inmates among them consistently chose, from the food available, those items that were low in nutrients. In a subsequent experiment, some of the violent inmates were placed on a diet high in nutrients. There was a steady improvement in their behavior over the four months of the experiment. These results confirm the link between poor nutrition and violent behavior.

Which one of the following, if true, most strengthens the argument?

(A) Some of the violent inmates who took part in the experiment had committed a large number of violent crimes.
(B) Dietary changes are easier and cheaper to implement than any other type of reform program in institutions for young offenders.
(C) Many young offenders have reported that they had consumed a low-nutrient food sometime in the days before they committed a violent crime.
(D) A further study investigated young offenders who chose a high-nutrient diet on their own and found that many of them were nonviolent.
(E) The violent inmates in the institution who were not placed on a high-nutrient diet did not show an improvement in behavior.

4. Renting cars from dealerships is less expensive than renting cars from national rental firms. But to take advantage of dealership rates, tourists must determine which local dealership offers rentals, and then pay for long taxi rides between the airport and those dealerships. So renting from dealerships rather than national rental firms is generally more worthwhile for local residents than for tourists.

Each of the following, if true, strengthens the argument EXCEPT:

(A) To encourage future business, many car dealerships drop off and pick up rental cars for local residents at no charge.
(B) Tourists renting cars from national rental firms almost never need to pay for taxi rides to or from the airport.
(C) Travel agents generally are unable to inform tourists of which local car dealerships offer rentals.
(D) Many local residents know of local car dealerships that offer low-priced rentals.
(E) For local residents, taxi rides to car dealerships from their homes or workplaces are usually no less expensive than taxi rides to national rental firms.

5. Everyone likes repertory theater. Actors like it because playing different roles each night decreases their level of boredom. Stagehands like it because changing sets every night means more overtime and, thus, higher pay. Theater managers like it because, if plays that reflect audience demand are chosen for production, most performances generate large revenues. It is evident, therefore, that more theaters should change to repertory.

The argument above would be strengthened if which one of the following were true?

(A) In a repertory theater, a large capital outlay is required at the beginning of each season.
(B) In a repertory theater, patrons need to pay overly close attention to the schedule in order to make their theater plans.
(C) In a repertory theater, storage space for sets for more than one production must be available.
(D) In a repertory theater, plays can be rescheduled to meet audience demand.
(E) In a repertory theater, some actors who change roles from night to night find it difficult to master all of the roles they play.

6. The supernova event of 1987 is interesting in that there is still no evidence of the neutron star that current theory says should have remained after a supernova of that size. This is in spite of the fact that many of the most sensitive instruments ever developed have searched for the tell-tale pulse of radiation that neutron stars emit. Thus, current theory is wrong in claiming that supernovas of a certain size always produce neutron stars.

Which one of the following, if true, most strengthens the argument?

(A) Most supernova remnants that astronomers have detected have a neutron star nearby.
(B) Sensitive astronomical instruments have detected neutron stars much farther away than the location of the 1987 supernova.
(C) The supernova of 1987 was the first that scientists were able to observe in progress.
(D) Several important features of the 1987 supernova are correctly predicted by the current theory.
(E) Some neutron stars are known to have come into existence by a cause other than a supernova explosion.

7. Historian: The Land Party achieved its only national victory in Banestria in 1935. It received most of its support that year in rural and semirural areas, where the bulk of Banestria's population lived at the time. The economic woes of the years surrounding that election hit agricultural and small business interests the hardest, and the Land Party specifically targeted those groups in 1935. I conclude that the success of the Land Party that year was due to the combination of the Land Party's specifically addressing the concerns of these groups and the depth of the economic problems people in these groups were facing.

Each of the following, if true, strengthens the historian's argument EXCEPT:

(A) In preceding elections, the Land Party made no attempt to address the interests of economically distressed urban groups.

(B) Voters are more likely to vote for a political party that focuses on their problems.

(C) The Land Party had most of its successes when there was economic distress in the agricultural sector.

(D) No other major party in Banestria specifically addressed the issues of people who lived in semirural areas in 1935.

(E) The greater the degree of economic distress someone is in, the more likely that person is to vote.

8. Therapist: Cognitive psychotherapy focuses on changing a patient's conscious beliefs. Thus, cognitive psychotherapy is likely to be more effective at helping patients overcome psychological problems than are forms of psychotherapy that focus on changing unconscious beliefs and desires, since only conscious beliefs are under the patient's direct conscious control.

Which one of the following, if true, would most strengthen the therapist's argument?

(A) Psychological problems are frequently caused by unconscious beliefs that could be changed with the aid of psychotherapy.

(B) It is difficult for any form of psychotherapy to be effective without focusing on mental states that are under the patient's direct conscious control.

(C) Cognitive psychotherapy is the only form of psychotherapy that focuses primarily on changing the patient's conscious beliefs.

(D) No form of psychotherapy that focuses on changing the patient's unconscious beliefs and desires can be effective unless it also helps change beliefs that are under the patient's direct conscious control.

(E) All of a patient's conscious beliefs are under the patient's conscious control, but other psychological states cannot be controlled effectively without the aid of psychotherapy.

9. There are 1.3 billion cows worldwide, and this population is growing to keep pace with the demand for meat and milk. These cows produce trillions of liters of methane gas yearly, and this methane contributes to global warming. The majority of the world's cows are given relatively low-quality diets even though cows produce less methane when they receive better-quality diets. Therefore, methane production from cows could be kept in check if cows were given better-quality diets.

Which one of the following, if true, adds the most support for the conclusion of the argument?

(A) Cows given good-quality diets produce much more meat and milk than they would produce otherwise.

(B) Carbon and hydrogen, the elements that make up methane, are found in abundance in the components of all types of cow feed.

(C) Most farmers would be willing to give their cows high-quality feed if the cost of that feed were lower.

(D) Worldwide, more methane is produced by cows raised for meat production than by those raised for milk production.

(E) Per liter, methane contributes more to global warming than does carbon dioxide, a gas that is thought to be the most significant contributor to global warming.

10. New evidence suggests that the collapse of Egypt's old kingdom some 4,000 years ago was caused by environmental catastrophe rather than internal social upheaval. Ocean sediments reveal a period of global cooling at the time, a condition generally associated with extended droughts. There were, no doubt, serious social problems in Egypt at the time, but they resulted from a severe dry spell.

Which one of the following, if true, would most strengthen the argument?

(A) Historically, most civilizations have succumbed to internal strife rather than external factors.

(B) The social problems in Egypt's old kingdom at the time of its collapse were serious enough to have caused the collapse.

(C) At the time of the collapse of the old kingdom, several isolated but well-established civilizations near Egypt underwent sudden declines.

(D) Egyptian records recovered from the time of the collapse explicitly refer to the deteriorating conditions of the society.

(E) Shortly after the collapse of the old kingdom, Egypt was thrust into a civil war that lasted most of the next two centuries.

Problem Set: Strengthen — Answers

1. **Correct Answer (C).** *Prep Test 45, Section 4, Question 7.*

   Element: Assumption

   The argument uses a *since premise, conclusion* structure to conclude that people can help reduce air pollution by choosing electric mowers over gasoline mowers. The argument supports this conclusion by claiming that a gasoline-powered mower emits as much air-polluting materials as an automobile and that an electric mower emits no air pollutants.

   This seems like a straightforward argument, but there is a slight disconnect between the premises and conclusion. The conclusion talks about reducing air pollution, but the premises talk about only one source of air pollution—the use of lawn mowers. The argument assumes that this is the only type of air pollution consumers should be concerned about with regard to lawn mowers. What about the air pollution produced through the manufacture of lawn mowers? Or the pollutants emitted when producing the power for an electric mower? Therefore, we should anticipate an answer choice that validates the assumption in the argument by stating that electric mowers do not significantly contribute to air pollution indirectly (i.e. in ways not related to their actual use).

   (A) Lawns help to clean the air, replacing pollutants with oxygen.

   This is irrelevant information. We are only concerned with which lawn mower produces less air pollution. (A) is a loser.

   (B) Electric lawn mowers are more expensive to purchase and maintain than are gasoline mowers.

   This too is irrelevant information. We are not concerned about which lawn mower is better value. We only care about which lawn mower produces less air pollution. (B) is a loser.

   (C) Producing the power to run an electric mower for an hour causes less air pollution than does running an automobile for an hour.

   This matches our anticipated answer choice. The argument states that running an automobile for an hour creates about as much air pollution as running a gasoline-powered lawn mower for an hour. If producing the power to run an electric mower for an hour creates less air pollution than running a car for an hour, then the electric mower may well produce less air pollution overall than the gasoline one. We can consider (C) a candidate.

   (D) Most manufacturers of gasoline lawn mowers are trying to redesign their mowers to reduce the emission of air pollutants.

   We are concerned with the current generation of mowers, not those of the future. This is a loser.

   (E) Lawn mowers are used for fewer hours per year than are automobiles.

   This is irrelevant information. We are not comparing lawn mowers in general with automobiles. We are trying to determine how much pollution electric and gas-powered lawn mowers produce. (E) is a loser.

   As (C) is the only candidate, it has to be the correct answer choice.

2. **Correct Answer (D).** *Prep Test 47, Section 1, Question 11.*

   Element: Assumption

   The word *so* indicates the conclusion that the use of a cash-flow statement is critical for all businesses. This is a strongly worded statement, and the premise does not seem strong enough to support it. The rest of the argument talks about the need for businesses to track nonmonthly expenses. However, the premises do not actually mention the role of a cash-flow statement. The assumption made by the argument is that a cash-flow statement helps business owners track nonmonthly expenses, and it is the only way to track these expenses. If there were another way to accurately track nonmonthly expenses, why would a cash-flow statement be critical for all businesses? We should anticipate a correct answer choice that validates this assumption.

(A) Only a cash-flow statement can accurately document all monthly expenses.

This is close to what we anticipated. However, we are concerned about whether a cash-flow statement is the only method for accurately documenting all nonmonthly expenses. While tracking monthly expenses may be important, the argument discusses how not tracking nonmonthly expenses can cause a business to over expand. (A) is a loser.

(B) Any business that has over expanded can benefit from the use of a cash-flow statement.

This may be true, but it does not strengthen the argument. The argument states that a cash-flow statement is critical for all businesses, and this includes businesses that have over expanded. (B) is a loser.

(C) When a business documents only monthly expenses it also documents only monthly revenue.

This is irrelevant information. The argument is concerned with nonmonthly expenses, not monthly revenue. (C) is a loser.

(D) A cash-flow statement is the only way to track both monthly expenses and expenses that are not monthly.

This matches our anticipated answer choice. It explicitly states that a cash-flow statement is the only way to track nonmonthly expenses. (D) is a candidate.

(E) When a business takes into account all expenses, not just monthly ones, it can make better decisions.

This answer choice does not strengthen the argument. The argument states that if a business does not track nonmonthly expenses, it will over expand (i.e. make poor business decisions). (E) is a loser.

As (D) is the only candidate, it has to be the correct answer choice.

---

3. **Correct Answer (E).** *Prep Test 41, Section 1, Question 12.*

Element: Causal Conclusion

The conclusion indicator *these results confirm* indicates that the last sentence, which is a restatement of the first one, is the conclusion. The first and last sentence use different expressions (*at the root of* and *the link between*) to indicate a causal relationship—Quality of Nutrition CAUSE Quality of Behavior. The evidence for this is the researchers' observation that when they gave inmates food with more nutrients, there was a steady improvement in behavior.

We should anticipate an answer choice that eliminates an *alternative cause* (for instance, that the inmates did not begin behaving better because of the possibility of early release), provides an example of *same cause, same effect* (such as an experiment at another institution that yielded similar results), or provides an example of *no cause, no effect* (such as a lack of improvement in inmates who did not undergo a change in diet).

(A) Some of the violent inmates who took part in the experiment had committed a large number

of violent crimes.

This is irrelevant information. The argument is not concerned with the number of violent crimes previously committed but rather with the effect of nutrition on behavior. (A) is a loser.

(B) Dietary changes are easier and cheaper to implement than any other type of reform program in institutions for young offenders.

This is a reason why inmates should be fed a different diet, but it does not strengthen the claim that Better Nutrition CAUSE Better Behavior. (B) is a loser.

(C) Many young offenders have reported that they had consumed a low-nutrient food sometime in the days before they committed a violent crime.

This matches one of our anticipated answer choices. It seems to be an example of *no cause, no effect*. (C) is a candidate.

(D) A further study investigated young offenders who chose a high-nutrient diet on their own and found that many of them were nonviolent.

This answer choice seems to be an example of *no cause, no effect*, but there are two problems. The first is that we have no information about the previous diets of the inmates who chose a high-nutrient diet. Additionally, we do not know if their behavior improved. Therefore, this answer choice does not demonstrate *no cause, no effect*. (D) is a loser.

(E) The violent inmates in the institution who were not placed on a high-nutrient diet did not show an improvement in behavior.

This matches one of our anticipated answer choices. The cause (a high-nutrient diet) is absent and so is the effect (an improvement in behavior). (E) is a candidate.

We now need to eliminate one of our two candidates. Looking back at (C), we can spot a couple of problems. First, this answer choice only discusses a specific low-nutrient food, which is different from a low-nutrient diet. An offender could have a high-nutrient diet and yet still consume a low-nutrient food. Second, we are looking at overall behavior during a period of time, not just one violent act days after a low-nutrient food was consumed. Therefore, (C) can be eliminated and we can select (E).

4. **Correct Answer (E).** *Prep Test 41, Section 3, Question 19.*

Element: Comparison

The word *so* indicates the conclusion that renting from a dealership is more beneficial for local residents than for tourists. The evidence for this is in the first two sentences, which state that renting cars from dealerships is cheaper, but tourists must be able to determine which dealerships offer rentals and then pay for long taxi rides between the airport and those dealerships. The argument compares local residents who rent from dealerships and tourists who rent from dealerships.

In order to strengthen this comparison, an answer choice must show why the comparison is appropriate, why one option (local residents who rent from dealerships) is favored, or why one option (tourists who rent from dealerships) is disfavored. Since this is a EXCEPT question, we should expect the four incorrect answer choices to strengthen the argument and the correct answer choice to not strengthen the argument.

(A) To encourage future business, many car dealerships drop off and pick up rental cars for local residents at no charge.

This strengthens the argument by showing that local residents do not have to take long taxi rides to rent cars from dealerships while tourists do. (A) is a loser.

(B) Tourists renting cars from national rental firms almost never need to pay for taxi rides to or from the airport.

This strengthens the argument by showing that tourists do not have to pay for taxi rides to or from the airport when renting from national rental firms (but they do when renting from car dealerships). (B) is a loser.

(C) Travel agents generally are unable to inform tourists of which local car dealerships offer rentals.

This answer choice strengthens the argument because it provides additional information to show that tourists face challenges in determining which local car dealerships offer rentals. (C) is therefore a loser.

(D) Many local residents know of local car dealerships that offer low-priced rentals.

This answer choice strengthens the argument. If local residents know which local car dealerships offer rentals, then they do not face the same challenges as tourists do, and renting from a car dealership is more worthwhile for them than it is for tourists. (D) is a loser.

(E) For local residents, taxi rides to car dealerships from their homes or workplaces are usually no less expensive than taxi rides to national rental firms.

This answer choice does not strengthen the argument. The fact that taxi rides to car dealerships are the same price or more expensive than rides to national rental firms does not support the conclusion that renting from car dealerships is more worthwhile for local residents than it is for tourists. This has to be the correct answer.

5. **Correct Answer (D).** *Prep Test 40, Section 3, Question 8.*

Element: Assumption

The phrase *it is evident, therefore* indicates that the argument's main conclusion is that more theaters should change to repertory. The subsidiary conclusion that everyone likes repertory theater is presented in the first sentence. This is supported by the premises that state that actors, stagehands, and theater managers all like repertory theater. However, the premise about theater managers is a bit different from the others—it involves a conditional statement. The claim is that theater managers like repertory theater because if plays that reflect audience demand are chosen, most performances generate large revenues. This can be diagrammed as follows:

Plays that Show Audience Demand Chosen $\overset{M}{\longrightarrow}$ Large Revenues

The conditional statement is important because it indicates that theater managers only like repertory theater if plays that reflect audience demand are chosen for production. However, since the subsidiary conclusion states that everyone likes repertory theaters, the argument makes the assumption that plays that reflect audience demand can be chosen for production. We can anticipate a correct answer choice that validates this assumption.

(A) In a repertory theater, a large capital outlay is required at the beginning of each season.

This would weaken the argument because it is a reason not to change to repertory theater. (A) is a loser.

(B) In a repertory theater, patrons need to pay overly close attention to the schedule in order to make their theater plans.

This provides another reason against changing to repertory theater. (B) is a loser.

(C) In a repertory theater, storage space for sets for more than one production must be available.

This is yet another reason against changing to repertory theater. This answer choice is a loser.

(D) In a repertory theater, plays can be rescheduled to meet audience demand.

This matches our anticipated answer choice. (D) states that the plays in question can be rescheduled to meet audience demand. This means that plays that reflect audience demand can be produced, and thus theater managers are sure to favor repertory theater. (D) is a candidate.

(E) In a repertory theater, some actors who change roles from night to night find it difficult to master all of the roles they play.

This is another reason why theaters should not change to repertory. (E) weakens the argument, so it is a loser.

As (D) is the only candidate, it has to be the correct answer choice.

6. **Correct Answer (B).** *Prep Test 51, Section 1, Question 24.*

Element: Fallacy

The argument concludes that the current theory is wrong in claiming that neutron stars are left behind by supernovas of a certain size. The argument's premise is that there is no evidence of a neutron star being produced by a supernova event in 1987, even though the most sensitive instruments ever developed have searched for the neutron star. While this may seem like a good argument, the argument actually commits an Absence of Evidence Fallacy by concluding that the neutron star does not exist because of a lack of evidence of its existence. We should anticipate a correct answer choice that fixes this fallacy. The answer will likely account for why the absence of evidence is actually strong evidence that the neutron star does not exist.

(A) Most supernova remnants that astronomers have detected have a neutron star nearby.

This would weaken the argument because it is evidence that the scientists' claim that a supernova is always accompanied by a neutron star is correct. (A) is a loser.

(B) Sensitive astronomical instruments have detected neutron stars much farther away than the location of the 1987 supernova.

This matches our anticipated answer choice. It is a reason for why the absence of evidence is actually evidence that the neutron star does not exist. If instruments have detected neutron stars farther away than the 1987 supernova, then these instruments should be able to detect the neutron star that would supposedly remain after the 1987 supernova. (B) is a candidate.

(C) The supernova of 1987 was the first that scientists were able to observe in progress.

This is irrelevant information. The fact that this was the first supernova observed in progress has nothing to do with the absence of the neutron star. (C) is a loser.

(D) Several important features of the 1987 supernova are correctly predicted by the current theory.

This is irrelevant information. The conclusion is that one aspect of the current theory is incorrect (i.e. that a supernova always produces a neutron star). (D) is a loser.

(E) **Some neutron stars are known to have come into existence by a cause other than a supernova explosion.**

This too is irrelevant information. The argument is about neutrons stars created by supernovas. (E) is a loser.

As (B) is the only candidate, it has to be the correct answer choice.

---

7. **Correct Answer (A).** *Prep Test 51.5, Section 2, Question 19.*

Element: Causal Conclusion

This historian concludes that the Land Party's victory in 1935 was due to its strategy of addressing the concerns of groups hit hardest by economic woes in Banestria. This is a causal conclusion that can be expressed as Land Party Strategy CAUSE Victory. The evidence for this is that the Land Party specifically targeted the rural and semirural areas where agricultural and small business interests were hit hardest economically, and it won the election. An answer choice that strengthens this causal conclusion must eliminate an *alternative cause* (for instance, that the party did not have a charismatic candidate), provide an example of *same cause, same effect* (such as another party that used the same strategy and won an election), or provide an example of *no cause, no effect* (such as another party that did not use the same strategy and lost an election).

This is a Strengthen EXCEPT question, meaning there are four incorrect answers that strengthen the argument and one correct answer that does not strengthen the argument.

(A) **In preceding elections, the Land Party made no attempt to address the interests of economically distressed urban groups.**

At first glance, this seems like it might be an example of *no cause, no effect*. However, this answer choice focuses on urban groups, not rural groups. The fact that the Land Party did not address the interests of urban groups does not strengthen (or weaken) the argument, as the conclusion is that the appeal to rural groups caused the party's victory. (A) is a candidate.

(B) **Voters are more likely to vote for a political party that focuses on their problems.**

This strengthens the argument by accounting for why the strategy of focusing on rural groups would result in support from that group. (B) is a loser.

(C) **The Land Party had most of its successes when there was economic distress in the agricultural sector.**

This strengthens the argument because the Land Party targeted agricultural groups at a time when they were facing economic problems. (C) is a loser.

(D) **No other major party in Banestria specifically addressed the issues of people who lived in semirural areas in 1935.**

This strengthens the argument by providing an example of *no cause, no effect*. The other major parties did not use the Land Party's strategy and did not win a national victory. (D) is a loser.

(E) **The greater the degree of economic distress someone is in, the more likely that person is to vote.**

This strengthens the argument. It accounts for why the Land Party's strategy was effective. (E) is a loser.

As (A) is the only candidate, it has to be the correct answer choice.

8. **Correct Answer (B).** *Prep Test 51.5, Section 3, Question 13.*

Element: Assumption

In this argument, the therapist concludes that cognitive psychotherapy is likely to be more effective at helping patients overcome problems than forms of psychotherapy that focus on changing unconscious beliefs. The reasoning for this is that cognitive psychotherapy focuses on changing a patient's conscious beliefs, and only conscious beliefs are under the patient's direct control. How exactly does being under a patient's direct control make a form of psychotherapy effective? The argument makes a major assumption here, as can be seen in the following outline:

P1: CT focuses on conscious beliefs.
P2: People can only control conscious beliefs.
A: (The ability to control conscious beliefs makes therapy effective.)
C: CT is more effective than other forms of therapy.

We should anticipate a correct answer choice that validates the assumption in the argument.

(A) Psychological problems are frequently caused by unconscious beliefs that could be changed with the aid of psychotherapy.

This would weaken the argument by invalidating the assumption. If unconscious beliefs can be changed, and doing so can help people overcome psychological problems, then cognitive psychotherapy cannot be more effective than other forms of therapy. (A) is a loser.

(B) It is difficult for any form of psychotherapy to be effective without focusing on mental states that are under the patient's direct conscious control.

This matches our anticipated answer choice. It expresses the assumption that needs to be made in order for the conclusion to be valid. (B) is a candidate.

(C) Cognitive psychotherapy is the only form of psychotherapy that focuses primarily on changing the patient's conscious beliefs.

For this answer choice to strengthen the argument, we would have to assume that a form of therapy that focuses on changing a patient's conscious beliefs is effective. As this is the assumption we are trying to validate, (C) is a loser.

(D) No form of psychotherapy that focuses on changing the patient's unconscious beliefs and desires can be effective unless it also helps change beliefs that are under the patient's direct conscious control.

This would not strengthen the argument. This answer choice can be rephrased as "A form of psychotherapy that focuses on changing one's unconscious beliefs cannot be effective if it does not change a patient's conscious beliefs." This would explain why forms of psychotherapy that focus on unconscious beliefs may not be effective, but it would not explain why cognitive psychotherapy, which focuses on conscious beliefs, is more or less effective. (D) is a loser.

(E) All of a patient's conscious beliefs are under the patient's conscious control, but other psychological states cannot be controlled effectively without the aid of psychotherapy.

This is irrelevant information. The fact that psychological states other than conscious beliefs cannot be controlled without the aid of psychotherapy does not strengthen the argument. (E) is a loser.

As (B) is the only candidate, it has to be the correct answer choice.

9. **Correct Answer (A).** *Prep Test 54, Section 2, Question 24.*

Element: Assumption

The word *therefore* indicates that the argument's conclusion is that if cows had better-quality diets, methane production from cows could be kept in check. The argument supports this by claiming that cows produce less methane when they have a better-quality diet. This seems like a simple, straightforward argument. There is no causal conclusion, major assumption, comparison, or fallacy. It is hard to anticipate an answer choice for this question, so let's go straight to the answer choices.

(A) Cows given good-quality diets produce much more meat and milk than they would produce otherwise.

At first, this answer choice seems irrelevant. Why would we care about meat and milk when we are focusing on methane production? However, this answer choice actually addresses a minor assumption required by the argument. If a good-quality diet made cows produce less meat and milk, we would need to have more cows in order to keep pace with the demand for meat and milk. Therefore, even if each cow produced less methane, an increase in the number of cows might prevent an overall decrease in methane production. This answer choice validates the assumption in the argument that changing the diet of cows to reduce methane production would not negatively affect meat and milk production. (A) is a candidate.

(B) Carbon and hydrogen, the elements that make up methane, are found in abundance in the components of all types of cow feed.

This answer choice does not strengthen the argument and may actually weaken it. If the components of methane were found in abundance in all types of cow feed, changing cows' diets would be less likely to limit methane production. (B) is a loser.

(C) Most farmers would be willing to give their cows high-quality feed if the cost of that feed were lower.

This is irrelevant information. The argument does not discuss the feasibility of giving cows high-quality feed, just whether doing so would keep methane production in check. (C) is a loser.

(D) Worldwide, more methane is produced by cows raised for meat production than by those raised for milk production.

This is irrelevant information. The argument does not differentiate between milk cows and beef cattle, so this is a loser.

(E) Per liter, methane contributes more to global warming than does carbon dioxide, a gas that is thought to be the most significant contributor to global warming.

This is irrelevant. The mention of global warming in the argument only serves as background information. The conclusion is about cow diets and methane production. (E) is a loser.

As (A) is the only candidate, it has to be the correct answer choice.

10. **Correct Answer (C).** *Prep Test 40, Section 3, Question 24.*

Element: Causal Conclusion

The phrase *they resulted from* indicates a causal conclusion. The causal conclusion, which restates the first sentence of the argument, is that Environmental Catastrophe CAUSE Old Kingdom Collapse. We should anticipate a correct answer choice that eliminates an *alternative cause* (for instance, that the Egyptians were not involved in a war), provides an example of *same cause, same effect* (such as another kingdom collapsing because of an environmental catastrophe), or provide an example of *no cause, no effect* (for instance, that Egypt thrived when there were no environmental catastrophes).

(A) Historically, most civilizations have succumbed to internal strife rather than external factors.

The fact that other civilizations succumbed to internal strife neither strengthens nor weakens the claim that Egypt's old kingdom collapsed due to an environmental catastrophe. (A) is a loser.

(B) The social problems in Egypt's old kingdom at the time of its collapse were serious enough to have caused the collapse.

This weakens the argument because it provides evidence that an *alternative cause* (social problems) led to the collapse of the old kingdom. (B) is a loser.

(C) At the time of the collapse of the old kingdom, several isolated but well-established civilizations near Egypt underwent sudden declines.

This matches one of our anticipated answer choices. It shows *same cause, same effect.* Other civilizations near Egypt (which were presumably affected by the same dry spell) also collapsed. This answer choice strengthens the argument, so we can consider it a candidate.

(D) Egyptian records recovered from the time of the collapse explicitly refer to the deteriorating conditions of the society.

This does not strengthen the argument. The conclusion is not about whether the collapse occurred but about what caused the collapse. (D) is a loser.

(E) Shortly after the collapse of the old kingdom, Egypt was thrust into a civil war that lasted most of the next two centuries.

This answer choice is irrelevant as it discusses what happened after the effect (the collapse of the old kingdom) occurred. (E) is a loser.

As (C) is the only candidate, it has to be the correct answer choice.

Weaken

PROCESS FAMILY

Strengthen
Weaken
Evaluation
Sufficient Assumption
Necessary Assumption
Paradox

Weaken

≈ 3.3 questions per test

Example Prompts

Which one of the following, if true, *most weakens* the argument?

If true, which one of the following *most undermines* the argument?

Which one of the following, if true, *is a response* A could make that *would counter* B's argument?

Take These Steps

Read the stimulus, which always includes an argument. Identify the main conclusion, subsidiary conclusions (if any), and premises. Does the argument contain a causal conclusion?

No → Does the argument include an assumption, comparison, or fallacy?

ASSUMPTION | COMPARISON | FALLACY

Yes →

Anticipate a statement that presents an alternative cause of the effect, has the same cause and no effect, has the same effect and no cause, or has reversed cause and effect.

Anticipate a statement that invalidates the assumption required by the argument.

Anticipate an explanation of why the comparison is inappropriate or incomplete.

Anticipate information that points out the error in reasoning and shows that it is sufficient to invalidate the argument.

Answer Choices

Correct Answer Choices	**Incorrect Answer Choices**
Statements that weaken the argument	Statements that do not weaken the argument
Statements that address a causal conclusion, assumption, comparison, or fallacy in the argument	Statements that strengthen the argument
	Irrelevant information

Weaken (W) questions are closely related to S questions. Instead of asking you to find the answer choice that strengthens the argument, W questions require that you select the answer choice that weakens it. Each answer choice presents new information that you must assume is true. Arguments always include one of the following elements (listed in order of frequency):

- Causal conclusion
- Logical fallacy
- Comparison
- Assumption

As mentioned in the S question section, the logical fallacy category can overlap somewhat with the others. However, this is not an issue when it comes to solving a W question. For example, the process for weakening an argument that contains a causal conclusion is the same whether or not it includes a Causal Reasoning Fallacy.

How to Solve Weaken Questions

The first step toward solving a W question is to determine how the argument's conclusion is supported by the premises. You must then identify an aspect of the argument that can be weakened. As arguments with causal conclusions, assumptions, or comparisons are the easiest to identify, you should check for these elements first.

If There Is a Causal Conclusion

As discussed in the previous section of this chapter, a causal conclusion is a conclusion in which a causal relationship is advanced. An argument does not need to commit a Causal Reasoning Fallacy to contain a causal conclusion, although this is usually the case. If a causal conclusion is present in the argument, the correct answer choice weakens the argument by presenting an *alternative cause*, an example of *same cause, no effect*, an example of *no cause, same effect*, or an example of *reversed cause and effect*. In W questions containing a causal conclusion, the correct answer choice tends to present an *alternative cause*. Consider the following:

> **In 2019, the Texas Tigers, a semiprofessional basketball team, signed Max Giovanni to its team. The team finished the 2019 season with an undefeated record and won the league championship. This was obviously a result of the team's addition of Max Giovanni, as Max's three-point shooting ability is the best in the league.**

This argument concludes that Addition of Max Giovanni CAUSE Record and Championship, as indicated by the phrase *as a result of*. The addition of this new player is the cause and the undefeated record and championship victory is the effect in this argument. If this were a real LSAT question, we would anticipate a correct answer choice that weakens the causal conclusion by presenting new information that falls into one of the three following categories:

Alternative Cause: The argument would be weakened if a different cause were presented as a possible reason for the intended effect. For example,

> **Hank Randall, the captain of the Texas Tigers, won the league's Most Valuable Player award this year and in the past three years.**

This suggests that the team's success was due to Hank Randall rather than Max Giovanni. Here, we have an alternative cause—it weakens the causal conclusion that Max Giovanni brought about the team's success.

Same Cause, No Effect: Introducing a case in which the cause was present but the effect was absent would weaken the argument. For example,

Last year, Max Giovanni was added to the Georgia Giants, which finished last in the league.

This example introduces a case in which the same cause (Max Giovanni being added to the team) is present but the effect (an undefeated record or league championship) is absent. This information would weaken the argument.

Same Effect, No Cause: Introducing a case in which the cause was missing but the effect occurred would weaken the argument. For example,

The Texas Tigers also had an undefeated record and won the league championship last year, before they ever acquired Max Giovanni.

This example introduces a case in which the same effect is present but the same cause is absent. This information would weaken the argument's causal conclusion.

Reversed Cause and Effect: Showing that the causal relationship is actually reversed (that instead of A CAUSE B, it is B CAUSE A) would weaken the argument. For example,

Max Giovanni only signed with the team after they had won the 2019 championship because he wanted to join the best team in the league.

This answer shows that the cause-and-effect relationship is reversed. It was the team's championship victory that caused Max Giovanni to join the team.

Let's look at an example:

Police commissioner: Last year our city experienced a 15 percent decrease in the rate of violent crime. At the beginning of that year a new mandatory sentencing law was enacted, which requires that all violent criminals serve time in prison. Since no other major policy changes were made last year, the drop in the crime rate must have been due to the new mandatory sentencing law.

Which one of the following, if true, most seriously weakens the police commissioner's argument?

(A) Studies of many other cities have shown a correlation between improving economic conditions and decreased crime rates.
(B) Prior to the enactment of the mandatory sentencing law, judges in the city had for many years already imposed unusually harsh penalties for some crimes.
(C) Last year, the city's overall crime rate decreased by only 5 percent.
(D) At the beginning of last year, the police department's definition of "violent crime" was broadened to include 2 crimes not previously classified as "violent."
(E) The city enacted a policy 2 years ago requiring that 100 new police officers be hired in each of the 3 subsequent years.

The argument uses the *since premise, conclusion* structure to conclude that New Sentencing Law CAUSE Crime Decrease, as indicated by the causal indicator *due to*. The evidence for this is a simple correlation between the law being enacted and a decline in the violent crime rate since it was enacted. This is a straightforward correlation-to-causation argument.

We should anticipate a correct answer choice that weakens the argument by weakening the causal conclusion. The correct answer choice probably presents an *alternative cause*—another factor that led to the decrease in violent crime. For example, more surveillance cameras may have been installed throughout the city or crime may be dropping nationwide. The correct answer choice may also show *same cause, no effect*, an example of which is another city that passed a similar law without seeing a corresponding drop in crime. We should also look for an answer choice that shows *same effect, no cause*—an example of a similar decrease in crime that occurred independently of a new sentencing law. Finally, the correct answer choice may show *reversed cause and effect*, meaning the decrease in crime caused the sentencing law to be enacted. However, this last option does not seem to work in this argument.

(A) **Studies of many other cities have shown a correlation between improving economic conditions and decreased crime rates.**

This is irrelevant information. The argument does not make any reference to the economic conditions of the city. (A) is a loser.

(B) **Prior to the enactment of the mandatory sentencing law, judges in the city had for many years already imposed unusually harsh penalties for some crimes.**

This answer choice tries to make it seem as if something similar to the new sentencing law was in place previously and, since the crime rate did not drop, the recent crime rate reduction must have been due to something else. However, *unusually harsh penalties* has a different meaning than *mandatory sentencing*, and *some crimes* does not necessarily mean *violent crimes*. (B) is a loser.

(C) **Last year, the city's overall crime rate decreased by only 5 percent.**

This is irrelevant information. The argument discusses the violent crime rate, not the overall crime rate. (C) is a loser.

(D) **At the beginning of last year, the police department's definition of "violent crime" was broadened to include 2 crimes not previously classified as "violent."**

Broadening the definition of *violent crime* to include crimes once considered to be nonviolent would actually increase the violent crime rate. (D) does not weaken the argument, so it is a loser.

(E) **The city enacted a policy 2 years ago requiring that 100 new police officers be hired in each of the 3 subsequent years.**

This matches one of our anticipated answer choices. If more police officers were hired over the last two years, it would make sense for the violent crime rate to drop. (E) weakens the argument by providing an *alternative cause*, so it has to be the correct answer choice.

If There Is an Assumption

When a significant assumption is necessary to make the conclusion of an argument valid, the correct answer choice exploits this logical gap to weaken the argument. As with S questions, it does not matter if the assumption is a true Questionable Assumption Fallacy. Once you have identified the assumption, you should anticipate a correct answer choice that provides new information that invalidates the assumption.

Let's look at an example:

Robert: The school board is considering adopting a year-round academic schedule that eliminates the traditional three-month summer vacation. This schedule should be adopted, since teachers need to cover more new material during the school year than they do now.

Samantha: The proposed schedule will not permit teachers to cover new material. Even though the schedule eliminates summer vacation, it adds six new two-week breaks, so the total number of school days will be about the same as before.

Which one of the following, if true, is a response Robert could make that would counter Samantha's argument?

(A) Teachers would be willing to accept elimination of the traditional three-month summer vacation as long as the total vacation time they are entitled to each year is not reduced.

(B) Most parents who work outside the home find it difficult to arrange adequate supervision for their school-age children over the traditional three-month summer vacation.

(C) In school districts that have adopted a year-round schedule that increases the number of school days per year, students show a deeper understanding and better retention of new material.

(D) Teachers spend no more than a day of class time reviewing old material when students have been away from school for only a few weeks, but have to spend up to a month of class time reviewing after a three-month summer vacation.

(E) Students prefer taking a long vacation from school during the summer to taking more frequent but shorter vacations spread throughout the year.

The stimulus features two authors, each with a separate argument, but the prompt only asks us to weaken Samantha's argument. We should begin by getting a grasp of Robert's argument. Robert concludes that a year-round schedule should be adopted by the school board as it would allow for more material to be covered. Samantha responds by claiming that there would not be an increase in the number of school days, so teachers would not be able to cover new material. Samantha introduces new and possibly irrelevant information here. Robert never claimed that a year-round academic year would result in an increase in the number of school days, and he does not say that additional days would be required to cover the new material. Samantha assumes that a year-round academic year would only allow teachers to cover new material if the number of days in the school year increased. In order for Robert to weaken Samantha's argument, he should invalidate this assumption by providing another reason why adapting a year-round academic year would allow teachers to cover more material.

(A) Teachers would be willing to accept elimination of the traditional three-month summer vacation as long as the total vacation time they are entitled to each year is not reduced.

This is irrelevant information. Neither argument discusses whether teachers would be willing to accept the elimination of the summer vacation. This answer choice does not weaken Samantha's argument, so it is a loser.

(B) Most parents who work outside the home find it difficult to arrange adequate supervision for their school-age children over the traditional three-month summer vacation.

This is irrelevant information—it does not weaken Samantha's argument. (B) is a loser.

(C) In school districts that have adopted a year-round schedule that increases the number of school days per year, students show a deeper understanding and better retention of new material.

This is an argument in favor of adopting a year-round schedule, but it does not address Samantha's claim that a year-round schedule would not increase the total numbers of days in the school year or her assumption that teachers would not be able to cover more material. (C) is a loser.

> **(D)** **Teachers spend no more than a day of class time reviewing old material when students have been away from school for only a few weeks, but have to spend up to a month of class time reviewing after a three-month summer vacation.**

This matches our anticipated answer choice. If teachers spent less time reviewing old material, they would have more time to cover new material. This invalidates Samantha's assumption that teachers would only be able to cover new material if the total number of days in the school year increased. (D) is a candidate.

> **(E)** **Students prefer taking a long vacation from school during the summer to taking more frequent but shorter vacations spread throughout the year.**

This answer choice introduces irrelevant information. Students' vacation preferences are not pertinent to an argument on how much material teachers could cover if a year-round schedule were adopted. (E) is a loser.

As (D) is the only candidate, it has to be the correct answer choice.

If There Is a Comparison

Chapter 5

Comparisons are more common in W questions than they are in S questions. When a comparison is made in a premise or conclusion, you should anticipate a correct answer choice that weakens the argument by explaining why the comparison is inappropriate (the objects of comparison are too dissimilar to be compared) or incomplete (insufficient information is provided about one of the objects of comparison).

Let's look at an example:

> Perry: Worker-owned businesses require workers to spend time on management decision-making and investment strategy, tasks that are not directly productive. Also, such businesses have less extensive divisions of labor than do investor-owned businesses. Such inefficiencies can lead to low profitability, and thus increase the risk for lenders. Therefore, lenders seeking to reduce their risk should not make loans to worker-owned businesses.
>
> Which one of the following, if true, most seriously weakens Perry's argument?
>
> (A) Businesses with the most extensive divisions of labor sometimes fail to make the fullest use of their most versatile employees' potential.
> (B) Lenders who specialize in high-risk loans are the largest source of loans for worker-owned businesses.
> (C) Investor-owned businesses are more likely than worker-owned businesses are to receive start-up loans.
> (D) Worker-owned businesses have traditionally obtained loans from cooperative lending institutions established by coalitions of worker-owned businesses.
> (E) In most worker-owned businesses, workers compensate for inefficiencies by working longer hours than do workers in investor-owned businesses.

The argument concludes that lenders seeking to reduce their risk should not make loans to worker-owned businesses. To support this conclusion, Perry states several disadvantages of worker-owned businesses, such as the amount of time spent on unproductive tasks and inefficient divisions of labor. Perry claims that these factors lead to low profitability, which is why lenders should not make loans to worker-owned businesses. During the course of the argument, Perry compares worker-owned businesses to investor-owned businesses. In making this comparison, Perry only focuses on the negatives of worker-owned businesses. This is an incomplete comparison and therefore an invalid argument. In order to weaken this comparative argument, we should select an answer choice that shows something positive about worker-owned businesses, as this would explain why worker-owned businesses may not be as risky as Perry concludes and why lenders should consider making loans to these businesses.

(A) Businesses with the most extensive divisions of labor sometimes fail to make the fullest use of their most versatile employees' potential.

This is a negative characteristic of businesses that are most likely investor-owned. However, we want to weaken the argument that lenders should not give loans to worker-owned businesses, not strengthen the argument that lenders should not give loans to investor-owned businesses. (A) is a loser.

(B) Lenders who specialize in high-risk loans are the largest source of loans for worker-owned businesses.

This is irrelevant information as the conclusion only mentions lenders who are seeking to reduce their risk. (B) is a loser.

(C) Investor-owned businesses are more likely than worker-owned businesses are to receive start-up loans.

This is irrelevant information. This answer choice does not explain why lenders should make loans to worker-owned businesses. (C) is a loser.

(D) Worker-owned businesses have traditionally obtained loans from cooperative lending institutions established by coalitions of worker-owned businesses.

The traditional source of loans for each type of businesses is irrelevant. We are looking for information that would weaken the claim that lenders who are seeking to reduce their risk should not make loans to worker-owned businesses. (D) is a loser.

(E) In most worker-owned businesses, workers compensate for inefficiencies by working longer hours than do workers in investor-owned businesses.

This matches one of our anticipated answer choices. It explains why worker-owned businesses may not be as bad as Perry thinks. Perry tries to show that these businesses have inefficiencies and that this leads to low profitability. If worker-owned businesses compensate for these inefficiencies, then Perry's premise is discredited, and there is no reason for lenders not to make loans to worker-owned businesses. To summarize, this answer choice shows that Perry's comparison is incomplete, and that there is an advantage (or not a disadvantage) to provide loans to worker-owned businesses. (E) has to be the correct answer choice.

If There Is a Fallacy

As with S questions, if the argument of a W question does not include a causal conclusion, assumption, or comparison, it must include a logical fallacy (most likely one of the Big Six). When there is an invalid argument in a W question, the correct answer usually involves exposing the fallacious reasoning used in the argument. Therefore, once you have identified the fallacy in the argument, you should anticipate a correct answer choice that exposes the error in reasoning, thus rendering the argument invalid, by presenting new information.

Let's look at an example:

Sickles found at one archaeological site had scratched blades, but those found at a second site did not. Since sickle blades always become scratched whenever they are used to harvest grain, this evidence shows that the sickles found at the first site were used to harvest grain, but the sickles found at the second site were not.

Which one of the following, if shown to be a realistic possibility, would undermine the argument?

(A) Some sickles that have not yet been found at the first site do not have scratched blades.
(B) The scratches on the blades of the sickles found at the first site resulted from something other than harvesting grain.
(C) Sickles at both sites had ritual uses whether or not those sickles were used to harvest grain.
(D) At the second site tools other than sickles were used to harvest grain.
(E) The sickles found at the first site were made by the same people who made the sickles found at the second site.

The phrase *this evidence shows that* indicates the conclusion that the sickles at the first site were used to harvest grain but the sickles at the second site were not. The evidence for this claim is the first premise, which states that the sickles at Site 1 had scratched blades while the sickles at Site 2 did not, and sickle blades always become scratched when they are used to harvest grain. This premise is actually a conditional statement, as indicated by the sufficient condition indicator *whenever* and the necessary condition indicator *always*. The conditional statement can be diagrammed as

Sickles Harvest Grain → Scratched Blades

This can be rephrased as "If sickles are used to harvest grain, then they become scratched." This argument commits a Conditional Reasoning Fallacy; specifically, flipped reasoning. The fact that all sickles used to harvest grain become scratched does not mean that all scratched sickles were used to harvest grain. We should anticipate a correct answer choice that exposes this fallacy by presenting new information; for instance, that the sickles were scratched not through harvesting grain, but through some other use.

(A) Some sickles that have not yet been found at the first site do not have scratched blades.

This is irrelevant information. The argument does not claim that all sickles at the first site were used to harvest grain, just that those with scratched blades were. (A) is a loser.

(B) The scratches on the blades of the sickles found at the first site resulted from something other than harvesting grain.

This matches our anticipated answer choice. The scratches on the blades (the necessary condition of the conditional statement) came about not through harvesting grain, but through some other use (a different sufficient condition). (B) is a candidate.

(C) Sickles at both sites had ritual uses whether or not those sickles were used to harvest grain.

This is irrelevant information. The strength of the argument is not affected by whether or not the sickles had ritual uses. (C) is a loser.

(D) At the second site tools other than sickles were used to harvest grain.

This actually strengthens the argument. If other tools at the second site were used to harvest grain, it would seem more likely that the sickles at that site were not used for that purpose. (D) is a loser.

(E) The sickles found at the first site were made by the same people who made the sickles found at the second site.

This is irrelevant information. Just because the sickles were made by the same people does not mean that they were made for the same (or different) purposes. We can consider this answer choice a loser.

We can select (B) because it is the only candidate.

Looking at the Answer Choices

The correct answer choice of a W question presents new information that undermines the argument's conclusion, either by attacking existing premises, providing evidence for a counter-premise, or exposing a weakness of the argument.

Incorrect answer choices often use the methods discussed in the previous section of this chapter to strengthen the argument. In addition, they frequently present irrelevant information. Answer choices containing irrelevant information neither strengthen nor weaken the argument, meaning that they can never be the correct answer choice.

Drill: Weaken

The following short arguments containing causal conclusions were featured in the previous section's Strengthen drill. For each, write four statements using each of the following methods to weaken an argument: provide an *alternative cause*, show *same cause, no effect*, show *same effect, no cause*, and show *reversed cause and effect*.

1. New research has shown that "joint cracking," or the routine bending of a person's joints to produce a cracking or popping sound, is responsible for the development of arthritis in that specific area in a person's later years. This was shown by survey data in which adults who suffer from arthritis of the hand were far more likely to report being frequent knuckle crackers in their 20s.

   _____

   _____

   _____

   _____

2. Over the last two years, Nation X has sponsored an aggressive ad campaign informing the public about the dangers of alcohol. This campaign contributed greatly to reducing alcohol consumption in the country. We can see this clearly because alcohol sales in the country are 15 percent lower this year than they were before the campaign.

   _____

   _____

   _____

   _____

3. The consumption of undercooked meat often leads to food poisoning or other acute illnesses. The neighborhood taco restaurant is known for employing cooks who do not know how to properly cook food or prepare meals. Therefore, Jerry's current food poisoning must have been caused by eating lunch at the restaurant that day.

   _____

   _____

   _____

   _____

1. **Causal Conclusion:** Joint Cracking CAUSE Arthritis

   Example of an Alternative Cause: Research has shown that people who do not consume enough calcium are more likely to develop arthritis later in life.

   Example of Same Cause, No Effect: The vast majority of people who crack their finger knuckles do not later develop arthritis of the hand.

   Example of Same Effect, No Cause: Millions of people with arthritis have never regularly cracked their joints.

   Example of Reversed Cause and Effect: People with arthritis find temporary relief in join cracking.

2. **Causal Conclusion:** Ad Campaign CAUSE Reduction in Alcohol Consumption

   Example of an Alternative Cause: Greater access to the Internet in the past two years has helped inform citizens about the dangers of drinking alcohol.

   Example of Same Cause, No Effect: A similar ad campaign was run in Country Z, which did not experience any reduction in alcohol consumption.

   Example of Same Effect, No Cause: Country X has seen decreasing rates of alcohol consumption each year for the past decade even though it did not run an ad campaign.

   Example of Reversed Cause and Effect: The ad campaign was only started in response to an decrease in alcohol consumption.

3. **Causal Conclusion:** Lunch at Taco Restaurant CAUSE Food Poisoning

   Example of an Alternative Cause: The breakfast Jerry ate this morning contained undercooked meat.

   Example of Same Cause, No Effect: None of the other lunch diners at the restaurant that day developed food poisoning.

   Example of Same Effect, No Cause: This was the first time Jerry ate Jerry at this restaurant, and Jerry regularly gets food poisoning.

   Example of Reversed Cause and Effect: Jerry ate lunch at the taco restaurant in the hope of curing his food poisoning.

1. Mayor: Local anti-tobacco activists are calling for expanded antismoking education programs paid for by revenue from heavily increased taxes on cigarettes sold in the city. Although the effectiveness of such education programs is debatable, there is strong evidence that the taxes themselves would produce the sought-after reduction in smoking. Surveys show that cigarette sales drop substantially in cities that impose stiff tax increases on cigarettes.

Which one of the following, if true, more undermines the reasoning in the argument?

(A) A city-imposed tax on cigarettes will substantially reduce the amount of smoking in the city if the tax is burdensome to the average cigarette consumer.

(B) Consumers are more likely to continue buying a product if its price increases due to higher taxes than if its price increases for some other reason.

(C) Usually, cigarette sales will increase substantially in the areas surrounding a city after that city imposes stiff taxes on cigarettes.

(D) People who are well informed about the effects of long-term tobacco use are significantly less likely to smoke than are people who are not informed.

(E) Antismoking education programs that are funded by taxes on cigarettes will tend to lose their funding if they are successful.

2. Commentator: Many people argue that the release of chlorofluorocarbons into the atmosphere is harming humans by damaging the ozone layer, thus allowing increased amounts of ultraviolet radiation to reach Earth. But 300,000 years ago a supernova greatly damaged the ozone layer, with no significant effect on our earliest ancestors. Because the supernova's disruption was much greater than the estimated effect of chlorofluorocarbons today, there is no reason to think that these chemicals in the atmosphere harm humans in this way.

Which one of the following, if true, would most seriously weaken the commentator's argument?

(A) Extraterrestrial influences on the ozone layer tend to occur less often than terrestrial ones.

(B) Natural events, such as the eruption of volcanoes, continue to damage the ozone layer today.

(C) Our earliest ancestors possessed genetic characteristics making them more resistant than we are to the harmful effects of ultraviolet radiation.

(D) The ozone layer regenerates at a slow rate, barring counteractive processes.

(E) Scientists have discovered that genetic changes occurred in our ancestors during the period in which the supernova affected Earth.

3. Scientists have shown that older bees, which usually forage outside the hive for food, tend to have larger brains than do younger bees, which usually do not forage but instead remain in the hive to tend to newly hatched bees. Since foraging requires greater cognitive ability than does tending to newly hatched bees, it appears that foraging leads to the increased brain size of older bees.

Which one of the following, if true, most seriously weakens the argument above?

(A) Bees that have foraged for a long time do not have significantly larger brains than do bees that have foraged for a shorter time.
(B) The brains of older bees that stop foraging to take on other responsibilities do not become smaller after they stop foraging.
(C) Those bees that travel a long distance to find food do not have significantly larger brains than do bees that locate food nearer the hive.
(D) In some species of bees, the brains of older bees are only marginally larger than those of younger bees.
(E) The brains of older bees that never learn to forage are the same size as those of their foraging counterparts of the same age.

4. A recent study of 10,000 people who were involved in automobile accidents found that a low percentage of those driving large automobiles at the time of their accidents were injured, but a high percentage of those who were driving small automobiles at the time of their accidents were injured. Thus, one is less likely to be injured in an automobile accident if one drives a large car rather than a small car.

Which one of the following, if true, most seriously weakens the argument?

(A) Most of the accidents analyzed in the study occurred in areas with very high speed limits.
(B) Most people who own small cars also drive large cars on occasion.
(C) Half of the study participants drove medium-sized cars at the time of their accidents.
(D) A large automobile is far more likely to be involved in an accident than is a small automobile.
(E) Only a small percentage of those people involved in an automobile accident are injured as a result.

5. Researcher: Hard water contains more calcium and magnesium than soft water contains. Thus, those who drink mostly soft water incur an increased risk of heart disease, stroke, and hypertension, for people being treated for these conditions tend to have lower levels of magnesium in their blood.

Which one of the following, if true, most undermines the researcher's argument?

(A) Magnesium deficiency is not uncommon, even in relatively prosperous countries with an otherwise generally adequate diet.

(B) Magnesium is needed to prevent sodium from increasing blood pressure.

(C) As people age, their ability to metabolize magnesium deteriorates.

(D) The ingestion of magnesium supplements inhibits the effectiveness of many medicines used to treat high blood pressure and heart disease.

(E) Compounds commonly used to treat hypertension and heart disease diminish the body's capacity to absorb and retain magnesium.

6. In the past, when there was no highway speed limit, the highway accident rate increased yearly, peaking a decade ago. At that time, the speed limit on highways was set at 90 kilometers per hour (kph) (55 miles per hour). Every year since the introduction of the highway speed limit, the highway accident rate has been at least 15 percent lower than that of its peak rate. Thus, setting the highway speed limit at 90 kph (55 mph) has reduced the highway accident rate by at least 15 percent.

Which one of the following, if true, most seriously weakens the argument?

(A) In the years prior to the introduction of the highway speed limit, many cars could go faster than 90 kph (55 mph).

(B) Ten years ago, at least 95 percent of all automobile accidents in the area occurred on roads with a speed limit of under 80 kph (50 mph).

(C) Although the speed limit on many highways is officially set at 90 kph (55 mph), most people typically drive faster than the speed limit.

(D) Thanks to changes in automobile design in the past ten years, drivers are better able to maintain control of their cars in dangerous situations.

(E) It was not until shortly after the introduction of the highway speed limit that most cars were equipped with features such as seat belts and airbags designed to prevent harm to passengers.

7. The Iliad and the Odyssey were both attributed to Homer in ancient times. But these two poems differ greatly in tone and vocabulary and in certain details of the fictional world they depict. So they are almost certainly not the work of the same poet.

Which one of the following statements, if true, most weakens the reasoning above?

(A) Several hymns that were also attributed to Homer in ancient times differ more from the Iliad in the respects mentioned than does the Odyssey.
(B) Both the Iliad and the Odyssey have come down to us in manuscripts that have suffered from minor copying errors and other textual corruptions.
(C) Works known to have been written by the same modern writer are as different from each other in the respects mentioned as are the Iliad and the Odyssey.
(D) Neither the Iliad nor the Odyssey taken by itself is completely consistent in all of the respects mentioned.
(E) Both the Iliad and the Odyssey were the result of an extended process of oral composition in which many poets were involved.

8. The number of applications for admission reported by North American Ph.D. programs in art history has declined in each of the last four years. We can conclude from this that interest among recent North American college and university graduates in choosing art history as a career has declined in the last four years.

Each of the following, if true, weakens the argument EXCEPT:

(A) The number of North American Ph.D. programs in art history that opted to report data about applications for admission has declined in each of the last four years.
(B) The average age of applicants for admission to North American Ph.D. programs in art history has increased in each of the last four years.
(C) The number of errors in data about applications for admission to North American Ph.D. programs in art history has increased substantially during the last four years.
(D) The number of North American employers willing to hire individuals without a Ph.D. for jobs in art history has increased in each of the last four years.
(E) The percentage of applications for admission received from outside North America by North American Ph.D. programs in art history has declined substantially in the last four years.

Problem Set: Weaken — Answers

1. **Correct Answer (C).** *Prep Test 52, Section 3, Question 6.*

   Element: Causal Conclusion

   The phrase *there is strong evidence that* indicates that the conclusion is that increased taxes would produce a reduction in smoking. The word *produce* indicates that this is a causal conclusion—that Increase Taxes on Cigarettes CAUSE Decrease Smoking. The evidence for this is survey data showing that cigarette sales drop substantially in cities that impose tax increases on cigarettes. This is a correlation-to-causation argument.

   We should anticipate a correct answer choice that presents an *alternative cause* (such as rules that limit where people can smoke), an example of *same cause, no effect* (for instance, that a city imposed the tax but did not see a reduction in smoking), an example of *same effect, no cause* (for instance, that a city experienced a decline in smoking rates without having increased taxes), or an example of *reversed cause and effect* (for instance, that the city will raise taxes to make up for revenue lost through a decline in smoking rates).

   (A) A city-imposed tax on cigarettes will substantially reduce the amount of smoking in the city if the tax is burdensome to the average cigarette consumer.

   If the tax is burdensome, which seems likely due to the phrase *heavily increased taxes*, then this would strengthen the causal relationship. Therefore, this answer choice is a loser.

   (B) Consumers are more likely to continue buying a product if its price increases due to higher taxes than if its price increases for some other reason.

   This is a relational statement. If consumers are more likely to buy a product that is more expensive due to higher taxes, they may still be less likely to buy the product than they were before the price increased. Therefore, this would not weaken the argument. (B) is a loser.

   (C) Usually, cigarette sales will increase substantially in the areas surrounding a city after that city imposes stiff taxes on cigarettes.

   This matches one of our anticipated answer choices. If cigarette sales increase substantially in the areas surrounding a city, then people are still buying cigarettes but going outside of the city to do so to avoid the tax. This would weaken the argument because people would not be smoking less after all. This would be an example of *same cause, no effect*, as the taxes will have been raised without reducing smoking. (C) is a candidate.

   (D) People who are well informed about the effects of long-term tobacco use are significantly less likely to smoke than are people who are not informed.

   This is irrelevant information. This demonstrates how effective an antismoking campaign may be, but that is not the issue in the argument. The issue is whether the tax increase will reduce smoking. This answer choice does not weaken the argument, so it is a loser.

   (E) Anti-smoking education programs that are funded by taxes on cigarettes will tend to lose their funding if they are successful.

   This too is irrelevant information. We are not concerned with how long antismoking education programs will continue to receive funding. (E) is a loser.

   As (C) is the only candidate, it has to be the correct answer choice.

2. Correct Answer (C). *Prep Test 45, Section 1, Question 2.*

Element: Comparison

The argument uses a *because premise, conclusion* structure to conclude that there is no reason to believe that increased exposure to ultraviolet radiation will harm humans. The argument supports this claim by comparing the current situation with a similar situation that occurred 300,000 years ago. The ozone layer was destroyed, but our earliest ancestors were not harmed. As sufficient information is provided to compare the two situations, we should anticipate a correct answer choice that shows that this comparison is inappropriate. This could be achieved by presenting new information showing that the situation 300,000 years ago was significantly different from the situation today.

(A) Extraterrestrial influences on the ozone layer tend to occur less often than terrestrial ones.

This is irrelevant information. The argument's conclusion has nothing to do with the classification of the influences on the ozone layer or the frequency with which they occur. (A) is a loser.

(B) Natural events, such as the eruption of volcanoes, continue to damage the ozone layer today.

This is irrelevant information. The argument's conclusion is not concerned with whether or not the ozone layer is in the process of being damaged. (B) is a loser.

(C) Our earliest ancestors possessed genetic characteristics making them more resistant than we are to the harmful effects of ultraviolet radiation.

This matches our anticipated answer choice. If a genetic difference made early humans more resistant to ultraviolet radiation than modern humans, it would be inappropriate to compare these two groups. (C) is a candidate.

(D) The ozone layer regenerates at a slow rate, barring counteractive processes.

This is irrelevant information. The regeneration of the ozone layer is not discussed in the argument. As this answer choice does not weaken the argument, it is a loser.

(E) Scientists have discovered that genetic changes occurred in our ancestors during the period in which the supernova affected Earth.

At first glance, this seems to weaken the argument. If our ancestors experienced genetic changes when exposed to solar radiation, then they may have been harmed by the radiation. However, the argument does not specify that these were harmful changes. It is equally possible that these changes may have benefited our early ancestors. This is a loser.

As (C) is the only candidate, it has to be the correct answer choice.

3. Correct Answer (E). *Prep Test 57, Section 2, Question 14.*

Element: Causal Conclusion

The argument uses a *since premise, conclusion* structure to conclude that foraging leads to the increased brain size of older bees, which can be expressed as Foraging CAUSE Larger Brain. The evidence behind this is a correlation; older bees usually have larger brains than younger bees, which do not forage.

We should anticipate a correct answer choice that presents an *alternative cause* (for instance, that bees' brains grow with age), an example of *same cause, no effect* (for instance, that some bees that forage have small brains), an example of *same effect, no cause* (for instance, that some large-brained bees never learned to forage), or an example of *reversed cause and effect* (for instance, that large brains allow bees to forage).

(A) Bees that have foraged for a long time do not have significantly larger brains than do bees that have foraged for a shorter time.

This matches one of our anticipated answer choices. If foraging increases brain size, would it not be true that bees that have foraged for a long time have significantly larger brains than bees that have foraged for a short time? This weakens the causal conclusion by showing *same cause*, *no effect*. (A) is a candidate.

(B) The brains of older bees that stop foraging to take on other responsibilities do not become smaller after they stop foraging.

This too matches one of our anticipated answer choices. The bees that stop foraging (*no cause*) still have a large brain (*same effect*). We will set this aside as a candidate.

(C) Those bees that travel a long distance to find food do not have significantly larger brains than do bees that locate food nearer the hive.

This is irrelevant information. The argument's conclusion is not that traveling long distances increases brain size but that foraging increases brain size. (C) is a loser.

(D) In some species of bees, the brains of older bees are only marginally larger than those of younger bees.

First, older bees still have larger brains than younger bees, even if marginally so. Second, this answer choice talks about some species of bees. The argument does not require that every species of bee follows the same pattern, as the argument uses terms like *usually* and *tend to*. Therefore, (D) is a loser.

(E) The brains of older bees that never learn to forage are the same size as those of their foraging counterparts of the same age.

This matches one of our anticipated answer choices. If older bees that never learn to forage have the same-sized brains as older bees that do forage, then there is no reason to think that foraging makes older bees' brains larger. This can be seen as *same effect, no cause* (larger brains, no foraging). (E) is a candidate.

We now need to eliminate one of our three candidates. Answer choices (A) and (B) have a similar problem. The argument states that foraging requires greater cognitive ability, which suggests that developing the ability to forage increases brain size. This does not mean that the brain continually increases in size with persistent foraging, as (A) suggests. Neither does it mean that the brain will shrink if a bee stops foraging, as is stated in (B). This leaves us with (E), which has to be the correct answer choice.

4. **Correct Answer (D).** *Prep Test 59, Section 3, Question 13.*

Element: Fallacy

The argument concludes that people are less likely to be injured in an automobile accident in a large car than they are in a small car. The argument's evidence is a study that shows that when involved in an accident, those driving small automobiles had a greater chance of being injured than those driving large automobiles. The argument commits a Sampling Fallacy. The sample (people involved in automobile accidents) is not representative of the general population of drivers. We should anticipate a correct answer choice that exposes this fallacy; for example, one that shows that small cars are less likely to be involved in accidents.

(A) Most of the accidents analyzed in the study occurred in areas with very high speed limits.

Where the accidents occurred is irrelevant as we have no information that either smaller or larger cars are better suited for certain speeds. This is a loser.

(B) Most people who own small cars also drive large cars on occasion.

This too is irrelevant information. If the same people drive both large and small vehicles, this does not weaken the argument. (B) is a loser.

(C) Half of the study participants drove medium-sized cars at the time of their accidents.

This is irrelevant information. Medium-sized cars are not mentioned in the argument. This answer choice is a loser.

(D) A large automobile is far more likely to be involved in an accident than is a small automobile.

This matches our anticipated answer choice. One is more likely to be involved in an accident (and therefore injured) while driving a large car, even if it is safer to be in a large car when an accident occurs. (D) is a candidate.

(E) Only a small percentage of those people involved in an automobile accident are injured as a result.

This applies equally to both large and small cars, so it is not relevant to our argument. (E) is a loser.

As (D) is the only candidate, it has to be the correct answer choice.

---

5. **Correct Answer (E).** *Prep Test 40, Section 1, Question 17.*

Element: Causal Conclusion

On its face, the argument seems to conclude that Drinking Mostly Water CAUSE Diseases. However, the argument implies that by drinking soft water, people will consume less magnesium, which is the reason there is an increased risk of heart disease, stroke, and hypertension. This means that the conclusion is actually as follows:

Drinking Soft Water CAUSE Low Magnesium CAUSE Diseases

In short, the actual cause of the increased risk of disease is the low levels of magnesium. We should anticipate a correct answer choice that presents an *alternative cause*, an example of *same cause, no effect*, an example of *same effect, no cause*, or an example of *reversed cause and effect*. Keep in mind that the correct answer choice may weaken either of the causal relationships in the conclusion (Drinking Soft Water CAUSE Low Magnesium or Low Magnesium CAUSE Diseases). For example, if it were true that people who drank soft water were much less likely to take multivitamins containing magnesium, this would be an *alternative cause* for the first causal relationship. Another example of a possible correct answer choice would be that people with very high magnesium uptake also have an increased risk of contracting those diseases. This would show *same effect, no cause* for the second causal relationship. There are many possible answers that can weaken part of this causal chain, and thus weaken the argument.

(A) Magnesium deficiency is not uncommon, even in relatively prosperous countries with an otherwise generally adequate diet.

Regardless of how common magnesium deficiency is, it can still lead to the diseases mentioned. This answer choice neither weakens nor strengthens the argument. (A) is a loser.

(B) Magnesium is needed to prevent sodium from increasing blood pressure.

This strengthens the argument. If magnesium were needed to prevent sodium from raising blood pressure, then low magnesium would lead to higher blood pressure. (B) is a loser.

(C) As people age, their ability to metabolize magnesium deteriorates.

This is irrelevant information. The argument makes no reference to age, nor would the fact that the ability to metabolize magnesium deteriorates with age weaken the argument. (C) is a loser.

(D) The ingestion of magnesium supplements inhibits the effectiveness of many medicines used to treat high blood pressure and heart disease.

This too is irrelevant information. This answer choice does not discuss the impact of taking magnesium supplements on medicines used to treat blood pressure and heart disease. (D) is a loser.

(E) Compounds commonly used to treat hypertension and heart disease diminish the body's capacity to absorb and retain magnesium.

This matches our anticipated answer choice. It suggests that the compound used to treat hypertension and heart disease lowers magnesium levels in the body. This is *reversed cause and effect*. Instead of Low Magnesium CAUSE Diseases, this answer choice suggests that Diseases CAUSE Low Magnesium by virtue of the common medications used to treat those diseases. This weakens the causal conclusion and therefore has to be the correct answer.

6. **Correct Answer (D).** *Prep Test 57, Section 2, Question 20.*

Element: Causal Conclusion

The argument concludes that setting the highway speed limit at 90 kph reduced the accident rate by at least 15 percent. This causal conclusion states that New Speed Limit CAUSE Less Accidents. The evidence for this causal conclusion is that every year since the introduction of the speed limit, the accident rate has been at least 15 percent lower than its peak rate a decade ago, just before the new speed limit was set.

We should anticipate a correct answer choice that presents an *alternative cause* (for instance, that heavy maintenance was done on the road to remove potholes and bumps), an example of *same cause*, *no effect* (for instance, that the same speed limit was imposed on a nearby highway, but the accident rate did not fall), an example of *same effect*, *no cause* (for instance, that the highway accident rate in another area has decreased without a new speed limit being imposed), or an example of *reversed cause and effect* (for instance, that the reduction in accidents caused the imposition of a new speed limit).

(A) In the years prior to the introduction of the highway speed limit, many cars could go faster than 90 kph (55 mph).

This would slightly strengthen the argument by showing that there were cars in the past that traveled faster than the current speed limit. (A) is a loser.

(B) Ten years ago, at least 95 percent of all automobile accidents in the area occurred on roads with a speed limit of under 80 kph (50 mph).

This is irrelevant information. The argument is concerned with accidents on highways, not accidents on other types of roads. (B) is a loser.

(C) Although the speed limit on many highways is officially set at 90 kph (55 mph), most people typically drive faster than the speed limit.

This answer choice appears to provide an example of *same cause*, *no effect*. However, even if most people do not follow the speed limit on other highways, this does not mean that the speed limit is ineffective. Perhaps people would drive even faster if the speed limit was not in effect. (C) is a loser.

(D) Thanks to changes in automobile design in the past ten years, drivers are better able to maintain control of their cars in dangerous situations.

This matches one of our anticipated answer choices. It presents an *alternative cause* for the decrease in the number of accidents—better automobile design. By showing that Better Design CAUSE Less Accidents may be the case, this answer choice weakens the argument. (D) is a candidate.

(E) It was not until shortly after the introduction of the highway speed limit that most cars were equipped with features such as seat belts and airbags designed to prevent harm to passengers.

At first glance, this answer choice suggests another *alternative cause*—better safety equipment. However, this equipment prevents in the course of an accident. It does not prevent accidents. (E) is a loser.

As (D) is the only candidate, it has to be the correct answer choice.

7. **Correct Answer (C).** *Prep Test 52, Section 1, Question 21.*

Element: Assumption

The argument here is that the *Iliad* and the *Odyssey* are almost certainly not the work of the same poet because the two poems differ greatly in tone, vocabulary, and certain details of the fictional worlds they depict. This argument is pretty straightforward, but it is based on a significant assumption. The fact that the two poems differ in certain ways does not necessarily mean they were written by different people. The argument makes the assumption that works by the same author are similar in terms of tone, vocabulary, and details. We should anticipate a correct answer choice that invalidates this assumption.

(A) Several hymns that were also attributed to Homer in ancient times differ more from the Iliad in the respects mentioned than does the Odyssey.

This seems like a good answer at first. If several hymns written by Homer differ more from the *Iliad* in the aspects mentioned than the *Odyssey* does, this shows that a writer does not need to be consistent in his or her writing. However, this answer choice does not discuss several hymns written by Homer, it talks about hymns attributed to Homer. It could very well be the case that Homer wrote only some, or none of them. (A) is a loser.

(B) Both the Iliad and the Odyssey have come down to us in manuscripts that have suffered from minor copying errors and other textual corruptions.

This also seems tempting at first. If there were minor errors, this could explain the difference between the two poems. However, minor copying errors would not explain differences in tone, vocabulary, and the details of the fictional world. (B) is a loser.

(C) Works known to have been written by the same modern writer are as different from each other in the respects mentioned as are the Iliad and the Odyssey.

This matches our anticipated answer choice. If works written by the same modern writer differ as much as the *Iliad* and *Odyssey*, the two poems could have been written by the same writer. This answer choice invalidates the key assumption in the argument, weakening the conclusion. Let's consider this a candidate.

(D) Neither the Iliad nor the Odyssey taken by itself is completely consistent in all of the respects mentioned.

This does not necessarily weaken the argument. While it may suggest why the works are not consistent when compared against each other, it may also suggest that each poem was written by multiple poets. (D) is a loser.

(E) Both the Iliad and the Odyssey were the result of an extended process of oral composition in which many poets were involved.

If many poets were involved in the creation of both poems, this would strengthen the claim that the poems were written by different authors. (E) is a loser.

As (C) is the only candidate, it has to be the correct answer choice.

8. **Correct Answer (B).** *Prep Test 40, Section 3, Question 26.*

Element: Fallacy

The argument concludes that the interest among recent North American college graduates in art history as a career has declined in the last four years, based on the premise that the number of applications for Ph.D. programs has declined in each of the last four years. This is an Equivocation Fallacy. The argument conflates applications for Ph.D. programs in North America and with interest in careers related to art history. To weaken this argument, an answer choice must expose this fallacy by showing that the number of Ph.D. program applications in North America is not representative of the number of people interested in art history as a career.

Since this is a Weaken EXCEPT question, we can expect four incorrect answer choices that weaken the argument and a correct answer choice that does not weaken the argument.

(A) The number of North American Ph.D. programs in art history that opted to report data about applications for admission has declined in each of the last four years.

This weakens the argument. It explains why the number of applicants is not the same as the number of people interested in art history careers—some Ph.D. programs are not reporting how many applications they receive. (A) is a loser.

(B) The average age of applicants for admission to North American Ph.D. programs in art history has increased in each of the last four years.

This does not seem to weaken the argument. There is no clear connection between the increase in the average age of applicants and the conclusion of the argument. (B) is a candidate.

(C) The number of errors in data about applications for admission to North American Ph.D. programs in art history has increased substantially during the last four years.

This weakens the argument. Like answer choice (A), this answer choice shows that the number of applications being reported may not tally with the actual number of applications submitted. (C) is a loser.

(D) The number of North American employers willing to hire individuals without a Ph.D. for jobs in art history has increased in each of the last four years.

This answer choice weakens the argument. It explains why the number of applications is not related to the level of interest in art history careers. (D) is a loser.

(E) The percentage of applications for admission received from outside North America by North American Ph.D. programs in art history has declined substantially in the last four years.

This weakens the argument by showing that there is not a clear relationship between the number of applications to North American Ph.D. programs and the level of interest in art history careers among graduates of North American universities. It could be the case that the decline in applications to these programs was entirely due to a decline in applications from outside North America, which has no relevance to the interest of North American college graduates in careers related to art history. (E) is a loser.

As (B) is the only candidate, it has to be the correct answer choice.

Evaluation

Evaluation

≈ 0.9 questions per test

Example Prompts

The answer to which one of the following questions is *most helpful in evaluating* the *truth* of the conclusion drawn in the argument?

Which one of the following would be *most important to know in evaluating* the argument's claim?

Take These Steps

Read the stimulus, which always includes an argument. Identify the main conclusion, subsidiary conclusions (if any), and premises. Does the argument contain a causal conclusion?

No →

Identify the underlying assumption that is required for the conclusion to be valid. Anticipate a question for which the answer validates or invalidates this assumption.

Yes ↓

Anticipate a question for which the answer either strengthens (by eliminating an *alternative cause*, providing an example of *same cause, same effect*, or providing an example of *no cause, no effect*) or weakens (by identifying an *alternative cause*, providing an example of *same cause, no effect*, providing an example of *no cause, same effect*, or identifying *reversed cause and effect*) the argument.

Answer Choices

Correct Answer Choices

Questions for which the answer would strengthen or weaken the argument

Questions for which the answer addresses a causal conclusion or an assumption in the argument

Incorrect Answer Choices

Questions for which the answer would neither strengthen nor weaken the arguments

Irrelevant information

In a way, Evaluation (E) questions are a hybrid of S and W questions. The prompt asks you to select the answer choice containing a direct or indirect question for which the answer would be most useful in evaluating the validity of the argument. In effect, the prompt requires you to identify a question for which the answer would either strengthen or weaken the argument. If the answer to a question does not strengthen or weaken the argument, it is not the correct answer choice. E questions can be very challenging. Fortunately, this question type is quite rare (although it has begun appearing more frequently in recent years), and you are unlikely to encounter more than one when taking the LSAT. The arguments always include one of the following elements (listed in order of frequency):

- Assumption
- Causal conclusion

How to Solve Evaluation Questions

The first step toward solving an E question is to identify the argument's conclusion and determine how the premises support it. You must then identify an element of the argument that can be either strengthened or weakened. This is likely the focus of the question in the correct answer choice. The process is simplified by the fact that the argument of an E question always includes a causal conclusion or an assumption. As a causal conclusion is easier to identify than an assumption, you should check for this element first.

If There Is a Causal Conclusion

As discussed in the previous sections of this chapter, a causal conclusion advances a causal relationship. For an E question, you must anticipate a correct answer choice that is a question for which the answer will either strengthen (by eliminating an *alternative cause*, providing an example of *same cause, same effect*, or providing an example of *no cause, no effect*) or weaken (by identifying an *alternative cause*, providing an example of *same cause, no effect*, providing an example of *no cause, same effect*, or providing an example of *reversed cause and effect*) the argument.

Let's look at an example:

> A recent study involved feeding a high-salt diet to a rat colony. A few months after the experiment began, standard tests of the rats' blood pressure revealed that about 25 percent of the colony had normal, healthy blood pressure, about 70 percent of the colony had high blood pressure, and 5 percent of the colony had extremely high blood pressure. The conclusion from these results is that high-salt diets are linked to high blood pressure in rats.
>
> The answer to which one of the following questions is most relevant to evaluating the conclusion drawn above?
>
> (A) How much more salt than is contained in a rat's normal diet was there in the high-salt diet?
> (B) Did the blood pressure have an adverse health effects on those rats that developed it?
> (C) What percentage of naturally occurring rat colonies feed on high-salt diets?
> (D) How many rats in the colony studied had abnormally high blood pressure before the study began?

(E) Have other species of rodents been used in experiments of the same kind?

The conclusion of the argument is that high-salt diets are linked to high blood pressure in rats. This is a causal conclusion that can be expressed as High Salt Diet CAUSE High Blood Pressure. The evidence for this conclusion is that after some rats were given a high-salt diet, 70 percent of them had high blood pressure and 5 percent had extremely high blood pressure.

We should anticipate a question for which the answer will either strengthen (by eliminating an *alternative cause*, providing an example of *same cause, same effect*, or providing an example of *no cause, no effect*) or weaken (by identifying an *alternative cause*, providing an example of *same cause, no effect*, providing an example of *no cause, same effect*, or providing an example of *reversed cause and effect*) the causal conclusion.

(A) How much more salt than is contained in a rat's normal diet was there in the high-salt diet?

The amount of additional salt in the high-salt diet is not relevant to the conclusion. The argument specifies the rats received a high-salt diet before concluding that this caused high blood pressure. This answer choice is a loser.

(B) Did the blood pressure have an adverse health effects on those rats that developed it?

The argument is about the relationship between high blood pressure and a high-salt diet. The health effects of high blood pressure are irrelevant. (B) is a loser.

(C) What percentage of naturally occurring rat colonies feed on high-salt diets?

Whether or not other rat colonies feed on high-salt diets would not affect the validity of the argument's conclusion. This information would not be relevant to the relationship between high-blood pressure and high-salt diets in rats. (C) is a loser.

(D) How many rats in the colony studied had abnormally high blood pressure before the study began?

This matches one of our anticipated answer choices. If many of the rats had abnormally high blood pressure before the study was conducted, then something other than the high-salt diet would have caused their high blood pressure, which would weaken the argument. If not, then the argument would be strengthened because it would be unlikely that something other than the diet caused the high blood pressure. As the answer to this question would eliminate or present an *alternative cause*, this answer choice is a candidate.

(E) Have other species of rodents been used in experiments of the same kind?

The argument is not concerned with other species of rodents, so this is irrelevant information. (E) is a loser.

As (D) is the only candidate, it has to be the correct answer choice.

If There Is an Assumption

If the argument does not include a causal conclusion, it must rely on a significant assumption in order to be valid. You must identify the logical gap in the argument, and then anticipate a correct answer choice that includes a question for which the answer validates or invalidates this assumption.

Let's look at an example:

> Advertisement: Most power hedge trimmers on the market do an adequate job of trimming hedges, but many power hedge trimmers are dangerous to operate and can cause serious injury when used by untrained operators. Bolter Industries' hedge trimmer has been tested by National Laboratories, the most trusted name in safety testing. So you know, if you buy a Bolter's, you are buying a power hedge trimmer whose safety is assured.
>
> The answer to which one of the following questions would be most useful in evaluating the truth of the conclusion drawn in the advertisement?
>
> (A) Has National Laboratories performed safety tests on other machines made by Bolter Industries?
> (B) How important to the average buyer of a power hedge trimmer is safety of operation?
> (C) What were the results of National Laboratories' tests of Bolter Industries' hedge trimmer?
> (D) Are there safer ways of trimming a hedge than using a power hedge trimmer?
> (E) Does any other power hedge trimmer on the market do a better job of trimming hedges than does Bolter Industries' hedge trimmer?

The advertisement concludes that Bolter's hedge trimmers' safety is assured. The evidence for this conclusion is that Bolter's hedge trimmers have been tested by National Laboratories, the most trusted name in safety testing. However, this argument is invalid unless a significant assumption is made. The argument assumes that Bolter's hedge trimmers passed the safety test. The argument can be outlined as follows:

P: Tested for safety
A: (Passed test)
_____
C: Safe

We should anticipate a correct answer choice that includes a question for which the answer could validate or invalidate this assumption (i.e. the cutters passed the test, or the cutters did not pass the test).

(A) Has National Laboratories performed safety tests on other machines made by Bolter Industries?

The answer to this question would not help us determine the validity of the argument. Whether or not National Laboratories has tested other machines is irrelevant to the conclusion that Bolter's trimmer is safe. (A) is a loser.

(B) How important to the average buyer of a power hedge trimmer is safety of operation?

The answer to this question would not help us determine the validity of the argument. Whether or not the average buyer thinks safety is important is unrelated to the safety of Bolter's trimmer. (B) is a loser.

(C) What were the results of National Laboratories' tests of Bolter Industries' hedge trimmer?

This matches our anticipated answer choice. If the results of the test were satisfactory, then the assumption is validated. If the results were not satisfactory, the assumption is invalidated. (C) is a candidate.

(D) Are there safer ways of trimming a hedge than using a power hedge trimmer?

The answer to this question would not help us determine the validity of the argument. The argument would neither be strengthened nor weakened if there were safer ways to trim a hedge. (D) is a loser.

(E) Does any other power hedge trimmer on the market do a better job of trimming hedges than does Bolter Industries' hedge trimmer?

The answer to this question would not help us determine the validity of the argument. The effectiveness of Bolter's hedge trimmer compared to those of other companies is not at issue here. (E) is a loser.

As (C) is the only candidate, it has to be the correct answer choice.

Looking at the Answer Choices

Correct answers to E questions are questions for which the answer either supports or undermines the argument's conclusion. This is the case whether or not the argument includes a causal conclusion.

Incorrect answer choices often include questions that are related to the content of the argument but do not actually address the validity of the conclusion. In other words, the answer to a question in an incorrect answer choice does not strengthen or weaken the argument. Often, incorrect answer choices introduce new information that is not relevant to the conclusion or include an equivocation of a key term or concept in the argument.

Drill: Evaluation

The following short arguments containing causal conclusions were featured in the Strengthen and Weaken drills of the previous sections. Two questions related to each argument have been provided. For each question, indicate whether the answer would help determine the validity of the argument. If applicable, specify how the argument would be strengthened/weakened.

1. New research has shown that "joint cracking," or the routine bending of a person's joints to produce a cracking or popping sound, is responsible for the development of arthritis in that specific area in a person's later years. This was shown by survey data in which adults who suffer from arthritis of the hand were far more likely to report being frequent knuckle crackers in their 20s.

   Question 1: Are some medications effective at treating the symptoms of arthritis?

   Does the answer help determine the validity of the argument? **(YES: □ / NO: □)**

   If **YES**, how does it strengthen/weaken the argument?
   Eliminates an Alternative Cause/Presents an Alternative Cause: □
   Example of Same Cause, Same Effect/Same Cause, No Effect: □
   Example of No Cause, No Effect/No Cause, Same Effect: □

   Question 2: Have most adults who suffer from arthritis injured their hands at some point in the past?

   Does the answer help determine the validity of the argument? **(YES: □ / NO: □)**

   If **YES**, how does it strengthen/weaken the argument?
   Eliminates an Alternative Cause/Presents an Alternative Cause: □
   Example of Same Cause, Same Effect/Same Cause, No Effect: □
   Example of No Cause, No Effect/No Cause, Same Effect: □

2. Over the last two years, Nation X has sponsored an aggressive ad campaign informing the public about the dangers of alcohol. This campaign contributed greatly to reducing alcohol consumption in the country. We can see this clearly because alcohol sales in the country are 15 percent lower this year than they were before the campaign.

   Question 1: Did the alcohol consumption rate decline by 15 percent during any period prior to the implementation of the ad campaign?

   Does the answer help determine the validity of the argument? **(YES: □ / NO: □)**

   If **YES**, how does it strengthen/weaken the argument?
   Eliminates an Alternative Cause/Presents an Alternative Cause: □
   Example of Same Cause, Same Effect/Same Cause, No Effect: □
   Example of No Cause, No Effect/No Cause, Same Effect: □

   Question 2: Which types of alcoholic beverages are most commonly consumed by the residents of Nation X?

   Does the answer help determine the validity of the argument? **(YES: □ / NO: □)**

   If **YES**, how does it strengthen/weaken the argument?
   Eliminates an Alternative Cause/Presents an Alternative Cause: □
   Example of Same Cause, Same Effect/Same Cause, No Effect: □

Example of No Cause, No Effect/No Cause, Same Effect: ☐

3. The consumption of undercooked meat often leads to food poisoning or other acute illnesses. The neighborhood taco restaurant is known for employing cooks who do not know how to properly cook food or prepare meals. Therefore, Jerry's current food poisoning must have been caused by eating lunch at the restaurant that day.

Question 1: Did Jerry get food poisoning when he ate at the taco restaurant on another day?

Does the answer help determine the validity of the argument? **(YES:** ☐ **/ NO:** ☐**)**

If **YES**, how does it strengthen/weaken the argument?
Eliminates an Alternative Cause/Presents an Alternative Cause: ☐
Example of Same Cause, Same Effect/Same Cause, No Effect: ☐
Example of No Cause, No Effect/No Cause, Same Effect: ☐

Question 2: How many employees does the taco restaurant currently assign to food preparation tasks?

Does the answer help determine the validity of the argument? **(YES:** ☐ **/ NO:** ☐**)**

If **YES**, how does it strengthen/weaken the argument?
Eliminates an Alternative Cause/Presents an Alternative Cause: ☐
Example of Same Cause, Same Effect/Same Cause, No Effect: ☐
Example of No Cause, No Effect/No Cause, Same Effect: ☐

1. **Causal Conclusion:** Joint Cracking CAUSE Arthritis

   Question 1:
   Does the answer help determine the validity of the argument? (**YES:** □ / **NO:** ■)

   If **YES**, how does it strengthen/weaken the argument?
   Eliminates an Alternative Cause/Presents an Alternative Cause: □
   Example of Same Cause, Same Effect/Same Cause, No Effect: □
   Example of No Cause, No Effect/No Cause, Same Effect: □

   Question 2:
   Does the answer help determine the validity of the argument? (**YES:** ■ / **NO:** □)

   If **YES**, how does it strengthen/weaken the argument?
   Eliminates an Alternative Cause/Presents an Alternative Cause: ■
   Example of Same Cause, Same Effect/Same Cause, No Effect: □
   Example of No Cause, No Effect/No Cause, Same Effect: □

2. **Causal Conclusion:** Ad Campaign CAUSE Reduction in Alcohol Consumption

   Question 1:
   Does the answer help determine the validity of the argument? (**YES:** ■ / **NO:** □)

   If **YES**, how does it strengthen/weaken the argument?
   Eliminates an Alternative Cause/Presents an Alternative Cause: □
   Example of Same Cause, Same Effect/Same Cause, No Effect: □
   Example of No Cause, No Effect/No Cause, Same Effect: ■

   Question 2:
   Does the answer help determine the validity of the argument? (**YES:** □ / **NO:** ■)

   If **YES**, how does it strengthen/weaken the argument?
   Eliminates an Alternative Cause/Presents an Alternative Cause: □
   Example of Same Cause, Same Effect/Same Cause, No Effect: □
   Example of No Cause, No Effect/No Cause, Same Effect: □

3. **Causal Conclusion:** Lunch at Taco Restaurant CAUSE Food Poisoning

   Question 1:
   Does the answer help determine the validity of the argument? (**YES:** ■ / **NO:** □)

   If **YES**, how does it strengthen/weaken the argument?
   Eliminates an Alternative Cause/Presents an Alternative Cause: □
   Example of Same Cause, Same Effect/Same Cause, No Effect: ■
   Example of No Cause, No Effect/No Cause, Same Effect: □

Question 2:

Does the answer help determine the validity of the argument? **(YES: □ / NO: ■)**

If **YES**, how does it strengthen/weaken the argument?

Eliminates an Alternative Cause/Presents an Alternative Cause: □

Example of Same Cause, Same Effect/Same Cause, No Effect: □

Example of No Cause, No Effect/No Cause, Same Effect: □

1. Between 1976 and 1985, chemical wastes were dumped into Cod Bay. Today, 3 percent of the bay's bluefin cod population have deformed fins, and wary customers have stopped buying the fish. In seeking financial reparations from companies that dumped the chemicals, representatives of Cod Bay's fishing industry have claimed that since the chemicals are known to cause genetic mutations, the deformity in the bluefin cod must have been caused by the presence of those chemicals in Cod Bay.

   The answer to each of the following questions would be helpful in evaluating the representatives' claim EXCEPT:

   (A) What is the incidence of deformed fins in bluefin cod that are not exposed to chemicals such as those dumped into Cod Bay?

   (B) What was the incidence of deformed fins in bluefin cod in Cod Bay before the chemical dumping began?

   (C) Has the consumption of the bluefin cod from Cod Bay that have deformed fins caused any health problems in the people who ate them?

   (D) Are bluefin cod prone to any naturally occurring diseases that can cause fin deformities of the same kind as those displayed by the bluefin cod of Cod Bay?

   (E) Are there gene-altering pollutants present in Cod Bay other than the chemical wastes that were dumped by the companies?

2. We already knew from thorough investigation that immediately prior to the accident, either the driver of the first vehicle changed lanes without signaling or the driver of the second vehicle was driving with excessive speed. Either of these actions would make a driver liable for the resulting accident. But further evidence has proved that the first vehicle's turn signal was not on, though the driver of that vehicle admits to having changed lanes. So the driver of the second vehicle is not liable for the accident.

   Which one of the following would be most important in evaluating the conclusion drawn above?

   (A) whether the second vehicle was being driven at excessive speed

   (B) whether the driver of the first vehicle knew that the turn signal was not on

   (C) whether any other vehicles were involved in the accident

   (D) whether the driver of the first vehicle was a reliable witness

   (E) whether the driver of the second vehicle would have seen the turn signal flashing had it been on

3. Eating garlic reduces the levels of cholesterol and triglycerides in the blood and so helps reduce the risk of cardiovascular disease. Evidence that eating garlic reduces these levels is that a group of patients taking a garlic tablet each day for four months showed a 12 percent reduction in cholesterol and a 17 percent reduction in triglycerides; over the same period, a group of similar patients taking a medically inert tablet showed only a 2 percent reduction in triglycerides and a 3 percent reduction in cholesterol.

It would be most important to determine which one of the following in evaluating an argument?

(A) whether the garlic tablets are readily available to the public
(B) what the diets of the two groups were during the period
(C) what effect taking the garlic tablet each day for a period of less than four months had on the levels of cholesterol and triglycerides
(D) whether large amounts of garlic are well tolerated by all patients
(E) whether the manufacturer of the garlic tablets cites the study in its advertising

1. **Correct Answer (C).** *Prep Test 45, Section 4, Question 11.*

Element: Causal Conclusion

The argument uses a *since premise, conclusion* structure to conclude that Chemical Dumping Cod Bay CAUSE Deformity Bluefin. The evidence for this causal conclusion is that chemicals were dumped into the bay over a nine-year period, and now 3 percent of the bay's bluefin cod have a deformity.

We need to consider what information could strengthen or weaken the argument. It seems odd that the argument states that there is a 3 percent deformity rate in bluefin cod but does not specify what a normal deformity rate is. The answer to a question about the normal deformity rate would either strengthen or weaken the argument. If the deformity rate is normally 3 percent, then the argument falls apart because the deformities are likely the result of natural causes (*alternative cause*). If the deformity rate is normally 0.1 percent, then the argument is strengthened because it is clear that natural factors are not the cause. It would also be useful to know whether bluefin tuna populations in other regions have similar deformity rates, and whether chemicals are being dumped in their habitats (*same cause, same effect*) or not (*no cause, same effect*).

Obviously, there are many possible questions that can strengthen (by eliminating an *alternative cause*, providing an example of *same cause, same effect*, or providing an example of *no cause, no effect*) or weaken (by identifying an *alternative cause*, providing an example of *same cause, no effect*, providing an example of *same cause, no effect*, or providing an example of *reversed cause and effect*) this argument. The prompt is an Evaluation EXCEPT question, meaning the four incorrect answer choice are questions for which the answer helps us determine the validity of the argument, and the correct answer is a question that does not.

(A) What is the incidence of deformed fins in bluefin cod that are not exposed to chemicals such as those dumped into Cod Bay?

The answer to this question would help us determine the validity of the argument. It may show *same effect, no cause* (which would weaken the causal conclusion) or *no cause, no effect* (which would strengthen the causal conclusion). (A) is a loser.

(B) What was the incidence of deformed fins in bluefin cod in Cod Bay before the chemical dumping began?

The answer to this question would help us determine the validity of the argument. It is similar to the previous answer choice in that it asks a question for which the answer may show *same effect, no cause* or *no cause, no effect*. (B) is a loser.

(C) Has the consumption of the bluefin cod from Cod Bay that have deformed fins caused any health problems in the people who ate them?

The answer to this question would not help us determine the validity of the argument. Whether or not consuming the deformed bluefin tuna causes heath problems has no relevance to the claim that Chemical Dumping Cod Bay CAUSE Deformity Bluefin. (C) is a candidate.

(D) Are bluefin cod prone to any naturally occurring diseases that can cause fin deformities of the same kind as those displayed by the bluefin cod of Cod Bay?

The answer to this question would help us determine the validity of the argument. It would either provide an *alternative cause* (a naturally occurring disease that can cause deformed fins) or eliminate this *alternative cause*. (D) is a loser.

(E) Are there gene-altering pollutants present in Cod Bay other than the chemical wastes that were dumped by the companies?

The answer to this question would help us determine the validity of the argument. Like the previous answer choice, this one presents a question for which the answer would either provide or eliminate an *alternative cause* (other pollutants). (E) is a loser.

As (C) is the only candidate, it has to be the correct answer choice.

2. **Correct Answer (A).** *Prep Test 51, Section 1, Question 2.*

Element: Assumption

The argument concludes that the driver of the second vehicle is not liable for the accident. This claim is supported by the premise that the first vehicle changed lanes without signaling, which makes that driver liable for the accident.

As this argument does not include a causal conclusion, we should look for an assumption. This argument assumes that just because one driver is liable, the other driver is not liable. As mentioned in Chapter 2, the phrase *either A or B* is not exclusive unless it is followed by the phrase *but not both*. Therefore, the first sentence of this argument does not preclude both drivers being liable.

The argument can be outlined as follows:

> P1: First Driver or Second Driver is Liable for Accident
> P2: First Driver Changed Lanes without Signaling
> SC: First Driver Is Liable
> A: (Only One Driver Is Liable)
> C: Second Driver Is Not Liable

We should anticipate a correct answer choice that validates or invalidates this assumption.

(A) whether the second vehicle was being driven at excessive speed

This matches our anticipated answer choice. If the second vehicle was being driven at excessive speed, then it is not the case that only one driver is liable. If the second vehicle was not being driven at excessive speed, then only the first driver is liable for the accident. As the answer to this question would validate or invalidate the assumption in the argument, it is a candidate.

(B) whether the driver of the first vehicle knew that the turn signal was not on

Whether or not the first driver was aware that the turn signal was not on would not strengthen or weaken the argument. (B) is a loser.

(C) whether any other vehicles were involved in the accident

Whether or not any other vehicles were involved is not relevant to whether or not the second driver is liable. (C) is a loser.

(D) whether the driver of the first vehicle was a reliable witness

Whether or not the driver of the first vehicle is reliable or unreliable would not strengthen or weaken the conclusion. (D) is a loser.

(E) whether the driver of the second vehicle would have seen the turn signal flashing had it been on

The argument does not discuss what would have happened if the second driver had seen a turn signal flashing. (E) is a loser.

As (A) is the only candidate, it has to be the correct answer choice.

3. **Correct Answer (B).** *Prep Test 49, Section 4, Question 2.*

Element: Causal Conclusion

The conclusion is that eating garlic reduces the levels of cholesterol and triglycerides in the blood, which reduces the risk of cardiovascular disease. This is indicated by the phrase *evidence that eating garlic reduces these levels is that.* This is a causal conclusion that can be expressed as Garlic CAUSE Lower Cholesterol AND Triglycerides CAUSE Less Risk of Cardiovascular Disease.

We should anticipated a question for which the answer either strengthens (by eliminating an *alternative cause*, providing an example of *same cause, same effect*, or providing an example of *no cause, no effect*) or weakens (by identifying an *alternative cause*, providing an example of *same cause, no effect*, providing an example of *no cause, same effect*, or providing an example of *reversed cause and effect*) the causal conclusion.

(A) whether the garlic tablets are readily available to the public

The answer to this question would not strengthen or weaken the causal conclusion. (A) is a loser.

(B) what the diets of the two groups were during the period

This matches one of our anticipated answer choices. If the group taking the tablet had a diet that lowered cholesterol and triglyceride levels, the argument would be weakened (through the presentation of an *alternative cause*). If the two groups had similar diets, the argument would be strengthened (through the elimination of an *alternative cause*). (B) is a candidate.

(C) what effect taking the garlic tablet each day for a period of less than four months had on the levels of cholesterol and triglycerides

The length of time one consumes garlic is not relevant to the argument. (C) is a loser.

(D) whether large amounts of garlic are well tolerated by all patients

The amount of garlic consumed is not discussed in the argument. This answer choice includes irrelevant information and is therefore a loser.

(E) whether the manufacturer of the garlic tablets cites the study in its advertising

Whether the manufacturer cites the study in its advertising is irrelevant to the conclusion of the argument. (E) is a loser.

As (B) is the only candidate, it has to be the correct answer choice.

Sufficient Assumption

PROCESS FAMILY

Strengthen
Weaken
Evaluation
Sufficient Assumption
Necessary Assumption
Paradox

Sufficient Assumption

≈ 2.6 questions per test

Example Prompts

Which one of the following is *an assumption* that would allow the conclusion to be *properly drawn*?

Which of the following, if *assumed*, allows the conclusion to be *properly inferred*?

The *conclusion drawn* by the argument *follows logically* if which one of the following is *assumed*?

Take These Steps

Read the stimulus, which always includes an argument. Identify the main conclusion, subsidiary conclusions (if any), and premises. Does the argument contain conditional statements?

Yes →

No ↓

Outline the argument and identify the fallacy. Anticipate a statement containing new information that eliminates the logical error in the argument, thereby connecting the conclusion to the premises to make a valid argument.

Outline the argument, diagramming the conditional statements. The conclusion and at least one premise are almost always an ALL or MOST statement. Anticipate an ALL or MOST statement that combines with one or more premises to create a logic chain from which the conclusion can be inferred (thereby making the argument valid). If a term appears in the conclusion but not in the premises, it always appears in the correct answer choice.

Answer Choices

Correct Answer Choices	Incorrect Answer Choices
Statements that, if assumed, make the argument valid	Statements that, if assumed, do not make the argument valid
Statements that include a term found in the conclusion but not in the premises (conditional arguments)	Statements that are necessarily true but do not validate the argument
Statements strong in logical force	Irrelevant information
	Statements weak in logical force

Sufficient Assumption (SA) questions ask you to select an answer choice that, if assumed to be true, guarantees that the argument is valid. Therefore, the correct answer choice of an SA question is termed a sufficient assumption—it is sufficient to validate the argument. SA questions always include an argument that is invalid on its own but valid if the sufficient assumption is assumed.

The sufficient assumption is often strong in logical force. This is because a strong statement is usually necessary to guarantee the validity of the conclusion and, therefore, the argument. Consider the following:

Helga is a formally trained gymnast. Therefore, she can do a backflip.

There is a significant gap in the logic of this argument. How do we know that Helga can do a backflip? An ALL statement such as the following would serve to guarantee the validity of the argument:

All formally trained gymnasts are able do backflips.

If all formally trained gymnasts are able to do backflips, then the conclusion must be valid that Helga, who is a formally trained gymnast, can do a backflip. The additional statement guarantees the validity of the conclusion.

Note that a weaker statement such as a SOME statement would fail to guarantee the validity of the argument. If not all formally trained gymnasts can do backflips, then it is possible that Helga cannot do a backflip.

How to Solve Sufficient Assumption Questions

The first step toward solving an SA question is to identify the argument's premises and conclusion. Next, determine how the conclusion is supported by the premises. After that, look for conditional statements in the argument.

If There Are Conditional Statements

Most SA questions include arguments containing conditional statements. You should begin by outlining the argument and diagramming the conditional statements. You should then attempt to determine the sufficient assumption. In effect, SA arguments containing conditional language include a Questionable Assumption Fallacy—the conclusion is an inference based on the ends of a logic chain, but one of the links of this chain is missing. You must find this missing link to make the argument valid. Note that SA questions hardly ever include an argument containing a Conditional Reasoning Fallacy (negated or flipped reasoning). The conclusion of an SA argument containing conditional language is almost always an ALL or MOST statement that can be inferred by combining the ends of a logic chain. The correct answer choice is a required link in this chain.

There is almost always a term in the conclusion that is not present in any of the premises. This term must be included in the sufficient assumption. Consider the following:

$$\frac{P: \cancel{Y} \rightarrow \cancel{X}}{C: X \rightarrow Z}$$

The term Z is included in the conclusion, but not in the premise. Therefore, the correct answer must use this term. Z is the necessary condition of the conclusion, which means the sufficient assumption should have Z as the necessary condition as well (if Z were the sufficient condition of the conclusion, it would also be the sufficient condition of the assumption). And because the conclusion is an ALL statement, the assumption must be an ALL statement as well. This is because you cannot combine an ALL statement with a SOME or MOST statement to infer an ALL statement. So, we now know the sufficient assumption must be as follows:

P: ~Y → ~X
SA: (? → Z)
C: X → Z

We now need to determine why X is the sufficient condition of the conclusion. If we find the contrapositive of the premise, we can see that the conclusion is based on combining the ends of a logic chain:

P: X → Y
SA: (? → Z)
C: X → Z

Once we have done this, it is easy to determine the sufficient condition of the sufficient assumption. In order for the conclusion to be valid, the sufficient assumption must be Y → Z. This allows us to create the logic chain X → Y → Z, and the ends of this chain can be combined to infer X → Z. Therefore, the assumption Y → Z guarantees the validity of the conclusion X → Z. Remember, the contrapositive of the sufficient assumption (~Z → ~Y) would also make X → Z a valid inference.

While the vast majority of arguments with conditional statements include a term in the conclusion that is not found in the premises, this is not always the case. For example,

P1: A → B
P2: C → D
SA: (B → C) or (A → C) or (B → D)
C: A → D

When both terms in the conclusion are included in the premises, the sufficient assumption either joins two premises together to create a logic chain or joins with one of the premises to create a logic chain. For the argument above, the sufficient assumption B → C can join with both premises to create the logic chain A → B → C → D, the sufficient assumption A → C can join with the second premise to create the logic chain A → C → D, and the third sufficient assumption can combine with the first premise to create the logic chain A → B → D. All three result in the valid inference A → D.

Of course, a conclusion based on the ends of a logic chain will not always be an ALL statement. It may be a MOST statement. As explained in Chapter 2, a MOST statement can be inferred when the necessary condition of a MOST statement is identical to the sufficient condition of an ALL statement, which creates a logic chain. The ends of this chain can be combined to infer a MOST Statement.

Let's look at an example:

Some students attending a small university with a well-known choir live off campus. From the fact that all music majors are members of the choir, a professor in the music department concluded that none of the students who live off campus is a music major.

The professor's conclusion is properly drawn if which one of the following is assumed?

(A) None of the students who live off campus is a member of the choir.
(B) None of the students who are music majors has failed to join the choir.
(C) Some of the students who do not live off campus are not music majors.
(D) All students who live on campus are music majors.
(E) All students who are members of the choir are music majors.

The professor's conclusion is that none of the students who live off campus is a music major. This argument can be outlined as follows:

P1: University ^{S}—^{S} Live Off-Campus
P2: Music Majors → Choir
_____
C: Live Off-Campus → ~~Music Major~~

Remember, *none* is a negative necessary indicator, so the necessary condition of the conclusion must be negated.

In this argument, the conclusion is not a valid inference drawn from the premises. SOME statements can only be combined with ALL statements when the statements have the same sufficient conditions. The ALL statement and SOME statement in the argument do not share any terms. Additionally, we know that it is impossible to infer an ALL statement from a SOME statement and a third statement. Therefore, the SOME statement can be ignored. It cannot be combined with the second premise or the sufficient assumption to infer Live Off-Campus → ~~Music Major~~.

This means that we must connect the second premise with the sufficient assumption. The term Live-Off Campus does not appear in the second premise, so it must appear in the sufficient assumption. As it is the sufficient condition of the conclusion, it must be the sufficient condition of the sufficient assumption. We can diagram this as follows:

P2: Music Majors → Choir
SA: (Live Off-Campus → ?)
_____
C: Live Off-Campus → ~~Music Major~~

The next step is to determine how we can connect Live Off-Campus with ~~Music Major~~. We can get ~~Music Major~~ by finding the contrapositive of the second premise, which gives us

P2: ~~Choir~~ → ~~Music Majors~~
SA: (Live Off-Campus → ?)
_____
C: Live Off-Campus → ~~Music Major~~

After we do this, it becomes clear that the necessary condition of the sufficient assumption is ~~Choir~~, as this creates the logic chain Live Off-Campus → ~~Choir~~ → ~~Music Major~~, from which we can infer Live Off-Campus → ~~Music Major~~.

We can anticipate a correct answer choice that expresses Live Off-Campus → ~~Choir~~ or its contrapositive, Choir → ~~Live Off-Campus~~.

(A) None of the students who live off campus is a member of the choir.

This matches our anticipated answer choice. *None* negates the second term in the statement, Choir. Therefore, this statement can be diagrammed as Live Off-Campus → ~~Choir~~. (A) is a candidate.

(B) None of the students who are music majors has failed to join the choir.

This can be diagrammed as Music Major → Choir, which does not match our anticipated answer and cannot be combined with either premise to infer Live Off-Campus → ~~Music Major~~. (B) is a loser.

(C) Some of the students who do not live off campus are not music majors.

This can be diagrammed as ~~Live Off-Campus~~ ^{S}—^{S} ~~Music Major~~. (C) is a loser.

(D) All students who live on campus are music majors.

This can be diagrammed as ~~Live Off Campus~~ → Music Major. (D) is a loser.

(E) All students who are members of the choir are music majors.

This can be diagrammed as Choir → Music Major. (E) is a loser.

As (A) is the only candidate, it has to be the correct answer choice.

Note: It is not always necessary to diagram every answer choice to see if it matches your anticipated answer. Often, it is possible to eliminate answer choices that do not include both of the terms you are looking for. For the example above, all of the incorrect answer choices could have been quickly eliminated using this method.

If There Are No Conditional Statements

On rare occasions, you may encounter SA questions that do not contain conditional language. In these questions, the argument includes a fallacy, most commonly a Questionable Assumption Fallacy—when the argument includes a significant logical gap that must be addressed. However, the other fallacies discussed in Chapter 4 (excluding Conditional Reasoning Fallacies and Strength Modifier Fallacies) may appear as well. The sufficient assumption presents new information that fixes the fallacy, making the argument valid.

The process for solving an SA question that does not contain conditional language is similar to that used for S questions. You must identify the fallacy in the argument and then anticipate a correct answer choice that fixes it, making the argument valid. Review the Strength question section of this chapter for information on how to fix each type of fallacy.

Let's look at an example:

> Physics professor: Some scientists claim that superheated plasma in which electrical resistance fails is a factor in causing so-called "ball lightning." If this were so, then such lightning would emit intense light and, since plasma has gaslike properties, would rise in the air. However, the instances of ball lightning that I observed were of low intensity and floated horizontally before vanishing. Thus, superheated plasma with failed electrical resistance is never a factor in causing ball lightning.
>
> The physics professor's conclusion follows logically if which one of the following is assumed?
>
> (A) Superheated plasma in which electrical resistance fails does not cause types of lightning other than ball lightning.
> (B) The phenomena observed by the physics professor were each observed by at least one other person.
> (C) Ball lightning can occur as the result of several different factors.
> (D) Superheating of gaslike substances causes bright light to be emitted.
> (E) All types of ball lightning have the same cause.

The argument concludes that superheated plasma with failed electrical resistance is never a factor in causing ball lightning. The evidence for this is that superheated plasma with failed electrical resistance would produce lightning that is intense and rises in the air, and that the ball lightning the professor has seen did not have these qualities. These premises support the fact that the ball lightning the professor has seen was not caused by superheated plasma with failed electrical resistance. However, the conclusion is far too strong, claiming that since some specific instances of ball lightning were not caused by superheated plasma with failed electrical resistance, then all instances of ball lightning are not caused by superheated plasma with failed electrical resistance. This is best viewed as a Sampling Fallacy. The sample the professor has based his conclusion on may not be representative of all cases of ball lightning. To fix this fallacy, the correct answer choice must show that the instances of ball lightning the professor witnessed are representative of all instances of ball lightning. The argument can be outlined as follows:

P1: Ball lightning caused by superheated plasma with failed electrical resistance has certain properties.
P2: The ball lightning I have witnessed does not have these properties.
SA: The ball lightning I have witnessed is representative of all ball lightning.
C: Ball lightning is never caused by superheated plasma with failed electrical resistance.

We should anticipate a correct answer choice that expresses this sufficient assumption.

(A) Superheated plasma in which electrical resistance fails does not cause types of lightning other than ball lightning.

This is irrelevant information as we are not concerned about types of lightning other than ball lightning. (A) is a loser.

(B) The phenomena observed by the physics professor were each observed by at least one other person.

This strengthens the argument by showing that the physics professor was not fabricating evidence, but (B) is not strong enough to guarantee that ball lightning is never caused by superheated plasma with failed electrical resistance. The ball lightning observed may not represent all cases of ball lightning. (B) is a loser.

(C) Ball lightning can occur as the result of several different factors.

If ball lightning is caused by several different factors, the argument is undermined because the possibility that there are other causes of ball lightning not observed by the physics professor has been introduced. (C) is a loser.

(D) Superheating of gaslike substances causes bright light to be emitted.

This is irrelevant information. This answer choice discusses gaslike substances in general. The argument is concerned with superheated plasma with failed electrical resistance. (D) is a loser.

(E) All types of ball lightning have the same cause.

This matches our anticipated answer choice. If all types of ball lightning have the same cause, and superheated plasma with failed electrical resistance was not the cause of the ball lightning observed by the professor, then this cannot be the cause of other instances of ball lightning. This answer choice shows that the sample of ball lighting observed by the professor is representative of all ball lighting, making the conclusion of the argument valid. (E) has to be the correct answer choice.

Looking at the Answer Choices

The correct answer is always a statement that presents new information that connects the premises of the argument to the conclusion, thereby making the argument valid. If the argument includes conditional statements, the correct answer choice is almost always an ALL or MOST statement that creates a logic chain with one or more of the premises. The conclusion is a valid inference based on the ends of this chain. This means that if a term that does not appear in any of the premises appears in the conclusion, it also appears in the sufficient assumption. Any answer choice that does not include both terms that appear in the sufficient assumption can be eliminated. If the argument does not contain conditional language, it must include a fallacy. In this case, the correct answer choice—a strong statement, usually—serves to fix the fallacy.

Incorrect answer choices often strengthen the argument but do not fully guarantee the validity of the conclusion. They can also be statements that are necessarily true in order for the argument to be valid but not sufficient on their own to make the argument valid (these statements are necessary assumptions, which are explained in the next section of this chapter). Incorrect answer choices for SA questions also commonly include irrelevant information.

Drill: Sufficient Assumption

Each short argument below contains conditional language. Diagram the conditional statements and provide a conditional statement that links the premises to the conclusion, validating the argument.

1. Unless we open our restaurant on Sundays, we will not be able to afford our rent. This is because every Sunday we are closed, we miss out on the lucrative "after Church" lunch crowd.

   Premise(s)
   +
   Assumption   (   )
   _____
   Conclusion

2. "Inner strength" requires the ability to overcome struggles. This is why the only way to prove you have real courage is to fight your fears. After all, if you are not able to fight through your fears, then you will never be able to overcome your struggles.

   Premise(s)
   +
   Assumption   (   )
   _____
   Conclusion

3. If a joint around a strong muscle is damaged, a person will not be able to exert the full force of that muscle. Therefore, for intense bodybuilding regimens, it is necessary to keep your joints healthy and lubricated.

   Premise(s)
   +
   Assumption   (   )
   _____
   Conclusion

1. **Unless we open our restaurant on Sundays, we will not be able to afford our rent. This is because every Sunday we are closed, we miss out on the lucrative "after Church" lunch crowd.**

Premise(s)	~~Business Open on Sunday~~ → ~~Lucrative Lunch Crowd~~
+	
Assumption	(~~Lucrative Lunch Crowd~~ → ~~Rent~~)
Conclusion	~~Business Open on Sunday~~ → Rent

To find the sufficient assumption, make ~~Rent~~, the new term in the conclusion, the necessary condition of the sufficient assumption. Next, determine how the conclusion's sufficient condition can lead to ~~Rent~~. This can be done by creating the logic chain ~~Business Open on Sunday~~ → ~~Lucrative Lunch Crowd~~ → ~~Rent~~. Therefore, the sufficient assumption is ~~Lucrative Lunch Crowd~~ → ~~Rent~~.

2. **"Inner strength" requires the ability to overcome struggles. This is why the only way to prove you have real courage is to fight your fears. After all, if you are not able to fight through your fears, then you will never be able to overcome your struggles.**

Premise(s)	Inner Strength → Overcome Struggles
+	~~Fight Fears~~ → ~~Overcome Struggles~~
Assumption	(Prove Real Courage → Inner Strength)
	Or (Prove Real Courage → Overcome Struggles)
Conclusion	Prove Real Courage → Fight Fears

To find the sufficient assumption, make Prove Real Courage, the new term in the conclusion, the sufficient condition of the sufficient assumption. Next, determine how the conclusion's sufficient condition can lead to Fight Fears. The contrapositive of the second premise is Overcome Struggles → Fight Fears. Therefore, anything that results in Overcome Struggles will trigger Fight Fears. This means that the sufficient assumption can be either Prove Real Courage → Overcome Struggles or Prove Real Courage → Inner Strength (which then necessitates Fight Fears).

3. **If a joint around a strong muscle is damaged, a person will not be able to exert the full force of that muscle. Therefore, for intense bodybuilding regimens, it is necessary to keep your joints healthy and lubricated.**

Premise(s)	Damaged Joints → ~~Full Force of Muscle~~
+	
Assumption	(Intense Bodybuilding Regimen → Full Force of Muscle)
Conclusion	Intense Bodybuilding Regimen → ~~Damaged Joints~~

To find the sufficient assumption, we take the new term from the conclusion's sufficient condition, Intense Bodybuilding Regimen, and insert it into the sufficient condition of the sufficient assumption. Next, we try to determine how we are able to get ~~Damaged Joints~~ on the necessary side. The contrapositive of the premise is Full Force of Muscle → ~~Damaged Joints~~. This means that Intense Bodybuilding Regimen → Full Force of Muscle is the sufficient assumption.

Note: The contrapositives of any of the above assumptions are also sufficient to make the arguments valid.

Chapter 5

Problem Set: Sufficient Assumption

1. Clearly, fitness consultants who smoke cigarettes cannot help their clients become healthier. If they do not care about their own health, they cannot really care for their clients' health, and if they do not care for their clients' health, they cannot help them to become healthier.

   The conclusion follows logically if which one of the following is assumed?

   (A) Anyone who does not care for his or her own health cannot help others become healthier.
   (B) Anyone who cares about the health of others can help others become healthier.
   (C) Anyone who does not care for the health of others cannot help them become healthier.
   (D) Anyone who does not smoke cares about the health of others.
   (E) Anyone who cares about his or her own health does not smoke.

2. Economist: A country's rapid emergence from an economic recession requires substantial new investment in that country's economy. Since people's confidence in the economic policies of their country is a precondition for any new investment, countries that put collective goals before individuals' goals cannot emerge quickly from an economic recession.

   Which one of the following, if assumed, enables the economist's conclusion to be properly drawn?

   (A) No new investment occurs in any country that does not emerge quickly from an economic recession.
   (B) Recessions in countries that put collective goals before individuals' goals tend not to affect the country's people's support for their government's policies.
   (C) If the people in a country that puts individuals' goals first are willing to make new investments in their country's economy, their country will emerge quickly from an economic recession.
   (D) People in countries that put collective goals before individuals' goals lack confidence in the economic policies of their countries.
   (E) A country's economic policies are the most significant factor determining whether that country's economy will experience a recession.

3. Paleontologists recently discovered teeth from several woolly mammoths on an isolated Arctic island where no mammoth fossils had previously been found. The teeth were 25 percent smaller on average than adult mammoth teeth that have been found elsewhere, but they are clearly adult mammoth teeth. Therefore, provided that the teeth are representative of their respective populations, woolly mammoths that lived on the island were smaller on average than those that lived elsewhere.

Which one of the following, if assumed, would allow the conclusion to be properly drawn?

(A) Neither tooth size nor overall body size is completely uniform among adult members of most species, including woolly mammoths.
(B) The tooth wear that naturally occurs in many animals over the course of their adult years did not result in a significant change in tooth size among adult woolly mammoths as they aged.
(C) Unusually small mammoth teeth found at locations other than the island have always been those of juvenile mammoths rather than adult mammoths.
(D) Tooth size among adult woolly mammoths was always directly proportional to the overall size of those mammoths.
(E) Woolly mammoths of the kind that lived on the island had the same number and variety of teeth as mammoths that lived elsewhere had.

4. Commentator: For a free market to function properly, each prospective buyer of an item must be able to contact a large number of independent prospective sellers and compare the prices charged for the item to what the item is worth. Thus, despite advertised prices and written estimates available from many of its individual businesses, the auto repair industry does not constitute a properly functioning free market.

The conclusion of the commentator's argument follows logically if which one of the following is assumed?

(A) People do not usually shop for auto repairs but instead take their autos to their regular repair shop out of habit.
(B) Some persons who are shopping for auto repairs cannot determine what these repairs are worth.
(C) Not all auto repair shops give customers written estimates.
(D) Many auto repair shops charge more for auto repairs than these repairs are worth.
(E) Because it is not regulated, the auto repair industry does not have standardized prices.

5. People who have doctorates in the liberal arts are interested in improving their intellects. Companies, however, rarely hire people who are not concerned with the financial gain that can be obtained by hard work in the business world. As a result, companies rarely hire people who have doctorates in the liberal arts.

The conclusion of the argument follows logically if which one of the following is assumed?

(A) Companies would hire people with doctorates in the liberal arts if such people were interested in the money available in the business world.

(B) Some people who are interested in the liberal arts do not care about money.

(C) The only people not interested in making money in the business world are people who are interested in improving their intellects.

(D) People with doctorates in the liberal arts are interested in employment in the business world.

(E) Only people not concerned with making money in the business world are interested in improving their intellects.

6. Criminologist: The main purpose of most criminal organizations is to generate profits. The ongoing revolutions in biotechnology and information technology promise to generate enormous profits. Therefore, criminal organizations try to become increasingly involved in these areas.

The conclusion of the criminologist's argument is properly inferred if which one of the following is assumed?

(A) If an organization tries to become increasingly involved in areas that promise to generate enormous profits, then the main purpose of that organization is to generate profits.

(B) At least some criminal organizations are or will at some point become aware that the ongoing revolutions in biotechnology and information technology promise to generate enormous profits.

(C) Criminal organizations are already heavily involved in any technological revolution that promises to generate enormous profits.

(D) Any organization whose main purpose is to generate profits will try to become increasingly involved in any technological revolution that promises to generate enormous profits.

(E) Most criminal organizations are willing to become involved in legal activities if those activities are sufficiently profitable.

7. The only preexisting recordings that are transferred onto compact discs are those that the record companies believe will sell well enough on compact disc to be profitable. So, most classic jazz recordings will not be transferred onto compact disc, because few classic jazz recordings are played on the radio.

The conclusion above follows logically if which one of the following is assumed?

(A) Few of the preexisting recordings that record companies believe can be profitably transferred to compact disc are classic jazz recordings.

(B) Few compact discs featuring classic jazz recordings are played on the radio.

(C) The only recordings that are played on the radio are ones that record companies believe can be profitably sold as compact discs.

(D) Most record companies are less interested in preserving classic jazz recordings than in making a profit.

(E) No recording that is not played on the radio is one that record companies believe would be profitable if transferred to compact disc.

1. **Correct Answer (E).** *Prep Test 47, Section 3, Question 21.*

The argument includes conditional statements. The word *clearly* indicates that the conclusion is that fitness consultants who smoke cigarettes cannot help their clients become healthier. The argument can be outlined as follows:

P1: ~~Care about Own Health~~ → ~~Care for Clients' Health~~
P2: ~~Care for Clients' Health~~ → ~~Help Clients Become Healthier~~
SA: (   )
C: Consultants Who Smoke → ~~Help Clients Become Healthier~~

Note that there are three similar yet different terms in the premises. In addition, the conclusion can be rephrased as "If you are a fitness consultant who smokes cigarettes, then you cannot help your clients become healthier."

The sufficient condition of the conclusion includes a term (Consultants Who Smoke) that does not appear in either of the premises. Therefore, we should move this term into the sufficient condition of the sufficient assumption. We then need to determine how the sufficient assumption could fit into a logic chain from which the conclusion could be inferred.

If we make the necessary condition of the sufficient assumption ~~Care about Own Health~~, we can connect this to the first premise to create the following logic chain:

Consultants Who Smoke → ~~Care about Own Health~~ → ~~Care for Clients' Health~~ → ~~Help Clients Become Healthier~~

If we make the necessary condition of the sufficient assumption ~~Care for Clients' Health~~, we can connect this to the second premise to create the following logic chain:

Consultants Who Smoke → ~~Care for Clients' Health~~ → ~~Help Clients Become Healthier~~

The conclusion becomes a valid inference if the ends of either of these logic chains are combined. Therefore, we should anticipate a correct answer choice that expresses Consultants Who Smoke → ~~Care about Own Health~~ or Consultants Who Smoke → ~~Care for Clients' Health~~ (or one of their contrapositives).

We know that the correct answer choice must include the term Consultants Who Smoke. We can quickly eliminate (A), (B), and (C) because they do not include this term.

(D) Anyone who does not smoke cares about the health of others.

This answer choice contains the phrases *anyone who does not smoke* (which is inclusive of *consultants*) and *health of others* (which is inclusive of *clients*). As broader terms that are inclusive of the specific terms in the argument have been used, we can diagram this answer choice using the specific terms. Doing so, we get ~~Consultants Who Smoke~~ → Care for Clients Health. As this cannot be combined with the premises to make the conclusion a valid inference, (D) is a loser.

(E) Anyone who cares about his or her own health does not smoke.

The broad term *anyone* is inclusive of the specific terms in the argument. The argument can be diagrammed as Care about Own Health → ~~Consultant Who Smokes~~, which is the contrapositive of Consultant Who Smokes→ ~~Care about Own Health~~, our anticipated answer choice. Therefore, (E) has to be the correct answer.

2. **Correct Answer (D).** *Prep Test 52, Section 3, Question 15.*

The argument includes conditional statements. A *since premise, conclusion* structure is used to conclude that countries that put collective goals before individual's goals cannot emerge quickly from an economic recession. The first premise uses the word *requires* to indicate that what follows is the necessary condition. The second premise uses the word *precondition* to indicate that the preceding clause is the necessary condition. The conclusion includes *cannot*, which negates the necessary condition. The argument can be outlined as follows:

P1: Rapid Emergence from Recession → New Investment
P2: New Investment → Confidence in Economic Policies
SA: (   )
C: Collective Before Individual → ~~Rapid Emergence from Recession~~

The term ~~Rapid Emergence from Recession~~ in the conclusion is not a new one, as it appears in the contrapositive of the first premise. However, Collective Before Individual is a new term. Therefore, it must be the sufficient condition of the sufficient assumption.

The next step is to determine how to create a logic chain from which the conclusion can be inferred. If the necessary condition of the sufficient assumption is ~~New Investment~~, we can join it with the contrapositive of the first premise to create the following logic chain:

Collective Before Individual → ~~New Investment~~ → ~~Rapid Emergence from Recession~~

If the necessary condition of the sufficient assumption is ~~Confidence in Economic Policies~~, we can join it with the contrapositives of the first and second premises to create the following logic chain:

Collective Before Individual → ~~Confidence in Economic Policies~~ → ~~New Investment~~ → ~~Rapid Emergence from Recession~~

The conclusion becomes a valid inference if the ends of either of these logic chains are combined. Therefore, we can anticipate a correct answer choice that expresses Collective Before Individual → ~~New Investment~~ or Collective Before Individual → ~~Confidence in Economic Policies~~ (or one of their contrapositives). As Collective Before Individual must appear in the sufficient assumption, we can eliminate (A), (C), and (E).

> **(B)** **Recessions in countries that put collective goals before individuals' goals tend not to affect the country's people's support for their government's policies.**

This answer choice includes the word *tend*, which means it is a MOST statement. We cannot combine a MOST statement with an ALL statement to infer an ALL statement. (B) is a loser.

> **(D)** **People in countries that put collective goals before individuals' goals lack confidence in the economic policies of their countries.**

This matches one of our anticipated answer choices. It can be diagrammed as Collective Before Individual → ~~Confidence in Economic Policies~~. (D) has to be the correct answer choice.

3. **Correct Answer (D).** *Prep Test 41, Section 3, Question 22.*

Fallacy: Composition

The argument does not include any conditional statements. It concludes that, if we assume recently discovered teeth are representative of their respective populations, the woolly mammoths that lived on a particular island were smaller than the woolly mammoths that lived elsewhere. This is supported by paleontologists' findings that the woolly mammoth teeth discovered on the island were 25 percent smaller than mammoth teeth found elsewhere. The argument can be outlined as follows:

P: Woolly mammoth teeth from the island are 25 percent smaller than average.

SA: (_____)

C: The woolly mammoths on the island were smaller than average.

Since the argument does not contain conditional language, we must identify the fallacy it includes. The argument assumes that a part of a whole (the teeth of a woolly mammoth) has the same quality (being 25 percent smaller than average) as the whole (the entire woolly mammoth). This is a Part-to-Whole Composition Fallacy.

To correct this fallacy, we must assume that the size of a woolly mammoth's teeth is proportionally representative of the size of its entire body. We should anticipate a correct answer choice that states this.

(A) Neither tooth size nor overall body size is completely uniform among adult members of most species, including woolly mammoths.

This would actually weaken the argument. If tooth size varies between individual woolly mammoths, then the teeth discovered may not be representative of all woolly mammoths on the island. (A) is a loser.

(B) The tooth wear that naturally occurs in many animals over the course of their adult years did not result in a significant change in tooth size among adult woolly mammoths as they aged.

This information strengthens the argument by eliminating the issue of tooth wear as a potential reason for why the teeth on the island are smaller than average. However, it is still possible that the size of a mammoth's teeth is not proportional to the size of its body. As this answer choice is not sufficient to make the argument valid, it is a loser.

(C) Unusually small mammoth teeth found at locations other than the island have always been those of juvenile mammoths rather than adult mammoths.

This answer choice includes irrelevant information. The argument specifies that the teeth come from adult mammoths, not juveniles. (C) is a loser.

(D) Tooth size among adult woolly mammoths was always directly proportional to the overall size of those mammoths.

This matches our anticipated answer choice. If tooth size is always directly proportional to the overall size of the mammoth, then teeth that are 25 percent smaller must be from mammoths that are 25 percent smaller. (D) is a candidate.

(E) Woolly mammoths of the kind that lived on the island had the same number and variety of teeth as mammoths that lived elsewhere had.

This answer choice includes irrelevant information. The number and variety of teeth is not an issue. (E) is a loser.

As (D) is the only candidate, it has to be the correct answer choice.

4. **Correct Answer (B).** *Prep Test 59, Section 2, Question 26.*

The argument includes conditional statements. It concludes that the auto repair industry is not a properly functioning free market. The commentator supports this argument by specifying two requirements of a free market: each buyer must have the ability to contact a large number of sellers and be able to compare the price charged with the actual value. The last sentence includes background information about the auto repair industry— many businesses have advertised prices and written estimates. This is not helpful for determining the sufficient assumption. The argument can be outlined as follows:

P: Free Market → Contact Many Sellers AND Compare Worth

SA: (_____)

C: Auto Repair Industry → ~~Free Market~~

The term ~~Free Market~~ in the conclusion is not a new one, as it appears in the contrapositive of the first premise. However, Auto Repair Industry is a new term. Therefore, it must be the sufficient condition of the sufficient assumption.

If we make the necessary condition of the sufficient assumption ~~Contact Many Sellers~~ OR ~~Compare Worth~~, we can use the first premise to create the following logic chain:

Auto Repair Industry → ~~Contact Many Sellers~~ OR ~~Compare Worth~~ → ~~Free Market~~

The conclusion becomes a valid inference if the ends of this chain are combined. Therefore, we can anticipate a correct answer choice that expresses Auto Repair Industry → ~~Contact Many Sellers~~ OR ~~Compare Worth~~ (or its contrapositive).

(A) People do not usually shop for auto repairs but instead take their autos to their regular repair shop out of habit.

This matches our anticipated answer choice. If people are not actively shopping around for different auto repair shops, then they are not contacting many sellers. This can be diagrammed as Auto Repair Industry → ~~Contact Many Sellers~~. Remember, only one of the terms from the disjunction in the sufficient assumption needs to be included to validate the argument. (A) is a candidate.

(B) Some persons who are shopping for auto repairs cannot determine what these repairs are worth.

This matches our anticipated answer choice. If people cannot determine what repairs are actually worth, then they are unable to accurately compare costs. This can be diagrammed as Auto Repair Industry → ~~Compare Worth~~. (B) is a candidate.

(C) Not all auto repair shops give customers written estimates.

It is not necessary to receive a written estimate to determine the worth of a good or service. (C) is a loser.

(D) Many auto repair shops charge more for auto repairs than these repairs are worth.

This answer choice does not match ~~Compare Worth~~ because it only states that many shops are charging more than the repairs are worth. This does not exclude the possibility of a buyer comparing the price of a service with its actual value. (D) is a loser.

(E) Because it is not regulated, the auto repair industry does not have standardized prices.

The fact that prices across the industry are not standardized does not prevent buyers from comparing price to value. (E) is a loser.

We now need to eliminate one of the two candidates. There is a slight problem with answer choice (A). It states that people do not usually contact multiple sellers out of habit. This does not mean that they are unable to contact many sellers. For this reason, we can eliminate (A) and select (B).

5. **Correct Answer (E).** *Prep Test 40, Section 3, Question 15.*

The argument includes conditional statements. It concludes that companies rarely hire people who have doctorates

Chapter 5 Process Family **387**

in the liberal arts. The evidence for this claim is that such people are interested in improving their intellect, and people who are not concerned with financial gain resulting from hard work are rarely hired by companies. The word *who*, which is a sufficient condition indicator, is used three times. The argument can be outlined as follows:

P1: Doctorate Liberal Arts → Interested Improving Intellect
P2: ~~People Concerned w/ Money~~ → Rarely Hired by Companies
SA: (   )
C: Doctorate Liberal Arts → Rarely Hired by Companies

Both of the terms in the argument appear in the premises. Therefore, the sufficient assumption cannot include one of these terms; rather, it is likely to join two premises together to create a logic chain from which the conclusion can be inferred. Doctorate Liberal Arts is the sufficient condition of the first premise and the conclusion, and Rarely Hired by Companies is the necessary condition of the second premise and the conclusion. If the sufficient assumption is Interested Improving Intellect → ~~People Concerned w/ Money~~, we can link the two premises to create the following logic chain:

Doctorate Liberal Arts → Interested Improving Intellect → ~~People Concerned w/ Money~~ → Rarely Hired by Companies

The conclusion becomes a valid inference if the ends of this chain are combined. Therefore, we should anticipate a correct answer choice that expresses Interested Improving Intellect → ~~People Concerned w/ Money~~ (or its contrapositive).

(A) Companies would hire people with doctorates in the liberal arts if such people were interested in the money available in the business world.

This answer choice can be diagrammed as Concerned w/ Money → ~~Rarely Hire~~, which is the negated version of the second premise. (A) is a loser.

(B) Some people who are interested in the liberal arts do not care about money.

If this were an ALL statement, it would match our anticipated answer choice. However, a SOME statement cannot be combined with an ALL statement to infer an ALL statement. (B) is a loser.

(C) The only people not interested in making money in the business world are people who are interested in improving their intellects.

The term *only* modifies *people*, which refers to *people who are interesting in improving their intellects* (making this the necessary condition). Therefore, this answer choice can be diagrammed as ~~People Concerned w/ Money~~ → Interested Improving Intellect. This is the flipped version of the sufficient assumption. (C) is a loser.

(D) People with doctorates in the liberal arts are interested in employment in the business world.

Although *people with doctorates in the liberal arts* can be expressed as Interested Improving Intellect, *interested in employment in the business world* is not a term that appears in the argument. Therefore, (D) is a loser.

(E) Only people not concerned with making money in the business world are interested in improving their intellects.

This matches our anticipated answer choice. The term *only* modifies *people*, which refers to *people not concerned with making money in the business world* (making this the necessary condition). This statement can be diagrammed as Interested Improving Intellect → ~~People Concerned w/ Money~~. (E) has to be the correct answer choice.

6. **Correct Answer (D).** *Prep Test 57, Section 2, Question 12.*

Fallacy: Questionable Assumption

Although the argument contains conditional indicator words such as *most*, *is*, and *will*, the statements do not express clear conditional relationships. Therefore, this argument does not include conditional statements. The criminologist concludes that criminal organizations will become increasingly involved in biotechnology and information technology. This conclusion is supported by the premise that most criminal organizations' main purpose is to generate profit and that these areas promise to generate profit. The argument can be outlined as follows:

> P1: Criminal organizations' main purpose is profit.
> P2: Tech areas promise to generate enormous profits.
> C: Criminal organizations will become increasingly involved in these areas.

This can be considered a Questionable Assumption Fallacy in that the criminologist assumes that if an organization has a main goal, then it will always pursue that goal. What if the organization is incapable of expanding into these areas? There are many reasons why criminal organizations may not try to become increasingly involved in the tech fields in question. We should anticipate a correct answer choice the fixes this fallacy.

(A) If an organization tries to become increasingly involved in areas that promise to generate enormous profits, then the main purpose of that organization is to generate profits.

This statement does not make the argument valid. We are looking for a statement that asserts that profit-oriented organizations always become increasingly involved in profitable areas. This answer choice is almost the flipped version of what we are looking for. (A) is a loser.

(B) At least some criminal organizations are or will at some point become aware that the ongoing revolutions in biotechnology and information technology promise to generate enormous profits.

This is necessary for the argument to be valid. However, it is not sufficient to validate the argument. It is possible that some organizations might realize that certain tech areas are profitable but still lack the capability to expand into them. (B) is a loser.

(C) Criminal organizations are already heavily involved in any technological revolution that promises to generate enormous profits.

The argument mentions becoming increasingly involved. Even if the organizations are heavily involved, this does not guarantee that they will become even more involved. (C) is a loser.

(D) Any organization whose main purpose is to generate profits will try to become increasingly involved in any technological revolution that promises to generate enormous profits.

This matches our anticipated answer choice. If we assume that any organization whose main purpose is to generate profits, such as the criminal organizations in our argument, will become increasingly involved in these areas, then the conclusion of the argument is valid. (D) is a candidate.

(E) Most criminal organizations are willing to become involved in legal activities if those activities are sufficiently profitable.

As with answer choice (B), this assumption is necessary for the argument but would not make the argument valid. It is necessary that criminal organizations are willing to become involved, but being willing does not mean that they will become involved. (E) is a loser.

As (D) is the only candidate, it has to be the correct answer choice.

7. **Correct Answer (E).** *Prep Test 45, Section 4, Question 22.*

The argument includes conditional statements. A *conclusion, because premise* structure is used to conclude that few jazz recordings are played on the radio. This is supported by two premises. The first is that the only recordings transferred onto discs are those believed to be profitable, and most classic jazz recordings will not be transferred onto discs. The word *only* in the first premise modifies *preexisting recordings*, which refers to *those that the record companies believe will sell well enough on compact disc to be profitable* (making this the necessary condition). Therefore, we can use the term Believed to be Profitable as the necessary condition and Transferred to Disc as the sufficient condition.

The second premise is included at the end of the last sentence, and it includes the word *few*, which normally indicates a SOME statement. However, the term *few* is used here in an uncommon way. Whereas "A few trees in the park are sycamores" would be diagrammed as Trees in Park ^{S}—^{S} Sycamores, the sentence "Few trees in the park are sycamores" can mean this or mean that most of the trees in the park are not sycamores, which can be diagrammed as Trees in Park ^{M}→ ~~Sycamores~~. In this way, the inclusion of *few* can create a Not MOST statement. So this premise can be diagrammed as either Classic Jazz ^{S}—^{S} Radio or Classic Jazz ^{M}→ ~~Radio~~. Because we are trying to connect create a logic chain with an ALL statement, it is better to treat this premise as a MOST statement.

The conclusion is a MOST statement that can be diagrammed as Classic Jazz ^{M}→ ~~Transferred to Disc~~.

Therefore, the argument can be outlined as follows:

> P1: Transferred to Disc → Believed to Be Profitable
> P2: Classic Jazz ^{M}→ ~~Radio~~
> SA: (_____)
> C: Classic Jazz ^{M}→ ~~Transferred to Disc~~

Classic Jazz is the sufficient condition of the second premise and conclusion, and ~~Transferred to Disc~~ is the sufficient condition of the contrapositive of the first premise and the necessary condition of the conclusion. As both terms in the conclusion appear in the premises, we need to find a way to connect the premises in a logic chain from which the conclusion can be inferred. We can do this if the sufficient assumption is ~~Radio~~ → ~~Believed to Be Profitable~~.

> P1: ~~Believed to be Profitable~~ → ~~Transferred to Disc~~
> P2: Classic Jazz ^{M}→ ~~Radio~~
> SA: (~~Radio~~ → ~~Believed to be Profitable~~) _____
> C: Classic Jazz ^{M}→ ~~Transferred to Disc~~

The second premise can be combined with the sufficient assumption to get a MOST statement because the necessary condition of the MOST statement matches the sufficient condition of the ALL statement. We get

> P2: Classic Jazz ^{M}→ ~~Radio~~
> SA: (~~Radio~~ → ~~Believed to Be Profitable~~) _____
> Inf: Classic Jazz ^{M}→ ~~Believed to Be Profitable~~

We can then combine this MOST statement inference with the first ALL statement premise in the exact same fashion:

> Inf: Classic Jazz ^{M}→ ~~Believed to Be Profitable~~
> P1: ~~Believed to Be Profitable~~ → ~~Transferred to Disc~~ _____
> C: Classic Jazz ^{M}→ ~~Transferred to Disc~~

This allows us to reach the conclusion of the argument. Therefore, by assuming ~~Radio~~ → ~~Believed to Be Profitable~~, we are able to validate the argument. We can anticipate this statement or its contrapositive as being the correct answer choice.

(A) Few of the preexisting recordings that record companies believe can be profitably transferred to compact disc are classic jazz recordings.

The word *few* here tells us that this answer choice is incorrect, as the correct answer must be an ALL statement. This answer choice can be diagrammed as Believed to Profitable $\overset{M}{\rightarrow}$ ~~Classic Jazz~~. (A) is a loser.

(B) Few compact discs featuring classic jazz recordings are played on the radio.

As with (A), the inclusion of *few* allows us to eliminate this answer choice. (B) is a loser.

(C) The only recordings that are played on the radio are ones that record companies believe can be profitably sold as compact discs.

The word *only* modifies *recordings*, which refers to *ones that record companies believe can be profitably sold*. Therefore, this statement can be diagrammed as Radio → Believed to Profitable, which is the negated version of our anticipated answer. (C) is a loser.

(D) Most record companies are less interested in preserving classic jazz recordings than in making a profit.

This answer choice includes irrelevant information. We are not concerned with record companies' level of interest in preserving classic jazz recordings. (D) is a loser.

(E) No recording that is not played on the radio is one that record companies believe would be profitable if transferred to compact disc.

This matches our anticipated answer choice. The word *no* is a negative necessary indicator that negates the second term in the statement. Therefore, this statement can be diagrammed as: ~~Radio~~ → ~~Believed to Profitable~~. (E) has to be the correct answer choice.

Necessary Assumption

PROCESS FAMILY

Strengthen
Weaken
Evaluation
Sufficient Assumption
Necessary Assumption
Paradox

Necessary Assumption
≈ 5.2 questions per test

Example Prompts

Which one of the following is *an assumption that is required* by the argument?

The argument *depends on assuming* which one of the following?

Which one of the following is *an assumption made* by the argument?

Take These Steps

Read the stimulus, which always includes an argument. Identify the main conclusion, subsidiary conclusions (if any), and premises. Does the argument contain a causal statement?

No → Does the argument include a fallacy?

Yes → Outline the argument and identify the fallacy. Anticipate a statement with new information that eliminates the logical error in the argument.

No → Outline the argument and identify a minor assumption or weakness in the argument. Anticipate a statement that addresses the assumption or weakness.

Yes → Anticipate a statement that eliminates an alternative cause of the effect, has the same cause and same effect, or has no same cause and no same effect.

Apply the (Un)Necessary Assumption Test when needed to confirm that an answer choice is correct or to eliminate a candidate.

Answer Choices

Correct Answer Choices	Incorrect Answer Choices
Statements that must be true in order for the argument to be valid	Statements that strengthen the argument but are not necessarily true
Statements weak in logical force	Statements that validate the argument but are not necessarily true
	Irrelevant information
	Statements strong in logical force

Necessary Assumption (NA) questions ask you to select an answer choice that must be true in order for the argument to be valid. As a result, the correct answer choice of an NA question is termed a necessary assumption. Unlike SA questions, NA questions generally do not include arguments with conditional statements. Another key difference is that the necessary assumption does not need to be sufficient to make the argument valid. In other words, the necessary assumption must be true in order for the argument to be valid but it does not have to guarantee that the argument is valid.

Necessary assumptions are usually weak in logical force. This is because it is easier for a valid argument to withstand a weak assumption than a strong one. Consider the following:

Helga is a formally trained gymnast. Therefore, she can to do a backflip.

As mentioned in the previous section of this chapter, the following statement is sufficient to make the argument valid:

All formally trained gymnasts are able to do backflips.

However, this statement is not necessarily true. It could be the case that only one formally trained gymnast—Helga—is able to do a backflip. A necessary assumption tends to be a SOME statement, such as

Some formally trained gymnasts are able to do backflips.

If Helga (a formally trained gymnast) is able to do a backflip, then it must be true that some (at least one) formally trained gymnasts can do backflips. Let's look at another example:

Researchers have recently discovered a cure for Disease X, called Cure A. Over the course of the next decade, Cure A could be synthesized, distributed, and sold to people all over the world. Therefore, Disease X will slowly be eradicated.

The following statements are necessary assumptions for this argument; that is, they must be true in order for the argument to be valid:

1. **Strains of Disease X will not become resistant to Cure A.**
2. **The cost of Cure A is not prohibitively expensive to many of the people infected with the disease.**
3. **A magical wizard will not cast a spell that makes Cure A ineffective against Disease X.**

Note that none of these assumptions is sufficient to make the argument valid. However, if the argument is to be valid, then all of these assumptions must be true.

The (Un)Necessary Assumption Test

A test can be used to determine if a statement is a necessary assumption. When a necessary assumption is logically negated, the argument is invalidated as well. Let's look at the logically negated versions of the necessary assumptions we identified for the previous example:

> This powerful method may be used with every NA question to double-check if you have selected the correct answer or to eliminate possible candidates.

Researchers have recently discovered a cure for Disease X, called Cure A. Over the course of the next decade, Cure A could be synthesized, distributed, and sold to people all over the world. Therefore, Disease X will slowly be eradicated.

1. **Strains of Disease X <u>will</u> become resistant to Cure A.**

2. **The cost of Cure A <u>is</u> prohibitively expensive to many of the people infected with the disease.**
3. **A magical wizard <u>will</u> cast a spell that makes Cure A ineffective against Disease X.**

Each of these logically negated statements would invalidate the argument. Therefore, they are necessary assumptions. By way of comparison, consider the statement *Cure A cures all diseases*. Is this a necessary assumption? The logically negated version of this statement is *Cure A does not cure all diseases*. This does not invalidate the argument. Cure A does not have to cure all diseases in order for the argument to be valid—it just has to cure Disease X. Thus, *Cure A cures all diseases* is not a necessary assumption.

Logically Negating Nonconditional Statements

In order to negate a nonconditional statement, you must find the logical opposite of the verb that immediately follows the subject. For example,

> **The man in the blue shoes is short.**

This sentence can be logically negated as follows:

> **The man in the blue shoes is not short.**

We must be careful not to logically negate this sentence as

> **The man in the blue shoes is tall.**

If we change an adjective (or any part of speech other than the verb), this means we have failed to logically negate the nonconditional statement. Let's consider another example:

> **My Uncle Lester plays the banjo.**

This sentence can be logically negated as

> **My Uncle Lester does not play the banjo.**

Logically Negating Conditional Statements Containing Strength Modifiers

When a statement contains a strength modifier, you should negate the strength modifier. If there is more than one strength modifier, negate the one that appears first. Consider the following:

> **The waitress from the restaurant *always* provides great service.**

The strength *modifier* is in italics. This statement can be negated as follows:

> **The waitress from the restaurant *does not always* provide great service.**

This is a *not all* statement, which, as discussed in Chapter 2, is equivalent to *some are not*. Therefore, this negated sentence can also be read as "The waitress from the restaurant sometimes does not provide great service."

While negating strength modifiers, we must bear in mind the range of each strength modifier. Review the following chart from Chapter 2:

Strength Modifier Category	Proportion
Strong (ALL)	100%
Strong (NO)	0%
Moderate (MOST)	50%< to 100%
Weak (SOME)	0%< to 100%
Weak (NOT ALL)	0% to <100%

The logical opposite of a modifier is the remaining range, from 0 to 100 percent. For example, an ALL statement indicates 100 percent, which means that a NOT ALL statement (0 to 99 percent) is the logical opposite. A SOME statement indicates 1 to 100 percent, which means that a NO statement (0 percent) is the logical opposite. The chart below contains some sets of logically negated strength modifiers:

Statement Type	Strength Modifier	Negated Strength Modifier
ALL (Quantity)	All	Not All
ALL (Degree)	Always	Not Always
MOST (Quantity)	Most	Less Than Half
MOST (Degree)	Probably	Probably Not OR Unlikely
SOME (Quantity)	Some	None
SOME (Degree)	Could	Cannot
NO (Quantity)	None	Some OR At Least One
NO (Quantity)	Never	Sometimes
NOT ALL (Quantity)	Not All	All

Logically Negating Conditional Statements that Do Not Contain Strength Modifiers

In order to logically negate a conditional statement, we must make the necessary condition no longer necessary. In other words, we must turn *if A then B* into *if A then not necessarily B*, which can be symbolized as A $\nrightarrow$ B. The conditional arrow is crossed out because A no longer guarantees B. B may still occur with A, but it is no longer necessary. For example,

> Convert complex conditional statements into "if ... then" statements to make them easier to negate.

If the supermarket has a sale, avocados will be cheap.

The negated version of this conditional statement is

If the supermarket has a sale, avocados will not necessarily be cheap.

The conditional statement has been logically negated because the necessary condition is no longer necessary.

The (Un)Necessary Assumption Test is useful for verifying that an answer choice is correct and for eliminating candidates. This test is time-consuming, though, so you should only use it when necessary.

How to Solve Necessary Assumption Questions

The first step toward solving an NA question is to identify the argument's premises and conclusion. Next, determine how the conclusion is supported by the premises. After that, check if the argument includes a causal statement.

If There Is a Causal Statement

The arguments of NA questions sometimes include a causal statement, either in a premise or in the conclusion. This type of language is rare but easy to identify, so you should always check for it first. A causal statement expresses a relationship in which Factor A causes Factor B. The argument thus necessarily assumes that no other factor can cause Factor B, that Factor A always causes Factor B, and that Factor B cannot occur without Factor A. When a causal statement is present in an NA argument, the correct answer choice almost always eliminates an *alternative cause*, provides an example of *same cause, same effect*, or provides an example of *no cause, no effect*. In this way, NA questions with causal statements are similar to S questions with causal statements. Note that NA questions tend to involve the elimination of an *alternative cause*.

Let's look at an example:

> Feathers recently taken from seabirds stuffed and preserved in the 1880s have been found to contain only half as much mercury as feathers recently taken from living birds of the same species. Since mercury that accumulates in a seabird's feathers as the feathers grow is derived from fish eaten by the bird, these results indicate that mercury levels in saltwater fish are higher now than they were 100 years ago.
>
> The argument depends on assuming that
>
> (A) the proportion of a seabird's diet consisting of fish was not as high, on average, in the 1880s as it is today
> (B) the amount of mercury in a saltwater fish depends on the amount of pollution in the ocean habitat of fish
> (C) mercury derived from fish is essential for the normal growth of a seabird's feathers
> (D) the stuffed seabirds whose feathers were tested for mercury were not fully grown
> (E) the process used to preserve birds in the 1880s did not substantially decrease the amount of mercury in the birds' feathers

The argument uses a *since premise, conclusion* structure to conclude that a study of seabird feathers from the 1880s indicates that mercury levels in saltwater fish are higher now than they were 100 years ago. The argument's evidence is that feathers taken from preserved seabirds have half as much mercury as feathers taken from living birds, and that mercury enters seabirds' systems on account of their fish diet and accumulates in their feathers. This second premise is a causal relationship, indicated by the word *derived*. The mercury in fish eaten by a bird CAUSE the mercury levels in the bird's feathers. This supports the argument because an increase in the effect (mercury in living birds' feathers) would follow from an increase in the cause (mercury in fish eaten by the birds). The argument can be outlined as follows:

P1: Feathers from living seabirds contain higher mercury levels than birds from the 1880s.

This argument includes a causal statement. Therefore, we should anticipate a correct answer choice that eliminates an *alternative cause*, provides an example of *same cause, same effect*, or provides an example of *no cause, no effect*. The most common category for NA questions is elimination of an *alternative cause*. For this argument, possible *alternative causes* are that the mercury levels were not caused by other seabird prey, that environmental degradation affected the seabirds directly, or that the laboratory results were inaccurate.

(A) the proportion of a seabird's diet consisting of fish was not as high, on average, in the 1880s as it is today

This matches one of our anticipated answer choices. A difference in diet is a possible cause of the difference in mercury levels. (A) is a candidate.

(B) the amount of mercury in a saltwater fish depends on the amount of pollution in the ocean habitat of fish

This answer includes irrelevant information. The argument is not concerned with how saltwater fish absorb mercury. Rather, the argument is concerns with the relative levels of mercury in saltwater fish now and 100 years ago. (B) is a loser.

(C) mercury derived from fish is essential for the normal growth of a seabird's feathers

This is irrelevant information. The argument is not concerned with whether mercury is beneficial or harmful to a seabird's feathers. (C) is a loser.

(D) the stuffed seabirds whose feathers were tested for mercury were not fully grown

This matches one of our anticipated answer choices. If mercury accumulates as the feathers grow, then the relative age of the birds would be important in determining the mercury levels in the fish. Age would thus be an *alternative cause*. (D) is a candidate.

(E) the process used to preserve birds in the 1880s did not substantially decrease the amount of mercury in the birds' feathers

This also matches one of our anticipated answer choices. If the process used to preserve the birds in the 1880s affected the amount of mercury in the birds' feathers, this could account for the differences in mercury levels. (E) is a candidate.

We now need to eliminate two candidates. On second reading, (A) is not what we are looking for. If birds from the 1880s ate less fish than birds today, that would present an *alternative cause*, not eliminate one. (D) also presents an *alternative cause*. If the birds from the 1880s were not fully grown, and mercury accumulates in feathers with age, this would provide an *alternative cause* for the difference in mercury levels. Therefore, (E) has to be the correct answer choice.

We can confirm this by performing the (Un)Necessary Assumption Test on the answer choices.

Answer choice (A) can be logically negated as follows:

the proportion of a seabird's diet consisting of fish *was* as high, on average, in the 1880s as it is today

This is actually a necessary assumption because it eliminates an *alternative cause* (a difference in diet). As the logically negated statement does not invalidate the argument, this answer choice has to be incorrect.

Answer choice (D) can be logically negated as follows:

the stuffed seabirds whose feathers were tested for mercury *were* fully grown

This is actually a necessary assumption because it eliminates an *alternative cause* (the birds from the 1880s were not fully grown). Therefore, this answer choice has to be incorrect.

Answer choice (E) can be logically negated as follows:

the process used in the 1880s *did* substantially decrease the amount of mercury in the birds' feathers

This invalidates the argument because it presents an *alternative cause*. So, we know this answer choice is correct.

If There Is a Fallacy

NA questions sometimes include flawed arguments. When the argument includes a fallacy, this calls for an approach that is almost identical to the one used to answer SA questions. You must identify the fallacy in the argument. Then you must look for an answer choice that fixes this error in reasoning. As with SA arguments, the most common fallacies in NA arguments are Questionable Assumption Fallacies.

The only difference between SA and NA questions containing fallacies is that the correct answer choice for an NA question is typically weak in logical force. Remember, the necessary assumption must be true in order for the argument to be valid. As a strong statement may possibly be false, such a statement is rarely the correct answer choice for an NA question. This means that answer choices that function as the sufficient assumption of an argument but are too strongly worded to be a necessary assumption are likely to be incorrect.

Let's look at an example:

> Consumer advocate: A recent study concluded that top-loading washing machines are superior overall to front-loaders. But front-loaders have the controls and access in front. This is more convenient for wheelchair users, some of whom find it highly inconvenient to remove laundry from top-loaders. So for some consumers front-loaders are superior.
>
> Which one of the following is an assumption upon which the consumer advocate's argument depends?
>
> (A) For some consumers the convenience of front-loaders outweighs the advantages of top-loaders in assessing which is superior.
> (B) Washing machines of a given type should be compared only with washing machines of that type.
> (C) Convenience is the only important factor in determining which type of washing machine is superior.
> (D) Retrieving clothes from a top-loader is convenient for people who do not use wheelchairs.
> (E) Retrieving clothes from front-loaders is inconvenient for people who are not wheelchair users.

The conclusion of the argument is that front-loading washing machines are superior to top-loading washing machines for some consumers. This is based on the premise that wheelchair users find it more convenient to use a front-loader than a top-loader. The conclusion is a SOME statement. Since some users must certainly be wheelchair users, this argument seems valid at first glance. However, the argument commits an Equivocation Fallacy. The premise states that wheelchair users find front-loading washing machines more convenient, while the conclusion states that these appliances are superior for some users. The terms *convenient* and *superior* are similar but not synonymous.

As we are dealing with an Equivocation Fallacy, we should anticipate information that shows that the two terms are distinct from one another. However, it is not necessary to equate convenience with superiority—such a claim would be too strong. Neither is it necessary to relate the assumption specifically to wheelchair users, as the conclusion only mentions some users. These may just be a subset of wheelchair users—the ones who find it highly inconvenient to remove laundry from top-loaders. We should look for an answer choice that states that some users find the convenience of front-loaders to override other factors in assessing superiority. To illustrate the point made previously about the difference between SA and NA questions containing flawed arguments, we will focus on only two of the answer choices.

(A) For some consumers the convenience of front-loaders outweighs the advantages of top-loaders in assessing which is superior.

This matches our anticipated answer choice. It must be the case that some users find that the convenience of front-loaders outweighs the advantages of top-loaders in assessing which type of appliance is superior. This fixes the Equivocation Fallacy by showing that, for some users, convenience determines superiority. In addition, this answer choice is weak in logical force, so it is suitable as a necessary assumption.

We can confirm this choice by applying the (Un)Necessary Assumption Test. (A) includes the strength modifier *some*, so it can be logically negated as follows:

For no consumer does the convenience of front-loaders outweigh the advantages of top-loaders in assessing which is superior.

If convenience does not outweigh the advantages of top-loaders for any consumers, then the argument is invalid (ignoring the fact that the fallacy itself already rendered the argument invalid). Therefore, (A) has to be the correct answer choice.

(C) Convenience is the only important factor in determining which type of washing machine is superior.

This answer choice fixes the fallacy in the argument. However, it is too strong to be the necessary assumption because of the term *only*. In fact, it is actually a sufficient assumption. The inclusion of the term *only* means that this statement does not necessarily have to be true in order for the argument to be valid. In other words, the argument could be valid if this statement was false.

We can confirm all this through the (Un)Necessary Assumption Test. (C) does not contain a strength modifier or conditional statement, so it can be logically negated as follows:

Convenience is not the only important factor in determining which type of washing machine is superior.

If convenience is not the only factor in determining which type of washing machine is superior, the argument is still valid. It does not matter if there are other factors, because the argument specifies that only some consumers find front-loaders superior because they are convenient. Therefore, (C) is incorrect.

If There Is No Causal Statement or Fallacy

Most arguments in NA questions contain neither a causal statement nor a fallacy. This makes it difficult to anticipate a correct answer choice. In some cases, the argument includes an assumption that is not significant enough to qualify as a Questionable Assumption Fallacy. In others, the argument includes a minor weakness such as the failure to address factors that, if true, would weaken the argument.

For this sort of question, it is often harder to anticipate an answer. You need to identify potential weaknesses in the argument and then anticipate a correct answer choice that eliminates this weakness while being necessarily true.

Let's look at an example:

> Many of those who are most opposed to cruelty to animals in the laboratory, in the slaughterhouse, or on the farm are people who truly love animals and who keep pets. The vast majority of domestic pets, however, are dogs and cats, and both of these species are usually fed meat. Therefore, many of those who are most opposed to cruelty to animals do, in fact, contribute to such cruelty.
>
> Which one of the following is an assumption made by the argument?
>
> (A) Loving pets requires loving all forms of animal life.
> (B) Many of those who are opposed to keeping dogs and cats as pets are also opposed to cruelty to animals.
> (C) Some people who work in laboratories, in slaughterhouses, or on farms are opposed to cruelty to animals.
> (D) Many popular pets are not usually fed meat.
> (E) Feeding meat to pets contributes to cruelty to animals.

The argument concludes that many of those who are most opposed to cruelty to animals actually contribute to such cruelty. This is based on the premise that these same people own domestic pets that are usually fed meat. This argument does not include a causal statement or a fallacy. However, it does seem to involve an assumption— that feeding meat to domestic pets contributes to cruelty to animals. If this assumption were not the case, the conclusion would be invalid. Therefore, we should anticipate a correct answer choice that validates this assumption with a weak statement.

(A) Loving pets requires loving all forms of animal life.

This is a very strongly worded statement. The argument says that many people who are opposed to animal cruelty love animals and keep pets. It is possible that these people would not condone the killing of animals for meat, but there is nothing to suggest you cannot love all forms of animal life and serve meat to your pets at the same time. This statement is not necessarily true. To confirm this, let's apply the (Un)Necessary Assumption Test. The logically negated version of this statement is as follows:

Loving pets does not require loving all forms of animal life.

This does not invalidate the argument. Therefore, (A) is a loser.

(B) Many of those who are opposed to keeping dogs and cats as pets are also opposed to cruelty to animals.

This answer choice is irrelevant, as we are only concerned with people who have domestic pets. (B) is a loser.

(C) Some people who work in laboratories, in slaughterhouses, or on farms are opposed to cruelty to animals.

This answer choice is irrelevant as it is not necessary to assume anything about where the animal lovers work. (C) is a loser.

(D) Many popular pets are not usually fed meat.

This answer choice also includes irrelevant information as the argument states that the majority of domestic pets are dogs and cats that eat meat. Additionally, assuming this would weaken the argument by offering an example of people who are opposed to animal cruelty and have a domestic pet that does not eat meat. (D) is a loser.

(E) Feeding meat to pets contributes to cruelty to animals.

This matches our anticipated answer choice. It is necessary that feeding meat to pets constitutes cruelty to animals in order for the argument to be valid. We can confirm this by applying the (Un)Necessary Assumption Test. (E) can be logically negated as follows:

Feeding meat to pets does not contribute to cruelty to animals.

This statement invalidates the argument, so (E) has to be correct.

Looking at the Answer Choices

The correct answer choice of an NA question must be true in order for the argument to be valid. Therefore, the correct answer choice is usually a weak statement. It presents new information that strengthens a causal statement, fixes a fallacy, or addresses a minor assumption or weakness in the argument. For many NA questions, it is difficult to anticipate a correct answer choice. Luckily, we can use the (Un)Necessary Assumption Test to verify a potential correct answer choice or eliminate an incorrect one. However, applying this test can be time-consuming, so it should only be done when necessary.

Incorrect answer choices tend to be statements that are strong in logical force. In many cases, these statements can function as a sufficient assumption—a statement that validates the argument but is not necessarily true. Other common types of incorrect answer choices are those that weaken an argument and those that include irrelevant information.

Drill: Necessary Assumption

Logically negate each of the following statements.

1. The greatest threat to domestic livestock is infectious disease.

2. Some qualified candidates never pass the bar exam.

3. The only way to avoid traffic is to take the highway.

4. The best man at a wedding should never make fun of the bride.

5. My best friend, Dennis, might make an appearance at the party.

6. The student with the highest grades in the school spoke to his peers about hard work and time management.

7. The case could be heard by the Supreme Court.

8. Unless we travel by car, we will not arrive at the theater on time.

9. Pinocchio's nose grew every time he told a lie.

10. The Wildcats' performance last night does not represent their true ability.

11. This weekend, I spent most of the time napping.

1. **The greatest threat to domestic livestock *is not* infectious disease.**

   The verb *is* should be negated to *is not*.

2. ***All* qualified candidates pass the bar exam.**

   This is a tricky one. The word *Some* should be negated to *No*, which gives us "No qualified candidates never pass the bar exam." The double negative is the logical equivalent of "All qualified candidates pass the bar exam." Note that only the first strength modifier should be negated.

3. **If we are to avoid traffic, we *do not necessarily* have to take the highway.**

   Conditional statements should be converted to the "if . . . then" form to make it easier to negate the statement. The word *only* modifies way, which refers to *taking the highway* (the necessary condition). This means that *avoiding traffic* is the sufficient condition. The statement can be reworded as "If we are to avoid traffic, we must take the highway." To negate a conditional statement, we must show that the necessary condition is not necessarily true.

4. **The best man at a wedding should *sometimes* make fun of the bride.**

   The word *never* is a strength modifier. It should be negated to *sometimes*.

5. **My best friend, Dennis, *will not make* an appearance at the party.**

   The verb *will make* should be negated to *will not make*.

6. **The student with the highest grades in the school *did not speak* to his peers about hard work and time management.**

   The verb *spoke* should be negated to *did not speak*.

7. **The case *could not be heard* by the Supreme Court.**

   The verb *could be heard* should be negated to *could not be heard*.

8. **If we are to arrive at the theater on time, we *do not necessarily* have to travel by car.**

   We should first convert the original *unless* statement to an "if . . . then" statement, which reads as "If we do not travel by car, we will not arrive at the theater on time." Since there is a negative in both the sufficient and necessary conditions, it is much simpler to covert this to its contrapositive, which is "If we are to arrive at the theater on time, we have to travel by car." Next, we should make the necessary condition unnecessary.

9. **Pinocchio's nose *did not grow every* time he told a lie.**

   The strength modifier *every* should be negated to *not every*. Note that when a strength modifier comes after a verb, it usually does not matter which one is negated. If we were to negate the verb in this statement, the outcome would be the same.

10. **The Wildcats' performance last night *represents* their true ability.**

    The verb *does not represent* should be negated to *represents*.

11. **This weekend, I spent *less than half* of the time napping.**

    The strength modifier *most* comes after the verb *spent*, so it does not matter which one is negated. If *most* is negated, we get "This weekend, I spent *less than half* of the time napping." If *spent* is negated, we get "This weekend, I *did not spend* most of the time napping." These two statements are logically equivalent.

Problem Set: Necessary Assumption

1. A reason Larson cannot do the assignment is that she has an unavoidable scheduling conflict. On the other hand, a reason Franks cannot do the assignment is that he does not quite have the assertiveness the task requires. So, the task must be assigned to Parker, the only supervisor in the shipping department other than Larson and Franks.

   The argument depends on assuming which one of the following?

   (A) Larson has the assertiveness the task requires.
   (B) The task cannot be assigned to anyone other than a supervisor in the shipping department.
   (C) Franks would be assigned the task if Franks had the assertiveness the task requires.
   (D) The task cannot be assigned to anyone who has any kind of scheduling conflict.
   (E) No one who is not a supervisor in the shipping department has the assertiveness this task requires.

2. Reducing stress lessens a person's sensitivity to pain. This is the conclusion reached by researchers who played extended audiotapes to patients before they underwent surgery and afterward while they were recovering. One tape consisted of conversation; the other consisted of music. Those who listened only to the latter tape required less anesthesia during surgery and fewer painkillers afterward than those who listened only to the former tape.

   Which one of the following is an assumption on which the researchers' reasoning depends?

   (A) All of the patients in the study listened to the same tape before surgery as they listened to after surgery.
   (B) Anticipating surgery is no less stressful than recovering from surgery.
   (C) Listening to music reduces stress.
   (D) The psychological effects of music are not changed by anesthesia or painkillers.
   (E) Both anesthesia and painkillers tend to reduce stress.

3. Museum visitor: The national government has mandated a 5 percent increase in the minimum wage paid to all workers. This mandate will adversely affect the museum-going public. The museum's revenue does not currently exceed its expenses, and since the mandate will significantly increase the museum's operating expenses, the museum will be forced either to raise admission fees or to decrease services.

Which one of the following is an assumption required by the museum visitor's argument?

(A) Some of the museum's employees are not paid significantly more than the minimum wage.
(B) The museum's revenue from admission fees has remained constant over the past five years.
(C) Some of the museum's employees are paid more than the current minimum wage.
(D) The annual number of visitors to the museum has increased steadily.
(E) Not all visitors to the museum are required to pay an admission fee.

4. In 1963, a young macaque monkey was observed venturing into a hot spring to retrieve food which had fallen in. Soon, other macaques began to enter the spring, and over a few years this behavior was adopted by the entire troop. Prior to 1963, no macaques had ever been observed in the hot spring; by 1990, the troop was regularly spending time there during the winters. Thus, these macaques are able to adopt and pass on new patterns of social behavior, and are not complete captives of their genetic heritage.

Which one of the following is an assumption required by the argument above?

(A) Mutations in the genetic heritage of a certain variety of macaques can occur over a time span as short as a few years or decades.
(B) New patterns of behavior that emerge in macaque populations over the course of a few years or decades are not necessarily genetically determined.
(C) Only when behaviors become typical among an animal population can we conclude that a genetic alteration has occurred in that variety or species.
(D) The social behaviors of macaques are completely independent of their genetic heritage.
(E) The macaques' new pattern of behavior will persist over several generations.

5. Reporter: A team of scientists has recently devised a new test that for the first time accurately diagnoses autism in children as young as 18 months old. When used to evaluate 16,000 children at their 18-month checkup, the test correctly diagnosed all 10 children later confirmed to be autistic, though it also wrongly identified 2 children as autistic. Autistic children can therefore now benefit much earlier in life than before from the treatments already available.

Which one of the following is an assumption on which the reporter's argument depends?

(A) No test intended for diagnosing autism at such an early age existed before the new test was devised.

(B) A diagnostic test that sometimes falsely gives a positive diagnosis can still provide a reasonable basis for treatment decisions.

(C) The new test can be used to evaluate all children, regardless of the level of development of their verbal skills.

(D) Those children incorrectly identified as autistic will not be adversely affected by treatments aimed at helping autistic children.

(E) There was no reliable evidence that autism could affect children so young until the advent of the new test.

6. Humanitarian considerations aside, sheer economics dictates that country X should institute, as country Y has done, a nationwide system of air and ground transportation for conveying seriously injured persons to specialized trauma centers. Timely access to the kind of medical care that only specialized centers can provide could save the lives of many people. The earnings of these people would result in a substantial increase in country X's gross national product, and the taxes paid on those earnings would substantially augment government revenues.

The argument depends on the assumption that

(A) lifetime per-capita income is roughly the same in country X as it is in country Y

(B) there are no specialized trauma centers in country X at present

(C) the treatment of seriously injured persons in trauma centers is not more costly than treatment elsewhere

(D) there would be a net increase in employment in country X if more persons survived serious injury

(E) most people seriously injured in automobile accidents in country X do not now receive treatment in specialized trauma centers

7. Repressors – people who unconsciously inhibit their display of emotion – exhibit significant increases in heart rate when they encounter emotion-provoking situations. Nonrepressors have similar physiological responses when they encounter such situations and consciously inhibit their display of emotion. Thus the very act of inhibiting displays of emotion, whether done consciously or unconsciously, causes a sharp rise in heart rate.

Which one of the following is an assumption required by the argument?

(A) Encountering an emotion-provoking situation is not sufficient to cause nonrepressors' heart rates to rise sharply.

(B) Nonrepressors can inhibit facial and bodily displays of emotion as well as repressors do.

(C) Despite their outward calm, repressors normally feel even more excited than do nonrepressors in an emotion-provoking situation.

(D) People who are ordinarily very emotional can refrain from feeling strong emotions when experimenters ask them to do so.

(E) In situations that do not tend to provoke emotions, the average heart rate of repressors is the same as that of nonrepressors.

8. Art critic: Abstract paintings are nonrepresentational, and so the only measure of their worth is their interplay of color, texture, and form. But for a painting to spur the viewer to political action, instances of social injustice must be not only represented, but also clearly comprehensible as such. Therefore, abstract painting can never be a politically significant art form.

Which one of the following is an assumption that is required by the art critic's argument?

(A) Abstract painting cannot stimulate people to act.

(B) Unless people view representations of social injustice, their political activity is insignificant.

(C) Only art that prompts people to counter social injustice is significant art.

(D) Paintings that fail to move a viewer to political action cannot be politically significant.

(E) The interplay of color, texture, and form is not a measure of the worth of representational paintings.

Problem Set: Necessary Assumption — Answers

1. **Correct Answer (B).** *Prep Test 45, Section 1, Question 3.*

Fallacy: Selection

The argument concludes that the task must be assigned to Parker because he is the only supervisor in the shipping department besides Larson and Franks, both of whom are unable to perform the task. This argument does not include a causal statement, but it commits a Selection Fallacy. We are told that Parker is the only supervisor in the shipping department, but why can the task not be assigned to someone else? This argument fails to explicitly state that Larson, Parker, and Franks are the only candidates for the task. We should anticipate a correct answer choice that fixes this fallacy, most likely by stating that only supervisors in the shipping department are able to do the assignment.

(A) Larson has the assertiveness the task requires.

This is irrelevant information because the argument has already stated that Larson is unavailable. The task will be assigned to Parker. (A) is a loser.

(B) The task cannot be assigned to anyone other than a supervisor in the shipping department.

This matches our anticipated answer choice. If the task must be assigned to a supervisor, this fixes the Selection Fallacy. (B) is a candidate.

(C) Franks would be assigned the task if Franks had the assertiveness the task requires.

This is not necessarily true. The argument states that Franks is not assertive enough for the task. An assumption about what would happen if he was assertive enough cannot be the necessary assumption. (C) is a loser.

(D) The task cannot be assigned to anyone who has any kind of scheduling conflict.

Larson's scheduling conflict is unavoidable, and this is stated as the reason why Larson cannot do the assignment. However, it is not necessarily true that everyone with a scheduling conflict is unable to do the assignment. (D) is a loser.

(E) No one who is not a supervisor in the shipping department has the assertiveness this task requires.

This is sufficient to fix the fallacy in the argument. If (E) were assumed, then it would be the case that only supervisors in the shipping department would be able to do the task, with Parker being the only supervisor available. However, this statement is too strong to be the necessary assumption. It does not necessarily have to be true in order for the argument to be valid. If someone who is not a supervisor in the shipping department is assertive enough, the argument could still be valid. Maybe there is another requirement for the task that makes Parker the only candidate. We can confirm this line of reasoning through the (Un)Necessary Assumption Test. By negating *no one* to *someone*, we get "Someone who is not a supervisor in the shipping department has the assertiveness this task requires." This does not invalidate the argument, so (E) is a loser.

As (B) is the only candidate, it has to be the correct answer choice. For confirmation, we can use the (Un) Necessary Assumption Test. When logically negated, (B) reads as "The task can be assigned to anyone other than a supervisor in the shipping department," which invalidates the argument.

2. **Correct Answer (C).** *Prep Test 52, Section 3, Question 9.*

Fallacy: Questionable Assumption

The argument concludes that reducing stress lessens a person's sensitivity to pain. The argument's evidence for this is that those who listened to music before and after surgery required less anesthesia and fewer painkillers than those who listened to normal conversations. This argument commits a Questionable Assumption Fallacy. It assumes that listening to music reduces stress (thereby making people less sensitive to pain). We should anticipate a correct answer choice that validates this assumption.

(A) All of the patients in the study listened to the same tape before surgery as they listened to after surgery.

This is a strong statement that does not have to be true in order for the argument to be valid. The patients could have listened to different tapes of music before and after surgery. (A) is a loser.

(B) Anticipating surgery is no less stressful than recovering from surgery.

This is irrelevant information. Whether anticipating surgery is more or less stressful than recovering from surgery has nothing to do with the conclusion of the argument. (B) is a loser.

(C) Listening to music reduces stress.

This matches our anticipated answer choice. The argument assumes that reducing stress lessens sensitivity to pain based on the fact that people who listened to music were less sensitive to pain. (C) states that listening to music reduces stress, making it a candidate.

(D) The psychological effects of music are not changed by anesthesia or painkillers.

This answer choice includes irrelevant information. Even if we assume that psychological effects include stress reduction, this statement would not need to be true for the argument to be valid and would not address the questionable assumption. Whether drugs affect the psychological effects of music does not matter in the context of this argument. (D) is a loser.

(E) Both anesthesia and painkillers tend to reduce stress.

Both groups received anesthesia and painkillers. The group that listened to music required less anesthesia and fewer painkillers. Whether these drugs reduce stress or not is irrelevant to argument. (E) is a loser.

As (C) is the only candidate, it has to be the correct answer choice. If we needed to, we could confirm this using the (Un)Necessary Assumption Test. (C) can be logically negated to read as "Listening to music does not reduce stress," which invalidates the argument.

3. **Correct Answer (A).** *Prep Test 54, Section 2, Question 9.*

The argument concludes that the 5 percent minimum wage increase will adversely affect the museum-going public. The evidence for this claim is that the museum's revenue does not exceed its expenses, the increase will significantly increase the museum's operating expenses, and the museum will be forced to either raise admission fees or to decrease services. The last statement is a subsidiary conclusion that has a *since premise, conclusion* structure. It directly supports the main conclusion that the museum-going public would be adversely affected. This NA question is unusual in that it includes conditional statements. It can be outlined as follows:

P1: Revenue does not exceed expenses.
P2: Wage Mandate → Increase in Expenses
_____
SC: Increase in Expenses → Raise Fees OR Decrease Services
_____
C: Wage Mandate → Adversely Affect Public

There may appear to be a Questionable Assumption here as there is no direct connection between Raise Fees OR Decrease Services and Adversely Affect Public. However, the fact that raising fees or decreasing services will adversely affect the public seems obvious, and it is reasonable for the argument to assume this. Therefore, the correct answer choice is unlikely to be related to this. For this reason, we can view the logic chain as follows:

Wage Mandate → Increase in Expenses → Raise Fees OR Decrease Services → Adversely Affect Public

The conclusion is a valid inference that has been derived through combining the ends of this chain. The argument does not include a causal statement and does not appear to include a fallacy. Therefore, we should anticipate a correct answer choice that addresses a minor assumption or weakness in the argument.

(A) Some of the museum's employees are not paid significantly more than the minimum wage.

This matches our anticipated answer choice. It eliminates a minor weakness in the argument. If all of the employees were paid significantly more than the minimum wage, the minimum wage increase would not increase operating expenses (and therefore not adversely affect the public). (A) is a candidate.

(B) The museum's revenue from admission fees has remained constant over the past five years.

This is irrelevant information. The argument states that admission fees may rise because of the wage increase. Whether or not fees have increased in the past does not affect the argument. (B) is a loser.

(C) Some of the museum's employees are paid more than the current minimum wage.

This is similar to answer choice (A), but it actually expresses the opposite idea. It also leaves out the term *significantly*. If a minority of employees were paid more than the minimum wage, then the majority would see their wage increase. We can confirm that this answer choice is incorrect using the (Un)Necessary Assumption Test. The statement can be logically negated to read as "None of the museum's employees are paid more than the current minimum wage" or "All of the museum's employees are not paid more than the current minimum wage." Neither of these statements would invalidate the argument. (C) is a loser.

(D) The annual number of visitors to the museum has increased steadily.

This does not necessarily need to be true in order for the argument to be valid. In addition, it may actually weaken the argument because an increase in visitors could offset increased operating expenses. (D) is a loser.

(E) Not all visitors to the museum are required to pay an admission fee.

This information is irrelevant. Whether or not all visitors were required to pay the admission fee would not affect the argument. (E) is a loser.

As (A) is the only candidate, it has to be the correct answer choice. This can be confirmed using the (Un)Necessary Assumption Test. After negating *some* to *none*, we must eliminate the double negative. The logically negated version of (A) therefore reads as "All of the museum's employees are paid significantly more than the minimum wage," which invalidates the argument.

4. **Correct Answer (B).** *Prep Test 42, Section 2, Question 14.*

The argument begins with the observation that a single macaque exhibited a certain behavior while retrieving food in 1963, after which the behavior became much more common throughout the monkey's entire troop. The behavior had not been observed prior to 1963. The argument concludes that the monkeys are able to adopt and pass on new patterns of social behavior and are not complete captives of their genetic heritage. In the context of the rest of the sentence, this phrase seems to mean that not all behaviors of macaque monkeys are genetically determined—they also exhibit learned behaviors, such as retrieving food from a hot spring. This argument does not include a causal statement or a fallacy. However, it does have a potential weakness. The monkey was first observed retrieving food from the hot spring in 1963, but what if this behavior has always been performed but not previously observed? Maybe it has become more common in recent years due to some other factor. We should anticipate a correct answer choice that addresses this potential weakness. It is likely to provide information indicating that the monkeys actually learned the behavior or that they are not born with the ability to figure out how to retrieve food from the hot spring on their own.

(A) Mutations in the genetic heritage of a certain variety of macaques can occur over a time span as short as a few years or decades.

This is irrelevant information. The argument rests on the idea that the behavior is not genetic in origin, so it does not matter how often mutations in genetic heritage may occur. (A) is a loser.

(B) New patterns of behavior that emerge in macaque populations over the course of a few years or decades are not necessarily genetically determined.

This is not our anticipated answer choice, but it is necessary for the argument to assume, and it eliminates the potential weakness in the argument. (B) clearly states that macaque populations acquire new behaviors that are not genetically determined over short periods of time. This is necessarily true if the monkeys learned how to gather food from a hot spring in 1963. (B) is a candidate.

(C) Only when behaviors become typical among an animal population can we conclude that a genetic alteration has occurred in that variety or species.

This is incorrect for two reasons. First, the argument concludes that regularly performed behaviors are learned, not that they are the result of genetic alteration. Second, this statement is far too strong to be a necessary assumption. (C) is a loser.

(D) The social behaviors of macaques are completely independent of their genetic heritage.

This statement is too strong to be a necessary assumption. The argument's validity does not hinge on all social behaviors being independent of their genetic heritage. It just requires that one behavior did not originate from the genetic heritage. (D) is a loser.

(E) The macaques' new pattern of behavior will persist over several generations.

This is irrelevant information. How long the behavior will persist for does not affect the argument. (E) is a loser.

As (B) is the only candidate, it has to be the correct answer choice. The (Un)Necessary Assumption Test confirms this. If we logically negate (B), it reads as "New patterns of behavior that emerge in macaque populations over the course of a few years or decades are genetically determined." This invalidates the argument.

5. **Correct Answer (B).** *Prep Test 41, Section 3, Question 17.*

The argument concludes that autistic children can now benefit much earlier in life from treatment. This is supported by the premise that new research shows that when a test evaluated 16,000 children during their 18-month checkup, the test correctly diagnosed 10 children as being autistic. However, two children were wrongly identified as being autistic. This is background information that does not necessarily weaken the conclusion, which only speaks to whether autistic children can benefit from treatment. The argument does not contain a causal statement or a fallacy. We should anticipate a correct answer choice that addresses a minor assumption or potential weakness of the argument.

(A) No test intended for diagnosing autism at such an early age existed before the new test was devised.

This is not necessarily true. The argument states that this is the first time a test has diagnosed autism accurately at that age. There may have been earlier tests that were intended to diagnose autism but which were inaccurate. (A) is a loser.

(B) A diagnostic test that sometimes falsely gives a positive diagnosis can still provide a reasonable basis for treatment decisions.

This matches our anticipated answer choice. The argument concludes that because of the new test, children can benefit from treatment. The test sometimes gives a false positive diagnosis, so it is necessary to assume that a test that gives false positive diagnoses can still provide a reasonable basis for treatment decisions. (B) eliminates the potential weakness that the diagnostic test might not be reliable because it sometimes gives false positives. (B) is a candidate.

(C) The new test can be used to evaluate all children, regardless of the level of development of their verbal skills.

This answer choice is too strong. The argument does not claim that the new test can be used to evaluate all children. In addition, this statement need not be true in order for the argument to be valid. (C) is a loser.

(D) Those children incorrectly identified as autistic will not be adversely affected by treatments aimed at helping autistic children.

This is irrelevant information. The argument concludes that autistic children will benefit. Whether or not nonautistic children are adversely affected does not affect the argument. (D) is a loser.

(E) There was no reliable evidence that autism could affect children so young until the advent of the new test.

The argument does not need to assume this because the test's importance depends on its ability to diagnose autism. Whether or not there was evidence the disease affected children so young is immaterial to the argument. (E) is a loser.

As (B) is the only candidate, it has to be the correct answer choice. We can confirm this using the Un(Necessary) Assumption Test. The logically negated version of (B) is "A diagnostic test . . . cannot provide a reasonable basis for treatment decisions," which would invalidate the argument.

6. **Correct Answer (D).** *Prep Test 52, Section 3, Question 13.*

The conclusion of this argument is that country X should institute a nationwide air and ground transportation system for conveying seriously injured persons to special trauma centers. The evidence for this claim is that this system would save lives, allowing the people who survive to contribute to country X's gross national product and pay taxes on their earnings. The argument can be outlined as follows:

P1: A transportation system would save lives.
P2: The earnings of these people contributes to GNP and tax revenue.
C: Economics dictates that country X build the transportation system.

There is no causal statement or fallacy in the argument, so we should anticipate a correct answer choice that addresses a minor assumption or potential weakness in the argument. For example, the argument assumes that the people using the system would earn money and pay taxes following their treatment.

(A) lifetime per-capita income is roughly the same in country X as it is in country Y

This is irrelevant information. The argument does not depend on country Y being similar to country X. (A) is a loser.

(B) there are no specialized trauma centers in country X at present

This weakens the argument. If there are no specialized trauma centers in country X, what would the nationwide system of air and ground transportation be used for? (B) is a loser.

(C) the treatment of seriously injured persons in trauma centers is not more costly than treatment elsewhere

The argument states that only specialized care centers can save the lives of many people. Therefore, it does not matter if these care centers are more costly or not. (C) is a loser.

(D) there would be a net increase in employment in country X if more persons survived serious injury

This matches our anticipated answer choice. If the system resulted in a net increase in employment because seriously injured people were able to return to work, then the assumption in the argument would be validated. This statement also needs to be true in order for the argument to be valid. (D) is a candidate.

(E) most people seriously injured in automobile accidents in country X do not now receive treatment in specialized trauma centers

This answer choice is about people injured in automobile accidents, a subset of seriously injured persons. What about people injured in other types of accidents? In addition, even if we focus on people involved in automobile accidents, the system is designed to ensure timely access to the centers. (E) is a loser.

As (D) is the only candidate, it has to be the correct answer choice. We can confirm this using the (Un)Necessary Assumption Test. Logically negating this statement involves converting it to an "if . . . then" statement and then negating the necessary condition, giving us "If more persons survived serious injury, there would not necessarily be a net increase in employment in country X," which invalidates the argument.

7. **Correct Answer (A).** *Prep Test 40, Section 3, Question 22.*

Element: Causal Relationship

The argument contains a causal conclusion that can be represented as Inhibiting Emotion CAUSE Heart Rate Increase. The argument's evidence for this is that both repressors (people who unconsciously inhibit their emotions) and nonrepressors (people who consciously inhibit their emotions) exhibit significant increases in heart rate when encountering emotion-provoking situations. We should anticipate a correct answer choice that eliminates an *alternative cause*, provides an example of *same cause, same effect*, or provides an example of *no cause, no effect*. The most obvious *alternative cause* for this argument is that the increase in heart rate was caused not by the inhibition of emotion during an emotion-provoking situation but by the emotion-provoking situation itself.

(A) Encountering an emotion-provoking situation is not sufficient to cause nonrepressors' heart rates to rise sharply.

This matches our anticipated answer choice. (A) is a candidate.

(B) Nonrepressors can inhibit facial and bodily displays of emotion as well as repressors do.

This is irrelevant information. How well people are able to inhibit their emotion is not an issue in this argument. (B) is a loser.

(C) Despite their outward calm, repressors normally feel even more excited than do nonrepressors in an emotion-provoking situation.

This is irrelevant information. Both repressors and nonrepressors exhibit similar physiological responses, so the amount of excitement one feels is immaterial to the argument. (C) is a loser.

(D) People who are ordinarily very emotional can refrain from feeling strong emotions when experimenters ask them to do so.

This is irrelevant information. It is unclear whether this answer choice addresses either of the groups. (D) is a loser.

(E) In situations that do not tend to provoke emotions, the average heart rate of repressors is the same as that of nonrepressors.

This eliminates the possibility that repressors and nonrepressors have different normal heart rates. However, the two groups do not need to be similar in this respect because both groups experienced an increase in heart rate. (E) is a loser.

As (A) is the only candidate, it has to be the correct answer choice. This can be confirmed using the (Un)Necessary Assumption Test. The logically negated version of (A) is "Encountering an emotion-provoking situation is sufficient to cause nonrepressors' heart rates to rise sharply," which invalidates the argument.

8. **Correct Answer (D).** *Prep Test 47, Section 3, Question 17.*

Fallacy: Questionable Assumption

The art critic's conclusion is that abstract painting can never be a politically significant art form. The argument contains many complex conditional statements indicated by words such as *are*, *must*, and *never*. This is uncommon for an NA question. The argument can be outlined as follows:

P1: Abstract Paintings → Nonrepresentational
P2: Spur Viewer to Political Action → Social Injustice Represented AND Comprehensible
C: Abstract Paintings → ~~Politically Significant Art~~

The argument commits a Questionable Assumption Fallacy, so we will solve it in much the same way as we would an SA question containing conditional statements. The term ~~Politically Significant Art~~ is a new term, so we should expect to see it in the necessary condition of the assumption. The term Abstract Paintings in the sufficient condition of the conclusion also appears in the sufficient condition of the first premise. If we find the contrapositive of the second premise, we get ~~Social Injustice Represented~~ OR ~~Comprehensible~~ → ~~Spur Viewer to Political Action~~. This results in the necessary condition of the first premise and the sufficient condition of the second premise being identical. If something is nonrepresentational, then it must be the case that it cannot adequately represent social injustice. Therefore, we can combine the first premise with the contrapositive of the second premise to get Abstract Paintings → Nonrepresentational → ~~Spur Viewer to Political Action~~. In order to reach the conclusion, the necessary assumption must be ~~Spur Viewer to Political Action~~ → ~~Politically Significant Art~~. This results in the following logic chain:

Abstract Paintings → Nonrepresentational → ~~Spur Viewer to Political Action~~ → ~~Politically Significant Art~~

The conclusion is a valid inference based on combining the end of this chain, so we should anticipate a correct answer choice that expresses ~~Spur Viewer to Political Action~~ → ~~Politically Significant Art~~ (or its contrapositive).

We can quickly eliminate (A), (C), and (E) because they do not include the new term present in the conclusion of the argument.

(B) Unless people view representations of social injustice, their political activity is insignificant.

This answer choice does not include the term Spur Viewer to Political Action. It can be diagrammed as ~~Social Injustice Represented~~ → ~~Politically Significant Art~~. (B) is a loser.

(D) Paintings that fail to move a viewer to political action cannot be politically significant.

This matches our anticipated answer choice. It can be diagrammed as ~~Spur Viewer to Political Action~~ → ~~Politically Significant Art~~. (D) has to be the correct answer choice. If we need to confirm this, we can use the (Un)Necessary Assumption Test. The logically negated statement reads as "If it is politically significant art, then it does not necessarily need to spur the viewer to political action." This would invalidate the argument.

Paradox

Chapter 5

PROCESS FAMILY

Strengthen
Weaken
Evaluation
Sufficient Assumption
Necessary Assumption
Paradox

Paradox
≈ 4.0 questions per test

Example Prompts

Which one of the following, if true, *most helps to resolve the paradox* described above?

Which one of the following, if true, *contributes most to an explanation of the phenomena* described?

Which one of the following, if true, *most helps to reconcile the discrepancy* described above?

Take These Steps

Read the stimulus, which always includes a fact pattern. Identify and summarize the claim and the unexpected result that arises from it.

Determine what the expected result of the claim would be.

Anticipate a correct answer choice that explains the unexpected result without invalidating the claim.

Answer Choices

Correct Answer Choices	Incorrect Answer Choices
Statements that explain the unexpected result without invalidating the claim	Statements that do not explain the unexpected result
	Statements that explain the unexpected result but invalidate the claim
	Statements that explain the expected result instead of the unexpected result
	Irrelevant information

Paradox (P) questions ask you to select an answer choice that explains an unexpected result. In this way, they are similar IMP questions that include an unusual circumstance. Unlike the other question types in the Process Family, P questions always include a stimulus with a fact pattern. Typically, a claim is made at the beginning or in the middle of the stimulus. At the end of the stimulus (usually in the last sentence), an unexpected result of this claim is presented. This is almost always indicated by the word *nevertheless*, *but*, *however*, *yet*, *surprisingly*, *paradoxically*, or *although*.

How to Solve Paradox Questions

The first step toward solving a P question is to carefully read the fact pattern. Next, identify and summarize the claim and the unexpected result that arises from it. Go on to extrapolate the expected result of the claim. Lastly, anticipate a correct answer choice that explains the unexpected result without invalidating the claim. Consider the following:

> **During the 1980s, the number of people employed in Nation X's agricultural sector decreased by 40 percent. Nevertheless, during this same time period, agricultural output increased substantially in Nation X.**

Claim	Unexpected Result	Expected Result
Agricultural employment in Nation X decreased by 40 percent.	Agricultural output in Nation X increased substantially.	Agricultural output in Nation X would decrease.

As the chart shows, the claim is that agricultural employment decreased by 40 percent. The unexpected result of this claim is that agricultural output increased. The expected result of the claim is that output would decrease.

There are a number of possible explanations for the increase in agricultural output. For example,

1. **The agricultural jobs were lost due to the introduction of more productive automated processes.**
2. **Nation X started growing crop Z during this time period, which requires much less labor but has higher yields than other crops grown in Nation X.**
3. **During the 1980s, newly developed pesticides substantially decreased the number of crops lost to insect infestation.**

There are many more possible explanations. It is often difficult to anticipate the specific reason that will appear in the correct answer choice. However, the anticipation process is useful because it can give you a general sense of what to look for when going through the answer choices. Note that given the number of possible explanations for an unexpected result, EXCEPT prompts are very common in P questions. In this case, the four incorrect answer choices include valid reasons for the unexpected result, while the correct answer choice does not.

Let's look at an example:

> Medical research has established that the Beta Diet is healthier than a more conventional diet. But on average, people who have followed the Beta Diet for several decades are much more likely to be in poor health than are people whose diet is more conventional.
>
> Which one of the following, if true, most helps to resolve the apparent conflict between the two statements above?
>
> (A) On average, people who have followed the Beta Diet for their entire lives are much

(B) The Beta Diet is used primarily as a treatment for a condition that adversely affects overall health.

(C) People of average health who switch from a conventional diet to the Beta Diet generally find that their health improves substantially as a result.

(D) The Beta Diet provides dramatic health benefits for some people but only minor benefits for others.

(E) Recent research has shown that a diet high in fruits, vegetables, and skim milk is even healthier than the Beta Diet.

As is the case with all P questions, the stimulus includes a fact pattern. The claim that the Beta Diet is healthier than a normal diet is stated in the first sentence. The unexpected result is that people who follow the Beta Diet are more likely to have poor health than those who follow a conventional diet. Based on the claim, we would expect people who follow the Beta diet to be healthier. We should anticipate a correct answer choice that explains the unexpected result without invalidating the claim. There are a number of possible explanations for the unexpected result. For example, people on the Beta Diet may use it as a substitute for exercise, or they may be unhealthier than other people to begin with.

(A) On average, people who have followed the Beta Diet for their entire lives are much more likely to have a variety of healthful habits than are people whose diet is more conventional.

This would explain the expected result, not the unexpected result. If people on the Beta Diet had healthful habits, they would be healthier than average. (A) is a loser.

(B) The Beta Diet is used primarily as a treatment for a condition that adversely affects overall health.

This would explain the unexpected result. If most of the people on the Beta Diet are using it to treat a chronic health condition, then it makes sense that they are less healthy on average than people who follow a more conventional diet. This answer choice seems to explain the unexpected result without invalidating the claim. (B) is a candidate.

(C) People of average health who switch from a conventional diet to the Beta Diet generally find that their health improves substantially as a result.

This answer choice explains the expected result. It presents evidence that the Beta Diet is healthy. (C) is a loser.

(D) The Beta Diet provides dramatic health benefits for some people but only minor benefits for others.

This answer choice explains the expected result. Whether the Beta diet provides dramatic or minor health benefits, it must still improve the health of people who follow it. (D) is a loser.

(E) Recent research has shown that a diet high in fruits, vegetables, and skim milk is even healthier than the Beta Diet.

This is irrelevant information. The fact that there may be even healthier diets than the Beta Diet does not relate to the comparison between people who have followed the Beta diet and people who have followed a conventional diet. (E) is a loser.

As (B) is the only candidate, it has to be the correct answer choice.

Looking at the Answer Choices

The correct answer choice is always a statement that explains the unexpected result without invalidating the claim.

Incorrect answer choices often explain the expected result rather than the unexpected result. And some provide an explanation for the unexpected result that invalidates the claim. For example, if the claim is that Car X is more reliable than other models and the unexpected result is that owners of Car X spend more than average on car repairs, an incorrect answer choice using this trick might state that Car X is unreliable. Students often struggle with this type of incorrect answer choice. Always keep in mind that if an answer choice invalidates the claim, it is incorrect. Meanwhile, some incorrect answer choices simply present irrelevant information.

Drill: Paradox

Read the stimulus below and determine whether each answer choice 1) explains the unexpected result and 2) invalidates the first claim.

Carrots are known to be one of the best sources of naturally occurring vitamin A. However, although farmers in Canada and the United States report increasing demand for carrots over the last decade, the number of people diagnosed with vitamin A deficiency in these countries has also increased in that time.

Each of the following, if true of Canada and the United States over the last decade, helps to resolve the apparent discrepancy above EXCEPT:

Answer Choices	Does it explain the unexpected result?	Does it invalidate the claim?
A. Weather conditions have caused a decrease in the availability of carrots.		
B. Instead of carrots, many people have begun purchasing Tofarrots, a tofu-based carrot substitute that lacks vitamin A.		
C. Public health organizations have run ad campaigns informing people about the health benefits of carrots.		
D. Carrot consumption has increased only among those demographic groups that have historically had vitamin A deficiency rates.		
E. The purchase of peeled and chopped carrots has become very popular, though carrots are known to lose their vitamins quickly once peeled.		
F. The population has significantly increased in every age group.		
G. Amid growing concern among the medical community about vitamin A deficiency, many doctors are now testing for it more often than they did in the past.		
H. The average person who buys carrots buys significantly fewer carrots than she or he did in the past.		
I. Certain cuisines that have become popular use many more vegetable ingredients, including carrots, than most cuisines that were previously popular.		

Drill: Paradox — Answers

Answer Choices	Does it explain the unexpected result?	Does it invalidate the claim?
A. Weather conditions have caused a decrease in the availability of carrots.	Yes	No
B. Instead of carrots, many people have begun purchasing Tofarrots, a tofu-based carrot substitute that lacks vitamin A.	Yes	Yes
C. Public health organizations have run ad campaigns informing people about the health benefits of carrots.	No	No
D. Carrot consumption has increased only among those demographic groups that have historically had vitamin A deficiency rates.	Yes	No
E. The purchase of peeled and chopped carrots has become very popular, though carrots are known to lose their vitamins quickly once peeled.	Yes	No
F. The population has significantly increased in every age group.	Yes	No
G. Amid growing concern among the medical community about vitamin A deficiency, many doctors are now testing for it more often than they did in the past.	Yes	No
H. The average person who buys carrots buys significantly fewer carrots than she or he did in the past.	Yes	Yes
I. Certain cuisines that have become popular use many more vegetable ingredients, including carrots, than most cuisines that were previously popular.	No	No

Problem Set: Paradox

1. Two randomly selected groups of 30 adults each were asked to write short stories on a particular topic. One group was told that the best stories would be awarded cash prizes, while the other group was not told of any prizes. Each story was evaluated by a team of judges who were given no indication of the group from which the story came. The stories submitted by those who thought they were competing for prizes were ranked on average significantly lower than the stories from the other group.

Which one of the following, if true, most helps to explain the difference in average ranking between the two groups' stories?

(A) The cash prizes were too small to motivate an average adult to make a significant effort to produce stories of high quality.

(B) People writing to win prizes show a greater than usual tendency to produce stereotypical stories that show little creativity.

(C) Most adults show little originality in writing stories on a topic suggested by someone else.

(D) The team of judges was biased in favor of stories that they judged to be more realistic.

(E) No one explained clearly to either group what standards would be used in judging their stories.

2. For one academic year all the students at a high school were observed. The aim was to test the hypothesis that studying more increased a student's chances of earning a higher grade. It turned out that the students who spent the most time studying did not earn grades as high as did many students who studied less. Nonetheless, the researchers concluded that the results of the observation supported the initial hypothesis.

Which one of the following, if true, most helps to explain why the researchers drew the conclusion described above?

(A) The students who spent the most time studying earned higher grades than did some students who studied for less time than the average.

(B) The students tended to get slightly lower grades as the academic year progressed.

(C) In each course, the more a student studied, the better his or her grade was in that course.

(D) The students who spent the least time studying tended to be students with no more than average involvement in extracurricular activities.

(E) Students who spent more time studying understood the course material better than other students did.

3. The cost of a semester's tuition at a certain university is based on the number of courses in which a student enrolls that semester. Although the cost per course at that university has not risen in four years, many of its students who could afford the tuition when they first enrolled now claim they can no longer afford it.

Each of the following, if true, helps to resolve the apparent discrepancy above EXCEPT:

(A) Faculty salaries at the university have risen slightly over the past four years.

(B) The number of courses per semester for which full-time students are required to enroll is higher this year than any time in the past.

(C) The cost of living in the vicinity of the university has risen over the last two years.

(D) The university awards new students a large number of scholarships that are renewed each year for the students who maintain high grade averages.

(E) The university has turned many of its part-time office jobs, for which students had generally been hired, into full-time, nonstudent positions.

4. Provinces and states with stringent car safety requirements, including required use of seat belts and annual safety inspections, have on average higher rates of accidents per kilometer driven than do provinces and states with less stringent requirements. Nevertheless, most highway safety experts agree that more stringent requirements do reduce accident rates.

Which one of the following, if true, most helps to reconcile the safety experts' belief with the apparently contrary evidence described above?

(A) Annual safety inspections ensure that car tires are replaced before they grow old.

(B) Drivers often become overconfident after their cars have passed a thorough safety inspection.

(C) The roads in provinces and states with stringent car safety requirements are far more congested and therefore dangerous than in other provinces and states.

(D) Psychological studies show that drivers who regularly wear seat belts often come to think of themselves as serious drivers, which for a few people discourages reckless driving.

(E) Provinces and states with stringent car safety requirements have, on average, many more kilometers of roads than do other provinces and states.

5. Most economists believe that reducing the price of any product generally stimulates demand for it. However, most wine merchants have found that reducing the price of domestic wines to make them more competitive with imported wines with which they were previously comparably priced is frequently followed by an increase in sales of those imported wines.

Which one of the following, if true, most helps to reconcile the belief of most economists with the consequences observed by most wine merchants?

(A) Economists' studies of the prices of grocery items and their rates of sales rarely cover alcoholic beverages.

(B) Few merchants of any kind have detailed knowledge of economic theories about the relationship between item prices and sales rates.

(C) Consumers are generally willing to forgo purchasing other items they desire in order to purchase a superior wine.

(D) Imported wines in all price ranges are comparable in quality to domestic wines that cost less.

(E) An increase in the demand for a consumer product is compatible with an increase in demand for a competing product.

6. There are two ways to manage an existing transportation infrastructure: continuous maintenance at adequate levels, and periodic radical reconstruction. Continuous maintenance dispenses with the need for radical reconstruction, and radical reconstruction is necessitated by failing to perform continuous maintenance. Over the long run, continuous maintenance is far less expensive; nevertheless, it almost never happens.

Which one of the following, if true, most contributes to an explanation of why the first alternative mentioned is almost never adopted?

(A) Since different parts of the transportation infrastructure are the responsibility of different levels of government, radical reconstruction projects are very difficult to coordinate efficiently.

(B) When funds for transportation infrastructure maintenance are scarce, they are typically distributed in proportion to the amount of traffic that is borne by different elements of the infrastructure.

(C) If continuous maintenance is performed at less-than-adequate levels, the need for radical reconstruction will often arise later than if maintenance had been restricted to responding to emergencies.

(D) Radical reconstruction projects are, in general, too costly to be paid for from current revenue.

(E) For long periods, the task of regular maintenance lacks urgency, since the consequences of neglecting it are very slow to manifest themselves.

1. **Correct Answer (B).** *Prep Test 57, Section 3, Question 4.*

The claim is expressed in the first two sentences of the stimulus. Two groups were asked to write short stories. One group was told that a cash prize would be given for the best story, while the second group heard nothing about a prize. The unexpected result is that the group not competing for a prize wrote better stories on average. The expected result is that the group competing for cash would write better stories. We should anticipate a correct answer choice that explains the unexpected result. For example, maybe the promise of a cash prize put stress on the members of the first group and this negatively affected their writing.

(A) The cash prizes were too small to motivate an average adult to make a significant effort to produce stories of high quality.

This would not explain the unexpected result but instead suggests that members of both groups would produce stories of similar quality. (A) is a loser.

(B) People writing to win prizes show a greater than usual tendency to produce stereotypical stories that show little creativity.

This matches our anticipated answer choice. The fact that people in the first group were most likely to write stereotypical stories would explain why their stories were worse on average. (B) is a candidate.

(C) Most adults show little originality in writing stories on a topic suggested by someone else.

This is irrelevant information because it can be applied to both groups. (C) is a loser.

(D) The team of judges was biased in favor of stories that they judged to be more realistic.

This is irrelevant information. There is no indication that the writing of one of the groups was more realistic. (D) is a loser.

(E) No one explained clearly to either group what standards would be used in judging their stories.

This is irrelevant information. If both groups were uncertain about the standards, neither group would have an advantage. (E) is a loser.

As (B) is the only candidate, it has to be the correct answer choice.

2. **Correct Answer (C).** *Prep Test 52, Section 1, Question 14.*

The claim here is the hypothesis that studying more increased a student's chances of earning a higher grade. The unexpected result is that many students who studied less earned higher grades than the students who spent the most time studying. The expected result is that students who studied the most would outperform students who studied less. We should anticipate a correct answer choice that explains this unexpected result. Perhaps the two groups took courses with different difficulty levels. In this scenario, students who studied more received higher grades than they would have otherwise, yet students who took easier courses and studied less still got higher grades.

(A) The students who spent the most time studying earned higher grades than did some students who studied for less time than the average.

This does not explain the unexpected result (that many students who studied less earned higher grades than the students who studied the most). (A) is a loser.

(B) The students tended to get slightly lower grades as the academic year progressed.

This is irrelevant information because it can be applied to both groups. (B) is a loser.

(C) In each course, the more a student studied, the better his or her grade was in that course.

This matches our anticipated answer choice. It introduces the idea that the students took different courses. Students in each course received better grades than they would have if they had studied less, but students in one course (presumably the easier one) who studied less received higher grades than students in the other course (presumably the harder one) who studied more. (C) is a candidate.

(D) The students who spent the least time studying tended to be students with no more than average involvement in extracurricular activities.

This is irrelevant information. We do not have any information about the grades of the students who studied the least. Neither do we know anything about the extracurricular activities of the students who studied the most. (D) is a loser.

(E) Students who spent more time studying understood the course material better than other students did.

This would explain the expected result, not the unexpected result. (E) is a loser.

As (C) is the only candidate, it has to be the correct answer choice.

3. **Correct Answer (A).** *Prep Test 45, Section 4, Question 15.*

The claim is that the cost per course at a university has not risen. The unexpected result is that many students who could previously afford tuition are now no longer able to afford it. The expected result is that, given that the cost per course has not risen, students who could previously afford it would still be able to. Note that there is an equivocation between the claim and the unexpected result. The claim is about the cost per course, while the unexpected result is about tuition. Perhaps the tuition fees are based on more than just the cost per course. Another possibility is that students are enrolling in more courses each semester, thus increasing the total amount of their tuition. This is a Paradox EXCEPT question—the incorrect answer choices explain the unexpected result and the correct answer choice does not.

(A) Faculty salaries at the university have risen slightly over the past four years.

This would not explain the unexpected result. Faculty salaries would presumably be a cost that is included in the cost per course for students. If the cost per course has not risen, the fact that faculty salaries have increased would not explain the unexpected result. (A) is a candidate.

(B) The number of courses per semester for which full-time students are required to enroll is higher this year than any time in the past.

This would explain the unexpected result. If students needed to take more courses per semester, the amount of tuition they pay would increase. (B) is a loser.

(C) The cost of living in the vicinity of the university has risen over the last two years.

This would explain the unexpected result. If the cost of living has increased, students have additional expenses, and these may make it harder for them to afford tuition. (C) is a loser.

(D) The university awards new students a large number of scholarships that are renewed each year for the students who maintain high grade averages.

This would also explain the unexpected result. If many students failed to have their scholarships renewed due to low grades, they might have trouble affording tuition. (D) is a loser.

(E) The university has turned many of its part-time office jobs, for which students had generally been hired, into full-time, nonstudent positions.

This would also explain the unexpected result. If many students earned money through part-time jobs that are no longer available, then they may no longer be able to afford tuition. (E) is a loser.

As (A) is the only candidate, it has to be the correct answer choice.

4. **Correct Answer (C).** *Prep Test 42, Section 4, Question 24.*

The claim is that areas with stringent car safety requirements have higher accident rates than areas with less stringent safety requirements. The unexpected result is that most safety experts still maintain that stringent requirements reduce accident rates. The expected result is that these experts would believe that stringent requirements do not reduce accidents. We should anticipate a correct answer choice that explains the unexpected result. Maybe the regions with more safety requirements are more dangerous to drive in.

(A) Annual safety inspections ensure that car tires are replaced before they grow old.

This does not explain the unexpected result. If safety inspections prevented drivers from continuing to use old tires, which could prevent accidents, why would areas with these requirements have more accidents? (A) is a loser.

(B) Drivers often become overconfident after their cars have passed a thorough safety inspection.

This would not explain the unexpected result because it accounts for why stringent safety requirements would produce more accidents. Therefore, (B) is a loser.

(C) The roads in provinces and states with stringent car safety requirements are far more congested and therefore dangerous than in other provinces and states.

This matches our anticipated answer choice. If the areas with stringent safety requirements were more dangerous, they would likely see more accidents than other areas (even after accounting for the reduction in accidents resulting from the safety requirements). (C) is a candidate.

(D) Psychological studies show that drivers who regularly wear seat belts often come to think of themselves as serious drivers, which for a few people discourages reckless driving.

This answer choice accounts for why safety requirements may reduce accidents, but it also provides evidence against the claim that areas with high safety requirements have higher accident rates. (D) is a loser.

(E) Provinces and states with stringent car safety requirements have, on average, many more kilometers of roads than do other provinces and states.

This is irrelevant information since the initial claim concerns accidents per kilometer. It does not matter which areas have more kilometers of roads. (E) is a loser.

As (C) is the only candidate, it has to be the correct answer choice.

5. **Correct Answer (E).** *Prep Test 52, Section 3, Question 22.*

The claim is that reducing the price of a product usually stimulates demand for it. The unexpected result is that merchants have found that decreasing the price of domestic wines is frequently followed by an increase in the sales of imported wines. The expected result is that lowering the prices of domestic wines would stimulate demand for them (not for another type). We should anticipate a correct answer choice that explains this unexpected result. This is a difficult question to anticipate a possible explanation for, so we will head straight to the answer choices.

(A) Economists' studies of the prices of grocery items and their rates of sales rarely cover alcoholic beverages.

This matches our anticipated answer choice. If economists hardly ever include the sale of alcoholic beverages in their studies, then they must be unaware that alcohol is an exception to the general rule. Let's consider (A) a candidate.

(B) Few merchants of any kind have detailed knowledge of economic theories about the relationship between item prices and sales rates.

This is irrelevant information. We are only concerned with the beliefs of economists and the relationship between decreasing the prices of domestic wines and increased sales of imported wines. (B) is a loser.

(C) Consumers are generally willing to forgo purchasing other items they desire in order to purchase a superior wine.

This is irrelevant information because we do not know which wines are superior. (C) is a loser.

(D) Imported wines in all price ranges are comparable in quality to domestic wines that cost less.

This would explain the expected result. If you are able to purchase comparable domestic wines at a cheaper price, it does not follow that imported wines would see an increase in demand. (D) is a loser.

(E) An increase in the demand for a consumer product is compatible with an increase in demand for a competing product.

This matches our anticipated answer choice. (E) exposes an assumption we had to make. The result expected to follow from decreasing a product's price is an increase in demand for that product. We assumed that sales of domestic wines did not increase and sales of imported wines increased. But looking back at the stimulus, this is not actually stated. So, it could be the case that lowering the price of domestic wines leads to an increase in sales of imported and domestic wines alike. (E) is a candidate.

We now have to eliminate one of our two candidates. Rereading (A), we can spot a problem. The stimulus clearly states that economists believe that reducing the price of any product generally stimulates demand for that product. Implying that alcoholic beverages are not included would invalidate the claim. Therefore, (E) has to be the correct answer choice.

6. **Correct Answer (E).** *Prep Test 52, Section 3, Question 20.*

The claim, which must be inferred from several statements, is that continuous maintenance should be performed. This is because continuous maintenance is far less expensive than radical reconstruction and performing continuous maintenance makes periodic radical reconstruction unnecessary. The unexpected result is that continuous maintenance is seldom carried out. The expected result is that it would be conducted often. We should anticipate a correct answer choice that explains the unexpected result. Maybe continuous maintenance is very difficult to perform or can only be handled by specialized personnel.

(A) Since different parts of the transportation infrastructure are the responsibility of different levels of government, radical reconstruction projects are very difficult to coordinate efficiently.

This answer choice is an explanation of the expected result. It accounts for why radical reconstruction is not a good option. (A) is a loser.

(B) When funds for transportation infrastructure maintenance are scarce, they are typically distributed in proportion to the amount of traffic that is borne by different elements of the infrastructure.

This is irrelevant information as it does not directly pertain to either option. (B) is a loser.

(C) If continuous maintenance is performed at less-than-adequate levels, the need for radical reconstruction will often arise later than if maintenance had been restricted to responding to emergencies.

This explains the expected result. It shows that continuous maintenance has benefits even if it is performed at less-than-adequate levels. (C) is a loser.

(D) Radical reconstruction projects are, in general, too costly to be paid for from current revenue.

This explains the expected result instead of the unexpected result. (D) is a loser.

(E) For long periods, the task of regular maintenance lacks urgency, since the consequences of neglecting it are very slow to manifest themselves.

This matches our anticipated answer choice. If neglecting continuous maintenance has consequences that are slow to manifest, it may be easy to neglect, hence the eventual need for radical reconstruction. (E) has to be the correct answer choice.

Key Takeaways

Example Prompts

S: Which one of the following, if true, most strengthens the argument?

S: Which one of the following, if true, most helps to support the argument?

W: Which one of the following, if true, most weakens the argument?

W: If true, which one of the following most undermines the argument?

E: The answer to which one of the following questions would be most helpful in evaluating the truth of the conclusion drawn in the argument?

E: Which one of the following would be most important to know in evaluating the argument's claim?

SA: Which of the following, if assumed, allows the conclusion to be properly inferred?

SA: Which one of the following is an assumption that would allow the conclusion to be properly drawn?

NA: Which one of the following is an assumption that is required by the argument?

NA: The argument depends on assuming which one of the following?

P: Which one of the following, if true, most helps to resolve the paradox described above?

P: Which one of the following, if true, contributes most to an explanation of the phenomena described?

Strengthen (S) – 14.03%
Weaken (W) – 6.52%
Evaluation (E) – 1.78%
Sufficient Assumption (SA) – 5.14%
Necessary Assumption (NA) – 10.28%
Paradox (P) – 7.90%

Sufficient Assumption: Information that, if assumed, guarantees the validity of the argument
Necessary Assumption: Information that must be true in order for the argument to be valid

 The prompt instructs you to apply the information in the answer choices to the stimulus. You must assume that each answer choice is true and then identify its effect on the stimulus.

The (Un)Necessary Assumption Test

If the negated answer choice invalidates the argument in the stimulus, then it must be the correct answer choice. If it does not invalidate the argument, it must be an incorrect answer choice.

For nonconditional statements, logically negate the first verb after the subject

For conditional statements with strength modifiers, logically negate the first strength modifier

For conditional statements without strength modifiers, logically negate the necessary condition

How to Strengthen or Weaken a Causal Statement

Strengthen	Weaken
Eliminate an Alternative Cause	Identify Alternative Cause
Same Cause, Same Effect	Same Cause, No Effect
No Cause, No Effect	Same Effect, No Cause
	Reversed Cause and Effect

Correct Answer Choices

S: Statements that strengthen the argument

W: Statements that weaken the argument

E: Questions for which the answer would strengthen or weaken the argument

SA: Statements that, if assumed, make the argument valid

NA: Statements that must be true in order for the argument to be valid

P: Statements that explain the unexpected result, without invalidating the claim

Incorrect Answers Choices

Does Not Strengthen: Statements that do not strengthen the argument (S)

Does Not Weaken: Statements that do not weaken the argument (W)

Neither Strengthens nor Weaken: Questions for which the answer does not strengthen or weaken the argument (E)

Does Not Validate: Statements that do not guarantee the argument's validity (SA)

Not Necessarily True: Statements that do not have to be true in order for the argument to be valid (NA)

Does Not Explain Result: Statements that do not explain the unexpected result in the argument (P)

Logical Force Errors: Statements that are too strong or weak (NA, SA)

Irrelevant Information: Information that does not pertain to the correct answer (S, W, E, NA, SA, P)

Chapter 6

Principle
Questions

Chapter 6: Principle Questions

HACKERS
LSAT *Logical Reasoning*

Principle Questions

A principle is a rule, often conditional in nature, that guides the evaluation or moral judgment of actions or behaviors in certain situations. Principles are generally broad and can be applied to many situations aside from the one presented in the stimulus or answer choice. An example is

If they want to be happy, people should meditate.

Here, the rule applies to people who want to be happy; it directs them to perform a specific action—meditation. Someone who wants to be happy but does not meditate violates this general principle. The words *should* and *ought* are regularly used in principle questions to indicate a duty or obligation that arises from a certain situation. Because principle questions are concerned with the evaluation or moral assessment of actions or behaviors, they also often include words such as *appropriate*, *justified*, *laudable*, *correct*, *wrong*, *morally right*, *duty*, *obligation*, *permissible*, and *forbidden*.

Principle questions are not a unique question type; rather, they are a subset of several question types discussed previously. Therefore, Principle questions can be solved using the basic methods explained in previous chapters, with some slight modifications. The most common types of Principle questions are Principle Strengthen, Principle Implication, and Principle Parallel Reasoning, although other types appear every now and then.

Principle questions almost always ask you to do one of three things:

1. Identify a principle that supports the argument in the stimulus (Principle Strengthen)
2. Identify a principle implied by the stimulus (Principle Implication)
3. Identify a principle in the stimulus and match it with one in an answer choice (Principle Parallel Reasoning)

Principle questions have begun to appear more frequently on the LSAT in recent years. Principle Strengthen questions are the most common type—you can expect to encounter two to four of these when you write the LSAT. Principle Implication questions are the next most common, with about one per exam administration. Finally, there is only a small chance that you will have to solve a Principle Parallel Reasoning question.

Principle Strengthen questions are generally similar to regular Strengthen questions. However, Principle Implication and Principle Parallel Reasoning questions can vary in terms of the wording and format of the stimulus or prompt.

Principle Strengthen

Principle Strengthen prompts are easy to identify because they include the following wordings, with minor variations:

"Which one of the following **principles**, if valid, **most helps to justify** the reasoning above?"

"Which one of the following **principles**, if valid, **most strongly supports** the argument?"

As in regular Strengthen questions, the stimulus always includes an argument. In a Principle Strengthen question, the conclusion is a judgment, and each answer choice states a principle. The correct answer choice includes a principle that provides support for the judgment, thereby strengthening the argument. Principle Strengthen questions almost always include an assumption. You should anticipate a correct answer choice that validates the assumption.

Let's look at an example:

> Mariah: Joanna has argued that Adam should not judge the essay contest because several of his classmates have entered the contest. However, the essays are not identified by author to the judge and, moreover, none of Adam's friends are classmates of his. Still, Adam has no experience in critiquing essays. Therefore, I agree with Joanna that Adam should not judge the contest.
>
> Which one of the following principles, if valid, most helps to justify Mariah's argument?
>
> (A) A suspicion of bias is insufficient grounds on which to disqualify someone from judging a contest.
> (B) Expertise should be the primary prerequisite for serving as a contest judge.
> (C) The ability of a judge to make objective decisions is more important than that judge's contest expertise.
> (D) In selecting a contest judge, fairness concerns should override concern for the appropriate expertise.
> (E) A contest judge, no matter how well qualified, cannot judge properly if the possibility of bias exists.

The conclusion is the judgment that Mariah agrees with Joanna that Adam should not judge the contest. What's interesting is that Mariah disagrees with Joanna's reason. Joanna feels that Adam should not be the judge because several of his classmates have entered the contest, but Mariah says this is not an issue because the essays are not identified by author and Adam's friends are not in his classes. Mariah's reason for agreeing that Adam should not be a judge is that he has no experience in critiquing essays. The argument can be outlined as follows:

P: Adam has no experience critiquing essays.
C (Judgment): Adam should not judge the essay contest.

This argument includes a logical gap. Why is it the case that because Adam has no experience, he should not judge the contest? Mariah is assuming the following principle:

A lack of experience should bar one from judging a contest.

We should anticipate a correct answer choice that validates this assumption.

(A) A suspicion of bias is insufficient grounds on which to disqualify someone from judging a contest.

This answer choice includes irrelevant information. The potential for bias was one of Joanna's concerns, not one of Mariah's. (A) is a loser.

(B) Expertise should be the primary prerequisite for serving as a contest judge.

This matches our anticipated answer choice. If expertise is the primary prerequisite for serving as a contest judge and Adam has no experience, then this strengthens Mariah's judgment that Adam should not judge the contest. (B) is a candidate.

(C) The ability of a judge to make objective decisions is more important than that judge's contest

expertise.

This does not strengthen the argument. We have no information regarding Adam's ability to make objective decisions. Additionally, Mariah's assumption is that expertise is very important. (C) is a loser.

   (D) In selecting a contest judge, fairness concerns should override concern for the appropriate expertise.

This does not strengthen the argument. Mariah considers appropriate expertise to be important. (D) is a loser.

   (E) A contest judge, no matter how well qualified, cannot judge properly if the possibility of bias exists.

This does not strengthen the argument. Mariah does not feel that there is any risk of bias. In addition, she believes that a judge's qualifications are important. (E) is a loser.

As (B) is the only candidate, it has to be the correct answer choice.

Principle Implication

Principle Implication questions usually include a fact pattern that does not contain an unusual circumstance or conditional language. Here are a few examples of Principle Implication prompts:

   "The situation described above **best illustrates** which one of the following **generalizations**?"
   "The argument's reasoning **most closely conforms** to which one of the following **principles**?"
   "Which of the following **propositions** is **best illustrated** by the passage?"
   "The facts stated above **most closely conform** to which one of the following **assessments**?"

The prompts for this question type have a greater variety of wordings than those of Principle Strengthen questions. However, each prompt requires you to perform the same basic task—identify the broad rule or generalization that is strongly implied by the stimulus. As in other Implication questions, the correct answers of Principle Implication questions are often weak in logical force.

> Principle Implication answer choices are more abstract than normal Implication answers as they express a broad rule or generalization.

Let's look at an example:

   A clear advantage of digital technology over traditional printing is that digital documents, being patterns of electronic signals rather than patterns of ink on paper, do not generate waste in the course of their production and use. However, because patterns of electronic signals are necessarily ephemeral, a digital document can easily be destroyed and lost forever.

   The statements above best illustrate which one of the following generalizations?

   (A) A property of a technology may constitute an advantage in one set of circumstances and a disadvantage in others.
   (B) What at first appears to be an advantage of a technology may create more problems than it solves.

(C) It is more important to be able to preserve information than it is for information to be easily accessible.

(D) Innovations in document storage technologies sometimes decrease, but never eliminate, the risk of destroying documents.

(E) Advances in technology can lead to increases in both convenience and environmental soundness.

The first proposition states an advantage of digital technology—waste is not generated because digital documents are electronic signals. The second proposition states a disadvantage—digital documents can easily be destroyed and lost forever because they are electronic signals. We should anticipate a correct answer choice that expresses a generalization that is implied by this fact pattern.

(A) A property of a technology may constitute an advantage in one set of circumstances and a disadvantage in others.

This matches our anticipated answer choice. The use of electronic signals is a property of digital technology that is an advantage (waste is not generated) and a disadvantage (documents can be lost forever). (A) is a candidate.

(B) What at first appears to be an advantage of a technology may create more problems than it solves.

This generalization does not accurately describe the stimulus, which does not imply that the advantages of digital technology are outweighed by the disadvantages. (B) is a loser.

(C) It is more important to be able to preserve information than it is for information to be easily accessible.

This is irrelevant information. This stimulus does address the issue of accessibility. (C) is a loser.

(D) Innovations in document storage technologies sometimes decrease, but never eliminate, the risk of destroying documents.

This is irrelevant information. The stimulus does not describe storage technologies that lessen the risk of documents being destroyed. (D) is a loser.

(E) Advances in technology can lead to increases in both convenience and environmental soundness.

This is irrelevant information. The stimulus does not address the issue of increases in convenience. (E) is a loser.

As (A) is the only candidate, it has to be the correct answer choice.

Principle Parallel Reasoning

Principle Parallel Reasoning questions can be divided into two basic categories. In the first type, the principle is stated explicitly in the stimulus. In the second type, the principle must be inferred from a situation described in the stimulus (the process is similar to that of finding an Abstract Paraphrase, which was discussed in Chapter 4). Once you have identified the principle, you must determine which answer choice expresses a judgment that conforms to this principle.

Principle Parallel Reasoning questions differ from regular Parallel Reasoning questions in that the stimulus may include a fact pattern. In addition, conditional statements are more likely to appear in a Principle Parallel Reasoning stimulus. Prompts for this question type vary the most among Principle question types in terms of wording.

Here are some examples of prompts in which the principle is explicitly stated in the stimulus:

> "**The principle** above, if established, would justify which one of the following **judgments**?"
> "Which one of the following **judgments most closely conforms to the principle** cited above?"
> "Which one of the following is **an application** of **the principle** above?"

Here are some examples of prompts in which the principle must be inferred from the stimulus:

> "Which one of the following **most closely conforms to the principle** underlying the passage above?"
> "Which one of the following arguments **illustrates a principle most similar to the principle illustrated** by the argument above?"

Let's look at an example:

> Some credit card companies allow cardholders to skip payments for up to six months under certain circumstances, but it is almost never in a cardholder's interest to do so. Finance charges accumulate during the skipped-payment period, and the cost to the cardholder is much greater in the long run.
>
> Which one of the following arguments illustrates a principle most similar to the principle underlying the argument above?
>
> (A) Although insecticides are effective in ridding the environment of insect pests, they often kill beneficial insects at the same time. Since these beneficial insects are so important, we must find other ways to combat insect pests.
> (B) Increasing the base salary of new employees is good for a company. Although the company's payroll will increase, it will be easier for the company to recruit new employees.
> (C) It is unwise to use highway maintenance funds for construction of new roads. There is some immediate benefit from new roads, but if these funds are not used for maintenance, the total maintenance cost will be greater in the long run.
> (D) It is better to invest in a used piece of equipment than to purchase a new one. Although used equipment requires more repairs and is sometimes more costly in the long run, buying a new machine requires a far greater initial outlay of capital.
> (E) Sports cars are impractical for most drivers. While there is undoubtedly a certain thrill associated with driving these cars, their small size makes them incapable of transporting any but the smallest amounts of cargo.

This stimulus includes an argument that does not contain conditional statements. The conclusion is that it is almost never in a cardholder's interest to skip payments. The evidence for this is that skipping payments results in an accumulation of finance charges, and the long-term cost to the cardholder is much greater. The principle is not explicitly stated, so we must infer what it is by creating an abstract paraphrase of the argument: "An option should not be chosen if its short-term advantages are outweighed by its long-term disadvantages." We should anticipate a correct answer choice that describes a situation that this principle applies to.

> **(A)** **Although insecticides are effective in ridding the environment of insect pests, they often kill beneficial insects at the same time. Since these beneficial insects are so important, we must find other ways to combat insect pests.**

This argument describes a situation in which advantages and disadvantages occur simultaneously. It does not compare short-term and long-term effects. This is a loser.

> **(B)** **Increasing the base salary of new employees is good for a company. Although the company's payroll will increase, it will be easier for the company to recruit new employees.**

This argument describes a situation in which there is a short-term disadvantage and a long-term advantage. (B) is a loser.

> **(C)** **It is unwise to use highway maintenance funds for construction of new roads. There is some immediate benefit from new roads, but if these funds are not used for maintenance, the total maintenance cost will be greater in the long run.**

This matches our anticipated answer choice. There is a short-term advantage (new roads) but a long-term disadvantage (increased maintenance costs). It specified that this situation should be avoided. (C) is a candidate.

> **(D)** **It is better to invest in a used piece of equipment than to purchase a new one. Although used equipment requires more repairs and is sometimes more costly in the long run, buying a new machine requires a far greater initial outlay of capital.**

This argument concludes that the short-term advantage is desirable despite its long-term disadvantages. (D) is another loser.

> **(E)** **Sports cars are impractical for most drivers. While there is undoubtedly a certain thrill associated with driving these cars, their small size makes them incapable of transporting any but the smallest amounts of cargo.**

This argument does not include a comparison between short-term and long-term effects. Thus, (E) is a loser.

As (C) is the only candidate, it has to be the correct answer choice.

Problem Set: Principle

1. Situation: Someone living in a cold climate buys a winter coat that is stylish but not warm in order to appear sophisticated.

   Analysis: People are sometimes willing to sacrifice sensual comfort or pleasure for the sake of appearances.

   The analysis provided for the situation above is most appropriate for which one of the following situations?

   (A) A person buys an automobile to commute to work even though public transportation is quick and reliable.

   (B) A parent buys a car seat for a young child because it is more colorful and more comfortable for the child than the other car seats on the market, though no safer.

   (C) A couple buys a particular wine even though their favorite wine is less expensive and better tasting because they think it will impress the dinner guests.

   (D) A person sets her thermostat at a low temperature during the winter because she is concerned about the environmental damage caused by using fossil fuels to heat her home.

   (E) An acrobat convinces the circus that employs him to purchase an expensive outfit for him so that he can wear it during his act to impress the audience.

2. Jablonski, who owns a car dealership, has donated cars to driver education programs at area schools for over five years. She found the statistics on car accidents to be disturbing, and she wanted to do something to encourage better driving in young drivers. Some members of the community have shown their support for this action by purchasing cars from Jablonski's dealership.

   Which one of the following propositions is best illustrated by the passage?

   (A) The only way to reduce traffic accidents is through driver education programs.

   (B) Altruistic actions sometimes have positive consequences for those who perform them.

   (C) Young drivers are the group most likely to benefit from the driver education programs.

   (D) It is usually in one's best interest to perform actions that benefit others.

   (E) An action must have broad community support if it is to be successful.

3. The human emotional response presents an apparent paradox. People believe that they can be genuinely moved only by those things and events that they believe to be actual, yet they have genuine emotional responses to what they know to be fictional.

Which one of the following situations most closely conforms to the principle cited above?

(A) Fred was watching a horror movie. Although he did not expect to be bothered by make-believe monsters, he nonetheless felt frightened when they appeared on the screen.

(B) Tamara was reading Hamlet. Although she knew that it was a work of fiction, she still made statements such as "Hamlet was born in Denmark" and "Hamlet was a prince."

(C) Raheem thought that his sister was in the hospital. Although he was mistaken, he was nevertheless genuinely worried when he believed she was there.

(D) Jeremy was upset by the actions that a writer attributed to a secret organization, although he considered it unlikely that the writer's account was accurate.

(E) Sandy was watching a film about World War II. Although the film's details were accurate, it was nevertheless difficult for Sandy to maintain interest in the characters.

4. In order to expand its mailing lists for e-mail advertising, the Outdoor Sports Company has been offering its customers financial incentives if they provide the e-mail addresses of their friends. However, offering such incentives is an unethical business practice because it encourages people to exploit their personal relationships for profit, which risks damaging the integrity of those relationships.

Which one of the following principles, if valid, most helps to justify the reasoning in the argument?

(A) It is unethical for people to exploit their personal relationships for profit if in doing so they risk damaging the integrity of those relationships.

(B) If it would be unethical to use information that was gathered in a particular way, then it is unethical to gather that information in the first place.

(C) It is an unethical business practice for a company to deliberately damage the integrity of its customers' personal relationships in any way.

(D) It is unethical to encourage people to engage in behavior that could damage the integrity of their personal relationships.

(E) Providing a friend's personal information to a company in exchange for a financial reward will almost certainly damage the integrity of one's personal relationship with that friend.

5. Sharon, a noted collector of fine glass, found a rare glass vase in a secondhand store in a small town she was visiting. The vase was priced at $10, but Sharon knew that it was worth at least $1,000. Saying nothing to the storekeeper about the value of the vase, Sharon bought the vase for $10. Weeks later the storekeeper read a newspaper article about Sharon's collection, which mentioned the vase and how she had acquired it. When the irate storekeeper later accused Sharon of taking advantage of him, Sharon replied that she had done nothing wrong.

Which one of the following principles, if established, most helps to justify Sharon's position?

(A) A seller is not obligated to inform a buyer of anything about the merchandise that the seller offers for sale except for the demanded price.

(B) It is the responsibility of the seller, not the buyer, to make sure that the amount of money a buyer gives a seller in exchange for merchandise matches the amount that the seller demands for that merchandise.

(C) A buyer's sole obligation to a seller is to pay in full the price that the seller demands for a piece of merchandise that the buyer acquires from the seller.

(D) It is the responsibility of the buyer, not the seller, to ascertain that the quality of a piece of merchandize satisfies the buyer's standards.

(E) The obligations that follow from any social relationship between two people who are well acquainted override any obligations that follow from an economic relationship between the two.

6. Commentator: In academic scholarship, sources are always cited, and methodology and theoretical assumptions are set out, so as to allow critical study, replication, and expansion of scholarship. In open-source software, the code in which the program is written can be viewed and modified by individual users for their purposes without getting permission from the producer or paying a fee. In contrast, the code of proprietary software is kept secret, and modifications can be made only by the producer, for a fee. This shows that open-source software better matches the values embodied in academic scholarship, and since scholarship is central to the mission of universities, universities should use only open-source software.

The commentator's reasoning most closely conforms to which one of the following principles?

(A) Whatever software tools are most advanced and can achieve the goals of academic scholarship are the ones that should alone be used in universities.

(B) Universities should use the type of software technology that is least expensive, as long as that type of software technology is adequate for the purposes of academic scholarship.

(C) Universities should choose the type of software technology that best matches the values embodied in the activities that are central to the mission of universities.

(D) The form of software technology that best matches the values embodied in the activities that are central to the mission of universities is the form of software technology that is most efficient for universities to use.

(E) A university should not pursue any activity that would block the achievement of the goals of academic scholarship at that university.

7. Essayist: One of the drawbacks of extreme personal and political freedom is that the free choices are often made for the worst. To expect people to thrive when they are given the freedom to make unwise decisions is frequently unrealistic. Once people see the destructive consequences of extreme freedom, they may prefer to establish totalitarian political regimes that allow virtually no freedom. Thus, one should not support political systems that allow extreme freedom.

Which one of the following principles, if valid, most helps to justify the essayist's reasoning?

(A) One should not support any political system that will inevitably lead to the establishment of a totalitarian political regime.

(B) One should not expect everyone to thrive even in a political system that maximizes people's freedom in the long run.

(C) One should support only those political systems that give people the freedom to make wise choices.

(D) One should not support any political system whose destructive consequences could lead people to prefer totalitarian political regimes.

(E) One should not support any political system that is based on unrealistic expectations about people's behavior under that system.

Problem Set: Principle — Answers

1. **Correct Answer (C).** *Prep Test 51.5, Section 3, Question 1.*

   Type: Principle Parallel Reasoning

   Note the format of the stimulus—a situation is provided and then an analysis is given. Although this type of stimulus is rare, it has begun to appear more frequently. When you see this type of stimulus, you can ignore the situation because the analysis explicitly states the principle. You must identify the answer choice that describes a situation that matches the principle. Therefore, we should anticipate a correct answer choice that describes a situation in which comfort or pleasure is sacrificed for appearances.

   (A) A person buys an automobile to commute to work even though public transportation is quick and reliable.

   Here, there is no sacrificing of sensual comfort or pleasure. Neither is there any indication that the automobile is being purchased for the sake of appearances. (A) is a loser.

   (B) A parent buys a car seat for a young child because it is more colorful and more comfortable for the child than the other car seats on the market, though no safer.

   No sacrifice for the sake of appearances is being made. (B) is a loser.

   (C) A couple buys a particular wine even though their favorite wine is less expensive and better tasting because they think it will impress the dinner guests.

   This matches our anticipated answer choice. A couple has decided not to purchase their favorite wine. Instead, they select a more expensive, less delicious one in order to impress their guests. (C) is a candidate.

   (D) A person sets her thermostat at a low temperature during the winter because she is concerned about the environmental damage caused by using fossil fuels to heat her home.

   This person sacrifices a sensual comfort, warmth, because she is concerned about environmental damage. She is not making the sacrifice for appearances. (D) is a loser.

   (E) An acrobat convinces the circus that employs him to purchase an expensive outfit for him so that he can wear it during his act to impress the audience.

   Neither the acrobat nor the circus is making a sacrifice. Therefore, it does not matter if the expensive outfit is purchased for the sake of appearances. (E) is a loser.

   As (C) is the only candidate, it has to be the correct answer choice.

2. **Correct Answer (B).** *Prep Test 51.5, Section 3, Question 6.*

   Type: Principle Implication

   The stimulus states that Jablonski donated cars to driver education programs because she wanted to help young drivers improve their driving skills. In support of this action, several members of the community have purchased cars from Jablonski's dealership. We can make a generalization based on this information—actions may result in unintended secondary benefits. We should anticipate a correct answer choice that expresses this through a weak statement.

(A) The only way to reduce traffic accidents is through driver education programs.

This is too strongly worded and does not include key details from the stimulus. Not only do we not know if driver education programs are effective at reducing traffic accidents, but we also cannot say that this is the only way to reduce accidents. (A) is a loser.

(B) Altruistic actions sometimes have positive consequences for those who perform them.

This matches our anticipated answer choice. Jablonski performed an altruistic action (donating cars in order to encourage better driving behavior) that resulted in positive consequences for her (people purchasing cars from the dealership). Also, (B) is weakly worded. It is a candidate.

(C) Young drivers are the group most likely to benefit from the driver education programs.

We have no knowledge of who is most likely to benefit from these programs. Additionally, this is not the principle that underlies the stimulus as it does not address the fact that members of the community have purchased cars from Jablonski's dealership. (C) is a loser.

(D) It is usually in one's best interest to perform actions that benefit others.

This is too strongly worded. We know that it is sometimes beneficial to perform actions that benefits others, but *usually* and *in one's best interest* are too strong for the situation. The stimulus only describes one person who has benefited from such actions. (D) is a loser.

(E) An action must have broad community support if it is to be successful.

This is too strong and mischaracterizes the stimulus. We have no information on whether Jablonski's initiative brought about better driving practices. Even if it did, we do not know whether broad community support was integral to its success. (E) is a loser.

As (B) is the only candidate, it has to be the correct answer choice.

3. **Correct Answer (A).** *Prep Test 47, Section 1, Question 5.*

Type: Principle Parallel Reasoning

The principle is explicitly stated in the stimulus—people believe they can be genuinely moved only by things they believe are real, but they have genuine emotional responses to what they know to be fictional. Note that this rule is dependent on a person having knowledge of whether something is real or fictional. If a person does not know whether something is real or fictional, this rule does not apply. We should anticipate a correct answer choice that describes a situation that this principle applies to.

(A) Fred was watching a horror movie. Although he did not expect to be bothered by make-believe monsters, he nonetheless felt frightened when they appeared on the screen.

This matches our anticipated answer choice. Fred did not think he would be frightened because the movie presented something that was not real. However, he felt afraid of the monsters despite knowing that they were fictional. (A) is a candidate.

(B) Tamara was reading Hamlet. Although she knew that it was a work of fiction, she still made statements such as "Hamlet was born in Denmark" and "Hamlet was a prince."

The statements made by Tamara are not emotional responses. (B) is a loser.

(C) Raheem thought that his sister was in the hospital. Although he was mistaken, he was nevertheless genuinely worried when he believed she was there.

In this situation, Raheem believed the situation was real, but it was not. Therefore, he was not genuinely worried about something he knew was fictional. (C) is a loser.

(D) Jeremy was upset by the actions that a writer attributed to a secret organization, although he considered it unlikely that the writer's account was accurate.

Jeremy is unsure whether the secret organization's actions are real or fictional, so the principle does not apply. (D) is a loser.

(E) Sandy was watching a film about World War II. Although the film's details were accurate, it was nevertheless difficult for Sandy to maintain interest in the characters.

Maintaining interest is not the same as an *emotional response*. In addition, Sandy felt no such response. (E) is a loser.

As (A) is the only candidate, it has to be the correct answer choice.

4. **Correct Answer (D).** *Prep Test 56, Section 2, Question 16.*

Type: Principle Strengthen

The argument uses a *conclusion, because premise* structure to conclude that offering financial incentives to customers who provide their friends' e-mail addresses is unethical because it encourages people to exploit their personal relationships for profit, in turn damaging the integrity of those relationships. This argument includes an assumption. Although it concludes that this practice in unethical, we have no information about what makes something unethical. Therefore, we should anticipate a correct answer choice that defines unethical behavior in a manner that applies to the situation described in the argument.

(A) It is unethical for people to exploit their personal relationships for profit if in doing so they risk damaging the integrity of those relationships.

This specifies behavior that is unethical for people to do with regard to their own personal relationships, but the argument is concerned with unethical business practices. (A) is a loser.

(B) If it would be unethical to use information that was gathered in a particular way, then it is unethical to gather that information in the first place.

This answer choice has the same problem as the argument—it does not state why the business practice is unethical. (B) is a loser.

(C) It is an unethical business practice for a company to deliberately damage the integrity of its customers' personal relationships in any way.

This answer choice refers to unethical business practices, but we have no information indicating that Outdoor Sports Company is deliberately damaging the integrity of its customers' personal relationships. That is, the company is not damaging any relationships in a direct manner. (C) is a loser.

(D) It is unethical to encourage people to engage in behavior that could damage the integrity of their personal relationships.

This matches our anticipated answer choice. If this principle were valid, then Outdoor Sports Company could be said to be engaging in an unethical business practice (encouraging people to engage in behavior that risks damaging the integrity of their personal relationships). (D) is a candidate.

(E) Providing a friend's personal information to a company in exchange for a financial reward will almost certainly damage the integrity of one's personal relationship with that friend.

This answer choice does not address why it is unethical to damage the integrity of personal relationships. (E) is a loser.

As (D) is the only candidate, it has to be the correct answer choice.

5. **Correct Answer (C).** *Prep Test 41, Section 1, Question 17.*

Type: Principle Strengthen

The prompt asks which principle would most help to strengthen Sharon's position, which is that she did nothing wrong. We know that she paid the price the shopkeeper asked for the vase, even though she knew the actual value was much higher. We should anticipate a correct answer choice that explains why Sharon has not done anything wrong.

(A) A seller is not obligated to inform a buyer of anything about the merchandise that the seller offers for sale except for the demanded price.

This answer choice does not explain why Sharon has done nothing wrong. It discusses what the seller is not obligated to do, but we are interested in what a buyer is or is not obligated to do. (A) is a loser.

(B) It is the responsibility of the seller, not the buyer, to make sure that the amount of money a buyer gives a seller in exchange for merchandise matches the amount that the seller demands for that merchandise.

This answer choice concerns what a seller should do. In addition, the amount Sharon paid matched the amount the seller demanded. (B) is a loser.

(C) A buyer's sole obligation to a seller is to pay in full the price that the seller demands for a piece of merchandise that the buyer acquires from the seller.

This matches our anticipated answer choice. If a buyer's sole obligation is to pay the full price a seller demands for an item, then the buyer has no other obligations. Since Sharon fulfilled her sole obligation, she has done nothing wrong. (C) is a candidate.

(D) It is the responsibility of the buyer, not the seller, to ascertain that the quality of a piece of merchandize satisfies the buyer's standards.

This is irrelevant information. In the stimulus, the quality of the merchandise is not at issue. (D) is a loser.

(E) The obligations that follow from any social relationship between two people who are well acquainted override any obligations that follow from an economic relationship between the two.

This is irrelevant information. The first sentence specifies that Sharon was just visiting the small town in which the store was located. Thus, it is unlikely that Sharon and the shopkeeper were well acquainted. (E) is a loser.

As (C) is the only candidate, it has to be the correct answer choice.

6. **Correct Answer (C).** *Prep Test 51.5, Section 3, Question 14.*

Type: Principle Implication

Although this is a Principle Implication Question, the stimulus includes an argument rather than a fact pattern. Note that this is very uncommon for this question type. As indicated by the *since premise*, *conclusion* structure, the argument concludes that universities should only use open-source software. The support for this claim is that open-source software better matches the values of academic scholarship, and scholarship is central to the mission of universities. What is the principle behind the claim that universities should use only open-source software? It seems to be that universities should choose products that match the values embodied in academic scholarship. We should anticipate a correct answer choice that expresses this principle.

(A) Whatever software tools are most advanced and can achieve the goals of academic scholarship are the ones that should alone be used in universities.

There is no indication that open-source software is either the most advanced or that it can achieve the goals of academic scholarship, which are not stated in the stimulus. (A) is a loser.

(B) Universities should use the type of software technology that is least expensive, as long as that type of software technology is adequate for the purposes of academic scholarship.

Even though open-source software seems to be less expensive than proprietary software, there is no indication that it is the least expensive type of software. Additionally, this answer choice runs into the same problem as (A). It refers to the purposes of academic scholarship, which are not stated. (B) is a loser.

(C) Universities should choose the type of software technology that best matches the values embodied in the activities that are central to the mission of universities.

This matches our anticipated answer choice. Universities should use open-source software because that technology matches the values embodied in academic scholarship, which is an activity central to the mission of universities. (C) is a candidate.

(D) The form of software technology that best matches the values embodied in the activities that are central to the mission of universities is the form of software technology that is most efficient for universities to use.

This is irrelevant information. The stimulus does not discuss the issue of software efficiency. (D) is a loser.

(E) A university should not pursue any activity that would block the achievement of the goals of academic scholarship at that university.

There are several issues with this answer choice. First, it confuses the values embodied in academic scholarship with the goals of academic scholarship. Second, even if proprietary software could be considered to be an activity that blocks the goals of academic scholarship, that would not necessarily mean that open-source software is the only type of software that should be used. (E) is a loser.

As (C) is the only candidate, it has to be the correct answer choice.

7. **Correct Answer (D).** *Prep Test 57, Section 3, Question 19.*

Type: Principle Strengthen

The argument can be outlined as follows:

P1: When people are given extreme freedom, they make bad decisions.
P2: The drawbacks of extreme freedom may lead people to prefer totalitarian regimes.
C: One should not support political systems that allow extreme freedom.

This argument relies on the assumption that the risk of people preferring a totalitarian regime is reason enough to not support political systems that allow extreme freedom (which may result in a preference for totalitarianism). We should anticipate a correct answer choice that validates this assumption.

(A) One should not support any political system that will inevitably lead to the establishment of a totalitarian political regime.

The use of *inevitably* makes this answer choice too strong. The essayist believes that a political system that allows extreme freedom may foster a popular preference for totalitarian regimes. (A) is a loser.

(B) One should not expect everyone to thrive even in a political system that maximizes people's freedom in the long run.

This answer choice would not strengthen the argument as it simply restates a premise. (B) is a loser.

(C) One should support only those political systems that give people the freedom to make wise choices.

While a political system that allows extreme freedom gives people the freedom to make unwise choices, it also presumably gives them the freedom to make wise choices. Therefore, (C) would weaken the argument that we should not support such a political system. (C) is a loser.

(D) One should not support any political system whose destructive consequences could lead people to prefer totalitarian political regimes.

This matches our anticipated answer choice. If we should not support any political system that leads to totalitarian regimes, then we should not support one that allows for extreme freedom because this results in a preference for totalitarian regimes. (D) is a candidate.

(E) One should not support any political system that is based on unrealistic expectations about people's behavior under that system.

This answer choice includes irrelevant information. The argument does not include any information related to unrealistic expectations about people's behavior under a political system that allows extreme freedom. (E) is a loser.

As (D) is the only candidate, it has to be the correct answer choice.

Chapter 7

Pacing and Test Day Preparedness

Chapter 7: Pacing and Test Day Preparedness

HACKERS
LSAT *Logical Reasoning*

Pacing and Test Day Preparedness

Pacing Strategy

General

An LR section may contain between 24 and 26 questions, although sections with 24 questions are rare. As the time allotted for each section is 35 minutes, you will have, on average, 1 minute and 25 seconds to answer each question if you complete the whole section. However, because the LR section tends to escalate in difficulty, it is unwise to allocate the same amount of time to each question.

LR sections become progressively more difficult, but this does not mean that each question is harder than the preceding one. For example, it is possible that question 6 will be more challenging than question 11.

There is a general pattern, however. Questions 1 to 7 tend to be relatively easy, questions 8 to 15 will likely be of moderate difficulty, and questions 16 to 24/26 are usually very difficult. You should keep this in mind when developing a pacing strategy.

Skipping Parallel Questions

As mentioned previously, PR questions are more time-consuming than other question types. Because of this, if you find yourself short on time while taking practice tests, you may want to consider simply guessing for PR questions on the actual test. As PR questions can take twice as long to complete as other question types, skipping one PR question may save enough time to attempt two other questions. Since every question on the LSAT has the same value, this is an effective strategy for some students.

This same strategy may also be used for PF questions, with slight modification. Read through the stimulus to check if you can quickly identify the fallacy. If you are able to do this immediately, go on to the answer choices as usual. If not, just make a guess and move on to save time for other questions.

Note that there will almost always be only one PR and one PF question per section, so there is a limit to how much time this strategy can save.

Selecting a Pacing Strategy

To achieve a high score on the LR section, you need to spend more time on the more difficult questions at the end of the section than on the easier ones at the beginning. You must also ensure that no question takes up so much of your time that you have to rush through other questions that you would have otherwise had a good chance of answering correctly. An effective pacing strategy will help you achieve the balance between speed and accuracy required to maximize your score. The strategy you choose should match your ability, and you should be flexible when applying it. Difficulty progression varies from administration to administration, so questions at the beginning or end of an LR section may be unusually difficult or easy. Here are some pacing strategies that are effective for different types of test-takers:

Pacing Strategy 1	
Question Pacing	**Who should follow this strategy?**
1. Complete the first 10 questions in 15 minutes. 2. Complete the next 10 questions in 19 minutes. 3. Use the final minute to guess the answers of the remaining 4-6 questions.	This pacing strategy is intended for test-takers who are only able to complete 15 to 20 questions in an LR section during a practice exam.

Pacing Strategy 2	
Question Pacing	**Who should follow this strategy?**
1. Complete the first 10 questions in 13 minutes. 2. Complete the next 10 questions in 17 minutes. 3. Work on the remaining 4-6 questions for 4 minutes. Focus on the shortest questions or the questions types that you are most comfortable with. 4. Use the final minute to guess the answers of the unanswered questions.	This pacing strategy is intended for test-takers who are able to complete all questions in an LR section with a low-to-moderate level of accuracy.

Pacing Strategy 3	
Question Pacing	**Who should follow this strategy?**
1. Complete the first 10 questions in 10 minutes. 2. Complete the next 10 questions in 15 minutes. 3. Complete the last 4-6 questions in 10 minutes.	This pacing strategy is intended for test-takers who are able to complete all questions in an LR section with a moderate-to-high level of accuracy.

Pacing Strategy 4	
Question Pacing	**Who should follow this strategy?**
1. Complete the first 15 questions in 15 minutes. 2. Complete the next 9-11 questions in 20 minutes.	This advanced pacing strategy is intended for students who are able to complete all questions in an LR section with a high level of accuracy.

The below table shows the approximate number of incorrect answers permitted for each score range. Note that this table assumes that your score on the LR section is similar to your scores on the other sections of the test.

Target Score	Number of Incorrect Answers
140	15-16 per LR section
145	13-14 per LR section
150	10-12 per LR section
155	8-9 per LR section
160	6-7 per LR section
165	4-5 per LR section
170	2-3 per LR section
175	1-2 per LR section
180	0-1 per LR section

Leading up to Test Day

A Month before the Test

By this point, you should have worked your way through most of this book and be aware of which question types you have the most difficulty with. The bulk of your remaining time before the test should be focused on improving in your weakest areas. Review the sections of this book that deal with the question types you are most likely to answer incorrectly. Keep in mind, though, that certain question types appear more frequently than others. You should pay more attention to the ones you will encounter most often. For example, if you are equally weak at Strengthen, Agree/Disagree, and Evaluation question types, the time you dedicate towards practicing these question types should be prioritized in that respective order, as Strengthen questions are more common than Agree/Disagree questions, which are more common than Evaluation Questions.

During this period, you should also attempt to complete at least one timed practice exam. The practice test at the end of this book is a great place to start, and the LSAC offers a free practice test on its website. Attempting a timed practice test is important because it helps you prepare mentally for the challenges of completing the LSAT in the actual test environment. It also gives you a chance to test the effectiveness of your chosen pacing strategy.

The Day before the Test

A day before to the exam, you should wake up as early as possible. This is to make it less likely that you will have trouble sleeping that night due to test anxiety.

During the day, print out your exam ticket and make sure you have a one-gallon (or smaller) clear plastic bag filled with the items needed during test day (see the Test Day Checklist later in this chapter). Note that you are not permitted to bring a bag that is larger or made out of non-transparent material into the testing center. You should also do everything possible to ensure that you are not stressed on the day of the exam. For example, arrange transportation to the testing center, and ensure that you are familiar with the route. Also, check you admission ticket for information about the center's policy regarding cell phones. As of 2019, all centers prohibit these devices, but the LSAC is developing a program to allow test-takers to store their cell phones at the center before the test begins.

Try not to study the day before the exam. You are unlikely to acquire any new information that will affect your exam performance at this point, and going over the material unnecessarily will likely stress you out. Instead, try to relax as much as possible. You will want to go to sleep early as most LSAT administrations start at 8:30 AM.

The Morning of the Test

It is best not to add anything new to your routine that may affect your test performance. For example, drinking coffee in the morning may keep you alert throughout the exam, but if you are not used to caffeine, you may feel uncomfortably jittery.

It may be helpful to read through one or two LR questions just before the exam to warm up. If you choose to do this, remember that you are not permitted to bring in any scratch paper or prep materials into the testing center itself.

For all test-takers, it is important that your appearance on the day of the test matches the photo you submitted to the LSAC. This is especially important for male test takers who have grown facial hair (or have shaved their facial hair) and thus look different from the photo in the admission ticket. There are even stories of students rushing to nearby stores to find a razor and shaving cream to shave so that they will be admitted into the test center.

Lastly, dress in layers. The testing center may be too cold (or too warm), and you want to make sure that you will not be uncomfortable during the exam.

Test Day Checklist

Bring the following items in a one-gallon clear plastic bag to the test center:

> You will be provided with a pen and scratch paper to use during the test.

1. LSAT admission ticket
2. Photo identification
3. Tissues (if needed)
4. Medication or feminine hygiene products (if needed)
5. Car or house keys (if needed)
6. Beverage in plastic container or juice box for breaks only (if needed)
7. Snack for breaks only (if needed)

Please check your admission ticket for a comprehensive list of allowed and prohibited items as this list is occasionally updated.

Chapter 8

Practice Test

Chapter 8: Practice Test

HACKERS
LSAT *Logical Reasoning*

Section 1

Time—35 minutes

25 Questions

Directions: Each question in this section is based on the reasoning provided in a brief passage. In answering the questions, you should not make assumptions that are by commonsense standards implausible, superfluous, or incompatible with the passage. For some questions, more than one of the choices could conceivably answer the question. However, you are to choose the best answer; that is, choose the response that most accurately and completely answers the question and mark that response on your answer sheet.

1. The editor of a magazine has pointed out several errors of spelling and grammar committed on a recent TV program. But she can hardly be trusted to pass judgment on such matters: similar errors have been found in her own magazine.

   The flawed reasoning in the argument above is most similar to that in which one of the following?

   (A) Your newspaper cannot be trusted with the prerogative to criticize the ethics of our company: you misspelled our president's name.
   (B) Your news program cannot be trusted to judge our hiring practices as unfair: you yourselves unfairly discriminate in hiring and promotion decisions.
   (C) Your regulatory agency cannot condemn our product as unsafe: selling it is allowed under an existing-product clause.
   (D) Your coach cannot be trusted to judge our swimming practices: he accepted a lucrative promotional deal from a soft-drink company.
   (E) Your teen magazine should not run this feature on problems afflicting modern high schools: your revenue depends on not alienating the high school audience.

2. Soaking dried beans overnight before cooking them reduces cooking time. However, cooking without presoaking yields plumper beans. Therefore, when a bean dish's quality is more important than the need to cook that dish quickly, beans should not be presoaked.

   Which one of the following is an assumption required by the argument?

   (A) Plumper beans enhance the quality of a dish.
   (B) There are no dishes whose quality improves with faster cooking.
   (C) A dish's appearance is as important as its taste.
   (D) None of the other ingredients in the dish need to be presoaked.
   (E) The plumper the bean, the better it tastes.

GO ON TO THE NEXT PAGE.

3. Durth: Increasingly, businesses use direct mail advertising instead of paying for advertising space in newspapers, in magazines, or on billboards. This practice is annoying and also immoral. Most direct mail advertisements are thrown out without ever being read, and the paper on which they are printed is wasted. If anyone else wasted this much paper, it would be considered unconscionable.

Which one of the following most accurately describes Durth's method of reasoning?

(A) presenting a specific counter-example to the contention that direct mail advertising is not immoral

(B) asserting that there would be very undesirable consequences if direct mail advertising became a more widespread practice than it is now

(C) claiming that direct mail advertising is immoral because one of its results would be deemed immoral in other contexts

(D) basing a conclusion on the claim that direct mail advertising is annoying to those who receive it

(E) asserting that other advertising methods do not have the negative effects of direct mail advertising

4. Among the various models of Delta vacuum cleaners, one cannot accurately predict how effectively a particular model cleans simply by determining how powerful its motor is. The efficiency of dust filtration systems varies significantly, even between models of Delta vacuum cleaners equipped with identically powerful motors.

The argument's conclusion is properly drawn if which one of the following is assumed?

(A) For each Delta vacuum cleaner, the efficiency of its dust filtration system has a significant impact on how effectively it cleans.

(B) One can accurately infer how powerful a Delta vacuum cleaner's motor is from the efficiency of the vacuum cleaner's dust filtration system.

(C) All Delta vacuum cleaners that clean equally effectively have identically powerful motors.

(D) For any two Delta vacuum cleaners with equally efficient dust filtration systems, the one with the more powerful motor cleans more effectively.

(E) One cannot accurately assess how effectively any Delta vacuum cleaner cleans without knowing how powerful that vacuum cleaner's motor is.

5. Many scientists believe that bipedal locomotion (walking on two feet) evolved in early hominids in response to the move from life in dense forests to life in open grasslands. Bipedalism would have allowed early hominids to see over tall grasses, helping them to locate food and to detect and avoid predators. However, because bipedalism also would have conferred substantial advantages upon early hominids who never left the forest—in gathering food found within standing reach of the forest floor, for example—debate continues concerning its origins. It may even have evolved, like the upright threat displays of many large apes, because it bettered an individual's odds of finding a mate.

Which one of the following statements is most supported by the information above?

(A) For early hominids, forest environments were generally more hospitable than grassland environments.
(B) Bipedal locomotion would have helped early hominids gather food.
(C) Bipedal locomotion actually would not be advantageous to hominids living in open grassland environments.
(D) Bipedal locomotion probably evolved among early hominids who exclusively inhabited forest environments.
(E) For early hominids, gathering food was more relevant to survival than was detecting and avoiding predators.

6. Mathematics teacher: Teaching students calculus before they attend university may significantly benefit them. Yet if students are taught calculus before they are ready for the level of abstraction involved, they may abandon the study of mathematics altogether. So if we are going to teach pre-university students calculus, we must make sure they can handle the level of abstraction involved.

Which one of the following principles most helps to justify the mathematics teacher's argument?

(A) Only those who, without losing motivation, can meet the cognitive challenges that new intellectual work involves should be introduced to it.
(B) Only those parts of university-level mathematics that are the most concrete should be taught to pre-university students.
(C) Cognitive tasks that require exceptional effort tend to undermine the motivation of those who attempt them.
(D) Teachers who teach university-level mathematics to pre-university students should be aware that students are likely to learn effectively only when the application of mathematics to concrete problems is shown.
(E) The level of abstraction involved in a topic should not be considered in determining whether that topic is appropriate for pre-university students.

GO ON TO THE NEXT PAGE.

7. In 1955, legislation in a certain country gave the government increased control over industrial workplace safety conditions. Among the high-risk industries in that country, the likelihood that a worker will suffer a serious injury has decreased since 1955. The legislation, therefore, has increased overall worker safety within high-risk industries.

Which one of the following, if true, most weakens the argument above?

(A) Because of technological innovation, most workplaces in the high-risk industries do not require as much unprotected interaction between workers and heavy machinery as they did in 1955.

(B) Most of the work-related injuries that occurred before 1955 were the result of worker carelessness.

(C) The annual number of work-related injuries has increased since the legislation took effect.

(D) The number of work-related injuries occurring within industries not considered high-risk has increased annually since 1955.

(E) Workplace safety conditions in all industries have improved steadily since 1955.

8. Economist: Historically, sunflower seed was one of the largest production crops in Kalotopia, and it continues to be a major source of income for several countries. The renewed growing of sunflowers would provide relief to Kalotopia's farming industry, which is quite unstable. Further, sunflower oil can provide a variety of products, both industrial and consumer, at little cost to Kalotopia's already fragile environment.

The economist's statements, if true, most strongly support which one of the following?

(A) Kalotopia's farming industry will deteriorate if sunflowers are not grown there.

(B) Stabilizing Kalotopia's farming industry would improve the economy without damaging the environment.

(C) Kalotopia's farming industry would be better off now if it had never ceased to grow any of the crops that historically were large production crops.

(D) A crop that was once a large production crop in Kalotopia would, if it were grown there again, benefit that country's farmers and general economy.

(E) Sunflower seed is a better crop for Kalotopia from both the environmental and the economic viewpoints than are most crops that could be grown there.

9. Several major earthquakes have occurred in a certain region over the last ten years. But a new earthquake prediction method promises to aid local civil defense officials in deciding exactly when to evacuate various towns. Detected before each of these major quakes were certain changes in the electric current in the earth's crust.

Which one of the following, if true, most weakens the argument?

(A) Scientists do not fully understand what brought about the changes in the electric current in the earth's crust that preceded each of the major quakes in the region over the last ten years.

(B) Most other earthquake prediction methods have been based on a weaker correlation than that found between the changes in the electric current in the earth's crust and the subsequent earthquakes.

(C) The frequency of major earthquakes in the region has increased over the last ten years.

(D) There is considerable variation in the length of time between the changes in the electric current and the subsequent earthquakes.

(E) There is presently only one station in the region that is capable of detecting the electric current in the earth's crust.

10. Unlike many machines that are perfectly useful in isolation from others, fax machines must work with other fax machines. Thus, in the fax industry, the proliferation of incompatible formats, which resulted from the large number of competing manufacturers, severely limited the usefulness—and hence the commercial viability—of fax technology until the manufacturers agreed to adopt a common format for their machines.

The information above provides the most support for which one of the following propositions?

(A) Whenever machines are dependent on other machines of the same type, competition among manufacturers is damaging to the industry.

(B) In some industries it is in the interest of competitors to cooperate to some extent with one another.

(C) The more competitors there are in a high-tech industry, the more they will have to cooperate in determining the basic design of their product.

(D) Some cooperation among manufacturers in the same industry is more beneficial than is pure competition.

(E) Cooperation is beneficial only in industries whose products depend on other products of the same type.

GO ON TO THE NEXT PAGE.

11. In comparing different methods by which a teacher's performance can be evaluated and educational outcomes improved, researchers found that a critique of teacher performance leads to enhanced educational outcomes if the critique is accompanied by the information that teacher performance is merely one of several factors that, in concert with other factors, determines the educational outcomes.

Which one of the following best illustrates the principle illustrated by the finding of the researchers?

(A) Children can usually be taught to master subject matter in which they have no interest if they believe that successfully mastering it will earn the respect of their peers.

(B) People are generally more willing to accept a negative characterization of a small group of people if they do not see themselves as members of the group being so characterized.

(C) An actor can more effectively evaluate the merits of her own performance if she can successfully convince herself that she is really evaluating the performance of another actor.

(D) The opinions reached by a social scientist in the study of a society can be considered as more reliable and objective if that social scientist is not a member of that society.

(E) It is easier to correct the mistakes of an athlete if it is made clear to him that the criticism is part of an overarching effort to rectify the shortcomings of the entire team on which he plays.

12. Critic: A novel cannot be of the highest quality unless most readers become emotionally engaged with the imaginary world it describes. Thus shifts of narrative point of view within a novel, either between first and third person or of some other sort, detract from the merit of the work, since such shifts tend to make most readers focus on the author.

Which one of the following is an assumption necessary for the critic's conclusion to be properly drawn?

(A) Most readers become emotionally engaged with the imaginary world described by a novel only if the novel is of the highest quality.

(B) A novel is generally not considered to be of high quality unless it successfully engages the imagination of most readers.

(C) Most readers cannot become emotionally involved with a novel's imaginary world if they focus on the author.

(D) Most readers regard a novel's narrative point of view as representing the perspective of the novel's author.

(E) Shifts in narrative point of view serve no literary purpose.

13. People aged 46 to 55 spend more money per capita than people of any other age group. So it is puzzling that when companies advertise consumer products on television, they focus almost exclusively on people aged 25 and under. Indeed, those who make decisions about television advertising think that the value of a television advertising slot depends entirely on the number of people aged 25 and under who can be expected to be watching at that time.

Which one of the following, if true, most helps to explain the puzzling facts stated above?

(A) The expense of television advertising slots makes it crucial for companies to target people who are most likely to purchase their products.

(B) Advertising slots during news programs almost always cost far less than advertising slots during popular sitcoms whose leading characters are young adults.

(C) When television executives decide which shows to renew, they do so primarily in terms of the shows' ratings among people aged 25 and under.

(D) Those who make decisions about television advertising believe that people older than 25 almost never change their buying habits.

(E) When companies advertise consumer products in print media, they focus primarily on people aged 26 and over.

14. Eighteenth-century moralist: You should never make an effort to acquire expensive new tastes, since they are a drain on your purse and in the course of acquiring them you may expose yourself to sensations that are obnoxious to you. Furthermore, the very effort that must be expended in their acquisition attests their superfluity.

The moralist's reasoning is most vulnerable to criticism on the grounds that the moralist

(A) draws a conclusion that simply restates a claim presented in support of that conclusion

(B) takes for granted that the acquisition of expensive tastes will lead to financial irresponsibility

(C) uses the inherently vague term "sensations" without providing a definition of that term

(D) mistakes a cause of acquisition of expensive tastes for an effect of acquisition of such tastes

(E) rejects trying to achieve a goal because of the cost of achieving it, without considering the benefits of achieving it

GO ON TO THE NEXT PAGE.

15. Zack's Coffeehouse schedules free poetry readings almost every Wednesday. Zack's offers half-priced coffee all day on every day that a poetry reading is scheduled.

Which one of the following can be properly inferred from the information above?

(A) Wednesday is the most common day on which Zack's offers half-priced coffee all day.
(B) Most free poetry readings given at Zack's are scheduled for Wednesdays.
(C) Free poetry readings are scheduled on almost every day that Zack's offers half-priced coffee all day.
(D) Zack's offers half-priced coffee all day on most if not all Wednesdays.
(E) On some Wednesdays Zack's does not offer half-priced coffee all day.

16. Philosopher: An event is intentional if it is a human action performed on the basis of a specific motivation. An event is random if it is not performed on the basis of a specific motivation and it is not explainable by normal physical processes.

Which one of the following inferences conforms most closely to the philosopher's position?

(A) Tarik left the keys untouched on the kitchen counter, but he did not do so on the basis of a specific motivation. Therefore, the keys' remaining on the kitchen counter was a random event.
(B) Ellis tore the envelope open in order to read its contents, but the envelope was empty. Nevertheless, because Ellis acted on the basis of a specific motivation, tearing the envelope open was an intentional event.
(C) Judith's hailing a cab distracted a driver in the left lane. She performed the action of hailing the cab on the basis of a specific motivation, so the driver's becoming distracted was an intentional event.
(D) Yasuko continued to breathe regularly throughout the time that she was asleep. This was a human action, but it was not performed on the basis of a specific motivation. Therefore, her breathing was a random event.
(E) Henry lost his hold on the wrench and dropped it because the handle was slippery. This was a human action and is explainable by normal physical processes, so it was an intentional event.

17. It is a mistake to conclude, as some have, that ancient people did not know what moral rights were simply because no known ancient language has an expression correctly translatable as "a moral right." This would be like saying that a person who discovers a wild fruit tree and returns repeatedly to harvest from it and study it has no idea what the fruit is until naming it or learning its name.

Which one of the following is an assumption required by the argument?

(A) To know the name of something is to know what that thing is.
(B) People who first discover what something is know it better than do people who merely know the name of the thing.
(C) The name or expression that is used to identify something cannot provide any information about the nature of the thing that is identified.
(D) A person who repeatedly harvests from a wild fruit tree and studies it has some idea of what the fruit is even before knowing a name for the fruit.
(E) One need not know what something is before one can name it.

18. There is little plausibility to the claim that it is absurd to criticize anyone for being critical. Obviously, people must assess one another and not all assessments will be positive. However, there is wisdom behind the injunction against being judgmental. To be judgmental is not merely to assess someone negatively, but to do so prior to a serious effort at understanding.

Which one of the following most accurately expresses the main conclusion drawn in the argument?

(A) To be judgmental is to assess someone negatively prior to making a serious effort at understanding.
(B) It is absurd to criticize anyone for being critical.
(C) There is some plausibility to the claim that it is absurd to criticize anyone for being critical.
(D) Not all assessments people make of one another will be positive.
(E) There is wisdom behind the injunction against being judgmental.

GO ON TO THE NEXT PAGE.

19. Even those who believe that the art of each age and culture has its own standards of beauty must admit that some painters are simply superior to others in the execution of their artistic visions. But this superiority must be measured in light of the artist's purposes, since the high merits, for example, of Jose Rey Toledo's work and his extraordinary artistic skills are not in doubt, despite the fact that his paintings do not literally resemble what they represent.

The claim that some painters are superior to others in the execution of their artistic visions plays which one of the following roles in the argument?

(A) It is a hypothesis that the argument attempts to refute.
(B) It is a generalization, one sort of objection to which the argument illustrates by giving an example.
(C) It is a claim that, according to the argument, is to be understood in a manner specified by the conclusion.
(D) It is a claim that the argument derives from another claim and that it uses to support its conclusion.
(E) It is a generalization that the argument uses to justify the relevance of the specific example it cites.

20. A study of rabbits in the 1940s convinced many biologists that parthenogenesis—reproduction without fertilization of an egg—sometimes occurs in mammals. However, the study's methods have since been shown to be flawed, and no other studies have succeeded in demonstrating mammalian parthenogenesis. Thus, since parthenogenesis is known to occur in a wide variety of nonmammalian vertebrates, there must be something about mammalian chromosomes that precludes the possibility of parthenogenesis.

A flaw in the reasoning of the argument is that the argument

(A) takes for granted that something that has not been proven to be true is for that reason shown to be false
(B) infers that a characteristic is shared by all nonmammalian vertebrate species merely because it is shared by some nonmammalian vertebrate species
(C) rules out an explanation of a phenomenon merely on the grounds that there is another explanation that can account for the phenomenon
(D) confuses a necessary condition for parthenogenesis with a sufficient condition for it
(E) assumes that the methods used in a study of one mammalian species were flawed merely because the study's findings cannot be generalized to all other mammalian species

21. Advertiser: Most TV shows depend on funding from advertisers and would be canceled without such funding. However, advertisers will not pay to have their commercials aired during a TV show unless many people watching the show buy the advertised products as a result. So if people generally fail to buy the products advertised during their favorite shows, these shows will soon be canceled. Thus, anyone who feels that a TV show is worth preserving ought to buy the products advertised during that show.

The advertiser's reasoning most closely conforms to which one of the following principles?

(A) If a TV show that one feels to be worth preserving would be canceled unless one took certain actions, then one ought to take those actions.

(B) If a TV show would be canceled unless many people took certain actions, then everyone who feels that the show is worth preserving ought to take those actions.

(C) If a TV show is worth preserving, then everyone should take whatever actions are necessary to prevent that show from being canceled.

(D) If one feels that a TV show is worth preserving, then one should take at least some actions to reduce the likelihood that the show will be canceled.

(E) If a TV show would be canceled unless many people took certain actions, then those who feel most strongly that it is worth preserving should take those actions.

22. Psychologist: It is well known that becoming angry often induces temporary incidents of high blood pressure. A recent study further showed, however, that people who are easily angered are significantly more likely to have permanently high blood pressure than are people who have more tranquil personalities. Coupled with the long-established fact that those with permanently high blood pressure are especially likely to have heart disease, the recent findings indicate that heart disease can result from psychological factors.

Which one of the following would, if true, most weaken the psychologist's argument?

(A) Those who are easily angered are less likely to recover fully from episodes of heart disease than are other people.

(B) Medication designed to control high blood pressure can greatly affect the moods of those who use it.

(C) People with permanently high blood pressure who have tranquil personalities virtually never develop heart disease.

(D) Those who discover that they have heart disease tend to become more easily frustrated by small difficulties.

(E) The physiological factors that cause permanently high blood pressure generally make people quick to anger.

GO ON TO THE NEXT PAGE.

23. A professor of business placed a case-study assignment for her class on her university's computer network. She later found out that instead of reading the assignment on the computer screen, 50 out of the 70 students printed it out on paper. Thus, it is not the case that books delivered via computer will make printed books obsolete.

Which one of the following, if true, most strengthens the argument?

(A) Several colleagues of the professor have found that, in their non-business courses, several of their students behave similarly in relation to assignments placed on the computer network.

(B) Studies consistently show that most computer users will print reading material that is more than a few pages in length rather than read it on the computer screen.

(C) Some people get impaired vision from long periods of reading printed matter on computer screens, even if they use high quality computer screens.

(D) Scanning technology is very poor, causing books delivered via computer to be full of errors unless editors carefully read the scanned versions.

(E) Books on cassette tape have only a small fraction of the sales of printed versions of the same books, though sales of videos of books that have been turned into movies remain strong.

24. Advertisement: Researchers studied a group of people trying to lose weight and discovered that those in the group who lost the most weight got more calories from protein than from carbohydrates and ate their biggest meal early in the day. So anyone who follows our diet, which provides more calories from protein than from anything else and which requires that breakfast be the biggest meal of the day, is sure to lose weight.

The reasoning in the advertisement is most vulnerable to criticism on the grounds that the advertisement overlooks the possibility that

(A) eating foods that derive a majority of their calories from carbohydrates tends to make one feel fuller than does eating foods that derive a majority of their calories from protein

(B) a few of the people in the group studied who lost significant amounts of weight got nearly all of their calories from carbohydrates and ate their biggest meal at night

(C) the people in the group studied who increased their activity levels lost more weight, on average, than those who did not, regardless of whether they got more calories from protein or from carbohydrates

(D) some people in the group studied lost no weight yet got more calories from protein than from carbohydrates and ate their biggest meal early in the day

(E) people who eat their biggest meal at night tend to snack more during the day and so tend to take in more total calories than do people who eat their biggest meal earlier in the day

25. Some twentieth-century art is great art. All great art involves original ideas, and any art that is not influential cannot be great art.

    Each of the following statements follows logically from the set of statements above EXCEPT:

    (A) Some influential art involves original ideas.
    (B) Some twentieth-century art involves original ideas.
    (C) Only art that involves original ideas is influential.
    (D) Only art that is influential and involves original ideas is great art.
    (E) Some twentieth-century art is influential and involves original ideas.

S T O P

IF YOU FINISH BEFORE TIME IS CALLED, YOU MAY CHECK YOUR WORK ON THIS SECTION ONLY. DO NOT WORK ON ANY OTHER SECTION IN THE TEST.

1.	B	6.	A	11.	E	16.	B	21.	B
2.	A	7.	A	12.	C	17.	D	22.	E
3.	C	8.	D	13.	D	18.	E	23.	B
4.	A	9.	D	14.	E	19.	C	24.	D
5.	B	10.	B	15.	D	20.	A	25.	C

1. Correct Answer (B). Question Type: Parallel Fallacy. Difficulty Level: 1 / 4

The conclusion of this argument is that the editor of the magazine cannot be trusted to pass judgment on spelling and grammar errors committed on a recent TV program. The evidence for this is that similar errors have been found in her own magazine. This is an Ad Hominem Fallacy; specifically, an attempt to nullify a source's advice on the grounds that that source's behavior has been inconsistent with the advice. The fact that the editor's magazine has failed to catch similar errors does not preclude the editor from being correct in her judgment of the errors on the TV program. The argument can be outlined as follows:

P1: The editor has pointed out mistakes on a TV program.
P2: Similar mistakes have been found in the editor's magazine.
C: The editor's comments on the TV program cannot be trusted.

We should anticipate a correct answer choice that includes the same type of Ad Hominem Fallacy.

(A) Your newspaper cannot be trusted with the prerogative to criticize the ethics of our company: you misspelled our president's name.

In this argument, the subject matter of the premise and the conclusion are different—misspelling someone's name is wholly unrelated to a criticism of corporate ethics. The arguments in (A) and in the stimulus have different flaws, so (A) is a loser.

(B) Your news program cannot be trusted to judge our hiring practices as unfair: you yourselves unfairly discriminate in hiring and promotion decisions.

This matches our anticipated answer choice. In (B), the argument concludes that the news program cannot be trusted to judge hiring practices because it has engaged in unfair hiring practices in the past. The fact that the news program has engaged in unfair hiring practices does not preclude it from being able to judge the hiring practices of another organization. (B) is a candidate.

(C) Your regulatory agency cannot condemn our product as unsafe: selling it is allowed under an existing-product clause.

The agency's past behavior is not criticized in this argument. (C) is a loser.

(D) Your coach cannot be trusted to judge our swimming practices: he accepted a lucrative promotional deal from a soft-drink company.

This is a different form of Ad Hominem Fallacy. In (D), the argument implies that the coach's judgment is biased because of a promotional deal he made with a soft-drink company. It does not claim that the judge's past behavior makes him unsuitable to judge the swimming practices. (D) is a loser.

(E) Your teen magazine should not run this feature on problems afflicting modern high schools: your revenue depends on not alienating the high school audience.

This argument does not contain a criticism of past behavior. (E) is a loser.

As (B) is the only candidate, it has to be the correct answer choice.

2. **Correct Answer (A).** Question Type: Necessary Assumption. Difficulty Level: 1 / 4

The argument concludes that beans should not be presoaked when the quality of a dish is more important than the need to prepare it quickly. The argument states that soaking beans overnight reduces cooking time, but beans that are not presoaked are plumper. However, nothing mentioned allows us to assume that using plumper beans raises the quality of a dish. The argument commits a Questionable Assumption Fallacy. It assumes that using plumper beans results in a higher-quality dish. The argument can be outlined as

> P1: Soaking dried beans overnight reduces cooking time.
> P2: Not soaking dried beans yields plumper beans.
> _____
> C: When dish quality is more important, beans should not be presoaked.

We should anticipate a correct answer choice that validates the assumption that using plumper beans improves the quality of a dish.

(A) Plumper beans enhance the quality of a dish.

This matches our anticipated answer choice. It clearly validates the assumption we identified in the argument. In addition, this statement must be true in order for the argument to be valid. (A) is a candidate.

(B) There are no dishes whose quality improves with faster cooking.

The argument does not need to assume this. Furthermore, (B) is irrelevant because it pertains to all dishes rather than just bean-based ones. (B) is a loser.

(C) A dish's appearance is as important as its taste.

This is irrelevant information as the appearance of a dish is not discussed in the argument. (C) is a loser.

(D) None of the other ingredients in the dish need to be presoaked.

This is irrelevant information because the argument only specifies what needs to be done with beans (not what needs to be done with any other ingredients). (D) is a loser.

(E) The plumper the bean, the better it tastes.

This matches our anticipated answer choice. If plumper beans taste better, then dishes containing them are likely to be higher in quality. (E) is a candidate.

We now need to eliminate a candidate. As this is an NA question, we can use the (Un)Necessary Assumption Test to do this.

(E) is a conditional statement. We can convert it into an "If . . . then" statement that reads as "If the bean is plumper, it tastes better." We need to logically negate the necessary assumption, which results in "If the bean is plumper, it does not necessarily taste better." This does not invalidate the argument as there may be other elements that determine a dish's quality other than taste.

(A) is a nonconditional statement, so we should logically negate the first verb after the subject, which results in

"Plumper beans do not enhance the quality of a dish." This statement invalidates the argument, so (A) has to be the correct answer choice.

3. **Correct Answer (C).** Question Type: Description. Difficulty Level: 1 / 4

This D question features a one-viewpoint argument that concludes that direct mail advertising is annoying and immoral. Durth supports this conclusion by positing that most of these advertisements are thrown away, which is a waste of paper. He then reasons that if anyone else wasted this much paper, it would be considered unconscionable. Durth is making a comparison between businesses wasting paper and individuals wasting paper; since it is unconscionable for individuals to waste paper, it must be unconscionable for businesses to do the same. The argument can be outlined as follows:

BI: Increasingly, businesses use direct mail for advertising.
P1: Most direct mail advertisements are thrown out, which is a waste of paper.
P2: If anyone else wasted paper in this manner, it would be considered unconscionable.
C: Direct mail advertisement is annoying and immoral.

This is a common argumentative structure: making a comparison or analogy. We should anticipate a correct answer choice that describes this structure.

(A) presenting a specific counter-example to the contention that direct mail advertising is not immoral

No counter-example is presented, and the argument concludes that direct mail advertising is immoral. (A) is a loser.

(B) asserting that there would be very undesirable consequences if direct mail advertising became a more widespread practice than it is now

This is implied by the argument but is never stated. For D questions, the correct answer choice must describe the argumentative structure. (B) is a loser.

(C) claiming that direct mail advertising is immoral because one of its results would be deemed immoral in other contexts

This matches our anticipated answer choice. The argument states that a result of direct mail advertising (i.e. paper wastage) is immoral in one context because it would be considered immoral in another context. This answer choice refers to the comparison made in the argument. (C) is a candidate.

(D) basing a conclusion on the claim that direct mail advertising is annoying to those who receive it

This line of reasoning is not employed in the argument. The fact that the practice is annoying is part of the conclusion; it is not part of a premise. (D) is a loser.

(E) asserting that other advertising methods do not have the negative effects of direct mail advertising

The argument does not discuss other advertising methods. (E) is a loser.

As (C) is the only candidate, it has to be the correct answer choice.

4. **Correct Answer (A).** Question Type: Sufficient Assumption. Difficulty Level: 1 / 4

The argument concludes that one cannot accurately predict how effectively a particular Delta vacuum cleaner model cleans simply by assessing motor power. The argument supports this by claiming that the efficiency of dust filtration systems varies significantly, even between models of vacuum cleans with equally powerful motors. The argument seems to imply that the efficiency of the dust filtration system is an important factor in determining the cleaning effectiveness of a vacuum cleaner model. However, this is not explicitly stated, resulting in a Questionable Assumption Fallacy. The argument can be outlined as follows:

P: The efficiency of dust filtration systems varies significantly.
A: (Dust filtration systems have a significant impact on cleaning ability.)
C: One cannot accurately predict a vacuum's effectiveness only by assessing motor power.

We should anticipate a correct answer choice that validates the argument by expressing this assumption.

(A) For each Delta vacuum cleaner, the efficiency of its dust filtration system has a significant impact on how effectively it cleans.

This matches our anticipated answer choice. If the dust filtration system significantly affects how effectively the vacuum cleans, then it must be the case that you cannot accurately predict its cleaning power just by assessing motor power. (A) is a candidate.

(B) One can accurately infer how powerful a Delta vacuum cleaner's motor is from the efficiency of the vacuum cleaner's dust filtration system.

We are looking for information that would show that something other than motor power has an effect on cleaning. This answer choice simply states that there is a relationship between dust filtration system efficiency and motor power. (B) is a loser.

(C) All Delta vacuum cleaners that clean equally effectively have identically powerful motors.

This would weaken the argument because it implies that cleaning effectiveness is determined only by motor power. (C) is a loser.

(D) For any two Delta vacuum cleaners with equally efficient dust filtration systems, the one with the more powerful motor cleans more effectively.

The argument implies that dust filtration system efficiency affects cleaning effectiveness, while this answer choice claims that motor power determines cleaning effectiveness when dust filtration systems are equally efficient. This answer choice does not address a situation in which dust filtration systems are not equally efficient. In such a scenario, the model with the most powerful motor may well clean more effectively. As (D) does not validate the argument, it is a loser.

(E) One cannot accurately assess how effectively any Delta vacuum cleaner cleans without knowing how powerful that vacuum cleaner's motor is.

This would weaken the argument because it provides evidence that motor power is the only significant factor in determining cleaning effectiveness. Therefore, (E) is a loser.

As (A) is the only candidate, it has to be the correct answer choice.

5. **Correct Answer (B).** Question Type: Implication. Difficulty Level: 2 / 4

The stimulus discusses the debate about whether bipedalism developed in open grasslands or in forests. The trait would have been advantageous to early hominids in both environments. In open grasslands, bipedalism would have enabled hominids to see over tall grass, allowing them to locate food and avoid predators. In forests, the trait would have made it easier to gather food. The stimulus does not include an incomplete argument, an unusual circumstance, or conditional language. Therefore, we should anticipate a correct answer choice that is a paraphrase of a proposition or a statement supported by the stimulus.

(A) For early hominids, forest environments were generally more hospitable than grassland environments.

This is irrelevant information. Nothing in the stimulus suggests that one environment was more hospitable than another. (A) is a loser.

(B) Bipedal locomotion would have helped early hominids gather food.

This matches one of our anticipated answer choices. The stimulus clearly states that bipedalism would have helped early hominids gather food in the forests. It also implies that it would have helped them do this in open grasslands. (B) is a candidate.

(C) Bipedal locomotion actually would not be advantageous to hominids living in open grassland environments.

This contradicts the stimulus, which states that bipedalism would have benefitted hominids living in open grassland environments. (C) is a loser.

(D) Bipedal locomotion probably evolved among early hominids who exclusively inhabited forest environments.

The stimulus does not take a position on whether this trait first evolved among hominids living in grasslands or in forests. (D) is a loser.

(E) For early hominids, gathering food was more relevant to survival than was detecting and avoiding predators.

The stimulus does not compare the importance of gathering food with that of detecting or avoiding predators. (E) is a loser.

As (B) is the only candidate, it has to be the correct answer choice.

---

6. **Correct Answer (A).** Question Type: Principle Strengthen. Difficulty Level: 1 / 4

The teacher's conclusion is a conditional statement that can be represented as Teach Students Calculus → Handle Level of Abstraction. The evidence for this is that if students are taught calculus before they are ready for the level of abstraction involved, they might abandon studying mathematics. The argument relies on the assumption that the risk of abandoning mathematics should be avoided. Otherwise, why should teachers be concerned about whether or not students can handle the level of abstraction involved in calculus before teaching it? The argument can be outlined as follows:

P: Students might abandon math if they are taught calculus before they are ready.
A: (The risk of abandoning math should be avoided.)
_____
C: Teach Students Calculus → Handle Level of Abstraction

We should anticipate a correct answer choice that states a principle that validates this assumption.

(A) Only those who, without losing motivation, can meet the cognitive challenges that new intellectual work involves should be introduced to it.

This matches our anticipated answer choice. Applied to the argument, this principle means that only students who can handle abstraction and will not lose motivation should be taught calculus. This directly relates to avoiding the risk of students abandoning math. (A) is a candidate.

(B) Only those parts of university-level mathematics that are the most concrete should be taught to pre-university students.

This is irrelevant information. We are not comparing different levels of mathematics courses. (B) is a loser.

(C) Cognitive tasks that require exceptional effort tend to undermine the motivation of those who attempt them.

This is simply a restatement of the argument's claim that teaching calculus to students before they are ready may discourage them from pursuing mathematics. We are looking for a principle that addresses the logical gap we identified in the argument. (C) is a loser.

(D) Teachers who teach university-level mathematics to pre-university students should be aware that students are likely to learn effectively only when the application of mathematics to concrete problems is shown.

This is irrelevant information. The argument does not discuss teacher awareness or the application of mathematics to concrete problems. (D) is a loser.

(E) The level of abstraction involved in a topic should not be considered in determining whether that topic is appropriate for pre-university students.

This answer choice weakens the argument. It contradicts the conclusion, which states that the level of abstraction should be considered when determining whether to teach a topic. (E) is a loser.

As (A) is the only candidate, it has to be the correct answer choice.

7. **Correct Answer (A).** Question Type: Weaken. Difficulty Level: 1 / 4

The argument concludes that specific legislation increased overall worker safety within high-risk industries. This is a causal conclusion, best represented as Legislation CAUSE Increased Safety. The evidence for this conclusion is that since the legislation was introduced in 1955, the likelihood that a worker will suffer a serious injury has decreased. The argument can be outlined as follows:

P: The incidence of injuries decreased after legislation.
C: Legislation CAUSE Increased Safety

We should anticipate a correct answer choice that weakens the argument by presenting an *alternative cause*, an example of *same cause, no effect*, an example of *same effect, no cause*, or an example of *reversed cause and effect*.

(A) Because of technological innovation, most workplaces in the high-risk industries do not require as much unprotected interaction between workers and heavy machinery as they did in 1955.

This matches one of our anticipated answer choices. It introduces an alternative cause of increased worker safety—technological innovation. If technological innovation reduced unprotected interactions between workers and with heavy machinery, then worker safety is likely to have increased. (A) is a candidate.

(B) Most of the work-related injuries that occurred before 1955 were the result of worker carelessness.

This does not weaken the argument. Whether the accidents prior to 1955 were avoidable or not does not affect the claim that the legislation has increased overall worker safety since 1955. (B) is a loser.

(C) The annual number of work-related injuries has increased since the legislation took effect.

This answer choice includes irrelevant information. It discusses work-related injuries in general, while the argument is about serious injuries in high-risk industries. (C) is a loser.

(D) The number of work-related injuries occurring within industries not considered high-risk has increased annually since 1955.

This answer choice includes irrelevant information. It discusses injuries in non-high-risk industries. (D) is a loser.

(E) Workplace safety conditions in all industries have improved steadily since 1955.

At first glance, this seems like an example of *same effect, no cause*. However, the argument states that the legislation increased control over *industrial workplace safety conditions*, which is not limited only to high-risk industries. Therefore, the legislation may have improved the safety conditions of all industries. (E) is a loser.

As (A) is the only candidate, it has to be the correct answer choice.

---

8. Correct Answer (D). Question Type: Implication. Difficulty Level: 1 / 4

This stimulus states that sunflowers were one of the largest crops in Kalotopia and that reintroducing sunflowers as a crop would provide relief to the farming industry. It would also lead to the manufacture of various products at little cost to Kalotopia's already fragile environment. This stimulus does not include an incomplete argument, unusual circumstance, or conditional language. Therefore, we should anticipate an answer choice that is a paraphrase of a proposition or a statement supported by the stimulus.

(A) Kalotopia's farming industry will deteriorate if sunflowers are not grown there.

This answer choice is strongly worded and is not directly supported by the argument. The farming industry is unstable and would benefit through renewed efforts to grow sunflowers. However, we cannot assert that if sunflowers are not grown, then the farming industry will deteriorate. (A) is a loser.

(B) Stabilizing Kalotopia's farming industry would improve the economy without damaging the environment.

Growing sunflowers would help stabilize the farming industry at little cost to the environment, but we do not know if all means of stabilizing the farming industry would have little or no cost to the environment. (B) is too broad and strongly worded, making it a loser.

(C) Kalotopia's farming industry would be better off now if it had never ceased to grow any of the crops that historically were large production crops.

This answer choice includes irrelevant information. We know nothing about any of Kalotopia's historically large production crops except sunflowers. We also lack information about the reasons why farmers stopped growing sunflowers. (C) is a loser.

(D) A crop that was once a large production crop in Kalotopia would, if it were grown there again, benefit that country's farmers and general economy.

This matches one of our anticipated answer choices. The stimulus states that sunflower seeds were once a large production crop in Kalotopia and that growing them there again would bring relief to the unstable farming community. Benefits would likely accrue to farmers and the general economy. (D) is supported by the stimulus, so it is a candidate.

(E) Sunflower seed is a better crop for Kalotopia from both the environmental and the economic viewpoints than are most crops that could be grown there.

This is far too strong of a statement. We know that sunflower seeds can provide some benefits at little cost, but we do not have enough information to make the claim that this crop is better than most crops in this regard. (E) is a loser.

As (D) is the only candidate, it has to be the correct answer choice.

9. **Correct Answer (D).** Question Type: Weaken. Difficulty Level: 2 / 4

The argument concludes that a new earthquake detection method will aid local officials in deciding exactly when to evacuate towns. The evidence for this is that each of the major earthquakes that hit a region was preceded by certain detectible changes in electric current. The argument assumes that being able to detect these changes in current will enable officials to determine exactly when to evacuate towns. The argument can be outlined as follows:

BI: Several major earthquakes have occurred in a certain region over the last 10 years.
P: A new method detects changes in electric current that occur before major earthquakes.
A: (The new method enables officials to determine when to evacuate.)
C: The new method will help aid local officials in deciding exactly when to evacuate.

We should anticipate a correct answer choice that weakens the argument by invalidating the assumption.

(A) Scientists do not fully understand what brought about the changes in the electric current in the earth's crust that preceded each of the major quakes in the region over the last ten years.

This is irrelevant information. Whether or not scientists understand the cause of the changes in current does not affect the ability of officials to use these changes to determine when to evacuate towns. (A) is a loser.

(B) Most other earthquake prediction methods have been based on a weaker correlation than that found between the changes in the electric current in the earth's crust and the subsequent earthquakes.

This strengthens the argument. If there is a stronger correlation between changes in electric current and subsequent earthquakes, then this method of prediction is more accurate. (B) is a loser.

(C) The frequency of major earthquakes in the region has increased over the last ten years.

The frequency of major earthquakes is irrelevant. (C) is a loser.

(D) There is considerable variation in the length of time between the changes in the electric current and the subsequent earthquakes.

This matches our anticipated answer choice. If there is considerable variation in the length of time between current changes and the earthquakes that follow, then this method would not help determine exactly when to evacuate a town. Officials would have no way of knowing how soon an earthquake would occur following a current change.

(D) is a candidate.

(E) There is presently only one station in the region that is capable of detecting the electric current in the earth's crust.

This is irrelevant information. The argument does not mention a need for multiple stations. (E) is a loser.

As (D) is the only candidate, it has to be the correct answer choice.

---

10. **Correct Answer (B).** Question Type: Principle Implication. Difficulty Level: 1 / 4

Unlike most IMP questions, this one includes an argument rather than a fact pattern. The conclusion is that the usefulness of fax machines was severely limited by the proliferation of incompatible formats resulting from the large number of competing manufacturers. This situation continued until manufacturers agreed to adopt a common format. The evidence for the conclusion is that fax machines must work with other fax machines to be useful. The argument can be outlined as follows:

P: Fax machines must work with other fax machines in order to be useful.
C: The usefulness of fax machines was limited until a common format was adopted.

We should anticipate a correct answer choice that states a principle that is supported by this argument. It may be something like "Sometimes it is beneficial to work with your competitors" or "Sometimes competition limits the usefulness of technology."

(A) Whenever machines are dependent on other machines of the same type, competition among manufacturers is damaging to the industry.

This is too strongly worded. We cannot say that the situation involving fax machines applies to all industries. (A) is a loser.

(B) In some industries it is in the interest of competitors to cooperate to some extent with one another.

This matches our anticipated answer choice. The word *some* indicates that this principle does not have to apply to all industries and may only apply to the fax machine industry. The argument provides an example of how cooperating to a certain extent with competitors is in the interest of manufacturers in the fax machine industry. We will consider (B) a candidate.

(C) The more competitors there are in a high-tech industry, the more they will have to cooperate in determining the basic design of their product.

This is irrelevant information. We do not know whether the fax industry is a high-tech industry, and it is unclear whether fax technology format can be considered basic product design. (C) is a loser.

(D) Some cooperation among manufacturers in the same industry is more beneficial than is pure competition.

This may appear to be a SOME statement, but it is actually an ALL statement. (D) can be reworded as "All manufacturers in the same industry would benefit more from some cooperation than from pure competition." This is too strongly worded. We know that some cooperation is better than pure competition within one specific industry, but we cannot say the same for other industries. (D) is a loser.

(E) Cooperation is beneficial only in industries whose products depend on other products of the

same type.

This statement is too strongly worded. We know that cooperation can be beneficial when products depend on one another, but we have no information to support the claim that this is the only case in which cooperation is beneficial. (E) is a loser.

As (B) is the only candidate, it has to be the correct answer choice.

11. **Correct Answer (E).** Question Type: Principle Parallel Reasoning. Difficulty Level: 2 / 4

In this Principle Parallel Reasoning question, the principle is not explicitly stated in the stimulus, so we need to extract it.

The findings of the researchers are that if a critique is accompanied by the information that teacher performance is one of several factors that determine educational outcome, the critique leads to enhanced educational outcomes. We can extract the following principle from this:

A better outcome will result if it is made clear that a critique is part of a larger framework.

We should anticipate a correct answer choice that expresses an argument that illustrates this principle.

(A) Children can usually be taught to master subject matter in which they have no interest if they believe that successfully mastering it will earn the respect of their peers.

This answer choice does not indicate that an individual critique is part of a larger framework. Instead, it focuses on the fact that the desire for peer respect can motivate students to master unappealing subject matter. (A) is a loser.

(B) People are generally more willing to accept a negative characterization of a small group of people if they do not see themselves as members of the group being so characterized.

This answer choice does not illustrate the principle we identified. It states that people are willing to accept criticism of a group if they do not consider themselves members of the group. (B) is a loser.

(C) An actor can more effectively evaluate the merits of her own performance if she can successfully convince herself that she is really evaluating the performance of another actor.

This answer choice discusses a situation in which people critique themselves, which does not match the principle. (C) is a loser.

(D) The opinions reached by a social scientist in the study of a society can be considered as more reliable and objective if that social scientist is not a member of that society.

This answer choice does not discuss the outcomes of critiques. Instead, it focuses on a criterion for judging the reliability and objectivity of opinions. (D) is a loser.

(E) It is easier to correct the mistakes of an athlete if it is made clear to him that the criticism is part of an overarching effort to rectify the shortcomings of the entire team on which he plays.

This matches our anticipated answer choice. It states that a critique will have a better outcome (i.e. mistakes will be easier to correct) if it is presented as part of an overarching effort to improve team performance. (E) has to be the correct answer choice.

12. **Correct Answer (C).** Question Type: Necessary Assumption. Difficulty Level: 2 / 4

The conclusion of the argument is that shifts of narrative point of view within a novel detract from the merit of the work. The argument supports this by saying that such shifts tend to make readers focus on the author and that, in order to be of the highest quality, a novel must emotionally engage readers with its imaginary world. The stimulus has multiple conditional statements, so we can solve it using the same method we use to solve SA questions containing conditional statements. We should assume that the conclusion is an inference drawn by connecting the ends of a logic chain, and that the necessary assumption is the missing link in the chain. The argument can be outlined as follows:

P1: ~~Most Readers Engage Emotionally w/ Imaginary World~~ → ~~Highest Quality~~
P2: Narrative Shifts → Tend to Make Most Readers Focus on Author
C: Narrative Shifts → ~~Highest Quality~~

Note that the phrase *detracts from the merit of the work* in the conclusion has been represented as ~~Highest Quality~~. As both terms in the conclusion appear in the premises, it is likely that the necessary assumption connects both premises to create a logic chain from which the conclusion can be inferred. Given that the conclusion has the sufficient condition Narrative Shifts and the necessary condition Highest Quality, the logic chain is likely to be

Narrative Shifts → Tend to Make Most Readers Focus on Author → [Necessary Assumption] → ~~Most Readers Engage Emotionally w/ Imaginary World~~ → ~~Highest Quality~~

Using the necessary assumption Tend to Make Most Readers Focus on Author → Most Readers Engage Emotionally w/ Imaginary World, we can create a chain from which the conclusion is inferable. We should anticipate a correct answer choice that expresses this statement (or its contrapositive). We can see that (C) is the only option that includes both terms, so let's look at this answer choice first.

(C) Most readers cannot become emotionally involved with a novel's imaginary world if they focus on the author.

This matches our anticipated answer choice. If readers focus on the author, they cannot become emotionally involved in the imaginary world. We can confirm this using the (Un)Necessary Assumption Test. (C) can be logically negated to read as "Less than half of readers cannot become emotionally involved with a novel's imaginary world if they focus on the author." This statement would invalidate the argument. If the majority of readers can become emotionally invested with a novel's imaginary world even if they focus on the author, then the conclusion that narrative shifts that make the reader focus on the author detract from the merit of a novel is invalid. (C) has to be the correct answer choice.

13. **Correct Answer (D).** Question Type: Paradox. Difficulty Level: 2 / 4

The claim presented in this stimulus is that people aged 46 to 55 spend more money per capita than people of any other age group. The unexpected result is that companies advertise almost exclusively to people 25 and under and that television producers believe that the value of an advertising slot depends entirely on the number of viewers among this age group. The expected result is that companies would advertise to people aged 46 to 55 because they spend more money per capita. We should anticipate a correct answer choice that explains the unexpected result without invalidating the claim.

(A) The expense of television advertising slots makes it crucial for companies to target people who are most likely to purchase their products.

This does not explain the unexpected result because we do not know if people aged 25 and under are more likely to purchase a company's products. (A) is a loser.

(B) Advertising slots during news programs almost always cost far less than advertising slots

during popular sitcoms whose leading characters are young adults.

This information is irrelevant as it does not explain why television advertisers prefer certain age groups over others. (B) is a loser.

(C) When television executives decide which shows to renew, they do so primarily in terms of the shows' ratings among people aged 25 and under.

This answer choice simply restates the unexpected result. As (C) does not explain the unexpected result, it is a loser.

(D) Those who make decisions about television advertising believe that people older than 25 almost never change their buying habits.

This matches our anticipated answer choice. If people older than 25 rarely changed their buying habits, they would be less receptive to advertising. Therefore, it would more effective for advertisers to focus on people 25 and under. As this answer choice explains the unexpected result without invalidating the claim, it is a candidate.

(E) When companies advertise consumer products in print media, they focus primarily on people aged 26 and over.

This explains the expected result—that advertisers would focus on the older age group. (E) is a loser.

As (D) is the only candidate, it has to be the correct answer choice.

---

14. **Correct Answer (E).** Question Type: Fallacy. Difficulty Level: 2 / 4

The conclusion of this argument is that one should never make an effort to acquire expensive new tastes. The reason for this, according to the 18th-century moralist, is that acquiring expensive tastes costs money, exposes one to undesirable sensations, and requires too much effort. The argument can be outlined as follows:

P1: Acquiring expensive tastes costs money.
P2: Acquiring expensive tastes exposes one to obnoxious sensations.
P3: The effort involved in acquiring expensive tastes shows their superfluity.
C: You should never make an effort to acquire expensive new tastes.

When considering this argument, you might wonder about the potential benefits of acquiring new tastes. This is the fallacy in the argument. The argument attempts to show that the disadvantages of acquiring new tastes outweigh the advantages. However, it never actually discusses the advantages. This is a Comparison Fallacy. We should anticipate a correct answer choice that expresses this fallacy.

(A) draws a conclusion that simply restates a claim presented in support of that conclusion

This answer choice describes a Circular Reasoning Fallacy. (A) is a loser.

(B) takes for granted that the acquisition of expensive tastes will lead to financial irresponsibility

If *financial irresponsibility* is synonymous with *a drain on your purse*, then this answer choice does not describe a fallacy. The fact that acquiring new tastes is a drain on one's purse is a premise of the argument. We must assume that all the premises are true. (B) is a loser.

(C) uses the inherently vague term "sensations" without providing a definition of that term

The term *sensations* is vague, but this is not a flaw in the argument. (C) is a loser.

(D) mistakes a cause of acquisition of expensive tastes for an effect of acquisition of such tastes

This answer choice describes a Causal Reasoning Fallacy. (D) is a loser.

(E) rejects trying to achieve a goal because of the cost of achieving it, without considering the benefits of achieving it

This matches our anticipated answer choice. The argument is flawed because it considers the cons but none of the pros of an option (making an effort to acquire a new taste). The argument makes an incomplete comparison. (E) has to be the correct answer choice.

---

15. **Correct Answer (D).** Question Type: Must Be True. Difficulty Level: 1 / 4

This stimulus includes multiple conditional statements. These can be diagrammed as follows:

S1: Wednesday ᴹ→ Free Poetry
S2: Free Poetry → Half Priced Coffee

Regarding the first statement, note that *almost every* is a moderate strength modifier that is similar to *almost all*.

Now, let's look for valid inferences. The necessary condition of the MOST statement is identical to the sufficient condition of the ALL statement. This means that the following MOST statement can be inferred:

Wednesday ᴹ→ Half Priced Coffee

We should anticipate an answer choice that matches this inference (or its contrapositive). It is also possible that the correct answer choice is a paraphrase of one of the statements or a weak statement supported by the stimulus.

(A) Wednesday is the most common day on which Zack's offers half-priced coffee all day.

This answer choice is not necessarily true. Zack's may offer half-priced coffee on days other than the ones when poetry readings are scheduled. (A) is a loser.

(B) Most free poetry readings given at Zack's are scheduled for Wednesdays.

This is not necessarily true. The fact that poetry readings are held on most Wednesdays does not preclude them from being held on other days of the week. (B) is a loser.

(C) Free poetry readings are scheduled on almost every day that Zack's offers half-priced coffee all day.

This is the flipped version of the second conditional statement. (C) is a loser.

(D) Zack's offers half-priced coffee all day on most if not all Wednesdays.

This matches one of our anticipated answer choices. It is the MOST statement we inferred from the two conditional statements in the stimulus. (D) is a candidate.

(E) On some Wednesdays Zack's does not offer half-priced coffee all day.

This statement is not necessarily true. The passage states that there are free poetry readings on almost every Wednesday and that half-priced coffee is offered when there is a poetry reading. However, it does not state that half-priced coffee is not offered on the Wednesdays when poetry readings are not held. (E) is a loser.

As (D) is the only candidate, it has to be the correct answer choice.

16. **Correct Answer (B).** Question Type: Principle Parallel Reasoning. Difficulty Level: 2 / 4

The principle is explicitly stated in the two conditional statements of the stimulus. These can be diagrammed as follows:

S1: Human Action w/ Specific Motivation → Intentional
S2: ~~Human Action w/ Specific Motivation~~ AND ~~Explainable by Physical Process~~ → Random

Since Intentional and Random are the necessary conditions of the conditional statements, we are able to make judgments about whether events are intentional or random. We are also able to make judgments about the necessary conditions of the contrapositives of these two statements (~~Human Action w/ Specific Motivation~~ / Explainable by Physical Process OR Human Action w/ Specific Motivation). We can eliminate any answer choice that does not make one of these judgments. Unfortunately, a quick scan of the answer choices reveals that we cannot eliminate any of them based on this. Therefore, we need to go through all of them, searching for the one that conforms with at least one of the rules of the principle in the stimulus.

(A) **Tarik left the keys untouched on the kitchen counter, but he did not do so on the basis of a specific motivation. Therefore, the keys' remaining on the kitchen counter was a random event.**

In order to conclude that something was a random event, it is necessary to establish that it was done without a specific motivation and is not explainable by normal physical processes. The latter is not specified in this answer choice. Therefore, (A) is a loser.

(B) **Ellis tore the envelope open in order to read its contents, but the envelope was empty. Nevertheless, because Ellis acted on the basis of a specific motivation, tearing the envelope open was an intentional event.**

This matches our anticipated answer choice. In order to conclude that something was an intentional event, it must be established that it was the result of a specific motivation. Even though Ellis did not achieve the results he was looking for, he still acted on the basis of a specific motivation. (B) is a candidate.

(C) **Judith's hailing a cab distracted a driver in the left lane. She performed the action of hailing the cab on the basis of a specific motivation, so the driver's becoming distracted was an intentional event.**

Judith's hailing of a cab was an intentional action, but she did not have the specific motivation of distracting the driver. (C) is a loser.

(D) **Yasuko continued to breathe regularly throughout the time that she was asleep. This was a human action, but it was not performed on the basis of a specific motivation. Therefore, her breathing was a random event.**

As we do not know whether Yasuko's breathing was the result of normal physical processes, we cannot conclude that it was a random event. (D) is a loser.

(E) **Henry lost his hold on the wrench and dropped it because the handle was slippery. This was a human action and is explainable by normal physical processes, so it was an intentional event.**

Henry's action was not performed on the basis of a specific motivation. The wrench slipped because the handle was slippery. Therefore, we cannot conclude that this was an intentional event. (E) is a loser.

As (B) is the only candidate, it has to be the correct answer choice.

17. **Correct Answer (D).** Question Type: Necessary Assumption. Difficulty Level: 3 / 4

The conclusion of the argument is that it is improper to conclude that ancient people did not have knowledge of moral rights just because no known ancient language had an expression that meant *a moral right*. This conclusion is supported by an analogy about a person who discovers a wild fruit tree and repeatedly harvests it. The argument states that the claim about ancient people is equivalent to saying that the person harvesting the fruit has no idea what the fruit is until naming it. The argument asserts that one can understand a concept without having a name for that concept. A possible outline of the argument is

P: Not knowing the name of a wild fruit tree does not stop the person who discovers that tree from returning to harvest and study it.

C: The conclusion is false that ancient people did not know what "moral rights" were simply because that term was not found in the language.

The argument does not include a causal statement or an obvious fallacy. However, it does rely on a minor assumption—that the person harvesting the fruit has some knowledge of what the fruit is even before naming it. If the person does not have this knowledge, then the analogy cannot function as a supporting premise of the claim that ancient people had knowledge of moral rights even if they had no name for this concept. We should anticipate a correct answer choice that validates this assumption.

(A) To know the name of something is to know what that thing is.

This does not need to be true in order for the argument to be valid. For confirmation, we can use the (Un)Necessary Assumption Test. (A) can be logically negated to read as "To know the name of something is not to know what that thing is." As this does not invalidate the argument, (A) is a loser.

(B) People who first discover what something is know it better than do people who merely know the name of the thing.

This is irrelevant information. The argument does not make this comparison. (B) is a loser.

(C) The name or expression that is used to identify something cannot provide any information about the nature of the thing that is identified.

This is irrelevant information. The argument does not discuss whether a name provides information about something. (C) is a loser.

(D) A person who repeatedly harvests from a wild fruit tree and studies it has some idea of what the fruit is even before knowing a name for the fruit.

This matches our anticipated answer choice. (D) validates the assumption in the argument and is necessarily true. For confirmation, we can use the (Un)Necessary Assumption Test. (D) can be logically negated to read as "A person who repeatedly harvests from a wild fruit tree and studies it does not have any idea of what the fruit is even before knowing a name for the fruit." If knowing the name of a thing is a prerequisite for understanding that thing, then the argument is invalid. (D) is a candidate.

(E) One need not know what something is before one can name it.

This is irrelevant information. The argument is not concerned with what is necessary before something can be named. (E) is a loser.

As (D) is the only candidate, it has to be the correct answer choice.

18. **Correct Answer (E).** Question Type: Main Point. Difficulty Level: 2 / 4

The conclusion indicator *obviously* or the counter-premise indictor *however* may indicate the conclusion of the argument. Remember, MP arguments commonly include conclusions marked by counter-premise indicators. The argument starts by positing that the opposing viewpoint (that it is absurd to criticize someone for being critical) has little plausibility. The argument then states that people must assess one another and that not all assessments are positive. This functions as a counter-premise as it supports the opposing viewpoint. The term *however* indicates a shift away from this opposing viewpoint. It therefore indicates the conclusion of the argument, that there is wisdom behind the injunction against being judgmental. The next sentence includes a premise to support this conclusion— being judgmental is not merely assessing someone negatively but doing so without serious effort. The argument can be outlined as follows:

Opposing Viewpoint: It is absurd to criticize someone for being critical.
BI: This viewpoint has little plausibility.
CP: People must sometimes assess negatively.
P: Being judgmental is not just assessing others negatively; it is assessing others negatively without taking the effort to understand.

C: There is wisdom in not being judgmental.

We should anticipate a correct answer choice that restates the conclusion.

(A) To be judgmental is to assess someone negatively prior to making a serious effort at understanding.

This answer choice restates a premise of the argument. (A) is a loser.

(B) It is absurd to criticize anyone for being critical.

This is a restatement of the opposing viewpoint. (B) is a loser.

(C) There is some plausibility to the claim that it is absurd to criticize anyone for being critical.

This answer choice inaccurately paraphrases the background information, using the term *some* instead of *little*. (C) is a loser.

(D) Not all assessments people make of one another will be positive.

This is a restatement of part of the counter-premise. (D) is a loser.

(E) There is wisdom behind the injunction against being judgmental.

This matches our anticipated answer choice. It is a restatement of the main conclusion. (E) has to be the correct answer choice.

19. **Correct Answer (C).** Question Type: Mini Description. Difficulty Level: 4 / 4

The claim presented in the prompt is located in the second half of the first sentence of the stimulus. This sentence begins by presenting the opposing viewpoint that each age and culture has its own aesthetic standards and ends with background information about how some painters are superior to others (the presented claim). The next sentence has a *conclusion, since premise* structure. The conclusion is that artistic superiority must be measured in light of artistic purpose. This is supported by a premise (an example, in this case) stating that the high merits of Jose Rey Toledo's work are not in doubt even though his paintings do not strictly resemble what they represent. The argument can be outlined as follows:

Chapter 8

Opposing Viewpoint: Art of each age and culture has its own standards of beauty.
BI: Holders of this viewpoint must admit that some artists are superior to others.
P: Toledo creates superior art, but his paintings do not resemble what they represent.
C: Artistic superiority must be measured in light of an artist's purposes.

The claim presented in the prompt is background information that is clarified in the conclusion. The term *background information* is not commonly used in MD answer choices, so we cannot simply scan the answer choices for this term. We should anticipate a correct answer choice that describes the claim's role in the argument.

(A) It is a hypothesis that the argument attempts to refute.

The argument does not attempt to refute the claim. Rather, it attempts to clarify the claim. (A) is a loser.

(B) It is a generalization, one sort of objection to which the argument illustrates by giving an example.

This claim is a generalization. However, the argument includes an example that illustrates the clarification of the generalization, not the generalization itself. (B) is a loser.

(C) It is a claim that, according to the argument, is to be understood in a manner specified by the conclusion.

This matches our anticipated answer choice. The claim is to be understood in the manner specified by the argument's conclusion. In other words, the conclusion clarifies the claim. (C) is a candidate.

(D) It is a claim that the argument derives from another claim and that it uses to support its conclusion.

The claim is neither derived from another claim nor used as a premise to advance the argument's conclusion. (D) is a loser.

(E) It is a generalization that the argument uses to justify the relevance of the specific example it cites.

While the claim is a generalization, it is not used to justify the relevance of the example. (E) is a loser.

As (C) is the only candidate, it has to be the correct answer choice.

20. **Correct Answer (A).** Question Type: Fallacy. Difficulty Level: 3 / 4

The argument concludes that there must be something about mammalian chromosomes that prevents reproduction without the fertilization of an egg (i.e. parthenogenesis). There are three supporting premises: a previous study showing mammalian parthenogenesis was flawed, no other studies have found evidence of mammalian parthenogenesis, and parthenogenesis occurs in a wide variety of nonmammalian vertebrates. The argument can be outlined as follows:

Opposing Viewpoint: Parthenogenesis sometimes occurs in mammals.
CP (supporting opposing viewpoint): Study of rabbits
P1: The study of rabbits is flawed.
P2: No other studies have shown mammalian parthenogenesis.
P3: Parthenogenesis occurs in a wide variety of nonmammalian vertebrates.
C: Something about mammalian chromosomes prevents parthenogenesis.

The argument commits an Absence of Evidence Fallacy. It concludes that mammalian parthenogenesis does not exist based on the fact that this process has not been proven to occur. We should anticipate a correct answer choice that describes this fallacy.

(A) takes for granted that something that has not been proven to be true is for that reason shown to be false

This matches our anticipated answer choice. It describes the Absence of Evidence Fallacy in the argument. (A) is a candidate.

(B) infers that a characteristic is shared by all nonmammalian vertebrate species merely because it is shared by some nonmammalian vertebrate species

This answer choice describes a Strength Modifier Fallacy. (B) is a loser.

(C) rules out an explanation of a phenomenon merely on the grounds that there is another explanation that can account for the phenomenon

This answer choice describes a Selection Fallacy. (C) is a loser.

(D) confuses a necessary condition for parthenogenesis with a sufficient condition for it

This answer choice describes a Conditional Reasoning Fallacy. (D) is a loser.

(E) assumes that the methods used in a study of one mammalian species were flawed merely because the study's findings cannot be generalized to all other mammalian species

This is irrelevant information. The argument does not discuss how or why the methods used in the study were flawed. (E) is a loser.

As (A) is the only candidate, it has to be the correct answer choice.

21. **Correct Answer (B).** Question Type: Principle Implication. Difficulty Level: 3 / 4

This IMP question includes an argument rather than the usual fact pattern. The argument's main conclusion is that anyone who feels that a TV show is worth preserving ought to buy the products advertised during the show. The reasoning for this is that most TV shows depend on funding from advertisers and that advertisers only air their commercials on TV shows if people watching the show buy their products. The subsidiary conclusion is that if people fail to buy the advertised products, the show will be canceled. The argument includes several conditional statements. It can be outlined as follows:

P1: ~~Advertiser Funding~~ $^{M}\!\!\to$ TV Show Canceled
P2: ~~Many People Who Watch Buy Products~~ → ~~Advertiser Funding~~
SC: ~~Many People Who Watch Buy Products~~ $^{M}\!\!\to$ TV Show Canceled
C: Person Feels TV Show Worth Preserving → Should Buy Products Advertised

We can find the principle inferred by the argument by combining the subsidiary conclusion and main conclusion. This gives us "If many people not undertaking an action (buying products) leads to an undesirable result (the cancelation of a show), then people who do not want that undesirable result should undertake the action." We should anticipate a correct answer choice that expresses this principle.

(A) If a TV show that one feels to be worth preserving would be canceled unless one took certain actions, then one ought to take those actions.

This is too strong. A TV show will be canceled not if a certain individual does not buy the advertised products, but if many people do not buy the products. (A) is a loser.

(B) If a TV show would be canceled unless many people took certain actions, then everyone who feels that the show is worth preserving ought to take those actions.

This matches our anticipated answer choice. If many people not taking an action leads to a show getting canceled, people who feel that the show is worth preserving should take the action. (B) is a candidate.

(C) If a TV show is worth preserving, then everyone should take whatever actions are necessary to prevent that show from being canceled.

The phrase *whatever actions* is too broad. The argument discusses a single, specific action. (C) is a loser.

(D) If one feels that a TV show is worth preserving, then one should take at least some actions to reduce the likelihood that the show will be canceled.

This is irrelevant information. (D) is about reducing the likelihood of a show being canceled, which is not discussed in the stimulus. And, again, the argument discusses a single, specific action. (D) is a loser.

(E) If a TV show would be canceled unless many people took certain actions, then those who feel most strongly that it is worth preserving should take those actions.

This answer choice is very similar to (B), except that it mischaracterizes the argument by using the phrase *those who feel most strongly*, which is not supported by the argument. (E) is a loser.

As (B) is the only candidate, it has to be the correct answer choice.

22. **Correct Answer (E).** Question Type: Weaken. Difficulty Level: 4 / 4

The argument concludes that recent findings indicate that heart disease can result from psychological factors. This is a causal conclusion. The argument can be outlined as follows:

P1: Temporary Anger CAUSE Temporary High Blood Pressure
P2: People who are easily angered are more likely to have high blood pressure.
A: (Easily Angered CAUSE High Blood Pressure)
P3: People with permanently high blood pressure are more likely to have heart disease.
A: (High Blood Pressure CAUSE Heart Disease)
_____
C: Psychological Factors (Anger) CAUSE Heart Disease

Four causal relationships are asserted here. The first is in the first premise. The second causal relationship is implied by the second premise—if there is a correlation between being easily angered and high blood pressure, then being easily angered causes high blood pressure. The third causal relationship is inferable from the correlation between having high blood pressure and having heart disease. The causal conclusion results from combining the causal relationships in the first and second assumption.

We should anticipated a correct answer choice that weakens the causal conclusion by presenting an *alternative cause*, an example of *same cause, no effect*, an example of *same effect, no cause*, or an example of *reversed cause and effect*. Note that the correct answer choice may weaken the causal conclusion indirectly by weakening one of the causal assumptions the conclusion is dependent on.

(A) Those who are easily angered are less likely to recover fully from episodes of heart disease than are other people.

This is irrelevant information as recovery from heart disease is not at issue in the argument. (A) is a loser.

(B) Medication designed to control high blood pressure can greatly affect the moods of those who use it.

This would not weaken the argument because it is unclear whether *moods of those who use it* refers to anger. (B) is a loser.

(C) People with permanently high blood pressure who have tranquil personalities virtually never develop heart disease.

This is irrelevant information. The argument is concerned not with people who have tranquil personalities but with those who are easily angered. (C) is a loser.

(D) Those who discover that they have heart disease tend to become more easily frustrated by small difficulties.

This matches one of our anticipated answer choices. It weakens the causal conclusion in a direct manner by providing an example of *reversed cause and effect*. (D) is a candidate.

(E) The physiological factors that cause permanently high blood pressure generally make people quick to anger.

This matches our anticipated answer choice. It provides an *alternative cause* for both high blood pressure and being quick to anger. (E) would explain the correlation between anger and high blood pressure in a way that eliminates a causal relationship between the two. (E) is a candidate.

We now need to eliminate one of the two candidates. Looking back at (D), a couple of problems become apparent. First, this answer choice only addresses a subset of people with heart disease—those who know they have the medical condition. Second, *easily frustrated* is different from *easily angered*. Therefore, we can eliminate (D) and select (E).

23. **Correct Answer (B).** Question Type: Strengthen. Difficulty Level: 2 / 4

The argument concludes that books delivered via computer will not make printed books obsolete. The evidence for this claim is that when a professor put a case-study assignment online, she found that 50 of 70 students printed it out on paper. The argument can be outlined as follows:

P: A professor placed a case-study online, and 50 out of 70 students printed it out.
C: Books delivered via computer will not make printed books obsolete.

The argument commits a Sampling Fallacy. It assumes that the sample group (students) is representative of computer users in general. We should anticipate a correct answer choice that addresses this fallacy.

(A) Several colleagues of the professor have found that, in their non-business courses, several of their students behave similarly in relation to assignments placed on the computer network.

This answer choice does not address the Sampling Fallacy we identified. Including evidence that several students in other classes behaved similarly does not resolve the issue that students may not be representative of computer users in general. (A) is a loser.

(B) Studies consistently show that most computer users will print reading material that is more than a few pages in length rather than read it on the computer screen.

This matches our anticipated answer choice. If most computer users behave in a manner similar to the students, then the students are representative of computer users in general. (B) is a candidate.

(C) Some people get impaired vision from long periods of reading printed matter on computer screens, even if they use high quality computer screens.

The phrase *some people* makes this statement too weakly worded to fix the Sampling Fallacy. In addition, impaired vision may also result from reading printed material for long periods of time. (C) is a loser.

(D) Scanning technology is very poor, causing books delivered via computer to be full of errors unless editors carefully read the scanned versions.

This answer choice seems to provide information that strengthens the claim that printed books will not become obsolete. However, there are two issues. First, it is not certain that if books delivered via computer contain errors, people will want to read printed books instead. Second, it may be the case that all books will be reviewed by editors, meaning that those delivered via computer will be error-free. (D) is a loser.

(E) Books on cassette tape have only a small fraction of the sales of printed versions of the same books, though sales of videos of books that have been turned into movies remain strong.

This is irrelevant information. Books on cassette tape are not discussed in the argument. (E) is a loser.

As (B) is the only candidate, it has to be the correct answer choice.

---

24. **Correct Answer (D).** Question Type: Fallacy. Difficulty Level: 3 / 4

The argument concludes that anyone who follows the advertisement's diet is sure to lose weight. The evidence for this is that the advertisement's diet is similar to a diet examined in a study. In the study, the people who followed the diet in question lost the most weight. The argument can be outlined as follows:

P1: In the study, the people who lost the most weight took in more calories from protein than carbohydrates and ate their biggest meal early in the day.
P2: Our diet provides more calories from protein and requires breakfast to be the biggest meal.
C: Anyone who follows our diet is sure to lose weight.

Note that the conclusion is that people who follow the diet are sure to lose weight. The argument includes a Strength Modifier Fallacy. The conclusion is an ALL statement that has been inferred from a SOME statement. The first premise does not state that all people who took in more calories from protein and ate their biggest meals early in the day lost the most weight. We should anticipate a correct answer choice that describes this fallacy.

(A) eating foods that derive a majority of their calories from carbohydrates tends to make one feel fuller than does eating foods that derive a majority of their calories from protein

This is irrelevant information. The argument is not concerned with how full one feels on account of one's diet. (A) is a loser.

(B) a few of the people in the group studied who lost significant amounts of weight got nearly all of their calories from carbohydrates and ate their biggest meal at night

This does not describe the fallacy in the argument. It is possible that some people who did not follow the diet also lost a significant amount of weight, while anyone who follows the diet is sure to lose weight. (B) is a loser.

(C) the people in the group studied who increased their activity levels lost more weight, on

average, than those who did not, regardless of whether they got more calories from protein or from carbohydrates

This is irrelevant information. The argument is concerned with following a diet, not with other factors that may cause weight loss. (C) is a loser.

(D) some people in the group studied lost no weight yet got more calories from protein than from carbohydrates and ate their biggest meal early in the day

This matches our anticipated answer choice. The fact that some people who took in more calories from protein and ate their biggest meals early in the day lost the most weight does not mean that other people who did the same did not lose weight. (D) is a candidate.

(E) people who eat their biggest meal at night tend to snack more during the day and so tend to take in more total calories than do people who eat their biggest meal earlier in the day

This does not describe the error of reasoning in the argument. It accounts for why another diet would not lead to weight loss. (E) is a loser.

As (D) is the only candidate, it has to be the correct answer choice.

25. **Correct Answer (C).** Question Type: Must Be True EXCEPT. Difficulty Level: 4 / 4

The stimulus is a fact pattern with multiple conditional statements and possible inferences. These can be diagrammed as follows:

Proposition 1: 20th Century Art ^{S}—^{S} Great Art
Proposition 2: Great Art $\rightarrow$ Original Ideas
Proposition 3: ~~Influential~~ $\rightarrow$ ~~Great Art~~

From propositions 1 and 2, we can infer that

Inference 1: 20th Century Art ^{S}—^{S} Original Ideas

From propositions 2 and 3, we can infer that

Inference 2: Original Ideas ^{S}—^{S} Influential

From propositions 1 and 3, we can infer that

Inference 3: 20th Century Art ^{S}—^{S} Influential

The prompt here asks you for an answer choice that does not necessarily have to be true, which means it could be false. Therefore, we should anticipate one correct answer that could be false and four incorrect answers that must be true. The incorrect answer choices are likely to include the inferences noted above (or their contrapositives).

(A) Some influential art involves original ideas.

This must be true because it is the second inference above. (A) is a loser.

(B) Some twentieth-century art involves original ideas.

This must be true because it is the first inference above. (B) is a loser.

(C) Only art that involves original ideas is influential.

This answer choice can be diagrammed as follows:

Influential → Original ideas

This could be false. We know that some influential art involves original ideas, but we cannot conclude that all influential art involves original ideas. (C) is a candidate.

(D) Only art that is influential and involves original ideas is great art.

This answer choice can be diagrammed as follows:

Great Art → Influential AND Original ideas

We know from the second and third propositions that great art must be both influential and involve original ideas. Therefore, (D) must be true. This is a loser.

(E) Some twentieth-century art is influential and involves original ideas.

If some 20th-century art is great art, and great art must be influential and involve original ideas, then it must be true that some 20th-century art has these qualities as well. (E) is a loser.

As (C) is the only candidate, it has to be the correct answer choice.

Section 2

Time—35 minutes

25 Questions

Directions: Each question in this section is based on the reasoning provided in a brief passage. In answering the questions, you should not make assumptions that are by commonsense standards implausible, superfluous, or incompatible with the passage. For some questions, more than one of the choices could conceivably answer the question. However, you are to choose the best answer; that is, choose the response that most accurately and completely answers the question and mark that response on your answer sheet.

1. Aristophanes' play *The Clouds*, which was written when the philosopher Socrates was in his mid-forties, portrays Socrates as an atheistic philosopher primarily concerned with issues in natural science. The only other surviving portrayals of Socrates were written after Socrates' death at age 70. They portrayed Socrates as having a religious dimension and a strong focus on ethical issues.

Which one of the following, if true, would most help to resolve the apparent discrepancy between Aristophanes' portrayal of Socrates and the other surviving portrayals?

(A) Aristophanes' portrayal of Socrates in *The Clouds* was unflattering, whereas the other portrayals were very flattering.
(B) Socrates' philosophical views and interests changed sometime after his mid-forties.
(C) Most of the philosophers who lived before Socrates were primarily concerned with natural science.
(D) Socrates was a much more controversial figure in the years before his death than he was in his mid-forties.
(E) Socrates had an influence on many subsequent philosophers who were primarily concerned with natural science.

2. Board member: The J Foundation, a philanthropic organization, gave you this grant on the condition that your resulting work not contain any material detrimental to the J Foundation's reputation. But your resulting work never mentions any of the laudable achievements of our foundation. Hence your work fails to meet the conditions under which the grant was made.

The reasoning in the board member's argument is vulnerable to criticism on the grounds that the argument

(A) takes for granted that a work that never mentions any laudable achievements cannot be of high intellectual value
(B) confuses a condition necessary for the receipt of a grant with a condition sufficient for the receipt of a grant
(C) presumes, without providing justification, that a work that does not mention a foundation's laudable achievements is harmful to that foundation's reputation
(D) fails to consider that recipients of a grant usually strive to meet a foundation's conditions
(E) fails to consider the possibility that the work that was produced with the aid of the grant may have met all conditions other than avoiding detriment to the J Foundation's reputation

GO ON TO THE NEXT PAGE.

3. Psychiatrist: Breaking any habit is difficult, especially when it involves an addictive substance. People who break a habit are more likely to be motivated by immediate concerns than by long-term ones. Therefore, people who succeed in breaking their addiction to smoking cigarettes are more likely to be motivated by the social pressure against smoking—which is an immediate concern—than by health concerns, since _____.

The conclusion of the psychiatrist's argument is most strongly supported if which one of the following completes the argument?

(A) a habit that involves an addictive substance is likely to pose a greater health threat than a habit that does not involve any addictive substance

(B) for most people who successfully quit smoking, smoking does not create an immediate health concern at the time they quit

(C) some courses of action that exacerbate health concerns can also relieve social pressure

(D) most people who succeed in quitting smoking succeed only after several attempts

(E) everyone who succeeds in quitting smoking is motivated either by social pressure or by health concerns

4. Cassie: In order to improve the quality of customer service provided by our real estate agency, we should reduce client loads—the number of clients each agent is expected to serve at one time.

Melvin: Although smaller client loads are desirable, reducing client loads at our agency is simply not feasible. We already find it very difficult to recruit enough qualified agents; recruiting even more agents, which would be necessary in order to reduce client loads, is out of the question.

Of the following, which one, if true, is the logically strongest counter that Cassie can make to Melvin's argument?

(A) Since reducing client loads would improve working conditions for agents, reducing client loads would help recruit additional qualified agents to the real estate agency.

(B) Many of the real estate agency's current clients have expressed strong support for efforts to reduce client loads.

(C) Several recently conducted studies of real estate agencies have shown that small client loads are strongly correlated with high customer satisfaction ratings.

(D) Hiring extra support staff for the real estate agency's main office would have many of the same beneficial effects as reducing client loads.

(E) Over the last several years, it has become increasingly challenging for the real estate agency to recruit enough qualified agents just to maintain current client loads.

5. The star-nosed mole has a nose that ends in a pair of several-pointed stars, or tentacles that are crucial for hunting, as moles are poor-sighted. These tentacles contain receptors that detect electric fields produced by other animals, enabling the moles to detect and catch suitable prey such as worms and insects.

Which one of the following is most strongly supported by the information above?

(A) Both worms and insects produce electric fields.
(B) The star-nosed mole does not rely at all on its eyesight for survival.
(C) The star-nosed mole does not rely at all on its sense of smell when hunting.
(D) Only animals that hunt have noses with tentacles that detect electric fields.
(E) The star-nosed mole does not produce an electric field.

6. In her recent book a psychologist described several cases that exhibit the following pattern: A child, denied something by its parent, initiates problematic behavior such as screaming; the behavior escalates until finally the exasperated parent acquiesces to the child's demand. At this point the child, having obtained the desired goal, stops the problematic behavior, to the parent's relief. This self-reinforcing pattern of misbehavior and accommodation is repeated with steadily increasing levels of misbehavior by the child.

The cases described by the psychologist illustrate each of the following generalizations EXCEPT:

(A) A child can develop problematic behavior patterns as a result of getting what it wants.
(B) A child and parent can mutually influence each other's behavior.
(C) Parents, by their choices, can inadvertently increase their child's level of misbehavior.
(D) A child can unintentionally influence a parent's behavior in ways contrary to the child's intended goals.
(E) A child can get what it wants by doing what its parent doesn't want it to do.

7. Scientist: In our study, chemical R did not cause cancer in laboratory rats. But we cannot conclude from this that chemical R is safe for humans. After all, many substances known to be carcinogenic to humans cause no cancer in rats; this is probably because some carcinogens cause cancer only via long-term exposure and rats are short lived.

Which one of the following most precisely describes the role played in the scientist's argument by the statement that chemical R did not cause cancer in laboratory rats?

(A) It is cited as evidence against the conclusion that chemical R is safe for humans.
(B) It is advanced to support the contention that test results obtained from laboratory rats cannot be extrapolated to humans.
(C) It illustrates the claim that rats are too short lived to be suitable as test subjects for the carcinogenic properties of substances to which humans are chronically exposed.
(D) It is used as evidence to support the hypothesis that chemical R causes cancer in humans via long-term exposure.
(E) It is cited as being insufficient to support the conclusion that chemical R is safe for humans.

GO ON TO THE NEXT PAGE.

8. Department store manager: There is absolutely no reason to offer our customers free gift wrapping again this holiday season. If most customers take the offer, it will be expensive and time-consuming for us. On the other hand, if only a few customers want it, there is no advantage in offering it.

Which one of the following is an assumption required by the department store manager's argument?

(A) Gift wrapping would cost the store more during this holiday season than in previous holiday seasons.
(B) Anything that slows down shoppers during the holiday season costs the store money.
(C) It would be to the store's advantage to charge customers for gift wrapping services.
(D) It would be expensive to inform customers about the free gift wrapping service.
(E) Either few customers would want free gift wrapping or most customers would want it.

9. Among people who have a history of chronic trouble falling asleep, some rely only on sleeping pills to help them fall asleep, and others practice behavior modification techniques and do not take sleeping pills. Those who rely only on behavior modification fall asleep more quickly than do those who rely only on sleeping pills, so behavior modification is more effective than are sleeping pills in helping people to fall asleep.

Which one of the following, if true, most weakens the argument?

(A) People who do not take sleeping pills spend at least as many total hours asleep each night as do the people who take sleeping pills.
(B) Most people who have trouble falling asleep and who use behavior modification techniques fall asleep more slowly than do most people who have no trouble falling asleep.
(C) Many people who use only behavior modification techniques to help them fall asleep have never used sleeping pills.
(D) The people who are the most likely to take sleeping pills rather than practice behavior modification techniques are those who have previously had the most trouble falling asleep.
(E) The people who are the most likely to practice behavior modification techniques rather than take sleeping pills are those who prefer not to use drugs if other treatments are available.

10. Lawyer: This witness acknowledges being present at the restaurant and watching when my client, a famous television personality, was assaulted. Yet the witness claims to recognize the assailant, but not my famous client. Therefore, the witness's testimony should be excluded.

The lawyer's conclusion follows logically if which one of the following is assumed?

(A) If a witness claims to recognize both parties involved in an assault, then the witness's testimony should be included.
(B) There are other witnesses who can identify the lawyer's client as present during the assault.
(C) It is impossible to determine whether the witness actually recognized the assailant.
(D) The testimony of a witness to an assault should be included only if the witness claims to recognize both parties involved in the assault.
(E) It is unlikely that anyone would fail to recognize the lawyer's client.

11. Biologist: Many paleontologists have suggested that the difficulty of adapting to ice ages was responsible for the evolution of the human brain. But this suggestion must be rejected, for most other animal species adapted to ice ages with no evolutionary changes to their brains.

The biologist's argument is most vulnerable to criticism on which one of the following grounds?

(A) It fails to address adequately the possibility that even if a condition is sufficient to produce an effect in a species, it may not be necessary to produce that effect in that species.
(B) It fails to address adequately the possibility that a condition can produce a change in a species even if it does not produce that change in other species.
(C) It overlooks the possibility that a condition that is needed to produce a change in one species is not needed to produce a similar change in other species.
(D) It presumes without warrant that human beings were presented with greater difficulties during ice ages than were individuals of most other species.
(E) It takes for granted that, if a condition coincided with the emergence of a certain phenomenon, that condition must have been causally responsible for the phenomenon.

GO ON TO THE NEXT PAGE.

12. The total number of book titles published annually in North America has approximately quadrupled since television first became available. Retail sales of new titles, as measured in copies, increased rapidly in the early days of television, though the rate of increase has slowed in recent years. Library circulation has been flat or declining in recent years.

Which one of the following is most strongly supported by the information above?

(A) Television has, over the years, brought about a reduction in the amount of per capita reading in North America.
(B) The introduction of television usually brings about a decrease in library use.
(C) Book publishers in North America now sell fewer copies per title than they sold in the early days of television.
(D) The availability of television does not always cause a decline in the annual number of book titles published or in the number of books sold.
(E) The introduction of television expanded the market for books in North America.

13. Botanist: It has long been believed that people with children or pets should keep poinsettia plants out of their homes. Although this belief has been encouraged by child-rearing books, which commonly list poinsettias as poisonous and therefore dangerous, it is mistaken. Our research has shown, conclusively, that poinsettias pose no risk to children or pets.

Which one of the following most accurately expresses the conclusion drawn in the botanist's argument?

(A) Child-rearing books should encourage people with children to put poinsettias in their homes.
(B) Poinsettias are not dangerously poisonous.
(C) According to many child-rearing books, poinsettias are dangerous.
(D) The belief that households with children or pets should not have poinsettias is mistaken.
(E) Poinsettias pose no risk to children or pets.

14. Archaeologist: An ancient stone building at our excavation site was composed of three kinds of stone—quartz, granite, and limestone. Of these, only limestone occurs naturally in the area. Most of the buildings at the site from the same time period had limestone as their only stone component, and most were human dwellings. Therefore, the building we are studying probably was not a dwelling.

Which one of the following, if true, would most strengthen the archaeologist's reasoning?

(A) Most of the buildings that were used as dwellings at the site were made, at least in part, of limestone.
(B) Most of the buildings at the site that were not dwellings were made, at least in part, from types of stone that do not occur naturally in the area.
(C) Most of the buildings that were built from stones not naturally occurring in the area were not built with both quartz and granite.
(D) Most of the buildings at the site were used as dwellings.
(E) No quartz has been discovered on the site other than that found in the building being studied.

15. Theodore will be able to file his tax return on time only in the event that he has an accountant prepare his tax return and the accountant does not ask Theodore for any additional documentation of his business expenses. If he does have an accountant prepare his return, the accountant will necessarily ask Theodore to provide this additional documentation. Therefore, Theodore will not be able to file on time.

The pattern of reasoning in which one of the following arguments most closely parallels the pattern of reasoning in the argument above?

(A) Given the demands of Timothy's job, his next free evening will occur next Friday. Since he spent a lot of money on his last evening out, he will probably decide to spend his next free evening at home. Therefore, Timothy will probably be at home next Friday evening.

(B) Tovah cannot attend the concert next week if she is away on business. If she misses that concert, she will not have another opportunity to attend a concert this month. Since she will be away on business, Tovah will not be able to attend a concert this month.

(C) Mark's children will not be content this weekend unless he lets them play video games some of the time. Mark will let them play video games, but only at times when he has no other activities planned. Therefore, unless Mark and his children take a break from planned activities, Mark's children will not be content this weekend.

(D) If Teresa is not seated in first class on her airline flight, she will be seated in business class. Therefore, since she cannot be seated in first class on that flight, she will necessarily be seated in business class.

(E) Susannah will have a relaxing vacation only if her children behave especially well and she does not start to suspect that they are planning some mischief. Since she will certainly start to suspect that they are planning some mischief if they behave especially well, Susannah's vacation cannot possibly be relaxing.

16. When a threat to life is common, as are automobile and industrial accidents, only unusual instances tend to be prominently reported by the news media. Instances of rare threats, such as product tampering, however, are seen as news by reporters and are universally reported in featured stories. People in general tend to estimate the risk of various threats by how frequently those threats come to their attention.

If the statements above are true, which one of the following is most strongly supported on the basis of them?

(A) Whether governmental action will be taken to lessen a common risk depends primarily on the prominence given to the risk by the news media.

(B) People tend to magnify the risk of a threat if the threat seems particularly dreadful or if those who would be affected have no control over it.

(C) Those who get their information primarily from the news media tend to overestimate the risk of uncommon threats relative to the risk of common threats.

(D) Reporters tend not to seek out information about long-range future threats but to concentrate their attention on the immediate past and future.

(E) The resources that are spent on avoiding product tampering are greater than the resources that are spent on avoiding threats that stem from the weather.

GO ON TO THE NEXT PAGE.

17. Real estate agent: Upon selling a home, the sellers are legally entitled to remove any items that are not permanent fixtures. Legally, large appliances like dishwashers are not permanent fixtures. However, since many prospective buyers of the home are likely to assume that large appliances in the home would be included with its purchase, sellers who will be keeping the appliances are morally obliged either to remove them before showing the home or to indicate in some other way that the appliances are not included.

Which one of the following principles, if valid, most helps to justify the real estate agent's argumentation?

(A) If a home's sellers will be keeping any belongings that prospective buyers of the home might assume would be included with the purchase of the home, the sellers are morally obliged to indicate clearly that those belongings are not included.

(B) A home's sellers are morally obliged to ensure that prospective buyers of the home do not assume that any large appliances are permanent fixtures in the home.

(C) A home's sellers are morally obliged to include with the sale of the home at least some of the appliances that are not permanent fixtures but were in the home when it was shown to prospective buyers.

(D) A home's sellers are morally obliged not to deliberately mislead any prospective buyers of their home about which belongings are included with the sale of the home and which are not.

(E) If a home's sellers have indicated in some way that a large appliance is included with the home's purchase, then they are morally obliged not to remove that appliance after showing the home.

18. Many parents rigorously organize their children's activities during playtime, thinking that doing so will enhance their children's cognitive development. But this belief is incorrect. To thoroughly structure a child's playtime and expect this to produce a creative and resourceful child would be like expecting a good novel to be produced by someone who was told exactly what the plot and characters must be.

The argument is most vulnerable to criticism on which one of the following grounds?

(A) It takes for granted that if something is conducive to a certain goal it cannot also be conducive to some other goal.

(B) It overlooks the possibility that many children enjoy rigorously organized playtime.

(C) It takes a necessary condition for something's enhancing a child's creativity and resourcefulness to be a sufficient condition for its doing so.

(D) It fails to consider the possibility that being able to write a good novel requires something more than creativity and resourcefulness.

(E) It fails to consider the possibility that something could enhance a child's overall cognitive development without enhancing the child's creativity and resourcefulness.

19. Bureaucrat: The primary, constant goal of an ideal bureaucracy is to define and classify all possible problems and set out regulations regarding each eventuality. Also, an ideal bureaucracy provides an appeal procedure for any complaint. If a complaint reveals an unanticipated problem, the regulations are expanded to cover the new issue, and for this reason an ideal bureaucracy will have an ever-expanding system of regulations.

Which one of the following is an assumption the bureaucrat's argument requires?

(A) An ideal bureaucracy will provide an appeal procedure for complaints even after it has defined and classified all possible problems and set out regulations regarding each eventuality.

(B) For each problem that an ideal bureaucracy has defined and classified, the bureaucracy has received at least one complaint revealing that problem.

(C) An ideal bureaucracy will never be permanently without complaints about problems that are not covered by that bureaucracy's regulations.

(D) An ideal bureaucracy can reach its primary goal if, but only if, its system of regulations is always expanding to cover problems that had not been anticipated.

(E) Any complaint that an ideal bureaucracy receives will reveal an unanticipated problem that the bureaucracy is capable of defining and classifying.

20. Scientists studying a common type of bacteria have discovered that most bacteria of that type are in hibernation at any given time. Some microbiologists have concluded from this that bacteria in general are usually in hibernation. This conclusion would be reasonable if all types of bacteria were rather similar. But, in fact, since bacteria are extremely diverse, it is unlikely that most types of bacteria hibernate regularly.

Which one of the following most accurately expresses the overall conclusion of the argument?

(A) Bacteria of most types are usually in hibernation.

(B) It is probably not true that most types of bacteria hibernate regularly.

(C) If bacteria are extremely diverse, it is unlikely that most types of bacteria hibernate regularly.

(D) The conclusion that bacteria in general are usually in hibernation would be reasonable if all types of bacteria were rather similar.

(E) It is likely that only one type of bacteria hibernates regularly.

GO ON TO THE NEXT PAGE.

21. Any student who is not required to hand in written homework based on the reading assignments in a course will not complete all of the reading assignments. Even highly motivated students will neglect their reading assignments if they are not required to hand in written homework. Therefore, if the students in a course are given several reading assignments and no written assignments, no student in that course will receive a high grade for the course.

The conclusion of the argument follows logically if which one of the following is assumed?

(A) No student who completes anything less than all of the reading assignments for a course will earn a high grade for that course.

(B) Any student who completes all of the reading and written assignments for a course will earn a high grade in that course.

(C) All highly motivated students who complete all of the reading assignments for a course will receive high grades for that course.

(D) If highly motivated students are required to hand in written homework on their reading assignments, then they will complete all of their reading assignments.

(E) Some highly motivated students will earn high grades in a course if they are required to hand in written homework on their reading assignments.

22. In a study, one group of volunteers was fed a high-protein, low-carbohydrate diet; another group was fed a low-protein, high-carbohydrate diet. Both diets contained the same number of calories, and each volunteer's diet prior to the experiment had contained moderate levels of proteins and carbohydrates. After ten days, those on the low-carbohydrate diet had lost more weight than those on the high-carbohydrate diet. Thus, the most effective way to lose body fat is to eat much protein and shun carbohydrates.

Which one of the following, if true, most weakens the argument above?

(A) A low-protein, high-carbohydrate diet causes the human body to retain water, the added weight of which largely compensates for the weight of any body fat lost, whereas a high-protein, low-carbohydrate diet does not.

(B) Many people who consume large quantities of protein nevertheless gain significant amounts of body fat.

(C) A high-protein, low-carbohydrate diet will often enable the human body to convert some body fat into muscle, without causing any significant overall weight loss.

(D) In the experiment, the volunteers on the high-carbohydrate diet engaged in regular exercise of a kind known to produce weight loss, and those on the low-carbohydrate diet did not.

(E) Many of the volunteers who had been on the low-carbohydrate diet eventually regained much of the weight they had lost on the diet after returning to their normal diets.

23. Essayist: Computers have the capacity to represent and to perform logical transformations on pieces of information. Since exactly the same applies to the human mind, the human mind is a type of computer.

The flawed pattern of reasoning in which one of the following most closely resembles the flawed pattern of reasoning in the essayist's argument?

(A) Often individual animals sacrifice their lives when the survival of their offspring or close relatives is threatened. It is probable, therefore, that there is a biological basis for the fact that human beings are similarly often willing to sacrifice their own well-being for the good of their community.

(B) In the plastic arts, such as sculpture or painting, no work can depend for its effectiveness upon a verbal narrative that explains it. Since the same can be said of poetry, we cannot consider this characteristic as a reasonable criterion for distinguishing the plastic arts from other arts.

(C) In any organism, the proper functioning of each component depends upon the proper functioning of every other component. Thus, communities belong to the category of organisms, since communities are invariably characterized by this same interdependence of components.

(D) Some vitamins require the presence in adequate amounts of some mineral in order to be fully beneficial to the body. Thus, since selenium is needed to make vitamin E fully active, anyone with a selenium deficiency will have a greater risk of contracting those diseases from which vitamin E provides some measure of protection.

(E) Friendship often involves obligations whose fulfillment can be painful or burdensome. The same can be said of various forms of cooperation that cannot strictly be called friendship. Thus cooperation, like friendship, can require that priority be given to goals other than mere self-interest.

24. It is popularly believed that a poem has whatever meaning is assigned to it by the reader. But objective evaluation of poetry is possible only if this popular belief is false; for the aesthetic value of a poem cannot be discussed unless it is possible for at least two readers to agree on the correct interpretation of the poem.

Which one of the following is an assumption required by the argument?

(A) Only if they find the same meaning in a poem can two people each judge that it has aesthetic value.

(B) If two readers agree about the meaning of a given poem, that ensures that an objective evaluation of the poem can be made.

(C) Discussion of a poem is possible only if it is false that a poem has whatever meaning is assigned to it by the reader.

(D) A given poem can be objectively evaluated only if the poem's aesthetic value can be discussed.

(E) Aesthetic evaluation of literature is best accomplished through discussion by more than two readers.

GO ON TO THE NEXT PAGE.

25. Dean: The mathematics department at our university has said that it should be given sole responsibility for teaching the course Statistics for the Social Sciences. But this course has no more mathematics in it than high school algebra does. The fact that a course has mathematics in it does not mean that it needs to be taught by a mathematics professor, any more than a course approaching its subject from a historical perspective must be taught by a history professor. Such demands by the mathematics department are therefore unjustified.

The dean's argument is most vulnerable to criticism on the grounds that it

(A) presumes, without providing justification, that expertise in a subject does not enable one to teach that subject well

(B) purports to refute a view by showing that one possible reason for that view is insufficient

(C) presumes, without providing justification, that most students are as knowledgeable about mathematics as they are about history

(D) fails to establish that mathematics professors are not capable of teaching Statistics for the Social Sciences effectively

(E) presumes, without providing justification, that any policies that apply to history courses must be justified with respect to mathematics courses

S T O P

IF YOU FINISH BEFORE TIME IS CALLED, YOU MAY CHECK YOUR WORK ON THIS SECTION ONLY. DO NOT WORK ON ANY OTHER SECTION IN THE TEST.

1.	B	6.	D	11.	B	16.	C	21.	A
2.	C	7.	E	12.	D	17.	A	22.	A
3.	B	8.	E	13.	D	18.	E	23.	C
4.	A	9.	D	14.	B	19.	C	24.	D
5.	A	10.	D	15.	E	20.	B	25.	B

1. **Correct Answer (B).** Question Type: Paradox. Difficulty Level: 1 / 4

The claim presented in this P question is that a description of Socrates written when he was alive portrays him as an atheistic philosopher primarily concerned with natural science. The unexpected result is that descriptions of Socrates written after his death portray him as having a religious dimension and being strongly concerned about ethical issues. The expected result is that the later portrayals would be similar to the earlier ones. We should anticipate a correct answer choice that explains the unexpected result without invalidating the claim.

> **(A) Aristophanes' portrayal of Socrates in *The Clouds* was unflattering, whereas the other portrayals were very flattering.**

This is irrelevant information. Whether portrayals of Socrates were flattering or unflattering does not explain the unexpected result. (A) is a loser.

> **(B) Socrates' philosophical views and interests changed sometime after his mid-forties.**

This matches our anticipated answer choice. Without invalidating the claim, (B) would explain why the later portrayals are different from the earlier ones. (B) is a candidate.

> **(C) Most of the philosophers who lived before Socrates were primarily concerned with natural science.**

This is irrelevant information because the argument does not mention what previous philosophers were concerned with. As (C) does not explain the unexpected result, it is a loser.

> **(D) Socrates was a much more controversial figure in the years before his death than he was in his mid-forties.**

This is irrelevant information. The argument does not discuss whether Socrates was a controversial figure, and this has no bearing on the unexpected result. (D) is a loser.

> **(E) Socrates had an influence on many subsequent philosophers who were primarily concerned with natural science.**

Again, this is irrelevant information. The influence of Socrates is not mentioned and has no relationship to the unexpected result. (E) is a loser.

As (B) is the only candidate, it has to be the correct answer choice.

2. **Correct Answer (C).** Question Type: Fallacy. Difficulty Level: 1 / 4

The board member concludes that the work in question fails to meet the conditions under which the grant was previously given. This is supported by two premises. The first states that the grant was given on the condition that the resulting work would not contain any material detrimental to the J Foundation's reputation. The second specifies that the resulting work fails to mention any of the foundation's laudable achievements. The argument can be outlined as follows:

> P1: The grant bars the work from containing any material detrimental to the foundation.
> P2: The work never mentions the laudable achievements of the foundation.
> C: The work fails to meet the conditions of the grant.

The board member commits a Questionable Assumption Fallacy. Just because laudable achievements were not mentioned, this does not necessarily mean that detrimental material was included. The argument assumes that the failure to mention achievements is detrimental to the foundation. We should anticipate a correct answer choice that describes this fallacy.

(A) **takes for granted that a work that never mentions any laudable achievements cannot be of high intellectual value**

This is irrelevant information. The argument is not concerned with high intellectual value. (A) is a loser.

(B) **confuses a condition necessary for the receipt of a grant with a condition sufficient for the receipt of a grant**

This answer choice describes a Conditional Reasoning Fallacy. (B) is a loser.

(C) **presumes, without providing justification, that a work that does not mention a foundation's laudable achievements is harmful to that foundation's reputation**

This matches our anticipated answer choice. The argument assumes that not mentioning laudable achievements is detrimental to the foundation. (C) is a candidate.

(D) **fails to consider that recipients of a grant usually strive to meet a foundation's conditions**

This is irrelevant information. The effort involved in meeting the foundation's conditions is not at issue here. (D) is a loser.

(E) **fails to consider the possibility that the work that was produced with the aid of the grant may have met all conditions other than avoiding detriment to the J Foundation's reputation**

This is irrelevant information. No other conditions are discussed in the argument. (E) is a loser.

As (C) is the only candidate, it has to be the correct answer choice.

---

3. **Correct Answer (B).** Question Type: Strengthen. Difficulty Level: 1 / 4

This is an unusual question. It appears to be an IMP question with an incomplete argument. However, the blank in the stimulus actually indicates a missing premise rather than a conclusion. Therefore, this is actually an S question. We must find the answer choice that supports the conclusion and, thereby, strengthens the argument.

The conclusion of the argument is that people who succeed in breaking their addiction to smoking cigarettes are more likely to be motivated by social pressure than by health concerns. This is supported by the premise that people who break a habit are more likely to be motivated by immediate concerns than by long-term concerns. The argument then specifies that social pressure is an immediate concern. The argument can be outlined as follows:

P1: People who break a habit are more likely to be motivated by immediate concerns than by long-term ones.

P2: _____

C: People who succeed in breaking an addition are more likely to be motivated by social pressure, which is an immediate concern, than by health concerns.

We should anticipate a correct answer choice that provides additional support for the conclusion. It probably specifies that health issues are long-term concerns or not immediate ones.

(A) a habit that involves an addictive substance is likely to pose a greater health threat than a habit that does not involve any addictive substance

This is irrelevant information. The argument does not discuss habits that do not involve addictive substances. (A) is a loser.

(B) for most people who successfully quit smoking, smoking does not create an immediate health concern at the time they quit

This matches our anticipated answer choice. If smoking does not create an immediate health concern for most people, then social pressure, which is an immediate concern, is more likely to motivate people to quit smoking. (B) is a candidate.

(C) some courses of action that exacerbate health concerns can also relieve social pressure

This does not strengthen the argument. The fact that some things that exacerbate health concerns relieve social pressure does not support the conclusion. (C) is a loser.

(D) most people who succeed in quitting smoking succeed only after several attempts

This is irrelevant information. The argument is not concerned with how many times people try to quit smoking. (D) is a loser.

(E) everyone who succeeds in quitting smoking is motivated either by social pressure or by health concerns

This does not strengthen the argument. It simply states that social pressure and health concerns are motivators. We need a premise that supports the conclusion that social pressure is a more common motivator. (E) is a loser.

As (B) is the only candidate, it has to be the correct answer choice.

4. **Correct Answer (A).** Question Type: Weaken. Difficulty Level: 1 / 4

This is an unusual question. It is a W question with two arguments in the stimulus. The prompt asks us to determine which answer choice includes information that Cassie can use to weaken Melvin's argument. Cassie's initial conclusion is that client loads should be reduced in order to improve the quality of customer service. Melvin responds by conceding that smaller client loads are desirable but noting that reducing client loads is not feasible. Melvin supports this by claiming that recruiting more agents would be necessary to reduce client loads, but it is already very difficult to recruit enough qualified agents. Melvin's argument can be outlined as follows:

P1: It is already difficult to find qualified agents.

P2: Recruiting more agents is necessary to reduce client loads.

C: Reducing client loads is not feasible.

There does not seem to be any obvious flaw in Melvin's argument. Therefore, we should anticipate a correct answer choice that points out a minor assumption or weakness in his argument.

(A) **Since reducing client loads would improve working conditions for agents, reducing client loads would help recruit additional qualified agents to the real estate agency.**

This matches one of our anticipated answer choices. It points out a minor weakness in Melvin's argument. Reducing client loads would improve working conditions, which would make it easier to hire agents (which would further reduce client loads). (A) is a candidate.

(B) **Many of the real estate agency's current clients have expressed strong support for efforts to reduce client loads.**

This would not weaken the argument. Whether or not clients support reduced client loads does not affect the feasibility of reducing client loads. (B) is a loser.

(C) **Several recently conducted studies of real estate agencies have shown that small client loads are strongly correlated with high customer satisfaction ratings.**

This supports Cassie's argument but does not weaken Melvin's argument. (C) is a loser.

(D) **Hiring extra support staff for the real estate agency's main office would have many of the same beneficial effects as reducing client loads.**

This is irrelevant information. Melvin does not discuss hiring support staff. Neither does he discuss any beneficial effects of hiring staff besides reducing client loads. (D) is a loser.

(E) **Over the last several years, it has become increasingly challenging for the real estate agency to recruit enough qualified agents just to maintain current client loads.**

This strengthens Melvin's argument because it lends further support to his claim that it is impossible to hire more agents. (E) is a loser.

As (A) is the only candidate, it has to be the correct answer choice.

5. **Correct Answer (A).** Question Type: Implication. Difficulty Level: 1 / 4

The stimulus claims that the star-nosed mole has a pair of tentacles that are crucial for hunting because the moles use these tentacles to detect electric fields produced by prey such as worms and insects. This question does not include an incomplete argument, an unusual circumstance, or conditional language. Therefore, we should anticipate a correct answer choice that is a paraphrase of a proposition or a statement supported by the stimulus. In this case, it is likely that the correct answer choice is related to the fact that worms and insects emit electric fields. This is an obvious inference that can be made based on the information in the stimulus.

(A) **Both worms and insects produce electric fields.**

This matches our anticipated answer choice. (A) is strongly supported by the stimulus, so it is a candidate.

(B) **The star-nosed mole does not rely at all on its eyesight for survival.**

The stimulus says that moles are poor-sighted, but this does not mean that they do not rely at all on eyesight for survival. (B) is too strongly worded, so it is a loser.

(C) **The star-nosed mole does not rely at all on its sense of smell when hunting.**

This is irrelevant information. The stimulus does not discuss the mole's sense of smell. (C) is a loser.

(D) Only animals that hunt have noses with tentacles that detect electric fields.

This is too strongly worded. The fact that moles use tentacles to detect electric fields does not preclude other animals from detecting electric fields in other ways. (D) is a loser.

(E) The star-nosed mole does not produce an electric field.

This is irrelevant information. The stimulus does not address this issue at all. (E) is a loser.

As (A) is the only candidate, it has to be the correct answer choice.

6. **Correct Answer (D).** Question Type: Principle Implication EXCEPT. Difficulty Level: 1 / 4

According to the stimulus, a recent book describes several cases that exhibit the same pattern: a child is denied something by a parent, the child behaves poorly, the parent gives in to the child's demand, and only then does the child cease behaving poorly. The severity of the misbehavior increases over time. This is an EXCEPT question, so we can expect four incorrect answer choices containing a principle implied by the stimulus and a correct answer choice lacking such a principle.

(A) A child can develop problematic behavior patterns as a result of getting what it wants.

This is a principle implied by the stimulus. The cases show that a child's behavior worsens when it gets what it wants. (A) is a loser.

(B) A child and parent can mutually influence each other's behavior.

This is a principle implied by the stimulus. The child's behavior results in the parent's acquiescence, and the parent's acquiescence results in the child acting up. (B) is a loser.

(C) Parents, by their choices, can inadvertently increase their child's level of misbehavior.

This is another principle implied by the stimulus. In this case, the parent inadvertently incentivizes the child to behave poorly by rewarding bad behavior. (C) is a loser.

(D) A child can unintentionally influence a parent's behavior in ways contrary to the child's intended goals.

This is not a principle implied by the stimulus. The child's behavior influences the parent precisely in accordance with the child's intended goals. (D) is a candidate.

(E) A child can get what it wants by doing what its parent doesn't want it to do.

This principle is implied by the stimulus. The parent does not want the child to engage in problematic behavior, but the child gets what he wants through problematic behavior. (E) is a loser.

As (D) is the only candidate, it has to be the correct answer choice.

7. **Correct Answer (E).** Question Type: Mini Description. Difficulty Level: 2 / 4

The claim presented in the prompt is located in the first sentence of the stimulus. The main conclusion is in the second sentence. The argument begins with the counter-premise that chemical R did not cause cancer in rats. This supports the implied opposing viewpoint that chemical R is safe for humans. The main conclusion states that we cannot know for certain whether this chemical is safe for humans. This is supported by the subsidiary conclusion

Chapter 8

that many substances known to cause cancer in humans do not cause cancer in rats. The evidence for the subsidiary conclusion is that some carcinogens cause cancer only as a result of long-term exposure, and rats are short lived. The argument can be outlined as follows:

> CP: Chemical R did not cause cancer in laboratory rats.
> Opposing Viewpoint: Chemical R is safe for humans.
> P1: Some carcinogens cause cancer only via long-term exposure.
> P2: Rats are short lived.
> _____
> SC: Many substances known to cause cancer in humans do not cause cancer in rats.
> C: The opposing viewpoint, that chemical R is safe for humans, is not certain.

We should anticipate a correct answer choice that states that the claim is a counter-premise supporting an opposing viewpoint.

(A) It is cited as evidence against the conclusion that chemical R is safe for humans.

The claim is evidence for the opposing viewpoint that chemical R is safe for humans. (A) is a loser.

(B) It is advanced to support the contention that test results obtained from laboratory rats cannot be extrapolated to humans.

The claim does not advance this contention. It supports the opposing viewpoint that chemical R is safe for humans. (B) is a loser.

(C) It illustrates the claim that rats are too short lived to be suitable as test subjects for the carcinogenic properties of substances to which humans are chronically exposed.

The claim is evidence for the opposing viewpoint. (C) is a loser.

(D) It is used as evidence to support the hypothesis that chemical R causes cancer in humans via long-term exposure.

The claim is used as evidence for the assertion that chemical R is safe for humans. Therefore, (D) is a loser.

(E) It is cited as being insufficient to support the conclusion that chemical R is safe for humans.

This matches our anticipated answer choice. The scientist argues that the fact that chemical R does not cause cancer in rats is insufficient to support the conclusion that chemical R is safe for humans. (E) has to be the correct answer choice.

---

8. **Correct Answer (E).** Question Type: Necessary Assumption. Difficulty Level: 1 / 4

The department store manager concludes that there is no reason to offer customers free gift wrapping during the holiday season. This is because if most customers take up the offer, gift wrapping will be expensive and time-consuming, and if only a few customers take up the offer, there is no advantage in offering it. The argument can be outlined as follows:

> P1: If most customers take up the offer of free gift wrapping, it will be expensive and time consuming.
> P2: If only a few customers take up the offer, there is no advantage to offering free gift wrapping.
> _____
> C: There is no reason to offer customers free gift wrapping.

The department store manager commits a Selection Fallacy by assuming that the list of options to select from is exhaustive. It is possible that a moderate number of customers will take up the offer. In that case, there may be a reason to provide free gift wrapping. We should anticipate a correct answer choice that eliminates this fallacy.

(A) Gift wrapping would cost the store more during this holiday season than in previous holiday seasons.

This statement is not necessarily true. The argument does not require that gift wrapping cost more this holiday season. (A) is a loser.

(B) Anything that slows down shoppers during the holiday season costs the store money.

This is not necessarily true. The argument only states that gift wrapping is time-consuming if most customers take up the offer. It is not necessary to assume that other things that slow down shoppers, such as typing in credit card PINs, cost the store money. (B) is a loser.

(C) It would be to the store's advantage to charge customers for gift wrapping services.

This is irrelevant information. The argument is about a free gift wrapping service. (C) is a loser.

(D) It would be expensive to inform customers about the free gift wrapping service.

This is not necessarily true. The argument does not require that it be expensive to inform customers about free gift wrapping. (D) is a loser.

(E) Either few customers would want free gift wrapping or most customers would want it.

This matches our anticipated answer choice. (E) eliminates the Selection Fallacy by clearly stating that there are two possible types of customers who would opt for the gift wrapping service—few would use it or most would use it. This is necessarily true for the argument to be valid. (E) has to be the correct answer choice.

9. **Correct Answer (D).** Question Type: Weaken. Difficulty Level: 2 / 4

The argument concludes that behavior modification is more effective than sleeping pills are for helping people fall asleep. The evidence for this is that those who rely only on behavior modification fall asleep more quickly than those who rely only on sleeping pills. The argument can be outlined as follows:

> BI: Some people who have trouble falling asleep take sleeping pills; others practice behavior modification.
> P: Those who rely on behavior modification fall asleep faster than those who take sleeping pills.
> C: Behavior modification is more effective than sleeping pills in helping people fall asleep.

This argument commits a Sampling Fallacy. It reaches a conclusion about both groups based on how each group responds to different treatments. We are not told that the members of each group are representative of people with a history of not being able to fall asleep. We should anticipate a correct answer choice that weakens the argument by exposing this fallacy.

(A) People who do not take sleeping pills spend at least as many total hours asleep each night as do the people who take sleeping pills.

This is irrelevant information. The argument has to do with people falling asleep, not with people staying asleep. (A) is a loser.

(B) Most people who have trouble falling asleep and who use behavior modification techniques fall asleep more slowly than do most people who have no trouble falling asleep.

This does not weaken the argument because it compares people who use behavior modification techniques to fall asleep with people who have no trouble falling asleep. The argument does not assert that behavior modification completely eliminates all issues related to falling asleep. (B) is a loser.

(C) Many people who use only behavior modification techniques to help them fall asleep have never used sleeping pills.

This introduces the possibility that some people who use behavior modification may benefit more from using sleeping pills. Regardless, (C) does not weaken the conclusion that people who do rely on behavior modification fall asleep more quickly than those who take sleeping pills. (C) is a loser.

(D) The people who are the most likely to take sleeping pills rather than practice behavior modification techniques are those who have previously had the most trouble falling asleep.

This matches our anticipated answer choice. If people who take sleeping pills have the most trouble falling asleep, then they are not representative of all people who have problems falling asleep. (D) is a candidate.

(E) The people who are the most likely to practice behavior modification techniques rather than take sleeping pills are those who prefer not to use drugs if other treatments are available.

This does not weaken the argument. Whether or not people prefer a particular treatment method does not affect the validity of the claim that one treatment method is more effective than the other. (E) is a loser.

As (D) is the only candidate, it has to be the correct answer choice.

---

10. **Correct Answer (D).** Question Type: Sufficient Assumption. Difficulty Level: 1 / 4

The lawyer concludes that the witness's testimony should be excluded on the basis that the witness recognizes the assailant but not the client. This argument seems to include a Questionable Assumption Fallacy. It can be outlined as follows:

P1: The witness was present while famous client was assaulted.
P2: The witness recognizes the assailant, but not the famous client.
SA: (   )
C: The witness's testimony should be excluded.

The argument assumes that because the witness did not recognize both the client and the assailant, his or her testimony should be excluded. We should anticipate a correct answer choice that expresses this assumption in a way that validates the argument.

(A) If a witness claims to recognize both parties involved in an assault, then the witness's testimony should be included.

This would not make the argument valid. The witness did not recognize both parties involved in the assault, so it is still unclear whether or not her or his testimony should be included. (A) is a loser.

(B) There are other witnesses who can identify the lawyer's client as present during the assault.

This is irrelevant information. Whether or not other witnesses were present has no bearing on the conclusion. As (B) does not validate the argument, it is a loser.

(C) It is impossible to determine whether the witness actually recognized the assailant.

This is irrelevant information. The argument does not question the truthfulness of the witness's claim. As (C) does not validate the argument, it is a loser.

(D) The testimony of a witness to an assault should be included only if the witness claims to recognize both parties involved in the assault.

This matches our anticipated answer choice. If the testimony of a witness should be included only if the witness recognized both parties in an assault, then this witness's testimony should be excluded because he or she did not recognize both parties. Accepting this assumption would make the argument valid. (D) is a candidate.

(E) It is unlikely that anyone would fail to recognize the lawyer's client.

This does not validate the argument. Whether is likely or unlikely that someone would fail to recognize the client does not affect the conclusion. (E) is a loser.

As (D) is the only candidate, it has to be the correct answer choice.

11. **Correct Answer (B).** Question Type: Fallacy. Difficulty Level: 2 / 4

The biologist concludes that an opposing viewpoint must be rejected. The opposing viewpoint is that the difficulty of adapting to ice ages caused the human brain to evolve. The biologist rejects this claim because most other animal species adapted to ice ages without their brains undergoing evolutionary changes. The argument can be outlined as follows:

Opposing Viewpoint: The human brain evolved through the difficulties of adapting to ice ages.
P: Most other animal species adapted to ice ages without their brains changing.
C: The opposing viewpoint must be rejected.

The argument commits a Strength Modifier Fallacy. A MOST statement premise is used to support an ALL statement conclusion (i.e. there is no possibility that humans evolved in this way). Remember, a conclusion cannot be stronger than the premise that supports it. We should look for an answer choice that describes this Strength Modifier Fallacy.

(A) It fails to address adequately the possibility that even if a condition is sufficient to produce an effect in a species, it may not be necessary to produce that effect in that species.

This answer choice describes a Conditional Reasoning Fallacy. (A) is a loser.

(B) It fails to address adequately the possibility that a condition can produce a change in a species even if it does not produce that change in other species.

This matches our anticipated answer choice. The biologist assumes that if a change does not occur in most species then it must not occur in all species, including humans. (B) is a candidate.

(C) It overlooks the possibility that a condition that is needed to produce a change in one species is not needed to produce a similar change in other species.

The argument does not state that the condition (difficulty adapting to ice ages) was needed in order for the human brain to evolve, only that it was responsible. (C) is a loser.

(D) It presumes without warrant that human beings were presented with greater difficulties during ice ages than were individuals of most other species.

This is irrelevant information. The argument does not claim that humans faced greater difficulties. (D) is a loser.

(E) It takes for granted that, if a condition coincided with the emergence of a certain

phenomenon, that condition must have been causally responsible for the phenomenon.

This answer describes a Causal Reasoning Fallacy. (E) is a loser.

As (B) is the only candidate, it has to be the correct answer choice.

---

12. **Correct Answer (D).** Question Type: Implication. Difficulty Level: 1 / 4

The stimulus states that since TV has become available, the number of books published annually has quadrupled. It also specifies that retail sales of books increased rapidly once TV was introduced, but the rate of increase has declined in recent years. Library circulation has been flat or declining. As the stimulus does not include an incomplete argument, unusual circumstance, or conditional language, we should anticipate a correct answer choice that is a paraphrase of a proposition or a statement supported by the stimulus.

(A) **Television has, over the years, brought about a reduction in the amount of per capita reading in North America.**

There are two issues with this answer choice. The first is that book sales have actually increased since TV was introduced. The second is that the stimulus does not discuss per capita reading levels—just book sales. (A) is a loser.

(B) **The introduction of television usually brings about a decrease in library use.**

The inclusion of *usually* makes this answer choice too strong. The stimulus only discusses the situation in North America. In addition, it suggests that in at least some parts of North America, library circulation has remained flat. (B) is a loser.

(C) **Book publishers in North America now sell fewer copies per title than they sold in the early days of television.**

This contradicts the stimulus, which states that book sales are currently increasing (though at a slower rate than in the early days of television). (C) is a loser.

(D) **The availability of television does not always cause a decline in the annual number of book titles published or in the number of books sold.**

This matches our anticipated answer choice. The stimulus states that the introduction of television did not bring about a decline in the annual number of books published or in the number of books sold. (D) is a candidate.

(E) **The introduction of television expanded the market for books in North America.**

This answer choice asserts a causal relationship between the introduction of television and the expansion of the book market. However, the stimulus simply shows a correlation between these two events. (E) is a loser.

As (D) is the only candidate, it has to be the correct answer choice.

---

13. **Correct Answer (D).** Question Type: Main Point. Difficulty Level: 2 / 4

The botanist starts by introducing the opposing viewpoint—that people with children or pets should keep poinsettia plants out of their homes. The botanist concedes that this belief has been encouraged by child-rearing books but concludes that it is mistaken. This is the main conclusion of the argument. The botanist supports this conclusion by pointing to research showing that poinsettias pose no risk to children or pets. The argument can be outlined as follows:

Opposing Viewpoint: Households with children or pets should not have poinsettias.
CP: This belief has been encouraged by child-rearing books.
P: Our research shows poinsettias pose no risk to children or pets.
C: The opposing viewpoint is mistaken.

We should anticipate a correct answer choice the restates the conclusion of the argument.

(A) Child-rearing books should encourage people with children to put poinsettias in their homes.

This is an inaccurate paraphrase of the conclusion. The botanist does not conclude that poinsettias should be put in homes with children, but rather that the belief that poinsettias should be kept out of these homes is mistaken. (A) is a loser.

(B) Poinsettias are not dangerously poisonous.

This is an inaccurate paraphrase of the premise. (B) is a loser.

(C) According to many child-rearing books, poinsettias are dangerous.

This is an inaccurate paraphrase of the counter-premise. (C) is a loser.

(D) The belief that households with children or pets should not have poinsettias is mistaken.

This matches our anticipated answer choice. It is a complete and accurate paraphrase of the conclusion. (D) is a candidate.

(E) Poinsettias pose no risk to children or pets.

This is a paraphrase of the premise. (E) is a loser.

As (D) is the only candidate, it has to be the correct answer choice.

14. Correct Answer (B). Question Type: Strengthen. Difficulty Level: 3 / 4

The argument concludes that the ancient stone building being studied was probably not used as a dwelling. The evidence for this is that of the three kinds of stone the building is made of, only limestone occurs naturally in the area. Most of the buildings at the site that date back to the same period had limestone as their only stone component, and most of these buildings were human dwellings. This argument can be outlined as follows:

P1: Specific Building → Multi Stone
P2: Naturally Occurring Stone → Limestone
P3: Building ^{M}→ Only Limestone Building
P4: Building ^{M}→ Human Dwelling
C: Specific Building ^{M}→ ~~Human Dwelling~~

This is a difficult question to anticipate a correct answer choice for. It does not include a causal conclusion or a comparison, which means that it likely contains an assumption or a fallacy. The presence of so many conditional statements containing strength modifiers suggests that it may have a Conditional Reasoning Fallacy or a Strength Modifier Fallacy. However, neither of these is apparent in the arguments.

As the conclusion introduces as new term, ~~Human Dwelling~~, it is possible that the argument includes an assumption. The correct answer choice may state that all multi stone buildings are not dwellings, or Multi Stone → ~~Human Dwelling~~. Combining this statement with the first premise gives us a logic chain from which the conclusion could be inferred. However, the correct answer choice may simply strengthen the argument without actually validating it.

(A) Most of the buildings that were used as dwellings at the site were made, at least in part, of limestone.

This does not strengthen the argument. In fact, (A) may weaken the argument by opening up the possibility that some dwellings were made of material that was not limestone. (A) is a loser.

(B) Most of the buildings at the site that were not dwellings were made, at least in part, from types of stone that do not occur naturally in the area.

This seems to strengthen the argument. If most buildings that were not dwellings were at least partly made from a type of stone other than limestone, then the claim that the one specific building that included stone that was not limestone was not a dwelling is strengthened. (B) is a candidate.

(C) Most of the buildings that were built from stones not naturally occurring in the area were not built with both quartz and granite.

This is irrelevant information. We have no information about buildings made from stones that do not naturally occur in the area. (C) is a loser.

(D) Most of the buildings at the site were used as dwellings.

This answer choice is simply a paraphrase of the last premise of the argument. It is slightly broader in that it does not refer to buildings at the site that date back to any specific time period. Still, (D) does not strengthen the argument, so it is a loser.

(E) No quartz has been discovered on the site other than that found in the building being studied.

This is irrelevant information. The fact that quartz has only been found in the building being studied does not strengthen or weaken argument. (E) is a loser.

As (B) is the only candidate, it has to be the correct answer choice.

---

15. **Correct Answer (E).** Question Type: Parallel Reasoning. Difficulty Level: 2 / 4

The argument concludes that Theodore will not be able to file his taxes on time. The reasoning for this is that Theodore will be able to file on time only if he has an accountant prepare his taxes and his accountant does not ask for additional documentation. The argument then states that the accountant will necessarily ask for additional documentation. This argument includes multiple conditional statements. It can be outlined as follows:

P1: File Tax Return on Time → Accountant AND ~~Asked for Additional Documentation~~
P2: Accountant → Asked for Additional Documentation
C: ~~File Tax Return on Time~~

This is a valid argument. To file on time, Theodore needs to meet two requirements, and meeting the first requirement makes it impossible to meet the second. Therefore, Theodore will not be able to fulfill both necessary conditions, and he will not be able to file his tax return on time.

We should anticipate a correct answer choice with the same argumentative structure. As the argument in the stimulus includes a conjunction, we can eliminate any answer choice that does not include one. We can quickly eliminate (A), (B), (C), and (D).

(E) **Susannah will have a relaxing vacation only if her children behave especially well and she does not start to suspect that they are planning some mischief. Since she will certainly start to suspect that they are planning some mischief if they behave especially well, Susannah's vacation cannot possibly be relaxing.**

This argument can be outlined as follows:

P1: Relaxing Vacation → Children Behave AND ~~Suspect Children Are Planning Mischief~~
P2: Children Behave → ~~Suspect Children Are Planning Mischief~~
_____
C: ~~Relaxing Vacation~~

This argument matches the argument in the stimulus perfectly. (E) has to be the correct answer choice.

16. **Correct Answer (C).** Question Type: Implication. Difficulty Level: 2 / 4

The stimulus states that only unusual instances of common life-threatening events are reported by the media, but rare threats are universally reported when they occur. The stimulus also states that people tend to estimate the risk of various threats by how frequently those threats come to their attention.

The stimulus does not include an incomplete argument or an unusual circumstance. Therefore, we should anticipate a correct answer choice that is a paraphrase of a proposition or a statement supported by the stimulus. The correct answer choice may well have something to do with the fact that people overestimate the existence of rare threats and underestimate the existence of common threats. Both of these ideas are strongly supported by the stimulus.

(A) **Whether governmental action will be taken to lessen a common risk depends primarily on the prominence given to the risk by the news media.**

This is irrelevant information. Governmental action is not discussed in the stimulus. (A) is a loser.

(B) **People tend to magnify the risk of a threat if the threat seems particularly dreadful or if those who would be affected have no control over it.**

This is irrelevant information. The stimulus does not discuss dreadful threats or threats that people have no control over. (B) is a loser.

(C) **Those who get their information primarily from the news media tend to overestimate the risk of uncommon threats relative to the risk of common threats.**

This matches one of our anticipated answer choices. It is strongly supported by the stimulus, which states that people assess the risk of threats by how commonly they come to their attention, and the media over-reports rare threats and under-reports common threats. (C) is a candidate.

(D) **Reporters tend not to seek out information about long-range future threats but to concentrate their attention on the immediate past and future.**

This is irrelevant information. The stimulus does not discuss long-range or short-range threats. (D) is a loser.

(E) **The resources that are spent on avoiding product tampering are greater than the resources that are spent on avoiding threats that stem from the weather.**

This is irrelevant information. The stimulus does not discuss the resources used to avoid specific threats. (E) is a loser.

As (C) is the only candidate, it has to be the correct answer choice.

17. **Correct Answer (A).** Question Type: Principle Strengthen. Difficulty Level: 2 / 4

The real estate agent concludes that sellers who intend to keep their home appliances are morally obliged either to remove them or indicate to buyers that the appliances are not included in the price of the house. The real estate agent supports this conclusion by claiming that buyers may assume that large appliances are permanent fixtures and, thus, come with the home. The argument can be outlined as follows:

P1: Home sellers must remove any items that are not permanent fixtures.
P2: Large appliances are not permanent fixtures.
P3: Many buyers would assume that large appliances in the home are part of the purchase.

C: Sellers who intend to keep large appliances should remove them or indicate that the appliances are not part of the purchase.

We should anticipate a correct answer choice that expresses a principle that provides support for the judgment expressed in the conclusion.

(A) If a home's sellers will be keeping any belongings that prospective buyers of the home might assume would be included with the purchase of the home, the sellers are morally obliged to indicate clearly that those belongings are not included.

This matches our anticipated answer choice. It presents a principle that strengthens the real estate agent's conclusion. If a home seller intends to keep a large appliance and a prospective buyer might assume that that the large appliance comes with the home, the seller is morally obliged to clearly indicate that that appliance is not included. (A) is a candidate.

(B) A home's sellers are morally obliged to ensure that prospective buyers of the home do not assume that any large appliances are permanent fixtures in the home.

This would not strengthen the argument because the argument concludes that a home seller is only morally obliged to indicate that an appliance is not included in the sale of a home. The seller is not required to stop a buyer from assuming this. (B) is a loser.

(C) A home's sellers are morally obliged to include with the sale of the home at least some of the appliances that are not permanent fixtures but were in the home when it was shown to prospective buyers.

This would also not strengthen the argument because the conclusion is that sellers should indicate that large appliances are not included, not that sellers must include such appliances. (C) is a loser.

(D) A home's sellers are morally obliged not to deliberately mislead any prospective buyers of their home about which belongings are included with the sale of the home and which are not.

This would not strengthen the argument because a seller who fails to indicate that an appliance is not included is not necessarily deliberately misleading prospective buyers. (D) is a loser.

(E) If a home's sellers have indicated in some way that a large appliance is included with the home's purchase, then they are morally obliged not to remove that appliance after showing the home.

This is irrelevant information. The argument is concerned with situations in which large appliances are not included in the sale of the home. There is no mention of situations in which a home seller indicates that an appliance is included. (E) is a loser.

As (A) is the only candidate, it has to be the correct answer choice.

18. **Correct Answer (E).** Question Type: Fallacy. Difficulty Level: 3 / 4

The argument concludes that a certain belief—that rigorously organizing children's activities during playtime will enhance their cognitive development—is incorrect. The argument supports this through the use of an analogy. Raising a child is compared to writing a book. The argument can be outlined as follows:

> Opposing Viewpoint: Organizing children's activities during playtime will enhance their cognitive development.
> P: Expecting this to produce a creative and resourceful child would be like expecting a good novel to be produced by someone who was told exactly what the plot and characters must be.
> C: The opposing viewpoint is incorrect.

Most times, when an F question contains an analogy, the argument includes a False Comparison Fallacy. However, in this question, another fallacy is committed before the analogy is made. The opposing viewpoint is about enhancing the cognitive development of a child, but the premise discusses producing a creative and resourceful child. This is an Equivocation Fallacy. A broad concept, *cognitive development*, undergoes a shift in meaning, becoming more specific. We should anticipate a correct answer choice that describes this fallacy.

(A) It takes for granted that if something is conducive to a certain goal it cannot also be conducive to some other goal.

The argument does not assume this because it never states that something is conducive to a certain goal. (A) is a loser.

(B) It overlooks the possibility that many children enjoy rigorously organized playtime.

This is irrelevant information. The argument is concerned not with enjoyment but with cognitive development. (B) is a loser.

(C) It takes a necessary condition for something's enhancing a child's creativity and resourcefulness to be a sufficient condition for its doing so.

This answer choice describes a Conditional Reasoning Fallacy. (C) is a loser.

(D) It fails to consider the possibility that being able to write a good novel requires something more than creativity and resourcefulness.

This describes a False Comparison Fallacy. Although the argument includes a comparison, it does not include this particular fallacy. (D) is a loser.

(E) It fails to consider the possibility that something could enhance a child's overall cognitive development without enhancing the child's creativity and resourcefulness.

This matches our anticipated answer choice. The argument assumes that *cognitive development* and *creativity and resourcefulness* are identical terms. This answer choice shows that there is more to cognitive development than just these two qualities. (E) has to be the correct answer choice.

19. **Correct Answer (C).** Question Type: Necessary Assumption. Difficulty Level: 4 / 4

The bureaucrat concludes that an ideal bureaucracy will have an ever-expanding system of regulations, which is indicated by the use of a *for this reason*, conclusion structure. The evidence for this conclusion is that the primary goal of an ideal bureaucracy is to define and classify all possibilities and come up with corresponding regulations. An ideal bureaucracy should also have an appeal procedure. If a complaint reveals a problem, regulations can be expanded to cover the issue. The argument can be outlined as follows:

P1: A constant goal of an ideal bureaucracy is to define all problems and impose regulations.

P2: An ideal bureaucracy provides an appeal procedure for any complaint.

P3: When a complaint reveals an unanticipated problem, regulations are expanded

C: An ideal bureaucracy will have an ever-expanding system of regulations.

The premises contain a small gap in logic. The last premise applies only to situations in which there are unanticipated problems. This means that if there are no unanticipated problems, regulations will not necessarily be expanded. Therefore, the argument must assume that complaints that reveal unanticipated problems will continue to arise. We should anticipate a correct answer choice that validates this assumption in a way that is necessarily true.

(A) An ideal bureaucracy will provide an appeal procedure for complaints even after it has defined and classified all possible problems and set out regulations regarding each eventuality.

This is not necessarily true. If there is a point at which all possible problems are covered by regulations, why would the system of regulations continue to expand? (A) is a loser.

(B) For each problem that an ideal bureaucracy has defined and classified, the bureaucracy has received at least one complaint revealing that problem.

This is too strongly worded to be necessarily true. There does not need to be at least one complaint for each problem that has been defined and classified. The bureaucracy may identify problems that it has not received complaints about. (B) is a loser.

(C) An ideal bureaucracy will never be permanently without complaints about problems that are not covered by that bureaucracy's regulations.

This matches our anticipated answer choice. We can confirm that this is the correct answer choice using the (Un)Necessary Assumption Test. This statement can be logically negated to read as "An ideal bureaucracy will sometimes be permanently without complaints about problems that are not covered by that bureaucracy's regulations." This would invalidate the argument. Without complaints, there is no need to expand regulations. (C) is a candidate.

(D) An ideal bureaucracy can reach its primary goal if, but only if, its system of regulations is always expanding to cover problems that had not been anticipated.

This is too strongly worded to be necessarily true. The argument does not need to assume that reaching the primary goal of classifying all problems requires that there is an ever-expanding network of regulations. There may be a limit to the amount of regulations, in which case all problems could be classified and covered. (D) is incorrect.

(E) Any complaint that an ideal bureaucracy receives will reveal an unanticipated problem that the bureaucracy is capable of defining and classifying.

This is too strongly worded to be necessarily true. It is not necessary that every complaint reveal a new problem, just that there is a constant stream of complaints that reveal unanticipated problems. (E) is a loser.

As (C) is the only candidate, it has to be the correct answer choice.

---

20. Correct Answer (B). Question Type: Main Point. Difficulty Level: 2 / 4

The conclusion of the argument is that it is unlikely that most types of bacteria hibernate regularly. As the claim that bacteria in general are usually in hibernation is the opposing viewpoint, the conclusion actually states that the opposing viewpoint is not true. The argument can be outlined as follows:

Opposing Viewpoint: Bacteria in general are usually in hibernation.
CP: It was discovered that most bacteria of a certain type are in hibernation at any given time.
P1: The opposing viewpoint would be true if all bacteria were similar.
P2: Not all bacteria are similar.
_____
C: It is unlikely that most types of bacteria hibernate regularly.

We should anticipate a correct answer choice that restates the conclusion.

(A) Bacteria of most types are usually in hibernation.

This is a paraphrase of the opposing viewpoint. (A) is a loser.

(B) It is probably not true that most types of bacteria hibernate regularly.

This matches our anticipated answer choice. It is a complete and accurate paraphrase of the conclusion. (B) is a candidate.

(C) If bacteria are extremely diverse, it is unlikely that most types of bacteria hibernate regularly.

This is an inaccurate paraphrase of the conclusion. It introduces an element (*if bacteria are extremely diverse*) that does not appear in the conclusion of the argument. (C) is a loser.

(D) The conclusion that bacteria in general are usually in hibernation would be reasonable if all types of bacteria were rather similar.

This is an inaccurate paraphrase of the conclusion. The conclusion does not state that the opposing viewpoint would be reasonable under specific circumstances. It clearly states that the opposing viewpoint is unlikely. (D) is a loser.

(E) It is likely that only one type of bacteria hibernates regularly.

This is irrelevant information as it is not stated or implied anywhere in the argument. (E) is a loser.

As (B) is the only candidate, it has to be the correct answer choice.

21. **Correct Answer (A).** Question Type: Sufficient Assumption. Difficulty Level: 3 / 4

The argument concludes that if students are given several reading assignments and no written assignments, no student in the course will receive a high grade. The argument includes multiple conditional statements. It can be outlined as follows:

P: ~~Written Assignment~~ → ~~Reading Assignments~~
C: ~~Written Assignment~~ → ~~High Grade~~

Note that the argument appears to have two premises. However, the second premise (*highly motivated students will neglect their reading assignments if they are not required to hand in written homework*) is actually covered by the first premise (all students will not complete reading assignments if not required to hand in written assignments). Therefore, we can express the two statements as a single premise (~~Written Assignment~~ → ~~Reading Assignments~~).

As the conclusion of the argument is an ALL statement, the sufficient assumption is likely to be an ALL statement that joins with the premise to create a logic chain. The conclusion includes a term that does not appear in the premise. As this term, ~~High Grade~~, is the necessary condition of the conclusion, it has to be the necessary condition of the sufficient assumption. If we make ~~Reading Assignments~~ the sufficient condition of the assumption, we get the following:

P: ~~Written Assignment~~ → ~~Reading Assignments~~
A: (~~Reading Assignments~~ → ~~High Grade~~)
C: ~~Written Assignment~~ → ~~High Grade~~

This results in the following logic chain:

~~Written Assignment~~ → ~~Reading Assignments~~ → ~~High Grade~~

As the conclusion is a valid inference based on combining the ends of the logic chain, we can anticipate a correct answer choice that expresses ~~Reading Assignments~~ → ~~High Grade~~ (or its contrapositive). Looking through the answer choices, we see that (D) does not include the term ~~High Grade~~. In addition, (E) is a SOME statement. These two answer choices can be eliminated.

(A) No student who completes anything less than all of the reading assignments for a course will earn a high grade for that course.

This statement matches our anticipated answer choice. It can be diagrammed as ~~Reading Assignments~~ → ~~High Grade~~. (A) is a candidate.

(B) Any student who completes all of the reading and written assignments for a course will earn a high grade in that course.

This statement can be diagrammed as Reading Assignments → High Grade. This is the negated version of the statement we anticipated. (B) is a loser.

(C) All highly motivated students who complete all of the reading assignments for a course will receive high grades for that course.

This statement can be diagrammed as ~~Highly Motivated Neglect Reading Assignment~~ → High Grade. This is a more specific negated version of the statement we anticipated. (C) is a loser.

As (A) is the only candidate, it has to be the correct answer choice.

---

22. **Correct Answer (A).** Question Type: Weaken. Difficulty Level: 3 / 4

The argument concludes that the most effective way to lose body fat is to consume a lot of protein and shun carbohydrates. The evidence for this comes from a study in which a group on a low-carbohydrate diet lost more weight a group on a high-carbohydrate diet. The argument can be outlined as follows:

P: In a study of two groups, the group on the low-carbohydrate diet lost more weight than the one on the high-carbohydrate diet, though the diets were identical in terms of calories.
C: Low-carbohydrate diets are the most effective way to lose body fat.

The argument includes an Equivocation Fallacy. The premise discusses weight loss, while the conclusion is about fat loss. This particular Equivocation Fallacy (weight/fat) has turned up on multiple administrations of the LSAT. We should anticipate a correct answer choice that exposes the fallacy.

(A) A low-protein, high-carbohydrate diet causes the human body to retain water, the added weight of which largely compensates for the weight of any body fat lost, whereas a high-protein, low-carbohydrate diet does not.

This matches our anticipated answer choice. (A) suggests that the low-protein diet caused water retention, which resulted in weight gain that offset losses in body fat. This was not an issue for those on the high-protein diet. (A) is a candidate.

(B) Many people who consume large quantities of protein nevertheless gain significant amounts of body fat.

The amount of protein consumed by the group on the high-protein diet is not discussed. In addition, the argument specifies that this group had a high-protein/low-carbohydrate diet. (B) does not mention anything about carbohydrates, so it is a loser.

(C) A high-protein, low-carbohydrate diet will often enable the human body to convert some body fat into muscle, without causing any significant overall weight loss.

This answer choice strengthens the argument. It implies that more fat would be lost than is indicated by the amount of weight lost. (C) is a loser.

(D) In the experiment, the volunteers on the high-carbohydrate diet engaged in regular exercise of a kind known to produce weight loss, and those on the low-carbohydrate diet did not.

This strengthens the argument. The people on the low-carbohydrate diet lost more weight than those on the high-carbohydrate diet. (D) is a loser.

(E) Many of the volunteers who had been on the low-carbohydrate diet eventually regained much of the weight they had lost on the diet after returning to their normal diets.

This is irrelevant information. The argument is concerned with the amount of weight lost while on the low-carbohydrate diet, not with what happens after a normal diet has been resumed. (E) is a loser.

As (A) is the only candidate, it has to be the correct answer choice.

---

23. **Correct Answer (C).** Question Type: Parallel Fallacy. Difficulty Level: 3 / 4

The essayist uses a *since premise, conclusion* structure to conclude that the human mind is a type of computer. The evidence for this is that human minds and computers both have the capacity to represent and logically transformation pieces of information. In other words, all computers have a certain capacity and since the human mind has the same capacity, it must be a computer. The argument can be outlined as follows:

P1: Computer → Capacity for Logical Transformations
P2: Human Mind → Capacity for Logical Transformations
C: Human Mind → Computer

An ALL statement can only be inferred when the sufficient condition of one ALL statement is identical of the necessary condition of another ALL statement, allowing for a logic chain to be formed. This is not the case here. When we find the contrapositives of the two premises, we end up with identical necessary conditions. This allows us to infer a SOME statement (~~Computer~~ ˢ—ˢ ~~Human Mind~~) but not an ALL statement. Therefore, we can view this argument as including either a Causal Reasoning Fallacy or a Strength Modifier Fallacy. Either way, the argument erroneously concludes that because two terms (Computer/Human Mind) share the same necessary condition, one (Human Mind) is a subcategory of the other (Computer). We should anticipate a correct answer choice that is an argument containing the same error in reasoning.

(A) Often individual animals sacrifice their lives when the survival of their offspring or close relatives is threatened. It is probable, therefore, that there is a biological basis for the fact that human beings are similarly often willing to sacrifice their own well-being for the good of their community.

This argument is not necessarily flawed. The premise shows evidence of a biological basis for animals sacrificing individual well-being for the good of the community, and the conclusion states that it is probable that there is a biological basis for humans sacrificing their own well-being. The category *animals* may be inclusive of human beings. It may be arguable *that survival of their offspring or close relatives* is different from *good of the community*, but this would be a different fallacy from the one in the stimulus. (A) is a loser.

(B) **In the plastic arts, such as sculpture or painting, no work can depend for its effectiveness upon a verbal narrative that explains it. Since the same can be said of poetry, we cannot consider this characteristic as a reasonable criterion for distinguishing the plastic arts from other arts.**

This conclusion does not state that one thing is a subcategory of another. Instead, it argues that a characteristic cannot be used to distinguish between two things. (B) is a loser.

(C) **In any organism, the proper functioning of each component depends upon the proper functioning of every other component. Thus, communities belong to the category of organisms, since communities are invariably characterized by this same interdependence of components.**

This argument can be outlined as follows:

P1: Organisms → Interdependence of Components
P2: Communities → Interdependence of Components
C: Communities → Organisms

This matches our anticipated answer choice. The conclusion is an ALL statement that is an invalid inference drawn from two ALL statement containing identical necessary conditions. The argument assumes that because Organisms and Communities share the same necessary condition, Communities is a subcategory of Organisms. (C) is a candidate.

(D) **Some vitamins require the presence in adequate amounts of some mineral in order to be fully beneficial to the body. Thus, since selenium is needed to make vitamin E fully active, anyone with a selenium deficiency will have a greater risk of contracting those diseases from which vitamin E provides some measure of protection.**

This answer choice can be diagrammed as follows:

P1: Vitamins ^{S}—^{S} Require Adequate Amount of Certain Mineral
P2: Vitamin E Fully Active → Selenium
C: Those with selenium deficiency will have greater risk of contracting certain diseases.

The conclusion is not a conditional statement. Therefore, this argument cannot include a Causal Reasoning or Strength Modifier Fallacy. (D) is a loser.

(E) **Friendship often involves obligations whose fulfillment can be painful or burdensome. The same can be said of various forms of cooperation that cannot strictly be called friendship. Thus cooperation, like friendship, can require that priority be given to goals other than mere self-interest.**

This answer choice can be diagramed as

P1: Friendship ^{S}—^{S} Involve Painful/Burdensome Obligation
P2: Cooperation ^{S}—^{S} Involve Painful/Burdensome Obligation
C: Cooperation ^{S}—^{S} Priority Given to Goals Other Than Self-Interest

This answer choice is wrong because the conclusion does not state that one thing is a subcategory of another. (E) is a loser.

As (C) is the only candidate, it has to be the correct answer choice.

24. **Correct Answer (D).** Question Type: Necessary Assumption. Difficulty Level: 4 / 4

The argument concludes that objective evaluation of poetry is possibly only if a certain popular belief is false. This popular belief is that a poem means whatever a reader thinks it means. The evidence for this conclusion is that the aesthetic value of a poem cannot be discussed unless it is possible for multiple readers to agree on a correct interpretation of the poem. The argument can be outlined as follows:

P1: The belief is that the meaning assigned to a poem determines its meaning.
P2: ~~Possibility of Readers Agreeing on Correct Interpretation~~ → ~~Aesthetic Value Discussed~~
C: Objective Evaluation of Poem → (Meaning Assigned Does Not Determine Poem's Meaning)

The argument functions like an argument in an SA question with multiple conditional statements. The necessary assumption must be an ALL statement that combines with the second premise to create a logic chain from which the conclusion can be inferred. Let's begin by finding the contrapositive of the second premise:

P1: The belief is that the meaning assigned to a poem determines its meaning.
P2: Aesthetic Value Discussed → Possibility of Readers Agreeing on Correct Interpretation
C: Objective Evaluation of Poem → (Meaning Assigned Does Not Determine Poem's Meaning)

It is possible to make the necessary conditions of the second premise and the conclusion match. Both of these terms directly contradict the belief stated in the first premise. Therefore, they can both be expressed as Belief Is False. Thus, the argument can be diagrammed as follows:

P1: The belief is that the meaning assigned to a poem determines its meaning.
P2: Aesthetic Value Discussed → Belief Is False
C: Objective Evaluation of Poem → Belief Is False

We can now create a logic chain with the second premise from which the conclusion can be inferred. The term Objective Evaluation of Poem is not included in the premise, so it will become the necessary condition of sufficient assumption. If we make the necessary condition of the sufficient assumption Aesthetic Value Discussed, we will end up with the following:

P1: The belief is that the meaning assigned to a poem determines its meaning.
P2: Aesthetic Value Discussed → Belief Is False
A: (Objective Evaluation of Poem → Aesthetic Value Discussed)
C: Objective Evaluation of Poem → Belief Is False

We can combine the sufficient assumption and first premise to create the following logic chain:

Objective Evaluation of Poem → Aesthetic Value Discussed → Belief Is False

As the conclusion is a valid inference based on combining the ends of the logic chain, we should anticipate a correct answer choice that expresses Objective Evaluation of Poem → Aesthetic Value Discussed. Quickly scanning the answer choices, we can see that the term Objective Evaluation of Poem only appears in (B) and (D). Therefore, we can eliminate (A), (C), and (E).

(B) If two readers agree about the meaning of a given poem, that ensures that an objective evaluation of the poem can be made.

This answer can be diagrammed as Belief Is False → Objective Evaluation of Poem. This is the flipped version of the argument's conclusion. As this is not necessarily true, (B) is a loser.

(D) A given poem can be objectively evaluated only if the poem's aesthetic value can be discussed.

This matches our anticipated answer choice. It can be diagrammed as Objective Evaluation of Poem → Aesthetic Value Discussed. We can confirm this is the correct answer choice using the (Un)Necessary Assumption Test. When we logically negate the statement, it reads as "If a given poem can be objectively evaluated, it does not necessarily mean that a poem's aesthetic value can be discussed." If this is the case, then readers do not need to agree on the meaning of a poem, and the popular belief is not necessarily false. The argument is, therefore, negated. (D) has to be the correct answer choice.

25. **Correct Answer (B).** Question Type: Fallacy. Difficulty Level: 3 / 4

The dean concludes that the demand by the mathematics department to be given the new course is unjustified. To support this conclusion, the dean makes an analogy involving a different academic discipline. He does this to show that a course does not need to be taught by a mathematics professor just because it involves mathematics. The argument can be outlined as follows:

> Opposing Viewpoint: The mathematics department should be given the new course.
> P1: The new course has no more mathematics in it than high school algebra.
> P2: A course with mathematics does not need to be taught by a mathematics professor, just as a course taking a historical perspective does not need to be taught by a history professor.
> ―――――――――――――――――――――――――――――――――――――
> C: The opposing viewpoint is unjustified.

The dean commits the third type of Absence of Evidence Fallacy (see Chapter 4). This involves claiming that something is false because a piece of evidence to support it is false. In the argument, the fact that mathematics is involved in the new course is the evidence to support the claim that it should be taught by the mathematics department. The dean dismisses this evidence using his analogy concerning the history department. However, eliminating one piece of evidence for a claim does not mean that the claim is false. We should anticipate a correct answer choice that describes this fallacy.

(A) presumes, without providing justification, that expertise in a subject does not enable one to teach that subject well

The dean does not argue that a mathematics professor cannot teach a mathematics course. (A) is a loser.

(B) purports to refute a view by showing that one possible reason for that view is insufficient

This matches our anticipated answer choice. It describes the specific Absence of Evidence Fallacy we identified. The dean concludes a view is unjustified because one possible reason for that view is insufficient. (B) is a candidate.

(C) presumes, without providing justification, that most students are as knowledgeable about mathematics as they are about history

The argument does not compare students' knowledge of the two subjects. (C) is a loser.

(D) fails to establish that mathematics professors are not capable of teaching Statistics for the Social Sciences effectively

The dean does not claim that mathematics professors are not capable of teaching the course effectively. (D) is a loser.

(E) presumes, without providing justification, that any policies that apply to history courses must be justified with respect to mathematics courses

The dean does not presume that any policy that applies to history courses also applies to mathematics courses. In addition, the dean does not discuss history courses. He mentions a presumably nonhistory course being taught from a historical perspective. (E) is a loser.

As (B) is the only candidate, it has to be the correct answer choice.

HACKERS
LSAT *Logical Reasoning*

Chapter 9

Question
Index

Question Index

Chapter 1

[Text]

Page 33. June 2003 (PT 40), Section 3, Question 7

Chapter 2

[Problem Set]

Q1. June 2003 (PT 40), Section 1, Question 24
Q2. October 2003 (PT 41), Section 1, Question 21
Q3. June 2009 (PT 57), Section 3, Question 20
Q4. June 2004 (PT 43), Section 2, Question 22
Q5. June 2003 (PT 40), Section 1, Question 22
Q6. June 2008 (PT 54), Section 2, Question 16

Chapter 3 – Must Be True

[Text]

Page 100. December 2004 (PT 45), Section 1, Question 22

[Drill]

Page 103. October 2005 (PT 47), Section 1, Question 18

[Problem Set]

Q1. December 2003 (PT 42), Section 2, Question 16
Q2. June 2009 (PT 57), Section 2, Question 25
Q3. June 2008 (PT 54), Section 2, Question 25
Q4. June 2003 (PT 40), Section 3, Question 11
Q5. December 2004 (PT 45), Section 1, Question 8
Q6. October 2003 (PT 41), Section 3, Question 25
Q7. June 2007 (PT 51.5), Section 3, Question 22

Chapter 3 – Implication

[Text]

Page 117. June 2007 (PT 51.5), Section 3, Question 10
Page 118. October 2003 (PT 41), Section 1, Question 11
Page 120. June 2008 (PT 54), Section 4, Question 5

[Drill]

Page 123. June 2009 (PT 57), Section 3, Question 23

[Problem Set]

Q1. October 2005 (PT 47), Section 3, Question 1
Q2. October 2004 (PT 44), Section 2, Question 2
Q3. September 2007 (PT 52), Section 3, Question 14
Q4. June 2007 (PT 51.5), Section 3, Question 16
Q5. September 2007 (PT 52), Section 1, Question 24
Q6. September 2007 (PT 52), Section 3, Question 23
Q7. June 2007 (PT 51.5), Section 2, Question 22
Q8. December 2009 (PT 59), Section 2, Question 24

Chapter 3 – Must Be False

[Drill]

Page 142. October 2003 (PT 41), Section 1, Question 7

[Problem Set]

Q1. October 2003 (PT 41), Section 3, Question 10
Q2. September 2007 (PT 52), Section 1, Question 18
Q3. December 2008 (PT 56), Section 3, Question 22

Chapter 4 – Main Point

[Text]

Page 156. September 2007 (PT 52), Section 3, Question 2
Page 158. June 2008 (PT 54), Section 4, Question 11

[Drill]

Page 161. December 2004 (PT 45), Section 1, Question 17

[Problem Set]

Q1. October 2003 (PT 41), Section 1, Question 5
Q2. October 2005 (PT 47), Section 3, Question 6
Q3. December 2003 (PT 42), Section 4, Question 10

Chapter 4 – Fallacy

[Text]

Page 170. December 2004 (PT 45), Section 4, Question 10
Page 172. June 2003 (PT 40), Section 3, Question 21
Page 174. December 2008 (PT 56), Section 2, Question 15
Page 176. December 2009 (PT 59), Section 2, Question 4
Page 178. September 2007 (PT 52), Section 1, Question 6
Page 179. December 2003 (PT 42), Section 4, Question 14
Page 181. October 2003 (PT 41), Section 3, Question 4
Page 183. October 2003 (PT 41), Section 1, Question 1
Page 184. December 2006 (PT 51), Section 3, Question 4
Page 186. October 2005 (PT 47), Section 3, Question 8
Page 188. October 2003 (PT 41), Section 3, Question 20
Page 190. June 2007 (PT 51.5), Section 2, Question 17
Page 191. June 2009 (PT 57), Section 3, Question 2
Page 193. December 2006 (PT 51), Section 1, Question 15

[Problem Set]

Q1. September 2007 (PT 52), Section 1, Question 2
Q2. June 2009 (PT 57), Section 3, Question 10
Q3. October 2003 (PT 41), Section 3, Question 13
Q4. September 2007 (PT 52), Section 3, Question 16
Q5. June 2008 (PT 54), Section 2, Question 15
Q6. December 2004 (PT 45), Section 1, Question 13
Q7. June 2003 (PT 40), Section 3, Question 19
Q8. December 2009 (PT 59), Section 3, Question 20
Q9. December 2005 (PT 48), Section 1, Question 17
Q10. October 2003 (PT 41), Section 1, Question 22
Q11. June 2008 (PT 54), Section 2, Question 22
Q12. June 2003 (PT 40), Section 3, Question 23
Q13. June 2009 (PT 57), Section 2, Question 26
Q14. June 2007 (PT 51.5), Section 3, Question 25
Q15. September 2006 (PT 50), Section 4, Question 22

Q3.   October 2003 (PT 41), Section 3, Question 22

Q4.   December 2009 (PT 59), Section 2, Question 26

Q5.   June 2003 (PT 40), Section 3, Question 15

Q6.   June 2009 (PT 57), Section 2, Question 12

Q7.   December 2004 (PT 45), Section 4, Question 22

Chapter 5 – Necessary Assumption

[Text]

Page 396.   June 2007 (PT 51.5), Section 3, Question 11

Page 398.   December 2003 (PT 42), Section 4, Question 13

Page 400.   June 2008 (PT 54), Section 2, Question 2

[Problem Set]

Q1.   December 2004 (PT 45), Section 1, Question 3

Q2.   September 2007 (PT 52), Section 3, Question 9

Q3.   June 2008 (PT 54), Section 2, Question 9

Q4.   December 2003 (PT 42), Section 2, Question 14

Q5.   October 2003 (PT 41), Section 3, Question 17

Q6.   September 2007 (PT 52), Section 3, Question 13

Q7.   June 2003 (PT 40), Section 3, Question 22

Q8.   October 2005 (PT 47), Section 3, Question 17

Chapter 5 – Paradox

[Text]

Page 418.   December 2009 (PT 59), Section 2, Question 11

[Drill]

Page 421.   October 2005 (PT 47), Section 3, Question 11

[Problem Set]

Q1.   June 2009 (PT 57), Section 3, Question 4

Q2.   September 2007 (PT 52), Section 1, Question 14

Q3.   December 2004 (PT 45), Section 4, Question 15

Q4.   December 2003 (PT 42), Section 4, Question 24

Q5.   September 2007 (PT 52), Section 3, Question 22

Q6.   September 2007 (PT 52), Section 3, Question 20

Chapter 6 – Principle

[Text]

Page 436.   December 2008 (PT 56), Section 3, Question 3

Page 437.   June 2008 (PT 54), Section 2, Question 8

Page 439.   December 2008 (PT 56), Section 2, Question 18

[Problem Set]

Q1.   June 2007 (PT 51.5), Section 3, Question 1

Q2.   June 2007 (PT 51.5), Section 3, Question 6

Q3.   October 2005 (PT 47), Section 1, Question 5

Q4.   December 2008 (PT 56), Section 2, Question 16

Q5.   October 2003 (PT 41), Section 1, Question 17

Q6.   June 2007 (PT 51.5), Section 3, Question 14

Q7.   June 2009 (PT 57), Section 3, Question 19

Chapter 8 – Practice Test

Page 459.   October 2008 (PT 55), Section 1

Page 495.   October 2008 (PT 55), Section 3